BUSINESS TODAY

BUSINESS

DAVID J. RACHMAN
DEPARTMENT OF MARKETING
BERNARD M. BARUCH COLLEGE
OF THE CITY UNIVERSITY OF NEW YORK

MICHAEL H. MESCON
DEAN, COLLEGE OF BUSINESS ADMINISTRATION
GEORGIA STATE UNIVERSITY

TODAY FOURTH EDITION

RANDOM HOUSE
BUSINESS DIVISION

NEW YORK

TO OUR WIVES,
BARBARA AND ENID

Fourth edition

98765432

Copyright © 1976, 1979, 1982, 1985 by Random House,
Inc.

Library of Congress Cataloging in Publication Data

Rachman, David J.
  Business today.

  Bibliography: p.
  Includes index.
  1. Business. 2. Management. I. Mescon,
Michael H. II. Title.
[HF5351.R26 1985]   658   84-16009

ISBN 0-394-33629-1

Manufactured in the United States of America by
Rand McNally & Co., Versailles, KY

Composition, color separations, art preparation by
York Graphic Services, Inc., York, PA.

Cover photograph by Alan Porter

DESIGNED BY BETTY BINNS GRAPHICS / MARTIN LUBIN

PREFACE

Business Today, Fourth Edition, like all previous editions of this book, shares with the instructor of the first college course in business an onerous responsibility—that of giving the student a concise understanding of the intricacies and interconnections of the machinery of the business world. Fundamental to the design and development of *Business Today* has been the conviction that it must provide an accurate, balanced, and realistic reflection of the ever-changing environment of business.

In the writing of this text, it has been important for the authors and publisher to understand not only how the business environment is changing, but also how the course for which this book is designed is changing. For this edition, surveys and interviews with over 422 professors of business have given us guidance in understanding the changing trends in the introductory business course's instructional methodology. These professors represent a highly qualified body of advisors, for it is they who have taught over 500,000 students using *Business Today* as their basic text. Their recommendations, as well as those of a distinguished editorial advisory panel of 31 experts selected from the academic and business communities, helped shape this fourth edition of *Business Today* into an energetic presentation of today's business scene.

The changes incorporated into this edition dramatically reflect the evolving nature of American business, from the supporting structure of a primarily industrially based economy to that of a rapidly growing service economy that is being powered into the future by the fast-paced growth of computer technology. Specifically, the significant changes in this edition are as follows:

Chapter organization

There are now 26 chapters in the text; six are designated "Component Chapters." The Component Chapters cover material not commonly found in texts intended for the Introduction to Business course. Alphabetically designated rather than numbered, the Component Chapters offer the instructor and the student an opportunity to investigate some important business functions that are components of major business areas; they require an understanding of material discussed in preceding chapters.

New chapters, revised chapters, and revision of key material

■ Included in this edition is a new chapter titled "International Business: America's Perspective." This chapter is intended to show the student the interdependence of the nation's economic and industrial engine with its global framework. In addition, further emphasis is given to the international dimension through a series of boxed features titled "International Business Today," which are dispersed throughout the text.

■ The treatment of business and data processing has been revised considerably for this edition. There are now two chapters concerned with this subject area. Chapter 17, "How Computers Are Used in Business," focuses on the utilization of computer technology by business. Component Chapter F, "How Computers Work," examines the amazing technology of the computer itself; when students gain a basic understanding of this topic, they will have further insight into possible inventive applications.

■ The material on business and the economic environment has been thoroughly revised in Chapter 3, "The American Economy: Triumphs and Challenges."

■ The chapter dealing with small business and franchises has been carefully revised to incorporate a more practical orientation. Its new title, "Small Business, Start-Ups, and Venture Capital," suggests other major changes that have also been made.

■ Component Chapter D, "Money and Banking," has been extensively revised to reflect the many changes that have occurred recently in this area.

■ Greater emphasis on technology has been incorporated into Chapter 6, "Production and Operations Management."

■ The material on consumer behavior, previously covered in a Component Chapter, has been merged into Chapter 9, "Introduction to Marketing."

Case material

There are two cases at the end of each chapter. Virtually all the cases are new to this edition, and nearly all are taken from actual business situations. They have been written so as to focus on specific pedagogical objectives.

In addition to the two cases following each chapter, a separate supplement of 20 extended cases is available to the instructor using *Business Today, Fourth Edition.*

Careers material

Retained in this edition are the careers grids for each of the functional areas of business. These grids can be found in Appendix I; they reflect current career trends in specific fields, including salary information, job descriptions, and future growth outlook. Additionally available is a separate careers supplement that contains self-assessment material and in-depth career information.

Lively examples and boxed features

A great deal of attention has been given to achieving a sensitive balance between sound, clear presentation of theory and interesting practical applications. Real-life examples have been selected that are recognizable to students, thus making illustrative points more understandable and memorable. Boxed material dispersed throughout the chapters provides practical, interesting, and relevant extensions of the chapter material. The series of boxes titled "Know These Laws" and "How It's Actually Done" provides an understanding of the mechanics of business, while the "International Business Today" and "High-Tech Horizon" boxes provide a perspective on the contemporary, albeit seemingly futuristic, environment of business.

Strong graphics program

Business Today, Fourth Edition reflects a firm belief that a text should have an attractive design that serves both to reinforce learning and to invite the reader's interest. Accordingly, we have designed illustrations and features to make their points both visually and verbally. Careful integration of these items into the overall format keeps them from interfering with text flow; almost all photos, illustrations, and boxed features appear at the top or the bottom of the page, so that there is a continuous flow of textual material from page to page—a factor we recognize as crucial to maintaining students' attention and concentration.

Supplementary materials available for use with *Business Today, Fourth Edition:* **Student Course Mastery Guide**, Lee Dahringer, *Emory University*, Stanley Garfunkel, *Queensborough Community College*, Dennis Guseman, *University of Northern Colorado*; **Careers Supplement**, Les Dlabay, *Lake Forest College*, Lester Schwartz, *Queens College*; **SIMEX: simulated exercises in business for microcomputers**; **Instructional Resource Materials**, Blaine Greenfield, *Bucks County Community College*, Karen Ross, *Georgia State University*, David Rachman, *Baruch College, City University of New York*; **Testing Materials and Services**, Stephen Cyrus, *Montclair State College*, Dolores Gioffre, *Montclair State College*, Edward Mirch, *West Valley College*, Shepherd Walker, *Montclair State College*.

Acknowledgments

We are grateful to have been assisted at many levels and stages of the development of *Business Today, Fourth Edition,* by a team of enthusiastic and talented individuals. Many of these people contributed insights gained from their experience in teaching from the previous edition of *Business Today;* others critiqued our new chapters and made recommendations for them; still others developed new material or contributed their editorial, design, production, or writing skills. We feel that the result of their efforts is a text which remains the best in the field.

We wish to acknowledge our tremendous debt to the academic advisors who analyzed the technical accuracy of the material in the functional areas of business. Their expert advice was invaluable. They are: John K. Ryans, Jr., Kent State University (international business and marketing); H. Ralph Todd, Jr., American River College, and Dewey E. Johnson, California State University, Fresno (small business); W. Jack Duncan, University of Alabama, Birmingham (management); James B. Dilworth, University of Alabama, Birmingham (production and operations management); Cheryl L. Maranto, University of Iowa (unions); Charles H. Fay, University of Kentucky (human resources management); James M. Higgins, Rollins College (human relations); William Locander, University of Tennessee, and Paul J. Londrigan, Charles S. Mott Community College (marketing); Lee Dahringer, Emory University (promotion); Robert Grau, Cuyahoga Community College, and Dale Lewison, University of Akron (wholesaling and retailing); Loretta Graziano, California State University at Hayward (international business); Thomas J. Hindelang, Drexel University (finance); George Head, American Institute for Property and Liability Underwriters (risk management and insurance); Robert K. Eskew, Purdue University (accounting and computers); Peter M. Ginter, University of Alabama, Birmingham (computers in business); Robert L. Goldberg, Northeastern University and John Hancock Distributors, Inc., James Lindberg, Mankato State University, and Andrew C. Rucks, University of Alabama, Birmingham (computers in business); John F. Steiner, California State University, Los Angeles, and Don Watson, University of South Florida (government and business); and Douglas Whitman, University of Kansas (business law).

We are similarly grateful to the following expert consultants who also scrutinized new material from its creation to final draft: William Glasgall, *Business Week* (business and the environment); Ronald Krieger, Chase Manhattan Bank (economics); Irene Pave, *Business Week* (business and minorities); William Petersen, Federal Reserve Bank (money and banking); Gary Slutsker, *Venture* (small business and entrepreneurs); Sean Strube, Council on Economic Priorities (business and the consumer); and Chris Welles, Columbia University (economics, business and society).

Joe Cappo of *Crain's Chicago Business* provided us with numerous examples and applications related to key academic concepts. We are indebted to him for putting his storehouse of ideas at our disposal. A special mention is also extended to Dewey E. Johnson, California State University, Fresno, and Thomas D. Kinsey, Moor Park College and Ergo Marketing and Advertising, who were contributing editors on the Perspectives in Small Business sections, and to John D. Shingleton, Michigan State University, who brought his vast experience to the task of researching material for the Careers section of the text.

Many academics were asked to appraise the first draft of *Business Today, Fourth Edition,* for currency, accuracy, and completeness of coverage. In this regard, we would like to thank: Wendell Armstrong, Central Virginia Community College; Blaine Greenfield, Bucks County Community College; Sandford B. Helman, Middlesex County Community College; Robert Higgins, Middlesex County Community College; Eric Kulp, Middlesex County Community College; Paul N. Loveday, University of Nevada; John W. Lloyd, Monroe Community College; Paul J. Londrigan, Charles S. Mott Community College; Edward C. Mirch, West Valley College; Cornelius Mitchell, New York City Technical College; Arthur Rochlin, Miami–Dade Community College; Floyd L. Rogers, North Harris County College; Terence Riddle, Central Virginia Community College; Ray Tewell, American River College; Gregory J. Worosz, Schoolcraft College.

Extensive as they are, the supplementary materials for *Business Today, Fourth Edition,* require a great deal of industry and creativity in the making. The authors of these materials have unfailingly met the demands of the task. Blaine Greenfield of Bucks County Community College has developed excellent instructor's materials for the text. The *Student Course Mastery Guide* has been updated and expanded by Lee Dahringer (Emory University), Stanley Garfunkel (Queensborough Community College), and Dennis Guseman (University of Northern Colorado). Stephen Cyrus, Dolores C. Gioffre, and Shepherd Walker (all of Montclair State College) and Edward Mirch (West Valley College) did a superb job of preparing the test items. We are also grateful to Les R. Dlabay (Lake Forest College) and Lester Schwartz, who prepared the *Careers in Business Today* supplement.

Before the revision of this text began, we looked to those individuals whose experience teaching *Business Today* from past editions had put them in the best position to help us to design the blueprint for *Business Today, Fourth Edition.* The following academics participated in our market research: Carole Adams, West Virginia Northern Community College; Robert Adkins, University of Southern Colorado; J. Ainsworth, Indiana University Southeast; Louis Alberto, Fairleigh Dickinson University; Emilio Alcon, Kapiolani Community College; Jane Anderson, Mount Wachusett Community College; Leonard Anderson, Olivet Nazarene College; Lincoln Anderson, Oxnard College; Larry Arp, Indiana University at Evansville; J.W. Autry, Tarleton State University; Al Barnhart, Mid Michigan Community College; Glen Barth, University of Montana; Charles Beene, Kilgore College; Milton Benz, Penn Valley Community College; William Bessey, Golden Gate University; William Bleisath, Charles S. Mott Community College; R.L. Bliss, Los Angeles Trade-Technical College; Leon Boghossian, Community College of Rhode Island; Arthur Boisselle, Pikes Peak Community College; Philip Bomeisl, Bergen Community College; Marion Boss, University of Southern Colorado; David Braun, West Los Angeles College; Lyle Brenna, Pikes Peak Community College; Templeton Briggs, Fullerton College; Janice Brundige, West Los Angeles College; John Buckley, Orange County Community College; Dorma Bullpit, Olympia Technical Community College; Dixie Burrell, Richland Community College; Al Campbell, Los Angeles Harbor College; Valeriano Cantu, Angelo State University; Bob Carroll, Vincennes University; Roberta Carter, Metro State College; Clarence Carver, Bucks County Community College; Y.C. Chang, University of Notre Dame; Robert Comerford, University of Rhode Island; Helene Corley, Oxnard College; Ron Courchone, Community College of Allegheny County; Doris Coy, College of the Canyons; C. Cramer, Los Angeles Trade-Technical College; Harold Craver, Kilgore College; Curtis Cremeans, Jackson Community College; Jack Crespin, Bergen Community College; the late Benjamin Cutler; Harris Dean, Lansing Community College; Jack Densen, Fullerton College; William Dickson, Green River Community College; Dale Dickson, Mesa College; John J. Doyle, Springfield College; Don Drennan, Abilene Christian University; Richard Drew, Mott Community College; Emmet Edwards, Indiana University—Evansville; Jack Egan, Jersey City State College; Ray Egan, Fort Steilacoom County College; Pat Ellebracht, Northeast Missouri State University; Thomas G. England, Slippery Rock State College; Barbara Erkkila, Fullerton College; Richard Fabris, Jersey City State College; Judd Faurer, Metro State College; David Finley, Charles S. Mott Community College; Robert Fishco, Middlesex Community College; Don Freeman, Pikes Peak Community College; Carl Fusco, State University of New York, Oneonta; Harold Gelderloos, Muskegon Community College; Gary Gibson, Maple Woods Community College; Marjorie Gilmore, Community College of Denver; Dolores C. Gioffre, Montclair State College; Paul Gonzalez, Champlain College; Lee Goode, Angelo State University; Robert Goodell, Fullerton College; Jean Goodwin, Holyoke Community College; Fred Gorczyk, Fairleigh Dickinson University; Doug Gordon, Arapahoe Community College; William Gorman, Fullerton College; Patricia Graber, Middlesex Community College; Steven Graham, Vincennes University; Blaine Greenfield, Bucks County Community College; Harold Grossman, Carl Sandburg College; Peter Gucciardo, Moorpark College; Sheila Gursh, Montclair State College; Luther Guynes, Los Angeles City College; Hal Hansen, Utah Tech College; J.J. Harrison, Parkersburg Community College; Larry Harrison, Kankakee Community College; James Hart, Elizabeth Community College; Joseph Hecht, Montclair State College; Gale Heiman, Aims College; Sandford Helman, Middlesex Community College; LeRoy Henry, Los Angeles Trade-Technical College; Wallace Hettle, Muskegon Community College; Robert Higgins, Middlesex Community College; Clarence Hill, Fullerton College; Nathan Himmelstein, Essex Community College; Charles Hinkle, University of Colorado; Kenneth Hirshl, Community College of Allegheny County; Charles Hobson, Indiana University, Gary; William Holda, Lansing Community College; Gary Holt, Tarrant County Junior College, N.E.; Marsha Homme, California State College; Robert Hughes, Richland College; Alvin Jackson, Bergen County Community College; Jack Jacques, University of North Colorado; Edward Johnson, Parkersburg Community College; Gene Johnson, Clark College; Marty Jonas, Berkshire Community College; William Kania, California State College; Francis M. Kauffman, Linn-Benton Community College; Jehan Kavoosi, Clarion State College; Marshall Keyser, Moorpark College; Fred Kiesner, Loyola Marymount University; Dan Kinker, Washburn University; Wayne Klemin, Central Washington University; Eric Kulp, Middlesex County Community College; Craig Kuhns, City College of San Francisco; Lawrence Lad, Southeastern Massachusetts University; James Lamprecht, Laramie County Community College; Don Landauer, Los Angeles City College; Karen Lawrence, Merritt College; John Leeper, Northeast Missouri State University; Edwin Leonard, Indiana University, Fort Wayne; Marvin Levine, Orange County Community College; Lincoln Lewis, Indiana University—Purdue University at Indianapolis; Robert Lewis, Indiana University—Purdue University at Indianapolis; Paul Listro, Community College of Rhode Island; Gerry Littlewood, Olympic College; Thomas Lloyd, Westmoreland County Community College; Paul J. Londrigan, Mott Community College; Jane Loprest, Bucks County Community College; Anthony Lucas, Community College of Allegheny County; Edith Luft, Orange County Community College; Edward Lyell, Metro State College; Sheldon Mador, Los Angeles Trade-Technical College; John Magnuson, State University of New York, Delhi; Al Mahrer, Community College of Denver; Daniel Masterson, Fullerton College; Carol J. Matteson, Slippery Rock State College; Michael Matukonis, State University of New York, Oneonta; Don McCauley, McLennan Community College; John McCullough, West Liberty State College; Judith McFatter, Rockland Community College; John McGinnis, Montclair State College; Margaret McGuire, State University of New York, Oneonta; James McKenzie, Tarrant County Junior College; Marion I. Meeker, Charles S. Mott Community College; Donald Mellon, Bergen Community College; Mark Mendenhall, Loyola Marymount University; David Miller, Fullerton College; Edward Mosher, Laramie County Community College; Norman Muller, Greenfield Community College; Robert Mullin, Orange County Community College; Lee Neuman, Bucks County Community College; Joyce Newton, Jackson Community College; Kay Norris, Bellevue Community College; Nick Nixon, Montana State University; John O'Brien, Fairleigh Dickinson University; Richard Olsen, Washburn University; Dora E. Orsini, West Liberty State College; Norman Pacula, College of Marin; Edward Palascak, University of Pittsburgh; R. Parroff, Elizabeth Community College; Lucille Parsons, Community College of Rhode Island; Marie Pietak, Bucks County Community College; Arnold Pisani, Berkshire Community College; John Polesky, Indiana University of Pennsylvania; Estella Pomroy, Parkersburg Community College; Robert Powell, Bucks County Community College; Frederick Puritz, State University of New York, Oneonta; Gerald Ramsey, Indiana University Southeast; Peter Replogle, Orange County Community College; Manuel Reynosa, Rio Hondo College; Jim Richardson, Angelo State University; Jerry Ridgley, University of Southern Colorado; James Robbins, Fairleigh Dickinson University; Pollis Robertson, Jackson Community College; Elizabeth Robinson, West Liberty State College; Ron Rose, Arapahoe Community College; Jack Ruterbusch, Charles S. Mott Community College; Bruce Rutter, Penn State University, Altoona; Cynthia Sadler, Northeast Missouri State University; Louis Salome, Bucks County Community College; Don Sandlin, East Los Angeles College; Duane Schechter, Muskegon Community College; Lawrence Schenck, Los Angeles City College; Martin Schwartz, Rockland Community College; Walter Scott, McLennan Community College; John Seely, Tulsa Junior College; Jennifer Shelly, College of the Sequoias; Patrick Shield, Rio Hondo College; Joseph Shott, Westmoreland County Community College; Gene Six, Mount San Antonio College; Patrick Skea, Bucks County Community College; William Small, Spokane Community College; Charles Smith, Spokane Falls Community College; John B. Smith, Bucks County Community College; Woodrow Smith, Los Angeles City College; Carl Sonntag, Pikes Peak Community College; Linda Spotts, Penn Valley Community College; M. Thomas Spraggins, Moorpark College; Richard Standish, Tulsa Junior College; George Stangler, Orange County Community College; William Stitt, Arapahoe Community College; John Sullivan, Bergen County Community College; Joseph Sullivan, North Shore Community College; Jack Sweeny, Fullerton College; Ron Tarullo, California State College; James Terada, Community College of Denver North; Claude Thomson, Longview Community College; Nancy Thomson, Northwest Missouri State University; Ray Trance, Community College of Allegheny County; Robert Ulbrich, Parkland College; Pamela Uzzolino, Montclair State College; Henry Vankowski, Bucks County Community College; Shepherd Walker, Montclair State College; Henry Warren, Biola College; Gene Watkins, Charles S. Mott Community College; Cathy Watson, Jackson Community College; Richard Wedell, Illinois State University; Robert Welsh, Greenfield Community College; Michael West, Maple Woods Community College; Jerry Wheat, Indiana University Southeast; Paul R. Williams, Charles S. Mott Community College; Steven Winter, Orange County Community College; John Wisen, Wenatchee Valley College; Geraldine Wolfe, Mount San Antonio College; William Wooldridge, University of Colorado, Boulder; Robert Youngquist, Mesa College; William Zahurak, Community College of Allegheny County.

We wish again to acknowledge our debt to the reviewers of *Business Today, Third Edition,* who have not already been mentioned: John G. Foster, Jr., Montgomery College; John Gelles, Ventura College; Milton Greenberg, American University; John W. Hamilton, Steven F. Austin State College; Lanny A. Karns, State University of New York—Oswego; Bernard V. Katz, formerly of Oakton Community College; Loren Lundgren, Forsyth Technical Institute; Craig C. Milnor, Clark College; G. Dean Palmer, formerly of the University of Northern Colorado; Mimi Will, Foothill College; Gene Wunder, Ball State University.

We are also grateful to those individuals who have made us aware of errors in this and the previous edition of the text. In every instance, we have corrected these errors in subsequent printings. **For the Third Edition:** John J. Balek, Morton College; Sandra M. Honig, Elms College; Ken Manko, Dekalb Community College; Donald Ryktarsyk, Schoolcraft College. **For the Fourth Edition:** John G. Foster, Jr., Montgomery College.

Finally, we would like to thank the following reviewers who wrote critiques of *Business Today, Fourth Edition,* from a marketing perspective: Les R. Dlabay, Lake Forest College; Roy Fox, Palm Beach Junior College South; John W. Lloyd, Monroe Community College; Noel C. Matthews, Front Range Community College; Stan Stone, Valencia Community College; Ron Young, Kalamazoo Valley Community College.

The editorial and design qualities of *Business Today, Fourth Edition,* reflect what we think are the best efforts by the best people.

We are especially grateful to project editor Elaine Rosenberg. She marshalled many staff and freelance people through the copyediting and production stages, and by her own careful, conscientious work successfully pulled this project together. We also thank these project editors: Judith Kromm, who helped us develop several of the chapters, and Elaine Romano, who wrote boxes, cases, and other features. We are grateful to Pat Cahalan and John Sturman, whose copyediting improved our prose, and Marion Corkett, who organized the reference citations.

We are also indebted to Valerie Raymond, Anne Mahoney, Lois Refkin, Janis Newman, and Alison Husting for their diligence and sound judgment in managing the manuscript review process and coordinating the ancillary materials that accompany the text.

Once again, we are indebted to the guiding spirit of Paul Donnelly; he brings a special inventive flair to so many aspects of this book. Thanks are also due to Suzanne Thibodeau and June Smith, whose sound management talents brought this book together smoothly and on schedule; and to Susan Badger for her helpful suggestions.

We owe the highest gratitude to special projects editor Susan Tucker. For three editions now her creativity, resourcefulness, and energy have astonished us. Her editorial skills, quickness, and dedication have been invaluable in developing this book.

We are again extremely grateful to Martin Lubin, David Skolkin, and Betty Binns of Betty Binns Graphics for their creative and persistent energy, which gave us a design that is both appropriate and unique. We gratefully acknowledge photo manager Kathy Bendo and picture researcher Barbara Salz, whose talents helped us communicate our message more strikingly. We also thank production manager Della Mancuso and production director Barbara Lauster for their patience, persistence, and long hours spent ironing the wrinkles out of this very complicated project. And finally, our thanks go to Casimir Psujek, Manager of Editorial Operations, and Production Associate Linda Goldfarb, who smoothly coordinated the production of the supplementary materials.

This book has benefited enormously from the inventive and creative talents of a number of writers who turned our ideas into words. We therefore salute the talents of Allen Boraiko, Mark Deitch, Betty Gatewood, Loretta Graziano, Eric Grevstad, Jack Hitt, Virginia Joyner, Roberta Meyer, Alice Shane, Harry Steinberg, Lawrence J. Tell, Heidi Thaens, and Elisa Turner.

Our very capable researchers were Naomi Bernstein and Pat Bear of For Your Information, Inc.

Without the expert typing of Barbara Hale this book would never have been published.

CONTENTS IN BRIEF

TO THE STUDENT: This book is designed for a flexible approach to its subject matter. At the beginning of the course, your instructor will decide on the sequence of chapters he or she plans to cover. Record this sequence on this Table of Contents, using the lines provided to the left of the chapter titles.

For more information on the content of the chapters, turn to the Detailed Table of Contents on page xii.

COURSE
CHAPTER
SEQUENCE

DETAILED CONTENTS

PART TWO

MANAGEMENT 121

PART THREE

MARKETING 251

PART FOUR

FINANCE 347

PART FIVE

TOOLS OF BUSINESS   461

PART SIX

THE ENVIRONMENT OF BUSINESS 535

PART ONE

FOCUS ON AMERICAN ENTERPRISE

Being a business leader today is quite a responsibility. Ask Robert Haas, president of Levi Strauss, the jeans maker. Haas worries about profit: sales are off at home because of competition from smaller designer-jeans firms, and they are off overseas because of the position of the American dollar. Haas also agonizes over possible layoffs because he feels a strong obligation to employees. And his feeling of social responsibility extends to the public at large: he has been known to pull commercials he found offensive.

As you'll learn in Part I, Haas' responsibilities are typical of those who manage business. The chapters in this Part survey business's goals, organization, and economic setting.

□ Chapter I, **Business and Its Social Responsibility,** tells of

the dual obligation managers face—making a profit while considering social goals.

☐ In Chapter 2, **Forms of Business Organization,** you'll see how large and small businesses are organized to compete.

☐ Chapter 3, **The American Economy: Triumphs and Challenges,** looks at the economic setting of businesses in this country.

☐ Component Chapter A, **International Business: America's Perspective,** presents the global context in which American businesses operate.

☐ Component Chapter B, **Small Business, Start-Ups and Venture Capital,** focuses on the special problems and satisfactions of the individual entrepreneur.

BUSINESS AND ITS SOCIAL RESPONSIBILITY

In recent years, American society has been going through explosive changes. We enjoyed unprecedented growth and prosperity for twenty-five years following World War II. In the early 1970s, shifts in the domestic and world economies disrupted this growth, and in the early 1980s we suffered the worst recession since the Great Depression of the 1930s. Though some of these economic difficulties now seem to have lessened, we no longer feel assured of the standard of living our parents took for granted, and we still face problems such as international competition and huge federal deficits. Yet a rush of technological progress has also brought us some undreamed-of amusements and conveniences: robots, video recorders, "smart" telephones, computers that flash us information in seconds.

These changes have not taken place without turmoil in American business. Managers, forced to adopt new techniques, have also had to tighten financial controls and sometimes even close plants or cut jobs. Now, more than ever, people are wondering what business's true responsibility is to the society it operates in. Should it concentrate on staying healthy by making profits? Or should it also strive for other goals—such as environmental protection, fairness to minorities, a square deal for consumers? In this chapter we'll outline some of these issues, and let you draw your own conclusions.

CHAPTER FOCUS

After reading the material in this chapter, you will be able to:
- enumerate the radical changes now under way in American business
- define business, and state the importance of the profit motive
- name the two forces that guide the free-market system, and discuss their operation today in theory and practice
- discuss the conflict between environmental responsibility and economic realities
- discuss at least three kinds of pollution and the provisions of at least ten laws to control the problem
- trace the recent history of the consumer movement, and cite the provisions of at least ten federal consumer laws
- state the provisions of two key federal antidiscrimination laws
- define affirmative action, quotas, and comparable worth

When he said "I hear America singing," poet Walt Whitman (1819–1892) must also have heard a great deal of background music—saws, hammers, drills, steam engines, whistles, and so on—all the racket of booming industrialization. But that was over a hundred years ago. If he were writing his poem today, he'd have to listen hard to hear anything at all, since many of our new industries hurtle along in an almost unearthly silence. Word processors absorb their data with restrained little clicks, computer display screens merely glow knowingly, and huge computers perform their mysterious functions with hardly a whirr or a whisper.

CHANGE AND AMERICAN BUSINESS

It's all part of an amazing transformation that has been taking place in American business during the last few years. That single world has now almost become two separate ones. One is the world of the traditional "smokestack" industries: automobiles, steel, rubber, shipbuilding, and other heavy manufacturing. The other is what is known as the high-technology, or "high-tech," industries: computers of endless variety and application, genetic engineering, telecommunications, fiber optics, lasers, and many more. The first sector—the smokestack industries—developed serious problems in the recession of the early 1980s. Stiff foreign competition arose in many market areas that the United States had formerly dominated, and some observers believed that managements in heavy manufacturing companies had been slow to innovate, allowing plants to lose efficiency. Though the recession had ended by the time this book was written, it remained questionable whether our heavy industry would ever regain the world dominance of its earlier days, and regions such as the Detroit metropolitan area, where local economies had depended on the big factories, still suffered from unemployment. But at the same time, high-tech industries were booming, and a wave of innovation was creating new ideas and products

almost daily. Although the early 1980s witnessed more bankruptcies than any time since the Great Depression, the same period also saw the birth of nearly a million new companies. New prosperity had come to parts of California, the Northeast, and other parts of the country where high-tech companies were concentrated. Even established service industries, such as retailing and banking, had been influenced by the new technologies.

How did these startling changes take place? Three decades ago, our economy was already in the process of a fundamental transition. Before World War II the majority of businesses had produced tangible *goods* such as cars, clothing, and industrial machinery, but after the war an increasing number of businesses began to produce *services* such as health care, communications, financial services, fast-food and other restaurant services, and research and consulting activities. Global upheavals—the 1970s energy crisis, the continued industrialization of Japan and other countries—both complicated and speeded the transition. But perhaps the most outstanding factor was a phenomenon, spurred by the spread of computers, that some observers have called the "information revolution." Recent studies indicate that fully *half* of the nation's economic activity now consists of the creation and processing of information.[1] This information includes not only the traditional kind that is exchanged in newspapers, books, letters, and reports. It also includes electronic information, such as the information that is beamed from one side of the world to the other as part of our mass-communications system. Electronic information now dominates industries such as contemporary banking: very few of the money transactions carried out by companies or individuals involve actual dollar bills or coins—most simply take place by electronically changing the numbers that are recorded in bank customers' accounts.

Electronic information is even used to guide many kinds of machinery and equipment, from assembly lines to nuclear submarines. Take, for example, the automobile industry, which some experts say is now almost 30 percent information-dependent. Not only do the secretarial, accounting, and marketing divisions of automobile manufacturers deal with information almost exclusively, but the production departments make heavy use of comput-

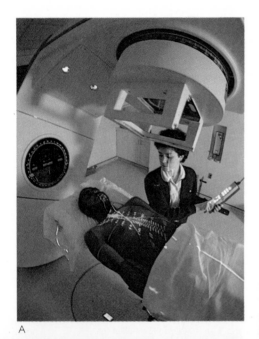

A

Science-fiction fantasies? No, these are all real innovations created by the high-tech tier of American business. **(A)** a linear accelerator used to give radiation therapy to a cancer patient; **(B)** a computer display of service quality data at a Bell Labs Switching Control Center (it is superimposed on a photo of a technician keeping tabs on the system's performance); **(C)** a video data storage disk being imprinted via a laser beam; **(D)** a prosthetic (artificial) arm, whose complex electronic gadgetry controls its movement as well as that of the realistic-looking hand.

B

C

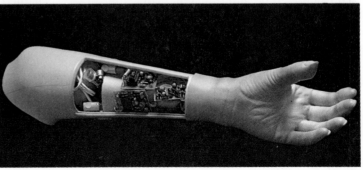

D

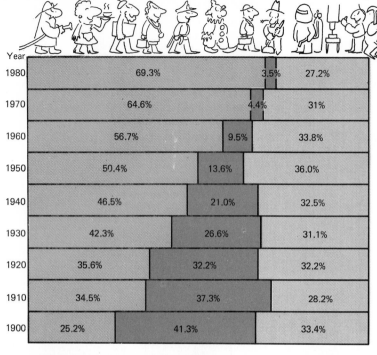

Year	Service industries	Agriculture	Manufacturing
1980	69.3%	3.5%	27.2%
1970	64.6%	4.4%	31%
1960	56.7%	9.5%	33.8%
1950	50.4%	13.6%	36.0%
1940	46.5%	21.0%	32.5%
1930	42.3%	26.6%	31.1%
1920	35.6%	32.2%	32.2%
1910	34.5%	37.3%	28.2%
1900	25.2%	41.3%	33.4%

Proportion of work force engaged in:

Service industries   Agriculture   Manufacturing

FIGURE I

THE OFFICE VERSUS THE FACTORY: The growing predominance of services in the U.S. economy

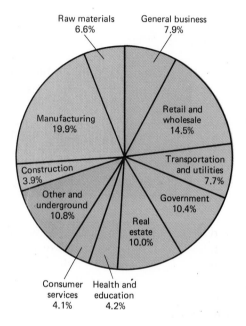

Raw materials 6.6%
General business 7.9%
Manufacturing 19.9%
Retail and wholesale 14.5%
Construction 3.9%
Transportation and utilities 7.7%
Other and underground 10.8%
Government 10.4%
Real estate 10.0%
Consumer services 4.1%
Health and education 4.2%

(Bar graph): In recent years, a growing proportion of the U.S. labor force has been employed in service industries (left) in comparison with those employed in manufacturing (right). Not since World War II has the goods-producing sector come close to providing 50 percent of U.S. employment. Recently, some of the workers who have been edged out of manufacturing have had trouble finding a solid footing elsewhere. (Pie chart): Major sectors of the economy, and their contribution to the U.S. gross national product (the total value of all goods and services produced by the economy).

erized information processing as well. A machine that tightens a bolt on an assembly line, say, is equipped with electronic sensors whose job is to take continual measurements of what that machine is doing. (A measurement, after all, is a piece of information!) Based on thousands of these tiny measurements, the sensor continually issues new "commands" (which are also information) to tell the machine what to do next—whether to continue doing the same thing or to change its activities, for example. In many parts of the assembly line, computers are stationed to check on what various machines are doing, and guide them through the steps

they must perform to turn out auto parts and assemble them into cars. Many of the finished cars themselves come equipped with their own microcomputers: these tiny computers go through the measurement/command cycle over and over again to control functions such as fuel consumption and air conditioning.[2]

All these changes have raised new questions about the roles business plays in our society. Traditionally, business has been our source of goods and services and a major source of jobs; it helps circulate money throughout the economy; it is a major taxpayer and thereby helps support regional, state, and federal governments; and it offers an opportunity for individuals to participate financially through investment in stocks and bonds.

Of course, business' responsibility does not end there. Businesses have also felt the tug of a range of social obligations, such as the need to maintain a clean and safe environment; the need to provide equal opportunity to minority and women employees; and the need to deal fairly with consumers by offering safe, high-quality products. But in the economic upheavals of the last decade, many businesses have been caught between their overall social responsibilities and their own, more immediate need to stay solvent and profitable. With tougher competition from abroad and technological changes, some businesses have taken measures that might be seen as harmful to their communities, such as closing a plant or outlet, laying off large numbers of workers, negotiating for concessions from unions, or cutting back on salaries and employee benefits. In some cases, businesses have cut spending on environmental protection, minority job programs, and other socially oriented actions.

There are many positions on the social role and responsibilities of business. Some observers have come to believe that a business discharges a large part of its social responsibility just by staying alive, thus enabling at least *some* local citizens to have jobs and put food on their tables. If business' primary service to society is to provide goods and services and to support the economy in general, then to what extent *should* it be responsible for keeping particular people employed, or to right social wrongs, or to maintain clean air and waterways? What is the real purpose of business, and where do its obligations end and government's begin? Our readers will form their own conclusions about these questions as they come up in many parts of this book.

In this chapter, we will look at some classic areas where conflict can arise between the needs of a business and the needs of the society around it: environmental protection, consumer issues, and fairness to minorities. But first, let's talk about what a business is, and how the profit motive functions as its operating principle.

BUSINESS AND OUR ECONOMIC SYSTEM

What is business? For our purposes, we can define **business** broadly as *all the work involved in providing people with goods and services for a profit.* This definition, of course, is very broad indeed, since that work can include an enormous variety of tasks.

THE ACTIVITIES INVOLVED IN BUSINESS

If you had an idea for the proverbial better mousetrap, you would have to do a great deal of practical work before your brainstorm could become a reality. First of all, you would have to acquire the necessary resources—wood and metal, tools, a workshop, and the like. Then you would have to organize the actual production—devising an efficient assembly process, training your workers, and supervising the operation. After this (assuming the world wasn't beating a path to your door), you would need to distribute your product to as many stores as possible, then make the public aware of its existence and superior qualities. Finally—or, actually, before you did anything else—you would have to find money to get the whole enterprise started. Equipment and materials must be bought, workers paid, distribution and advertising paid for—before you could sell a single mousetrap.

This sequence of tasks, needless to say, is a simplified outline of the kinds of activity involved in business. In general terms, though, it is typical of businesses of all sizes, whatever the nature of the enterprise. An ice-cream company offers a product. An airline offers a service. But both need to acquire resources, produce what they intend to sell, advertise it, and make it available to customers.

The estimated 16 million American businesses come in all forms and sizes, from General Motors Corporation, which has over 1 million shareholders, 700,000 employees, and $41 billion in assets, to the one-man hot-dog cart on a busy street corner.[3] And the business scene is a constantly changing one. New products and services are forever being offered by entrepreneurs looking to make a million. Most don't make it, but people keep trying.

BUSINESS AS A PROFIT-MAKING ACTIVITY

We described business as all the work involved in providing people with goods and services *for a profit.* The last three words are important. **Profit,** simply put, is *the money left over from all sums received from sales after expenses have been deducted.* If it costs you

$1.00 to produce one of your mousetraps and you sell it for $1.50, your profit is fifty cents (before taxes, of course).

The element of profit is the foundation of our economic system. It is, indeed, the whole point—the "bottom line" for most business activities and enterprises. The American economic system is based on the idea that the owner of a business is entitled to keep whatever profits the business produces. It takes effort, after all, to put a desirable product or service into a useful form and then sell it to people. Furthermore, the owner may have to take a considerable financial risk. Most businesses need a substantial investment to get started, and if a new venture doesn't succeed (and most don't), whoever financed it stands to lose a great deal of money. It seems only fair, therefore, that someone who makes the effort and takes the financial risk should be rewarded with the profits.

At this point we must note that not all businesses exist to make a profit. As we'll see, it is the nature of the American system to provide goods and services for which there is a sizable demand or for which a relatively small number of people are willing to spend a large sum of money. But some small segments of society have needs that profit-oriented businesses can't afford to supply at prices that these markets can pay. Therefore, our society supports a number of nonprofit businesses, such as the Rand Corporation and Goodwill Industries. In other respects, these enterprises are much like profit-directed businesses.

THE FREE-MARKET SYSTEM

In view of the importance of the profit motive, it is essential to understand *how* businesses make their profits. To begin with, our country's business life is based on what economists call a **free-market system.** In essence, this means that *if you have something to sell*—whether it's a product like that better mousetrap or a service—*you're free to charge any price and to sell to anyone willing to pay that price.* Conversely, as a consumer you're free to buy whatever you want and can afford, from whomever you choose.

In practice, of course, there are numerous exceptions to this principle and we'll discuss them shortly. Nevertheless, there are two forces that can be said to dominate the operation of any free market: *competition* and *supply and demand.*

How competition operates

If you set out to sell a product or service in today's society, chances are that someone else not too far away is selling something similar. And since potential customers are free to shop where they please, you will have to compete with your rival for their business. How can you go about this? One obvious strategy is to charge lower prices.

COMPETITION KEEPS PRICES DOWN   If your rival is selling blue jeans, say, for $28 a pair, you may try offering them for $25. The catch, of course, is that you'll get $3 less for each pair you sell and you'll still have to cover the same expenses—buying the jeans from the manufacturer, paying rent on your store, and so forth. How, then, can you charge less and still make a worthwhile profit? The answer—you hope—is that the lower price will attract more customers. Thus even though you make less money on each pair of jeans, you'll sell more of them and so come out with a good overall profit.

In real life, needless to say, things do not always work out so logically. But more often than not, the choices offered by the free-market system do benefit both the customer and the business owner—just as they're supposed to in theory. This basic head-on type of competition tends to keep prices down, which is obviously good for the buying public. At the same time, it holds out the promise of great profits to the business that can sell more units of whatever its product or service happens to be.

COMPETITION ENCOURAGES EFFICIENCY   In addition, the nature of the free market is to encourage other forms of competition that serve the interests of both the business community and the society at large. A business owner may be able to lower prices without having to settle for a smaller profit per unit if ways can be found to improve efficiency and reduce operating costs. The merchant selling blue jeans, for example, may find that rearranging the store's layout makes it possible to display more items in the same amount of space or that a new lighting system cuts the electric bills. Likewise, someone who refinishes furniture for a living may discover that dipping a table or chair in a large vat of chemical solvents removes the old finish faster—and thus more economically—than doing the same job by hand.

COMPETITION PROMOTES QUALITY   Instead of cutting prices, a business may decide to compete for customers by offering higher-quality goods or services than its rivals. The price may also be higher, but those customers who can afford it will probably be willing to pay the extra amount. (Indeed, the snob appeal of high prices, plush surroundings, and prestigious brand names can be a vital advantage in some markets.) Thus although a business that deals in luxury goods will not attract as many customers as, say, an average discount store, it will make more money per item and may well end up with an equal or even greater total profit. A particular benefit of this competitive approach is that it provides a practical incentive for businesses to maintain high standards of quality and increases the choices available to customers of different income levels.

COMPETITION ENCOURAGES INNOVATION   The free-market system not only encourages variety in the price range for a given category of products or services but also encourages an immense variety in the *types* of goods and services offered to the public. Changes in popular taste, technology, and the like are constantly creating new business opportunities—and free enterprise, like nature, abhors a vacuum. The possibility of profit—however remote it may be—almost invariably attracts entrepreneurs willing to risk their time or money. The result is an astonishing diversity of businesses: virtually anything you might want to buy—any product or service, no matter how obscure—is probably sold somewhere. (And if it isn't, you may have a profitable idea yourself.)

Supply and demand

As we have seen, prices in a free-market system are influenced by the competitive strategies of rival businesses. Price levels are not determined solely by the decisions of business managers, however. Price levels usually respond to forces of supply and demand. In economic terms **supply** refers to *the quanti-* *ties of a good or service that producers are willing to provide at various prices;* **demand** refers to *the amounts of a good or service that consumers are willing to buy at that time, at different prices.*

In basic terms, the theory of supply and demand holds that when people want a good or service very much, they will be willing to pay a higher price for it; and when the price rises, manufacturers will be willing to supply it in greater quantity. People will usually have to pay more for something they want that's in short supply (as anyone who's tried to buy a shovel immediately after a heavy snowfall knows); but if the product is widely available, the sellers will have to settle for lower prices. In other words, supply and demand are continuously reacting to one another, and the balance between them at any given moment is reflected by the current price on the open market. Thus the price of a product may drop, not because a businessperson is trying to lure customers away from the competition, but because consumer demand for the product has fallen off.

In broad terms, the forces of supply and demand combine with the profit motive in a free-market system to regulate what is produced and in what amounts. For example, a farmer in Maine might increase the amount of potatoes he plants in response to reports that a drought had damaged the potato crop in Idaho. Or a mining company, reacting to reports of increased demand for jet aircraft (which require large amounts of titanium), might decide to increase production of titanium or to open a second mine. Conversely, if reports indicated that the airlines weren't spending much on new equipment, the mine owner might delay developing more capacity and might even lay off workers. And the potato farmer in Maine might decide to plant some of his land to parsnips if the news from Idaho was that a bumper potato crop was expected. The result of all this—in theory, at least—is that the consumers will get what they want and the producers will earn a profit by keeping tabs on public demand.

How "free" is our free-market system?

The principles of supply and demand, competition, and the profit motive govern most areas of business. On paper they combine to form a balanced, self regulating system in which business and consumers, acting freely, meet each other's needs and the society's natural and human resources are used most efficiently. But theory is one thing and practice another. In reality, our free-market system is not totally free—not for the business owner or the worker or the consumer.

HOW THE GOVERNMENT LIMITS FREE ENTERPRISE Our government limits free enterprise in many ways. For instance, we don't get to keep all our profits. Whether we speak of corporate earnings, stock dividends, personal wages, or winnings from a lottery, the government takes a sizable portion in taxes. Nor

Business people cannot always sell without any constraints or restrictions. In New York City, street vendors may be ticketed for selling without a permit.

is there unrestricted freedom of action in the marketplace. As a consumer, for instance, you can't buy most medications without a doctor's prescription; you can't buy alcohol without a certificate proving that you're old enough; and you can't even get married without a license!

As for selling, whether you're a department-store owner or a street vendor, you can't legally do business without a tax permit. If you run a restaurant, you need a certificate from the board of health. You can't practice medicine, sell stock, or drive a cab without a variety of licenses. In many industries you can't sell your own services as a worker without joining a union. And you can't legally hold any job at all without a Social Security number.

Furthermore, businesses are not free to set prices without restrictions. It is not permitted, for example, for two firms to get together and fix prices at an artificially high level. Conversely, in many states, liquor stores are barred from selling their wares for *less* than the authorized minimum price.

THREATS TO FREE COMPETITION   In a system in which profit and growth are the accepted goals of private enterprise, it is inevitable that some companies may become so powerful that rivals offer little or no real competition. Unless restrictions are imposed, the result could be a **monopoly,** a situation in which *one company dominates a particular industry or market, fixes prices, and restrains free entry or activity in that market.* By definition, monopolies are contrary to the principle of competition.

True monopolies are prohibited by federal law and have been a subject of continuing governmental concern since the turn of the century. (Some monopolies, such as utilities, are legal, but are regulated.) But a related situation persists in which *a few large companies dominate an industry.* This concentration of power is called an **oligopoly.** Examples are the oil industry, which is dominated by eight large companies, and aluminum, an industry in which three companies produce 62 percent of the country's supply.[4]

Some experts believe that oligopolies may be nearly as effective as monopolies in suppressing price competition and other free-market activities, and that they may suppress technological innovation. But even oligopolies are constrained by the forces of supply and demand. There are plentiful substitutes for aluminum, a fact that limits the prices producers can set. And oil companies must contend with competition from alternative fuels as well as strong efforts by conservationists. Moreover, foreign sellers are ready to seize markets from domestic "oligopolists" that push prices too high.

New trends in the free-market system

When President Ronald Reagan took office in 1981, he made a promise to "get government off the backs" of the American people. By this he clearly meant continuing a trend that had already begun: the trend toward **deregulation,** or *the removal or relaxing of some of the rules and restrictions affecting business.* Advocates of deregulation believe that this policy can foster competition and productivity, and can boost overall economic growth.

An argument for reduced government intervention can, for example, be made in the case of the troubled American automobile industry. Although there is little doubt that the trio of General Motors, Ford, and Chrysler dominate *domestic* auto production, the rapid growth in sales of imported cars has subjected the "Big Three" to far more competition than is comfortable. The growth of international trade and the entry of foreign competitors into American markets have erased the dominant position held by some American companies, so there may be less reason to fear domestic monopolies and concentrations of power than there once was.

Deregulation has had drastic effects on certain industries that were previously controlled and protected by the federal government. The air travel industry, for example, has undergone great upheavals since it was deregulated in 1978, and it will probably be years before it stabilizes again. Suddenly, the big airlines found themselves forced to compete more actively with one another for the customer's dollar. Government-approved fare standards were lifted: airline rates now had to reflect more accurately what the average traveler was willing to spend. On the other hand, the airlines were freed to try to boost profits another way: now, they could focus their efforts on the most popular passenger routes, such as the flights between "hub" cities like New York, Chicago, Los Angeles, Washington, and a few other major metropolitan areas. (Previously,

government had had a strong say in determining which airlines flew where, and in making sure that many of the smaller cities received service.) As of this writing, the effects of deregulation have been disastrous for some of the major air carriers, but beneficial for consumers and for several of the smaller commuter airlines that have emerged. Similar turmoil has recently developed in the bus and trucking industries.

Several other industries have felt (or will soon feel) the noticeably brisker climate of deregulation. Times have changed in the banking industry, where interest-rate ceilings have been lifted, and where the banks must now compete with large diversified corporations such as Sears and American Express. A new wind is also blowing in the communications industry: as of this writing, the head of the Federal Communications Commission, Mark Fowler, has shown himself an avowed foe of *all* regulations in that field. And hot controversy has been boiling up in the natural gas industry, which will be fully deregulated in 1986, and which has become a battleground as consumer groups all over the country organize to retain government control over gas prices.

Obviously, the move toward deregulation does not please everyone. While it has pushed ahead in many areas of business, it has met strong resistance in the fields of health, safety, and consumer protection. In fact, after a brief period of tentative rollbacks, government agency spending and regulatory efforts are on the rise once again in these areas, thanks in part to a renewed consumer protection movement. Americans may well want government off their backs, but they do not necessarily want to dismantle *all* regulations—as we'll see when we look at environmental protection, the subject of our next section.

BUSINESS AND THE ENVIRONMENT

The biggest environmental disaster of the early 1980s actually began some twelve years earlier, in 1971, when a waste hauler named Russell Bliss sprayed oil on the roads of several Missouri communities, including the small river town of Times Beach. Bliss, who had been paid by a chemical plant to dispose of its waste oil, believed that he was helping the townspeople by spraying the oil to keep the dust down. Instead, in the words of the Missouri Assistant Attorney General, he was spreading "a trail of sickness and death."[5] The oil, it turned out, contained large amounts of the chemical dioxin, a substance that is highly toxic in laboratory animals, but whose effects on humans are not fully known. The contamination threat was confirmed in December 1982, when investigators from the Environmental Protection Agency (EPA) took soil samples in Times Beach and other suspected contamination sites in Missouri. A few days later, the Meramec River overflowed, flooding Times Beach and producing an unprecedented double disaster. When the water was finally cleared away, a second set of soil samples showed that dioxin levels were still dangerously high. At that point, the Environmental Protection Agency decided to step in and, for $33.7 million, buy out the entire town and relocate its residents.

The Times Beach tragedy was not the first incident of industrial toxic wastes disrupting an American community's life. And the indiscriminate dumping of hazardous chemicals on land is not the only form of pollution endangering the public health. Of equal consequence are the problems posed by the dumping of wastes into the nation's waterways, the pollution of the air by noxious fumes and dust, the transportation and disposal of radioactive wastes, and a number of other problems. These problems have been recognized for many years; they began to be the subject of widespread public concern in the 1960s, when large numbers of people became concerned about the effects of our way of life on the *quality* of our life. At that time, writers like Rachel Carson, who is the author of *Silent Spring,* helped to arouse the public to the fact that pesticides, oil spills, and smog threaten all forms of life, including our own.[6] **Ecology**—*the pattern of relationships among living things and the water, air, soil, and nutrients that support them*—became a popular "cause," and environmentally minded citizens began to attack the sources of **pollution,** which is defined as *all the threats to the environment caused by human activities in an industrial society.*

POLLUTION, GOVERNMENT, AND BUSINESS: THE ESTABLISHMENT OF THE EPA

In 1963, federal, state, and local governments began to enact laws and regulations aimed at reducing pollution. (A brief summary of major federal legislation appears on the next page.) But the bedrock legislation on which all federal efforts to control pollution rest is the **National Environmental Quality Act of 1970.** This act *established the Council on Environmental Quality and assigned to it the power to coordinate all federal environmental programs.* Later that same year, the **Environmental Protection Agency (EPA)** was *created to carry out the council's policies.* The 1970 act requires every federal agency to present to the EPA an "environmental impact statement" explaining just how any federal project—a highway, for example—might affect the environment before any final decision is made to go ahead with it.

After some initial conflict, the EPA and industry established a relatively smooth working relationship; their willingness to work together and reach compromises when possible brought about considerable advances in pollution control. But the economic problems that began with the oil crises of the 1970s, and continued into the recession of the early 1980s, set the stage for renewed debate. When the Reagan administration took over in 1981, environmental concerns did not always mesh with the nation's energy goals (for example, burning coal instead of oil would produce more air pollution, but would also reduce our dependence on imported oil), or with its immediate economic needs (keeping a pollution-spreading factory open might be undesirable environmentally, but it would also help reduce unemployment). The administration's announced policy was to ease federal regulations on industry—in effect, curtailing the power of the EPA—and to transfer much of the burden of environmental protection to state and local governments and to industry itself. In 1983, EPA head William Ruckelshaus also stressed *risk assessment* as the key to regulatory decision-making. This approach means establishing procedures whereby the health threat posed by a given industrial pollutant is carefully weighed against the economic cost of limiting or eliminating the offending manufacturer.

MAJOR FEDERAL ENVIRONMENTAL LEGISLATION

National Environmental Policy Act, 1969 Established Environmental Protection Agency; consolidated federal activities under it. Established Council on Environmental Quality to advise President on environmental policy and to review environmental impact statements.

AIR POLLUTION

Clean Air Act, 1963 Authorized assistance to state and local governments in formulating control programs. Authorized limited federal action in correcting specific pollution problems.

Clean Air Act Amendments (Motor Vehicle Air Pollution Control Act), 1965 Authorized federal standards for auto exhaust emission. Standards set for 1968 models and thereafter.

Air Quality Act, 1967 Authorized federal government to establish air quality control regions and to set maximum permissible pollution levels. Required states and localities to carry out approved control programs or else give way to federal controls.

Clean Air Act Amendments, 1970 Authorized EPA to establish nationwide air pollution standards and to limit the discharge of six principal pollutants into the lower atmosphere. Authorized citizens to take legal action to require EPA to implement its standards against undiscovered offenders.

Clean Air Act Amendments, 1977 Postponed auto emission requirements. Required use of scrubbers in new coal-fired power plants. Directed EPA to establish a system to prevent deterioration of air quality in clean areas.

SOLID WASTE POLLUTION

Solid Waste Disposal Act, 1965 Authorized research and assistance to state and local control programs.

Resource Recovery Act, 1970 Subsidized construction of pilot recycling plants; authorized development of nationwide control programs.

Resource Conservation and Recovery Act, 1976 Directed the EPA to regulate hazardous waste management, from generation through disposal.

Surface Mining and Reclamation Act, 1976 Controlled strip mining and restoration of reclaimed land.

WATER POLLUTION

Refuse Act, 1899 Prohibited dumping of debris into navigable waters without a permit. Extended by court decision to industrial discharges.

Federal Water Pollution Control Act, 1956 Authorized grants to states for water pollution control. Gave federal government limited authority to correct specific pollution problems.

Water Quality Act, 1965 Provided for adoption of water quality standards by states, subject to federal approval.

Water Quality Improvement Act, 1970 Provided for federal cleanup of oil spills. Strengthened federal authority over water pollution control.

Federal Water Pollution Control Act Amendments, 1972 Authorized EPA to set water quality and effluent standards; provided for enforcement and research.

Safe Drinking Water Act, 1974 Set standards for drinking water quality.

Clean Water Act, 1977 Ordered control of toxic pollutants by 1984 with best available technology economically feasible.

OTHER POLLUTANTS

Federal Insecticide, Fungicide and Rodenticide Act, 1947 To protect farmers, prohibited fraudulent claims by salespersons. Required registration of poisonous products.

Federal Insecticide, Fungicide and Rodenticide Amendments, 1967, 1972 Provided new authority to license users of pesticides.

Pesticide Control Act, 1972 Required all pesticides shipped in interstate commerce to be certified as effective for their stated purposes and harmless to crops, animal feed, animal life, and humans.

Noise Control Act, 1972 Required EPA to set noise standards for major sources of noise and to advise Federal Aviation Administration on standards for airplane noise.

Federal Environmental Pesticide Control Act Amendments, 1975 Set 1977 deadline (not met) for registration, classification, and licensing of many pesticides.

Toxic Substances Control Act, 1976 Required testing of chemicals; authorized EPA to restrict the use of harmful substances.

Comprehensive Environmental Response, Compensation, and Liability Act, 1980 Commonly called "Superfund Act"; created a trust fund (paid for in part by toxic-chemical manufacturers) to clean up hazardous waste sites.

AIR POLLUTION

The air we breathe is threatened by two forms of pollution—dust particles and gaseous discharges. The EPA estimates that approximately 155 million tons of pollutants spill into the air each year, and each type of pollutant has a different effect. For example, hydrocarbons (gases released when fossil fuels are burned) combine with sunlight under certain atmospheric conditions to produce smog—which burns the eyes, sears the throat, and distresses those who suffer from asthma, bronchitis, and emphysema. Hydrocarbon emissions have been reduced somewhat by the use of catalytic converters on cars.

Acid rain

Gaseous sulfur dioxide, approximately 70 percent of which is discharged from the smokestacks of coal-burning factories and electric utilities, is believed to be one cause of "acid rain." The sulfur dioxide reacts with the air to form acids that can destroy aquatic life and damage crops. Emissions from coal-burning power plants in Midwestern states, in particular, have been blamed for damage to lakes and forests in southeastern Canada and the northeastern United States. The problem has grown more critical since the energy crisis, during which Congress encouraged utilities to burn more coal for electrical power, instead of burning more costly oil and natural gas. In 1984 the EPA was planning to launch more studies of acid rain, raising the budget for research and lake cleanups to $115 million. And there was debate over whether the ratepayers of individual utilities should bear the costs for air cleanup, or whether ratepayers in an entire region—such as all the states east of the Mississippi—should pay a pollution levy to support a scrubber program (a scrubber is a device added to smokestacks to control their emissions).

The greenhouse effect

Burning coal may have a price advantage over burning oil or gas, but it offers no protection against another environmental threat known as the "greenhouse effect." Scientists have long discussed the possibility that carbon dioxide gas, released into the atmosphere by burning fossil fuels, might eventually form a kind of thermal blanket around the earth. This thermal blanket would act like a greenhouse, trapping the sun's heat and preventing the earth's surface from cooling. Dramatic changes in the earth's climate would result, including a general increase in temperature and, perhaps, global flooding if the polar icecaps should melt. No proof is yet available as to when we may be likely to feel this temperature change; nevertheless, the threat of the greenhouse effect may serve as a warning about our capacity for massive environmental disruption.[7]

Airborne carcinogens

An air-pollution problem with more immediate implications is posed by the airborne carcinogens that are emitted by manufacturing processes and breathed by the general public. These toxins, according to environmentalists, are responsible for up to 20,000 cancer deaths each year.[8] The EPA so far has issued definitive standards for controlling four known carcinogens—but many others, including arsenic, benzene, and certain radioactive substances, remain unregulated.

Arsenic emissions were at the center of an important test case for the EPA's new policy of risk assessment. The ASARCO, Inc., copper-smelting plant in Tacoma, Washington, was found to be emitting arsenic at a rate that noticeably increased the risk of lung cancer in nearby residents. In response, the EPA proposed a set of emission controls that would bring the lung cancer risk down to "acceptable" levels. For ASARCO to comply with these standards would cost them $5 million; more likely, however, was the possibility that the plant would simply close down, leaving 575 Tacoma area workers out of jobs. The EPA launched an extensive campaign to inform Tacoma citizens about both sides of the issue, and it held a series of hearings to ascertain public opinion. ASARCO has begun to spend $5 million to erect huge exhaust hoods to reduce arsenic-related cancer deaths in the area, in compliance with the EPA's tentative proposal. But the EPA could order the company to cut emissions further in an attempt to eliminate all such deaths—a proposal that ASARCO officials say would cost more than

$100 million to put into effect. At this point, EPA chief Ruckelshaus must make the final decision on whether or not to go ahead with the more stringent standards.[9]

WATER POLLUTION

The basis for the EPA's water-pollution control activity is the Clean Water Act of 1972. Only about 30 percent of all municipal sewage systems have complied with EPA requirements, mostly because they lack the funds to do so. Because taxpayers have been increasingly resistant to financing large capital improvements such as sewage-treatment plants, it is unlikely that the EPA's optimistic goal of zero polluting discharges by 1985 will be met. In 1983, the EPA proposed new clean-water rules aimed at chemicals and plastics manufacturers, who are the leading dischargers of toxic wastes into the nation's waterways. The proposed rules, scheduled to go into effect in 1984, would require manufacturers to install pollution-control equipment capable of treating waste waters before they are dumped into public sewers.

Industrial toxic wastes remain one of the foremost threats to our fresh water supply, because they can leak into the ground water. And even if all waste-water discharge were eliminated, our ground water would still be endangered by leakage from the millions of tons of hazardous substances that have been buried in the ground or dumped in inadequate storage sites. (Toxic waste disposal will be discussed in greater detail in the next section.) Already, several hundred cases of ground-water pollution have been reported, and ground-water pollution will certainly be the EPA's primary clean-water concern for years to come.[10] Other ground-water problems include pollution by fertilizers and other agricultural wastes, and the spendthrift use of water, which has dangerously lowered water-table heights in some areas.

LAND POLLUTION: TOXIC WASTES

The disposal of industrial toxic wastes is probably the single greatest environmental threat facing America today. Times Beach, Missouri, was a partic-ularly dramatic example of the possible dangers of toxic wastes, but it was by no means an isolated case: in fact, soil samples at twenty-five other sites in Missouri alone have shown dioxin levels well above EPA safety standards.[11] Recent studies indicate that American industry produces some 450 million metric tons of hazardous wastes each year. And a large portion—some estimates reach as high as 90 percent—of these wastes are disposed of unsafely.

For years, most wastes were routinely dumped in landfills, whose protective barriers (if any) could not be counted on to prevent dangerous chemicals from leaking into the soil and, eventually, into the water supply. Thus far, industry has not been totally cooperative with the EPA in cleaning up dump sites that already exist; one reason has been the difficulty in keeping up with the EPA's shifting policies. Industry has, however, begun to take steps to reduce future hazardous waste contamination. More companies are now treating their wastes to limit toxicity before sending them to public dumps, or else they are dumping in their own controlled and environmentally sound sites. And fewer companies are leaving their wastes to independent disposal firms, which are notorious for illegal dumping. In addition, manufacturers are trying out several other methods of eliminating or neutralizing their hazardous by-products. Some use high-temperature incineration, some recycle wastes, some give their wastes to other companies that can use them (getting wastes *they* can use in return), some neutralize wastes biologically, and some have redesigned their manufacturing processes so as not to produce the wastes in the first place.

OTHER ENVIRONMENTAL PROBLEMS

There are a number of other pressing business-related environmental problems, including three that have gained special prominence in recent years: radioactive wastes, occupational hazards, and wilderness preservation.

Radioactive wastes

Radioactive wastes actually cover a number of separate but related problems. There is a danger of air-

A

B

C

D

Environmental pollution: ugly and unhealthy. In some of its forms, pollution may be causing permanent damage to the biosphere—that part of our planet that is capable of supporting life. (A) noise pollution: a Chinese Airlines passenger jet revs up for takeoff; (B) water pollution: waste chemicals leak into the Norwalk River in Connecticut; (C) air pollution: black smoke from a sugar beet processing plant near Clarksburg, California; (D) toxic waste pollution: at a factory near Phoenixville, Pennsylvania, a technician in protective garb gathers samples for testing.

borne radiation in plants such as uranium mills. In addition, low-level radiation is emitted by the by-products of science laboratories and hospitals engaged in nuclear medicine. At present, only three commercial burial dump sites in America are equipped to handle low-level nuclear wastes, and a major crisis nearly occurred when two of them temporarily shut down in 1979. Congress then passed legislation requiring the states to band together to create several new regional dumps by 1986. Few states, however, have been willing to play host to such facilities, and as they squabble over location sites, it seems unlikely that the congressional deadline will be met.[12]

Another radiation pollution problem involves the deadly high-level residue from the nation's seventy-nine nuclear power generators. Up to now, the plants themselves have been storing these radiated wastes, but they will run out of room within the next few years. Congress has set a long-term timetable for the Department of Energy to construct permanent storage facilities in caverns thousands of feet underground. Meanwhile, a temporary facility is planned, but once again, the chief obstacle will be finding a suitable site. Strong opposition can be expected from environmentalists and from the residents in whatever communities are chosen. Chances are that negotiations over site selection and payment may add even more time and money onto a project that was already scheduled to take twenty years and cost $15 billion.[13]

Occupational hazards

In the years following World War II, when many of America's chemical manufacturers were enjoying major growth spurts, their workers were routinely exposed to substances whose toxic properties have only recently been recognized. No one suspected the hazards of dioxin, for example, until Dow Chemical employees broke out in chloracne, a severe skin disease. Whether or not dioxin also causes cancer may not be decided for years to come; the effects of certain carcinogens can take decades before they show themselves.

Asbestos is one substance whose dangers are now well known. Commonly used as insulation and fire protection in houses and buildings, asbestos fibers, when inhaled, can cause cancer and lung diseases.[14] The hazards are such that the U.S. Department of Labor's Occupational Safety and Health Administration (OSHA) has issued an emergency notice to protect the 375,000 workers in several industries who are regularly exposed to asbestos.[15]

Wilderness preservation

Wilderness preservation became a hotly debated topic under the Reagan administration's first Secretary of the Interior, James Watt. Watt favored opening up protected government-owned lands to coal mining, and using large segments of undeveloped coastline for petroleum drilling. Along with the many industrialists who supported him, Watt viewed these rich regions as a potential solution to the country's energy problems and its dependence on foreign oil. Most of Watt's land-use proposals were defeated in Congress. But the question his policies raised remains: much as we value our wilderness areas, how do we weigh their intangible worth against our real needs for natural resources in an economic crisis? This may be one of the most difficult environmental decisions we will have to make in the years ahead.

BUSINESS AND THE CONSUMER

One of the earliest consumer-oriented exposés of shoddy business practices was Upton Sinclair's book about the meat-packing industry, *The Jungle,* published in 1906.[16] When the modern-day consumer protection movement emerged more than a half-century later, in the 1960s, another book, Ralph Nader's *Unsafe at Any Speed,* led the advance.[17] Nader shocked the American public with his scathing attack on General Motors and, in particular, the dangerously designed Chevrolet Corvair. Following Nader's lead, other exposés revealed that many other companies were marketing poorly designed, unsafe, or unhealthful products. In response to the consumer movement, a number of businesses created their own consumer-affairs departments to handle customer complaints, while state and local agencies set up bureaus to provide consumer infor-

AN UNFORGETTABLE DRIVING EXPERIENCE

The consumer protection movement has had an impact on the auto industry. Today, the fellow who's been stuck with a lemon may not necessarily be a loser—if he lives in one of the twenty or so states that have passed "lemon laws." Connecticut's 1982 law was the first, and most others are similar. They generally entitle a dissatisfied buyer to a refund or a replacement from the auto maker under certain conditions (for example, if a major problem persists even after four repair attempts, or if the car is out of service for at least thirty days during the first year).

Health and safety remain important concerns, but the key current issues involve basic economics. Citizens in various parts of the country have banded together to fight the deregulation of natural gas prices and the expected rise in telephone rates that may follow from the breakup of AT&T. The Telecommunications Research and Action Center in Washington, D.C., is coordinating national protests against higher phone bills, while the Citizen/Labor Energy Coalition is organizing community, church, labor, farm, and senior citizens' groups against natural gas decontrol. Fair Share, a consumer organization in Massachusetts, holds regular town meetings that the governor of the state attends. This group has been so persuasive that now many of the gas companies in Massachusetts have come out against deregulation.[18]

Members of Congress, too, can be swayed by a movement of this size and intensity. Many analysts feel that the rising tide of consumerism played a part in Congress's 1982 approval of Federal Trade Commission (FTC) regulation of the funeral industry. Similarly, in 1983 Congress refused to enact legislation, desired by the powerful American Medical Association, that would prevent the FTC from regulating the practice of medicine within the provisions of the FTC Act. Congressional investigations into consumer complaints have also increased in the latter part of Reagan's term in office.

mation and assistance. In 1972, the **Consumer Product Safety Commission** was created *to monitor the safety of products sold to consumers,* excluding automobiles, drugs, foods, medical devices, and a few other items already monitored by other agencies. (The table on the next page lists major federal consumer legislation.) But attempts to create a federal agency that could intervene on the consumer's behalf have failed repeatedly, mainly because of strong opposition from business.

After its heyday in the late 1960s and early 1970s, the consumer movement seemed to lose momentum for several years. But it has revived in the 1980s to protest the Reagan administration's program of rolling back government restraints on business. And this revival seems to have broader-based popular support than did the consumer activist groups that led the movement a decade ago.

BUSINESS AND WORKERS: THE PROBLEM OF MINORITY DISCRIMINATION

So far we've talked about the responsibilities of business in connection with issues that concern all Americans—protecting the environment and responding to the needs of consumers. But what about the responsibility businesses bear specifically to the people who work for them? This is a topic that we'll highlight in several of our later chapters. In Chapter 8 we'll discuss health insurance plans, pensions, and safety measures that businesses set up for their workers. In Component Chapter C we'll survey management efforts to make workers' jobs more satisfying. And in Chapter 7 we'll see how unions and

MAJOR FEDERAL CONSUMER LEGISLATION

FOOD AND DRUG

Pure Food and Drug Law, 1906 Forbade adulteration and misbranding of food/drugs in interstate commerce.

Meat Inspection Act, 1907 Authorized Dept. of Agriculture to inspect slaughtering, packing, and canning plants.

Federal Food, Drug, and Cosmetic Act, 1938 Added cosmetics and therapeutic products to FDA's jurisdiction. Broadened definition of misbranding to include "false and misleading" labeling.

Delaney Amendment to the Food, Drug, and Cosmetic Act, 1958 Prohibited use as food additive of any chemical found to induce cancer.

Kefauver-Harris Drug Amendments to Food and Drug Act, 1962 Required manufacturer to test safety and effectiveness of drugs before marketing and to include common or generic name of drug on label.

Wholesome Meat Act, 1967 Strengthened standards for inspection of slaughterhouses of red meat animals.

PROTECTION AGAINST MISBRANDING AND FALSE OR HARMFUL ADVERTISING

Wheeler-Lea Act, 1938 Enlarged Federal Trade Commission's powers to cover deceptive practices in commerce, and false advertising of foods, drugs, cosmetics.

Wool Products Labeling Act, 1939 Required fabric labeling, percent of fabric components, manufacturer's name.

Fur Products Labeling Act, 1951 Required that fur labels name animals of origin.

Textile Fiber Products Identification Act, 1958 Prohibited misbranding and false advertising of fiber products not covered in the Wool or Fur Labeling Acts.

Federal Hazardous Substances Labeling Act, 1960 Required warning labels to appear on items containing dangerous household chemicals.

Fair Packaging and Labeling Act, 1966 Required honest, informative package labeling. FTC, in 1972, required that labels show: origin of product, quantity of contents, representation of servings, uses, and/or applications.

Public Health Cigarette Smoking Act, 1970 Banned cigarette advertising on radio and TV; strengthened required warning on packaging.

PRODUCT SAFETY

Flammable Fabrics Act, 1953 Prohibited interstate shipment of apparel or fabric made of dangerously flammable materials.

Traffic and Motor Vehicle Safety Act, 1966 Required manufacturers to notify purchasers of new cars of safety defects discovered after manufacture and delivery.

Child Protection and Toy Safety Act, 1969 Provided greater protection from children's toys with dangerous mechanical or electrical hazards.

Poison Prevention Packaging Act, 1970 Required manufacturers to use safety packaging on products that may be harmful to children.

Consumer Product Safety Act, 1972 Created Consumer Product Safety Commission, an independent federal agency. CPSC is empowered to set safety standards for certain products, such as power lawnmowers and children's toys; to require warning labels on unsafe products; and to order recalls of hazardous products.

CREDIT PROTECTION

Truth-in-Lending Act (Consumer Protection Credit Act), 1968 Required creditors to inform individuals obtaining credit of the amount of the financing charge and the percentage rate of interest charged annually. Limited credit cardholders' liability in unauthorized use.

Fair Credit Reporting Act, 1970 Required agencies reporting consumer credit data to follow procedures assuring accuracy of their information. Required users of this information, upon withholding credit, to inform consumer of source of this information.

Magnuson-Moss Warranty Act, 1975 Required all warranties to be written in ordinary language, contain all terms and conditions of the warranty and be made available prior to purchase to facilitate comparison shopping.

Fair Debt Collection Practices Act, 1978 Prohibited deceptive and unfair debt collection practices: calling at inconvenient or unusual times; harassing, oppressing or abusing any person; making false statements when collecting debts.

Home Mortgage Disclosure Act, 1975 Required banks and savings and loan associations to compile and make public information on mortgage loans that they make and the locations of those loans.

management negotiate to establish wages, working hours, and workplace conditions. Here we will take up the important problem of job discrimination against minorities.

WHAT ARE MINORITIES?

In a sociological sense, a **minority** is a *category of people that society at large singles out for discriminatory, or selective, unfavorable treatment.* Historically, blacks have perhaps suffered the most severe discrimination: it was not until World War I that blacks in large numbers worked next to whites in factory assembly lines. Because they were the last to be hired, they were often the first to be fired under the seniority-protection rules that prevailed in most businesses. But many Spanish-surnamed Americans have also been assigned to low-paying, menial jobs, as have many women. (Women are actually a *majority* numerically speaking, but they are a *minority* in the sense that they have suffered discrimination.) Job discrimination against minorities has been a "vicious cycle." Because they could not hope for better jobs, many minority-group members have had little incentive to seek education. And because they have not had an adequate education, many have not been able to qualify for those jobs that have been available to them.

WHAT IS BEING DONE TO IMPROVE JOB OPPORTUNITIES FOR MINORITIES?

Discrimination runs counter to our American ideal of equal opportunity for all citizens. So when blacks, women, Spanish-speaking people, and other minorities have presented demands for fair treatment, they have found many sectors of American society willing to move toward change.

Government action

The keystone of the nation's commitment to equal opportunity for all Americans is the **Civil Rights Act of 1964,** which *forbids discrimination in employment.* The act established an **Equal Employment Opportunities Commission (EEOC),** *a government organization whose goal is to counter job discrimination.*

Its aim is to help bring minority-group members into the mainstream of the American economy. The EEOC investigates complaints of job-related discrimination and files legal charges against discriminatory companies. Sometimes the settlements include back-pay awards for individuals or groups victimized by unfair practices and plans for future hiring and promotion practices. In recent years, the EEOC's enforcement policies have been eased, in keeping with the governmental trend toward loosening restrictions on business.

Another important piece of antidiscrimination legislation is the **Equal Pay Act of 1963,** which *requires that all workers performing the same job must be paid at the same rate.* This act was especially beneficial to women, many of whom have long earned less than men who did similar work.

Business's response

The 1964 Civil Rights Act imposed on business the primary responsibility for ending patterns of job discrimination. So did a federal executive order that was binding on companies doing business with the government, a group that includes most major firms. Recognizing that patterns of bias were too deeply embedded to be combated merely by pledges of future change, the government required businesses to set up **affirmative action** programs to *actively recruit members of minority groups and train them for jobs, based on some demonstration of availability.*

In carrying out affirmative action plans, businesses walk a tightrope. On the one hand, they must make visible progress toward providing genuine equal career opportunities. On the other hand, they must not establish **quotas,** *fixed numbers of minority members to be hired*—except where previous discrimination has been proven. Recent court decisions have ruled that quotas discriminate against others who are new to the job market, and that they are thus unconstitutional. Indeed, the basic principles of affirmative action (or "reverse discrimination," as opponents have labeled it) have touched off a variety of legal challenges all over the country. Until a definitive policy is established, the future course of government-mandated equal-opportunity programs remains uncertain. As it is, some of the gains in minority employment brought about by affirmative action in the 1960s and 1970s have been under-

FIGURE 2

LOW INCOME, HIGH UNEMPLOYMENT:
Minority disadvantage means social costs

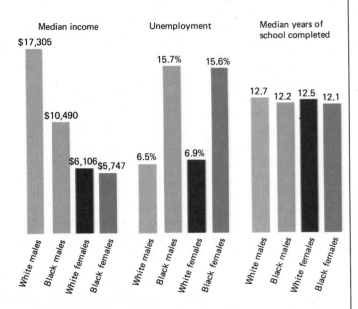

Our society has changed in recent years, but minorities are still at a significant disadvantage, particularly in tough times when the government cuts back job and training programs and the "last hired" are frequently the "first fired." There's no quick fix for minority problems, but forward-looking businesses are joining the search for long-term solutions.

cut by the widespread job layoffs accompanying the economic changes of the 1980s. Black workers hired under affirmative action often have less seniority on their jobs than their white counterparts; as a result, when layoffs occur, the minority workers have been the first to go in some cases.

While the courts alternately defend and chip away at affirmative action, a new concept in minority employment has been gathering momentum. This is the concept of "comparable worth": parity in pay scales for all workers whose jobs require equally demanding training and skills. Comparable worth, as a doctrine, grew out of the failure of the Equal Pay Act of 1963 to fully close the gap between what the average male worker is paid and what the average working woman receives. According to law, men and women at the same job had to be paid equally; but this did not alter the fact that most women work in traditionally low-paying jobs, such as secretary,

nurse, and grade-school teacher. According to the doctrine of comparable worth, women in these jobs should receive the same level of pay that men in equally demanding, but more lucrative, fields receive. (A common comparison is between a low-paid nurse and a higher-paid sanitation worker.)

In October 1983, a legal precedent for comparable worth was established when a federal judge in Tacoma, Washington, ruled that the state of Washington was guilty of discriminating against its female employees. If this ruling stands, it will be a major victory for the feminist movement and a watershed case in the struggle for equal employment opportunities for women. Opponents argue, however, that the comparable worth concept cannot be enforced without disrupting the nation's entire employment system and, in the process, forcing some industries into bankruptcy. They also question whether anyone can weigh the skills and demands of different jobs on the same scale.

THE CORPORATION IN SOCIETY

Despite the pressures of the rapidly changing business environment, many businesses continue making efforts to be responsive to the needs of the larger society. One indicator of new business attitudes is the growing number of companies submitting themselves to voluntary **environmental audits.** These audits are thorough *investigations of a firm's pollution, waste management, and worker safety situations, performed on a contract basis by outside specialists, or internally by teams of trained company employees.* The auditors use the latest laboratory technology, capable of identifying hazardous substances in minute quantities, and they often submit the companies to more stringent investigation than the EPA, OSHA, and state investigators do. In fact, environmental audits are in such demand that the companies who specialize in these studies are now viewed as a booming industry. Client companies hire these auditing firms not only to analyze their own pollution problems, but also to check up on other firms they may be interested in acquiring.[19]

How will businesses cope with social responsibility issues in the future? According to management expert John Diebold, it is likely that more corporations will build noneconomic goals—such as product safety, occupational health, and equal employment—into their planning processes by 1990. Chief corporate executives will spend even more time dealing with external relations than they do now. They will solicit more input from shareholders and customers, and work more closely with the government to push for rules and legislation that will be beneficial to business *and* the community.[20]

Other observers have asked, however, whether it is truly desirable to allow corporations, rather than the government, to set social policy. Corporations, after all, are private organizations, not accountable to the public; the government is composed, at least in part, of elected officials whom the public can remove from office. Some critics also question whether business should not be left alone to do what it does best—make profits—without having its efforts diluted by the sometimes-conflicting claims of more socially oriented goals. Each of us must form his or her own opinion about these issues. More evidence, concerning both sides of the argument, will emerge in the chapters that follow.

CHAPTER REVIEW

At present, the American economy is in the middle of a basic transition from goods- to service-based business. The reasons for this include the energy crisis, overseas competition in the manufacturing sector, and "high-tech" innovations. Now, the old smokestack industries exist side by side with the new high-tech enterprises. All this rapid change is being fueled by the "information revolution"—that is, the use of computers—making it possible to eliminate both people and paperwork from many processes and transactions.

Since business plays such a central role in our everyday lives, our society, and our environment, business also has certain social responsibilities. Unfortunately, these often conflict with the profit motive, which business sees as its guiding force.

Business is broadly defined as all the work involved in providing people with goods and services for a profit. The belief that the owner of a business is entitled to keep whatever profits the business generates is fundamental to the American economic system.

In theory, American business is part of a free-market system, in which the seller of a product or service is free to charge any price for it and to sell it to anyone willing to pay that price. In practice, however, our system is modified by two forces—competition and supply and demand. Increased competition generally encourages low prices, efficiency, quality, and variety. The theory of supply and demand holds that the supply of a product tends to increase when consumer demand is high and to decrease when demand is low. Free enterprise is also limited by the government, which taxes profits, and by the existence of monopolies and oligopolies, which limit competition. Since the late 1970s, there has been a growing trend toward deregulation, which greatly increases competition.

In recent years, business has begun to play a more active role in attacking three major areas of social concern: environmental protection, consumer protection, and the equal treatment of minorities. Public concern about the effects of water, air, and land pollution has spurred government and business to try to dispose of wastes properly and to clean up polluted areas. In spite of some progress, many problems remain. These include the greater number and wider dispersal of pollutants as well as their effects on public health. The consumer movement has also led to the development of products that are safer and better value. However, the Reagan administration has tended to support industry's side in these issues.

There has also been progress toward reducing economic discrimination against minorities and women: federal laws and regulations have resulted in increased efforts by business to broaden hiring and promotion opportunities. A new concept in the struggle for fair employment—comparable worth—demands pay parity for all workers whose jobs require similar training and skills.

Businesses are increasingly trying to respond to society's needs—for example, by making environmental audits and by recognizing non-economic goals such as product safety, occupational health, and equal employment.

KEY WORDS

Page numbers follow key words.

REVIEW QUESTIONS

1. Explain "the change from goods- to service-oriented business." What does it involve? Why is it happening?

2. What is the "information revolution"? List several ways in which it is altering procedures in business and industry.

3. What is business and what activities does it involve?

4. Define profit. Why is profit fundamental to American business?

5. What is a free-market system? Name the two forces that dominate its operation and explain how these forces work.

6. Explain why our free-market system is not completely free. Give examples to support your answer.

7. List and give examples of three types of pollution. What has been done to protect the environment from the dangers of pollution? What remains to be done?

8. Keeping in mind the importance of competition in our economic system, in what way do you think the consumer movement might actually benefit business?

9. Sociologically speaking, what is a minority? In what ways is business legally accountable for helping to achieve equal opportunity?

CASE 1

FOR SALE: INSURANCE, AND THE GRAND OLE OPRY

Most businesses recognize that they are part of a larger community, and make charitable contributions toward the welfare of that community. Frequently, cultural activities and the arts are recipients of such funding. You've probably seen a music or dance performance on public television and been informed that it was sponsored by some corporation or another.

But you probably weren't aware that Tennessee's Grand Ole Opry, home of country music, was owned and nurtured by a corporation—the National Life and Accident Insurance Company of Nashville. In 1982, National Life was bought out by American General Corporation of Houston, and the new owner decided to put the Opry up for sale. The Opry could bring in an estimated $200 to $300 million, and would go far in reducing the huge debt American General had incurred to buy National Life.

The story of the Opry is an interesting one. The Opry began in 1925, when National Life started broadcasting a barn dance live. Since the 1960s, the popularity of country music has grown steadily, and with it the renown of the Opry—the "mother church of country music," as one of its stars, Tom T. Hall, calls it. Today, the broadcast goes out to thirty-four states, and the barn has grown into a complex of facilities known as "Opryland USA." The industries that have sprouted up around it—200 music publishing houses and dozens of recording studios—are the mainstay of Nashville's economy.

The Opry never earned much money for National Life, for the company always stressed quality over profit. But rarely has corporate sponsorship of the arts reaped such goodwill benefits to the sponsoring company. National Life salesmen would knock on doors saying "I'm with the Grand Ole Opry, and I want to sell you insurance." This beginning earned them a warmer welcome in the home of country-music fans than could any advertising ploy. The relationship between National Life and the country-music world was captured by Minnie Pearl's comment, "They were my family."

Tennesseans and country-music pilgrims alike are reluctant to see the Opry come under the knife of bottom-line-oriented management. The *Nashville Tennessean* newspaper expressed the fear that a new owner might "milk the facility for exorbitant profits," and spoke of potential "ripoffs and exploita-tion." To preserve the Opry's character, Opry fans, through the governor of Tennessee, are pressing American General to sell only to local interests. One offer was made by ten Tennesseans, but it failed to go through. First Boston, the investment bank that is handling the sale, has received many other offers, but most of them aren't local.[21]

1. In this story there are a number of different parties, each of whom is faced with a problem. What is the problem that faces American General? What is the problem facing residents of Nashville and fans of the Opry? What is the problem that faces First Boston?

2. What alternative actions have been tried by each of these parties? What other alternatives are open to each party?

3. Think about the situation a little more. Families strive to stay together; they do not define their relationships according to the shifting winds of profitability. But companies exist to make a profit. More important, companies can be bought and sold. Do you believe that a corporation is responsible for continuing the community relationships it has built, into the far future?

4. If you were a shareholder in American General (let's say, someone who didn't happen to like country music), would you feel that your company was responsible for subsidizing the "mother church of country music"?

5. How would you feel if you were the public relations manager of American General?

6. Construct a solution: think up a plan of action that American General could take, that would help enable American General to reduce its debt but would at the same time help to keep the Opry a going concern.

CASE 2

SANTA BARBARA VS. THE OIL INDUSTRY

Santa Barbara—it's like a Technicolor movie. The camera pans from the sparkling Pacific to the shore, glancing rapidly at an old Spanish mission, tropical greenery, resort hotels, and elegant homes nestled in the foothills. Sweeping back toward the shore, the camera encounters tanned vacationers basking on the sand and frolicking in the water. But wait! What are those futuristic towers spoiling the view on the horizon? They are oil rigs, and Santa Barbara is certainly not happy about them.

This is the general scenario—a natural treasure is being threatened by the discovery and exploitation of a valuable natural resource. Actually, companies have been drilling for oil near Santa Barbara for decades, but in October 1982 they struck it big— somewhere between 300 million and 1 billion barrels—in a field known as the Santa Maria Basin some 3 miles offshore. Now, at least fifteen companies are rushing to get in on the action, and the number of oil rigs has boomed.

These companies don't take their investments lightly. One of the largest is Standard Oil Company of California (Socal). Together with its partner, Phillips Petroleum Company, Socal has paid the government $333 million to lease a tract measuring 9 square miles—in fact, the largest lease in the world. On top of that, the partners are spending about $1 million a day on the drilling. They go to incredible lengths to keep their discoveries secret, and their competitors spare no effort in spying, by boat and by helicopter, for clues that might reveal the best drilling sites and depths. Meanwhile, Santa Barbara becomes less and less like paradise.

Some people might say, "We all appreciate natural beauty, but oil is a necessity—our economy depends on it. Besides, it's not an either/or proposition. You can bring in the oil and still preserve the environment." Socal, for one, has installed the most up-to-date and costliest safeguards into its rigs to prevent blowouts, and there's even an organization supported by all the drillers, called Operation Clean Seas, which stands by to deal with any possible spills. But the situation is not a simple one. Here are some of the complications:

■ Current production from the Santa Maria Basin is being hauled by tankers, and there is talk of building a pipeline. A serious spill is more likely to come from either of these than from a rig.

■ Cleaning up an oil spill is more or less feasible when it happens in shallow water near sandy beaches. But rough, open seas make clean-ups impossible, and if oil were to spill onto a rocky coast, like the one north of Santa Barbara, it would stay there.

■ Even without oil spills, the activity of the rigs, tankers, and other equipment is already disrupting the environment and the habitats of regional wildlife, including sea lions, sea otters, and whales.

Thus far we have Santa Barbara's concerns for its natural beauty, ecology, and tourist business pitted against the interests of the oil companies and "business" in general. The situation becomes more complex when we bring in the state, which, like most of us, is apparently having some money trouble. Through the sale of leases on state-owned drilling sites near Santa Barbara, California's governor hopes to revive the health of his treasury. He faces only one major hurdle—the review of his plan by the California Coastal Commission, an independent agency that has served as governmental watchdog over offshore drilling activities. The governor hopes to deal with this commission by, in effect, wiping it out and transferring its authority to his own office.

The upshot is that Santa Barbara County, which opposes the governor, has filed suit to halt the state's sale of leases, claiming that the environmental threat has not been sufficiently explored. Santa Barbara County hopes at least to slow development down. In addition, the city of Santa Barbara has joined other coastal cities in the Channel Islands Alliance, which is dedicated to fighting the governor's plan. Their battle may be made more difficult by a recent Supreme Court ruling, which holds that the federal government need not consider the objections of affected states when the Department of the Interior offers oil- or gas-drilling leases on the continental shelf. There is one bright note for the environmentalists, however: Shortly after his appointment in November 1983, William Clark, who replaced James Watt as Secretary of the Interior, indefinitely postponed two oil-lease sales. This move may signal a positive change in administration policies toward environmental concerns.[22]

1. Once California's oil is used up, as it eventually will be, the damage will have been done and there will still be shortages. Develop an argument for doing away with the drilling entirely. Consider the implications for the country's economic system, energy sources, and lifestyle.

2. What might the oil companies have to say against the plan you have suggested? What would be their best arguments? Do they have a legitimate obligation to their investors?

3. "The people who boost environmentalism are already rich, as a rule. They can afford to be generous—because they don't have to worry about finding jobs, or about supporting industries that can create new opportunities." Is there something to be said for this viewpoint? Consider the pros and cons.

4. Do you think the governor has an obligation to make use of the state's resources? He might claim, for example, that California's well-known and excellent state-supported colleges cost a great deal, as do other state programs, such as aid to dependent children. Weigh the issues from this angle.

FORMS OF BUSINESS ORGANIZATION 2

You are a young research chemist who has just developed a promising "gene machine"—a device that manufactures DNA, the living raw material for all biotechnology. You've set up shop in your garage, and you now need more lab space, more materials, and more money to launch your new business. As a businessperson, you now have several options. You can continue to go it alone, enlarging your business but still running it yourself. You can take on a partner—perhaps someone whose skills in marketing or finance complement your scientific expertise. Or you can turn yourself into a small corporation, raising capital by selling stock in your enterprise.

The entrepreneur faced with such a decision needs to know something about all three of these forms of business organization: how to set them up legally and what their advantages are. (And these three forms are not the only possibilities, as we shall see: for example, our entrepreneur might also decide to join with another company in an arrangement known as a joint venture.) Whatever structure is ultimately chosen, the decision will have important consequences for the new business. In this chapter, we'll look at all the major forms of business organization—and some of the tough questions a businessperson faces in choosing among them.

CHAPTER FOCUS

After reading the material in this chapter, you will be able to:
- distinguish the three basic forms of business organization
- list the advantages and disadvantages of those three forms
- define and give examples of seven types of corporation
- describe how corporations are organized and at least two means of challenging that organization
- distinguish vertical, horizontal, and conglomerate mergers
- list five other forms of business organization, and state at least one advantage of each

On January 8, 1982, American Telephone and Telegraph astonished the world's business community when it made a deal with the Department of Justice, approved by the courts, for a reorganization of the company. AT&T, known affectionately as "Ma Bell," had been the largest publicly held corporation in America, with 3.2 million stockholders, 1 million employees and $152 billion in assets; it supplied 80 percent of America's 182 million telephone subscribers with every related service and product. Now, in the largest antitrust suit in history, it was being asked to reduce itself to a smaller version—while creating from itself seven independent companies charged with handling the nation's local telephone services. Opponents of the breakup feared it would raise local phone costs, which Ma Bell had subsidized with profits from long-distance service, and that it would cause telephone service to suffer. "We're going to be sorry that we tampered with a system that was functioning well," said Senator Barry Goldwater, normally a supporter of deregulation and competitive markets.[1] But others hoped the breakup would help lower long-distance costs and free the new, leaner AT&T to break into the tempting computer and telecommunications markets. The breakup went into effect on January 1, 1984. The eventual outcome? As of this writing, it was still too early to tell, but there would surely be profound changes in this mammoth corporation.

- What exactly is a corporation, and what do we mean when we say that the old AT&T had 3.2 million stockholders?

- How is this way of structuring a business different from the *sole proprietorship* and the *partnership,* the two other forms of business organization that are most commonly seen in this country?

- Why might a woman with a small computer software business, for example, start her enterprise as a sole proprietorship, and why might she eventually find it wise to switch to the corporate form?

- Why might two recent business-school graduates decide that partnership is the best format for their new advertising and public relations agency?

These are the types of questions we will explore in this chapter. As we'll see, each of these three basic forms of business organization has key advantages and disadvantages, and offers its employees a distinct working environment with its own risks and rewards. Each represents a different approach to business in terms of internal structure, legal status, average size, and fields to which it is best suited.

SOLE PROPRIETORSHIPS

In Washington, D.C., a successful attorney and management consultant gave up a secure career to open a supermarket, of all things, in the inner-city area. Why? Because Roy Littlejohn thought he could operate a profitable business and perform a social service at the same time. And he seems to have succeeded where the chain supermarkets failed. He did it by rehabilitating a site that he already owned and turning it into a so-called "box store," a no-frills, limited-assortment supermarket where customers serve themselves directly from the shipping cartons and bag their own groceries. As a former attorney for the U.S. Civil Rights Commission and one-time executive director of a Model Inner City Community program, Littlejohn had some knowledge of the area he would be serving before he opened his doors for business. He knew, for instance, that the high cost of delivering food to the center city had driven many chain supermarkets to the more accessible suburbs, because the higher costs whittled away their already low profit margins. He also knew that the poor residents of the inner city liked to feel that they were getting the best, and they would put up with limited hours and services in order to get nationally branded products at bargain prices. With this information plus $60,000 and advice sought from consultants who knew the grocery business, Littlejohn set up his first store. After only a few months' operation, the store was taking in $20,000 a week, which was well above the estimated breakeven point of $12,000 to $15,000. By keeping labor costs at a minimum, Littlejohn has managed to squeeze out an impressive 2 to 3 percent profit on sales, compared with the average supermarket profit of a little less than 1.5 percent. Is it worth the effort? Apparently it is: Littlejohn expected to open at least three more box stores before long.[2]

Roy Littlejohn is just one of the hundreds of thousands of Americans who each year embark on new business ventures. Like most new businesses, his enterprise is of the type known as the **sole proprietorship**—*a business owned by just one person*. Associated closely with the ideals of individual initiative, self-reliance, and hard work, the sole proprietorship has a special place in American history and tradition. It also has the practical advantage of being the easiest form of business to start with limited funds. In essence, all you have to do is start selling your goods or services, and you are a business. It is no surprise, then, that the sole proprietorship is the most common type of business in the United States—accounting for nearly 76 percent of the country's 16.2 million business enterprises in the government's most recent survey.[3] (Figure 1 shows the number of businesses in each organizational category, along with their respective profits.) The lines of business in which the sole proprietorship is often the chosen form are agriculture, retailing, and services, both professional—legal, medical, accounting—and manual—laundries and repair shops.

ADVANTAGES OF SOLE PROPRIETORSHIP

The sole proprietorship has a number of advantages.

EASE OF ESTABLISHMENT The first and most concrete advantage, as we have said, is that it is relatively easy to establish. The financial investment need not be large, and there's far less legal red tape to deal with than in other forms of business.

INDEPENDENCE Perhaps most important, though, is the emotional factor: sole proprietors have the satisfaction of working for themselves. Making their own decisions and seeing the results of their efforts, they are spared the all-too-common sensation of being a small cog in a much larger organization. And, of course, since they get all the profits—assuming there *are* profits—they know exactly how well they're doing. It is for the sake of such personal rewards that many corporate executives abandon secure, high-salaried jobs to start their own businesses.

FLEXIBILITY Another major advantage of the sole proprietorship is flexibility of organization and management. Proprietors can decide for themselves what hours to work, whom to hire, what prices to charge, whether to expand, and whether to shut down. If small enough, the business may not have to deal with unions, equal employment opportunity agencies, or minimum wage regulations. Sole proprietors can make all the major decisions without consulting anyone.

SECRECY A parallel advantage to flexibility is secrecy. Sole proprietors never have to reveal their plans or intentions to anyone else. Their financial data may also remain strictly confidential (except to the Inter-

FIGURE 1

THE THREE MAIN TYPES OF BUSINESS:
How many are there? How much money do they make?

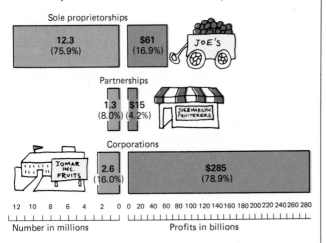

Sole proprietorships
12.3 (75.9%) $61 (16.9%)   JOE'S

Partnerships
1.3 (8.0%) $15 (4.2%)   JOE&MARILYN FRUITERERS

Corporations
JOMAR INC. FRUITS   2.6 (16.0%) $285 (78.9%)

12 10 8 6 4 2 0   0 20 40 60 80 100 120 140 160 180 200 220 240 260 280
Number in millions   Profits in billions

As you can see, sole proprietorships are the most common type of business in the United States, accounting for more than three of every four enterprises. However, less than one in every four dollars of profit earned by American business comes from sole proprietorships. Which type of business appears to be the most successful in terms of money earned?

nal Revenue Service). They are far less vulnerable than other businesses to spying from competitors.

TAX ADVANTAGES Furthermore, small sole proprietorships have the theoretical advantage of tax savings, since proprietors pay taxes only on the personal income they earn from their businesses. And as the business grows and becomes more profitable, the owner has the option of incorporating to obtain other kinds of tax advantages without giving up ownership.

Finally, self-employed people are permitted to set up so-called Keogh accounts, in which they can bank some of their earnings for their own pensions. They do not have to pay income tax on that money until they begin to draw on that money for income—at which time they will probably be in a much lower tax bracket. Meanwhile, the interest they earn is compounded tax-free.

DISADVANTAGES OF SOLE PROPRIETORSHIP

There are some disadvantages in choosing the sole proprietorship.

LIMITED POTENTIAL FOR PROFITABILITY Most businesses owned by one person tend to be small, and their profitability is limited. In a recent government estimate, about 71 percent of all sole proprietorships grossed less than $25,000 a year (less than $500 a week). Only 0.2 percent grossed more than $1 million a year.[4] Since proprietorships are not publicly owned, they do not report their incomes publicly, so we do not know what the largest sole proprietorship is or what it earns.

Few manufacturing companies are proprietorships. This type of business requires a big investment and a large work force with specialized skills, which a single individual generally cannot afford. High start-up costs and operating expenses also hold down the number of sole proprietorships in finance, insurance, and real estate.

MANAGEMENT PROBLEMS Beyond these problems of size and profit, the main advantage of sole proprietorships can also be a major disadvantage: the prosperity of the business depends on the talents and

managerial skills of one person. If these are limited, the sole proprietor is frequently too emotionally involved in the business to be able to admit it and seek aid. He or she may be unwilling to concede that qualified help is needed and may thus be unwilling to pay for it. Of course, a proprietor is often simply unable to pay for talent. But even if he or she is willing and can afford to hire outside help, the proprietor is often reluctant to share managerial or creative responsibility. A capable outsider will not stay on the job for long without such responsibilities.

FINANCIAL PROBLEMS A major cause of business failure among sole proprietorships, poor management does nothing for these businesses' credit standing. A small business often has difficulty borrowing money from banks and frequently must pay a higher rate of interest to get money. (Banks charge lower interest to large corporations that are regular customers and safer credit risks.) This difficulty puts sole proprietorships at a great disadvantage.

LIABILITY Another major disadvantage of a proprietorship is what is legally termed **unlimited liability.** This means that *any damages or debt that can be attributed to the business can also be attached to the owner.* The two have no separate legal existence. Take the case of a man who owns a small, unincorporated flower shop. If his business slows down and he suffers big operating losses, he is personally liable for those losses. His home might even be taken to satisfy a business debt.

LIMITED LIFE A final disadvantage is that proprietorships have a limited life. It is difficult for the owner to arrange for the company to outlive him or to be carried on by someone else if he or she is temporarily unable to run the business alone. Generally, successful proprietors who want to make sure that their businesses grow and carry on after them think of forming a partnership or corporation or of merging with a larger business.

PARTNERSHIPS

A **partnership** is *a legal association of two or more persons in a business, as co-owners of that business.* It combines the skills of several people, each of whom has a direct interest in the success of the business. The partnership can give its members some of the freedom and flexibility of a sole proprietorship—yet it may also help eliminate some of a sole proprietorship's headaches.

Take, for example, the partnership that Jan Levine and John Vasil set up to help small businesses adapt to computerization more painlessly. When small-business managers decide to computerize their business, as more and more do today to keep up with their competitors, they are often faced with the maddening problem of having to work with several different sets of people. First they may have to hire a consultant to tell them which computer to buy; next they may have to choose one vendor out of dozens available; then they may have to engage a professional to teach them how to use their new machine; and finally they may have to subcontract a maintenance crew. Levine and Vasil proposed to supply all these services in one simple package. Their company, Network 1, takes advantage of both partners' talents: Levine's background in small business and Vasil's experience as a computer consultant. And it eases the burden of the small-business operator who is fighting the obstacles to computerization that block his or her path.[5]

Business partnerships like Levine and Vasil's have been fairly common for many years. Today there are many small partnerships—the two-chair barbershop, the two-lawyer office. And there are many huge partnerships, often representing alliances of many professionals. Many law and accounting firms have hundreds of partners, though only the names of the main partners appear on the firm's shingle.

ADVANTAGES OF PARTNERSHIP

PROFIT POTENTIAL Like proprietorships, partnerships are easy to form. But a partnership often has the potential to create far more wealth than a sole proprietorship: the combination of skills can vastly enhance a firm's profitability. Five lawyers working in partnership can bring in far more business than five lawyers working separately. Likewise, an advertising copywriter, an artist, and a marketing director—as in the "three-name agencies" such as Doyle Dane Bernbach and Wells Rich Green—can do much more business if they pool their talents than they could if they were working alone.

INCENTIVES FOR TALENTED EMPLOYEES A partnership can be a "high-performance" arrangement. In fields such as accounting, law, and finance, the prospect of becoming a partner in an established firm can attract talented people to the company. Being asked to become a partner occasionally requires investing a substantial sum in the business, but the prestige and subsequent rewards of partnership strongly motivate people to excel in a very competitive environment.

LEGAL AND FINANCIAL ADVANTAGES Partnerships often enjoy the benefits of having a definite legal standing: usually the partners have entered into a specific legal agreement—and even if they have not done so, there is generally an implied agreement that a court would uphold if a legal question arose. (Sole proprietorships, by contrast, are not initiated with a specific legal agreement.) Moreover, partnerships generally have high credit ratings—for the simple reason that the typical partnership has several talented owners, most of whom have unlimited personal liability for debts incurred by the partnership. Thus, a partnership can raise the money it needs to do business more easily than a proprietorship can.

DISADVANTAGES OF PARTNERSHIP

LIABILITY A fundamental drawback of the partnership arrangement is unlimited liability. Medical partnerships, for instance, can suffer financial disaster if they are hit with malpractice suits—which have mushroomed in recent years, both in number and in the size of the financial settlements involved. A number of precedent-setting suits against accountants and lawyers have made those professions equally aware of the hazards of unlimited liability, and thus of the partnership arrangement itself. (There is a type of partnership that is specially set up to limit the liability of some of the partners. A **limited,** or **special, partner** is *a partner whose liability for his or her firm's debts is limited to the amount of his or her investment;* in a **limited partnership,** the organi-

Who will be "top banana"? Prospective partners may have conflicting ideas as to which one is best suited for that particular job.

zation *has at least one limited partner* as well as its **general partner** or **partners**—*partners who have unlimited liability for the firm's debts.*)

INTERPERSONAL PROBLEMS Another severe disadvantage of partnerships is that conflict among partners can wreck the company. The Beatles, an extraordinarily successful rock group in the 1960s, broke up in 1970 because the four partners had developed different career ambitions and interests. Paul McCartney wanted to do more personal appearances, while John Lennon was primarily interested in making records. George Harrison and Ringo Starr, the other two partners, wanted to pursue more personal interests.[6]

From another point of view, a large partnership has the disadvantage of being extremely competitive. Except for its clerical staff, a large partnership, broadly speaking, has two kinds of personnel— partners and aspiring partners. The junior employees are in competition with each other for a limited number of partnership slots, so they must work long and hard to convince the partners of their superior ability. Even if they do become partners, they continue competing for the best accounts.

MANAGEMENT DIFFICULTIES A third major disadvantage is the practical limit on the number of managing partners. If many partners have an equal say in running the business, management can easily be ineffective; many large partnerships are forced to name a managing partner. One single manager may not be enough, however, for an enterprise such as a large industrial firm. Such a firm may operate better as a corporation. As we will see below, a corporation has the advantage of being run by a management system that fans out from the top levels to the lower rungs of the ladder, with decreasing responsibility the farther down the employee is. This structure makes it easier to set and execute policy.

THE PARTNERSHIP'S LIFE SPAN It might seem that still another disadvantage of partnerships would be that

THE THREE MAJOR FORMS OF BUSINESS ORGANIZATION: HOW THEY COMPARE

SOLE PROPRIETORSHIP

Chief characteristics: Single owner; no legal requirements.
Advantages: Little capital needed to begin. Owner in complete control, and benefits from flexibility, secrecy and tax savings.
Disadvantages: Talent pool restricted. Liability unrestricted. Credit difficult to obtain, business has limited life span.

PARTNERSHIP

Chief characteristics: At least two owners; written agreements usual though not necessary.
Advantages: Easy to form. Can bring together many skilled persons. Good credit obtainable.
Disadvantages: General partners have unlimited liability. Ever-present danger of conflict between partners. Built-in size limitations. Life span somewhat restricted.

CORPORATION

Chief characteristics: May have few or many owners (stockholders). Incorporated by law under formal charter with bylaws.
Advantages: Owners have limited liability. Investment liquidity. Corporation has unlimited life span.
Disadvantages: Public disclosure often required. Cost of incorporation can be high. Heavy tax burden on small corporation.

they die with the death of the last partner. In fact, however, this is more a theoretical than a practical disadvantage. Many partnerships provide for the firm's survival after the founding partners have died. Thus the New York law firm of Sullivan & Cromwell continues to do business under that name, although Mr. Sullivan and Mr. Cromwell have been dead for many years.

CORPORATIONS

It is easy enough to imagine a one-person business operation: one person can sell ice cream in the park or handicrafts at a fair. He or she can paint houses, repair old clocks, or whatever. But try to imagine one person manufacturing a million automobiles or refining a billion gallons of gasoline. In a very important sense, these things *are* actually done by one "person," for, in the abstract realm of the law, General Motors and Exxon are very much like two individual people—not "just plain folks," to be sure, but people in the legal definition.

How is this so, and what are we really saying here? Legally, General Motors and Exxon have many of the same rights and duties as an individual person. The form of organization that embodies these attributes is the **corporation**—a body that Webster's New Collegiate Dictionary tells us *is "authorized by law to act as a private person . . . and legally endowed with various rights and duties,"* among them to *receive, own, and transfer property, to make contracts, and to sue and be sued.*[7] A corporation may own tremendous wealth—more than most private individuals do in this country: it can raise large amounts of permanent capital by selling **stock** or *shares of ownership* to public investors. By concentrating resources in this way, it offers its **shareholders** (*people who own parts of the company*) a chance to profit if it succeeds. It can also assume tremendous liabilities—but it is the corporation that is liable in full, rather than any one of the private individuals who share ownership in it. And this is perhaps the greatest advantage the corporation offers; if it fails, each shareholder has to pay only a limited penalty. *The legal responsibility of shareholders of a corporation for damages or debt only to the extent of their investments* is called **limited liability.**

A corporation, then, is

1. an artificial person
2. with an unlimited life span
3. empowered by a state to carry on a specific line of business
4. owned by shareholders (stockholders) who are
5. liable for damages only to the extent of their holdings.

No brief definition begins to convey the importance of the corporate form of business in the American economy. Of all the types of business organization, the corporation is by far the most significant in terms of money, size, and power.

A few statistics will serve as illustration: according to the most recent statistics, corporations in the United States accounted for more than 88 percent of all money taken in by business firms—$5.6 trillion out of $6.3 trillion. More than 33 percent of this total was accounted for by firms engaged in manufacturing. The largest corporation in 1982, Exxon, had sales of over $97 billion. In 1982, 294 corporations had sales greater than $1 billion. The largest 500 corporations in sales took in over $1.7 trillion. Assets of the 500 largest corporations totaled just over $1.3 trillion.[8]

These corporate giants are almost all publicly owned—that is, shares of their stock can be bought by anyone. The relationship between stockholders and company is central to the enormous strength of the modern corporation. Ownership and management are separate: so, in theory at least, if the owners wish to get rid of the managers, the organization will still survive. Conversely, because a stockholder's shares can be bequeathed or sold to someone else in the case of his or her death, whole generations of stockholders can come and go, but the company remains (so long as it's economically sound). This is

why, as we have said, the corporation has an unlimited life span, which gives it unlimited potential for growth.

Large corporations represent the most powerful, fastest-growing segment of the national economy, but their power also extends beyond the economic sphere to the political and social spheres. To understand American business—and, indeed, the society that sustains it—it is essential to understand the American corporation.

TYPES OF CORPORATION

Most discussion in a course on business centers on large business corporations such as General Motors, U.S. Steel, and Procter & Gamble. But several kinds of corporations play important roles in American society, and you should be aware of the differences among them. Table 1 summarizes the seven principal types of corporations.

There are two major distinctions to keep in mind. First, not all corporations sell shares on the open market. Of the ones listed in the table, only public and quasi-public corporations do so. The others are private corporations that withhold their stock from public sale, preferring to finance any expansion out of their own earnings or to borrow

TABLE I   Classification of Corporations

TYPE	DEFINITION	EXAMPLE
Open corporation (public corporation)	Carries on business to make a profit for its owners, the shareholders, persons, or institutions with enough money to purchase a share.	General Motors
Closed corporation (private corporation)	Profit-making business, but with few owners and no open market for its shares.	Gallo Wines
Municipal corporation	City or township that carries on governmental functions under charters granted by state.	New York City
Government-owned corporation	Federal, state, or local business that functions for the public welfare; all shares are government-owned.	Tennessee Valley Authority
Quasi-public corporation	Business owned partly by the government, partly by private investors; or owned by investors, but subsidized by the government; usually a high-risk venture, but important to society.	Comsat (Communications Satellite Corporation)
Nonprofit corporation	Service institution incorporated for reasons of limited liability.	Harvard University
Single-person corporation	Individual who incorporates to escape high personal income tax rates.	Movie stars, athletes, and authors

from some other source. A corporation whose shares are owned by fewer than 500 persons or has less than $1 million in assets is not required to disclose its finances to the general public. Thus, a private corporation's executives are assured of complete control over their operations.

Second, not all corporations are profit-making institutions. Numerous nonprofit organizations incorporate, chiefly for the rights that a corporate charter grants. Some of these organizations are owned by the government; others are formed to pursue goals in areas such as social service and the arts.

STRUCTURE OF THE CORPORATION

The initial voting shareholders of a newly formed corporation elect a board of directors, who replace the original incorporators. (Of course, the original incorporators frequently serve on the board.) Depending on the size of the company, there can be from three to about thirty-five directors; it is usual to have from fifteen to twenty-five. The directors, in turn, select the top officers of the company. The result is the basic structure shown in Figure 2.

The shareholders

Theoretically the voting shareholders are the ultimate governing body of the corporation, and in practice, they do have some say in how the corporation is run. At least once a year, all the owners of voting shares are invited to a meeting.to choose directors for the company and to select independent accountants who will certify the accuracy of the company's financial statements. In many corporations the shareholders form too large and scattered a group to attend the annual meeting personally, so instead most vote by **proxy,** *a slip of paper authorizing management to vote on their behalf either for or against the nominees for the board of directors and any resolutions on the agenda.* Voting by proxy does not entitle a shareholder to nominate other directors or to propose new resolutions. Most stockholders in large corporations—where the stockholders may number in the millions—generally accept the recommendations of management; they may own the corporation, but

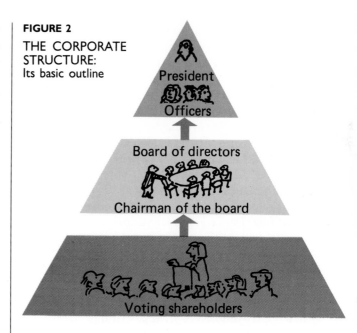

FIGURE 2

THE CORPORATE STRUCTURE: Its basic outline

Shareholders are the basis of the corporate structure: it is because of their capital investment that the company can function. The shareholders elect a Board of Directors (some or all of whom may be shareholders). The Board, in turn, elects a chairman to speak for them. The directors also elect the corporate officers to carry out their policies and decisions. Officers can be members of the board, or may simply be hired employees.

they don't manage it. Indeed, the more stockholders there are, the less real influence each one has on the corporation.

The board of directors

As a practical matter, the **board of directors,** which represents the shareholders, has *the ultimate authority in guiding corporate affairs and making general policy.* Typically, the board has the power to vote on major management decisions such as authorizing money to build a new factory, develop a new product line, or buy a new subsidiary.

The board's actual involvement in running a corporation varies from one company to another. Often, the board acts simply as a "rubber stamp" tending to follow management's recommendations: this is common in situations where a majority of the board members are also managers, and also in situations where management ensures that outside board members who are friendly toward management's interests will be chosen. But sometimes the chief executive and the board clash. During a 1982 board meeting of World Airways, for example, when the company's chief executive officer and majority stockholder Edward J. Daly was absent, the board revised the rules, stripped Daly of his chief executive status and appointed Brian A. Cooke to replace him. In turn Daly tried to fire Cooke and regain his position, threatening a lawsuit against his own board. Daly died in January, 1984; but while the struggle had sapped the company of its leadership, only a few moderate board members had tried to correct the company's mounting losses, which had reached $107 million as of this writing.[9]

The officers

The top officers of a corporation are selected by the directors, are responsible to them for carrying out the board's policies, and can be removed by them. Officers below top rank, including most vice-presidents, are generally appointed by the chief officer and approved by the board. But the real power in a corporation usually lies with the **chief executive officer,** or **CEO,** who *is responsible for setting down the policies of the company, under the direction of the board, and for supervising the officers who carry out those policies.* The chief executive officer may also be the chairman of the board, the president of the corporation, or both.

CHALLENGES TO CORPORATE MANAGEMENT

Although corporate executives are accountable to the board of directors, and ultimately to the shareholders, challenges to their authority have traditionally been relatively few and nonthreatening. But in recent years, this pattern has changed, and corporate managers are increasingly being called upon to answer for the way they run their business. Stockholders have sparked disputes on public policy, and

internal battles have recently made front-page headlines.

Stockholder activism

Years ago, shareholders' meetings were quiet affairs where company executives voted to reelect themselves while the few shareholders who showed up ate their box lunches placidly. But in the 1960s, some stockholders began pressing board members to account for their activities in areas such as minority hiring and the manufacture of weapons. Most of the time, these dissident stockholders (stockholders who did not agree with their management's policies) were allowed to have their say, but were seen by management as only a nuisance. Their proposals were typically ignored or voted down; even when the activists did manage to apply pressure successfully, they rarely got anything out of management other than disclosure of equal employment practices or lists of investments in controversial countries like South Africa.

But since then, stockholder activism has increased, and has come to take up considerable time at annual meetings. The Securities and Exchange Commission (SEC) has reacted by tightening the rules: as of January 1, 1984, only stockholders with 1 percent or $1,000 worth of company stock are permitted to bring up an issue before the other stockholders. Some companies like IBM—which claims that a single resolution costs the company $15,000 in expenses—have praised this new restriction, but activist stockholders view it as a defeat for corporate democracy. Other SEC restrictions have practically excluded small stockholders from taking unpopular issues before the full body. As a result, many activist stockholders have banded together to concentrate on putting just a few carefully selected proposals before just a few companies. Large stockholders, like the Presbyterian Church (which has assets exceeding $1 billion), have said that the new restrictions will force them to register their complaints by more radical actions, such as selling off their holdings in the companies.[10]

Proxy fights and tender offers

More serious challenges arise when there are attempts to take control of the corporation away from one group of managers. Such attempts can take the form of proxy fights or tender offers—both aimed at seizing control from the board of directors and top managers.

In a **tender offer,** *some specific outside person or group offers to buy all or a great deal of a company's stock at a higher price than it would bring on the open market.* Such takeover attempts are often hostile and are met by counterassaults. The management of the target company may wage a public relations campaign—for example, to convince its stockholders of moral or practical reasons *not* to sell at the attractive prices the attackers are offering. In another standard defense, the threatened company tries to buy a small company in the aggressor's industry—so that if the aggressor were to succeed in the takeover, it might be subject to antitrust action by the government.

A recent famous incident involving tender offers was the Bendix–Martin Marietta battle of 1982: Bendix offered to buy 15.8 million shares of Marietta at an inflated price, and Marietta returned with the previously unheard-of counterattack of bidding on 11.9 million shares of Bendix! (Marietta's response was a good example of what came to be known as the "Pac-Man defense": if a hostile company attempts a takeover, the target company turns around and threatens to gobble the raiders up.) The promised result was mutually assured destruction. If Bendix moved to buy, so would Marietta, and many analysts thought the two companies would simply collapse under the debt. But as the deal began to go through, two other companies—Allied Corporation and United Technologies—joined the battle. In the end, Marietta retained its independence and Bendix—the original aggressor—was itself devoured by Allied, one of the newcomers.[11]

Recently, there has also been an increasing incidence of **proxy fights,** *struggles between management and a group of dissident shareholders for shareholder support to control the company or gain greater influence over it.* Some proxy fights are waged by companies trying to control other companies' boards; but nowadays they are more often waged by investors who are discouraged about management's financial policies. In the spring of 1983, for example, a lone stockholder in the giant GAF Corporation managed to corral enough support to pry the company's chairman, Jesse Werner, from the position he had held since the 1960s. GAF's proxy fight made many executives anxious because it seemed possible that it might herald a new trend. Traditionally, heavyweight institutional investors had sided with management during such affairs,[12] but this time the institutional investors were backing GAF's lone crusader, and it seemed possible that institutional investors might back the dissidents in future proxy fights too.

ADVANTAGES OF THE CORPORATION

The corporation has certain significant advantages.

LIMITED LIABILITY As we have mentioned previously, the main advantage of a corporation is its limited liability. This feature guarantees that the people who invest in the company will not lose more than the amount of their investment if the company fails or causes injury.

LIQUIDITY Another important advantage is that an investment in a publicly held corporation is **liquid:** it can be *easily converted to cash,* by being bought and sold on stock exchanges (see Chapter 15). Liquidity enables corporations to raise far larger sums than can be raised by unincorporated business enterprises. They have the option of issuing new stocks; they can also sell bonds, which they must redeem with interest. (For more on bonds, see Chapter 14.)

UNLIMITED LIFE SPAN As we also mentioned earlier, a corporation's unlimited life span is another important advantage. It allows a firm to make long-range plans and thus recruit, train, and motivate the best talent.

For all these reasons, no other business form can match the success of the corporation in bringing together money, resources, and talent; in accumulating assets; and in creating wealth.

DISADVANTAGES OF THE CORPORATION

Corporations are not without some disadvantages.

PUBLIC DISCLOSURE REQUIREMENTS In the case of large, publicly owned companies, about the only serious disadvantage of operating as an incorporated entity is the tangle of government regulations requiring that the company publicly disclose its finances and certain corporate operations. Having to disclose its profit margins can increase a corporation's vulnerability to competition.

COSTS OF INCORPORATION It may be difficult, however, to *become* a public corporation in the first place: going public can be complicated and expensive. In addition to charter fees and lawyers' fees, the cost of making a public stock offering can be $125,000 or higher; the printing bill alone for all the documents that are required by the SEC, and the cost of distributing them to investors, can run to $25,000 or more, depending on the number of prospective investors. (It should be pointed out that these difficulties occur only with the establishing of a *public* corporation; becoming a *private* corporation is relatively simple and inexpensive.)

HIGH TAXES Second, although the tax rates for small corporations have gone down in recent years, incorporated businesses are still taxed more heavily than unincorporated ones; all corporations pay a tax of 46 percent on net income over $100,000 a year. In addition, shareholders, who may well be members of a single family in small corporations, must pay income taxes on their dividends.

Large corporations claim that they are unfairly taxed, but this claim is vigorously disputed by their critics, who say that corporations expend great effort and talent arranging business transactions so as to minimize taxable income. Especially criticized are corporations that do business in "tax-shelter" countries like Panama, the Bahamas, and Bermuda, which have no income taxes. According to opponents, such corporations have a far lower actual tax rate than do small corporations or individuals.

MERGERS AND CONGLOMERATES

Although companies commonly expand from within, in many instances companies choose to acquire other companies as a means of growth. The most common form of acquisition *is the sale of one company to another company, with the purchasing company remaining dominant.* This form of business combination is called a **merger.** In a classic example, General Motors absorbed the Chevrolet Corporation in 1919 and GM remained dominant. Another form of merger involves an interested outsider, such as an investment bank, which brings together two or more companies to form an entirely new company. This type of combination is called an *amalgamation.* In 1917, for instance, the Pontiac, Olds, Buick, and Cadillac corporations amalgamated to form General Motors.

Before the 1960s two great waves of mergers in American business history stirred public debate. Each was marked by a different kind of merger. The first great wave was the creation of monopolistic industrial trusts between 1881 and 1911, such as the enormous oil and steel trusts founded by John D. Rockefeller and J. P. Morgan, respectively. These trusts were **horizontal mergers,** or *combinations of competing companies performing the same functions.* The purpose of a horizontal merger is to achieve economies of scale and to prevent cutthroat competition. The rise of a government antitrust movement and the dissolution of Standard Oil in 1911 ended this wave, although in recent years, as we'll see below, the horizontal merger has reappeared in a new form.

A second great wave occurred in the boom decade of the 1920s. This era was marked by the growth of **vertical mergers,** in which *a company involved in one phase of a business absorbs or joins a company involved in another phase of that business.* The aim of a vertical merger may be to guarantee a supplier or a customer. In 1930, the Radio Corporation of America (now RCA), which owns the National Broadcasting Company (NBC), fashioned a vertical merger when it bought the Victor Talking Machine Company in order to acquire the performing contracts of Victor recording artists for NBC radio stations. Similarly, when oil-refining companies began buying oil fields to ensure a supply of crude oil, and gas stations to ensure sales outlets, they were expanding vertically. The Great Depression in the early 1930s greatly slowed down this trend because there was less cash available to finance acquisitions.

MERGERS TODAY

After the days of prosperity in the 1970s—a time when almost every business succeeded—mergers took on a new tone. In more recent years, a number of big companies have tried to merge with other companies because of worries about economic safety: it often makes more financial sense to buy an existing company than to start a new one. The merger, for example, has provided a solution to sister companies on the verge of bankruptcy. The ailing Acme-Cleveland Company merged with Numex Corporation, a machine-tools firm that had come within dollars of filing for bankruptcy.[13] The two hope the marriage will help them profit more together than they would apart.

More recently, LTV Corporation and Republic Steel Corporation, the third- and fourth-largest American steel producers, announced plans that sent shock waves through the antitrust division of the Justice Department. The two steel companies intended to unite and form the second-largest steel producer in the country. And in 1984, several of the largest oil companies in the country, suspecting it might be easier to find oil on Wall Street than in the ground (as world oil supplies dwindle), were looking around for takeover targets among the other oil companies. Years ago such horizontal mergers would have been unthinkable, but the recession and the new trend toward deregulation may eventually force even the Justice Department to favor practicality over principle. In mid-1984, the Justice Department approved the Republic-LTV merger on condition that Republic sell two of its plants to other producers; this condition was imposed with the purpose of maintaining competition.

Conglomerate mergers

In some cases, two or more companies merge with the intention of providing each other with a diversity of operations and safeguarding their income regardless of economic troubles. Such a *union of two or more corporations whose operations are unrelated* is called a **conglomerate merger.** In 1983, for example, Esmark Inc., the billion-dollar business that produces Swift Foods and Playtex personal prod-

ucts, joined forces with Norton Simon, another giant that owns Avis car rental, Max Factor cosmetics, Hunt and Wesson foods, and the Somerset whiskey distributor. Conglomerate mergers offer tempting benefits: massive expansions of markets, a consolidation of management, and a better chance in foreign countries. Yet not all are productive: when U.S. Steel acquired Marathon Oil, for example, it was accused of neglecting its basic business, and Baldwin United's acquisition of MGIC dragged Baldwin into bankruptcy.

New trends in conglomerates

Remember Sears, Roebuck and Co., America's number-one retailer, famous for its mail-order catalogue? It's not just the department store that it used to be. Today, through mergers with firms like Dean Witter Reynolds, Sears also offers a full line of investment and banking services: insurance, savings programs, and loans and mortgages. And other companies have recently been expanding by taking on new financial services, too, partly because of the recent deregulation of banks (see Component Chapter D) and partly because some financial experts believe Americans will start to save more money now that inflation has eased. Prudential Insurance Company got into the brokerage business when it teamed up with Bache and Company; but the most actively merger-minded firm has been American Express, which has moved in with a brokerage firm (Shearson Loeb Rhodes Inc.), several European and Latin American banks, a major marketer of mutual funds, a life insurance firm (Investors Diversified Services Inc.) and even a cable television organization (Warner Amex Cable Communication).

THE MOVE TOWARD DIVESTITURES

Nowadays, many large companies are **divesting themselves of,** or *selling off,* some of their businesses for economic reasons. The slump that began in the mid-1970s has kept profits down in most industries. As a result, the conglomerates have not had the cash to pay off their debts or to finance internal changes that might raise profits. The operations that are

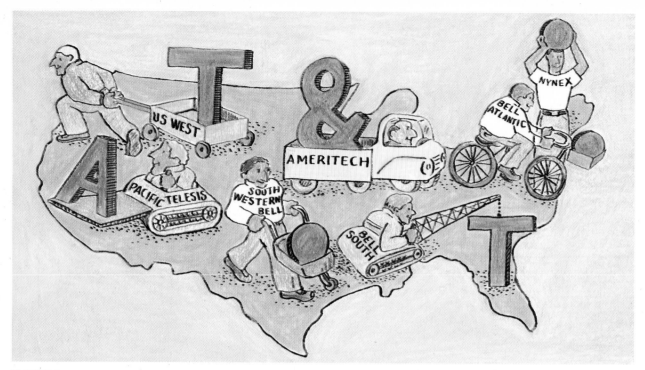

FIGURE 3
A NEW ERA:
The AT&T divestiture

The breakup of AT&T—that is, the parent company's decision to divest itself of its seven regional holding companies—has caused chaos in the phone business. Now the newly independent regionals are scrambling for cover, trying to keep their systems profitable without having the parent company's resources to fall back on. For consumers, local phone rates may rise, since the cost of local service will no longer be subsidized by profits from AT&T's lucrative long-distance operations. But the change may look good to investors, since the regionals are now free to explore new ideas that may lead to new growth.

being shed are chiefly the ones that are least related to the parent company's primary business, as well as those that have been only marginally profitable. Commonly, companies have seen the value of their stock rise dramatically after announcing the intention of selling their secondary operations.

Greyhound Corporation, for instance, has spent the last two years getting rid of more than twenty of the unrelated operations it acquired during the prosperous 1960s and early 1970s. Now that the company no longer deals in such businesses as yarn manufacturing, insurance, and car rentals, decision making has been streamlined. Fare changes, once decided every two to three months in loud, angry committee meetings and consultations, are now made by pricing specialists who have their fingers on the pulse of the market.[14]

OTHER TYPES OF BUSINESS ORGANIZATION

While most business organizations tend to be sole proprietorships, partnerships, or corporations, there are other forms in which businesses can be organized.

JOINT VENTURES, TECHNICAL PARTNERSHIPS, AND SYNDICATES

Sometimes competing companies pool their resources on a project that is mutually beneficial. On the Alaskan pipeline, for example—the most expensive enterprise ever financed by the private sector—

eight oil companies footed the $9.3 billion bill. The unexpected oil shortage and price hikes since the pipeline was begun in 1969 have made the project a profitable decision. The Alaska pipeline is an example of a **joint venture,** or *a company established for the cooperation of two or more companies in accomplishing a specific task.* Nowadays, joint ventures are becoming more popular as production and manufacturing become more complex and the many projects present too much risk for one firm to bear alone.

Joint ventures are often formed to bring together companies whose expertise in different areas can contribute to the total success of a particular project. Many motion pictures are now the product of joint ventures; made-for-television movies are often created through a joint venture between a film studio with money and a local TV station with production equipment.

Similar to the joint venture is the **technical partnership,** an arrangement whereby *one company buys a chunk of another company's stock so that the two can team up on new technologies and products.* Some of the most vigorous and mutually beneficial of such partnerships have occurred among high-technology companies. After the initial boom in the various segments of computer technology, for example, competition began to get tough. Some companies failed, and the survivors realized that not only technological advances, but also cooperation, would be necessary for success. In 1983, when it became clear that telephone technology would be central to national computer communication, International Business Machines (IBM) bought 15 percent of the stock of Rolm Corporation. IBM, a giant in computer and communications technology, needed Rolm, a manufacturer of telephone systems. IBM now uses its link with Rolm to improve its overall sales of equipment, and Rolm has IBM to boost its research and development, sales force, and market expansion.[15]

Unlike joint ventures, which establish a specific organization for an indefinite period of time, **syndicates** are *temporary associations of two or more firms, usually for mutual investment.* Banks often form syndicates in order to share the risk of a particularly large loan request. The syndicate hires no permanent staff, nor does it open an office; and once the loan has been repaid, the syndicate disbands.

COOPERATIVES

In the last few years, sales at Ocean Spray, a fifty-year-old cranberry-growing concern, have nearly doubled, from $235 million to $417 million. Such a record would be envied by any company, but Ocean Spray is not a company. It is a **cooperative,** which is *an association of people or small companies with similar products, services, or interests, formed to obtain greater bargaining power and other economies of scale.* Like large companies, co-ops can buy and sell things in quantity, but instead of distributing a share of the profits to stockholders, co-ops divide all profits among their members, who pay an annual membership fee. In a sense, then, a co-op combines the freedom of the proprietorship with the financial power of the corporation.

The co-op's latest incarnation has been at the less traditional end of the spectrum—the frontier of high technology. Two major research and development cooperatives—Microelectronics and Computer Cooperatives (MCC) and Semiconductor Research Corporation (SRC)—have gathered together research-and-development divisions of major corporations (at MCC) and universities (at SRC), with the goal of matching some of the technological advances achieved by foreign cooperatives abroad. MCC particularly hopes to put America back on top in microchip technology, an area where we have fallen behind the Japanese. Although some antitrust questions have arisen over the idea of joining so many companies together for one purpose, supporters argue that companies need this kind of research pool to compete abroad and to cut costs. One MCC executive foresees that companies may buy as much as $100 million in microtechnology research, at the bargain-basement price of $15 million.[16]

FRANCHISES

As we mentioned earlier, owning your own business has some major disadvantages, and yet a lot of people would rather work fourteen hours a day, seven days a week for themselves than eight hours a day, five days a week for a large corporation. For many of them, buying a franchise brings together the best

JOINT VENTURES FOR COOPERATION: AN ALTERNATIVE TO COMPETING WITH FOREIGN BUSINESS

As we've noted in Chapter 1, it's tough sometimes to beat our foreign rivals. Instead, why not join them in enterprises that can do both sides good? That's what some American companies are doing now, using the joint venture. In 1983, General Motors and Toyota decided to combine their resources and reopen an old GM plant in Fremont, California. The plant will build subcompact cars with both domestic and imported parts. The management will be primarily Japanese and the labor American. The costs will be divided equally, with Toyota contributing $150 million and GM contributing $30 million plus the $120 million plant. Both companies can reap many benefits from this limited association. GM hopes to provide a subcompact with little investment and cost, and learn from Toyota's famous manufacturing techniques. For Toyota, favorable visibility among U.S. manufacturers might ease the hostility many American businessmen feel toward their Japanese competitors. And because Toyota is putting up most of the hard capital, it will get not only half the profits but most of the revenues from sales of auto parts.

Critics of the plan—most notably GM's twin competition in Detroit—have attacked the plan as monopolistic and full of problems such as potential price-fixing. One Chrysler Corporation executive testified in Congress that the two companies would lock up half

A historic agreement: Roger B. Smith, Chairman of General Motors, and Eiji Toyada, Chairman of Toyota, shake hands on a deal to pool their resources.

the American auto market, and wondered aloud if they would therefore be subject to antitrust action. Yet such joint ventures seem to be on the rise. For all their complaints, Chrysler managers didn't shrink from opening their own talks with Volkswagenwerk about a joint venture to design and build a car. AMC has cut a deal with Renault, and Mitsubishi has set up an arrangement with Amco to sell Amco's plastic composites at home. Mitsubishi gets to closely examine Amco's superior materials technology, and Amco gets a rare opportunity to gain a foothold in the closed-door Japanese marketplace.

SOURCE: *The New York Times*, March 20, 1983; *Wall Street Journal*, May 10, 1983; *Wall Street Journal*, February 15, 1983; *Wall Street Journal*, June 10, 1983; *Newsweek*, April 25, 1983, p. 63.

of both worlds—independence and a measure of security. The **franchise operation** *brings a corporation with a famous product,* like Carvel ice cream, *together with an individual or group desiring to start a small business. Both the agreement and the individual business* are known as a **franchise.** *The* **franchisor** (the corporation) *grants the* **franchisee** (the person) *the exclusive right to use the franchisor's name in a certain territory, usually in exchange for an initial fee plus monthly royalty*

payments. The franchise operation enables a corporation to establish outlets for its product or service without making enormous capital investments. And it enables individuals to go into business with far less risk than independent operators would face, and to deal in a nationally advertised product or service. Franchises are likely to remain an important form of business organization for many years to come; we discuss them in Component Chapter B.

CHAPTER REVIEW

Sole proprietorships, partnerships, and corporations are the major forms of business organizations in the United States. Nearly 78 percent of American business enterprises are sole proprietorships. Most proprietorships are small and concentrated in retailing and farming. Proprietors enjoy the advantage of working for themselves. But they cannot always recruit talented help, and they are burdened by unlimited liability.

A second form of business organization, the partnership, is important because it includes many service businesses. Partnerships combine the talents of several partners and often enjoy good profits. Potential handicaps include conflicts among partners and lack of management flexibility. A limited partnership lets many people share a large, often risky investment, providing a tax shelter and the hope of long-term capital gains.

The most important form of business organization today, in terms of wealth and power, is the corporation. Its stockholders have limited liability. It is organized under a board of directors, who are elected by stockholders and who, in turn, elect the top corporate officers. There are many kinds of corporations, including nonprofit corporations, private corporations, and public corporations. Public corporations issue stock on the open market.

Corporations have many advantages, such as liquidity and the ability to combine relatively large amounts of money, resources, and talent. The disadvantages of going public include public disclosure of finances and of some operations, the expense of incorporating, and, in some cases, high taxes. In the early 1980s, shareholder activism became so common, costly, and time-consuming that the SEC had to restrict it. Interference and takeover attempts by other companies owning stock in a corporation are potentially even more serious challenges to corporate operations. The SEC is considering steps to calm these storms also.

In the past hundred years, many corporations have grown to giant size by merging with unrelated companies. The 1960s saw a wave of conglomerate mergers, but in the 1970s many of these conglomerates divested themselves of the very companies they had purchased. In the 1980s, the trend toward acquisition will probably be selective, taking place only if acquisition is less costly than self-generated growth.

Other business organizations include joint ventures, in which two or more companies establish a new company to pursue a mutual goal; technical partnerships, in which one company buys a chunk of another's stock so that the two can team up on new technologies and products; and syndicates, temporary associations of two or more firms for mutual investment.

Cooperatives and franchises combine the advantages of the other forms. Cooperatives generally give their members greater buying or selling power by joint action that does not deprive members of their independence. The recent boom in co-ops has brought protests from corporations, who say co-ops enjoy unfair advantages. Franchises, too, allow people to go into business for themselves, but with a large organization behind them to provide financial and managerial assistance.

KEY WORDS

sole proprietorship (29)

unlimited liability (30)

partnership (30)

limited (special) partner (31)

limited partnership (31)

general partner(s) (32)

corporation (33)

stock (33)

shareholders (33)

limited liability (33)

proxy (35)

board of directors (35)

chief executive officer (CEO) (36)

tender offer (37)

proxy fights (37)

liquid (37)

merger (38)

horizontal mergers (38)

vertical mergers (38)

conglomerate mergers (39)

divesting (39)

joint venture (41)

technical partnership (41)

syndicates (41)

cooperative (41)

franchise operation (42)

franchise (42)

franchisor (42)

franchisee (42)

REVIEW QUESTIONS

1. What is a sole proprietorship? Why is it the most common type of business in the United States?

2. What are the advantages and disadvantages of sole proprietorships?

3. Define a partnership. In what fields are partnerships typical?

4. Discuss the advantages and disadvantages of partnerships.

5. What is a limited partnership? What advantages are sought by the partners?

6. List five characteristics that distinguish the corporation from other types of businesses.

7. What three groups are responsible for running a public corporation? What role does each play?

8. What are some of the challenges that face corporate management today? What advantages and disadvantages do these challenges present?

9. What is a conglomerate? Why have many large corporations found diversification to be an ineffective strategy in today's economy?

10. What is a cooperative? What are its advantages? Why are some corporations critical of cooperatives?

11. What is a franchise operation? How does it benefit both the small-business owner and the corporation?

CASE 1

A TWENTY-FOUR-TABLE DREAM

Like a lot of people, Pat Rogers and Bob Barbero dreamed of opening a restaurant. Just a little place—a dozen or two tables—but with great food and chic decor. Unlike most of the people who have this dream, however, Rogers and Barbero actually *did* open their small restaurant in New York City after nine months of hard work.

Rogers and Barbero's restaurant, which opened in the fall of 1983, faces an uphill battle. Most new restaurants in New York fail—60 percent in their first year. They fail, like most small businesses, for two reasons: they are undercapitalized and their owners lack experience in the business.

Setting up a restaurant is an expensive proposition, as Rogers and Barbero quickly discovered. When their doors opened, they had spent $350,000, most of it borrowed. Each had put his life savings into the venture ($25,000 apiece); they borrowed $200,000 from friends and relatives and obtained a bank loan of $100,000. If this sounds like a lot of money for a twenty-four-table restaurant, consider some of the expenses Rogers and Barbero faced. Rent in New York is high. And the space the partners found was "raw"—it had been a pawnshop, and the interior had to be rebuilt from scratch. A kitchen had to be put in, and restaurant appliances and fixtures are costly. Restrooms had to be built. Tables and chairs, linens, silverware, dishes, and ashtrays had to be purchased. Menus had to be printed. A sign had to be ordered for the exterior of the restaurant. As the bills poured in before they had even served their first customer, Rogers and Barbero watched their funds dwindle.

Another important expense was a liquor license. This took seven months to obtain from the state liquor authority and cost $5,250. After the partners paid this fee, three weeks before their restaurant was to open, Barbero found that he had $88 left in the bank. And the two still owed money to the lawyer who had obtained their license.

Given these difficulties, it's fortunate that Rogers and Barbero had some restaurant experience before they launched their venture. Rogers had worked in several restaurants, and most recently had been a restaurant manager. Barbero had worked in the same restaurant as waiter and maître d'hôtel. Having worked together before also meant that they were well acquainted enough that they thought they would be able to work well together as partners. So far, the mishaps that have occurred—during construction, a wall caved in, some scaffolding collapsed, and equipment they ordered did not fit—have not caused a major falling-out between the two.

Rogers and Barbero, at this writing, seem to have launched one of the fortunate 40 percent of New York restaurants that survive their first year. Business is good, although both say it could be better. "At this point," Rogers says, "what you do is worry."[17]

1. What are the advantages of running a restaurant as a partnership? The disadvantages?

2. Do you think starting the restaurant would have been easier if there had been more partners? Why or why not?

3. How might Rogers and Barbero resolve disagreements so as to preserve their partnership?

4. If you wanted to open a restaurant, what kind of person would you seek as a partner?

5. If Rogers and Barbero wanted to become a corporation, would you advise them to do so or not? Explain your answer.

6. In your judgment, will this venture be a success? Why or why not?

CASE 2

AN ATTEMPT TO MAKE GULF GULP

Proxy fights involving large companies often shape up as David-vs.-Goliath battles, with the big corporations forced to dodge the missiles fired by a puny challenger. Such was the situation in 1983 when Mesa Petroleum, of Amarillo, Texas, sought to change the direction of mighty Gulf Oil Corporation.

Gulf's problem was how to head off the attack by Mesa and its aggressive CEO, T. Boone Pickens, Jr. In August 1983, Pickens began to buy up Gulf stock. Eventually he accumulated 13 percent of the huge company's shares. Pickens's aim was to stage a proxy fight that would force Gulf's management to give shareholders a better deal. In Pickens's view, Gulf's poor management was keeping its stock artificially low. Specifically, Pickens argued that Gulf should put some of its oil and gas reserves into a royalty trust—a step that would channel income and tax benefits from the reserves directly to shareholders rather than to the company. If this were done, Gulf stock would rise—perhaps even double—in value.

Gulf's response to Pickens's challenge was swift. Gulf's chairman, James E. Lee, asked shareholders to approve moving the company's incorporation from Pennsylvania to Delaware. Under Delaware laws governing elections to corporate boards of directors, Pickens probably could not have been elected. Gulf also took its case to the banks that were backing Mesa's share-buying maneuver, and persuaded four banks to withdraw from the deal. Gulf executives also publicly grumbled about Pickens's motives in challenging Gulf's

management. Pickens, they pointed out, was something of a corporate "sharenapper": his specialty was buying up enough stock in a company to scare its management, then selling the same stock back to the company at a higher price—thus making a handsome profit. (Pickens stated publicly that he did not intend to do this in Gulf's case, however.) Finally, Gulf executives argued that Pickens's ideas about how the company should be run were wrong. Harold Hammer, a top manager at Gulf, called the royalty trust proposal "a dumb idea that would mutilate Gulf Oil."

For his part, Pickens denied that he was trying to make a fast buck or to shoot down Gulf's management. "I am fighting as an investor to create value for Gulf shareholders," he said, "and I am shocked at the hostile reaction of Gulf."[18]

1. How did Pickens stand to gain if he won the proxy fight?

2. Do you sympathize with the Gulf management? Why or why not?

3. Do you think that buying a large amount of a company's stock in order to scare its management into buying it back is a good business practice?

4. If you were a Gulf shareholder, how would you react to Pickens's challenge?

5. Do you think the proxy fight may have done Gulf some good? Why or why not?

6. Do you think that proxy fights contribute to or interfere with business productivity? Explain.

THE AMERICAN ECONOMY: TRIUMPHS AND CHALLENGES 3

Business A maintains a model training program for unemployed black teenagers; on the other hand, business B is unconcerned about minority hiring. Business A is a giant chemical corporation that has annual earnings of over $3 billion; business B, a health-food store, provides a modest living for its sole owner. Clearly, these firms differ greatly when you look at them from the standpoints of social responsibility (which we discussed in Chapter 1) and organizational structure (discussed in Chapter 2). Yet they both fit comfortably in the American economic system.

What exactly is an **economic system**? Simply put, it's *a way of distributing a society's resources*—all the goods and services required to produce and market what people need. Different countries have different systems; as you read in Chapter 1, the U.S. economy is primarily a free-market system based on competition and supply and demand. In this chapter we'll take a close look at how the American system works.

CHAPTER FOCUS

After reading this chapter, you will be able to:

- cite one example from American industry that shows the workings of competition
- distinguish macroeconomics from microeconmics
- draw supply and demand curves, and point to the market price of a good by examining those curves
- name at least three factors that make ours a mixed economy rather than a true free-market system
- explain the basic concepts of macroeconomics, including circular flow and the multiplier effect
- discuss the role of capital, human resources, organization, and entrepreneurs in U.S. economic growth
- relate fiscal policy to unemployment, and cite one possible limitation of that policy
- define inflation, describe the sources of it, and outline recent steps to control it

Q.: What do you have in your pocket that's worth several hundred dollars?

A. *(Your first thought)*: Nothing—I'm not that rich!

But what about your pocket calculator? Just over a decade ago, your $10 calculator might have been worth $300 or $400; its manufacturers made it using a high-cost production process, and it had very limited sales. Now they produce it inexpensively in huge quantities, and market it using highly competitive mass-merchandising techniques.

The way the pocket calculator went so quickly from an unusual status symbol to an everyday household product is one of the great business success stories of our time. It's a story that *ends* with millions of consumers enjoying a product that makes their lives easier, that can be bought almost anywhere at a low price, and that comes in a wide variety of forms to suit customers' convenience. It also ends with many manufacturers earning a profit by making these calculators available to the public. But it's a story that *begins* with one Japanese company that put a new technology to a new use for a profit.

What were the key stages in the story? The initial manufacturer made only a few units, and sold them at a high price for a high profit. At that price, not too many customers could afford them—but plenty of other manufacturers were attracted by those high profit margins. Thus, more and more aspiring calculator makers entered the field. As a result, the price of calculators started to drop: as more and more calculators came onto the market, manufacturers found it necessary to cut their prices to find more buyers. Meanwhile, because they saw rich profit opportunities (and were also under heavy competitive pressures to reduce costs), manufacturers also pushed to find ways to produce the calculators even more cheaply. Their efforts resulted in advances in silicon-chip technology, and thanks to those advances, the industry remained profitable despite the continual slashing of its sales prices. And that is how the reliable $10 calculator, available at your drugstore, got where it is today.[1]

STUDYING ECONOMIC SYSTEMS

In our society, as the pocket calculator story shows, free competition and the chance to make profits can encourage businesses to try to make new items, of good quality, available to large numbers of people at affordable prices. The free market is one characteristic aspect of our **economic system**—*the way in which our society provides people with the goods and services they desire* (both the means of organizing people for producing those goods, and the means for making the goods available). Different societies have different economic systems. In one society, the central government might simply command citizens to build Factory X, produce 9 million bushels of foodstuff Y, and so on, on pain of punishment: in fact, a more complex version of just such a system exists in the Soviet Union. In another society, members might fish, grow corn, and weave cloth out of a sense of social duty, doing these things for the common good; this is, in fact, how the economic systems of some very primitive societies work. In our society, though, the prospect of private profit motivates businesspeople to find ways to make pocket calculators and other things available. In fact, it usually motivates many businesspeople, resulting in competition for sales and profits.

KEY ECONOMIC QUESTIONS

Our economic system may be compared to a huge tapestry, woven from the thousands of different goods and services that are available in this country—computers, haircuts, McDonald's hamburgers, college educations, space shuttles, intercontinental ballistic missiles, steel furnaces, taxicabs, and everything else. As consumers, we're all interested in one very basic question regarding each product or service—namely, can I afford to buy it? How much is it going to cost me? But businesspeople are interested in slightly different questions, too: Can I afford to *produce* it? Will it net me an attractive profit? Whenever the businessperson's answer to this question is "yes," he or she may set out to try to make that item available.

PLANNED ECONOMIES

As you might guess, given the number of nations in today's world and the complexities of economics, you won't find the same economic system everywhere. Indeed there are many different ways of distributing a society's resources.

It's common to divide economic systems into two main categories. One is capitalism. Because of the importance of the market mechanism in capitalist economies, they are often known as *market economies*. In this type of system, the pursuit of private profit through competition is regarded as a worthwhile goal that ultimately benefits society as a whole. Countries having market economies include the United States, Canada, France, West Germany, and Japan.

The second main type of economic system is socialism. Socialist economies are characterized by: (1) public ownership of the factors of production and (2) planned resource allocation. The latter feature is so important in these systems that they are frequently called *planned economies*. In a planned economy, social equality is a major goal, and private profit and competition are generally regarded as wasteful and exploitative. Planned economies are found in many European countries (from Sweden to the Soviet Union to Yugoslavia), in Africa (Algeria and Tanzania), Asia (China), and Latin America (Cuba).

Capitalism has been adapted in one way or another by the various market economies; the modified form found in the United States is different from the West German system, for instance. The range of socialist economies is much wider. In democratic countries such as Sweden, the state owns only strategic industries and services: transportation networks, banks, mines, communications, and such industries as chemicals and steel. Private ownership is widespread, although taxes are quite high so that the state can absorb the costs of all medical care, education, subsidized housing, and other social services. Much of the economic planning in Sweden is decentralized and rests with local councils of workers and managers.

At the other socialist extreme is the Soviet Union. There almost all factors of production are under state control. Private ownership is restricted largely to personal and household items. Resource allocation is handled through rigid centralized planning by a handful of government officials, who decide what goods to produce, how to produce them, and to whom they should be distributed.

Planned economies have both advantages and disadvantages compared with market economies. Because of their commitment to social welfare, there is more equality—less of a gap between the wealthy and the poor. Unemployment and inflation can more easily be controlled. (Some planned economies are more successful at this practice than others, however. In Britain, which considers itself a socialist nation, unemployment is very high. In the Soviet Union, where the state is everyone's employer, it is nonexistent.) On the other hand, without the spur of the profit motive and competition, there is little incentive to increase efficiency and productivity in planned economies. A major failure of the Soviet Union has been the government's inability to improve agricultural productivity. Russian farmers working on government-owned farms have not been producing adequate supplies of food. Therefore the nation with the largest amount of tillable land ironically has had to import wheat.

Businesses are the core of our economic system because they "deliver the goods." If you are a businessperson, understanding economics is a practical necessity: it can help you make better business decisions, so your business will have a better chance of staying healthy and maybe even growing.

MICROECONOMICS AND MACROECONOMICS

Let's suppose you are thinking of starting your own business, and you are looking at the economic considerations that will affect your enterprise. You will need to think about two types of questions.

First, you will need to determine whether you can turn a profit on your product. You will have to analyze:

1. How much it will cost you to produce and deliver the product (what you will have to pay for parts, labor, fuel, and so on).
2. How much you will be able to charge for the product (based on the competition and other factors).

This type of analysis, which *studies the costs and revenues of individual enterprises,* is called **microeconomics.**

Next, you will want to get an idea of how much of your product you can sell. To a large extent this will depend on how prosperous your potential customers are—are *they* making enough profit or wages to spend some of it on your goods? *The study of large groups of economic actors* (such as a whole country), *and of the ways they interact with each other and depend on each other,* is called **macroeconomics.**

In this chapter and the next one we'll take a closer look at how our economic system operates, and at how the health of the economy affects business. Until the mid-1960s our economy was relatively self-sufficient, and was not greatly affected by the economic status of other countries in the world; this chapter will focus on that closed system. From the mid-1960s to the present, our economy has become increasingly linked to economic activities elsewhere on the globe; we will look at those links in the next chapter.

THE "MICRO" LEVEL: PRICES AND PROFITS ON INDIVIDUAL ITEMS

We've seen that in order to analyze the profit potential of any product, the businessperson needs to forecast both the cost and the selling price of that product. Let's say, for example, that you're a sweater wholesaler, and you're wondering whether you should buy some Angora sweaters to sell to retailers. You have figured that in order to cover your overhead costs (rent, electricity, and so on) and leave a margin of profit on each sweater you buy, you would need to sell the Angora sweaters in reasonable quantity at a price of $20 apiece. But the department stores and boutiques to which you sell will also need to mark up the sweaters to meet *their* overhead and profit margin. Judging from the final market these retailers face, will you be able to sell the Angora sweaters to them at $20? If not, should you forget about Angora and test the Shetland market?

HOW AN INDIVIDUAL PRICE IS SET

Prices are not established one-sidedly. Of course the sweater wholesaler could just make a pricing decision and slap on a price sticker, but he might not sell many sweaters if he didn't take the buyer into consideration. The retailer knows it will be easier to sell more of a particular sweater to her customers if that sweater is priced at $40 instead of $60. If she can price it at $30, the quantity demanded will be even higher. In this way, the customer's willingness to pay is communicated to the retailer, and then translated to the wholesaler in terms of the retailer's willingness to pay.

Demand

The relationship between price and quantity in demand is often shown on a graph. Figure 1 is a graph illustrating the demand for Angora sweaters on October 1. A range of prices is listed vertically at the left, with the lowest at the bottom and the highest at the top. Quantity (in thousands) is given hori-

FIGURE 1

A SIMPLE DEMAND CURVE:
Demand for angora sweaters on October 1

FIGURE 2

A SIMPLE SUPPLY CURVE:
Supply of angora sweaters on October 1

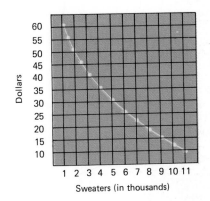

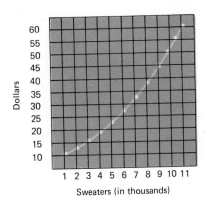

A demand curve slopes *downward* to the right. That's not too surprising: the more a producer charges for an item, the fewer units people will be willing to buy.

A supply curve slopes *upward* to the right. This isn't too surprising either: the higher the price producers can charge, the more units they'll want to produce!

zontally along the bottom, with the lowest at left and the highest at right. The points on the graph indicate that, on October 1, there would be 1,000 buyers for these sweaters if they were priced at $60, 2,000 if they cost $55, and so on. The *line that describes the relationship between price and the quantity demanded* is a **demand curve.** (This line is not necessarily curved; it may be a straight line.)

Supply

Now let's think about what's going on in the mind of the sweater manufacturer. He will want to sell more sweaters—that is, the quantity supplied will be greater—if each sells for $50 than if the price is $25.

As we noted in Chapter 1, **supply** is defined as the *producer's* (or seller's) *ability and willingness to sell or produce specific quantities of a good in a given time period.* In general, the *amount of a good that is supplied*

increases as the price rises, other things being equal. The relationship between price and quantity supplied can also be depicted graphically. Figure 2 is a graph illustrating the supply of Angora sweaters on October 1, again with prices at left and quantity along the bottom. The points on the graph indicate that manufacturers would be willing to supply 1,000 sweaters at $10, 2,000 at $15, and so on. *The line tracing the relationship between price and the quantity supplied* is called a **supply curve.**

Equilibrium and market price

We have examined the buying behavior of suppliers (sweater manufacturers) and demanders (sweater sellers) at a variety of prices. But we know that in reality, goods sell at a single price. How do the intentions of buyers and sellers interact to arrive at such a price?

FIGURE 3

HOW SUPPLY AND DEMAND INTERACT:
Supply and demand, angora sweaters, October 1

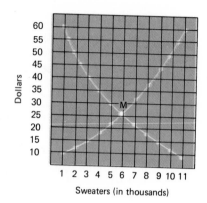

Sweaters (in thousands)

In a free-market system, prices aren't set by the government. They aren't even set by the producers alone—without any input from consumers. Instead, there's an interaction between the quantities producers are willing to sell and the quantities consumers are willing to buy. (These two quantities are represented by the supply and demand curves here.)

There's only *one* price where the two curves intersect. And that's the market price.

Figure 3 is a graph combining the demand and supply curves for Angora sweaters on October 1. As before, prices are shown at the left and quantities along the bottom. Note that the demand curve and the supply curve intersect at point M—where the price is $25. Only here do the intentions of buyers and sellers coincide. If the price were $50, sellers would be glad to supply about 9,750 sweaters; but buyers would purchase only 2,000. If the price were $20, buyers would take 7,500 sweaters; but manufacturers would supply only 4,500. If the price were $25, however, manufacturers would supply 6,000 sweaters and buyers would purchase 6,000. In other words, at the price of $25 we arrive at a balance, or *point of equilibrium, between supply and demand;* the price at this point is known as the **market price.** Note that this intersection represents both a specific

amount of money—$25 in our example—*and* a specific quantity of goods—here, this quantity is 6,000.

As you can see, it's the mutual interaction of demand and supply—in this instance the interaction between consumers and manufacturers—that determines the market price. No outside interference is necessary.

HOW PRICES AFFECT WHOLE INDUSTRIES

As we saw with pocket calculators, price affects the supply of a product by helping businesspeople to decide not only which products to produce in their factories and how much of each product to produce, but even which industries to invest in. New factories and new companies came into existence because the going price of calculators signaled high profit potential to managers and investors. These signals sprang largely from the behavior of consumers, who chose not to buy the bulky and expensive old mechanical calculators. When a consumer freely decides how to allocate his or her money among alternative purchases, we may think of each dollar spent as a "vote" for the output of that industry—consumers are actually "voting" for the amount of resources that shall be invested in various industries.

PRICES AND LABOR DECISIONS

After an industry such as manufacturing electronic calculators has attracted the investment it needs to start up, it must then attract workers in order to produce something. Price is also the way our economic system sends signals from demanders of labor to potential workers—the suppliers of labor. Workers use the price of work, whether measured in terms of hours (wages) or years (salary), to choose among different available jobs, just as they use price to choose between different sweaters. Karen, a recent college graduate, has been evaluating the price of labor during her month-long job search. All she has been able to find are typist and receptionist positions paying an average of $175 a week. But in the classified section of the newspaper she has seen many ads for computer programmers, who earn as much as $250 per week. She thus decides to take a special six-week course in programming, figuring that her future earnings will more than make up the cost of the course.

Karen has chosen to get more schooling rather than sell her labor at $175 a week. Thus, she has withdrawn herself from the supply of labor in the clerical field and will eventually add herself to the supply of labor in the programming field. *Price* is what helps her decide that $175 is not a high enough price for her labor: she decides to try to get a higher price in another field.

LIMITATIONS ON THE FREE-MARKET ECONOMY

Of course, our economic system isn't always as efficient in delivering goods as it has been with pocket calculators. In order for the system to work at its best, buyers and sellers require complete information about products and their prices. Cheaper sweaters may be available across town, but if buyers don't know about it, they can't change their demand patterns. Some businesses may be getting a higher price for furniture, but if other businesses don't find out about it, they won't get the signal to invest more in furniture production and to raise prices. Further, technological change is quite limited in the production of sweaters and furniture; the drastic price reductions possible for high-tech items are not always possible for other types of product.

OLIGOPOLY

There is not always enough competition to motivate each enterprise to provide the best product at the lowest cost. Some items, such as oil and aluminum, are produced not by many smaller firms but by a handful of huge firms, and the result tends to be less competition. *A market dominated by just a few producers* is called an **oligopoly.** Although the law prohibits oligopolists from agreeing on prices with each other, they generally charge about the same price rather than try to undercut each other.

A number of factors help prevent the development of oligopolies. In many instances, if prices in

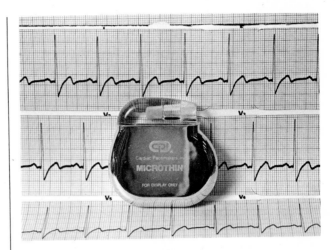

Should free competition apply to the medical technology industry? Not long ago, the government would have paid for this cardiac pacemaker; but now Uncle Sam has changed the rules. Hospitals must hold costs down, and manufacturers may try to lower prices to compete for the hospitals' business. Would you feel safe with a cut-rate pacemaker? In this area, the free-market approach may not be good for our health.

one industry are higher than consumers wish to pay, those consumers can find substitute goods or services from other industries at more acceptable prices. Furthermore, the lines that mark the boundaries of a single industry are often blurred; in addition, an industry that has concentrated power within a country (such as the auto industry in the United States) often faces competition from elsewhere on the globe that significantly reduces its total clout. And not all economists agree that even a single company with no major competitors is always likely to jack up prices higher than they would prevail in a freely competitive situation. Even the mere *threat* of future competition, some theorists believe, can be enough to keep a company's prices down. In view of all these factors, oligopoly may be more of a theoretical threat than a real one.

Suppliers of labor as well as products sometimes behave in an oligopolistic fashion in our economic system. For example, if everyone wanted to supply his labor as a carpenter, this competition would soon

Public goods are goods and services that can't be provided to one citizen without being supplied to others. What public goods do you see here? What goods are provided by private enterprise?

lead to a fall in the price of carpentry services. Instead, carpenters join together in the form of labor unions and agree not to work for less than a particular price. They are able to obtain this higher price by limiting the supply of carpentry services—that is, by limiting the number of union carpenters.

MODIFIED CAPITALISM

Eighteenth-century philosophers such as Adam Smith described an economic system they called **pure capitalism** in which *all production and allocation decisions would be made by private holders of property or money, on the basis of prices set by the free market.* In our society, however, we have agreed that it is sometimes in everyone's best interests for the government to intervene in the free-market economy. Because in our system *the government can use its power to change prices or change the way resources are allocated,* our system may be called **modified capitalism.**

Public goods

The government's impact on the workings of supply and demand in our system takes many forms. For example, if the government didn't take your tax money and demand national security for you, what would your demand for missiles be? Perhaps you would have no incentive to spend any of your income on defense; if you chose to vote none of your dollars for that purpose but your neighbors did, you would be just as well protected. Similarly, it might

not be practical for our society to rely on individual demand to provide police and fire protection, to build roads, or to launch satellites. Instead, the government steps in and supplies these **public goods**—*goods or services that cannot be provided to one citizen without being supplied to others.*

Economic externalities

Clean air is a public good because no one can stop me from breathing it even if I refuse to contribute my share to cleaning it up. But let's look at this point from a slightly different angle. Some people can enjoy the benefits of polluting the air (through the electricity, steel, or chemicals they buy) without paying for the costs of dirty air (such as lung disease or acid rain). **Economic externalities** are said to exist when *the costs or benefits of one person's economic choices are imposed on others.* As we all know, the government penalizes and regulates business activities that involve negative externalities such as pollution. But the government also helps subsidize activities with positive externalities, such as education: when I advance my education, some rewards spill over to society in general.

Transfer payments

Finally, our society recognizes that some individuals—especially children and the handicapped—are not capable of supplying enough labor to the free market to assure themselves a decent standard of living. We could each "demand" adequate care for

those individuals who have no other means of support by making voluntary contributions toward their welfare; but instead of this free-market solution, we have chosen to let the government intervene. In essence, the government collects our contributions in the form of taxes, and distributes them in the form of payments such as Social Security, food stamps, welfare, and unemployment compensation. Economists call these allocations **transfer payments:** they are *payments to individuals that are not made in return for goods and services.*

MICROECONOMICS AND THE BUSINESSPERSON

The concepts we have discussed in this section are part of every decision maker's thoughts when he or she evaluates the future profit potential of a business. Is the market environment of my business relatively similar to pure capitalism? Or can my firm expect to encounter a relatively high degree of government regulation, due to externalities (such as environmental pollution) or other public interests (such as consumer-affairs issues) that are associated with my industry? Will my firm be competing with many small firms that may try aggressive price cutting, or will the market be dominated by a few major corporations that will tend to charge about the same price? Is there a free flow of information about prices to buyers and sellers, or has limited information caused prices to settle at other-than-equilibrium levels? With these microeconomic questions in mind, a businessperson is better able to make supply decisions that will keep his or her enterprise in sound financial health.

THE "MACRO" LEVEL: PARTS AND THE WHOLE

Microeconomics is a useful tool for understanding supply and demand decisions and their effect on consumer spending, production, and labor in our society. The price mechanism helps to explain why there are many fast-food outlets but relatively few gourmet restaurants; many auto dealers but fewer horse suppliers; many buyers of (people with a demand for) computer programmers, but fewer buyers of (people with a demand for) ukulele players. But we also need to understand our economic delivery system as more than just a big collection of points where many little supply and demand curves intersect. A tapestry is a collection of points of thread of different colors; but because those points relate to each other in a complex pattern, the total effect is greater than the sum of its parts.

Macroeconomics helps us view our national economic tapestry as a whole: it lets us examine the weave of the tapestry—the pattern that links all the equilibrium points of the many individual markets. Macroeconomics helps business decision makers determine whether that tapestry is becoming rich and elegant or bare and worn; whether its offerings of products, jobs, and investment opportunities will be plush or thin.

THE CIRCULAR FLOW

Perhaps the most important conceptual tool in macroeconomics is the concept of the circular flow, a way of imagining the movement of money and goods within the economy. The **circular-flow con-**

FIGURE 4

THE CIRCULAR FLOW:
How money, goods, and services move through our
economy

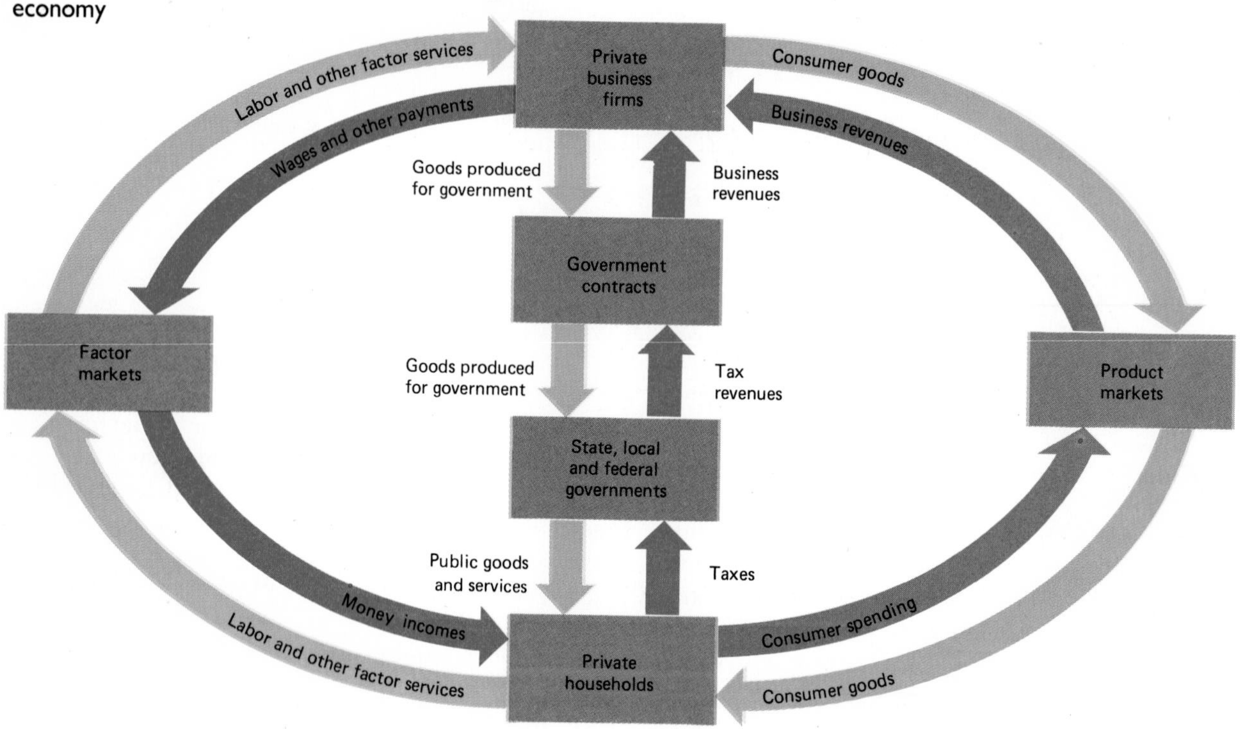

If you look at our economy as a giant circulatory
system, you can think of businesses and consumer
households as two vital organs—almost like the heart
and the lungs. Each needs the other to keep going.

How does the system work, in the very simplest
terms? Consumer households pay money for the goods
and services businesses provide. With this money,
businesses pay for raw materials—but they also need
a labor force to produce their goods and services. This
force comes out of the consumer households. Thus,
there's a circular pattern here (you can see it in the
oval pathways around the edge of the diagram).

Meanwhile, the government is involved in the
system as well. It buys goods and services, as well as
labor. (You can see government's role if you look at
the straight-line pathways in the center.)

cept is useful for examining the relationships
among economic actors—businesses, households,
and governments (federal, state, and local). Just as
the bloodstream carries oxygen in one direction and
carbon dioxide in the other, *the economy carries goods
and services one way and money the other,* as shown in
Figure 4. Specifically:

1. Goods and services flow from businesses to households; households generate a return flow of
money in compensation for these goods. (Goods
and services also flow from businesses to other
businesses, and money flows back the same way.)

2. Governments provide goods and services (such as
roads, courts, and education) to households and
businesses. Households and businesses send a return flow of money in the form of taxes.

3. At the same time, households provide services to
businesses in the form of labor, and receive a return flow of money in the form of wages and salaries.

FIGURE 5

THE MULTIPLIER EFFECT:
All economic decisions ripple through the system.

If, say, 75 percent of each additional amount of revenue is spent in each cycle, we could have a series of spending cycles like this:

Hypothetical spending cycles	Amount	Cumulative increase
First cycle: government buys $100 billion worth of missiles	$100.00 billion	$100.00 billion
Second cycle: missile workers have more income, buy new boats	75.00 billion	175.00 billion
Third cycle: boat builders have more income, spend it on beer	56.25 billion	231.25 billion
Fourth cycle: brewery workers have more income, buy new cars	42.19 billion	273.44 billion
Fifth cycle: auto workers have more income, spend it on air travel	31.64 billion	305.08 billion
Sixth cycle: airline personnel have more income, spend it on bicycles	23.73 billion	328.81 billion
. . .	. . .	. . .
nth cycle and beyond:		400.00 billion

Households, which provide workers, are producers as well as consumers; businesses are consumers (of labor) as well as producers. We also see that money has different names (tax, pay, purchase), depending on what goods and services it is being exchanged for—that is, what items are flowing in the opposite direction.

THE MULTIPLIER EFFECT

The circular-flow diagram shows that each economic actor and activity is linked to all others. Because of these interrelationships, any change in one part of the economic system creates some changes elsewhere in the economy. For example, if the government decides to buy one more missile, some missile workers will have more income. If some of these workers decide to spend the extra income on new boats, boat builders will have more income. The boat builders, in turn, might spend this income on beer, and the brewers, in turn, might spend it on cars. This *pattern whereby all economic decisions ripple through the system* is known as the **multiplier effect.**

The multiplier effect operates in the downward direction as well. If a business needs fewer delivery trucks, truck assembly workers will have less income. The truck assembly workers may choose to cut back

HOW IT'S ACTUALLY DONE

HOW IS THE GNP MEASURED?

The GNP measures each component only once. For instance, goods are evaluated at their market price only. A pair of shoes may cost the manufacturer $20, the wholesaler $25, a department store $35, and an individual consumer $50. But the net result of all this business activity is $50, not $20 + $25 + $35 + $50 = $130.

Only current production is used to estimate GNP. The 1984 GNP, for example, does not include automobiles sold in that year but manufactured in 1983; those cars were included in the 1983 GNP.

on air travel, and airline personnel with less income may choose to buy fewer bicycles. Money never stays in one place, and every market decision has an impact, no matter how small, on other markets.

ECONOMIC GROWTH AND ECONOMIC SETBACKS

Economists also use a concept known as the **gross national product (GNP),** *a dollar figure that lumps together the total dollar value of the goods and services produced by the economy over a given period of time.* The gross national product is useful for comparing one year's total value of goods and services produced to another's, or for comparing one nation's output to another's. Although the market value of the goods and services produced fails to reflect many aspects of our economic activity (what impact was there on our natural resources? how fairly were those goods and services distributed?), a rising GNP is considered very important by economists and politicians, and often by voters.

It is possible that the GNP will not change from one year to the next—the system can hum along producing goods and services of the same total value, adjusted for inflation. (We will discuss inflation later in this chapter.) However, with all the economy's interconnected parts, some change is likely, whether a growth or a decline in total output. Economists spend much of their efforts trying to figure out why (and predict when) economic growth and decline occur. As you can guess, most of our society would like to put this knowledge to use by encouraging the forces for growth and inhibiting the forces causing decline.

THE HISTORY OF OUR ECONOMY'S GROWTH

Americans have enjoyed the output of a rapidly growing economy since World War II—indeed, since settlers first made this territory into a nation. A large part of our economic wealth arose from our abundance of land. The land attracted many settlers because it was so good for farming; and with fertile, flat terrain, and adequate rainfall, the settlers soon grew more prosperous than the people of the Old World they had left behind. In the early nineteenth century, the economic significance of industry began to overshadow farming; we began to rely more on our plentiful rivers and harbors, and our rich deposits of coal, oil, iron, and copper.

Our excellent natural resources paved the way for the development of abundant capital to increase that growth. **Capital** includes *the tools—such as machines, vehicles, and buildings—that make the outputs of labor and resources more valuable. But it also includes the funds necessary to buy those tools.* If a society had to consume everything it produced just to stay alive, nothing could be put aside to increase future production. But if a farmer can grow more corn than his family needs to eat, he can use the surplus as seed to increase the next crop, or to feed workers who build tractors. This process of *capital accumulation* was aided in the American economy by our surplus of savings over consumption, as well as by our cultural heritage. Saving played an important role in the European tradition; it contributed to Americans' motivation to put something aside today, for the tools to buy tomorrow.

Human resources

By the mid-nineteenth century, we had accumulated enough capital in the form of factories to productively employ a large amount of labor, or *human resources*, in addition to our natural resources. A nation that still consisted largely of independent farmers could not provide an adequate labor supply for heavy industrialization. But millions of new workers came to the United States from abroad.

As we are all aware, not all these workers arrived voluntarily. Slaves were brought from Africa to the South; they were put to work on plantations to extract maximum harvests from the cotton fields. But in the North, the machines that turned that cotton into textiles were worked by massive waves of immigrants who came willingly from one part of Europe after another. This vastly expanded pool of

Technological change in the auto industry: **(A)** man welds car, **(B)** robot welds car, **(C)** man builds robot. Although robots may displace humans in some areas, they also provide jobs for those people who build and repair them.

SOME KEY ECONOMIC TERMS

All economic systems revolve around **factors of production**—*the resources the society uses to produce goods and services.* There are three main types. One, **land,** includes *not only the surface of the earth but also its minerals, timber, and water.* The second, **labor,** consists of *human resources used to produce goods and services.* The third factor of production is **capital**—*all the machines, tools and buildings used to produce goods and services.*

And all economic systems involve two kinds of markets: **product markets**—*any place where finished goods and services are bought and sold*—and **factor markets**—*any place where factors of production (land, labor, or capital) are bought and sold.*

labor allowed for large leaps in our national output.

A nation cannot grow forever by finding more natural resources and attracting more workers; thus, our *extensive* growth eventually slowed. But *intensive* growth gradually appeared as we made better use of the labor force. Many of the newly arrived immigrants were unskilled and illiterate, but education policy of their new land meant that their children all received an education, and many were trained in a skill. If a society gives workers more knowledge, they will be able to use machines in a more complex way and to follow more complex instructions, yielding manufactured goods of greater value; this process is often known as *investing in human capital.* In the late twentieth century, our physical capital is so abundant and our natural resources so limited that we are beginning to appreciate the importance of improving our human resources if we are to continue to grow.

Technological gains

Technology is probably most responsible for the leap in the productivity of labor in our economy during the past century. Output per worker is much higher at steel mills and textile mills than at blacksmiths' shops and spinning looms. The steam engine, electricity, and now the computer all make workers much more productive in their tasks. Technology itself is labor: technical knowledge is a packaged form of the work put in by some engineer, scientist, craftsperson, or just plain tinkerer, who has struggled to find a more efficient way of doing something. And each of these innovators, in the process of seeking a new technique, relies on all the technical knowledge that innovators have accumulated for centuries before.

Organization

Organization is a type of technology that is essential for using human resources more efficiently. We hear a lot about the sophisticated, computer-based management techniques that are becoming widespread today, but we may forget that organizational technology has a long history of development. *Interchangeable parts*, a concept pioneered by Eli Whitney in the muskets he designed, allowed factories to use relatively inexperienced workers rather than craftspeople to assemble manufactured goods. Henry Ford's *assembly line* represented another leap in organizational productivity, by bringing the parts to the worker. (See Chapter 6.) Later, *corporate organizations* were able to enhance their productivity by substituting the labor of professional managers for the more traditional pattern of decision making by the corporation's owners. Finally, great advances in our nation's transportation resulted when technology and organization teamed up. The crisscrossing of the nation, first with rail and canal networks, then with highways and air routes, allowed producers to combine human and natural resources more efficiently, and distribute the output to consumers.

Entrepreneurs

Much planning is needed to bring together just the right blend of human and natural resources, technology, and capital so as to fill business and consumer needs. The people who undertake this planning and organizing work are called **entrepreneurs.** Entrepreneurs are *individuals who undertake to start and build business enterprises.* More important, entrepreneurs finance these efforts with their own money. If the decisions are poor and the output can't be sold for a profit, they lose their money. Thus, an important part of entrepreneurship is *risk.* On the other hand, the entrepreneur reaps the profit if the venture is successful; in this way, our economy provides an incentive to apply one's labor and capital to risky ventures.

Most of our huge corporations today owe their existence to individual entrepreneurs who saw an opportunity to provide the economy with something that was lacking. In the nineteenth century, for instance, the steel industry matured through the organizational efforts of Andrew Carnegie; the oil industry became an integrated giant under the hand of John D. Rockefeller; Andrew Mellon founded the aluminum industry; and J. P. Morgan pioneered a financial conglomerate to provide capital to these entrepreneurs. In the twentieth century, Henry Ford revolutionized factories, labor relations, and transportation with his mass-produced automobile; and later in the century, Thomas Watson's International Business Machines computerized many aspects of our society and brought much social change. In some of today's large corporations it is difficult to observe entrepreneurship, since these corporations essentially work by allowing committees of managers to pursue opportunities using the capital of shareholders. Nevertheless, growth means innovation, innovation means risk, and risk means entrepreneurship—if we are to grow, we must have entrepreneurs. In dynamic industries, particularly in high-tech areas, today's entrepreneurs are busy building their small companies into the IBMs and Fords of tomorrow.

SETBACKS IN ECONOMIC GROWTH

Although our economic history includes periods of impressive growth, we have also had many setbacks—periods when our total output either stood still or actually declined. Economic decline is a complex and worrisome phenomenon, because once consumers start to buy less, factories must produce less; factories must lay off workers who in turn buy less; and so on. Despite the best efforts of economists, we do not fully understand what causes these setbacks nor what cures them.

Unemployment

Unemployment was a serious problem not only in the 1981–1982 recession, but also in the depressions that occurred in the 1830s, in the 1870s, and in 1890, and of course in the Great Depression of the 1930s, set off by the stock-market crash of October 1929.

During the Great Depression, unemployment affected as much as 25 percent of the labor force. Today's federal system of social welfare programs did not exist then, so the families of most of the unemployed went hungry. Since that time, we have progressed both in maintaining higher levels of employment and in providing support services to the unemployed. However, unemployment is still a threat in certain industries and for certain groups, especially among minority youth first entering the labor force. Unemployment is a waste of human resources, and represents a drain on public budgets and on the life savings of individual families.

Can unemployment be curbed?

Economists and politicians have given much attention to reducing unemployment and its effects. For much of the post–World War II period, they placed

1750

Population
1,170,800

National wealth
$750,000,000

1869

Population
43,500,000

GNP
$7.4 billion

Per capita income
$170

1900

Population
76,000,000

GNP
$18.7 billion

Per capita income
$246

By 1750, our population had grown to over a million (excluding Native American Indians). The concept of a "gross national product" was not in use at that time, but the wealth of the country was estimated at $750,000,000.

After the Revolutionary War, entrepreneurs began to amass money for reinvestment, and by the time of the Civil War the GNP had grown to $7.4 billion.

By 1900, the population had almost doubled. GNP had more than doubled, thanks to the expansion of industries made possible by the railroads, and the growth of the West.

their faith in the philosophy of John Maynard Keynes, which developed in response to the Great Depression. Keynes recommended a governmental policy known as **fiscal policy,** *the use of government revenue and spending to help control the economy.* He believed that during the inevitable lags in private spending (which, as we have seen, have multiplier effects, causing a downward spiral), the government should step in and spend large amounts of money. The government could spend money on goods and services of any type: on public works such as road repair and hospitals; on payments to or training for the jobless; or even on defense or war. This extra spending could not be financed by tax collections, however, for that would cut private spending a corresponding amount; instead, the government would have to borrow money, thus increasing the national debt and—as more recent economists have realized—possibly "crowding out" private borrowers.

The high unemployment of the early 1980s has raised many questions about the efficacy of fiscal policy. However, there is no agreement on the answers. Some believe the solution is even more federal spending. Others disagree.

1929

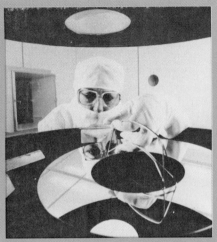

1982

FIGURE 6

AN OVERNIGHT SUCCESS STORY:
Growth of the American economy

Population
121,700,000

GNP
$103.1 billion

Per capita income
$847

Population
231,997,000

GNP
$3,073 billion

Per capita income
$11,107

By 1929, America had come of age as an industrial power. Its population numbered more than 121 million (the majority now city dwellers), and the GNP had shot up to over $103 billion.

In 1982, the population was still growing, though at a slower rate. GNP and per capita income had both mushroomed. Some sectors (notably high-tech) were booming, but trouble brewed for heavy manufacturing.

THE IMPACT OF INFLATION

Whenever *price increases are widespread through the economy for any reason*, we have a situation known as **inflation.** Although inflation was quite slow for most of the post–World War II period, it rose gradually through the 1970s, and then soared to double-digit levels (10 percent or more) in the late 1970s and early 1980s. Inflation is a sign that the economy is "heating up," so in its early stages it is usually associated with economic prosperity. But the problem feeds on itself: when goods cost more, workers demand higher wages, and this causes producers to charge more, further overheating the economy. Indeed, at an inflation rate of 10 percent, you must double your income every seven years just to keep up.

Even if you do keep up, continual price increases create a climate of uncertainty about the future that changes people's behavior and distorts the economy. Inflation encourages people to buy "before the price goes up"—even if they have to borrow money today—rather than to save for tomorrow. Thus, there is an increase in the demand for credit (borrowing), and a decrease in the supply of credit (saving); this pushes the price of credit (interest rates on loans) way up. Businesses are less likely to risk investing in new production facilities when they must borrow at high rates. Individuals are less likely to invest for fixed rates of return, fearing that inflation will exceed that return. They have less incentive to plan for long-term items, such as retirement or children's education, since the future cost of these things, and the future value of savings, is unknown. There is incentive for people to put their money in "real" things—houses, land, jewels, Oriental carpets: such items are not denominated in shaky dollars, the way bonds and other investment vehicles are. Buying real estate and "collectibles" such as jewels does not greatly increase the flow of goods and services in the economy, nor does it increase the nation's productivity in supplying such goods.

WHAT CAUSES INFLATION?

Some economists have traditionally explained inflation as "too many dollars chasing too few goods"— *demand-pull* inflation. If there are many people who want to buy, and not enough items for sale, people will pay higher prices. Economists illustrate this with a very simple experiment: put ten people in a room with ten chairs and ten dollars ($1 each to each person). If each person tries to buy a chair, the price will be bid up to $1 a chair. Now give each person $2, but don't put any more chairs in the room. The price of a chair will be bid up to $2, the inevitable result of people's having more spending power without more goods to spend it on.

But can't the economy avoid inflation by producing more chairs? Sometimes inflation develops when there is a recession—when workers and factories are lying idle. Recession is not unusual in developing countries, some of which are experiencing inflation at rates well above 100 percent annually even though factories are shut down and unemployment is higher than 25 percent. Other theories are needed to explain inflation in such situations.

"Cost-push" inflation: how higher costs contribute to inflation

Economists theorize that manufacturers raise prices if they find they have to pay more for inputs such as wages, energy, and machines. The steps businesses must take to comply with government regulation (such as buying pollution-control equipment or hiring safety inspectors), for example, have significantly raised the cost of doing business over the past two decades. Regulation is believed to cause higher prices for two reasons. First, the cost of compliance is passed along to the consumer; and second, regulation forces companies to spend funds on safety, pollution control, and other measures, so that they have less money to spend on modernizing and increasing efficiency.

Business costs have also increased because we have experienced a slowdown in productivity. During the 1950s and 1960s, when productivity grew rapidly, workers got used to healthy annual increases; greater productivity meant manufacturers could pay more in wages without increasing prices. But then productivity slowed. Workers were still accustomed to yearly raises, and manufacturers had to pass these raises on to the consumer in the form of higher prices. Unfortunately, these higher prices ate up wage increases, causing wage demands to accelerate even more.

The role of excess money in inflation

In a stable economy, if the price of one item (such as energy) goes up, the price of other things must go down to offset it. That is, if people spend more of their income on energy, they will have less left over to buy clothes, and clothing manufacturers will cut their prices because they are selling less. Thus, it seems that inflation is impossible given a stable money supply.

But what if more money is somehow put into people's hands to support a higher level of spending? For example, suppose the price of energy goes up and people are finding it very painful to cut back their spending. What if the government tries to increase its popularity by printing more money—thus allowing us to spend more dollars on foreign oil, say, without spending fewer dollars at home? Generally, if an increase in paper money is not accompanied by an increase in *real* output, creation of excess money will cause the price of goods to be bid up to match the amount of new money.

INFLATION AND THE VIETNAM WAR Just such an inflationary situation occurred during the 1970s. Let's say a government wants to buy a lot of guns and bombs to wage war, but it doesn't want to lose popularity with the people by taxing them to pay for these military expenditures. It finances military spending by printing new money. This, in effect, means the government starts up new factories for guns without slowing down the factories that produce food and clothing for the citizens. Can the economy supply the labor, the transportation, the steel, and the energy required to fire up the military sector without slowing down the consumer sector? If it can't, these two sets of producers compete for inputs, bid up prices, and thus spark inflation. That's what happened as a result of the war in Vietnam.

EXCESS GOVERNMENT SPENDING Another source of excess money-supply creation during the past two inflationary decades has been overuse of fiscal policy. We have already seen that when there is unemployment, people expect the government to step in and spend a lot of new money. It was originally believed that the government should offset this by running a budget *surplus* during good years. By taxing more than it spends during prosperous times, the government would absorb excess dollars, pay back debt, and slow down consumer spending—thus countering any tendency toward inflation. But somehow the good times were never good enough, politicians were always inclined to spend more and tax less, and so we have had a federal budget surplus in only one of the past twenty-five years. Since there was a deficit in each of the other years, a lot of new money, and inflationary pressure, has been released into the system.

RECENT ATTEMPTS TO CONTROL INFLATION

By the late 1970s and early 1980s, many economists, politicians, and voters had become convinced that the only way to stop inflation was to reduce the rate of growth of the money supply. However, many others feared that this tactic would cause even more economic problems. They maintain that it would be like increasing the number of chairs in the room from ten to twenty, but only increasing the number of dollars to fifteen. At $1 apiece, only fifteen chairs would be sold. A price decrease (to 75 cents each) would be necessary to sell all twenty. Since in real life producers are rarely willing to lower prices, five chairs would most likely go unsold. This means unemployment and lost profit for the producers of those five chairs, which, as we have seen, could easily spiral into a recession. The policy of controlling money-supply growth seems to have slowed down inflation in the early 1980s, but its merits are still being debated. (We will consider this issue again in Component Chapter D.)

In grappling with the inflation-recession question over the past years, we have learned that the answers are not independent of what is happening in other parts of the globe. Our military budget depends in part on events elsewhere in the world; likewise, the price of the energy and other natural resources that our factories use depends on the actions of foreign suppliers. We can even purchase many finished goods abroad for less than we can make them at home, and while these imports have helped hold down inflation, they have also meant fewer jobs for Americans in certain industries. In the following chapter, we will explore these links between the U.S. economy and events in all corners of the world.

CHAPTER REVIEW

In about a decade, the pocket-calculator industry grew from little more than an idea into a multi-million-dollar business, and the price of an individual calculator fell from about $400 to about $10. This phenomenon shows how the chance to make profits can encourage businesses to make good-quality items widely available at affordable prices. It typifies the ideal operation of our economic system, which is based on free competition and the profit incentive (by contrast, for instance, to government regulation, as in the Soviet Union, or a sense of social duty, as in primitive societies).

A businessperson must understand both microeconomics and macroeconomics in order to make sound business decisions. Microeconomics involves studying the costs and revenues of individual enterprises. Macroeconomics, on the other hand, is the study of large economic forces and the ways they interact with and depend on one another.

Prices of individual items are set at the "micro" level, through the use of demand and supply curves. The demand curve reflects the increasingly greater demand that an item generates as its price declines. Correspondingly, the supply curve indicates the increasing production (supply) that an item generates as its price rises. By combining the supply and demand curves, the marketplace establishes a point of equilibrium that is the ideal price.

Pricing influences not only producers but also investors. But basically it is consumers who, through their "votes" on whether and what to buy, shape the allocation of resources and production of goods. They also, indirectly, influence the supply of labor since, other things being equal, a higher price (in pay or salary) will attract more workers than a lower one.

The American economy is not controlled entirely by marketplace decisions, however. Coalitions of manufacturers (oligopolies) and workers (unions) limit the free movement of market forces. So do society's needs for things the free market cannot supply, such as public goods and economic externalities. This is where the government steps in, supplying public goods and services, regulating business, and making transfer payments. Because it is influenced by a mixture of market and non-market forces, the economic system of the United States is known as modified capitalism. Effective businesspeople must be aware of these factors and of how they affect their firms.

At the macroeconomic level, the concept of circular flow illustrates the interrelationships among businesses, households, and governments; all economic decisions thus ripple through the system (the multiplier effect). This flow is measured in terms of the gross national product (GNP), which indicates a nation's economic growth and provides a comparison with the output of other nations, although it does not measure all goods and services or the quality of life.

The phenomenal economic growth of the United States rested on its rich natural assets, skilled human resources, and abundant capital. Initially, Americans made themselves into a nation of independent farmers, expanded to the Pacific coast, and began to build a transportation network. This extensive growth became intensive in the mid-nineteenth century, when rapid industrialization began to attract many new immigrants. Technology, organization, and entrepreneurship—as exemplified by Henry Ford, Andrew Carnegie, John D. Rockefeller, and others—then took over.

But the unprecedented booms that resulted were marked by periodic "busts," the worst of which was the Great Depression of the 1930s. It led economists and others to seek ways in which recessions, depressions, and their effects (such as unemployment and inflation) might be controlled. Influential among these thinkers was John Maynard Keynes, who felt that government spending could serve to mitigate unemployment and warm up a cooling economy. This fiscal policy came into question during the recession of the early 1980s, but no clear-cut solution has been found to use in its place.

By the late 1970s, inflation, which indicates an economic warming trend, rose to double-digit annual rates—which is far *too* warm. Such a trend discourages saving and investment, spurs short-term spending, increases the demand for goods and credit, and, as it feeds on itself, increasingly distorts the economy. Although economists explain it as "too many dollars chasing too few goods," no one knows exactly what causes it. It can stem from curbs on supply, which may be due to shortages or increased costs of labor, equipment, raw materials, and so on. Declines in productivity also play a role. An especially important spur to inflation is an increase in the supply of money (as when the government prints excess money to enhance its popularity or finance military outlays or when it imposes less taxes than the total amount it spends).

During the early 1980s, many Americans became convinced that the only way to stop inflation was to stop creating excess money. Although this policy has, in fact, stemmed inflation, it has also caused unemployment in some industries, and raised many new questions regarding future economic policy.

KEY WORDS

economic system (48)
microeconomics (50)
macroeconomics (50)
demand curve (51)·
supply (51)
supply curve (51)
market price (52)
oligopoly (53)
pure capitalism (54)
modified capitalism (54)
public goods (54)
economic externalities (54)
transfer payments (55)
circular flow (55–56)
multiplier effect (57)
gross national product (GNP) (58)

capital (59)
factors of production (60)
land (60)
labor (60)
product markets (60)
factor markets (60)
entrepreneurs (61)
fiscal policy (62)
inflation (63)

REVIEW QUESTIONS

1. How does the pocket-calculator industry exemplify the ideal operation of our economic system?

2. Describe the subject matter of microeconomics and explain its value to the businessperson.

3. Define the demand curve, the supply curve, and market price.

4. Name at least three factors that inevitably prevent a true free-market economy.

5. Our system is actually a form of modified capitalism. What benefits does this, as opposed to pure capitalism, ensure for the average citizen?

6. What do we learn from macroeconomics? What is the circular flow? The multiplier effect?

7. What major change in the American economy appeared during the mid-nineteenth century, and what were some of its effects?

8. Explain the relationships between money-supply growth and inflation. Describe the ripple effects that occur when people must pay more and more for basic necessities.

CASE 1

A GLOOMY SCENARIO IN THE PAPERBACK INDUSTRY

During the 1970s, the paperback book industry was every manager's dream. Conglomerates were bidding high prices to own paperback publishers, and editors were bidding astronomical prices for everything from romantic novels to "how-to"s. A record was set in 1979 when Bantam paid $3.2 million for rights to publish *Princess Daisy*, by Judith Krantz.

But during the early 1980s, the industry was having a hard time living up to these glowing expectations. A number of factors were pushing costs higher and sales lower. For one thing, consumers seemed to be reading less. For another, the spectacular success of romance novels (one *billion* have been sold during the past ten years) and humorous "non-books" (such as the flood of cartoon books about cats) had begun to pinch the market for other types of paperbacks. Meanwhile, people in all parts of the book business, from bookstore owners to paper suppliers, were demanding a larger cut of the profit pie. And of course book companies were paying the price for the excitement of the preceding ten years: authors' and agents' fees had climbed high.

Traditionally, the profitability of the paperback industry has depended on mass sales. The classic economics of book publishing work somewhat as follows. In this business, margins—the difference between costs and revenues—have always been quite thin. But if a book is a blockbuster, then its profits zoom: that thin profit is multiplied by the tens of thousands of units that are sold. What's more, printing a several thousand copies has not usually cost too much more than printing just a few hundred—at least up to now. In either case, the company still incurs the same relatively large *fixed costs*, such as setting the book up on the printing press. Once the book sells enough copies to cover its basic fixed costs, the additional sales are almost pure profit: *variable costs*, for additional paper and other items, are relatively low.

But in the past few years the cost of paper has skyrocketed, adding heavily to variable costs and cutting sharply into the margins of the paperback industry. Why not raise prices to cover the increased cost of paper? This is the most obvious strategy, and it was the first resort of most publishers. But they soon found that there was a limit to workable price increases. They encountered heavy customer resistance to prices above a certain level.

For mass-market paperbacks (those of standard size and shape), this so-called "resistance point" seemed to be at $3. Charge more than $3, and demand suddenly falls off. Even though consumers are aware of price rises in general, they seem to think that paperbacks are worth $3 and no more. Added to the price problem are sociological problems: whole categories of consumers, such as blue-collar males, are no longer buying books in significant quantities.

In 1983, the failure of four paperback companies (later absorption into larger firms) was fresh in the memory of paperback industry executives. More casualties among the eight remaining paperback majors are expected.[2]

1. What economic situations are likely to create profit problems for a product that has a price resistance point? Which of these cost-price squeezers are likely to have an impact on all industries, and which are likely to affect only certain industries?

2. It has been said that consumers "vote with their dollars" in our economy. How is this pattern reflected in the fate of the paperback industry?

3. Try to draw an imaginary demand curve for a paperback science fiction title. First draw a vertical and a horizontal axis, and label them "price" and "quantity," respectively. Now pick a point on the price axis and label it $2.50, and follow it with points labeled $2.75, $3.00, $3.25, and $3.50. Next, try putting in a series of points representing demand at these prices. To do this, start at $2.50 and indicate how many thousand copies you think people would buy. Go on to the other prices and do the same for each one. Will people demand more books or fewer at $2.50? What happens after $3.00? (Hint: Your graph should reflect the fact that demand falls off sharply.) Connect up the points, and you have a demand curve.

4. Pretend that you're a manager in one of the remaining paperback companies. What will you do to buck the trend and restore profitability to your firm? Some of your strategies should be directed toward raising sales, and others toward lowering costs. What subjects in your book list will sell the best?

MEAD PAPER'S PRODUCTIVITY PROBLEM

During the recession years of 1981–82, Mead, one of the nation's major paper makers, wasn't surprised to see sales and profits tumble. At the end of the recession, sales picked up again but profits . . . that was another challenge. During the lean years, Mead had lowered its prices to encourage sales. So had most of its competitors. Pulling out of the recession, most firms in the paper industry had excess capacity: they could not sell everything their factories could produce, and so they couldn't keep their machines humming at full speed. Thus, they needed to encourage sales—and therefore they were reluctant to raise prices. The bottom line: low profits, at that point in the cycle.

When business starts to pick up at the end of a recession, most firms do not immediately go out and hire more workers. Instead, they find ways of getting more output from each worker. Accounting clerks are urged to find time to enter more pieces of data during their workday; secretaries are urged to find time to type more letters. At some point, current employees will no longer be able to handle the increased workload, and the firm will need to hire more workers; but until that point, the company has increased its output without increasing the dollar costs of its inputs (here, workers' salaries). That is, it has increased its *productivity*. It is quite common for productivity to rise after a recession.

Mead's managers knew that since they wouldn't be able to raise prices after the recession, the only way they could increase profits would be by increasing productivity more than their competitors. A common strategy for productivity-minded managers is to take a critical look at older plants. Mead had a plant in Chillicothe, Ohio, with some machines that dated as far back as 1906. As in many parts of the smokestack sector, funds for maintenance and repair had been allowed to run low at this plant. One manager called the policy "baling wire and twine maintenance"; the atmosphere was so gloomy that workers seemed to walk around with their heads down. A decision to close the plant entirely, and shift output to a higher-productivity facility, would not have been surprising.

But Mead executives sharpened their pencils and took a closer look at the economic value of their Chillicothe assets. The plant had a good water supply (essential to paper production); it was located in an area of good hardwood forests; it possessed an experienced labor force; and it was within overnight trucking distance of a number of major markets, including Chicago and St. Louis. Why not put some effort into keeping the plant open and making it work?

The first step was to install a new $125,000 machine that could double the output of the five machines it had replaced. Electronic controls replaced hand-operated valves and cranks. Tighter quality controls were implemented to produce more tons of salable paper for each ton of wood—increasing productivity by getting more output from the same input. In the plant's carbonless copying paper operation, the paper yield per ton of wood pulp rose from the low 70 percent range to the mid-80s. After a lengthy information and education program, Mead was able to negotiate new work rules with its unions. Now, workers are assigned to tasks as a team rather than being shuffled individually from job to job, workmate to workmate. Overall, the plant now turns out a ton of paper with thirteen hours of employee effort, compared to twenty-one employee hours only two years ago.

Mead also had some very new plants, and they presented a different problem entirely. Since these plants already had the latest in automation, productivity gains could only come from human effort and organization. Here, Mead took the innovative step of involving the production workers themselves in the drive for productivity—to take advantage of their intimate knowledge of the manufacturing process and its problems. First of all, to inspire cooperation, the managers began to refer to the workers as "members," rather than "employees." The workers help select new members, and they are encouraged to offer ideas on how to improve product quality and get the job done more efficiently. At times, it seemed that human relations improvements weren't going to compensate for the workers' lack of technical proficiency. But eventually, Mead's newer plants were able to produce at costs 20 to 30 percent lower than the older plants, and Mead estimates that they are the lowest-cost plants in the industry.

Mead found that there's no single secret to improving productivity. "It's a lot of little base hits," says the company's chairman and chief executive. "Eliminate a little waste from each process," says another executive. Today, Mead feels that it is poised for higher profits. The company must still contend with high interest rates, and with weak exports due to recession abroad and the high dollar. But Mead is glad to be in an industry where the U.S. has a competitive advantage (abundant forests), rather than in an industry, like steel or autos, where the competitive edge is held abroad.[3]

1. What microeconomic decisions is a firm sometimes faced with, that are affected by the macroeconomic situation? In what ways do you think the macroeconomy may at times be affected by the micro decisions of individual managers? Cite examples from the Mead story.

2. If a manager were able to make predictions about future trends in the economy, how would it help him run his business?

3. Old plants differ from new plants in many ways. What key business concept allows companies to make comparisons between the value to the firm of such different assets? How can it decide which assets to keep and which to get rid of?

4. If you were a manager at a competing paper manufacturer, what strategies would you consider to increase your productivity?

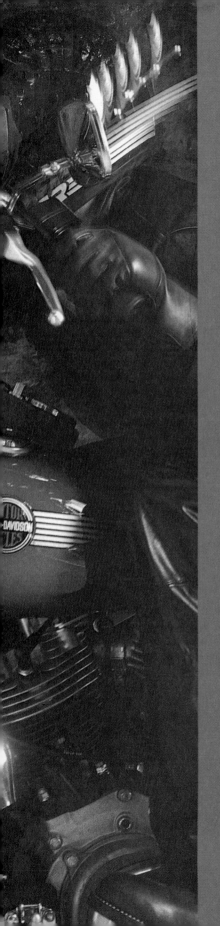

INTERNATIONAL BUSINESS: AMERICA'S PERSPECTIVE

When David Liederman gets up in the morning, he heads straight for the financial pages of the newspaper to check out the standing of the Swiss franc. But David isn't a currency speculator. He's the owner of David's Cookies, and every year he uses Swiss francs to buy millions of dollars' worth of Swiss chocolates. Fluctuations of a point or two in the dollar-franc exchange rate could mean the difference between big profits and a disastrous loss.

David's anxious monitoring of a foreign country's currency is only one example of the ways U.S. businesspeople are enmeshed in international concerns. Today, we buy more foreign products and we sell more products to foreigners; and when the world economy trembles, we tremble. Now, more than ever, U.S. businesses operate in a global environment. We'll look at the challenges of this environment in this chapter.

CHAPTER FOCUS

After reading the material in this chapter, you will be able to:

- list the major postwar developments that have affected American trade with the world
- discuss at least four factors that have made Japan America's chief economic rival
- describe trends in Pacific Rim countries, Western Europe, and Latin America that are affecting international business
- cite the arguments for and against protectionism in world trade
- cite the arguments for and against a national industrial policy
- distinguish the balance of trade from the balance of payments
- list the advantages and disadvantages of a strong American dollar in foreign exchange
- describe the factors contributing to the world banking crisis of the early 1980s

The workers at the Tultex Company, in an area of Virginia's Blue Ridge Mountains known as the "sweatsuit capital of the world," are part of the international business scene, although they don't know it. Like almost every other American mass-market clothing producer, Tultex is competing with cheap foreign imports. Tultex, as it happens, is doing well. Luckily for the company, sweatsuits are a bulky product: they're an item not all foreign producers are eager to ship, since some cost advantages are lost through shipping costs. Luckily also, the U.S. government helps protect domestic clothing makers by limiting garment imports to an annual quota, and many foreign nations fill their quota with items that have a bigger price tag than sweatsuits. Tultex also has an unusual ability to keep costs low. It gets top productivity out of its knitting machines: though the machines are old, they are still clanking out three shifts a day. The firm is still family-run, so its managers are under less pressure to make short-term profits than are the salaried managers who run many American firms. The rural labor force lives well on wages lower than the U.S. industry average. And the firm is leaping ahead of its Asian rivals with new, sophisticated computer-controlled cutting, dyeing, and spinning equipment.[1]

Today, fully 70 percent of U.S. products are in competition with goods that are made just as well in other countries. And not every U.S. business is in as good a position as Tultex. Many U.S. companies are operating at less than maximum productivity: they use outmoded equipment and pay high wages, and their managers often choose not to reinvest profits for long-run improvements. Our "smokestack" industries, in particular, have declined: we import 18 percent of our cars and 18 percent of the steel we use, while 19 percent of our auto workers were on indefinite layoffs in 1983, and 42 percent of steel-plant capacity was lying idle.[2]

It is true that the American economy can still claim its share of international successes. One out of five of our manufacturing jobs produces for export, and fully one-third of our agricultural output is exported.[3] Moreover, although we confront increasing competition in high-technology areas and have to work harder than ever to maintain markets, U.S. goods are highly competitive in telecommunications, aerospace, computers, petrochemicals, lasers, genetic engineering, medical equipment, pharmaceuticals, electrical machinery, and office equipment. But the distribution of job opportunities in these high-tech areas is uneven—workers who lose their jobs in older industries generally lack the skills that are in demand in newer ones. Many policy analysts believe we may be headed, at least temporarily, for a "two-tier" (two-layer) economy, where some individuals, companies, and regions will face rosy prospects, while others will suffer an ongoing economic slump unless and until they can adapt.

In the past, the United States was not heavily oriented toward world trade. Yet, because of the sheer size of our country and of the manufacturing sector of our economy, we were one of the major producers of goods sold worldwide.[4] How did our position in the world economy change, and what are some of the problems we now face? Let's look at the recent history of the world economy, and then discuss some of the key political and financial issues connected with world trade today.

WORLD TRADE IN RECENT HISTORY

In recent decades, the world has seen a boom in international trade unlike any other in history. Between 1961 and 1981, both U.S. foreign trade and world trade tripled in "real," or inflation-adjusted, terms. And this trade expansion was accompanied by a new flourishing of **foreign direct investment**— *the purchase of productive plant and equipment outside one's own country.* Most of today's large corporations earn a hefty portion of their revenues from their overseas ventures. And many nations owe a large share of their gross national product to the output of firms located beyond their borders.

POSTWAR DEVELOPMENT AND THE MULTINATIONAL CORPORATIONS

Some of this international business activity was originally generated by American companies. The trend began after World War II, when the economies of most European countries were so devastated that they could provide neither consumers' basic needs

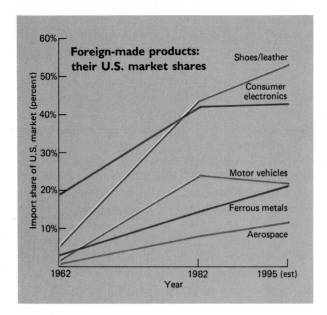

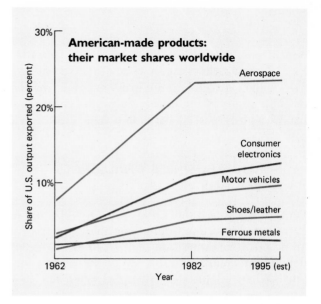

FIGURE I

JOCKEYING FOR POSITION IN GLOBAL TRADE:
American versus foreign manufactures, in five representative product areas

Some foreign imports, such as shoes and clothing, have flooded U.S. markets in the last twenty years— while U.S. exports of these items have grown only modestly. In other product areas, such as aerospace, our exports have zoomed and we have also retained most of our domestic market. Possible reasons for **these patterns include low foreign labor costs versus high domestic labor costs; the "high dollar"; unique U.S. expertise in aerospace engineering; and recent innovations in the U.S. electronics industry. (A forecast of the future is also shown.)**

Source: Interindustry Forecasting Project, University of Maryland

nor the goods businesses needed to rebuild. The U.S. government hatched the idea of providing funds to help the European countries get back on their feet. As expected, Europeans spent most of the funds provided by this "Marshall Plan" on American goods. In the 1950s, some American firms did a brisk business in Western Europe selling everything from machines to luxury goods: the United States accounted for approximately 16 percent of world trade during that decade[5] (compared to just over 11 percent today).[6] And certain U.S. firms decided to set up subsidiary companies in Western Europe to hold on to that huge and reviving market.

The Marshall Plan was so successful in Western Europe that the United States turned its attention to the developing countries of Africa, Latin America, and Asia: here, the goal was to help build industries where they had never existed before. The United States gave these developing countries some direct foreign aid. But the developing countries' economic problems turned out to be much more complex than Western Europe's, and so help from banks was also needed. The result was the establishment of the **World Bank** (officially the International Bank for Reconstruction and Development), *a multilateral development agency with more than 140 member countries, located in Washington, D.C.* When we say that the World Bank was multilateral, we mean that many countries were lenders of funds for development. Nonetheless, much money flowed back from the developing countries to the American companies that were selling them much-needed consumption and investment goods. And just as in Western Europe, certain American businesses opened up factories and sales offices in these nations.

The growth of U.S. **multinational corporations,** *firms with operations in a variety of countries,* was striking. In 1956, fully forty-two of the world's fifty largest firms were U.S.-owned.[7] In 1968, the Frenchman Jean-Jacques Servan-Schreiber's famous book *The American Challenge* noted that the second largest economy in the world, after the United States, was U.S. business interests in Europe![8] Even today, twenty-one out of the world's fifty largest industrial companies are American, and 40 percent of all the world's businesses owned by noncitizens are owned by Americans.[9] In 1980 Exxon, the world's largest company, had sales of $103 billion, exceeding the gross national product of 150 nations in the world—including Saudi Arabia, Czechoslovakia, Austria, and Argentina.[10]

FOREIGN BUSINESS CHALLENGES AMERICANS

Perhaps it was not until OPEC (the Organization of Petroleum Exporting Countries) tripled the price of oil in 1973 that Americans truly realized how interdependent we are with the rest of the world economy. When oil prices quadrupled again in 1979, Americans were forced to spend an ever-larger share of their income abroad. And, as if that weren't enough, during the 1970s American consumers began to decide that foreign products, from shoes to cars, were more attractive than American goods— because they were cheaper. Your favorite brand of shirt suddenly was "made in Singapore"; your shoes were "made in Brazil"; your office equipment at work was "made in Germany"; and you could afford another TV because it was "made in Taiwan." When you found yourself trading in your car for one "made in Japan," you looked around and noticed that one in four cars on the road in the United States were imports. Imported goods now represent 19 percent of total American consumption, compared to just 9 percent in 1970.[11]

It may have been inevitable that our economy should become more closely linked to foreign economies, as fast-developing transportation and communications technology slashed the time, expense, and risk of shipping goods from one part of the globe to the other. But why were foreign businesses so skillfully generating jobs for foreign workers, while U.S. unemployment climbed? Did the foreign businesses have some kind of business savvy that we lacked? Let's see what they were doing differently.

"JAPAN, INC."

In 1979, RCA felt that it did not have the $200 million it would need to develop a videocassette recorder (VCR). Two Japanese firms, Sony and Matsushita, operating from a different management philosophy, and backed by tight linkages to the Japanese banking community, were able to devote their long-term resources to such an innovation, and now they alone dominate the huge and growing world VCR market.[12]

A slightly different story is that of the American auto makers. Unlike RCA, they have made a gigantic effort in their market: they vowed to meet their Japanese competition by 1985 with an $80 billion investment plan that would be no less monumental than the U.S. space program. But as of this writing, one year before that goal, it seems that making a competitive small car in the United States is still harder than landing someone on the moon.[13] Japan's unique productivity and quality standards have proved difficult to match. Japanese productivity yields a cost advantage of $1,500 to $2,000 per car, even after shipping costs. And in the future, American auto makers will have to contend with some impressive new design features still on the Japanese drawing board: windshields that sense rain and automatically turn on the wipers; transmissions that change from automatic to manual at the flip of a switch; stereo speakers built into molded head restraints; and ceramic engines controlled by optical fibers instead of by wiring.[14]

The Japanese system of organization

Japan's formula for economic success developed after World War II, when most Japanese citizens lived at a level of extreme poverty. Strikes were commonplace in factories, and the nation's leaders searched for a better way to organize production to meet the people's needs. The result was Japan's unique system of industrial organization, in which workers gain lifetime security and a role in decision making, in exchange for high productivity and complete devotion to the company. Japanese workers' dedication is evident early each morning when production workers arrive, dressed in the company uniform, to set up their tools, exercise, and sing the company song. In order to help keep productivity high, many Japanese workers work a half-day on Saturday; they take less than half of their allowable vacation days and almost no sick days. They also allow themselves to be transferred to a different task in a different branch of the company—without question—if that's where they're needed.

But Japanese quality and productivity derive not only from workers' sacrifices but also from their role in making production planning decisions. Groups of workers known as quality circles meet on company time to discuss ways to cut costs, eliminate defects, and generally perform their tasks more efficiently. (A **quality circle** is *a regularly scheduled meeting of about five to fifteen workers who usually work in the same area to identify and solve quality, safety, and production problems.*) Quality-circle members receive special training for their role, and management listens seriously to their conclusions. The worker knows best what the problems are on his part of the production line, they believe. Quality circles work well because employment security is guaranteed, so workers do not fear that production efficiencies will put them out of a job. One reason Japan has been able to use robots extensively in its factories is that its workers know they will be retrained rather than laid off: workers adapt readily to the robots because they do not pose a threat. And instead of relying on quality inspectors, Japanese workers are responsible for their own quality control. In fact, they achieve a far lower rate of defects on the production line than do American workers. (We explore these and other Japanese production innovations, such as the "just-in-time" system of keeping inventories at a bare minimum, in Chapter 6.)

The uniqueness of Japanese business organization extends to management as well. In hard times, rather than laying off workers, managers in many of Japan's largest companies take cuts in their salaries. Managers spend years in factories and sales offices getting to know their businesses intimately. Indeed, in Japan there are few executive suites: managers' desks are generally located in large open areas along with their staffs'. Some observers believe that Japanese executives have a very different set of values and approaches than their American counterparts.[15] Economist Robert Reich has suggested that there may be a trend in American management toward "paper entrepreneurialism": because they tend to be judged on the basis of short-term—even quarterly—profits, managers devote more resources to buying up other companies than they do to investing in new plants and machinery.[16] Japa-

nese executives tend to design policies with an eye to their companies' long-run financial health. Since Japanese managers plan for the long term, they are able to invest quite heavily in research and development, and in new plant and equipment. And they pursue new markets aggressively until they flourish, rather than merely testing the waters and pulling out if a quick profit can't be made.

The government-business relationship in Japan

Many observers of the Japanese business scene believe that the nation's tremendous economic success is partly due to the policies of its government. The Japanese government does not directly subsidize Japanese business. It does, however, organize opportunities for Japanese executives in each industry to get together and discuss their plans for the future, and it often helps Japanese companies in their negotiations overseas. (American executives, by contrast, are prohibited by our antitrust laws from getting together with competitors to fix prices, restrain trade, and so on.) Companies do compete fiercely in Japan. But they also meet under the guidance of MITI (the Japanese Ministry of International Trade and Industry) to eliminate the unproductive aspects of their rivalry. For example, they may undertake joint research and development projects to achieve technological innovations at a lower cost to each. Smaller firms may form "export cartels" to compete with foreign giants. (A **cartel** is *an association of producers that attempts to control a market by limiting output and dividing market shares among the members.*) And when there is excess production, firms may form "production cartels," so that they can divide up the cutbacks fairly rather than continuing to overproduce.

The harmonious relations among Japanese workers, managers, and government agencies have earned the country the title "Japan, Inc." But this spirit of cooperation was not designed by clever modern industrial psychologists; it is rooted in Japan's ancient social customs and homogeneous society (most Japanese people are of similar ancestry and have a similar cultural background). The Japanese islands have been overcrowded for centuries, creating a culture that emphasizes getting along

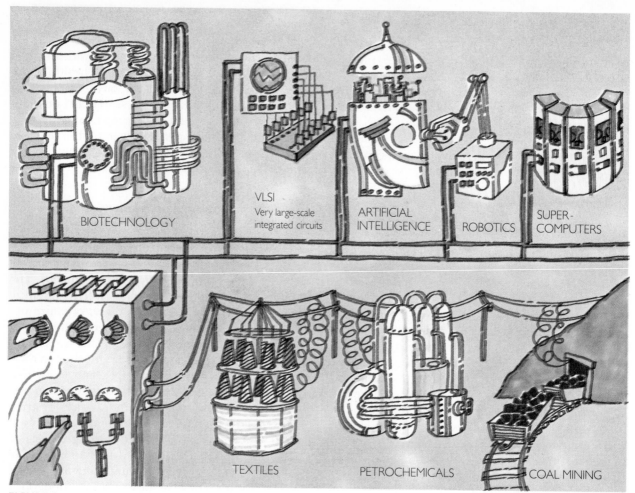

FIGURE 2

HOW THE GOVERNMENT HELPS INDUSTRIES IN JAPAN:
Growing industries receive support, declining industries fade without struggle

The tradition of having the government keep its nose out of business, long popular in the United States, finds less favor in Japan. There, the government sometimes plays an almost grandfatherly role, helping to shepherd some of the nation's enterprises along the road to prosperity. Backing from the Ministry of International Trade and Industry (MITI), for example, actively encourages certain industries by smoothing out risks: if MITI approves a given program for research and development, banks will be more likely to support it with loans. The kindly grandfather also eases the decline of industries that are less needed. The government cushions layoffs by supervising transfers and retraining programs; it also oversees cooperative decision-making among companies within an ailing industry to ease the impact of cutbacks.

with the group. Also, until the late 1800s, Japan's socioeconomic system was a feudal one (the country was governed by a handful of powerful families): the culture reinforced the traditional values of loyalty and obedience to authority. Many of Japan's largest firms, particularly the trading companies, began as feudal family commercial empires. Their modern counterpart is the **zaibatsu,** *an informal group of Japanese companies, often in different sectors of the economy, bound together by personal and business ties.*

America's vast frontier, on the other hand, allowed a high value on self-reliance and individuality. We now have a culture that stresses the individual and competition; these attitudes are reflected in our frequent lawsuits, and in our tendency to put career before company, rights before duties. Our society is also much less homogeneous than Japan's: our population includes people of many different ethnic and cultural backgrounds. We may learn much from the Japanese, but some experts believe we cannot expect to transplant techniques successfully from one cultural environment to another.

OTHER MAJOR COMPETITORS ABROAD

Remarkable as Japan is, it is not, of course, our only major competitor. Western Europe, Latin America, and the countries of the Pacific Rim also play key roles in world trade today.

The countries of the Pacific Rim

In recent years, the Japanese have carefully watched the booming economic growth of their neighbors in the Pacific Rim. Taiwan, South Korea, Hong Kong, Singapore, and other nations in this region have been following Japan's model of export-led growth, and succeeding quite well at it. Their low labor costs (averaging around $1.50 an hour compared to $7.50 in the United States) have enabled them to find mass markets for their manufactured consumer goods.[17] Now that Japanese wage rates have risen close to U.S. levels, the Pacific Rim countries are starting to take over Japan's export markets for textiles, televisions, and even steel. But Japanese industrialists are not just sitting by: instead, they are shifting their focus to more sophisticated exports that require higher-skilled and higher-paid workers.

Social democracy in Western Europe

Since 1950, while the U.S. economy grew only 3 percent a year, most Western European economies grew at an average annual rate of 6 percent.[18] The area's postwar growth was helped greatly by the **European Economic Community (EEC),** often called the Common Market, *a grouping of European countries that provides for free trade and labor mobility among members, and a common tariff to outsiders.* (We will discuss free trade and tariffs later in this chapter.) The EEC developed during the period when those nations were overcoming the economic barriers that divided them from each other on the continent, and it helped them become competitive worldwide.

Western Europe has a unique brand of socialism, known as "social democracy." For most Western European countries, this policy means widespread welfare benefits such as nationalized health care, plus government ownership of principal industries such as telephones, energy, and steel. On the job, it means a high degree of "industrial democracy," or worker participation in decision making. Firms are generally not free to lay off workers without negotiating with the government and/or unions, despite stagnation in old manufacturing industries such as steel and textiles. But in recent years, many industries and companies in socialized Western European countries have performed poorly. In some of these countries, there is a trend away from socialism: in 1984, the government of France approved a tough plan to strengthen inefficient state-owned industries—including steel and shipbuilding—by cutting jobs. Some Western European governments provide aid to "national champions," or leading firms in strategic industries such as computers and mass transit, in hopes that they will become globally competitive. Some governments sponsored the development of a whole new technological area, such as videotex (Prestel) in Great Britain, and have gone on to lead the United States and the world in those fields.[19]

Meanwhile, some observers believe that Western European managers are still too narrowly nationalistic in their thinking. Wisse Dekker, president and chairman of Philips, the Dutch electronics giant, believes that only global corporations will be competitive in the future, since huge markets are necessary to support the huge expenditures behind technological innovations. If Western European firms don't join together to serve a single integrated regional market, Dekker says, they will lose out to other firms with broader horizons. To help make his vision a reality, he is arranging many technology-sharing joint ventures with firms from other European countries. A joint venture was formed with AT&T to bring "Ma Bell" technology to Europe.[20]

Industrialization in Latin America

Most of the nations in the Western Hemisphere have found themselves importing many of their manufactured goods from the United States, and exporting primarily raw materials—natural resources and agricultural products. This position has generally been regarded as an unfavorable one; some observers believe it has been a factor in these countries' relatively low levels of material wealth.

Over the past two decades, most Latin American nations have sought to industrialize and become less dependent on foreign products. Doing so, however, requires a huge amount of capital. Some of the needed capital has come from exports of valuable natural resources, such as Mexico's and Venezuela's petroleum, and some has come from foreign investors, as in Brazil and Argentina; but much of it has been borrowed. As these loans are coming due, many nations find themselves unable to repay.

THE UNITED STATES FIGHTS ON

Despite the damaging effects of the recession of the early 1980s on some of our industries, we are still a major industrial power, particularly in industries which focus on advanced technology, and which have a high research and development component. The U.S. economy provides an excellent environment for technological sophistication and innovation. We have an abundant supply of highly trained engineers, and of venture capital to finance their work. Furthermore, we have an individualistic, entrepreneurial atmosphere that tolerates, even encourages, risk taking. (It was partly the influence of this environment that made it possible for Apple Computer to grow from its garage start-up to the Fortune 500 in just six years.) Innovative businesses are one of the brightest parts of our employment picture: job growth is fast in data processing and health care—services affiliated with rapidly advancing technologies.

At the same time, however, America is gradually shutting down parts of its manufacturing sector; it is getting some of its manufactured goods by trading with nations that can produce these items for less than we can. Some experts have suggested that short-sighted management is partly to blame; they believe U.S. managers should have invested more resources in research and development, and should have tried harder to increase productivity. American companies also pay high wages. In 1982, the average hourly wage in the U.S. auto industry was $19.43; it was $12.94 in West Germany and $7.22 in Japan. On average, our steelworkers earned $22.74, while those in West Germany earned $11.51, and in Japan, $10.18.[21] Japan and West Germany are now two of our biggest suppliers. And an increasing share of our steel imports come from Brazil, South

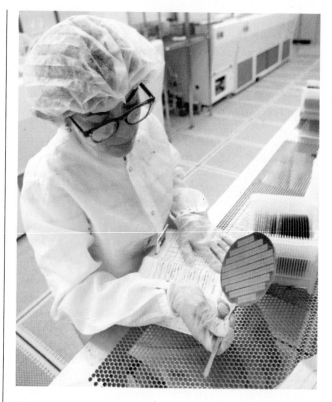

There's heartbreak as well as success in Silicon Valley (shown here, a technician helping to build microchip wafers in a Silicon Valley plant). Some companies may spend years (and millions) perfecting their new technology, only to have overseas competitors copy the finished product and undersell the originator. Some companies' research simply fails to pay off—as at Southern Biotech, which was involved in genetic engineering. Some companies get left behind, like Digital Equipment Corporation, which led the way in minicomputers but is still struggling with micros; some established giants fail to elbow their way into the developing action—like Xerox, which led in office copiers but has not been able to do well in office automation.

Korea, Argentina, Taiwan, and even Trinidad and Tobago—nations with low wage scales that even the efficient Japanese and West Germans can't match.

Economists Barry Bluestone and Bennett Harrison have labeled this trend the "deindustrialization of America."[22] For many of us, the problem is only something to read about: we continue to enjoy a steady supply of manufactured goods—most of them at relatively affordable prices. But the deindustrialization of our heavy manufacturing is a

FIGURE 3

OUR SMOKESTACK INDUSTRIES: WHY ARE THEY FAILING?

How do American business executives feel about the failing smokestack industries? Should these industries be "rescued" through government bailouts? *Business Week* **magazine had pollster Louis Harris & Associates ask 600 high-level executives about this issue. Ominously, the respondents were badly split: though 43 percent blamed the decline on high labor costs, 22 percent cited poor management. These results suggest that many members of the business community would not support government intervention—even at the price of higher unemployment and higher costs for basic materials and products.**

frightening problem for Americans who live in factory towns; even the local butcher will go out of business if unemployed steelworkers can't afford much meat. Amid these changes in our international economic standing, many observers feel strongly that we should take measures to shield our domestic industries from foreign competition. Today, there is renewed debate over a question that has been argued for centuries: the question of protectionism versus free trade.

PROTECTIONISM VERSUS FREE TRADE

Historically, not all governments have encouraged foreign trade. Some have favored **protectionism** (*government policies aimed at shielding a country's own industries against foreign competition*). For example, they have set up **tariffs** (*special taxes on imports*) and **quotas** (*fixed limits on the quantity of imports a nation will allow for a specific good*). In the eighteenth cen-

tury, King George argued that Britain's industries must be protected so that the nation's gold reserves would be used to support its armies abroad, not wasted to import goods that Britain could make itself. In that same century, Alexander Hamilton argued that the young United States of America must protect its infant industries, or America would forever be a cotton-and-tobacco-exporting nation, dependent on Britain for manufactured goods. (Latin American nations used this same argument two centuries later, when they erected barriers to American goods so their own industries could mature.)

Yet during the period after World War II, there was considerable support for the basic **principle of free trade:** *the idea that each nation ultimately gets more if it trades freely, for it is exchanging the goods it produces most efficiently for goods it produces less efficiently.* New international trade institutions developed. The **General Agreement on Tariffs and Trade (GATT),** for example, was established after World War II by representatives from the world's major trading nations; it is *a multinational agreement that sponsors negotiations for lower tariffs and encourages the elimination of nontar-*

iff barriers to imports (such as quotas). The new arrangements outlined in this agreement were designed to promote world trade by defining fair and unfair trading practices. The major trading nations also devised the **International Monetary Fund (IMF),** a sister institution to the World Bank. The IMF is *an organization whose purpose is to smooth the exchange of one nation's currency for another's in payments for foreign goods.* Much of the world's postwar economic vitality has been credited to the GATT and the IMF.

THE CURRENT PUSH FOR PROTECTIONISM

After World War II, the GATT proved extremely effective at minimizing tariffs, cutting down on import quotas and other nontariff barriers, and help-ing to promote free, nondiscriminatory international trade. In recent years, however, protectionist pressures have risen again, and the United States now has voluntary quotas on steel, textiles, footwear, and televisions; in fact, there is some sort of protection—quotas, tariff-rate quotas, bilateral agreements, voluntary restraints—on a large proportion of our imports. Of the total goods that were imported into the United States in 1983, 67 percent paid duty on a value basis.[23]

Many groups have pushed in particular for protectionist measures against Japan. Japan has been accused of **dumping**—*charging less for certain products abroad than at home* (which may include selling them below cost). Though dumping may make some imported goods available at lower prices to American consumers, it may hurt our manufacturers—by undercutting the prices of our domestic goods.

"KEEP OUT" VERSUS "COME IN":
Protectionist and free-trade policies in U.S.–Japan marketing

Some U.S. goods and services are welcomed by Japan, others are discouraged or even turned away at the door. It's puzzling, perhaps—yet we do the same thing, limiting certain Japanese items while accepting others in high volume. The complex reasons involve politics as well as economics.

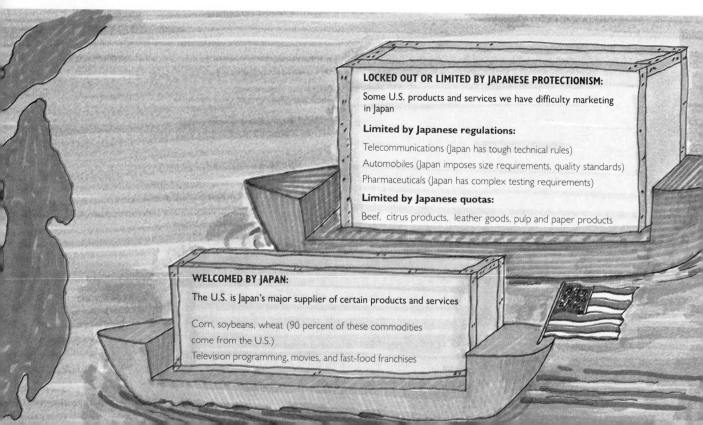

LOCKED OUT OR LIMITED BY JAPANESE PROTECTIONISM:
Some U.S. products and services we have difficulty marketing in Japan

Limited by Japanese regulations:

Telecommunications (Japan has tough technical rules)
Automobiles (Japan imposes size requirements, quality standards)
Pharmaceuticals (Japan has complex testing requirements)

Limited by Japanese quotas:

Beef, citrus products, leather goods, pulp and paper products

WELCOMED BY JAPAN:
The U.S. is Japan's major supplier of certain products and services

Corn, soybeans, wheat (90 percent of these commodities come from the U.S.)
Television programming, movies, and fast-food franchises

Japan has also been accused of using its complicated wholesale channels to discourage the importation of foreign goods; some observers believe Japan uses its banking formalities, its public-health laws, and the laws regarding merchandise that is brought in through its customs, for the same purpose.

Many nations have set up trade barriers in the interest not only of industrial employment, but also national security. For example, a number of observers believe that the United States would be militarily vulnerable if we allowed our steel and shipbuilding industries, however inefficient, to wither away. Similarly, we have imposed trade barriers on some of our exports that have possible military applications (such as computer technology), attempting to prevent these goods and technologies from getting into the hands of potential enemies. Many businesses object to such export controls as ineffective and counterproductive. For instance, when the Soviet Union was denied access to our own Caterpillar equipment for the construction of its gas pipeline in 1978, it did business with the Japanese firm Komatsu—which didn't help our companies.[24]

Are protectionist measures effective?

It is not unusual for trade barriers to fail to achieve their purpose. In January 1983, when the United States and China failed to reach agreement on the size of Chinese textile imports and broke off negotiations, China struck back by reducing its imports of our cotton, synthetic fibers, soybeans, and wheat.[25] Both nations lose in such a situation. Inefficient domestic producers survive and can charge higher prices, because their foreign competitors are either adding on a tariff or raising prices on quota-limited sales. Though a poll taken in 1983 by Opinion Research Corporation showed that 69 percent of Americans support import barriers, some experts believe protectionism can be seen as a 'hidden tax" on the consumer because it encourages prices to stay high.[26]

Deindustrialization and protectionism

Should we let the deindustrialization of our heavy manufacturing continue, or should we adopt protectionist measures in the hope of reversing the

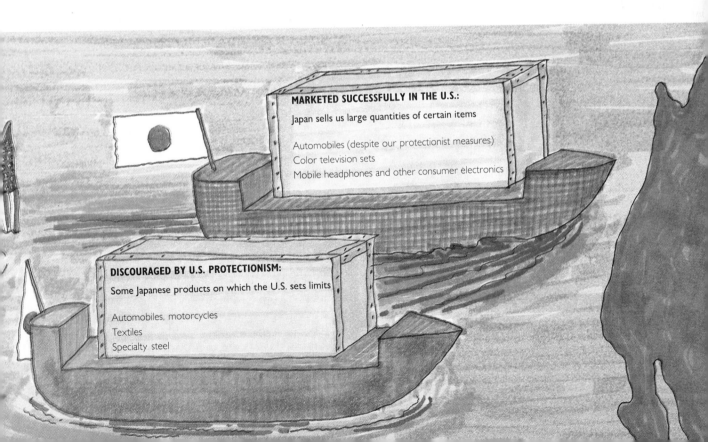

MARKETED SUCCESSFULLY IN THE U.S.:

Japan sells us large quantities of certain items

Automobiles (despite our protectionist measures)
Color television sets
Mobile headphones and other consumer electronics

DISCOURAGED BY U.S. PROTECTIONISM:

Some Japanese products on which the U.S. sets limits

Automobiles, motorcycles
Textiles
Specialty steel

trend? Chrysler chairman Lee Iacocca has warned that we should not let the smokestack industries wither. He believes that it would be very undesirable for us to become a nation of fast-food chains and insurance companies. Testifying before the House of Representatives, Iacocca exclaimed, "We're going to find ourselves armed to the teeth and with nothing left to defend but drive-in banks, video arcades, and McDonald's hamburger stands."[27] Others, however, think we should not try to protect our basic heavy industries. Herbert Stein, who was Chief Economic Adviser to President Richard Nixon, says, "If the most efficient way for the U.S. to get steel is to produce tapes of *Dallas* and sell them to the Japanese, then producing tapes of *Dallas* is our basic industry."[28] According to this viewpoint, focusing America's resources on inefficient steel production could lower our high standard of living; and that outcome would be even more undesirable than losing our steel industry.

THE QUESTION OF INDUSTRIAL POLICY

In addition to protectionist measures, many different plans have been proposed for helping America compete more effectively in world markets. Some experts blame our industries' failure to invest adequately in modernization on an excess of government involvement. Complying with government regulations costs money, these experts point out; meanwhile, profits are also being eaten up by inflation and taxes. These observers think that the government should cut down on regulations; such an approach could free up more corporate funds for new investment in plant and equipment (particularly automation).

Until recently, the United States has not been export-oriented, because the domestic market was still growing. Now, however, the domestic market has reached a plateau: the population is no longer expanding at prior rates. Noting this, some observers believe our government should become *more* involved in international trade, not less. They point out that Japan and many Western European countries, whose domestic markets have always been small, have for decades had a strong "export mentality": those countries have tended to be more aware of the wide range of government programs to aid exporters, offering the exporters everything from pep talks to tax advantages—plus subsidized loans to pay for research and to help foreign customers finance their purchases. Consider Airbus. A short time ago, U.S.-made commercial jet aircraft manufacturers commanded 90 percent of the world's business. But today, our three commercial aircraft companies (Boeing, McDonnell Douglas, and Lockheed) are in heavy competition with Airbus Industrie, a collaboration of the British, French, West German, and Spanish governments. With huge government subsidies for research and to cover operating losses, Airbus increased its share of the widebody aircraft market from 3 percent to more than 50 percent in five years.[29] Another example of government support is the "domestic content" laws of Canada and some Latin American countries, requiring foreign manufacturers within a country to buy parts and raw materials from the local economy.

Not everyone agrees that such heavy government participation is ethical: some Americans believe that these government policies involve unfair trading practices. Nor do all observers believe that the "export mentality" could take hold in the United States: people in our culture may not have the deep awareness of global interdependence that the Japanese and Western Europeans do. Nevertheless, many experts believe our government should undertake export promotion activities on a grand scale—and soon. In 1984, many Americans were calling for a national "industrial policy" to solve our industrial problems.

How would industrial policy work?

"Industrial policy" is an idea with many interpretations. Supporters of industrial policy emphasize that they do not want the government to bail out lagging industries on a large scale. As they point out, such measures (which economist Lester Thurow has called "lemon socialism"[30]) haven't worked for European governments that have tried to help their smokestack industries. Instead, those in favor of industrial policy want to see our government provide aid "with strings attached": if the government offered incentives that would persuade large but sick industries ("sunset" industries) to slim down to an appropriate size, those industries might function better than they would if they continued to hobble

DATA PROCESSING AND THE PROTECTIONIST DEBATE

Could computerized information be a commodity, to be protected like clothing or cars? That's just what is happening right now, in what many American companies consider a worrisome expansion of global protectionism.

■ Brazil, for example, is trying to develop a data-processing industry of its own by preventing IBM and other U.S. multinationals from hooking into Brazilian data bases by satellite.

■ Canada is forcing banks to do some of their data processing in that country by restricting the common banking practice of sending daily records to London or New York, where they are processed and returned by the opening of business the next day.

■ The French government is exploring ways to tax imported computer programs on the basis of their actual commercial value, not the value of the small amounts of computer tape that carry them.

■ India tried to tax *Time* magazine for the stories that were filed (that is, telecommunicated) from its New Delhi bureau.

■ Information is even restricted for political reasons. In August 1982, for example, President Reagan seized on the computer connection as a way to penalize Western European firms that were helping the Russians to build a trans-Siberian pipeline. The president required Dresser Industries, a giant oil- and gas-equipment maker, to "flip the switch" on its French subsidiary's computer link to the United States. Without access to Dresser's technical data base, the French subsidiary was paralyzed and lost sales.

A GROWING TRADE ITEM

Information has one characteristic that makes it an ideal commodity for international trade: its high value per unit of transportation costs. The value of digitally stored information derives mainly from the labor of the engineers who design the computer systems, and of the key punchers who enter the data—and this labor has a high price tag. Transporting information, on the other hand, is cheap. It requires no trucks, ships, planes, or trains: all it takes is a long-distance phone call, which can be efficiently routed through worldwide networks of satellites and computer terminals.

And indeed, the international transmission of computerized information—"transborder data flows," as data-processing professionals say—has become increasingly common. A company may, for example, choose to use lower-wage foreign workers for the labor-intensive task of inputting large quantities of detail into a computer. Or, the far-flung subsidiaries of a global corporation may need to communicate with each other regarding the goods and payments that flow between them. Or, a firm may acquire information in one country and need to use it in another. For example, if an American giftware company wants to send its catalogue to all the American Express cardholders in Britain, it could buy American Express's mailing list of British customers and have it telecommunicated from a British computer to a U.S. computer.

TO PROTECT OR NOT TO PROTECT?

Will governments start putting tariffs on the value of the computer-channeled information that comes in from foreign lands, the same way they put tariffs on the bananas unloaded at their ports? To many American managers, this prospect would be a nightmare for international trade, and they are urging the U.S. government to hang tough and resist other nations' moves in this direction. Managers from other nations, however, claim that the American business community is taking this position merely because we got there first—U.S. firms account for 80 percent of all the data processing that is done worldwide. The foreign managers feel we are trying to avoid losing the data-processing industry as we've lost the automobile, steel, and consumer electronics industries. These foreign nations view high technology as their best hope for growth and jobs, and they are determined to create a high-tech sector however necessary. Governments—both in the United States and elsewhere—now recognize that data transmission is the lifeblood of the modern corporation. For all these reasons, the battle lines on "transborder data flows" are drawn. We may be in for future "information wars."

Would Silicon Valley have ever boomed if it had been up to the government to decide which new industries deserved support? Probably not, because bureaucrats don't like to take chances: they favor a safe course that will keep them out of trouble. We owe Silicon Valley's success to the American individualist tradition of dreaming big and backing long shots. America has built its companies on private entrepreneurship; the United States also has the world's largest pool of private venture capital to back risky new businesses.

along inefficiently with government support. If such old, inefficient industries shrink, these experts believe, some resources will be left idle. Certain newer business sectors, such as high-technology industries, will absorb these unused resources. The government should try to predict which newer business sectors will soak up resources, and should target these "sunrise" industries for special government assistance as well. Other industrial-policy measures that have been suggested include relaxation of antitrust rules to allow joint research and development ventures, extensions on existing research and development tax credits, patents granted to private researchers for discoveries made in federal laboratories, and import relief (protectionist measures). Industrial policy also attempts to single out key industries for development: France, for example, wants to be the leader in high-speed transportation, and it has targeted that area for attention.

Objections to industrial policy

Opponents of industrial policy, who include economists of all political persuasions, shudder at the idea of the government's allocating capital in the economy. Can we assume, they ask, that a civil servant will have better judgment about an industry than an investor who has risked his or her hard-earned funds on that industry, or a manager whose livelihood is at stake? These critics point out that our culture has always had a strong tradition of individ-

ualism and entrepreneurship; they believe that solutions that involve the government in a parental role wouldn't work.

For example, Charles L. Schultze, a liberal Democrat who was chairman of the Council of Economic Advisers under President Jimmy Carter, does not think that government in this country would be able to identify "winning" industries or industrial structures. And he fears that the U.S. political system would let industrial policy turn into a "pork barrel," with every region and interest group getting a share of the money, regardless of merit. Under industrial policy, he argues, a systematic program of assistance to weakening industries would be little more than a "universal protector of inefficiency."

CAN WE DO WELL IN THE WORLD ECONOMY WITHOUT GOVERNMENT ASSISTANCE?

It may be that deliberate government policies to aid our industries will not be necessary. Already, the workings of the free market have enabled us to adjust to the new global economic trends to some extent. Some American companies have taken steps to improve their productivity—slimming down by cutting jobs, merging with other companies, or slashing labor costs. Some U.S. corporations are teaming up with foreign companies in joint ventures designed to share technology in strong countries, and penetrate

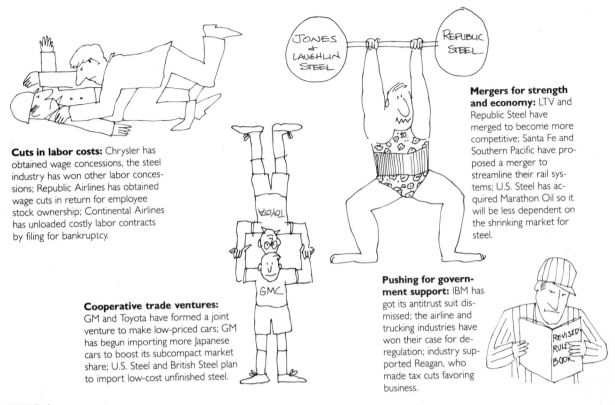

Cuts in labor costs: Chrysler has obtained wage concessions, the steel industry has won other labor concessions; Republic Airlines has obtained wage cuts in return for employee stock ownership; Continental Airlines has unloaded costly labor contracts by filing for bankruptcy.

Cooperative trade ventures: GM and Toyota have formed a joint venture to make low-priced cars; GM has begun importing more Japanese cars to boost its subcompact market share; U.S. Steel and British Steel plan to import low-cost unfinished steel.

Mergers for strength and economy: LTV and Republic Steel have merged to become more competitive; Santa Fe and Southern Pacific have proposed a merger to streamline their rail systems; U.S. Steel has acquired Marathon Oil so it will be less dependent on the shrinking market for steel.

Pushing for government support: IBM has got its antitrust suit dismissed; the airline and trucking industries have won their case for deregulation; industry supported Reagan, who made tax cuts favoring business.

FIGURE 4

GETTING IN SHAPE:
Steps U.S. businesses have taken for stronger competitiveness

Perhaps American business doesn't need a governmental industrial policy: it seems to be finding many answers on its own. Some U.S. businesses have been able to get around constraints that lower competitiveness. By cutting wages, pooling resources, joining with efficient foreign companies, and undoing regulatory restrictions, they are getting into fighting trim.

import barriers in weak countries. U.S. Steel opened talks in 1983 with British Steel to import low-cost unfinished steel to compete with foreign producers; and GM made plans to import more Japanese cars itself to gain a larger share of the market for subcompacts. Foreign investors are being welcomed to invest on American soil: Nissan's new small-truck plant in Smyrna, Tennessee, will allow Americans to buy Japanese pickup trucks and will provide jobs for Americans. And Japan now allows direct American investment in Japanese industry: in 1983, Campbell's Soup and Pfizer bought out Japanese companies with which they had earlier formed joint ventures. Such developments may help ease the economic strain of foreign competition.

FINANCIAL ISSUES IN INTERNATIONAL TRADE

We have looked at a number of issues in international trade. A major factor we haven't yet examined is money. Money and financing complicate our international position.

THE UNITED STATES' BALANCE OF TRADE

Periodically, just as a company calculates its assets and liabilities, every country makes a tally of its **trade balance,** *the relationship between the value of the goods it exports and those it imports.* In general, a nation strives for some balance between these two quantities. If the country has a trade deficit, it has spent more money abroad on goods than it has been able to earn abroad from selling its products.

In part because of our negative balance in the particular area of energy (foreign oil), the U.S. balance of trade has shown a deficit every year except two since 1971—thanks to our appetite for foreign oil and consumer goods, and the lagging competitiveness of our manufactured goods in foreign markets. In 1983 our balance-of-trade deficit reached $69.4 billion, and it is expected to climb to $100 billion in 1984.[31] One cause of this huge trade imbalance was the fact that the recession ended earlier in the United States than overseas: though American consumers were able to start spending freely, other nations could afford few of our goods. Moreover, in 1983 it was very expensive for foreigners to purchase the dollars necessary to buy American goods. (We will explore the reasons for this later.) But it should be noted that our trade with certain specific countries contributes largely to this situation: we have relatively large deficits with Canada and Japan. Were it not for our energy purchases and our imbalance with Japan, we would be nearly in balance.

The major countries and regions with which we have a *positive* balance of trade are Western Europe, Eastern Europe, Netherlands, and Saudi Arabia. Those with which we have a *negative* balance are Japan, Canada, Latin America, Taiwan, and Sub-Sahara Africa. Our balance is *positive* where these major products are concerned: business services, agriculture—wheat and corn, and high technology. Our balance is *negative* for these major products: oil, automobiles, and consumer goods.[32]

Because there are many ways to spend money in a foreign economy, economists track several kinds of external balances. Instead of buying an imported car or coat, you could take a vacation in Europe and spend your money in foreign hotels, restaurants, and museums. Another way to spend money abroad is to invest it—you could buy some stock in a Japanese company, or buy a factory in Hong Kong. Or you could lend your money in a foreign country, as do many U.S. banks and American buyers of foreign bonds. When all these various international movements of funds are accounted for along with trade in goods and services, the overall tally is known as the *balance of payments*. This balance tallies

international trade in services, such as tourism, transportation, and investment income—profits, interest, dividends, royalties, and fees. It also tallies merchandise; and it tallies transfer payments, such as economic and military aid. The United States has had problems with its balance of payments for decades—for a variety of reasons ranging from military involvements to our enthusiasm for travel.

The movement of exchange rates

Every time a Japanese trading company buys a ton of American soybeans to make soy sauce, it must obtain U.S. dollars to pay the American farmer. It can exchange Japanese yen for dollars at one of the international banks that buy and sell **foreign exchange,** *foreign currency that is traded for the equivalent value in domestic currency.* The number of yen, francs, or pounds that must be exchanged for every dollar, mark, or lira is known as the *exchange rate* between those two currencies. On February 27, 1984, 1 dollar was worth 233.25 Japanese yen; or, 1 Japanese yen was worth .4287 U.S. cent.

Flexible (floating) exchange rates

We operate under a **flexible exchange rate system, or floating exchange rate system:** that is, *the values of all currencies are determined by supply and demand,* as reflected in foreign exchange markets around the world (in banks and elsewhere).

For example, suppose France has a trade deficit. Many French people may trade in their francs for foreign currencies to spend abroad, but not so many foreigners will be calling banks to buy francs in order to shop or invest in France. In this situation, the French franc is to the banker what day-old pastry is to the baker—something you had better sell for less, so that you won't be stuck with it. Trade deficits, in other words, can push a nation's currency down. In the same way, a trade surplus can push it up; as everyone rushes to buy West German marks so they can pick up a Mercedes, Porsche, or BMW, the price of the West German mark rises.

Exchange rates change rapidly because supply and demand are always changing. The relationships among the rates are determined in part by what is happening in local economies. If Italy's economy is suffering from severe inflation and unemployment, for example, the value of Italian currency will be low

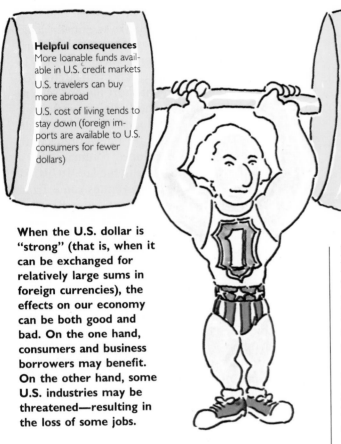

Helpful consequences
More loanable funds available in U.S. credit markets

U.S. travelers can buy more abroad

U.S. cost of living tends to stay down (foreign imports are available to U.S. consumers for fewer dollars)

Harmful consequences
U.S. exports suffer (U.S. goods are priced high in foreign countries)

Jobs lost in U.S. industries producing for export

Low-priced foreign imports compete with U.S.-made products

Jobs lost in U.S. industries whose domestic sales are undercut by foreign imports

FIGURE 5

A STRONG U.S. DOLLAR: GOOD OR BAD?
Consequences of the dollar's strength

When the U.S. dollar is "strong" (that is, when it can be exchanged for relatively large sums in foreign currencies), the effects on our economy can be both good and bad. On the one hand, consumers and business borrowers may benefit. On the other hand, some U.S. industries may be threatened—resulting in the loss of some jobs.

in comparison to that of countries that are not in economic turmoil (such as Germany or Japan).

The high dollar and its consequences

Between 1980 and 1983, the dollar rose 36 percent against other major currencies. The British pound lost 40 percent of its value against the dollar; the West German mark hit a nine-year low, and all-time lows against the dollar were recorded for the French franc, the Swedish krona, the Italian lira, the Dutch guilder, and the Spanish peseta.[33]

What did this mean? Although individuals demand a foreign currency primarily for the purpose of buying goods in that country, it is also possible to simply hold the foreign currency in a bank account and earn interest on it. Recently, interest rates in the United States have been significantly higher than interest rates in other nations. In order to earn this high rate of interest, many foreigners

have been exchanging their own currencies for dollars, and then investing at interest just as if they were dollar-earning Americans. Dollars go up in price when many people rush to buy them and there is a limited supply. An increase in the price, or exchange rate, of the dollar means that it takes more units of foreign currency to purchase each dollar.

The economic effects of the high dollar are both helpful and harmful. One positive effect is the increase in funds available in the United States for lending, which we have sorely needed to match our economy's huge increase in borrowing—the borrowing that has been done by the government to finance the deficit in the federal budget. When the government spends more on defense or social welfare than it receives in taxes, it has to borrow from the savings of the people, made available through bank loans. If foreign investors were not willing to place their money in the U.S. economy, there might be less loan money left for businesses to expand; or, loan money might only be available at extremely high rates.

American travelers also benefit from the dollar's rising exchange rate. Each dollar buys more francs, yen, or pounds, which means the tourist can buy more meals in good restaurants and more (foreign-currency-priced) souvenirs with the same amount of dollars. Finally, the high dollar helps keep down the cost of living in the United States. We can now buy foreign imports with fewer dollars; moreover, cheaper imports exert pressure on U.S. manufacturers to maintain or reduce their prices on capital equipment and some consumer goods.[34]

Despite all these short-run advantages of the

high dollar, there are serious long-run drawbacks. Since it becomes expensive for foreigners to purchase the dollars needed to import U.S. goods, foreigners are less inclined to buy our exports. Being unable to sell exports means losing the jobs that went into producing those exports. At the same time, Americans are more tempted by the bargains provided by yen-priced or mark-priced goods, so Americans import more of these foreign goods. When we buy imports instead of domestic goods, we threaten the jobs that are performed to produce those goods at home. Since, as mentioned above, U.S. producers have already been falling behind their foreign competitors in productivity and quality, this additional handicap is making it very difficult for U.S. manufacturing industries to stay healthy. Not only are the U.S. manufacturers having trouble competing in overseas markets, they have difficulty competing in their own home markets.

As we saw in an example above, a French trade deficit would push down the value of the French franc. You may be wondering, then, why the U.S. trade deficit isn't pushing down the value of the U.S. dollar. As long as U.S. interest rates stay high and foreigners have confidence in U.S. investments, it seems that there will be a strong demand for the dollar despite our weak trade position. On the other hand, as soon as one of the pieces of the puzzle changes, the dollar may come crashing down—with disruptive effects on businesses, which plan their activities around particular international price levels.

America's trading partners are not at all happy about the high dollar. Though the high dollar gives a nice boost to these foreign countries' exports, they feel compelled to either keep their own interest rates high or watch all their nations' loanable funds be sucked up by the United States.

THE PROBLEMS OF OUR GLOBAL BANKS

During the 1970s many OPEC nations quickly amassed more wealth than they could spend all at once. Their natural reaction was to put it in the bank—mostly in the huge New York banks. It was not hard for the banks to find borrowers, since many countries, including the United States, sud-

denly found themselves short of the cash that they needed to pay their oil bills. Banks essentially acted as the matchmakers between borrowers (oil importers) and lenders (oil exporters), earning profits in exchange for absorbing risk. The banks charged higher interest rates to capital-short nations such as Brazil, Argentina, Mexico, the Philippines, Poland, Nigeria, Zaire, Peru, and Indonesia than they could get from domestic borrowers: the interest rates were higher because the less developed countries had a greater risk of defaulting. During the late 1970s, 51 percent of Citibank's annual revenues came from foreign loans, including 5 percent from Brazil.[35] Some bankers, notably Citibank's Walter Wriston, believed that "petrodollar recycling" would work: the less developed countries, they argued, would not go out of business or disappear.

The world banking crisis of 1982

The situation began to approach crisis proportions in 1982: bankers' confidence was shaken when borrowers threatened default, and the possibility of U.S. government intervention was discussed. Many unfavorable circumstances occurred at the same time. First, the recession had cut the earnings of debtor nations, since countries that bought those debtor nations' products had less money to spend. Not only did these debtor nations sell less, but they were forced to sell at lower prices, since natural resources and agricultural goods tend to fall sharply in price when they are in surplus. Perhaps most important, interest rates were quite high around the world, and most developing nations had borrowed short-term at variable rates. (With a variable-rate loan, your bank may periodically change the interest rate it is charging you every 90 days, in accord with current market levels.) With higher interest bills and lower earnings to pay them with, many debtors had to increase their borrowings just to keep up with the interest that was falling due on old loans. For example, in August 1982, Mexico declared that it simply would not have the cash to make its next payment. Many other nations either fell behind in their payments or projected a shortfall in funds in the near future.

As long as the banks kept renewing old loans and approving new ones, they would not need to declare these loans formally in default. Many of the smaller regional banks were not interested in risking any more money in these countries. But in order to raise enough money to prevent a default, every bank already involved would have to commit its share. So the U.S. Department of the Treasury stepped in and provided what amounted to an emergency loan until the banks could reach their own emergency-loan agreement on commercial terms (which frequently meant even higher interest rates than before).

The other debt-burdened nations have had to rely on the International Monetary Fund to provide the emergency loans. It is the policy of the IMF to make its loans dependent on a nation's agreement to change the excessive spending habits that caused the problem in the first place—particularly to restrain inflation, which topped 200 percent a year in Brazil, Argentina, and Mexico. The concept of IMF lending is that the funds should be invested in projects that generate the wealth to repay them. The problem is, however, that less developed countries often spend loan money for current consumption: nations with great poverty strongly resist the idea of cutting back their meager consumption in time of recession. Nevertheless, the debtor nations knew that commercial bankers would resist funding them if they failed to get the IMF seal of approval. The IMF has had a very difficult time reaching agreements with some of these governments, and in some cases the governments have been unable to reach the targets they had agreed on, and have been denied new loans.

What lies ahead for world banking?

The debt crisis is everyone's problem, whether or not we are aware of it. Some less developed nations now lack the hard currency they need to import the basic goods that keep their economies afloat, and their overseas suppliers are unwilling to extend them credit. Thus, U.S. companies lose the business they used to do with these countries (in the past, a hefty 40 percent of U.S. exports went to developing countries). In addition, consumers are affected by the increased risk now carried by the banks: if banks' overall costs go up, the banks may charge consumers more for loans and services. But some observers feel that the banks are overcharging these nations, and that a cut in interest rates would help solve the problem.

To date, despite widespread predictions of a collapse, no serious signals of a coming disaster have yet developed. Early in 1984, when Argentina seemed unlikely to make interest payments on the $8.6 billion lent by American banks, other Latin American countries plus an international banking consortium put together a $500 million short-term loan package to tide Argentina over temporarily. Even if a major crisis of confidence did occur, the Federal Reserve System (the federal agency that governs the U.S. banking system) could be relied on to step in. Some experts feel that a big collapse is still possible, even likely; but it remains to be seen whether the danger of collapse has increased or is now less threatening.

CHAPTER REVIEW

Since the end of World War II, American business outside the United States has expanded enormously, not only in foreign trade but also in foreign direct investment. This trend, which began with the Marshall Plan, spurred the growth of huge multinational corporations and gave rise to new institutions (such as the World Bank) designed to improve the climate for international trade.

During the 1970s, Americans became sharply aware of the interdependence of the world economy, first because of OPEC's oil-price increases and also because of the many foreign-made consumer products that poured into the country. It soon became clear that this process was contributing to unemployment at home.

At present, America's chief economic rival is Japan, whose strength stems from exceptional productivity, very high quality standards, and great technical creativity—none of which the United States has been able to match. These advantages are based on Japan's particular system of industrial organization as well as the close cooperation between Japanese business and government. They also rest on centuries of history and tradition that have given rise to a profoundly different cultural environment from ours. We may be able to learn from Japan, but we may be unable to adopt its ways successfully.

The countries of the Pacific Rim have begun to pose problems for both the U.S. and Japanese economies because their very low labor costs allow them to undersell their rivals. In Western Europe, the advantages of social democracy and the European Economic Community enabled some economies to grow twice as fast as the United States', though many industries in these countries have been performing poorly in recent years. The Latin American countries have borrowed huge amounts of capital to help them industrialize, and some of them are unable to repay these loans.

Despite its problems, U.S. industry is still a strong competitor in the world market, especially in the area of high tech. And at home, innovative technological businesses are thriving. But the picture is less bright for the old smokestack industries, largely because their products can be made for less elsewhere. The result has been deindustrialization, which is causing hardship in many American factory towns.

The principle of free trade, which became popular after World War II and was promoted by the GATT and the IMF, seemed to work during the postwar economic boom. When the world economy began to worsen, however, there were increasing calls for a return to protectionism. In addition, many experts are now calling for a government-implemented industrial policy to ease America's transition from a manufacturing to a service economy. Their critics say that this goes against our traditions and probably would not work.

Since 1971, the United States has shown a balance-of-trade deficit in every year but two. In 1983, this deficit reached a staggering $69.4 billion. The combined tally of every type of trade balance (merchandise, tourism, investment, and so on) is known as the balance of payments.

Foreign exchange rests on a system of floating exchange rates, which vary from moment to moment. And when the dollar is extremely high, as it has been in recent years, the effects are both good and bad. There is more money available for borrowing and Americans can buy more overseas, but domestic goods become harder to sell outside the United States because they are too costly. Also, the long-range implications of a high dollar, such as our weak trading position, are causing concern.

After the OPEC nations invested heavily in U.S. banks during the 1970s, these banks loaned billions of dollars to developing countries. These nations must often borrow merely to pay their interest, and their actual default—and collapse of the entire world's banking system—is a strong possibility. While overspending by the borrowing nations is partly to blame for this crisis, some experts argue that the banks have brought it about through extremely high interest rates.

KEY WORDS

foreign direct investment (72)

World Bank (73)

multinational corporations (73)

quality circle (75)

cartel (75)

zaibatsu (76)

European Economic Community (EEC) (77)

protectionism (79)

tariffs (79)

quotas (79)

principle of free trade (79)

General Agreement on Tariffs and Trade (GATT) (79)

International Monetary Fund (IMF) (79)

dumping (80)

trade balance (86)

foreign exchange (86)

flexible (floating) exchange rate system (86)

REVIEW QUESTIONS

1. Explain how the United States became so heavily involved in foreign trade after World War II. What is a multinational corporation? Give an example and describe.

2. In what ways has Japanese industry proved superior to ours? What are the reasons for Japan's success? Why may we be unable to transplant its methods here?

3. What are the arguments for and against protectionism? What is stopping the American government from simply banning the importation of Japanese cars?

4. Describe the role of the World Bank, the GATT, and the IMF in international trade.

5. What is a national industrial policy? Discuss the arguments for and against it.

6. Explain the nature of trade balances and the balance of payments. Why is the United States facing problems in this area?

7. What is a floating exchange rate and what are the difficulties associated with it?

8. What is the "high dollar" and how did it come about? Outline the advantages and disadvantages of this economic condition.

9. "Petrodollar recycling" by large U.S. banks has caused some serious problems. Describe them and their possible consequences.

CASE I

PROTECTIONISM IN THE RUBBER-BAND MARKET

If you can never find a rubber band when you need one, you may be surprised to know that 75 billion rubber bands are sold in the United States each year. In 1980 imports held only 10 percent of the market, but by 1983 their market share climbed to 25 percent. This was bad news for four American manufacturers—one of which is B. F. Goodrich—who have traditionally dominated this $55-million-a-year business.

A fierce battle for the business of the big rubber-band consumers is unfolding. The target market is not the people who put a rubber band around their wrist when they have to remember something, but the big users. The newspaper industry uses a huge quantity of rubber bands for home delivery. *The Wall Street Journal* alone uses about 50,000 pounds a year, at about $1.70 a pound.

The nation's largest rubber-band user is the U.S. Postal Service. Thus it was bad news for American manufacturers in July 1983 when the Post Office placed its first order ever for foreign-made rubber bands—$316,000 worth. In the past, foreign producers did not make bands strong enough to meet the Post Office's needs. But today, overseas competitors can meet its quality specifications, and at 20 percent less than the price charged by American manufacturers. Says a spokesperson for one U.S. firm, "They're selling the darn stuff as cheap as we can make it."

What do observers say about how the foreign manufacturers manage to sell so cheaply? First, some experts say that foreign producers use filler materials rather than pure rubber. Some American manufacturers accuse foreign companies of exploiting child labor. Other Americans suspect their overseas competitors of industrial spying in an effort to gain access to American firms' technology. American firms also claim that foreign suppliers are less reliable than American companies in terms of quality specifications and delivery dates. American rubber-band firms are doing their best to keep their costs and prices down, but they fear that low-priced foreign rubber bands will continue to make inroads into their markets.[36]

1. If the U.S. rubber-band industry continues to lose sales to foreign companies, what will happen to the number of jobs it provides? to profits? to

the reinvestment that profits make possible?

2. What protection might rubber-band manufacturers ask the U.S. government for?

3. If tariffs or quotas were used to protect the rubber-band market from foreign imports, what would be the effect on consumer prices? Would this policy be justifiable?

4. How does the consumers' view of protectionism differ from the view of workers, managers, and investors in the industry that is seeking protection? How should government resolve this controversy?

5. If the U.S. rubber-band industry were crippled by foreign imports, would there be a significant effect on our national security or economic strength? Why or why not? Can you think of another industry that is more critical to our national security and that is facing a similar problem? Identify it and describe the situation.

CASE 2

DE BEERS, THE INTERNATIONAL DIAMOND CARTEL

One of the most international businesses in the world is the diamond trade. A single company, De Beers Consolidated Mines Limited, dominates the world market for this commodity. Eighty percent of the world's uncut diamonds pass through the hands of this South African company, founded in 1888 by Cecil Rhodes.

We saw in Chapter 3 how supply and demand interact in the free market to set a price. There is one single world market for

wholesale diamonds; and there is one world price. That price is determined by total world demand and whatever De Beers says is the supply. How can one company manage to control the supply of diamonds that come to it from such a far-flung network. De Beers has managed this feat for more than half a century, though at one point in the early 1980s it looked as though De Beers were losing its iron grip on the world diamond supply.

De Beers essentially operates as a cartel—an agreement among producers to limit the amount of a product they will make available to the market, in order to hold up its price. (OPEC is the most well-known cartel.) There are not too many diamond-producing nations in the world, and most of these have exclusive arrangements with De Beers to market their diamonds—at a 25 percent commission. Thus, the world's wholesale diamond buyers have no one to buy from but De Beers. And they must buy according to De Beers' established procedures: they must bid on a whole box of raw diamonds, sight unseen and without recourse, or they will never be invited to another De Beers diamond sale. Does selling diamonds sound like a profitable business for De Beers? It is; in a good year, earnings are 60 percent of revenue.

De Beers does provide a service for the world's diamond miners and merchants. Cartels keep prices stable and high. Diamond miners generally want to sell their entire output right away, but selling too many diamonds at once can cause the price to fall. If they sell to De Beers, they will be paid immediately, but their diamonds will not necessarily get onto the market soon. If supply is outpacing demand, some of those diamonds will stay in De Beers' inventory until the market can absorb them without a drop in price. And diamond demanders can't get a cheaper price somewhere else, because almost every diamond that comes out of the earth gets sold to De Beers. Do business with one of the independents, and you risk being cut off by De Beers.

In 1981, a combination of factors threatened the existence of this long-stable empire. Demand dropped and supply leaped—the precise formula for a price collapse. At the same time, a key diamond-producing nation balked at its arrangements with the cartel in a revolt that could have been contagious. De Beers responded with bold and risky moves, relying on its network of entrenched allies, and sometimes on questionable ethics. But two years later, the "luster" of the diamond business was restored.

The drop in demand was caused by the world economic recession and high interest rates: people had less money to spend. To protect the cartel, De Beers began to restrict supplies, holding as much as 60 percent of production off the market. By the end of 1982, the inventory of diamonds in De Beers' vaults had risen to $1.7 billion from $570 million in 1979. Such a huge inventory of diamonds strained even De Beers' resources. Earnings in 1982 were down 73 percent, and the company reduced its dividend for the first time since 1944.

The leap in supply came from a huge new diamond discovery, at the Argyle mine in Western Australia. The Argyle mine's estimated 1985 production is one-quarter of world production, and thus it would swamp the market if De Beers were not able to keep it under control. Most of the investment partners in Argyle had long-standing links to De Beers, and were willing to sign up the company as their exclusive marketing agent. Not to leave anything to chance, De Beers' public relations staff arranged free first-class tours of De Beers' facilities for a group of Australian journalists. But an Argyle minority partner raised a public cry that De Beers had undervalued a sample of Australian diamonds. The anti-De Beers mood was even expressed by the nation's Prime Minister in a speech to the Australian Parliament. But the company managed to save the day with an innovative agreement—and a little help from its friend Sir Charles Court, the premier of the state of Western Australia. In that mineral-rich country, the state government has the major say in mining matters. The negotiations resulted in some concessions. By the terms of the agreement, De Beers would no longer control production levels at Argyle, and for the first time De Beers gave the producer the right to sell 25 percent of its industrial diamonds and 5 percent of its gems outside the cartel.

Keeping Zaire in the fold was more difficult. That country, with its huge diamond output, had long been considered the key unit in the cartel. Zaire had been voicing dissatisfaction with its De Beers arrangement since the late 1970s, and had pressed harder as its own financial troubles worsened. De Beers offered Zaire a "carrot" to maintain the agreement: a 5 percent cut in its commission and a $10 million loan to upgrade Zaire's worn production facilities. De Beers also used a "stick"—reminding Zaire how hard time it would be for Zaire to find lenders and diamond buyers if it broke from the cartel. Zaire did go independent, and it did find a cold shoulder everywhere it turned. Once Zaire pulled out, De Beers flooded the world market with its inventory of the type of diamond mined in Zaire, causing the price to fall by two-thirds. De Beers stated that this move was motivated by economics, not revenge: with Zaire out of the cartel, there was no need to hold such inventories and no incentive to protect the price of this type of diamond. After breaking with the cartel, Zaire also experienced a huge rash of diamond smuggling. De Beers denies any role in encouraging smuggling, but did purchase the smuggled diamonds once they found their way out of the country. Two years after trying to go it alone, Zaire broke relations with its independent diamond dealers and signed up again with De Beers.[37]

1. Do you think Australia got a good deal from De Beers? One writer suggested that the Argyle agreement is merely a "PR ploy" for De Beers, giving all the power to the producer and tying it to the cartel in name only. Why would it be in De Beers' interest to do so?

2. Why is there always an incentive for cartels to break up? What do you see as the role of one strong cartel leader? How does Saudi Arabia play the "De Beers" role for the oil business? The Soviet Union is one of the world's largest diamond producers. Why do you think they too abide by the De Beers cartel, particularly in light of their strong opposition to the South African apartheid regime?

3. Diamonds are an investment as long as their price steadily increases. In times of high inflation, people believe that gems and other "real" assets hold their value better than paper assets. But when interest rates climb, people sell their diamonds to shift into interest-bearing bonds and certificates. Explain the relationship between inflation, interest rates and the supply, demand, and price of diamonds. What impact do interest rates have on the supply decisions of a diamond cartel?

4. Why do you think there is little protectionism for the diamond business in the U.S. or in most nations? Why do governments feel differently about trade in goods that are not produced in that country? About trade in luxury goods?

5. An international business such as diamonds or oil must be able to operate within the highly varied business climates of many different countries. What impact does internationalizing a business have on the job duties of a company's lawyer? an accountant? a marketing manager? a personnel manager? a public relations manager? Can you think of other jobs that might differ between the domestic and the international context?

SMALL BUSINESS, START-UPS, AND VENTURE CAPITAL

It's 5:32 P.M., and you, the proprietor of a small business, are pondering the events of the day. You've just received a bill for $2,500 worth of business forms—the same amount that cost you $1,800 the last time you ordered. (There must be a way to cut back on paperwork somewhere.) Your community has just decided to split its Yellow Pages into two volumes—one for businesses and one for consumers. You think you should be listed in both. (But are two ads worth the money? And how large should they be?) Your state sales taxes are due, but several of your biggest customers haven't yet paid for the goods they've ordered. (How can you get people to pay on time?) And yet your newest product seems about to take off: orders are pouring in, and the customers love it. (The demand for your coffee-fudge ice-cream cake is exceeding your most optimistic expectations.) It's been another day in the life of that peculiar animal, the entrepreneur.

Every year, many Americans launch their own entrepreneurial enterprises, attracted by the prospect of being independent and running their own show. In this chapter, we'll consider small businesses, start-up companies, and other entrepreneurial ventures.

CHAPTER FOCUS

After reading the material in this chapter, you will be able to:

- define entrepreneurship, and cite four qualities that characterize the successful entrepreneur
- define small business, and list five common categories of small business
- list four important functions of small business in the economy
- enumerate small business's advantages and disadvantages in the marketplace
- cite five services the Small Business Administration provides
- name at least five ways of financing small businesses
- debate the pros and cons of franchise operations

They are nationwide giants today, but they started small like every other business. Delta Airlines, IBM, and McDonald's: here's where it all began.

 One of the most dynamic forces in American business today is the enthusiasm and drive of the **entrepreneur**—*the person who starts or takes over a business, and takes the financial and personal risks involved in keeping it going.* Without entrepreneurs, there would *be* no business. We tend to forget that however large and impressive a business may be today, it was once merely an idea in someone's head— perhaps an idea that was laughed at in its time. Many a familiar product—from Dodge cars to Levi's

jeans to Post Toasties—still carries the name of the fearless soul who launched a business with a clever idea.

Today, we see entrepreneurs at work in many different arenas. The most familiar of these might be called the "classic" small business, a company with a relatively small volume of sales and few employees—your corner dry cleaner, for example, or the neighborhood pizza parlor. Then there are businesses that start out small but grow over the years: Pepperidge Farm, for example, which one woman with a good bread recipe started in the 1930s, is a multimillion-dollar division of the Campbell Soup Company today.[1] And there are "start-up companies," which aim at outgrowing their small-business status as quickly as possible. Start-up companies are no Mom-and-Pop enterprises. Often founded by a group of entrepreneurs rather than by one individual, they obtain a sizable supply of investment capital, and attempt to introduce new products or services quickly and find a large and lucrative market. Start-up companies operate most frequently in high-tech fields, such as computers, medicine, energy, and robotics.

But whatever the setting in which entrepreneurs work and whatever the scale of the fledgling business, people who succeed as entrepreneurs usually share certain personal characteristics. Among the most important is vision—and the stick-to-itiveness to make the vision a reality. Arthur Jones, the inventor of Nautilus exercise machines, worked on his good idea for *twenty-two years* before it paid off. (While perfecting his machine, he earned his living from importing wild animals and producing TV shows—two other entrepreneurial activities.)[2] It also helps if you love your field—be it exercise equipment or automobiles. Terry Ehrich, for example, a self-described "auto addict," bought *Hemmings Motor News,* an advertising monthly for old-car buffs, and increased its circulation more than fivefold. Since then he has acquired other publications.[3]

Successful entrepreneurs also are willing to take the advice of other experts. Herman and Sidney Swartz, whose family shoe company had been barely turning a profit, listened to their advertising manager, Len Kanzer, who suggested that they promote their boots as fashion rather than as heavy-duty work wear. The result was a huge success for the company, now known as Timberland.[4] And finally, entrepreneurs are typically resilient men and women who regard difficulty as a challenge and learn from their mistakes. (Even Henry Ford had two business failures before he founded the Ford Motor Company.) In this spirit, Adam Osborne, whose Osborne Computer Company filed for bankruptcy in 1983, remarked: "You've got to fail some of the time or you aren't trying hard enough. . . . You can't be the kind of person who takes failure hard and be an entrepreneur."[5]

Since most entrepreneurs start small, we'll begin this chapter with a consideration of small business—what it is, what it contributes to the economy, what its problems are. Then we'll look at other arenas in which entrepreneurs work, the start-up company and the corporate entrepreneurial unit. We'll also look at franchising, in which a company can create a big business by cloning itself and selling identical small businesses in many different locations.

SMALL BUSINESSES

Every year, thousands of hopeful entrepreneurs launch new businesses. If they have done their homework—that is, come up with a good product or service and obtained enough financing to see themselves through the first difficult months (or years)—they may make a go of it. One who did was Pat Duncan, who founded the Great American Puzzle Factory, a manufacturer of jigsaw puzzles, in 1976. With a single specialized product, Duncan's business has sales of more than $2 million a year.[6] Someone else who did well with a simple idea is Debbi Fields, whose Mrs. Fields Cookies, founded in 1978, has grown from $200,000 in annual sales to $30 million— a sum that means her business has outgrown the "small" category.[7]

Just when is a business a *small* business? According to the **Small Business Administration (SBA),** *an agency of the federal government that offers loans and provides other services to small firms,* a **small business** is one that is *independently owned and operated and is not dominant in its field.* In addition, it must meet the following criteria:

Type of Business	SBA Ceiling
Service	$8 million annual sales
Retail	$7.5 million annual sales
Wholesale	$22 million annual sales
General construction	$9.5 million annual sales
Manufacturing	1,500 employees (yearly average)

THE WOMAN ENTREPRENEUR

Until recently, most American entrepreneurs were men. Discrimination against women in business, the demands of caring for families, and lack of business training had kept the number of women entrepreneurs small. Now, however, businesses owned by women account for more than $40 billion in annual revenues, and this figure is likely to continue rising throughout the 1980s. As Carolyn Doppelt Gray, an official of the Small Business Administration, has noted, "The 1970s was the decade of women entering management, and the 1980s is turning out to be the decade of the woman entrepreneur."

What are some of the factors behind this trend? For one thing, as more women earn advanced degrees in business and enter the corporate world, they are finding obstacles. Women are still excluded from most executive suites. Charlotte Taylor, a management consultant, has noted, "In the 1970s women believed if they got an MBA and worked hard they could become chairman of the board. Now they've found out that isn't going to happen. So they go out on their own."

In the past, most women entrepreneurs worked in "women's" fields—cosmetics and clothing, for example. But this is changing. Consider ASK Computer Systems, a $22-million-a-year computer software business. It was founded in 1973 by Sandra Kurtzig, who was then a housewife with degrees in math and engineering. When Kurtzig founded the business, her first product was software that let weekly newspapers keep tabs on their newspaper carriers—and her office was a bedroom at home, with a shoebox under the bed to hold the company's cash. After she succeeded with the newspaper software system, she hired several bright computer-science graduates to develop additional programs. When these were marketed and sold, ASK began to grow. It now has 200 employees, and Sandra Kurtzig owns $66.9 million of stock.

Another woman who gambled successfully on her own entrepreneurial ability is Barbara Proctor, the head of Proctor and Gardner Advertising in Chicago. (Gardner is Proctor's maiden name; she decided to put it on her corporate masthead so that it would sound less like a woman's business. As she put it, "Clients assumed a Mr. Gardner was sitting back there manning the ship with everything under control.") Proctor decided to go into business for herself after being fired from her job as copy supervisor in another ad agency. The reason? She, a black woman, refused to write a shaving-cream commercial that featured a "foam-in"—parodying the civil rights sit-ins of that time.

Confident that she could run an agency with higher ethical standards, she obtained an $80,000 loan from the Small Business Administration and set up shop. She has stuck to her principles, stressing a positive, "warm" approach in her ads and refusing to accept accounts for cigarettes or alcohol. Proctor and Gardner now has thirty employees and billings of more than $12 million a year.

Of course, many women who start their own businesses fail, just as men often do. They still face hurdles in the business world, especially problems in raising money: the banking and finance world is still dominated by men, and old attitudes die hard. Most businesses owned by women are still quite small.

But the situation is changing: there are likely to be many more Sandra Kurtzigs and Barbara Proctors in the years ahead.

SOURCE: Earl C. Gottschalk, Jr., "More Women Start Up Their Own Businesses, With Major Successes," *The Wall Street Journal*, May 17, 1983.

As you can see, the sizes of the first four types of business are measured in sales dollars, but the size of a manufacturing business is measured in number of employees. This is because sales figures don't really tell much about the size of a manufacturing operation. The costs of raw materials and components vary so widely that there is no direct relationship between staff size and sales volume. A firm with fewer than 250 employees, for example, could be manufacturing intricate and expensive medical equipment with sales exceeding $30 million. In terms of sales, this would not be a small business, but with only 250 people employed, it could hardly be called large. The relationship between the number of employees and total sales is more direct in retail and wholesale businesses, construction, and service operations.

According to the Small Business Administration, over 98 percent of the nation's businesses are small firms—more than 13 million in all[8]—and they account for 46.5 percent of the gross national product.[9] Moreover, despite inflation, recession, and high interest rates of recent years, which have caused a number of firms to go under, small business is a growing sector of the economy. Small firms are so important to the nation's future that the White House held a conference on small business in January 1980. The attendees—more than 25,000 men and women—developed lobbying strategies to win approval of such measures as a graduated income tax for corporations and a reduction in the paperwork required for a government loan.

As a result of this conference, small-business owners became more involved in the political process than they had before. Leaders in the small-business community began lobbying for legislation favorable to small business, and a number of victories have been achieved since 1980. One has been a series of reductions in the capital gains tax to entice more investors into sharing the high risks of starting new businesses. Another has been legislation that requires the federal government to pay its bills to outside contractors within forty-five days. Some legislators, like Representative Ed Zschau from "Silicon Valley" in California, are entrepreneurs in their own right; they and the "Atari Democrats," legislators oriented toward encouraging high-technology industries, have helped push for changes favorable to

COMMON TYPES OF SMALL BUSINESSES

Small businesses, as we've noted, can be grouped into five large classes.

Service businesses offer specialized and often technical services to customers and business owners. Examples are hairdressers, TV repair shops, dry cleaners, and travel agencies.

Retail businesses sell products directly to the consumer. Bookstores, pet shops, and florists are typical retail outlets. A retail business will often combine with a service business at one location, as in the case of a typewriter and office-machines dealer.

Wholesalers employ capital, raised in many ways, to buy finished products from a manufacturer and resell them to retailers, who in turn sell them to consumers or to industrial users.

General construction firms build or rebuild homes, industrial buildings, and other structures.

Manufacturing firms buy raw materials and components and produce finished products. Because operating costs and risks are high, relatively few small-business entrepreneurs start manufacturing firms without help from wealthy investors.

The satisfactions of shaping one's own enterprise: increasing numbers of women are starting their own firms today.

small and small-but-growing business. In most states, moreover, 1982 and 1983 saw a huge grass-roots movement to encourage small businesses. The states wanted to create their own local "Silicon Valleys," with entrepreneurs who (the states hoped) would create instant wealth and bigger tax receipts for the region.

THE IMPORTANCE OF SMALL BUSINESS: PROVIDING JOBS

Here's a question whose answer may surprise you. What class of organizations represents the nation's largest employer? Oil companies? No. Government agencies? Wrong again. The answer is small businesses. Believe it or not, about 60 percent of all new jobs in the United States are generated by small businesses.[10] Though the vast majority of the jobs small businesses create are low-paying service positions such as sales clerk, waiter, or waitress, these nevertheless are jobs that help put bread on people's tables.

BRINGING OUT NEW PRODUCTS AND SERVICES

Another important way small businesses contribute to economic growth is by fostering innovation. Among the contributions small businesses have made to our comfort and convenience are the safety razor, the self-winding wristwatch, the helicopter, stainless steel, and the plain-paper copier.

SUPPLYING THE NEEDS OF LARGE CORPORATIONS

Besides providing new products and services and new jobs, small businesses fill an important role in the operation of large corporations. General Motors, for example, buys goods from more than 32,000 small companies, more than 50 percent of which have fewer than 100 employees. Typical of small-business specialization are establishments serving the garment industry, such as the shrinkers, who preshrink for clothing manufacturers, and the weavers, who reweave finished garments with minute flaws so that they can be sold as first-quality

goods rather than as seconds. And small retail outlets, of course, are important in selling the products of the giant corporations, from corn flakes to rubber bands to automobiles (General Motors sells its cars through some 10,000 independent dealers). In short, large and small companies are in many cases interdependent, with each needing the other to an equal degree.

PROVIDING SPECIALIZED SERVICES

Finally, many small businesses in our society exist because they meet consumers' needs for specialized personal services. (Small firms that *don't* fill a need disappear quickly!) If you want to rent a Santa Claus suit, buy an odd piece of sheet music, or get your watch fixed, you naturally turn to the costume shop, the music store, or the jeweler—all likely to be small businesses.

Today, affluent consumers have "custom" tastes. They often seek out the individual or the different item. Some small businesses have thus become successful meeting some pretty far-fetched "needs." In New York City, for example, you can buy small chocolate replicas of yourself or a friend—$22.50 for a box of twelve.[11] In Boston, a retail shop called Hog Wild sells everything related to pigs: greeting cards, mugs, stuffed animals, and so on. Perhaps their most unusual product is a device they call an "oinkolator"—a "dieter's alarm system" that consists of a tape recording of pig noises that plays whenever the refrigerator door is opened. The market for chocolate people or "oinkolators" may be small, but businesses that offer such unique products can often find a niche in a well-to-do market.

RUNNING A SMALL BUSINESS

Many is the tired soul who has plunged starry-eyed into a new small enterprise, only to find himself or herself routinely working twelve-hour days week in, week out—with no boss to blame it on! Nitty-gritty detail can come to dominate the life of the small-business owner. Not only is he or she doing the actual work to put out the venture's product or serv-

Running your own business is a lot less simple than it looks "on paper."

ice—gourmet cooking, cabinetmaking, legal consulting, or whatever—he or she may also have to function as secretary, personnel manager, financial planner, public relations department, and janitor, all rolled into one.

Some of these may be areas in which the small-business owner has little or no formal training. Still, these skills can be learned. In most small businesses, the overall routines that must be followed to start up and operate the business are fairly standard. At the end of each unit in this book, you will find a special section titled "Perspectives on Small Business," which explores these routines in detail. We're also going to give an overview here.

STARTING UP

First, the entrepreneur must choose whether to establish the business in the form of a sole proprietorship, a partnership, or a corporation, bearing in mind some of the considerations we have mentioned in Chapter 2. For each type of organization, certain legal formalities will then have to be carried out.

■ The sole proprietorship can be started simply by rounding up some bank checks, some invoices, and the cash to pay a month's rent—but you must also obtain a business license, and there *may* be other legal details as well.

■ To start a partnership, you will have to have two legal instruments: a *partnership agreement*, which spells out the basic outlines of your arrangement with your partner, and a *buy/sell agreement*, which defines what will happen if one of the partners dies.

■ For a corporation, you will have to choose the state in which you want to incorporate, file incorporation papers,

form a board of directors, name officers, and also set up a *stock redemption plan*, which serves the same functions as the buy/sell agreement in a partnership. You may also want to think about setting up a *Subchapter S corporation* instead of a regular type of corporation. The Subchapter S corporation has the limited-liability advantages of a corporation, but also the simpler tax structure of a partnership. (For more on the legal and other arrangements necessary to start a small business, see "Perspectives on Small Business: A Preliminary Overview," at the end of Part 1.)

MANAGING THE BUSINESS

There's no room for vagueness when you are managing a small enterprise. Just like a manager in a large company, you must make business plans, organize your staff (if you have any), delegate responsibilities, motivate and direct your people, and monitor the outfit's daily activities—and you must be as specific as possible at all times. Exactly how many units can you produce and deliver by the end of this month? Will you or your partner negotiate with the outside supplier who is coming this Thursday? Does your assistant know which particular tasks he must get done this week? Can you account for all of this month's mileage on your delivery truck? If you don't ask yourself detailed questions like these, you may find your profit margin disappearing—and not quite know why.

Special planning problems

The wise entrepreneur determines that a need exists for a certain product or service *before* rushing in to supply it. No amount of hard work can make a

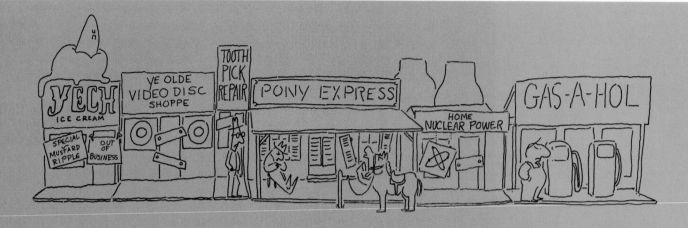

WHY SMALL BUSINESSES FAIL: Some top reasons

The following is a list of causes pinpointed by SCORE, the Service Corps of Retired Executives that operates under the direction of the Small Business Administration.

- Plunging in without first testing the waters on a small scale.
- Underpricing goods or services.
- Underestimating how much time it will take to build a market.
- Starting with too little capital.
- Starting with too much capital and being careless in its use.
- Going into business with little or no experience and without first learning something about it.
- Borrowing money without planning just how and when to pay it back.
- Attempting to do too much business with too little capital.
- Not allowing for setbacks and unexpected expenses.
- Buying too much on capital.
- Extending credit too freely.
- Expanding credit too rapidly.
- Failing to keep complete, accurate records, so that the proprietor drifts into trouble without realizing.
- Carrying habits of personal extravagance into the business.
- Mistaking the freedom of being in business for oneself, for liberty to work or not according to whim.

bad idea work: the health-food store in a meat-and-potatoes neighborhood and the new-wave club in a retirement community are probably doomed from the beginning.

A second management shortcoming is the inability to deal with problems as they arise. A small business is vulnerable, especially when it is new and does not have a list of steady customers.

- What does the entrepreneur do if one of his or her suppliers suddenly goes out of business? (Can another supplier be located quickly?)
- What if the neighborhood suddenly starts to change—even for the better? An influx of wealthier neighbors can

cause such a steep increase in rent that the business must move. Also, tough competition may move into the neighborhood along with the fatter pocketbooks. (Does the owner have an alternative location staked out?)

- What if the company manufactures or sells a fashion item and suddenly the fashion changes? (Can the company switch quickly from making hand-painted T-shirts to making some other kind of shirts?)
- What if the product or service of the small business is so successful that corporate giants start offering it? (Can the small business become a supplier to the large one?)

Such problems are often difficult for the owners of small businesses, most of whom have no special training in general management—and many of whom are so caught up in the everyday concerns of running the shop that they have little time for important long-range planning.

Growing pains

Management problems may also arise when a small business begins to succeed. Although this may sound puzzling, it is an all-too-familiar outcome when an entrepreneur—fundamentally an "idea person"—assumes the role of manager. Many entrepreneurs, however brilliantly they have launched the new company, lack the skills needed to manage its operations over the long run. The person who is good at the start-up phase may not be able to delegate work well, or may have problems figuring out how to expand the business.

An example of a company with "growing pains" is TSR Hobbies Inc., the brainchild of Gary Gygax, the inventor of the Dungeons and Dragons video game. Although the company has grown spectacularly (from $1 million annual sales in 1978 to $22 million in 1982), it has been beset with problems. When it expanded by introducing new games, several were flops. Quality control also broke down, and thousands of printed game boards and instruction booklets had to be thrown away because of errors. The company's computer system failed to indicate when inventory was low, and TSR had no product to ship to its customers. To remedy these and similar problems, TSR has hired more experienced managers to run its various divisions.[12]

We'll talk about management for businesses of all sizes in Chapters 4–8, and in Component Chapter C. For more on managing a small business, you may wish to turn to "Perspectives on Small Business: Management Aspects," at the end of Part 2.

MARKETING FOR A SMALL BUSINESS

Small-business owners simply can't afford to waste money, so they must be sure every dollar spent on marketing is used the most effective way.

■ Setting prices, for example, requires analyzing your competition, your area, your shipping arrangements, and your profit-margin requirements with a critical eye; you may also need to apply special pricing methods, depending on whether yours is a retail operation, a wholesale outfit, a business that specializes in high-volume selling, or a service business (see Chapter 10 for explanations of these concepts).

■ Guiding your product to success, moreover, means you must know exactly where it is in its product life cycle: many businesses fail, for example, because they hang onto a product after it has entered the "decline" phase of the cycle (see Chapter 10).

■ And—last but not least—selling requires you to know some key tricks, especially tricks for using your advertising budget to the fullest. The small business may profit particularly, for example, from newspaper advertising; from running ads in special-interest magazines such as boating magazines; and from direct mail, which allows you to easily target potential customers. The key is: some advertising methods can get you lots of sales; some are almost wasted if they are used for small enterprises. (You'll learn more about basic approaches to advertising in Chapter 11.)

Watch out: marketing competition ahead

The fact that small businesses fill real needs in our society does not guarantee their success. If the opportunity to make a profit exists, and if the job can be done on a large scale, the chances are good that some corporation will enter into competition with "Mom and Pop."

Take, for example, the case of Tech Hi Fi. Founded by a group of MIT students in 1967, Tech grew rapidly: it was an era in which the market for stereo systems was expanding fast, and Tech stocked good-quality equipment and hired experienced salespeople. But the growing market for stereo equipment attracted discounters—Crazy Eddie stores and a host of others—who could do business on a larger scale and underprice Tech. The big companies didn't use highly experienced salespeople; thus, they could cut costs and prices. They also knew more about advertising: Crazy Eddie, for example, became well known for a series of TV commercials featuring a wild-eyed man raving about his "insane" prices. And the big competitors were able to stock a wider selection of goods, thus making it more likely that customers who went there would find what they wanted. Tech Hi Fi, which emphasized quality stereo components, lost customers to retailers who sold lower-priced one-piece stereo sets designed to look like furniture. In 1983, Tech Hi Fi was forced to try discounting in the hope of bolstering sales.[13]

One way small businesses can compete successfully with larger ones is by carving out a specialized niche in the market and by responding to local demand. It should be noted that they can also respond *quickly*: if a demand for broccoli pizzas or spinach pizzas arises tomorrow, the small restaurant can make them up almost as quickly as "Pop" can run out to the supermarket for the new ingredients and "Mom" can think of a way to incorporate them into the old family recipe. A chain, on the other hand, would probably not get wind of the new demand for months and would then need time to study the feasibility of vegetable pizza, formulate a new recipe, order ingredients in quantity, ship them to each outlet, and so on.

We'll discuss these basic marketing concepts in more detail in Chapters 9–12. And if you are interested in finding out how these concepts apply to small businesses in particular, you may wish to read "Perspectives on Small Business: Marketing Aspects," at the end of Part 3.

HOW SMALL BUSINESSES ARE FINANCED

Most people who launch small businesses do so, at least in part, with their own savings. The second most common source of funds is bank loans, although banks are often reluctant to back risky new ventures and may demand a high rate of interest for doing so. Other entrepreneurs borrow from friends or private investors.

Financial help from the SBA

Loans are also available from the Small Business Administration. The SBA, established by Congress in 1953, not only extends loans to small businesses, but also helps firms obtain bank loans by guaranteeing repayment if the business should fail. The SBA provides a number of other services as well. Chief among these are counseling and management ad-

vice, which the SBA makes available through publications and consulting services. A small business can also receive SBA help in preparing bids on government contracts. And the SBA has special programs to aid minority and women entrepreneurs.

In 1982 and early 1983, high interest rates and the Reagan administration's lack of enthusiasm for direct SBA lending drastically cut the number of direct SBA loans made to entrepreneurs. By late 1983, it seemed likely that the SBA would be making few direct loans in the near future, but would concentrate instead on providing guarantees for loans obtained from private lenders such as banks. Entrepreneurs were typically required to put up at least part of the money involved in the funding themselves—often between one-third and one-fourth—and often to pledge real estate and other assets to secure the loans.

Nevertheless, despite these restrictions, SBA-guaranteed loans still offer some important advantages. They can be approved quickly, sometimes in just a few days; and on average the borrower can have eight years to repay, instead of the one to three years typical of all-private loans. In 1983, the SBA's Section 503 loan program was very active; under it, 445 certified local development companies (LDCs) across the country were authorized to issue bonds backed by the U.S. Treasury. In fiscal 1983, the Section 503 program made $270 million worth of loans.

Coping with financial problems

Obtaining funds has become a particular problem in the past few years, as interest rates have gone up sharply. A prime rate of 11 or 12 percent can be tough for any business; small businesses are often asked to pay a rate several points *above* the prime. Thus, when big business can borrow at a prime rate of 11 percent, a small business may be forced to pay 13 or even 15 percent. With banking deregulation, banks competing for big-business loans may even offer their favored big customers rates significantly below the prime. This means that small businesses are at an ever greater disadvantage when it comes to raising money.

Though financing a small business may be difficult, it's not impossible. There are tried-and-true

These are some important services the SBA provides:

Helping small businesses deal with the federal government   The SBA serves as an advocate for small businesses that are having trouble dealing with the government.

Loans   The SBA offers ▪ direct loans to small businesses that meet its size requirements, and even to people who are thinking of going into business; ▪ loans to minorities, handicapped people, and other special categories; ▪ loans to firms that have suffered natural disasters or are in trouble due to government construction; ▪ loans to local development companies, which are formed by citizens, and which aim to fund local companies and boost local economies.

Loan guarantees   The SBA offers guaranty loans (SBA guarantees up to 90 percent of a bank loan): ▪ guarantees for all kinds of small-business loans; ▪ guarantees for seasonal financing; ▪ short-term financing guarantees for small firms that have government contracts.

SBICs (Small Business Investment Companies)   The SBA licenses, regulates, and provides financial assistance to publicly and privately owned and operated SBICs, whose major function is to invest in small enterprises that meet their investment criteria.

Counseling for management problems   The SBA offers ▪ counseling by SCORE (Service Corps of Retired Executives) and ACE (Active Corps of Executives); ▪ SBIs (Small Business Institutes) at schools of business administration; ▪ SBDCs (Small Business Development Centers) at universities and community colleges; ▪ counseling for small-business managers in international trade.

Courses in managing small businesses   The SBA offers ▪ Business Management Courses; ▪ Pre-Business workshops for prospective business owners.

Procurement assistance   The SBA helps direct government contracts and subcontracts to small businesses.

Special programs for minority-owned small businesses   The SBA ▪ helps minorities with capital development and government procurement; ▪ conducts an ongoing campaign for women's businesses.

methods of improving your chances, which every small entrepreneur should know about.

▪ You can, for instance, overcome the tough initial problem of obtaining credit from suppliers who don't know you if you start by setting up a collateral loan, and make some special arrangements with some of your customers as well. (Perhaps you can ship COD so you can get some cash early on, for example.)

▪ Later on, you can ease your financial situation by negotiating liberal payment terms with your vendors—also by paying your bills promptly.

▪ Similarly, if you need a short-term loan, there are approaches you should know—such as contacting the bank manager first, and also applying at two banks simultaneously for the same loan. (This procedure *isn't* illegal or unethical—for reasons we explain in the "Perspectives on Small Business" section at the end of Part 4.)

▪ Your own credit terms for your customers are an important part of your financial planning. Should you extend credit to Company X? Ask your bank—they can call Company X's bank and find out for you.

▪ If you need long-term financing, you should know the right and the wrong ways to look for outside investors, the pros and cons of mortgaging your home to help finance your business, and the ins and outs of obtaining financing via your accounts receivable.

All these financial concepts may seem unfamiliar now, but you will become comfortable with them when you read Chapters 13 and 14. And if you are interested in reading more about the special problems of financing a small business, you may wish to read "Perspectives on Small Business: Financial Aspects," at the end of Part 4.

USING BUSINESS TOOLS IN THE SMALL VENTURE

Meanwhile, you need to work out with your accountant the most effective way to make sure all your records and financial questions are dealt with thoroughly. Choosing an accountant is an important decision you will have to make thoughtfully. And setting up a suitable system of record keeping is probably *the* most crucial procedure you will establish when you start your business.

Today, when small-business owners set up systems of record keeping, they "hire" a mechanical "employee"—a computer—to help them. In the old days, a doctor might have planned to have a secretary type each patient's name and address on a card: after each office visit, the secretary would type onto the card the date of the visit, the type of service the doctor had rendered that day (a physical exam or a chest X-ray, for example), and the fee. Later, the secretary would have typed out a bill using information from this card; later still, the patient might have requested help filling out an insurance form, which would have required a third look at the original card and a third trip to the typewriter. But now, using a computer, the doctor can have all this information entered just once, and the computer will issue bills and fill out insurance forms whenever necessary. Furthermore, the doctor can add up monthly revenues, make a count of active patient accounts, rebill late payers, and manipulate the information in the files in many other ways—in a fraction of the time it would have taken to carry out these procedures "by hand."

The desk-top microcomputers, or personal computers, that many small-business owners are finding particularly useful for their record-keeping and information-processing needs have been going through a rapid technological evolution. Almost every month, faster and less expensive models have appeared. Yet though the computer manufacturers keep thinking up new "bells and whistles" to make these machines even more convenient, all the machines run according to the same basic principles. We talk about these principles in Chapter 17 and Component Chapter F. In Chapter 16, we discuss the methods of accounting that underlie the record-keeping techniques used by all businesses. If you wish to read more about the small-business aspects of these topics, you may find it helpful to turn to the section titled "Perspectives on Small Business: Using Business Tools," at the end of Part 5.

THE BUSINESS ENVIRONMENT

No business operates in a vacuum or under a glass dome—and like all other enterprises, small businesses are subject to the pressures and requirements of our society's legal and governmental systems. If you need a trademark, a company brand, or a pat-

ent, or if you are thinking of becoming incorporated, you will definitely need legal help—and there may be many other situations in which you will have to work with a lawyer. When you *choose* a lawyer you'll need to ask some key questions to find out whether he or she is experienced in working with small enterprises; when you *work with* that lawyer you'll need to know how attorneys operate and what they can and cannot do for a business.

Likewise, you'll be coping with government regulations—many of which were written with larger businesses in mind but nonetheless apply to small business too. Sometimes regulations intended to remedy one set of problems end up causing others. But not all your relations with the U.S. government are likely to involve conflict. You may, for example, find yourself applying to the SBA for more than financial help: the SBA can help small businesses put themselves into position to obtain government procurement contracts (Uncle Sam can be a good customer for a small enterprise), and it can also offer seminars and individual counseling for small-business management problems—and special aid for minority-run small businesses.

These comments touch on some fundamental concepts that we discuss in Chapters 18 and 19. You may also wish to know more about their specific application to small business; if you do, turn to "Perspectives on Small Business: Legal and Governmental Environment," at the end of Part 6.

START-UP COMPANIES

Entrepreneurship of a particularly exciting sort is responsible for the **start-up company,** *a business based on the introduction of a new product with a view to rapid growth and return on investment.* Most start-up companies are founded to produce new products. Most of these are sophisticated high-tech products or services, often in fields such as computers, robots, and electronic devices. But some are deliberately and successfully low-tech—such as Cabbage Patch dolls (originally made by a small company), rent-a-picnic services, and many other items as varied as the human imagination. The start-up company, in contrast to most other new businesses, usually needs

INTERNATIONAL BUSINESS TODAY

A HELPING HAND FROM UNCLE SAM: HOW SMALL BUSINESSES CAN BOOST THEIR EXPORT OPPORTUNITIES

As we noted in Component Chapter A, the United States has a continuing problem with its negative trade balance: as a nation, we continue to import far more goods than we are able to sell abroad. Small business should be playing an important part in increasing exports. The federal government has estimated that as many as 20,000 U.S. firms that could be selling goods overseas are not.

For many small businesses, the mechanics of exporting goods seem forbiddingly complex. How can a business find out which countries want its products? How is payment arranged internationally, and how can a U.S. firm be sure that it will be paid? And how can a novice exporter deal with shipping regulations, customs, tariffs, and other rules of the export game?

Help is on the way from the federal government. Several agencies have recently made special efforts to assist the company new to selling abroad. For example:

■ Operation Opportunity, a program sponsored jointly by the Agriculture and Commerce departments and the Small Business Administration, now produces a "video conference" on the subject to which small businesses can subscribe. A reference book accompanies the conference.

■ The Small Business Administration has set up a series of informative regional meetings called "Exporting: Your Passport to Profit." The SBA also offers loan guarantees for companies that wish to sell overseas.

■ The Commerce Department's Office of Export Counseling can provide statistical profiles and other information on a particular product's likely sales appeal in a given foreign country. It can also check on the reliability of any foreign company that wants to buy American goods.

■ The Export-Import Bank can provide guidance on how small firms can combine their efforts to make foreign sales, as allowed by a new federal law. The "Ex-Im" Bank also has a new program to help finance small-business exports.

■ The Overseas Private Investment Corporation can supply loans and insurance to companies that need them for export trade.

■ The Export Trading Act of 1982 has made possible the creation of export trading companies to search out international business opportunities in both imports and exports.

---

substantial amounts of capital to begin operations: imagine, for example, the complex and expensive equipment that is needed to produce a computer or a robot. As we shall see below, investment groups known as venture-capital firms specialize in providing cash to start-up companies, with the hope that once the start-up firm's new product hits the market, it will quickly recover its initial investment many times over.

The late 1970s and early 1980s saw a dramatic increase in the number of start-up companies. In fact, even in the recession year of 1982, in which 25,346 businesses went under, 566,942 new businesses were started—a significant number of them start-up ventures.[14] Why the start-up boom? We are witnessing a new wave of product development that is largely the result of post–World War II scientific discoveries that only began to find commercial applications in the early 1980s. Innovations such as silicon microchips, genetic engineering, laser technology, and robotics are examples of the entry of this new science into the marketplace.

Not all start-up companies succeed, of course, but when they do they often do so spectacularly. Apple Computer, for example, went from a two-person operation to a Fortune 500 company in only six years. This kind of growth is a good omen for the American economy, promising jobs and even creating entirely new (and spin-off) industries. Start-up companies are remarkably efficient, producing a valuable product in a short time—providing a stimulus to the economy and often outdistancing foreign competition. Thus, start-ups are a hopeful development in a national economy that has been severely challenged by products from abroad.

FINANCING THE START-UP COMPANY: VENTURE CAPITAL

When start-up entrepreneurs look for financial backing, they particularly hope to attract venture capital. **Venture capital** is *money invested in new, fledgling, or struggling small businesses by groups of investment specialists so that these small companies will grow larger and more profitable, and so that the venture capitalists can then sell their interest in the company at profits commensurate with the large risk.* Venture-capital groups do not simply lend money to a small business as a bank would. Instead, they provide capital in return for an ownership interest, which may amount to half of the stock or even more. Hence, bringing in a venture-capital group may mean that the entrepreneur will have to give up a certain amount of control over the enterprise. What often happens is that the venture-capital group buys part of the stock cheap—say, at $2 a share; then, when the company goes public,

A

C

B

Entrepreneurially minded? Your chances are best if you have special skills, intense drive, or a strong desire to be your own boss. Success is also more likely if your parents were entrepreneurs, if you are under 40, and if you have a partner. (A and B) Two who've made it: Myra Evans, founder of Manhattan's first Italian ice-cream parlor, and teenage computer whiz Will Harvey, creator of interactive musical software for personal computers. (C and D) Four who hope to get there: Stan Leitner with his Litestar "carcycle," and (left to right) David Thompson, Scott Weber, and Bruce Ferguson, developers of a privately financed propulsion system for launching satellites from the space shuttle.

they sell at a much higher price and make a big capital gain.

The investment funds available to venture-capital firms come from corporations, wealthy individuals, pension funds, and other pools of capital, such as university endowments. Because the goal of venture-capital investors is to make a considerable profit, these firms look specifically for start-up businesses that have the potential for rapid growth. (If you want to open a bowling alley or set up a plant to manufacture shoelaces, you should not turn to a venture-capital firm.)

Venture capitalists were not discouraged by the recession of the early 1980s; they continued to back start-up companies during that period, assuming that by the time their companies were ready to go public (a stage we'll discuss later in this chapter), the economy would probably have turned around. After the economy had begun to bounce back, venture capital continued to boom: it had grown fourfold since 1980, reaching $4.1 billion in 1983.[15]

In recent years, venture capital has been heavily invested in high-technology firms. In fact, venture capital largely financed the development of California's Silicon Valley. Venture-capital firms have also been strongly attracted to genetic engineering labs. What makes venture-capital firms so ready to risk large sums of money on untried businesses is the chance of making a fabulous return. For example, when Telerate, a company that electronically sends

D

securities price quotations to money managers, went public in 1983, its investors saw their $75 million stake in the firm jump instantly to $740 million.[16] Of course, not every new high-tech enterprise comes through with such glittering returns. But venture-capital firms, once thought of as investors who liked to live dangerously, have been joined in the field by some once-conservative corporations, such as insurance companies and banks, eager to get in on the start-up bonanza.

SBICs and venture capital

Venture capital may also come from **Small Business Investment Companies (SBICs),** which were set up after the passage of the Small Business Investment Act of 1958. Since then, groups of investors have formed more than 400 SBICs across the country. SBICs, like venture-capital firms, *invest in high-risk businesses that promise growth; however, most of their funds go to existing companies rather than new ventures.*

Big businesses enter the venture-capital arena

Yet another source of venture capital is big business. A good number of large corporations have departments that are devoted to finding good venture-capital investments. Increasingly, businesses are beginning to realize that venture capital—if invested carefully—can bring big financial rewards. Among the twenty largest venture-capital investors in 1982, for example, were departments or subsidiaries of such giants as Allstate, First National Bank of Chicago, General Electric, Citicorp, and Bankers Trust.[17]

The large corporation's interest may go beyond making a profitable investment, however; sometimes smaller companies that are particularly successful are eventually acquired by the larger company.

GOING PUBLIC

Venture capital may get a start-up company going, but once the ambitious new firm is in operation, it will need additional funds, especially if it is to grow rapidly. Many companies raise money by selling shares in their operation to the general public—or "going public," as it is known. The bull market that began in August 1982 and was still continuing as of this writing encouraged emerging companies to use new issues of stock as a major source of funding. By the end of 1983, new issues had raised $11 billion for companies ranging from high-tech firms to savings and loans to franchised businesses (a topic we'll discuss later in this chapter), and many of these were start-up companies. The Securities and Exchange Commission's Regulation D, established in 1979, made it easier for small companies to go public: it allows them to use a "short form" stock-registration statement, so they can make small offerings without the red tape involved in most public stock issues. (We will discuss the process of going public in detail in Chapter 14 and 15.)

FRANCHISING

The **franchise operation** *brings a corporation with a product*—sometimes a famous one such as Midas Mufflers or Kentucky Fried Chicken—*together with an individual or group desiring to start a small business.* Franchising is a major part of the small-business community and a rapidly growing sector of the U.S. economy; by 1983, sales had grown to $400 billion, and nearly one of every three dollars of retail sales was made by a franchise.[18]

Both the agreement and the business go by the name of "franchise." The franchisor (the corporation) grants the franchisee (the small-business owner) the exclusive right to use the franchisor's name in a certain territory, usually in exchange for an initial fee plus monthly payments. The franchise operation enables a corporation to establish outlets for its product or service without making enormous capital investments. At the same time, it enables an individual to set up a business with far less risk than an independent operator would face.

FRANCHISING: A QUICK LOOK AT THE PAST

Franchising began in the nineteenth century when such companies as Singer and International Harvester established dealerships throughout the world.

The bright side

The franchisor can offer you...
- A tested management system
- A name customers already know
- Financial advice and assistance—for supplies, credit, insurance
- Training: how to operate and advertise the business
- Performance records for other outlets (which you can use to assess *your* progress)

And you get some autonomy, too!

FIGURE I

THE TWO SIDES OF FRANCHISING

anchising has some important luses." But don't forget, there are awbacks to consider too.

The dark side

The franchisor . . .
- Will exercise total control over how you operate your business—he'll tell you when and how to change your product or your prices, and even how to decorate the place
- May charge you a monthly payment or royalty (if your outlet does poorly, most of your profit may go to him)
- May charge you a lot of money just to get the franchise in the first place—and may even try to lure you into a business that's badly conceived
- May allow territorial conflicts with other outlets

Remember, too, that you'll probably have to work long hours—and you won't really be your own boss

---

In this century, Coca-Cola, General Motors, and Metropolitan Life, among others, use franchises to distribute or sell their products. Franchising grew most rapidly in the consumer-product boom years of the 1960s. The fastest-growing franchise operations then were hotels and motels like Holiday Inns and Quality Courts Motor Inns, and fast-food establishments like Baskin-Robbins, McDonald's, and Dunkin' Donuts.

The latest trend in franchising has been diversification. Franchising has moved into a variety of new areas, including real estate, dental care, and video. Whether these new franchise operations will succeed remains to be seen. One large dental-care franchise, DentCare, failed spectacularly in 1982.[19] Even so, others have been quick to join the field, for example Omnidentrix (which is headed by an ex-president of Mister Donut). Other franchise efforts have also failed recently, even some that have the backing of a celebrity name—like the Joe Namath and Arthur Treacher restaurant chains.

The growth in fast-food franchises slowed in the early 1970s, but more recently it has picked up again, thanks largely to Americans' increasing fondness for eating out. The economic slump of the early 1980s was also partly responsible for the renewed interest in franchising in general. According to franchise consultant Donald D. Boroian, during times of high unemployment people are more likely to buy franchises. "Losing a job can force the issue," he says. "They will even remortgage their homes to buy franchises."

WHAT ARE THE ADVANTAGES OF FRANCHISING?

The Small Business Administration says that the two most common reasons small businesses fail are lack of money and lack of know-how. Franchising helps to solve both of these problems, lending some "big-company" clout to the small-time operator.

Help on the financial end

Before offering financial help to prospective franchisees, the franchisor weeds out those whose own finances are in unacceptably bad shape: a franchisor will not grant a franchise unless the prospective franchisee has enough money for start-up costs. (The franchisor, unlike many independent proprietors, has enough experience to estimate start-up costs realistically.) But once accepted, the franchisee has the advantage of being able to buy supplies and to obtain credit and insurance at low cost.

Training

Besides financial aid and advice, the franchisor gives a new franchisee all-important training in how to run a business. McDonald's "Hamburger University" in Illinois gives a nineteen-day course to owners and operators leading to a "Bachelor of Hamburgerology, with a minor in French fries." By offering this course, McDonald's is also able to teach standard procedures to each operator and thus maintain its distinctive image.[20] Many franchise organizations offer advice on advertising, taxes, and other business matters, as well as instructions in the routine day-to-day operation of the franchise.

WHAT ARE THE DISADVANTAGES OF FRANCHISING?

Although franchising offers many advantages to small-business people, it does have disadvantages, and franchises are not the right sort of enterprise for everyone—as we'll see.

Financial "strings"

Chief among the disadvantages is the monthly payment or royalty that must be paid to the franchisor. If the outlet does poorly (if a restaurant is in an area of severe unemployment, for example), most of the profit may end up going to the franchisor. (Franchise arrangements involving a monthly percentage rather than a flat payment do not present this problem.)

Shady deals

Fly-by-night franchisors who have no credit of their own may tempt "Mom and Pop" to borrow from the bank, turn over the money for a franchise, then get "stuck" with an ill-conceived business.

Tight controls by the franchisor

Another drawback of franchises is that they allow individual operators very little independence. Franchisors can prescribe virtually every aspect of the business, down to the details of employees' uniforms and the color of the walls. Franchisees may be required to buy the products they sell directly from the franchisor—at whatever price the latter feels like charging. (This requirement led franchisees of Nutri/Systems, a chain of weight-loss centers, to sue the franchisor in 1983, charging that they were being hurt by the high prices Nutri/Systems demanded for its diet food products.)[21] Franchisors can also make important decisions (changes in the product or its price, for example) without consulting franchisees.

Individuals who find the idea of a franchise attractive should study a franchise project carefully before they sign up. Will the business be so tightly controlled that they end up feeling like mere employees? Will they be willing to work the long, late hours and seven-day weeks required by some businesses, such as food-service operations? Does the franchise contract offer adequate protection against territorial conflicts with the franchisor's other outlets? What are the provisions for selling the franchise if the franchisee should decide to get out? Although franchises can offer the small-business person a good way to set up shop, they should be approached with the careful thought and planning that any new business venture demands.

CHAPTER REVIEW

The vitality of American business depends on the spirit of the entrepreneur—the person who starts a business and takes the financial and personal risks required to keep it going. The fruits of entrepreneurial activity range from the corner store to the national corporation that started small. Most entrepreneurs begin by running their own shows; others form start-up companies, which aim for the big time right away; still others work through corporate entrepreneurial units or franchise operations.

A small business is one that is independently owned and operated and not dominant in its field. Such businesses can be grouped into five classes: service, retail, wholesale, general construction, and manufacturing. They account for over 98 percent of the nation's businesses and are our largest employer.

Although the recession of the early 1980s hit small business hard, the future looks brighter. Efforts to extend tax breaks, encourage investors, and simplify the job of doing business with the government have created a more comfortable climate for small business.

Small businesses are an important source of innovation and new jobs, so they contribute to economic growth. As suppliers, they fill the needs of large corporations (whose products are sold, in turn, by other small businesses in the form of retail outlets). Small businesses are also important in our society as suppliers of specialized services.

Starting and running a small business involves extensive planning, many details, and multiple skills. Beyond mere logistics, the entrepreneur must consider the need for a given product or service and plan strategies to recruit suppliers, attract customers, outwit competitors, and deal with unforeseen complications as well as day-to-day problems.

Small businesses can often compete successfully in the marketplace by keeping overhead low and by responding to local demand. Effective management and marketing are essential. When small firms fail (and most new ones do), the failure is usually the result of poor management or inadequate financing.

The Small Business Administration (SBA) is the federal agency charged with serving the needs of small firms. It guarantees and provides loans (although direct loans have been cut drastically under the Reagan administration) and supplies management counseling to small businesses.

Financing a small business can be difficult, especially in view of high interest rates, the more favorable terms available to big business, and the small business's sales tax liability. Small-business owners can use new high-tech equipment, such as microcomputers, to improve the efficiency of their operations.

Start-up companies, unlike most other new businesses, usually need very large amounts of capital to begin operations. These funds are often advanced by venture-capital firms, which support new businesses in the hope that they will grow rapidly and yield substantial returns. Most venture-capital firms confine their investments to manufacturing enterprises with large growth potential, such as high-technology companies. Venture-capital investments have increased sharply in recent years and are likely to continue to rise.

Another source of venture capital is big business, which is often on the lookout for good investments. Some large firms try to encourage entrepreneurship within their own organizations.

A franchise brings together a corporation with a nationally promoted product and an individual who wants to start a small business. A franchise offers an opportunity to go into business without many of the risks an individual proprietor takes. Franchisees, however, must be prepared to run their businesses under the tight control of the franchisor.

KEY WORDS

entrepreneur (96)
Small Business Administration (SBA) (97)
small business (97)
start-up company (106)
venture capital (108)
Small Business Investment Companies (SBICs) (110)
franchise operation (110)

REVIEW QUESTIONS

1. What qualities usually characterize successful entrepreneurs, and why?

2. What class of organizations creates the most new jobs in the United States?

3. How has Congress tried to create a more favorable climate for entrepreneurship?

4. Explain the SBA's ceilings on small businesses. Why are manufacturing firms judged by different criteria than others?

5. Why is small business so vital to the American economy?

6. What advantages does small business have over big business?

7. Why do most new small businesses fail, and how might such failures be avoided?

8. What are the principal sources of financing for small businesses?

9. What are the motives that encourage big businesses to support start-up companies and corporate entrepreneurial units?

10. How does a franchise operation work, and what are some of its advantages and disadvantages for the franchisee?

CASE 1

MOVING AHEAD WITH AVANTI

Avanti Motor Company is a small manufacturer of luxury automobiles. The Avanti car, originally developed by Studebaker, was produced for nearly twenty years at a small plant in South Bend, Indiana. The company's chief executive, Nate Altman, was satisfied to see 200 cars leave the factory each year, each custom-designed for a knowledgeable, well-to-do auto buff. The Avanti had a dedicated, if tiny, following among the kind of customer who wants a stylish and distinctive sports car.

In 1976, Nate Altman died. After prolonged negotiations, his brother Arnold agreed to sell the company to Stephen Blake, a young real estate developer and car dealer. Although Blake had considerable difficulty arranging financing—more than thirty banks turned him down—he was eventually able to obtain a bank loan with the backing of the Indiana Economic Development Authority. When Blake took charge of the company, he decided to change its course. His problem: how to build more and better Avantis—without losing loyal customers or causing production problems.

Blake's first step was to upgrade the car. He brought in a new engineering team to improve the Avanti's suspension system, steering, and brakes—all of which had been virtually unchanged for twenty years. He planned the introduction of a new chassis in 1985. The new Avanti envisioned by Blake would be about 20 percent more expensive, with a base price of about $30,000. To sell people on the new, improved car, Blake launched a major effort to publicize the car. He sought out media coverage, even entering the Avanti in the twenty-four-hour endurance race in Daytona, Florida. Blake's plan was to attract young, performance-oriented sports-car fans who might have overlooked the Avanti or dismissed it as old-fashioned.

To match the increased demand that he hoped for, Blake planned to expand production dramatically. Instead of 200 cars a year, he planned to produce 600. To achieve this expansion, Blake followed the advice of consultants and streamlined the production process—cutting production time by a third. He also asked workers to put in overtime, which they were generally willing to do.

Finally, Blake planned to make it easier for customers to buy an Avanti. He increased the number of dealerships about threefold (now there are twenty-two). Before Blake's day, a prospective customer who wanted to take the car for a test drive often had to travel to the plant in South Bend!

But Blake's efforts have come up against several problems. Veteran workers, understandably, have resisted changes in their duties and in the way the plant is run.

After new work rules were introduced and a few employees were fired for poor performance, a unionization drive got under way. Although the United Auto Workers was not voted into the plant, some workers are still grumbling, and Blake may see further unionization efforts.

And some customers have also complained about the new regime at Avanti. Under the previous management, Avanti pampered its wealthy customers. For example, a representative of the plant would often pick up a customer's car when it needed factory service—even if the customer lived several hours away. Customers could also count on being loaned another Avanti while their own was in the shop. Blake has discontinued both of these services, and some Avanti customers are displeased.

Despite these problems, however, Avanti has already increased production 50 percent, and there is a three-month backlog in orders. For the moment, Blake's new strategy seems to be paying off.[22]

1. Why do problems often develop when a person with little industry experience, like Stephen Blake, takes charge of a company in a specialized field?

2. Why do you think Avanti was able to succeed for twenty years by producing such a small number of cars? Do you think increasing production by 200 percent is a good idea or a poor one?

3. What steps might Blake take to increase worker satisfaction with new work rules and production techniques? Do you think that the workers are likely to vote in a union? Why or why not?

4. Is Blake's decision to cut back on customer service a good one? Explain your answer.

5. Do you think Blake's management is a case of entrepreneurial energy revitalizing an aging company, or of a brash newcomer trying to accomplish too much too soon?

6. If you were running Avanti, would you want to increase production even more? If you decided to expand, what would some of the risks be?

CASE 2

LSI: CAN THIS TINY START-UP COMPANY COMPETE AGAINST THE GIANTS?

LSI Logic Corporation, of Milpitas, California, is a manufacturer of silicon chips—the tiny but powerful components now used in small computers, video games, and many other high-tech consumer products. LSI is one of the sixty or so creative and aggressive new companies whose chips have given the Silicon Valley its name. In this superheated competitive environment, some companies are destined to fail—but others will be America's future high-tech giants.

The question currently facing LSI is: is the time ripe to go public? If it does so successfully, it will gain a welcome infusion of new capital. But it will also find itself competing against a number of corporate giants. The stakes are high in entering this market. How can LSI—a company only a few years old—hope to make headway in a crowded and ruthlessly competitive market?

LSI can take comfort from the fact that some other small chip makers have successfully taken the public-offering plunge already. For example, VLSI Technology Inc., or VTI, went public early in 1983. Eager investors quickly snapped up 4.4 million shares of its stock. In little more than a week, the three-year-old VTI, which had yet to turn a profit, was worth $66 million. Since investors seem ready to pounce on nearly any promising high-tech venture, LSI would probably find a similar reception. Being greeted with open arms by investors is not enough, however. Many a new company has failed after a year or two as a public venture. To succeed, the new company must have a good product and a good management team. How does LSI measure up?

LSI's current product is a relatively simple integrated circuit known as a read-only memory (ROM) chip. Its ROM chip sales are booming. But LSI is staking its future on what are known as semicustom chips—that is, basic chips of fairly standard design that can be customized in various ways to suit a customer's needs. This combination of mass production and customizing allows LSI to produce a customized chip cheaply (for as much as $15,000 to $20,000 less than other methods) and quickly (orders can be filled in four to six weeks). Low cost and speed, of course, are all-important in the silicon-chip market. The drawback to the plan is that this procedure makes chips easy to design and produce. Competitors using the same techniques can move in quickly.

LSI is fortunate in another respect: its managers are highly experienced and well known in their field. LSI's chief executive, Wilfred J. Corrigan, was president of Fairchild Camera and Instrument Corporation (now the semiconductor subsidiary of Schlumberger Ltd.). LSI is also fortunate to have started with a sizable venture-capital nest egg, so that it has been able to gear up its initial production effectively.

With industry experts predicting that the semicustom chip may be *the* product to make or break Silicon Valley firms in the late 1980s, LSI seems ready to pit itself against formidable competitors. The next few years should see whether it, like VTI, will make a successful transition from a struggling entrepreneurial firm to a publicly held corporation.[23]

1. Should LSI go public? What would the advantages be? The disadvantages?

2. What are LSI's strong points? What special niches can it fill?

3. Why is foreign competition so important a factor in LSI's success or failure?

4. If you were a video-game manufacturer, would you rather buy chips from LSI or from a Japanese firm? Can you think of any drawbacks in letting a Japanese firm become familiar with the design of your products, especially innovative ones?

5. How can small firms like LSI attract top management people, and why is good management so important to them?

6. In what ways is LSI's situation representative of the opportunities and problems facing the start-up company?

PERSPECTIVES ON SMALL BUSINESS A PRELIMINARY OVERVIEW

Small businesses are a vital part of the American economy. In Component Chapter B we gave an overview of some of the most important facts about small business. We talked about the criteria a business must meet to be considered a small business, and the five common types of small business: service, retail, wholesale, general construction, and manufacturing. We looked at the interdependence of small and big business, and at some of the special strengths of small business—such as the ability to fill needs of specialized and local markets, and the opportunity to develop new markets and products.

We are going to explore some of the unique concerns of small business in a series of special sections—one at the end of each part of this book. Here, we begin by considering the processes involved in starting one.

STARTING A SMALL BUSINESS: THE FIRST STEPS

Before you decide to start a small business, you need to analyze yourself. Are you the kind of person who is really ready to run your own business? The answer is probably yes if you are a self-starter, a good organizer, a risk taker and decision maker, if you are willing to work long hours, and if you like to take satisfaction in your own achievements. The fact that you are in college shows that you have all or some of these characteristics.

Once you have decided to start a small business, your first major task will be to choose one of the five major legal forms of business—sole proprietorship, partnership, limited partnership, a standard corporation, or a Subchapter S corporation. With the assistance of a group of specialists—an attorney, an accountant (CPA), an insurance broker, and a banker—you will need to evaluate each form carefully and choose the one best suited to your needs. Then you will need to go through certain specific procedures as follows.

Starting a sole proprietorship

Legally, the sole proprietorship is the easiest form to implement. For the simple cost of invoices, bank checks, a business license, and one month's rent, you're an entrepreneur.

One key detail: unless you use your own name, you will need to file the name of your business with your local county government. You are then required to publish that name in the local newspapers three times and do so every five years if you want to keep the name of your business. This procedure is called making a **Fictitious Business Name Statement.**

There are just a few other details. If your product or service involves a state sales tax, you will need a certificate to collect taxes—or be exempt from them if you're eligible. (Your state's Board of Equalization will provide the necessary information.) Also, unless you're planning to operate a part-time business, you may be required to pay a security deposit to guarantee that these taxes will be paid in the event of financial difficulties.

Starting a partnership

Two legal instruments or agreements are important in this form of business: the partnership agreement and the buy/sell agreement.

The **partnership agreement** *specifies the partnership's purpose, the duties of the partners, the percentage of ownership of each partner in the business, how the profit will be split, the amount of income to be paid to each partner,* and the method by which the income will be paid. The document must either be drafted by an attorney or reviewed by one.

The **buy/sell agreement** *prevents the termination of the business at the death of one of the partners.* Why is it important? Upon the death of one of the partners, the deceased partner's husband, wife or estate inherits the deceased partner's interest in the business. This *could* present a problem if the heir started to become a liability to the business. The buy/sell agreement solves this problem: under its provisions, the heir of the deceased partner must accept payment for his or her share of the business. The agreement must be signed and agreed to by all partners and their heirs. A properly written buy/sell agreement will ensure a smooth transfer of the ownership of the business at the death of one of the partners so that the business can continue without interruption.

The agreement must contain a formula for determining the current dollar value of the business. Also, you will need to fund the agreement with enough cash to allow execution of the plan upon death of one of the partners. If sufficient funds are not available to pay inheritance taxes, the government would be forced to sell the business to raise the money. If the cash is not available, you should purchase life insurance in the amount of the current value of the business to fund the plan. This keeps both the government and the heirs happy and guarantees that the business will continue to operate. Three parties, apart from the heirs, should be involved in every buy/sell agreement: (1) a qualified business attorney, (2) a CPA, and (3) a business life insurance agent (CLU).

In a partnership, liability is by far the most serious handicap. You should never enter into a partnership unless you have given careful attention to the liability aspects, particularly crossover liability, which holds each partner responsible for all the business and personal actions of the other partner. Crossover liability provides an element of risk since limited partnerships and corporations are available at little extra cost. While most established partnerships today have purchased very large and quite expensive liability insurance, few small businesses can afford such plans.

Starting a limited partnership

This form is ideal for any new small business venture where one person runs the business and agrees to be solely responsible for its operations, profits, and losses, and other individuals want to invest, with no risk beyond their investment. The *person who runs the business* is called the **general partner** or **managing partner.** The others are called **limited partners** and *they participate in the profits or losses of the business, but their liability is limited to the amount of their investment.* To use this form of business, you will need a business attorney to draft a limited partnership agreement to ensure the correct protection. A major advantage of a limited partnership to the general partner is that the investors or limited partners may not interfere in partnership decisions unless the business is being grossly mismanaged. As you will see, this is quite different from a corporation.

A special form of limited partnership is called the **research limited partnership.** This form has the same liability protection as a limited partnership; however, it receives special tax considerations from the Internal Revenue Service (IRS). Any new business that requires research and the development of a new product to start up could qualify for this form of partnership. So discuss your new business idea with your attorney and CPA to see if your venture might fall into this category.

Starting a standard corporation

We've discussed the corporate form of business in Chapter 2, but we'll add some additional points here.

It's very easy to attract investors in the corporate form of business. Investors can buy and sell shares in the corporation by any legal means available, and each investor is liable only for the amount of his or her investment. However, it's crucial to note that investors in a corporation (no matter how small their ownership position) are usually involved in all the internal decisions, as opposed to the passive role of the investor in the limited partnership. This is a major point of consideration.

Incorporation also offers a number of tax advantages, including full tax-free medical and accident insurance; tax-free sick pay; tax-free group life insurance coverage up to $50,000; tax-free business-related meals, lodging, and education; and IRS-approved pension and profit-sharing plans that allow the corporation to shelter up to 25 percent of its profits. Under some IRS-approved "defined benefit" programs, even more money can be tax-sheltered in a retirement plan. Last but not least, it's important to note that the corporation may accumulate earnings for a specific purpose, and these earnings are not taxable to the shareholders until they are distributed. The reason why the earnings are being retained must be recorded in the minutes of the regular corporation meetings to receive this benefit.

The corporation is the most complex form of business organization. It involves compliance with more governmental regulations and payment of more legal and accounting fees than any other form. However, the liability protection and excellent tax benefits are sufficient incentive for most investors.

Incorporation involves some tax disadvantages as well. The business is taxed at the corporate rate, and the shareholders are then taxed again when the profits are distributed as dividends. This double burden of taxation falls especially heavily on the small corporation.

In our discussion of partnerships, we mentioned the need for a buy/sell agreement. The corporate form requires a similar instrument, normally called a **stock redemption plan,** which *serves the same function as the buy/sell agreement.* Again, you will need the same legal, accounting, and insurance expertise. The same basic rules should apply.

Starting a Subchapter S Corporation

This hybrid form of business offers all the limited-liability advantages of the corporation, the investor mobility that a corporation allows, and most of the corporation's basic fringe benefits. But there are radical tax differences between the regular corporation and the Subchapter S corporation. A Subchapter S corporation is taxed the same way as a partnership: all the profits and losses are passed on to the shareholders (whether they are distributed or not), and shareholders pay taxes on their share of the profits or losses according to each individual's tax schedule.

Any standard corporation can switch to a Subchapter S corporation with little trouble. However, the IRS places very serious limitations on reverting from a Subchapter S to a standard corporation. There would be some remarkable tax advantages if a corporation could switch back and forth at will, primarily due to the method of reporting profits and losses to the IRS under each form. So when you choose one version, plan to stick with it awhile, and have a very legitimate reason (other than tax avoidance) to change to the other.

Here are some of the basic restrictions of a Subchapter S corporation. You should consult with your accountant to discover all the many fine points.

1. It must have no more than thirty-five shareholders.

2. It must have only individuals or estates as shareholders.

3. It must have only one class of stock.

4. It must not have a nonresident alien as a shareholder.

5. It must not be a member of an affiliated group eligible to file a consolidated return.

6. It must be a domestic corporation (organized under the laws of the United States or of a state or territory).

7. No more than 25 percent of the gross receipts of the corporation may come from rents, royalties, interest, dividends, annuities, gains from stocks, or securities.

8. All shareholders must consent to Subchapter S election.

The Subchapter S corporation is ideal for two or more individuals who seek the limited-liability umbrella of a corporation and the simple tax structure of a partnership.

Which form is right for you? You'll have to think through the decision carefully—as carefully as you consider all other decisions involved in starting your own small business.

PART TWO

MANAGEMENT

Can the makers of Band-Aids, Baby Shampoo, and Tylenol succeed at selling implantable lenses, surgical lasers, and advanced diagnostic equipment? That's the question Johnson & Johnson now faces after its takeover of several high-tech firms. The answer may depend on whether J & J can shift management gears. Staffing is a problem—not enough experts are available. So is corporate structure—J & J's is so decentralized that cooperation is difficult. The most important stumbling block, though, may be managers' attitudes: their jealousy and turf-consciousness make it hard for them to share research and marketing expertise.

J & J will have to apply not Band-Aids but solid management principles to get its staff to work together. Those principles are the subject of Part 2.

☐ In Chapter 4, **The Process of Management,** we discuss the four basic functions of management.

☐ Chapter 5, **Internal Organization,** tells how managers group employees and distribute work for maximum efficiency.

☐ Chapter 6 describes the process of **Production and Operations Management**—how resources are actually converted into the form in which the business will sell them.

☐ In Chapter 7, **Management and Unions,** you'll read about how unions and management negotiate.

☐ Chapter 8 is about **Human Resources Management.** It describes methods of recruiting, compensating, and evaluating staff.

☐ Component Chapter C, **Human Relations: Motivation and Morale,** looks at the factors affecting workers' performance and attitudes.

THE PROCESS OF MANAGEMENT

"WANTED: A person who has the technical background to understand good factory layout and to use a small computer; the financial background to comprehend a profit-and-loss statement and to project future needs for capital; and the human-relations background to communicate well with subordinates and superiors. In short, a highly qualified manager—a person who knows how to combine technical knowledge, financial savvy, and interpersonal skills to keep a company running smoothly."

Today, more than ever, companies need people with specialized knowledge: experts in automation, energy conservation, telecommunications, and a host of other rapidly changing fields. But technical know-how alone is not enough to make a good manager. Managers also need to be able to understand and interpret many different kinds of information—ranging from computer printouts of sales and inventory to competitors' annual reports. And they need the skills to plan, to make decisions, and to adjust those plans and decisions to reflect changing circumstances. In this chapter we will examine what managers do and what skills they need.

CHAPTER FOCUS

After reading the material in this chapter, you will be able to:

- define management, and enumerate its four functions
- distinguish short-range from long-range plans, and list three types of each
- describe one modern system and one technique that aid planning
- state the difference between division of labor by task and by authority
- distinguish motivation from leadership
- cite three leadership styles, and explain why no one style is best
- enumerate the steps in the control cycle
- describe the work of the three levels of management
- distinguish the three types of managerial skills, and discuss the need for managerial survival skills
- define corporate culture, and list four common types

At the Harley-Davidson Motor Company in late 1982, management faced a tough challenge. America's last motorcycle manufacturer had some impressive points in its favor, including fiercely loyal customers who identified with the product (nicknamed the "hog"); an extra 45 percent tariff protection from imports (to be phased out over five years); and the boundless energy of the founder's grandson, who had arranged to buy the company back from AMF, the conglomerate that his father sold it to. But the forces that Harley-Davidson had to overcome were even more formidable. Under AMF's management the product had stagnated: the motorcycles carried a high price tag, but their design was antiquated and their quality was shoddy. Inevitably, the Japanese manufacturers of lightweight bikes had noticed that the heavyweight V-engine market was ripe for the taking. They had swooped in with advanced design features, stiff quality control, and heavy price cutting, and between 1980 and 1982, Harley-Davidson had lost one-third of its market share and racked up big losses.

What was to be done? First, Harley-Davidson's new management team started by tackling the design problem, and they came up with a better product that they could produce more cheaply. But that was only the beginning. They still had to find a sizable chunk of money to finance the new bike; hire the skilled workers to produce it; keep those workers turning out the product at a steady clip; continually check and recheck to make sure budgets, quotas and schedules were being met—and keep a watchful eye on the competition and possible changes in the marketplace. The management was geared up to fight—but it remains to be seen whether they will win.[1]

Harley-Davidson's ordeal resembles what many other companies are coping with in the United States today. Jolted by a tight economy and aggressive foreign competition, managers in autos, machine tools, textiles, and countless other fields now see they must make some big changes—fast—in their traditional ways of running their businesses. It is still essential for managers to carry out the four basic functions of management—planning, organizing, directing, and controlling. But these days, survival also means staying flexible and being ready to try innovative approaches. And innovative ideas *are* circulating. If the last few years have brought worry and insecurity to American business, they have also brought a wave of new theories about management—plus a number of new methods for solving practical management problems. We will discuss many of these new theories and methods in this chapter and the ones that follow.

WHAT IS MANAGEMENT?

We define **management** as the *process of coordinating resources to meet an objective,* and we say that all the people who work toward meeting that objective form an organization. An **organization** is, simply, *a group of people who have a common objective.*

There are certain basic principles of coordination that can be applied to the management of virtually every type of organization, whatever its size or purpose—an auto plant, a city government, a baseball team, a student typing service. Whenever people work together to achieve a goal, they make decisions about who will do what when, and what money and other resources are to be used when. And that's management.

As this emergency medical crew demonstrates, good management means being ready to cope with almost any event. Coordination and teamwork count too: here, they may even save a trauma victim's life.

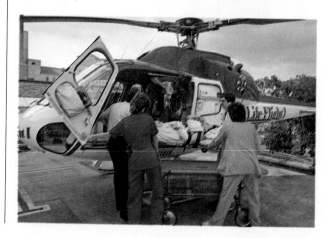

DAILY MANAGEMENT QUESTIONS

Even the smallest organization may have big management problems. For example, picture yourself at the end of a long school year as your concerns turn from passing final exams to earning enough money for fall tuition and expenses. Summer jobs are scarce. But you and a friend believe there is a pressing need in your community for a gourmet picnic-catering service.

Having decided to go into business as Chic Picnique Caterers, you must now deal with a number of basic managerial questions:

- How will you find customers and advertise your service?
- What menus will you offer and how will you price them?
- Where will you get your materials and equipment—basic ingredients, kitchen tools and appliances, delivery and serving equipment?
- Where will you get the start-up money to pay for them?

You and your partner develop a plan of action. As an accounting major, you agree to handle billing, bookkeeping, and purchasing. Your partner, a marketing major, will do the selling and promotion. With your parents as cosigners, you take out a $500 personal loan from the local bank. Your partner designs and places a small ad in the weekly newspaper, and together you distribute leaflets to homes throughout the community. Soon, calls for your service begin to come in, and your new business is launched.

After a while, if business becomes good enough, you may want to hire a few classmates to help out—and at this point things start to get complicated. You and your partner will find yourselves spending less time actually preparing your gourmet picnics, and more time making decisions about such things as scheduling jobs, supervising workers, collecting and paying bills, attracting new business, and so forth. You may even want a personal computer to make better use of all the information you accumulate—to keep up on who owes you and whom you owe, to analyze which promotions and which menus are most profitable, and (you hope) to process repeat orders in a snap. In short, you will have a typical set of management problems claiming an ever-greater portion of your time and energy.

THE FOUR FUNCTIONS OF MANAGEMENT

The activities managers perform can be subdivided into four functions of management: *planning, organizing, directing, and controlling.* We'll take a look at these in the sections that follow.

THE PLANNING FUNCTION

There's no doubt that planning is the first management function, on which all the others depend. When a manager **plans,** he or she *establishes objectives for the organization and tries to determine the best ways to accomplish them.*

The planning for the 1984 Los Angeles Olympics, for instance, began in 1979, when the Organizing Committee's newly hired president, Peter Ueberroth, stepped into his empty office. Ueberroth had one foremost objective fixed in his mind—that the Olympics should be funded entirely from private sources, and should at least break even. Taxpayers had become increasingly concerned over the enormous financial burden the Olympics had become: in 1983, the Canadians had yet to pay off $1 billion in debt from the 1976 games in Montreal. Ueberroth chose a "no-frills" strategy to achieve his objective, budgeting an expenditure of only 5 percent of what the Russians spent in 1980. Then he set about detailed tactical planning, with two key aims: to avoid new construction wherever possible, and to get as much revenue as possible from corporate sponsorship.

"We decided not to hammer a nail," Ueberroth explained, regarding his decision to rent existing facilities for housing and for the events themselves, wherever possible. He determined that only two major new facilities, for swimming and cycling events, needed to be built—and authorized their construction under the sponsorship of McDonald's and the Southland Corporation, owner of 7-Eleven Stores. Ueberroth's primary tactic for reaping the greatest benefit from corporate sponsors was to keep the number of sponsors down to thirty firms. In this way, the exposure the corporate sponsors receive will have real promotional value to them. That value, moreover, was not left to chance, but was a key component of the plan: Ueberroth studied the promotional value of corporate sponsorship for each of the products and services that would be connected with the Olympics (such as TV rights, beverages, air transportation, and camera supplies), and used this information to drive a very hard bargain with prospective sponsors. Each of the thirty corporate sponsors will pay a minimum of $4 million, and will also provide their services to the games, as applicable. For instance, AT&T will provide help with communications, and IBM with computerization. And ABC paid $225 million for U.S. rights to televise the games.

Ueberroth's other major concern was to plan the spectacle itself. And here the critical element was *logistics* (moving things and people from place to place, as efficiently as possible). Athletes, administrators, and ticket-holding spectators must be transported from hotels to Olympic sites and back again without bringing the ordinary business of the city to a grinding halt. With twenty-three sites from Ventura County, 84 miles north of Los Angeles, to San Diego County, 110 miles south, and with an expected 400,000 to 600,000 daily visitors swelling Los Angeles' population to 3.6 million, this end of the planning required the coordination of a huge quantity of detail, so computers were rolled in. The stakes were high—if Ueberroth let too many logistical snarls develop, he might wind up blowing the budget, angering the people of Los Angeles, and leaving the spectators stranded.

By early 1984, every one of the twenty-three sites had been set up—not only on schedule but under budget. Ueberroth's plan seems on the way to total success. If so, then the Los Angeles games will show that they not only can do without public funding but also will come out slightly in the black.[2]

SHORT-RANGE AND LONG-RANGE PLANS

In any organization's strategy it is possible to distinguish two different "time frames" for planning—short range and long range. **Short-range plans** *cover* *the kinds of situations that are likely to come up month by month, and sometimes weekly or daily.* **Long-range plans** *tend to be geared to a two- to five-year span, and in some cases longer.*

Short-range plans

Short-range plans tend to be quite specific. For example, one type of short-range plan, the **procedure**, *tells employees exactly what steps to take in a given situation* (such as moving raw materials from the receiving platform of the factory to the beginning of the assembly line). Similarly detailed are **practices**, *methods for handling specific problems* (an employee's alcoholism), and **rules**, procedures *covering one situation only* (an employee's loss of his or her ID card).

A familiar and very important type of short-range plan is the **budget**, *a plan that expresses in numerical terms* (usually dollars) *how the resources of a company can be distributed to attain a desired profit.* There are a number of tricky variables a manager must think over in preparing a budget. In order to increase profits, should the company simply cut costs—for example, by laying off workers? The alternative may be an appealing one, but it can backfire if it reduces the quality of the company's product or service enough to drive away customers. We'll talk more about budgets in Chapter 16.

Long-range plans

Possibly the most important type of long-range plan is the **statement of purpose**, which *answers the fundamental question, "What is the overall purpose of the organization?"* Or, for a profit-making enterprise, *"What business is it in?"* (For example, is it a root-beer company or a general soft-drink manufacturer?) Also important are **objectives**—*broad goals.* (For example, a business will have profit as one of its objectives, but it may also have other objectives, such as producing a high-quality product or gaining large numbers of customers.) And a third key type of long-range plan consists of **policies**—*guidelines for activity* that help organization members meet the organization's objectives.

MANAGEMENT BY OBJECTIVES

Management by objectives (MBO) is a technique introduced during the 1950s as an aid to planning. It stresses goals for all management levels, by clearly *communicating the goals of the organization to subordinate managers and giving each manager the opportunity to structure personal goals and work procedures to mesh with the organization's objectives.* An MBO program has four phases:

1. The overall goals of the organization are clearly communicated to all participants in the program. It is best if these long-range goals are worked out by upper management in conjunction with unit managers.

2. Unit managers meet with subordinate managers and discuss goals. From this discussion each management person works out personal goals that mesh with the goals of the organization. These should be measurable and written up for later review.

3. At frequent intervals superior and subordinate meet and discuss performance. Each manager's performance is measured against the standards established during the previous conference.

4. Superior and subordinate hold periodic (annual, semiannual, or quarterly) meetings to get an overview of whether long-range goals are being met. The cycle is then refined and repeated. Figure 1 illustrates this cycle.

FIGURE 1

MANAGEMENT BY OBJECTIVES:
Combining worker goals with those of the organization

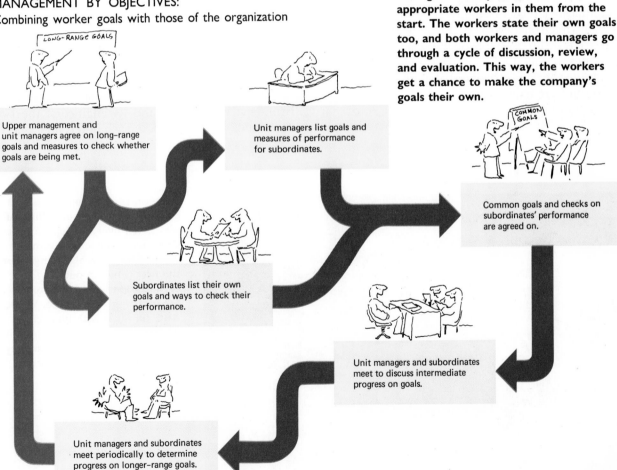

In the **MBO** system, managers state their goals clearly and involve the appropriate workers in them from the start. The workers state their own goals too, and both workers and managers go through a cycle of discussion, review, and evaluation. This way, the workers get a chance to make the company's goals their own.

Upper management and unit managers agree on long-range goals and measures to check whether goals are being met.

Unit managers list goals and measures of performance for subordinates.

Common goals and checks on subordinates' performance are agreed on.

Subordinates list their own goals and ways to check their performance.

Unit managers and subordinates meet to discuss intermediate progress on goals.

Unit managers and subordinates meet periodically to determine progress on longer-range goals.

PLANNING FOR CHANGE IN A FAST-PACED ENVIRONMENT

Planning is just as important when a company is reaching its peak as when it is down in the dumps. In fact, today's business environment changes so rapidly that highs can soon turn into lows—a lesson that Warner's Atari division learned.

In 1982, Atari was harvesting the fruits of its pioneering role in the home video-game industry. Sales growth was more than doubling, market share was 75 percent, and profits were providing more than half of the parent company's earnings. But all this glory disappeared almost overnight. By mid-1983, the company had announced successive quarterly losses and watched the value of its stock sink by more than half—and wondered how it had gotten off the track so fast. Management moved in with a multifaceted plan to lay off 2,000 blue-collar and 1,000 white-collar workers (many of them recently hired), transfer assembly operations from new U.S. facilities to Asia, merge the video-game and home-computer lines; overhaul distribution channels; and introduce an array of new products. This strategy did help to position Atari more advantageously for the future. But better planning at the outset might have helped prevent the dramatic reversal in Atari's fortunes.

One of Atari's main problems was competition. In the early years of the video-game industry, demand grew faster than the handful of suppliers could keep up with. Atari, the technological leader, could sell virtually anything it produced. But suddenly the number of competitors exploded, particularly in game cartridges, which provided a considerable share of Atari's revenue. Many of the competitors were staffed with former Atari game designers who had fled from the firm's uneven compensation policy. Atari's management had failed to foresee that competition would develop, and refused to take it seriously when it arrived. Competitors cut into Atari's profits by unleashing a severe round of price slashing, and cut into sales by releasing game innovations that ended Atari's trend-setting role.

Another big mistake: by failing to keep lines of communication open both inside and outside the company, Atari's management had ignored many signals that should have alerted them to these developments. There was a dangerous split between the firm's marketing staff and its engineers: the two departments did not talk to each other, and as a re-

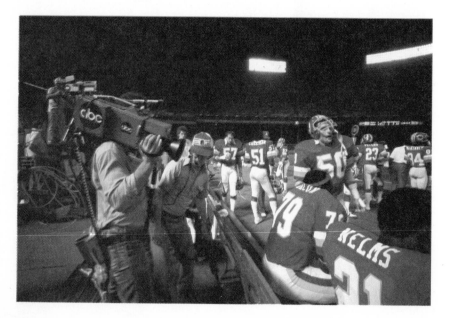

Sometimes one long-range goal conflicts with another. When ABC was taken over by Capital Cities Communications, Inc., some viewers feared a big change. For the first time, an outside organization would control one of broadcasting's Big Three. Would ABC continue with its exciting shows and formats? Or would its innovative programming strategy be preempted by the "bottom line"?

"Sorry, we can't give you the paper clip order yet. The boss is still collecting data."

Regardless of advanced technologies, it's *people* who make decisions.

sult, new product ideas were allowed to sit in desk drawers for years while similar innovations earned millions for competitors.

Unfortunately, Atari's 1983 cost-cutting plan seemed primarily aimed at stopping the short-term loss of cash, and late in that year many observers saw no improvement in the cold war between the firm's marketing and engineering departments. Some improvement in the company's external communications should result from Atari's recent restructuring of its relationships with its distributors. In January 1984, Atari realigned its management team and created Atari Products Company, a new division responsible for research and development, software development, sales and marketing, product engineering and manufacturing. These changes were

aimed at turning Atari around. But Atari will not survive over the long run if it does not constantly monitor signals from the market, so it can stay on track when the business environment changes.[3]

MANAGEMENT INFORMATION SYSTEMS (MIS): THE KEY TO EFFECTIVE PLANNING

As the Atari story shows, keeping in touch with changes in the business environment may be the key to future profits—even survival—for American firms. Markets change, as U.S. and world-wide consumers alter their tastes and spending patterns. Technology changes, as researchers come up with new materials and production methods. Even the value of money changes, as inflation and interest rates notch up and down and the value of the U.S. dollar varies in terms of foreign currencies.

Managers constantly need to collect and evaluate information about such changes, and to do this they must have open communication channels so that data can flow from many sources to the decision makers who need them. Sources of crucial information may be external (customers, distributors, competitors, consultants) or internal (staff specialists; company data on trends, sales, costs and inventory). The managers who use this information work in many areas: they include managers who make decisions about what shall be sold, managers who decide how it shall be produced, managers who decide what prices shall be charged, and others. All these managers need a carefully planned and organized **management information system (MIS),** *a system for providing timely and effective information to support management decision-making.*

In many modern corporations, the problem is not how to get enough information, but how to sort through the massive overload of information so that what a manager receives is meaningful and up to date. If managers were hit all at once by the entire flow of information that comes from all sources, they would be buried and unable to interpret the data quickly enough to take appropriate action. Thus, many companies use computer-based information systems to organize, manipulate, and distribute information. It is important to remember, though, that computers are only a tool for processing information—they will store and extract data as we instruct them to, but they cannot tell us what information we should ask for or what form it should take. The manager must determine what type of data he or she wishes to extract from the universe of potential information, and what to do with this information.

Perhaps the most important recent change in the management function is managers' increased involvement in information-processing systems of all kinds. "Stand-alone" personal microcomputers, for example, have been much in the news. These amazingly powerful machines, about the size of a TV set, can help managers manipulate data instantaneously. And terminals that are used not on a "stand-alone" basis, but "on-line" (hooked up) with the firm's central data-processing facility, have also appeared in executive suites. The manager does not have to have years of technical computer training to use these machines: special software packages that the nonprogrammer can easily use have begun to appear. Some of these packages are designed for applications such as budgeting and forecasting, where managers must often explore outcomes under alternative assumptions; others are used for up-to-the-minute analysis of cash flow and inventory. Even the manager who does not have a terminal of his or her own is increasingly expected to talk to staff members who design the company's data-processing systems so that these experts can make sure the manager gets the right information, at the right time, in the right format.

Because the impact of the computer is expanding in so many aspects of business, information systems will be discussed in many chapters in this book—including two (Chapter 17 and Component Chapter F) devoted entirely to computers.

THE ORGANIZING FUNCTION

Suppose the managers of an organization have made their plans. What question must they tackle next? They have to figure out how to accomplish all their goals by using the resources at their disposal. The most important resource is their employees.

The managers must think through all the activities employees must carry out, from programming the organization's computers (if it has any) to driving its trucks to mailing its letters. And they must get together a staff capable of doing these things. This aspect of management—*the process of arranging resources, primarily people, to carry out the organization's plans*—is called **organizing.**

Organizing is particularly challenging in that the organization is likely to undergo constant change. Old staff members may leave and new ones arrive. The public's tastes and interests may change so that the organization has to change its goals. Shifting political and economic trends may mean cutbacks, rearrangements, or perhaps expansion. Every month (even every week) the organization presents a new picture, and so management's organizing tasks are never complete.

THE DIVISION OF LABOR

The main problem the manager faces in organizing is figuring out the division of labor that will be best suited to the goals of the organization. Labor may be divided in two different ways—according to task and according to authority—and the manager has to structure the organization with both these dimensions in mind.

Dividing labor by task

In 1776 the Scottish economist Adam Smith designed a classic study demonstrating something we take for granted today. He showed that *dividing labor by task enables a group of workers to achieve far more than the same number of workers could achieve without it.* The labor process Smith studied was the manufacture of pins. What Smith found was that if each of ten workers went through every step needed to make a pin, the best worker could make a maximum of 20 pins a day, and some could make only a single pin. Even if every worker could make 20 pins, the final tally would be only 200 pins a day. But if each worker performed only a few steps—and no one made a pin from start to finish—ten workers could manufacture a total of 48,000 pins a day! There was no question about it: dividing up the job into a series of steps was by far the best plan.

Dividing labor by task works well because each individual worker only needs certain specific skills. When the worker repeatedly performs the same specialized task, skills are enhanced and the worker is able to perform the task more quickly; furthermore, less preparation or set-up time is necessary when the worker does not shift from task to task. Modern technology has carried the advantages of Adam Smith's vision one step further: it has encouraged the invention of machines that can perform these specialized tasks at rates that greatly exceed human efficiency.

But although division of labor is still a central organizing principle of both manufacturing and administrative operations, some organizations are modifying this approach to make it more appropriate to modern workers' needs and abilities. In Adam Smith's day, industrial workers were used to the less rigid routines of the farm, and the factory had to impose strict discipline on them. The modern organization, by contrast, is peopled with individuals who already know how to cope with the structured life of a complex metropolis; they have been familiar with machines since childhood, and their education has trained them to analyze information and make decisions. If you demand of such workers nothing more than simple repetition, many managers find, the workers may rebel against you—and you may waste the true value of the person you are paying. Thus the classic division of labor is now evolving into new forms. Innovative managers are experimenting with new approaches, such as allowing teams of workers to decide for themselves how to break down a complex task, and allowing them to share responsibility for the final product. We discuss some new approaches in Component Chapter C.

Dividing labor by authority

If the managers can divide up the organization's labor process by task, they will have made a good start toward reaching their goals. But the organization will function even more smoothly if the workers know not only what to do and when to do it, but also who is looking over their shoulders to make sure they do it right. In most organizations, certain employees are held accountable for work done by other people. If the workers do not complete their tasks properly or on time, those who are responsible for the work must take the blame. President Harry Truman kept a famous sign on his desk that read: "The Buck Stops Here." He knew that in any organization—including the United States government—there is always a point of ultimate accountability, right at the top. But certain people below the top must have accountability too, and part of management's job is to plan the way this accountability is distributed.

How can a person who is responsible for the work of others actually get those people to do their jobs? By being given a certain amount of authority. **Authority** is a form of power; it is *power granted by the organization and acknowledged by the employees.* A supervisor must have the authority to modify the work slightly to achieve greater efficiency. He or she must also have the authority to reward or penalize workers according to how well they perform their jobs. So when managers work out divisions of labor for an organization, they must be sure to grant the right amount of authority to those workers who will need it to do their jobs. For example, managers must determine which decisions they can allow assembly-line supervisors to make without consulting higher-level managers, and then make sure the assembly-line workers see their supervisors making these decisions.

In this area too, technological changes have brought changes to management methods. With new electronic monitoring systems that put better information about production processes into the hands of the production supervisor, management is tending to push more decision-making authority downward—to the floor-supervisor level. Upper-level production managers, meanwhile, may spend less time making direct production decisions, and more time preparing lower-level production staff to make those decisions for themselves. Upper-level managers may also spend more time analyzing electronic data to check on the floor supervisors' progress.

These points, of course, are just the highlights of the complicated process of formulating a division of labor in an organization. We talk more about this aspect of the manager's job in Chapter 5. We also talk about **staffing,** the process of *matching the right people with the right jobs,* in Chapter 8.

THE DIRECTING FUNCTION

Through the process of organizing, then, managers plan the tasks their employees are *supposed* to do. But even if managers set up a magnificently logical organizational plan, not all things will necessarily happen the way they have in mind. Far from it. The results may be very unsatisfactory unless the managers also spend time on a third type of management activity—directing.

Directing is a complex management function whose primary aim is *getting people to work effectively and willingly*. It consists of two different but related processes. First, it involves **motivating**—the process of *giving employees a reason to do the job and to put forth their best performance*. Second, it involves **leading,** the process of *showing employees how to do the job*, both through actual demonstration of specific tasks and through the manager's own behavior and attitude.

LEADERSHIP STYLES

One of the favorite topics of political commentators and newspaper columnists is the "leadership style" of whoever happens to occupy the White House. A president may be attacked for being overly formal or too informal, for overusing his presidential influence by leaning on people or for failing to mobilize effectively the powers of the presidency. But the president of the United States is not the only manager with a leadership style. Every manager, from the brawling, cursing baseball manager to the urbane, statesman-like university chancellor, has a leadership style.

Three types of leader

You can learn something about leadership by examining the methods different leaders use to get results and the specific ways they exercise authority. While virtually all leaders have their own individual characteristics, we can identify three broad categories of leadership style:

THE AUTOCRATIC STYLE This leader uses authority in a straightforward manner by simply issuing orders. His or her preference for making decisions without consulting others is highly effective when quick decisions are critical, *if* the leader indeed has the

Robert A. Pritzker, President, Marmon Group:
"I tell my people, 'Don't play games. Don't lie to me. Don't lie for me. Don't do me any favors. Play it straight.'"[4]

James F. Beré, Chairman, Borg-Warner:
"The job of the top executive is not to make decisions. It is to put good people in place and judge if they are making good decisions. You give them the power. When they come in and say 'How should I do something?' I say, 'That's your problem.'"[5]

power to enforce those decisions. There are drawbacks to this management style, however. In some instances, the manager could be more objective, or motivate workers better, if he or she were more open to subordinates' input.

THE DEMOCRATIC, OR PARTICIPATIVE, STYLE Group participation is emphasized here. The democratic leader encourages a free flow of communication, while making it clear that he or she has the final say. This approach, which requires relatively little supervision, is useful when the workers are highly skilled professionals. But it has weaknesses: the group may be slow to arrive at decisions, and the leader may end up having less control over subordinates.

THE LAISSEZ-FAIRE STYLE The French term *laissez faire* can be roughly translated as "leave it alone," or, more roughly, "hands off." In this style, the manager leads by taking the role of consultant, providing encouragement for employees' ideas, and offering insights or opinions when asked. This approach encourages group members to express themselves creatively, but it may fail if the group's goals do not match the organization's.

Situational management

There is no "best" way to carry out any of the basic management functions—planning, organizing, directing, and controlling. All three styles of leadership work sometimes, but no style works every time. The best approach to take depends on the leader's personality, the workers' skills and backgrounds, and the problems the company is facing at that particular moment. Even though a company may start out under one system of management, there are a number of *contingencies* (possible events) that may cause the firm's situation to change—for example, it may start making new products, or start making the old ones in a new way. *Management that emphasizes adapting general principles to the actual needs of one's own business,* called **situational** or **contingency management,** is now considered highly important by many management experts and theorists.

NEW THEORIES OF LEADERSHIP

Today, corporations are keenly aware that organizational change must keep up with technological changes, and they count on leaders to guide the or-

Quentin T. Wiles, working chairman of five corporations:
"Most of my time is spent making sure people know what their jobs are.'"[6]

John J. Byrne, Chairman, Geico Corp.:
"[Winnie the] Pooh is an unlikely leader, but his very unlikeliness puts him in the leadership role time after time. He's a relaxed realist who never thrusts himself forward, and it's surprising how often it works."[7]

ganization through these difficult transitions. Thus, there is a renewed interest in many American corporations in just what it takes to be a leader.

Young companies and mature ones: contrasting leadership needs

Part of today's debate about leadership focuses on two contrasting types of organizational goals and two types of individuals: the young, innovative high-growth (often high-technology) firm, staffed with risk-seeking entrepreneurial types, and the mature company that is faced with defending its market share and cutting its costs, and is staffed with administrators who are trained to be "risk-averse" (to avoid risks). Leadership problems in these alternative business environments have been in the news recently. In 1983, for example, many of Intel Corporation's most creative engineers and executives left to take jobs with competitors and spin-off companies when hard times took away Intel's entrepreneurial atmosphere. Similarly, when Polaroid passed out of a stage of frequent new-product introductions around the same time, many of the brightest people left, complaining of a loss of excitement and glamour.[8]

Did poor leadership cause these firms to lose their best talent? Or was their leadership good at building sales but less effective at maintaining profits? Perhaps there is a real distinction between those leaders who are good at breaking new ground and those who are good at keeping a healthy company on course. If so, a young organization should not hire leaders from mature companies, and a mature company should not keep all its past "performers."[9] These questions require much research; it was partly to deal with them that Matsushita (makers of Panasonic products) endowed a professorial chair in leadership at Harvard Business School in 1981.

The psychology of the leader

Another current question is: are there universal qualities that make good leaders in any setting? Recent research suggest that true leaders have certain thought and behavior patterns that are different from those of the everyday manager. First, the true leader seems to be a person who tends to focus his or her energies on a concrete, original objective, and draws inspiration from visualizing that goal in great detail. This ability to conceptualize, and to see the *unobvious*, exists—some researchers believe—in the true leader's subconscious mind: he or she does not suppress ideas and associations (as many of us do) but rather allows impressions to "bubble up," no matter how irrelevant or trivial they may at first seem.

Second, the leader is able to share this vision with others, and by doing so, to inspire them too. Subordinates who have a lofty ideal perform much better than those who don't have a sense of purpose, or those who transfer their loyalty to each passing corporate fad.

Finally, the true leader understands that there will be failures along the way. The ability to tolerate failure frees him or her to try every means to reach the objective, and not to shy away from possibilities that may not work. Failure is less threatening to the true leader, for this type of person engages in much less blaming of self and others than most people do. Of course, this theory raises further questions. How can we identify such leaders? Are they born that way, or can they be "trained"?[10] Future research may shed some light on these questions.

THE CONTROLLING FUNCTION

A fourth, very crucial management function is known as controlling—a word that is often a source of confusion because it suggests some sort or restriction, as when a leash controls a dog. In management, **controlling** is not solely a restrictive process. It is *the process of ensuring that organizational objectives are actually being attained and correcting deviations if they are not.*

When managers control, they compare where they are with where they should be and take any necessary corrective action. Managers determine where they are by getting reports from subordinates, coworkers, superiors, and sources outside the organization. They determine where they should be by referring to the plans and objectives they have set up. They then take corrective action, if needed—by replanning, reorganizing, or redirecting. Controlling is the management function that pinpoints flaws in the other three functions. If the managers of an organization maintain a continuous control process, they can make at least some mistakes without seriously hurting the organization.

THE CYCLE OF CONTROLLING

As a first step in the control cycle in any organization, managers must set **standards**—*goals against which performance can be measured later*. In business, control standards are expressed in a number of ways. Here are some of them:

- lateness in minutes per week (the managers might, for example, decide that employees should not be more than ten minutes late to work and should not be late more than one day a week)

- profitability (for example, the managers might set a standard of a 20 percent profit to be derived from a certain product)

- units produced or sold per week

- employee turnover (percentage of work force leaving the firm in a given period)

Next, the managers must establish a **feedback system** whereby *they will receive reports on a regular basis*—perhaps daily or weekly. Today many companies use progress reports that come from a computerized monitoring system. But progress reports from the people who are doing or supervising the work are still important too. Supervisory managers may complain, "All I do is make out reports. I don't have time to do any work." But making out reports *is* part of their work. Without supervisors' participation in the control feedback system, the company would have a harder time functioning effectively.

In Figure 2, the production managers' report shows that only 1,800 cars were produced, 200 short of the standard. Why was production not up to par? To find out the answer, the managers must take a look at the feedback they have been getting on other aspects of the operation. Suppose, for example, they

FIGURE 2

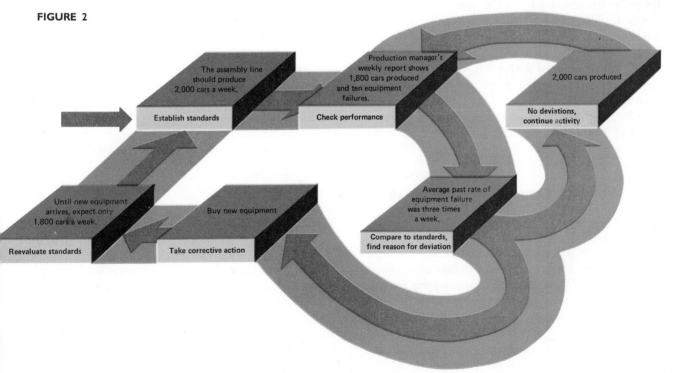

THE CONTROL CYCLE IN AUTOMOBILE PRODUCTION

FIGURE 3

THE MANAGEMENT HIERARCHY

Top management

JOB TITLES AT THIS LEVEL INCLUDE:

President
Premier
Vice-president
General
Chairman of the board

Middle management

JOB TITLES AT THIS LEVEL INCLUDE:

Head of accounting
Factory manager
Army captain
Cardinal

Supervisory management

JOB TITLES AT THIS LEVEL INCLUDE:

Foreman
Supervisor
Sergeant
Pastor
Chairman of history
   department

check the weekly report on the performance of the machines that are used in the production line. They find that the average number of equipment breakdowns is three per week (this, in other words, can be taken as the standard). Yet in the week that only 1,800 Cadillacs rolled off the assembly line, the sheet-metal presses broke down ten times. Now the managers know why fewer cars were produced that week, and their best corrective action in this case would probably be to replace the machinery. Of course, until the new equipment arrived, they would also have to revise the production standard downward to 1,800 units to allow for the defective machinery.

THE MANAGEMENT HIERARCHY

In any organized group, no matter how complicated, the managerial staff consists basically of three different levels of people; the **top,** or **upper, managers,** *who have the most power and responsibility;* the **middle managers,** *who have somewhat less power and responsibility;* and the **supervisory,** or **operating, managers,** *whose power and responsibility are limited to a narrow segment of the organization.* These three levels form a **hierarchy**—a *structure with a top, middle, and*

bottom—which can be represented as a pyramid, as shown in Figure 3. There are quite a number of managers at the bottom level, a smaller number of managers at the middle level, and just a few managers, or in many cases only one, at the very top.

On the surface, management hierarchies may seem to differ because the titles of managers' jobs vary from one organization to another. But such differences are often misleading. Three executives in three similar corporations, for instance, may have different titles—senior vice president, executive vice president, and president—but actually perform the same jobs within their companies. In Figure 4, we show the tasks that are typically performed by managers at each level of the hierarchy.

MANAGERIAL SKILLS

Is there a managerial "type" of person? We have all known the person who has been managing groups of people ever since childhood—starting with the leader of the neighborhood gang. But you don't have to be a "born manager" to learn some managerial skills or to sharpen the ones you already have. Most people, at some point in their lives, find themselves with new responsibilities—sometimes heavy

WHO DOES THE PLANNING?

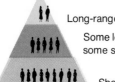

Long-range planning

Some long-range,
some short-range planning

Short-range planning

Not surprisingly, top managers are usually the ones responsible for long-range planning, while middle managers and supervisory managers are more involved with planning over the short range. Of course, there is a good deal of overlap.

The chief difference between planning by a company president and planning by an assembly-line supervisor is the complexity of the problems which confront them. The president deals with thousands of people, millions of dollars, and years of time, while the supervisor handles only a few people, over a short time, on a much smaller budget. Both managers plan in order to influence the future—but for the president the future is far more difficult to predict, and the losses will be much greater if his or her predictions do not come true. Working as a top manager can be very stressful.

WHO DOES THE ORGANIZING?

Organizing the whole structure
Staffing upper-level positions

Organizing individual divisions

Training new workers
Evaluating workers' progress

Generally, it is the top managers who establish the organizational structure for an enterprise as a whole, and staff upper-level positions. Middle managers do the same thing—but usually just for one division. Supervisors seldom set up organizational structure, but they may still have important responsibilities in the organizing area— such as training new workers and evaluating their progress.

WHO DIRECTS THE WORKERS?

Planning motivational devices
(e.g. bonuses)

Implementing motivational programs

Dealing with day-to-day motivation

Directing begins at the top and is then mirrored downward. But the closer a manager gets to the "action"—the work itself—the more time-consuming, demanding and crucial directing becomes. For example, the first-line supervisor spends most of the time trying to motivate workers to churn out their daily quotas of whatever the department is charged with producing. The first-line supervisor is on the "firing line" all the time— contending frequently with such problems as worker lateness, illness, disagreements and grievances against the organization. Top management, by contrast, is and should be interested in the "big picture"—the methods to be used in motivating the organization as a whole, such as wage scales and bonuses.

WHO DOES THE CONTROLLING?

Setting overall control systems and standards

Setting specific goals, getting routine
feedback, solving routine problems

Getting progress reports
Solving day-to-day difficulties

Top management usually establishes the control systems and standards—such as market-share targets—that measure the performance of the organization as a whole. These standards are then translated into more specific goals—such as sales quotas—for middle management and the other managers down the line. Like directing, controlling is particularly important on the middle and lower management levels. Middle management receives most of the routine feedback and solves most routine problems before they become serious enough to draw the attention—and the wrath—of upper management. Supervisory managers collect daily and weekly progress information to pass on to middle managers, and they try to handle any difficulties that are due to employees' poor work habits or practices.

THEORY Z: THE JAPANESE APPROACH TO MANAGEMENT

What makes a company function well from day to day? One of the important factors—a factor we'll be discussing often in this book—is the relationship between managers and workers. Management expert Douglas McGregor used to say that there were two kinds of bosses: the "Theory X" boss, who believes that workers are basically lazy and untrustworthy, and the "Theory Y" boss, who believes in the workers and wants to help them perform the best they can. Now, UCLA management professor William Ouchi has added "Theory Z." The observations Ouchi makes in his book *Theory Z* are based in part on the distinctive style of management that is practiced in Japanese companies.

LIFETIME EMPLOYMENT

The Japanese strive to create a family spirit among all employees of the firm, from top to bottom. They believe that when an employee partakes of a company-

wide sense of identity and belonging, he or she is more likely to perform job tasks conscientiously and will try more enthusiastically to achieve a perfect final product. Though we often hear accounts of Japanese workers getting together to exercise or sing the company song, the most important motivator of this family feeling is a very practical one—a lifetime employment policy. Even when sales are down, workers at most large Japanese companies know they will never be laid off, and thus have good reason to feel that their own long-term fate is tied to the company's.

COLLECTIVE DECISION-MAKING

If the employee gets a sense of practical belonging from the lifetime job security system, he or she also gets a sense of psychological belonging from the way Japanese companies make decisions. Unlike American managers, who are expected to act forcefully and make decisions on their own (and accept the consequences), Japanese managers make decisions in groups. With each person able to cast a veto—sometimes as many as sixty or eighty people may be included—it takes time for the group to work out a decision

ones—that make them feel the need to develop managerial skills.

Basically, managerial skills fall into three areas: technical skills, human skills, and conceptual skills.

TECHNICAL SKILLS

A person who is able to operate a machine, prepare a financial statement, program a computer, or pass a football has a **technical skill.** That is, he or she is *able to perform the mechanics of a particular job.* Managers such as production supervisors must often understand a technical skill well enough to train workers in their jobs. In certain companies, executives

without technical skills can manage nonproduction workers who have technical skills in programming, engineering, or accounting. But even here, most managers have to have some technical skills—such as scheduling techniques and the ability to read computer printouts.

Technical skills are sometimes not readily transferable from one industry to another, whereas general management skills can often be applied to a wide range of industries. If you're trained to operate textile-cutting machines, you probably would be unable to use your skills in the restaurant business. If you're an executive who runs a garment business, however, you might be able to use your general management skills in different enterprises.

INTERNATIONAL BUSINESS TODAY

everyone can live with. The advantage of this process of collective compromise is that once an agreement has been reached, no one in the group will try to sabotage it out of disappointment or frustration.

PROMOTION AND CAREER PATHS

Promotions come infrequently in Japanese companies—in some companies, only at ten-year intervals—so managers are much less likely to feel their colleagues are getting ahead of them. (The American manager's push to get on the "fast track" wouldn't make sense in a Japanese company.) Moreover, Japanese executives do not specialize in specific functional areas such as sales, finance, or production: they are moved from one department to the next so that they are familiar with, and have a sense of identification with, all of the company's internal workings.

THEORY Z IN THE UNITED STATES

Can the group-oriented Japanese approach to management be made to work in this country? As we noted in Component Chapter A, our cultural background is very different from Japan's. Surviving in a small,

densely populated, resource-poor land has made teamwork and compromise essential for the Japanese; we, on the other hand, have had a tradition of individualism and self-reliance since pioneer days. Getting thirty or forty hard-driving American executives to build a decision by collective compromise might tie an American company in knots. Yet, as Ouchi notes, some U.S. firms are already using at least some Japanese management practices. Intel Corporation has encouraged a collective approach by dividing employees into project teams; Procter & Gamble uses partially self-governing work groups in some of its plants; and Hewlett-Packard kept worker turnover down during economic slumps by making sure *all* employees—not just the "low men on the totem pole"—had to give up some working hours and privileges. These days, as we face tougher foreign competition and resources such as energy become more expensive, it might help many companies to imitate the corporate teamwork of the Japanese.

SOURCE: Christopher Byron, "An Attractive Japanese Export: The XYZs of Management Theory Challenge American Bosses," *Time*, March 2, 1983, p. 74.

HUMAN SKILLS

Human skills are all the *skills that are required in order to understand other people and to interact effectively with them.* Managers' human skills are most needed when directing, but they need them in countless other situations too—since their main job is getting things done through people. This is true even if the manager is the boss and can fire anyone at will; after all, anxious employees don't always do good work.

One human skill all managers must have is the ability to **communicate,** that is, to *transfer information.* In any organization, communication is the thread that weaves everything together. It keeps internal operations running smoothly and it also fos-

ters good relations with people outside the organization. Successful communication is a two-way street. A manager should always be attuned to the way people are reacting to what's being said and, above all, listen to what they have to say in return. There are two chief forms of communication: oral and written.

Oral communication

This very direct form of communication generally takes up a substantial part of any business day. Within the firm, there are meetings, presentations, conferences, informal chats with superiors and subordinates—and all these require effective oral communication. Outside the firm, sales talks, interviews, speeches, and press conferences require managers to use oral communication to achieve organizational goals.

Written communication

Within an organization, especially a large one, memos, letters, progress reports, policy statements, and other forms of written communication are constantly moving back and forth. A company's plans, long-range and short-range, must be recorded in the form of policy directives, summaries of high-level meetings, budget statements, rulebooks, and any number of other written documents. Likewise, the organizing function relies on staff charts and written job descriptions; the directing function proceeds largely through memos; and the controlling function, as we noted earlier, depends heavily on written reports. At the same time, written communication is essential in presenting an organization to the outside world. Letters, press releases, annual reports, sales brochures, advertisements—all these play a direct role in shaping a company's public image.

The ability to communicate effectively on paper is thus a valuable skill at all levels of management. Appendix II discusses at length the written presentation of business information, but these points also deserve emphasis here:

■ The message must be suitable for its audience. In explaining how a windmill works, for instance, you would use one style of writing for an elementary-school magazine, and quite a different one for a sales brochure directed to potential buyers.

■ It must be readable. Long, needlessly complex sentences will only slow the reader and camouflage the message you're trying to put across.

■ It must be objective. If care is not taken to balance the message, the reader may easily reject it as biased and unreliable.

CONCEPTUAL SKILLS AND DECISION MAKING

Conceptual skill is *the ability to understand the relationship of parts to the whole.* Managers must be able to imagine the long-range effects their plans may have not only on their employees, but also on other company plans. In a large corporation, managers can lose sight of the forest amid all the trees. Even in a small business there are any number of factors that have to be organized and kept track of, and a manager who wants things to run smoothly must have a clear understanding of their relationship to each other and to the business as a whole.

The decision-making process is a managerial activity that takes conceptual skill. Researchers have closely observed decision-making and broken it down into its component parts, which we illustrate here with a situation in a publishing house.

1. Keeping watch for problems: First, the decision maker must continually scan his or her area of responsibility for problems.
   Tuesday morning: Our book project seems to be going OK. The authors are handing in their manuscripts on time, the editors are getting their rewrites done, and the designers are making sketches for the pictures. *Tuesday afternoon:* Editor Jane Weissberg has missed her deadline for rewrites on three chapters.

2. Identifying the problem and pinpointing goals for the solution: After spotting a problem on the horizon, the decision maker determines the nature of the problem and the objective involved in solving the problem.
   ■ What has caused Jane to slow down? She says she's having trouble finding time to carry out all parts of her assignment—rewriting the chapters, thinking up picture ideas, and checking everything with the authors—in the time allowed.
   ■ What's our objective? Do we want to punish Jane? Or is our goal simply to get the work done somehow?

3. Finding possible courses of action: Next, the decision maker must figure out what choices are possible. Choices can range all the way from doing nothing at all to making drastic changes, with an array of adjustments in between.
   What are our choices? We can:
   ■ Ignore the problem and hope Jane finds a way to solve it herself.
   ■ Yell at Jane.
   ■ Talk to Jane quietly—see if there are other problems, such as a noisy office mate, that she hasn't mentioned.
   ■ Solve the problem by adding time: look for more time in the schedule so Jane can have an extra day for each chapter.

- Solve the problem by adding manpower: assign part of the task—maybe the picture ideas—to another editor.

4. Examining the options: The decision maker must evaluate these choices, looking at each from the point of view of the objective and projecting its consequences.

   Which choices will help us get the work done?

   - Yelling or ignoring the problem *might* work—but they are risky because they don't lead clearly to a solution.
   - Talking to Jane *might* help—but it may not solve the problem fast enough to keep us on schedule.
   - *Do* we have extra time in the schedule? (Unfortunately, we find we don't.)
   - *Do* we have another editor with some free time? (Fortunately, yes.)

5. Choosing a course of action: Finally, the choice that compares most favorably must actually be implemented.

   Looking for another person to help is probably the most productive choice. Meanwhile, a chat with Jane may also help us prevent this type of problem from happening again.

SURVIVAL SKILLS FOR TODAY'S MANAGERS

In today's rapidly changing business climate, companies must often rapidly modify the ways their workers and machines get things done—and consequently, there is a great demand for managers who have both the human skills *and* the technical skills to make these changes. Business schools are trying hard to respond to this need. Students who already have a technical background are encouraged to take courses in practical interpersonal skills, covering topics such as how to manage time, how to run a meeting, and how to deal with problem employees. For students lacking technical skills, the business schools offer training in analytical and theoretical techniques such as operations research, econometrics, and information systems that will be useful in any functional area of management the student chooses to enter.[12]

CORPORATE CULTURE: A TOOL FOR MODERN MANAGEMENT

There remains one final variable in the equation for successful management: a complicated factor that is often called the "corporate culture." In formal terms, **corporate culture** *comprises the beliefs, values, attitudes, and expectations that are held by the employees of an organization and that make up its unique character.* Less formally, a corporation's culture is the "feel" of the place—its atmosphere, attitudes, traditions, style of dress, and social style—whether it's "laid back" or "button-down." The corporate culture is the mysterious factor that determines why a certain mix of management policies and styles "works" in a particular organization. And it is the factor that endures over time, even if the organization changes its specific outputs.

The corporate culture serves as a guidepost by which employees can judge what the company wants from them, how they should approach problems, and what types of solutions will be acceptable in that company. The book *In Search of Excellence*, by Thomas Peters and Robert Waterman, concluded that a strong corporate culture is *the* common characteristic of highly successful companies such as IBM, GE, and McDonald's.[11] Another research team has suggested that there may be four common types of corporate culture:

- *The macho/tough guy culture,* which rewards aggressiveness and demands immediate results, and is found most commonly in unpredictable industries such as entertainment.

- *The work hard/play hard culture,* which rallies around promotions, contests, and the image of the supersalesperson, and is common in sales-oriented firms such as retailers.

- *The "bet-your-company" culture,* which is found in high-stakes, slow-feedback firms, and is appropriate in industries with large but infrequent payoffs such as oil and aerospace.

- *The process culture,* which is seen in low-risk, slow-feedback organizations, and is often favored in industries such as financial services where the need for technical perfection means emphasis on procedure rather than product.[12]

A manager who understands the culture of his or her corporation has an extremely powerful tool for designing policies likely to get results in that organization. If you know your company's culture, it will be much easier to act on decisions fast; knowing the culture can also provide a sense of stability in times of great change. *Not* knowing the culture can lead an otherwise intelligent policy to fail if it is inconsistent with the culture. Managers should also be able to recognize organizations that have no corporate culture; in those firms, managers can only fit policies to workers' styles on a hit-or-miss basis.

CHAPTER REVIEW

Management—the process of coordinating resources to meet an objective—comprises four basic functions: planning, organizing, directing, and controlling. The managers and those who work under them make up an organization—a group of people sharing and working toward a common goal.

When managers plan, they establish objectives for the organization and try to find the best ways to achieve them. Short-range (day, week, month) plans take four basic forms: procedure, practices, rules, and budget. Long-range (two to five years) plans include an organization's statement of purpose, broad objectives, and general policies. Plans must be based on information, and today there is far more of that than managers can easily handle. Therefore they often depend on a central computer-based management information system (MIS) to organize, manipulate, and distribute data. Other useful new tools include "stand-alone" personal microcomputers and "on-line" computer terminals with associated software.

When managers organize, they arrange resources to carry out plans. Organizing requires division of labor. Dividing a large job into smaller components is called dividing labor by task. Dividing a job into a hierarchy based on responsibility is called dividing labor by authority.

When managers direct, they get people to do their assigned jobs. This function has two interrelated aspects: motivating and leading. Motivating employees means giving them a reason for doing the job as well as they can. Leading is usually based on one of three styles of leadership: autocratic, democratic, or laissez-faire. Although different leadership styles may be suited to young vs. mature companies, it is believed that there are some "true" leaders, who seem to share a number of characteristic gifts.

When managers control, they make sure that objectives are actually being attained or, if they are not, take corrective measures. The controlling cycle involves establishing standards, checking performance, comparing performance with the standard, and correcting problems.

All large organizations have hierarchies: top management, middle management, and supervisory or operating management. People throughout this hierarchy need overall managerial expertise as well as technical, human, and conceptual skills. Technical skill involves the mechanics of a job, whether it is operating a machine or programming a computer. Human skill is largely a matter of effective interaction and communication. Oral communication must be clear and comprehensible to the listener; written communication must be suitable, readable, and objective. Conceptual skill is the ability to see each part in relation to the whole. To ride out the sudden storms of today's business climate, a manager also needs survival skills—the human and technical know-how to expedite quick changes.

Corporate culture comprises the beliefs, values, attitudes, and expectations that are held by the employees of an organization and make up its unique character. This is the "feel" of the place, which determines the particular mix of management policies and styles that will be most effective.

KEY WORDS

management (124)
organization (124)
plans (125)
short-range plans (126)
long-range plans (126)
procedure (126)
practices (126)
rules (126)
budget (126)

REVIEW QUESTIONS

1. Grandma's Homemade Pasta Products has sold successfully to hotels and restaurants for decades. Now the Japanese-owned Luscious Larmen Ltd., with its high-tech noodle machines and freeze-dried dumplings, is cutting deep into sales. How should Grandma's management respond?

2. Name the two general types of plans used by organizations and give several examples of each.

3. How has modern technology helped managers to cope with the information explosion? For an imaginary business, tell how "MIS Made the Mission Possible."

4. Discuss the two processes involved in directing.

5. Identify the three broad leadership styles. What are the advantages and disadvantages of each? Is there a "best" style? Explain your answer.

6. What are the steps in a typical control cycle?

7. Name the three levels of the management hierarchy and the four basic types of management skills. Outline your own ideas on what makes a good manager and a good leader.

8. Why are human and conceptual skills important to managers at all levels?

9. What are managerial survival skills, and why have they become important?

10. The corporate culture of firm A, a quiet, conservative bank, contrasts sharply with that of firm B, a company that runs aerobic dance classes throughout the city. Imagine two firms that fit these descriptions and speculate on how you, as company president, would run either organization.

CASE 1

MEAD GOES HIGH-TECH

Mead Corporation, which we met in one of the cases for Chapter 3, is a large manufacturer of paper, lumber, and corrugated cardboard. In the late 1960s Mead's management, looking ahead, realized that computers were likely to be increasingly important in the publishing industry—a field that paper companies like to keep up with. Mead decided to devote some of its corporate resources to developing computerized information services. Mead's first service, called Lexis, was (and still is) a system in which users pay a fee for a computer telephone link with Mead Data Central—which in turn supplies all manner of information about federal regulations, court decisions, case law, and scholarly articles.

But it's not easy for a big smoke-stack company like Mead to jump into the fast-paced, competitive world of computer services. Mead's managers found this out in short order. First, they lost money. Developing Lexis took six years and $27 million—all before any profits materialized. Mead's managers, seeing millions melting away year after year, were understandably worried. Tension developed within the company as pro- and anti-Lexis factions debated the new division's fate. As James W. McSwiney, Mead's former chairman and CEO, put it, "There wasn't a day that we didn't question the project." A second problem was that rapid developments in the computer field tempted the company to involve itself in all sorts of other high-tech ventures, such as a computer-aided service to identify industrial pollutants and an ink-jet printing operation. Mead seemed in danger of spreading itself too thin in this highly competitive market.

Mead addressed its first problem—the unprofitability of Lexis—with a highly creative marketing strategy. Although no one questioned the usefulness of Lexis in aiding legal research, Mead found that its potential customers—primarily older lawyers—were resistant to the idea of using computers. The company's solution? Sell Lexis to law schools. Law students, familiar with the service, would come to rely on it—and eventually would form a powerful lobby group for its acceptance in their firms. Mead promptly sold Lexis to more than 150 law schools throughout the country. The problem with this solution, of course, was that it took time. By 1977, however, Lexis did become profitable, and it has been doing well ever since. Mead's long-range gamble proved successful.

Mead's other big problem—too wide a range of services—was also skillfully solved. Success with Lexis led Mead's managers to decide to concentrate on information services such as Nexis, which provides more general news and research materials, including wire-service reports, the text of major newspapers, magazines, and newsletters, and reference works, such as the *Encyclopaedia Britannica*. Mead acquired the New York Times Company's information service, and introduced Lexpat, a patent-search service. And it got plans on the drawing board for financial and scientific information services. Mead's high-tech services that were not directly related to information were scrapped.

Mead's computer-information division is a success story: it's now considerably *more* profitable than the rest of the company. But it still faces some big decisions. One of the biggest is how to tie in with customers' computer systems. Initially, Mead's services were available only through its own terminals, which customers would lease. Recently, the company has allowed customers who own IBM computers to link up with Mead's services using their own machines. Mead's managers are now pondering whether to allow other makes of computer access to their systems, and if so, which of the many other computers now on the market to choose. Jack W. Simpson, the head of Mead's information services, sees expansion ahead. "When people wonder what to do with their new computer," he says, "we will supply the answer."[13]

1. Describe the debate that developed among Mead's managers: name the long-range and short-range plans that conflicted with each other.

2. When managers create plans, one of the most important questions they must ask is, "What business are we in?" How did this question apply to Mead's new products and services?

3. Were the Lexis managers right to stick to their guns?

4. Why was the law-school strategy so effective?

5. Should Mead allow access by other popular computers besides IBM? Why or why not?

6. Do you think Mead should plow profits into other new high-tech products? Should Mead try to make computers itself?

7. How else might Mead market its services so as to overcome the general public's "fear of computers"?

8. If you were a top manager at a paper-products company, what other high-tech products or services would you want to consider developing?

CULTURE SHOCK

AT&T—or "Ma Bell," as the company was known—was until recently one of America's established corporate giants. As might be predicted, the company's culture was highly traditional. Decisions were reached slowly and painstakingly, after memos circulated up and down the chain of command. Meetings were many and lengthy. Rules, written and unwritten, governed employee behavior. The manager who broke the rules might earn a rap on the knuckles from "Ma."

Enter Bill Buehler. After nineteen years with the Bell System's Pacific Telephone Company, Buehler was promoted to head of General Business Systems, the new Bell division that would market small-business phone systems after the breakup of AT&T in 1984. Buehler's task involved supervising 3,000 people in twenty-seven branches across the country. His goal was to *sell* telephone systems—something the old Bell system, as a regulated monopoly, had never had to do, but that was now extremely important if the company was to do battle with GTE and other competitors.

When he took his new position, Buehler was given considerable freedom to reorganize his division as he saw fit. And reorganize he did. Discarding Bell's old dignified and proper way of doing things, he put his salespeople on the highest commission-based compensation plan in AT&T's history. (This meant that a salesperson's take-home pay was much more closely related to his or her sales performance.) He posted a sales board prominently in every office, so that each person's performance was constantly on public view. In place of detailed sales plans, he handed out a typed sheet of inspirational goals (taken in part from Peters and Waterman's book *In Search of Excellence*) as guidelines for the sales force. He let his employees know that they would either measure up or lose their jobs: each salesperson's work would be evaluated monthly, and those who performed poorly would be fired. "If a salesman can't meet quota," Buehler said, "he doesn't belong here."

Buehler's approach, understandably, rocked the boat. More than a third of his sales force quit, was transferred, or was fired. Not only his tough standards raised eyebrows: his style of management was unlike anything Bell had ever seen. Junior employees in branch offices who had never seen an AT&T vice-president suddenly found themselves eating their brown-bag lunches in Buehler's company. But although he was willing to listen to his subordinates, Buehler demanded strict obedience once he reached a decision. "If I found one of my managers trying to sabotage any decision I made, I'd cut his neck off," he said.

Because of (or perhaps in spite of) Buehler's somewhat abrasive style, sales in the General Business Systems division, after a few troubled initial months, began to climb. His salespeople began to exceed their quotas, taking home $40,000 and more per year. As they shifted into high gear, they began to make demands on Buehler: that customers be guaranteed prompter delivery, that paperwork be reduced, that customer bids be approved more quickly. Buehler responded, keeping up his end of the high-performance bargain.

And so it went for a while—about a year. Then, instead of being recognized for his sales achievements, Buehler found himself transferred from his job into a planning position at Bell. Buehler's own boss, who had hired him and given him the autonomy to shape General Business Systems, resigned from the company. And top management at Bell decided to give the GBS command to a colleague of Buehler's, who had run another division at Bell in a more traditional way. Apparently, in the clash of corporate cultures, Buehler's freewheeling style has been squelched.[14]

1. In what ways did Buehler's management style conflict with AT&T's? Which style do you think is more suitable for the situation that the company now finds itself in?

2. Do you think that the problem was simply a clash in culture? What else might have been involved?

3. How might Buehler's management style have stimulated the entrepreneurial skills of his sales force?

4. Buehler's methods, such as posting sales results and evaluating each salesperson monthly, seemed effective in this setting. In what kinds of management situations would such techniques *not* be appropriate?

5. How would you feel if you worked for Buehler? Do you agree with Buehler's demand for total obedience from his subordinates? Explain your answer.

6. How would you introduce new management ideas into a traditional corporate culture? Are there ways in which friction could be kept to a minimum?

INTERNAL ORGANIZATION 5

Picture a General Motors car and what do you see? Probably something big and expensive. And if you studied the internal organization of GM, you would see the same thing: America's leading car manufacturer has been organized around five car divisions, with design, engineering, and marketing staffs directed by the top of the corporate hierarchy.

In 1983, Roger B. Smith, the chairman of GM, decided that he wanted to increase GM's share of the small-car market. Smith proposed a radical change in GM's internal organization: he planned to cut the number of divisions at GM from five to two, and to reduce the total number of large-model cars that the company manufactured. The Chevrolet-Pontiac division would build only small cars; all larger models would be produced at the Buick-Oldsmobile-Cadillac division. Managers would also be held more accountable, on an individual basis, for profit and performance: a manager might gain more power, but he or she would also take more of the blame if things went wrong.[1]

If Smith's plan works, it will reinforce a conviction of many business analysts and corporate executives: to succeed in today's economy, companies have to focus on their internal structure. In this chapter, we will see how the various parts of an organization relate to each other—and how this pattern shapes not only the organization's day-to-day functioning, but its ability to meet long-range goals.

CHAPTER FOCUS

After reading the material in this chapter, you will be able to:
- read an organization chart
- describe appropriate situations for different types of departmentation
- point to the benefits and difficulties of establishing a chain of command by delegating authority
- cite the merits of centralized versus decentralized authority
- distinguish between line and line-and-staff organization
- define three major new approaches to organizational structure
- list advantages and disadvantages of the informal organization

What happens when a trail-blazing conglomerate finds that certain tried-and-true management methods don't always work—and that newer, more fashionable methods have their pitfalls, too? TRW Inc., a leader in management technology, has had to "tough it out" and learn by trial and error. A Cleveland-based giant that includes a high-tech complex in Redondo Beach, California, TRW represents an alliance between space-age technology and conventional manufacturing. Originally started by two Hughes Aircraft veterans in the 1950s as an aircraft-manufacturing company, TRW has since distinguished itself as the producer of the Apollo moon module, the *Pioneer II,* and, more recently, spy satellites dubbed "the absolute outer edge of technology." The conglomerate also manufactures commercial electronics systems, such as computer software and automated teller machines.[1]

TRW's most recent blunder occurred at their Vidar division, which produces commercial digital telephone switches. Vidar took a whopping $43.5 million loss that caused half the division to shut down. Analysts blamed a number of factors. There were external factors: unforeseen competition had arisen, and the booming market in digital switches had taken a nose-dive when high interest rates shattered the home-building industry. But there were internal factors as well. First, design engineers had failed to consult manufacturing divisions about the procedures that would be needed to produce their designs. Second, LSI Productions, a fast-growing TRW division that produces electrical components for television and medical equipment, had been withholding crucial expertise from other divisions, fearing that top engineering talent would be relocated to the digital telephone project—even though the parent company had tried to guard against such a "brain drain" by doing heavy outside recruiting and controlling the transfer of engineers to new commercial operations. Meanwhile, other parts of TRW were having internal difficulties too. Some factions wanted to take risks and go all out for technological progress, some favored cautious strategic planning; some wanted to see teamwork, some preferred autonomy.[2]

The Vidar disaster was a classic failure in **internal organization**—*that aspect of management which deals with the inner structure of authority and responsibility in a company.* For years, internal organization has been one of the areas in the field of management that has changed the least. But today, rumblings of change are shaking the traditional structure of many companies—and in some companies, these rumblings have become minor earthquakes. In the sections that follow, we'll look at the major issues that are developing in internal organization today. We'll also see how some companies, including TRW, are responding to these questions.

WHAT INTERNAL ORGANIZATION IS ALL ABOUT

What does organizing really mean? Basically it means deciding, first, who will do each of the tasks that must be performed and, second, who will be responsible for seeing that particular tasks get done properly. The result of these decisions is a **structured organization**—*a group of people working together in a carefully planned manner to achieve a certain goal.*

As an example, let's take a look at Glenn Wood's business—hardly comparable in size to the complex, multidivision TRW Inc., yet an excellent example of how internal organization fundamentally works in any company. Glenn Wood's small but very successful business, Wood Brothers' Race Shop, in Stuart, Virginia, is home base for three special automobiles—Thunderbirds—that are driven 200 miles per hour on weekends on professional stock-car racing circuits. The Wood brothers (Glenn and his younger brother, Leonard) have been producing racing cars that have won championships for over thirty-four years.

That kind of success doesn't happen by chance. In part, of course, it's the result of a lot of technical skill and mechanical know-how. But it's also the result of a lot of good management. Glenn Wood, in his grease-stained overalls, is just as much a manager as the corporate executive in a three-piece suit.

As a manager, Glenn performs all the management functions we described in the last chapter: *planning* the goal of his organization (to make championship racing cars) and the strategies to achieve it (what parts to buy from Lincoln-Mercury or other suppliers; what assembly schedule to follow); *directing* the business's other members; *controlling* their day-to-day work (to see that no major snags develop); and *organizing*.

In the structured organization Glenn has set up, Leonard serves as chief mechanic, a title that scarcely does him justice. Under his direction the cars are regularly taken apart and rebuilt from the inside out by Glenn's sons Eddie and Len, after which Leonard fine-tunes and tinkers with things until he's satisfied. Similarly, Eddie Wood's job is to seal and smooth the cars' sheet-metal exteriors after Leonard has gone over every inch in his never-ending battle against wind resistance. And Len works with Leonard on the engines after they are built or rebuilt in a nearby town by Tommy Turner—again according to Leonard's precise specifications—and then brought over to the Woods' shop to be installed. The company's books are kept by Kim Wood, Glenn's daughter.

This type of structured organization is typical of almost every business and of nonbusiness work groups and organizations of all kinds. A surgical team of doctors, nurses, and technicians—each with a number of tasks to perform—must work with a degree of coordination that obviously does not spring up by itself. A movie crew on location may look like a bewildering collection of trucks and equipment and people milling around by the dozens. But amid the seeming chaos is a director who organizes the activities of actors, camera operators, lighting and sound technicians, and a host of other people with specific jobs—and a movie gets made. Even a family bakery where Mom makes the pies, Pop drives the delivery truck, and Sonny works behind the counter is a structured organization, in which the essential tasks are divided among the family members. Glenn Wood, in explaining the success of his shop, has said, "There ain't no secret. Everybody always does the best they can."[3] They have a little help from someone with a knack for organizing.

THE FORMAL ORGANIZATION AND THE ORGANIZATION CHART

When a person who is setting up a structured organization makes a written description of the way the organization is supposed to work or draws a diagram of it, he or she is "formalizing" the organization plan. In other words, the person is recording the plan in a form that can be seen by other people and can be passed on from one generation of managers to their successors. *Organizations that have a formal record describing their structural plan* are often called **formal organizations.**

Usually the formal record is a chart known as the **organization chart,** *a diagram that shows how work is divided and where authority lies.* It is kept in the top executive's files and may also be posted on a wall for all the workers to look at. Since you're likely to be seeing organization charts—or finding yourself on one—in the future, it will be worth the effort to learn to read them clearly.

For the Wood Brothers' Race Shop, the organization chart would look like the one in Figure 1. In this chart the boxes show the division of labor—all the jobs that have to be done to produce a championship racing car and who does each one. The placement of the boxes and the lines connecting them show authority and responsibility—who takes orders from whom, which workers function as equals, who is responsible for seeing that a certain job is done right. Eddie, Len, and Tommy, whose boxes are on the same row, are equals in the Wood Brothers' organization. The lines going up from their boxes to Leonard's on the row above indicate that he's the one who gives them instructions and oversees their work. Although Kim's box is on the same row as Leonard's, the fact that she, as bookkeeper, has no authority over Eddie, Len, and Tommy is indicated by the absence of any lines from their boxes to hers. The placement of Glenn's box at the top of the chart and the lines leading from it show that he has ultimate authority and responsibility. He directly supervises both Kim and Leonard, and through Leonard, he indirectly supervises Eddie, Len, and Tommy as well.

For larger businesses, many of the boxes in the organization chart represent not individual workers

FIGURE 1
ORGANIZATION CHART
OF THE WOOD BROTHERS' RACE SHOP

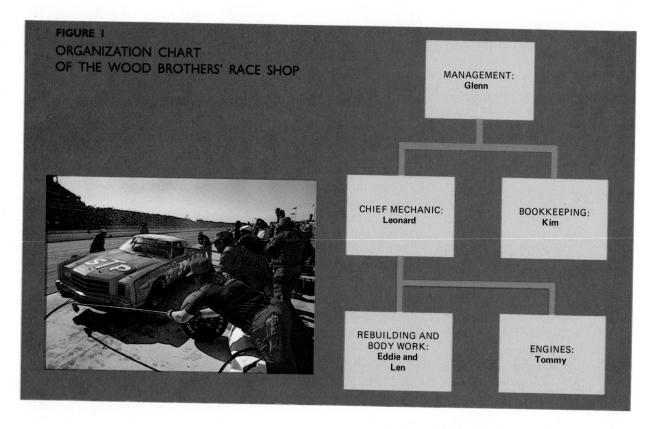

but groups of workers performing the same function, as well as several levels of management. Figure 2 shows a typical organization chart for a large company.

THE STRUCTURE MUST FIT THE SITUATION

At least at first glance, many organization charts look very similar—like a pyramid. A large number of boxes on the lowest rows lead up to fewer and fewer boxes on the higher rows, and ultimately to one box at the top. But a closer look should reveal differences in the way the charts are set up, reflecting the differences in the way various businesses need to operate. In other words, there is no one best type of organization chart because there is no one type of structure that is best for every formal organization.

In the sections that follow, we shall be discuss-

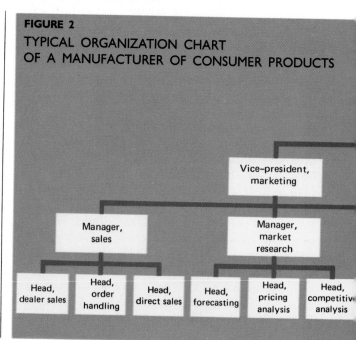

FIGURE 2
TYPICAL ORGANIZATION CHART
OF A MANUFACTURER OF CONSUMER PRODUCTS

ing different types of organizational structures and the questions managers must answer to decide what structure is best for their enterprise and the particular situation and contingencies it faces.

DEPARTMENTATION: WHAT IT IS AND WHY IT'S NECESSARY

Suppose you were trying to set up a fairly good-sized organization. One of the first questions you'd have to deal with would be this: Is there any way I can divide the people into separate groups, giving specific tasks to each so that they'll all help the organization achieve its goals? The way you answered this question would appear on your organization chart. Each *group or section of people working together in a specific area* is called a **department;** *the process of establishing departments* is known as **departmentation.** One approach, **departmentation by function,** consists of *grouping workers together according to their activities.* In a typical manufacturing business, departments may be set up to carry out the functions of

production, finance, and marketing. For a retail store, the departments might be publicity (advertising, window display, and so forth), merchandising (acquiring and selling of the store's goods), general services (store security, customer service, and the like), and finance. The functional departments set up by a large commercial airline might include the following sections: engineering, maintenance, ground services (food preparation, terminal management), flight operations, sales, advertising, and finance.

But as we pointed out in the last section, these typical ways of dividing up departments by functions cannot be automatically applied like a formula. Different companies should, and of course often do, develop departmentation patterns to suit the particular functions that must be carried out in their business. *Time* magazine, for example, has four principal divisions: editorial, advertising, production, and circulation. Each department works more or less independently, with its own functions, its own managers and personnel, its own budget, work schedules, and so on (see Figure 3). And the principal divisions are themselves divided into specialized departments. At the New York headquarters, members of the edito-

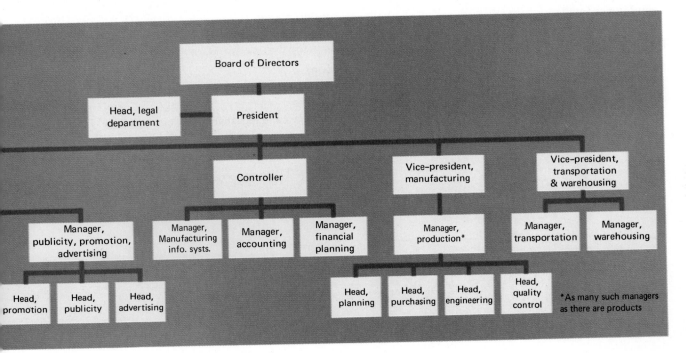

rial staff are assigned to individual units specializing in such topics as business and finance, medicine, sports, and a dozen or more other categories. Likewise, a salesperson in the New York advertising department might specialize in selling space to insurance companies, say, or airlines or tobacco companies. There is some contact between departments, of course, but only on certain levels and for specific purposes. The director of advertising, for instance, might consult with the production director on the number of four-color advertising pages, but an individual salesperson would have no direct dealings with anyone on the production staff.

A second approach to departmentation is **departmentation by territory**—*grouping an organization's personnel by physical location.* This method is commonly used when an organization is spread over a wide geographic area and when differences between even small areas are important enough to merit special attention.

Time magazine's operations, for example, are departmentalized by territory as well as by function, at least in the editorial and advertising divisions (see Figure 4). *Time* has several divisional advertising managers, as well as submanagers for most major American cities. At the same time, the magazine maintains a totally separate editorial network, with

reporters in various bureaus across the country whose job is chiefly to cover local or regional news. Both the advertising and editorial staffs in regional offices are inevitably less specialized in their duties than those in New York, where more people are available. An advertising salesperson in the St. Louis office, for example, will deal with advertisers of all kinds rather than just one industry, and a reporter in the Cleveland bureau may cover a train derailment on Monday, an election Tuesday, an art exhibit Wednesday, and a labor dispute Thursday. Departmentalizing by territory may have several advantages for a large organization. For example:

■ it allows greater responsiveness to local customs, styles, product preferences and the like;

■ it makes it easier to tie in the promotion of a product or service with local celebrities and events;

■ it allows a firm to take advantage of such local economies as a low price for a key raw material;

■ and local or regional offices provide excellent training ground for the company's future top-level managers.

It's important to note, however, that it isn't necessary for a company to be departmentalized by territory just because it does business across a large geographical area. Today's facilities for high-speed communication allow executives at a corporate

FIGURE 3

DEPARTMENTATION BY FUNCTION:

Time has four major divisions.

FIGURE 4

DEPARTMENTATION BY TERRITORY:

Time magazine has advertising and editorial divisions in many different cities.

headquarters to oversee the operations of far-flung branch offices with an efficiency that was impossible only a generation ago.

An organization may find it desirable to *group activities along product lines,* an approach known as **departmentation by product.** *Time,* for instance, is not the only magazine published by Time Inc. *Fortune, Sports Illustrated, Life, Money, Discover,* and *People* can all be thought of as different product lines, produced by different divisions of the same corporation (see Figure 5). Each of these publications has its own editorial and advertising staffs, as well as its own production and circulation departments.

AUTHORITY AND RESPONSIBILITY

Suppose you've set up departments or otherwise divided the work of your organization. The next question you must face is how to distribute authority and responsibility. Except in the very smallest busi-

nesses, this kind of distribution is necessary because there is just too much work for any one person to oversee and control. In a manufacturing firm organized into functional departments the president might **delegate,** or *assign,* authority over production workers and responsibility for making the product well and on schedule to the head of the production department.

SETTING UP THE CHAIN OF COMMAND

The systematic delegation of authority in an organization requires ranking employees differently. The *relationship between different levels of employees* is usually referred to as the **chain of command.** In a typical manufacturing firm the different levels of employees might be workers, department heads, and the firm's president. Three chains of command in the firm run as follows: from the production workers to the production department head to the presi-

FIGURE 5

DEPARTMENTATION BY PRODUCT:

TIME Incorporated publishes seven different magazines.

dent; from the sales staff to the marketing department head to the president; and from the accountants and bookkeepers to the finance department head to the president. A person at any point in the chain of command is answerable to those above him or her on the chain and has responsibility for and authority over those below (that is, he or she can give orders, or "commands").

Delegation and accountability

On paper, setting up a chain of command is a fairly simple, straightforward matter. In practice, though, it can become a far more complicated task, as it involves the interaction of real human beings. First of all, the planners have to deal with the sometimes tricky question of the *degree* to which those at the top will be held accountable for the performance of their subordinates. For example, the rules of the U.S. Navy spell out with unusual clarity responsibility for work that is delegated. The captain is always directly accountable for the work of his crew and his ship, even if he is asleep, ill, or not even aboard. More than one captain has been removed from command for life because of a collision that was traced to a lowly seaman who fell asleep on watch.

In businesses, the chairman of the board is technically accountable for poor work done by an employee who comes to work with a hangover. In actual practice, of course, it is rare for top management to be blamed directly for the mistakes of workers. It is common practice, however, to hold a manager fully accountable for the work done by people directly under his or her supervision. A manager is usually held answerable for attaining objectives assigned to his or her department. A national sales manager, for example, may be fired if the company does not meet its sales expectations.

Balancing authority and responsibility

A second major consideration in setting up a chain of command is determining how much authority *must* be given to someone who is going to be responsible for something, so that he or she will be able to do the job properly. The most common error in delegation is failing to give the recipient (or delegate) enough authority to carry out assigned duties and responsibilities. The following situations illustrate this point:

1. A worker is told to drill a round hole but is not given the authority to get a drill from the company toolbox.
2. A salesperson is responsible for keeping customers happy but has to go through an elaborate company procedure to handle an exchange of merchandise.
3. A manager is made responsible for increasing production but is not given the authority to hire, fire, raise salaries, or rearrange work.

Delegation will not work in these situations unless the employee either is more resourceful than usual or acts without formal authority.

Clearly, authority and responsibility must be balanced for delegation to be effective. Returning to our Navy example for a moment, we may note that the Navy does balance the captain's enormous responsibility with very broad authority. A captain at sea has authority over his crew that stops just short of the power of life and death.

Inducing employees to accept authority—and to give it up

Two other related points should be made about delegations of authority. The first is that duties, responsibility, and authority must be assigned to a willing recipient. The word "willing" is important here. If a worker or lower-level manager does not accept the assignment, there can be no delegation.

By the same token, of course, the leaders themselves must also accept the idea of delegation, which inevitably means giving up some portion of their control over things. For some, this turns out to be easier said than done—especially when it runs counter to the habits of a lifetime.

SPAN OF MANAGEMENT

The *number of people a manager directly supervises* is called a **span of management** or **span of control.** When a large number of people report directly to a manager, he or she has a wide span of management.

When only a few people report, the span is narrow. There is no formula for determining the ideal span of management. Estimates of how many persons a manager can effectively supervise vary considerably. Several factors affect the number. These include the manager's personal skill and leadership ability, the skill of the workers, the motivation of the workers, and the nature of the job.

In general, highly skilled workers require less supervision than the less skilled. The manager of an organization made up almost exclusively of professionals can have a wide span of management. The work of a large number of scientists can be coordinated by a single manager.

CENTRALIZATION VS. DECENTRALIZATION

For many years the typical American corporation was *a highly centralized operation, with most of the authority and responsibility concentrated at the top.* Such a company is often referred to as a **tall organization,** because of the many levels in its hierarchy and the narrow span of management at each level. The U.S. Army, for example, would come under the heading of a tall, or centralized, organization. Virtually all important decisions are made by the generals and colonels at the top. There are also many levels separating a general from a private; and while the general may be responsible for thousands of men, his actual span of management is quite small since he directly supervises only a few colonels.

But there have also been certain *organizations that are quite decentralized, characterized by wider spans of management and a greater delegation of authority to people in middle-management positions.* Because its hierarchy has relatively few levels, such an organization is commonly known as a **flat organization.** The Roman Catholic Church is a good example of a flat, or decentralized, organization. The pope directly supervises many cardinals, who supervise numerous archbishops and bishops, and each bishop in turn may have authority over hundreds of priests. There are thus only three levels between a parish priest and the pope, and while a priest is expected to follow the general policies laid down by his superiors,

he has considerable authority in managing the affairs of his own parish.

THE CURRENT TREND TOWARD DECENTRALIZATION

Corporations are doing a lot of soul-searching these days over the way they structure their organizations, and some highly centralized (tall) companies are restructuring their organizations to move some of this power downward and outward. The reasons are complex; but one factor is the current flurry of mergers and acquisitions of new (and sometimes unrelated) businesses that we noted in Chapter 2. Today's conglomerates require fluid internal structures: they need to be able to accommodate and control new businesses, but they must also be able to protect these new businesses from the interference of senior officers who may know nothing about them. Some conglomerates may also want to keep their subsidiaries intact and self-governing so that they can function on their own if they are sold.

Internal structures are also being challenged today by the pressures businesses are feeling to boost productivity and encourage innovation; as noted in Component Chapter B, many companies even have corporate entrepreneurs on their payrolls. The corporate entrepreneur is often a division head who may have started his or her own product line; now, this new product line has become a business, existing as a separate entity under the corporate umbrella. Furthermore, the shifts in organizational power we mentioned in Chapter 4 tend to give more encouragement to middle-level innovators, and less to top-level managers who spend most of their time on long-range planning, and may be prone to obsessing about checks and balances. Risk taking is in fashion, and the "doers" closest to the marketplace—engineers, salespeople, plant managers—are riding high on the crest of decentralization.

THE SHRINKING OF MIDDLE MANAGEMENT

What happens when decentralization, with its decreasing layers of authority, reduces the need for middle managers? A few companies, out of courtesy

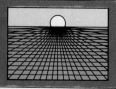
A SHOCK WAVE HITS THE COMPANY'S STRUCTURE: THE IMPACT OF COMPUTERIZED INFORMATION SYSTEMS

What happens to a company's internal structure when computer systems alter the flow of information within the organization?

Suppose a top executive decides to bypass her usual information-gathering channels to learn how sales are going in her division or to get recent marketing surveys in her field. She now may be able to call information up from her own desk-top executive information system, so she doesn't have to rely upon as many people to collect, interpret, and analyze data as were needed in the past—the computer does all that. As a result, her department is about a third the size it once was.

Her desk-top computer also liberates her from dependence on the company's central data-processing department—which might have delivered the information weeks later, in a complicated, possibly unworkable format. Many executives prefer running these desk-top systems themselves. Working at the terminal gives them new ideas and a better feel for their business. They can use special computer programs, designed for these desk-top systems, to test theories, challenge assumptions, and analyze information in a variety of ways.

Staff people may be among the first to lose jobs when computers take over, but senior officers whose main function is information gathering become vulnerable to cutbacks, too. Also vulnerable are data-processing managers, whose influence as keepers of corporate information has waned; so are employees in the controller's office, whose main skills lie in the area of locating and tallying figures. Computerization may also erode the authority of managers with highly developed technical skills: when the computer has the final word, the boss is in no position to demand that subordinates defer to his or her opinions.

In some cases the new executive information systems terrify underlings, who fear that the boss is keeping tabs on them. At one multinational oil company, a research chief used his own information system to keep track of five laboratory directors and monitor their projects under development. The lab directors viewed such check-ups as an erosion of their autonomy, and promptly threatened to resign. They were, quite simply, unaccustomed to being monitored.

Most resentful of executive information systems are harassed higher-ups who don't have access to the same information as their peers. But this technology scares just about everyone. In the old days, managers' errors could be easily concealed by associates or subordinates with an interest in protecting one another. Today, though, managers may find themselves tied up just fielding questions provoked by the boss's computer. To illustrate how these systems expose incompetence, there's a story about a chief operating officer of an oil-equipment company, who discovered via his computer system that a pricing policy for one of his company's products was far below competitors' prices. Analysis revealed that his company could have made several million dollars more by bringing its prices closer to the competition's. His reaction was, "If I can find this out in an afternoon or two, where was the manager of this division? What was he doing all year?" Even though the manager wasn't fired, his career was severely damaged.

At Westinghouse, the system stripped managers of their standard excuse: "I haven't received that report in the mail yet." A senior executive surprised a Baltimore operating official by calling to inquire about some recent figures. The official said he hadn't seen the numbers yet. "Why haven't you seen them?" the senior executive demanded angrily. "You've had them for two days, and I'm looking at them right now!"

Yet while executive information systems can be threatening to headquarters people, they can also create opportunities, sometimes spurring managers on to more fruitful performances. At one bank, the president was known to be at his terminal by 7:30 A.M., and by 8:00 A.M. would be on the telephone calling his managers. The managers scrambled to keep up with him; but their concern turned into professional pride as the detailed knowledge they accumulated became impressive to clients and enabled them to better monitor their subordinates.

SOURCE: Mary Bralove, "Direct Data: Some Chief Executives Bypass, and Irk, Staffs in Getting Information," *The Wall Street Journal,* January 12, 1983.

Lower-level managers have to be aggressive.

to veteran employees, create busywork or assign them monitoring functions. But in the uncertain economic climate of the 1980s, lean management boosts profits. The multilayered corporation that prospered in the 1950s, 1960s, and 1970s is now viewed as a dinosaur. Hence, some of today's companies have trimmed payrolls to weed out mediocre performers. Standards of performance are tougher: there's more reliance upon quotas, ratings, testing. Xerox now seeks an across-the-board efficiency upgrading of 30 percent to 50 percent; Chrysler engineers must now test their products, so it is harder for them to blame design failures on defective parts (which come from other departments).[4]

Another reason middle management is shrinking is that today, the very purpose of management is changing. Formerly, corporations rewarded analysts and planners for minimizing risk and safeguarding against questionable decisions. Now, though, the emphasis is shifting to identifying new prospects and acting on them boldly: thus, Chrysler instituted new guidelines decreeing that no more than five executives could stand between a new idea and senior officers.[5]

LINE AND STAFF ORGANIZATION

Essentially, the simple chain-of-command system we've been looking at represents what is known as **line organization,** so called because it *establishes a clear line of authority flowing from the top downward through every subordinate position.* Line organization is the simplest and most common structure for authority relationships: everyone knows who is responsible to whom, and the location of ultimate authority is easily identified. (See Figure 6.)

THE PROS AND CONS OF LINE ORGANIZATION

Enterprises that are structured according to line organization enjoy a number of practical advantages. The existence of line authority tends to speed decision making because managers know in which areas they can make decisions. It also simplifies discipline. Channels for communication are direct and

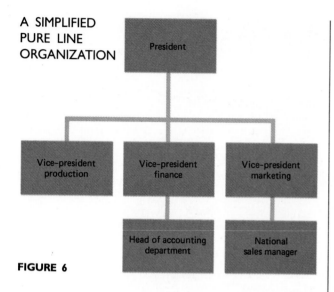

A SIMPLIFIED PURE LINE ORGANIZATION

President

Vice-president production

Vice-president finance

Vice-president marketing

Head of accounting department

National sales manager

FIGURE 6

easily located. The simplicity of line organization sometimes results in lower expenses.

On the other hand, the nature of line organization also carries at least three important disadvantages. First, it concentrates most decision-making power at the upper levels of management, so subordinates may have trouble learning the skills needed to occupy top positions. Second, the technical complexity of a firm's activities may require specialized knowledge that its top management does not have. Third, growth can extend the chain of command to the point where communication and decision making take too long.

ADDING A STAFF COMPONENT

Because of these disadvantages, which become magnified as a line organization grows larger, management planners developed a more elaborate system known as the **line-and-staff organization.** This form of organization *has a clear chain of command from the top downward, but it also includes various auxiliary groupings of people who come under the heading of staff.* Traditionally, the line organization manages the primary activities of the organization. The **staff organization** *supplements the line organization by providing advice and specialized services.*

Persons in the staff organization are not in the line organization's main chain of command. On an organization chart, a staff position is connected to

the line organization by a dotted line or is simply left unconnected. In the formal organization chart shown in Figure 7, the legal department has staff authority with respect to the vice-presidents and the head of the accounting department. It can give them advice on the law and request that they comply with this advice. Since the legal department has specialized knowledge about the law, the managers of the line organization will probably follow its suggestions. The decision to accept or reject the legal staff's advice, however, is up to the line managers. The legal staff is connected to the president of the organization by a solid line because it is directly responsible to the president. If the legal staff feels that its advice should be followed by one of the vice-presidents, it must go to the president, who can order compliance. Note also that the head of accounting may use the services of the legal staff but that the national sales manager must go through the marketing vice-president to get legal advice.

WHEN LINE-BASED ORGANIZATION ISN'T ENOUGH: FUNCTIONAL ORGANIZATION

In certain businesses the nature of the work to be done dictates that *specialists should be given direct authority in their particular area of expertise.* This system is known as **functional organization.** In the television and movie industries, for example, there are studio supervisors for such personnel as actors, musicians, sound engineers, and camera operators. When one of these people—an actor, say—is working on a particular show, he is also responsible to the director. The actor thus seems to have two bosses. In practice, however, only one boss is in charge at any given time: the director when a film is being made, and the studio supervisor when the actor is between projects.

PROJECT MANAGEMENT

As rigid organizational structures fall away and corporations become fluid in structure, systems increasingly change to suit specific company needs. Some

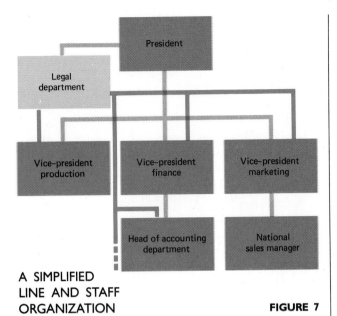

A SIMPLIFIED
LINE AND STAFF
ORGANIZATION   **FIGURE 7**

companies have set up temporary project management teams that disband when projects are completed. Managers receive periodic retraining to update their skills and maintain their flexibility so that they can be assigned in this way. IBM has been successfully pursuing these methods for some time, for problem solving, and also for developing markets in such high-potential areas as robotics, remote computing services, and analytical instruments.

A classic example of the use of the project management team occurred at Apple Computer Inc., the personal-computer pioneer that built "Lisa," a machine designed for computer-illiterate managers and administrators. In 1979, Apple management decided to produce an office machine that anyone could use—including businesspeople who had neither the time nor desire to understand computers. The system they had in mind was similar to "Smalltalk" (also known as "Star"), a revolutionary computer developed by Xerox in the 1970s. Apple formed a separate corporate entity, Personal Office Systems, and assembled a team of 96 engineers and marketing specialists that grew to 200 before the project was completed in 1982.

Normally, "design by committee" is unworkable, but no one person in the Personal Office Systems group had enough experience to be the sole planner. So, the core group was broken up into smaller units to plan the design, each person working in his or her own area of expertise and submitting results to the larger group. Differences in opinion were ironed out by testing design ideas on Apple employees. Once the team had worked out a time schedule and the basic design was agreed upon, each engineer set up a work schedule. Lisa was designed and tested throughout 1980 and built in 1981–82; it went public with much fanfare in January 1983, carrying a $10,000 price tag. It was an attractive item—a technological wonder that novices could learn to run in half an hour (it normally takes twenty hours to learn to use the Apple II computer).[6]

Lisa's marketing capabilities were not as carefully conceived as its design. Its prospects were soon threatened by Macintosh, a more inexpensive Apple spin-off of Lisa technology that promised to be competitive, and both Lisa and Macintosh faced being upstaged by IBM's personal computers. Nonetheless, Lisa itself was a ground-breaking product, and a testimonial to what the project management team can achieve.

MATRIX STRUCTURE

In organizations with the familiar vertical lines of authority, orders are always sent down the chain of command, and decisions are always passed upward. Too often, however, different departments in an organization have conflicting needs or priorities that can only be resolved by a higher-level executive, who may well have a dozen more important things to worry about.

The idea behind the matrix structure is to push decision making downward, in the belief that some conflicts can often be better handled at a lower level. If, for instance, the marketing director for a particular product wanted to build up inventory in anticipation of rising demand, while the manufacturing director for the same product wanted to *reduce* inventory in order to keep costs down, the problem would normally be passed up the ladder to be decided by an executive with authority over both functions. In a matrix structure, however, the decision would be sent down to a manager who's actually subordinate to both the marketing and manufacturing directors—but who also understands the situation in detail. The manager in effect would play a media-

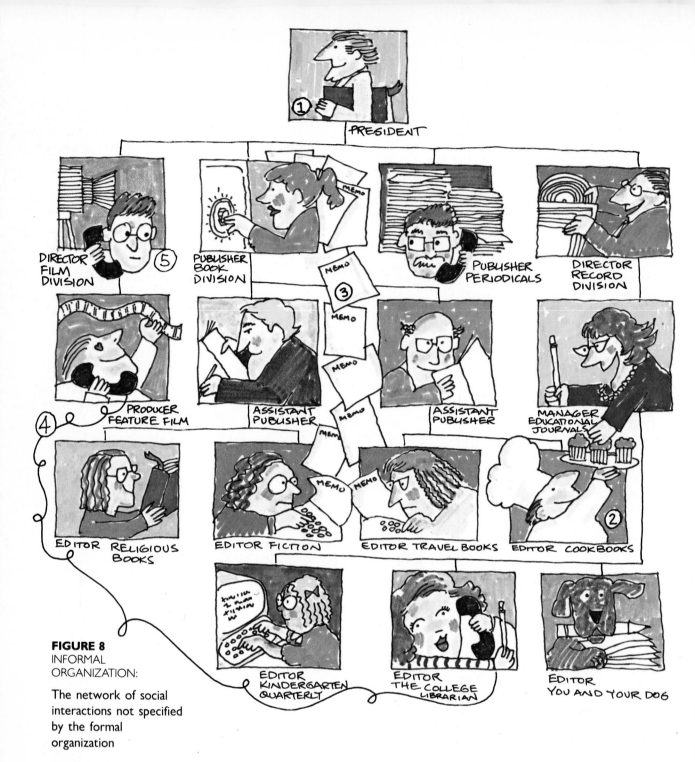

FIGURE 8
INFORMAL
ORGANIZATION:

The network of social
interactions not specified
by the formal
organization

1 The editor of religious books and the president both attend the Second Avenue Christian Science Church.

2 The editor of cookbooks is a close personal friend and old fraternity brother of the publisher of the periodical division and recently influenced him to promote another friend to manager of educational journals.

3 The editor of fiction and the editor of travel books bypass the assistant publishers, whom they view as male chauvinist pigs, to enlist the aid of the publisher of the book division in getting raises.

4 The producer of feature films is engaged to the editor of *The College Librarian*.

5 The director of the film division and the publisher of the periodical division disagree with the president's fiscal policies and collaborate against him.

tor's role, trying to balance the marketing and manufacturing goals and come up with a solution that was acceptable to both bosses.

THE INFORMAL ORGANIZATION

All organization charts, whether traditional or innovative, are similar in one respect: they show the formal relationships of people in a company and what they are expected to do *as employees*. What the charts do not do—what they cannot do—is illustrate the **informal organization**—*the network of social interactions that are not specified by the formal organization, but that develop on a personal level among the workers at a company.*

The "grapevine" is one of the best known examples of informal organizational structure. It is an unofficial way of relaying news that bypasses the formal chain of command. It may pass on either personal or business information. But the informal organization does more than spread rumors; it strongly influences the distribution of power. While the formal organization spells out who *should* have power, the informal organization sometimes reveals who actually *has* it. The informal organization and the formal organization may be the same, but this isn't always the case because the authority delegated by the formal organization depends at least in part on the consent of employees. If workers strongly disapprove of the organization's choice of a manager, it is unlikely that the manager will be effective.

CHAPTER REVIEW

When managers set up a structured internal organization, they divide the labor of the organization among people or groups of people and set up lines of authority and responsibility. They formalize this organization by recording it on an organization chart.

Most organizations group workers by their activities. Departmentation may be according to function, territory, product, or other criteria. Each system has both advantages and disadvantages, and organizations often use more than one method simultaneously.

Effective distribution of authority and responsibility is crucial to an organization's success. Management must consider whether the span of management should be wide or narrow, whether delegation balances authority and responsibility, and who has accountability in the chain of command.

Management must also decide whether to set up an organization based on line or line-and-staff authority. And it must determine whether to centralize or decentralize its internal operations.

Huge, highly centralized companies and conglomerates have begun to decentralize so as to (1) remain fluid, efficient, and productive and (2) keep their subdivisions self-governing and free from high-level interference. One unfortunate effect of decentralization is the shrinking of middle management. As the mammoth, multilayered corporation fades into history, fewer middle managers are needed; those that remain are likely to have production as well as planning and data-gathering responsibilities.

The simple chain-of-command system represents line organization; this is sometimes augmented by staff (services linked to but outside of the chain of command). As corporations decentralize, planning and advisory staff divisions tend to be trimmed.

New approaches to organizational structure include functional organization, the project-management system, and matrix structure.

The informal organization, or unofficial network of social interactions, operates in all known organizations. It can bypass the formal organization's system of communication and upset its distribution of authority. The negative aspects of the informal organization can be minimized by good management and by giving workers a say in designing the formal organization.

KEY WORDS

internal organization (148)
structured organization (148)
formal organization (149)
organization chart (149)
department (151)
departmentation (151)
departmentation by function (151)
departmentation by territory (152)

REVIEW QUESTIONS

1. What are the functions of an organization chart? What can happen in an organization that doesn't have one?

2. Describe a situation in which it would be best for an organization to set up departments by territory.

3. What is the most common error managers make in delegating responsibility? Suggest an example from your own experience.

4. Why would you expect a manager of a group of nuclear physicists to have a wide span of management?

5. Describe the characteristics of tall organizations and flat organizations. Is the U.S. Navy a tall organization or a flat one? What about the Roman Catholic Church? Explain your answers.

6. Describe a situation in which it would be a big mistake for an organization to decentralize.

7. Discuss the ways in which the role of middle management has changed and outline difficulties facing today's middle managers.

8. What are the benefits and costs of a pure line organization? A line-and-staff organization? Why would a large company want to cut back on staff positions?

9. Discuss matrix structure. How does it work?

10. How might a manager use the informal organization to good effect?

CASE I

NEW STEPS UP THE CORPORATE LADDER

What do most of today's MBAs from the top business schools hope to do? The answer is the same as it has always been: they want to climb the corporate ladder. But today, getting to the top may require a different set of steps than in previous years. Nowadays, graduates with a sharp eye on business trends are competing for line jobs, not staff positions. Those who will make it to the top will be the people who can help their companies produce products more efficiently.

This shift in the corporate jobs that are considered desirable reflects another basic shift in the way today's companies do business. In the 1950s, when the economy was expanding, marketing jobs were the ones to get. In the 1960s, a booming stock market and the rise of conglomerates opened doors for financial experts, the people who could make the best deals. Then, in the 1970s, managers spent their time dealing with the government, so those who knew how to fight battles in the courtroom were in demand. Today's economy and world market conditions call for a different type of expert. "Many businesses have to become low-cost producers to survive," says Parker Llewellyn, Placement Director of Harvard Business School. "If you are in a job where you can help do that, you increase your corporate leverage." In other words, if you want to get ahead, save the company's money.

The kinds of jobs that focus on manufacturing efficiency tend to be jobs in operations, where cutting costs and solving production problems are the goals. In today's economy, companies run by managers who "grew up with the core of the business" are among the best run: this important point was made by management experts T. Peters and R. Waterman in their book *In Search of Excellence*. Knowing this, today's ambitious young MBAs are looking for line jobs. At FMC Corporation, for example, where 90 percent of new talented recruits used to take staff positions, 40 percent are now being hired for line jobs and, according to a recent survey by executive recruiters Heidrick and Struggles, operations does seem to be the route to the top.[7]

1. What kinds of experience will new MBAs miss by taking line jobs?

2. If production management is the most important thing to know about, which area of business do you think is second in importance when it comes to saving money for the company? Why?

3. If you were hiring new recruits for a company in today's economy, what personal qualities would you look for?

4. What long-term consequences might there be for corporations that put most of their best new employees in line positions?

CASE 2

A STRUCTURELESS ORGANIZATION?

Can a company that employs 3,000 people operate without a hierarchy—without middle-management executives and organization charts, with "associates" instead of bosses? At W. L. Gore & Associates the answer is yes.

The company's product is Gore-Tex, a synthetic fiber made from the chemical compound known as Teflon. Gore-Tex cannot be penetrated by sunlight, chemicals, heat, or cold. Not surprisingly, it was the fiber chosen for astronauts' space suits, but its uses on earth have proven even more marketable. Hikers and campers are attracted to the high-quality clothing, tents, sleeping bags, and other outdoor products that are made from Gore-Tex. The fiber is also used in antipollution filters, on electrical cables, and in the human body for synthetic blood-vessel grafts.

The man behind the success of W. L. Gore is its founder and chairman, Wilbert L. Gore. In 1958, after working at DuPont for seventeen years, Gore quit his job and started his own company.

Gore did not want to build a highly structured organization. His goal was to hire talented people who would be committed to outstanding performance. Those looking for traditionally charted lines of authority need not apply. Gore believes that "groups respond to recognized authority or to individual commitment. If you are going to have a lot of change in an organization, you better get a commitment. In the process, natural leaders will evolve."

Such a philosophy, Gore has found, is best expressed in an organization that has an unusual structure. The only officers at Gore are the chairman, the president, the vice-president, and the secretary-treasurer. Everyone else is an "associate." The company is family-held and family-run. Gore's son, Robert, is president and his wife, Viere, is secretary-treasurer. Chairman Bill Gore and his son have an excellent working relationship, which some Gore associates believe is the key to the system.

But for Bill Gore, the system works because of the way he has set it up. People work best together when they're in groups of no more than 200, he believes—that way, they can maintain effective communication. Thus, Gore's 3,000 employees work in 28 small plants. Viewed purely in terms of its operating efficiency, this decentralized plant system would seem a wasteful way to run a business. But Gore maintains that productivity and creativity thrive in the small-plant atmosphere.

Gore's associates are carefully chosen. New employees are recruited by "sponsors" within the company who help set the new associates' salary. Bill Gore calls his staff "the brightest, hardest-working people I have ever seen anywhere," and he rewards them well for their efforts. "As much as 15 percent of each associate's salary goes into an employee stock-ownership plan."

Has Bill Gore's philosophy yielded success? Does his company's style of organization produce more than employee satisfaction? At Gore, the answer is a solid yes. Sales in 1983 ran between $140 and $170 million, and with a growth rate of 30 to 40 percent annually, Bill Gore need not defend his structureless organization to anyone.[8]

1. Is it really true that there is no organization chart at Gore? Explain your answer.

2. What kinds of businesses do you think are particularly suited to an organization like that of Gore-Tex? Could such an arrangement work in an automobile assembly plant?

3. What is there in the nature and quality of the employees at W. L. Gore & Associates that makes them particularly well suited to an unstructured organization? Do you think such an organization would work in a company that used unskilled or blue-collar workers?

4. What motivating strategies does Gore use to keep his employees highly productive? What other strategies might he use?

5. If Gore went public, what problems would he create for an organization of his type?

6. Can you think of any disadvantages to working for such a structureless organization?

PRODUCTION AND OPERATIONS MANAGEMENT

Henry Ford revolutionized production management by breaking down auto assembly into small steps on a moving line. Ford could do this because he offered Americans one standard product—a black Model A. Times have changed. Consider the problems of Hewlett-Packard, which offers one computer in 6 million versions! How does it keep all the parts it needs on hand without bankrupting itself on warehousing costs? And how does it ensure a smooth flow of parts from suppliers to assembly line to shipping?

The company found the answers in a new production technique—the "just in time" method. Stocks of parts are kept to no more than what is needed for one day of production. As a circuit board or microchip goes onto the assembly line, it is automatically reordered for the next day's production. The assembly process has been carefully designed to take no more than 20 hours. Hewlett-Packard's use of the "just in time" method is typical of the dramatic changes taking place in production management today—the subject of this chapter.

CHAPTER FOCUS

After reading the material in this chapter, you will be able to:
- cite the three technological advances that made mass production possible
- list at least four ways in which automation is being used in American industry
- enumerate examples of mass production in service industries
- cite at least three factors managers must consider in choosing plant location
- distinguish between an analytic and synthetic production process
- define the five basic steps in production control
- discuss new directions in production and inventory control, including PERT, CPM, and MRP
- describe three methods American industry is using to improve quality and productivity

At John Deere and Company's new tractor plant in Waterloo, Iowa, a conveyor belt sends freshly cut gears humming toward the assembly area. At one point, a mechanized arm seizes a roughly cut cogwheel. Moving away from the belt, the arm inserts the gear into a shaving device where it is polished smooth. At the other end of the device, another arm retrieves a finished gear and replaces it on the belt. Before this modernized plant opened, several paid laborers would have polished the unfinished gears. Today, though, the polishing job is done more precisely and cheaply by computer-controlled machines and robots.[1]

And this seemingly minor innovation may be just a glimpse of things to come. Across the Pacific Ocean, near Nagoya, Japan, Tsunehiko ("Tony") Yamazaki, owner of a machine tool company, picks up his telephone to send a new product design from his office computer to a remote factory, some 20 miles away. There, 34 robots and 65 computer-controlled machines receive their new "instructions." Immediately, electronic foremen, tooling robots, mechanical arms, computer-guided parts carriers, and automatic welders and inspectors hum into operation. Yamazaki's factory does employ 215 people to tend the machines and robots. This factory, which produces $250 million worth of machine tools annually, would need more than ten times that number of people to do the same without automation.[2]

What do these startling new developments mean to American industry? To some commentators, robots in the factory represent a new class of labor, sometimes called the "steel-collar worker." Many experts have compared their arrival to the Industrial Revolution in England 150 years ago. Seeing that the use of robots and computers has become an industrial way of life in Japan, some U.S. manufacturers have concluded that they too will have to adopt these methods in order to compete. American management is retooling its factories to accommodate the new technology, while Wall Street soothsayers warn them of tidal waves of innovation, revolutions in the workplace, and major changes in our entire economy.

But in reality, robotics, automation, and computers are just the most recent additions to a series of technological advances that stretch far back in this country's history. There have been other milestones in the history of **production,** or *the process of converting resources into a form in which people need or want them.* When all the current excitement dies down, the "steel-collar worker" may take its place as just one more step in the development of our manufacturing capacity.

MASS PRODUCTION AND AUTOMATION

Mass production, *the manufacture of goods in great quantities,* has long been the organizational keystone of many American industries. It has cut prices, made products available to more people, and contributed significantly to the United States' high standard of living. It was made possible by three earlier technological advances. The first of these, **mechanization,** is *the use of machines to do work previously done by people.* An innovation of the last century's Industrial Revolution, mechanization had an impact everywhere. The pages of books like this one, for example, were once sewn together by hand. Mechanization replaced those hands with a binding machine and, as a consequence, dramatically increased the number of books published. Similarly, in transportation, the collective labor of thousands of people and animals was replaced by the mighty locomotive engine.

Adding to mechanization's effectiveness was **standardization,** or *the production of uniform goods.* By making products and their parts of the same shape, size, weight, and quality, businesses can market popular products in tremendous quantities. (Cassette tapes are a good example.) The mass-production technique with the most wide-ranging influence, however, is the **assembly line,** *the manufacturing technique in which the item being put together moves along a conveyor belt, past a number of different work stations where each worker performs a certain task.* Henry Ford, the assembly line's originator, reduced the time required to build his Model T chassis from $12\frac{1}{2}$ hours to just $1\frac{1}{2}$. The cost also dropped impressively, from

$12,000 to $290. Even today, while robots are filling in where workers once did, they stand before a conveyor belt. Each one is performing its specific function—adding a new part, or making an adjustment to a product that is moving down the familiar assembly line.

THE DEVELOPMENT OF AUTOMATION

Mechanization, as we have seen, is aimed at eliminating as much manual labor as possible from the production process. Its natural extension, **automation,** is *the process of performing a mechanical operation with either the absolute minimum of human intervention, or complete automatic control.* In automated production, people are necessary to put the machines into operation and sometimes to monitor or regulate them and inspect their output. Beyond that, the machines are automatic: essentially, they run themselves.

In recent years, automation has achieved a prominent place in production methods among advanced industrial nations, especially Japan, because it cuts costs and raises quality. It is largely responsible for Japan's increased share in the U.S. automobile market. To date, only a handful of American industries have refitted their factories for advanced automation systems. But because of Japan's growing strength in newer markets, the message to American management is clear: automation is essential if the United States hopes to regain its superior position in the world marketplace.

"Hard" and "flexible" automation

One of the most recent changes in this field has been the development of "flexible" automation as an alternative to "hard" automation. **Hard automation** is *the use of specialized equipment that repeats the same operation over and over.* Since hard automation usually involves producing one unchangeable product design in large volume, its applications in many of today's markets are limited. The costs of hard automation are high, because it requires building specialized equipment for each of the operations involved in making a single item. Moreover, significant cost-effectiveness occurs only after long production on a massive scale. **Flexible automation** (also called **soft automation**), on the other hand, allows automated machines to perform more than one function: it involves the *use of computer-controlled machines that can adapt to different versions of the same operation.* With soft automation, changing from one product design to another requires only a few different signals from the computer, not a complete refitting of the machinery. This flexibility allows managers to create different types of products in the same factory. Volume can be smaller, and quality can be higher—though the cost is not necessarily inflated. Plants can be smaller, and they can be built closer to key markets. One General Electric plant produces over 1 million electric meters a year. Thanks to flexible automation, this plant can immediately program and produce any one of 2,000 variations of these meters.[3] Such flexibility suits today's entrepreneurial atmosphere: using soft automation, producers can outmaneuver less agile competitors by moving swiftly into profitable new fields—and move out when those fields begin to decline.

Computer-aided design and manufacturing (CAD/CAM)

A recent production innovation that will greatly complement the capabilities of flexible automation is **computer-aided design (CAD),** which, as the name suggests, is *the use of computer graphics in the design of products.* Computer-created three-dimensional images and calculations rapidly performed on the computer allow engineers to test products without ever building preliminary models. Computer-aided designs can be subjected electronically to temperature variations, various seam stresses, and even artificial accidents. CAD saves time, and it improves quality: now, a product can be perfected even before it's built.

Computer-aided manufacture (CAM) is *the use of computers to control production machines.* Using the same principle as soft automation, CAM issues instructions to a machine tool from a computer. It increases output, speed, accuracy, and dependability. **CAD/CAM,** *the combination of computer-aided design and manufacturing,* reduces costly time and labor involved in the design and production of items. CAD/CAM makes way for newer and faster changes, customized products, and shorter production runs.

General Motors computer scientist David Warn uses computer-aided design (CAD) to simulate the appearance and aerodynamics of a car under development.

The factory of the future

Robots and CAD/CAM can be integrated with other applications of computers that plan and schedule materials and other broad aspects of manufacturing. Plants that have incorporated these features are said to use "computer-integrated manufacturing"; the overall concept has been called "the factory of the future." Actually, in a few locations this type of production is the factory of the present. For example, at Fanuc, Ltd., in Japan, a small crew works by day with machines to manufacture parts for robots and machine tools. But by night, the factory— in an isolated pine forest beneath Mount Fuji—works alone. Unattended carts whizz along preprogrammed routes in the twilight. Some robots unload

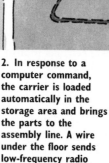

1. A fully automated flexible manufacturing system (FMS) can handle an unprecedented variety of operations. This process—which involves computer-aided design and computer-aided manufacture (CAD/CAM)—begins with an electronic drafting board that transmits data to the electronic "foreman" of the system (see item 7).

2. In response to a computer command, the carrier is loaded automatically in the storage area and brings the parts to the assembly line. A wire under the floor sends low-frequency radio signals that establish the carrier's path.

3. Managers can keep track of the robots' work without ever entering the plant: they simply consult remote terminals for daily output data.

4. A programmed pick-and-place robot picks up metal blanks from the carrier, fits them into the lathe, and places them on the conveyor belt.

5. The various machining tools needed for this operation are supplied by a revolving holder. The central controller directs the lathe to choose the appropriate tool for each cutting step.

raw materials, while others work them into shapes that can be used by the computer-controlled machining center. In the machining center, simple shapes are cut, tooled, and remodeled in a complex process that yields the pieces needed to build the final part. One person stationed in a corner monitors the plant's activity throughout the night on closed-circuit television screens. If anything goes wrong, this person can correct the problem; or, he or she can reroute the production process so that it goes around the failing section, simply by typing the proper commands onto a computer keyboard.[4]

MASS PRODUCTION IN SERVICE OPERATIONS

Though mass production has made its greatest strides in the manufacturing sector of American industry, its potential for application to service industries has not been lost on many of America's most famous entrepreneurs. Some services, of course, may never be suited to mass production: the mind shrinks, for example, from the image of a patient on a hospital assembly line, with robot-doctors performing the segmented steps of a standardized appendectomy. But other service industries have used the mass-production principles ingeniously, standardizing the steps to be performed just as in a Model T factory, and developing procedures and equipment to perform each step efficiently.

Perhaps the most famous service-industry entrepreneur to have adopted mass-production techniques is Ray Kroc, "father" of Ronald McDonald and creator of the nation's first successful hamburger chain. Kroc was able to cut overall costs (thus, he could expand fast) and save time (thus, he could serve more customers). In the early days, when McDonald's was a novelty, many customers went there simply to have the amazing experience of getting a burger, fries, and a soft drink in about a minute instead of the 15 minutes customary in most diners.

What was Kroc's secret? He broke down the chain into its component links and then standardized the links. Ovens, pots and pans, wrappers, even the golden arches of the hamburger stands were all uniformly designed and purchased in bulk. All the restaurants' more complicated functions—inventory, advertising, and purchasing—were con-

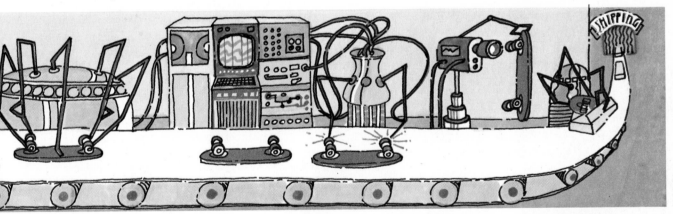

6. An assembly robot joins the parts together. Because assembly operations are often quite complex, robots of this type are more difficult to develop than some of the other kinds.

7. A programmable controller directs the whole system.

8. A welding robot, which fixes the parts in place, is a good example of flexible automation in action: the robot has been programmed to make all the different welds required on this product.

9. An inspector robot, armed with a camera plus a semiconductor chip, checks the finished item against standards. U.S. manufacturers excel in this area: their robot "inspectors" easily outperform humans.

10. Another pick-and-place robot puts the finished products on a carrier, which will bring them to shipping. If trouble arises anywhere along the line, lights or alarms will bring human help.

trolled at a centralized headquarters. Meanwhile, at the restaurants themselves, the making of a hamburger had been scientifically segmented. At peak hours, like lunch, one person flipped the burger, another applied the mayonnaise and catsup, another put on the lettuce and onion, and a final one folded the completed burger in a wrapper.

Similar mass-production principles can be found in other service industries—hotel chains, car rental agencies, even real estate firms like Century 21. Essential to all these industries is the use of computers for information processing: branches scattered across the country are controlled by a centralized information bank at headquarters. One of the most visible examples of this concept is the airline reservation system: all airline companies and travel agents can tap into a common information bank to give potential passengers immediate confirmation of flights available.

ISSUES IN PRODUCTION MANAGEMENT

How to organize the process of assembling the product is the concern of the production or operations manager. Like other types of management, production management involves the basic functions of planning, organizing, directing, and controlling. But in addition, the production manager must actually see to the creation of the product or service, a complex process that usually involves the careful coordination of raw materials, machinery, and many different kinds of workers.

It's easy to visualize this process in the production of goods, or tangible items such as shirts or hot dogs. (The word *tangible* simply means "touchable.") To produce a shirt, the resources that are converted are cloth, thread, and buttons; the form that people need or want is the shirt. It's a little harder to visualize the process in the production of services, or of *intangible* items such as television programs. But when we realize that a TV program is essentially the end product of combining resources such as writers' and actors' talents, plus other resources such as scenery and costumes, we can see that producing it is in some ways not very different from producing a shirt.

CHOOSING A LOCATION

When managers choose a site for a plant, they must consider several factors in order to avoid serious and costly problems. The most important considerations are the availability of labor and low-cost supplies, access to transportation, and the attitude of the surrounding community.

Mass-production principles applied to people-moving: every day, some 60,000 passengers and guests are moved along this Automated Guideway Transit System (a conveyor belt for people) at Atlanta's airline terminal. The system is essential for the airport's efficient operation.

Take the labor question, for instance. Highly technical firms, which need highly trained mathematicians, engineers, and computer scientists, put down roots near university communities such as Boston and San Francisco. If, on the other hand, most of the jobs in a plant can be filled by unskilled workers, managers can choose locations where this type of labor is available at a relatively low cost.

Or take the question of access to transportation and resources. Chicago's outstanding port and rail facilities are the reason it has become a machine-manufacturing center. Denver is in the midst of a wealth of natural resources—low-sulfur coal fields in Montana, uranium deposits in New Mexico, the oil- and gas-rich Rockies, and the oil-shale deposits of western Colorado. Denver's generally pleasant weather, beautiful scenery, and rich natural resources are even more attractive now that the city has upgraded its public school system, improved its roads and communications, and ensured the quality of public services. It was not always like this. Not too long ago, Colorado, like many Western states, would prosper when a few towns boomed, and would fade when they turned to ghost towns. Now, Denver's diverse economy—in which service workers, government employees, high-tech engineers, and research scientists flourish—provides an attractive environment for business newcomers.

DECIDING HOW TO PRODUCE THE PRODUCT

After a decision has been made about what to produce, the long-range production planner must deal with the question of how to produce it as efficiently, quickly, and cheaply as possible. There are two basic types of production processes used by manufacturers—the analytic process and the synthetic process. Each is appropriate for certain types of products, and each has its own particular problems and challenges.

The analytic process

The **analytic process** involves *breaking down a raw material into one or more different products, which may or may not resemble the original material in form and func-*

tion. One familiar example is oil refining. This process takes crude oil pumped from the well and extracts gasoline, kerosene, lubricating oil, and home fuel oil from it. Meat packing is another analytic process: the packer divides a steer into hide, bone, steaks, and so on. The challenge in every analytic process is to make full use of the raw material and to use each element as profitably as possible. Many companies now make valuable goods out of what used to be considered waste by-products. For example, many of the largest meat-packing firms are also leather producers.

The synthetic process

The synthetic process involves *combining two or more materials to form a single product.* Steel manufacturing is a synthetic process by which iron (extracted from ore by analysis) is combined with small quantities of minerals at high temperatures to make steel. Likewise, glass is made by heating sand (silica) and an alkali (for example, potash) together. And most plastics are formed by combining complex hydrocarbons derived from petroleum. The particular challenge in synthetic processing is to use the smallest possible amount of raw materials to produce the finished product. Clothing makers, for example, must carefully plan the way patterns are laid out for cutting, so that as little cloth as possible becomes useless scrap.

Timing of production

Some processes (such as making steel from ore) are economical only if long, continuous runs are made. Other types of process (such as the machine-sewing of shirts) can be started and stopped with few problems. Generally, processes that are more continuous require a heavier initial investment, but they also offer a greater opportunity for long-term economies. These longer runs, often used in the manufacture of televisions, radios, and cars, are examples of **repetitive manufacturing,** or *the production of discrete (separate) items in large volume.* Repetitive manufacturing usually employs hard automation. Its main advantage is the fact that the company can stockpile parts and products prior to sale, thus saving on **setup costs,** *the expenses incurred each time a manufacturer begins a production run.* But the heavy costs of maintaining large lots and storage facilities, and the system's inflexibility, have led many managers to look at the advantages of flexible automation. With its swift adaptability to the ups and downs of rapidly changing markets, flexible automation can turn old-fashioned factories into what General Motors calls its flexible automation plants—"factories with a future."

PURCHASING AND INVENTORY CONTROL

Manufacturing companies need supplies, or inventory, of components from which to make their products. (**Inventory** is defined as *goods held on hand for the production process or for sales to final customers.*) Many companies need a fairly sizable inventory of products to achieve economies of scale and meet customer demand quickly.

If inventory were not tracked, workers might waste time searching for a particular part; or the purchasing department might not know when certain supplies were low or used up. Even worse, the sales department might wreck relationships with customers by promising products that were unavailable. Every manufacturer, therefore, needs a system of **inventory control**—some way of *determining the right quantity of various items to have on hand and keeping track of their location and use within the plant.* Inventory control systems are applied to both types of supplies on hand: the **materials inventory,** or *stock of items needed for production,* and the **merchandise inventory,** or *stock of finished products.* In this discussion we'll concentrate on materials inventory.

How large should the materials inventory be?

The basic choice in purchasing materials for inventory is whether to buy small amounts frequently, or to buy large amounts once in a while. The first method, called **hand-to-mouth buying,** is used when *a manufacturer uses certain materials continuously and buys often in relatively small quantities.* The second choice is **forward buying,** *the purchase of a large enough quantity of materials to fill a manufacturer's needs for a long time.* Hand-to-mouth buying has its advantages: weekly purchases are generally more flexible; less money is tied up in storing materials; and costs drop when prices fall. But it also has disadvantages: the plant may be out of needed material at a critical stage in production; and worse, hand-to-mouth buying means losing the economies of scale that the company can get by buying in bulk.

Although inventory-control managers may be tempted to head off shortages by stockpiling everything the plant may use, this approach is not practical. Hoarding materials wastes cash reserves, produces added costs in warehousing and security, and yields little from the investment. Obviously, though, whittling down needed surpluses through overeager hand-to-mouth buying involves its own dangers. Every order must allow for **lead time,** *the period that elapses between the placement of a purchase order and the receipt of materials from a supplier.* Lead time varies considerably according to the materials that are used, and according to many other conditions, all of which can change without notice. The challenge facing the inventory-control manager is to find a delicate balance among these many considerations, so as to maintain an inventory that's large enough to keep production as high as possible, yet small enough to keep costs at a minimum.

PRODUCTION CONTROL

Production control is a complex coordinating process in which *the manager coordinates labor, materials, and machinery to make the finished product and maintains a smooth work flow so that orders can be filled efficiently and economically.*

Production control can be difficult. The manufacture of complex products is not a simple procedure that consists of adding part A to part B to part C and so forth until a product emerges ready to ship. Automobiles, for example, are assembled from subunits that vary from car to car. A system is needed to ensure that the correct engine, the right tires, and the proper chrome trim reach each car at the precise point in the assembly process at which they are to be added. Goods must thus move from storage to the assembly line with precision. And the problem is complicated in some instances because the subunits may have to be manufactured almost simultaneously on subassembly lines.

More and more manufacturers are using computers in production control. Computers can keep track of production timing and help to determine raw-material needs. In many cases, the actual overall scheduling of production is based on computer-derived programs.

Production-control procedures vary from company to company. In most manufacturing processes, however, we can identify five basic steps in production control: planning, routing, scheduling, dispatching, and follow-up and control. To illustrate the five steps, we will follow the production process of a hypothetical small company that manufactures wooden tables. It just received a rush order for 500 white and 500 unpainted tables.

Planning

As the first step in production-control planning for this order, the production manager makes a list of all the resources needed to fill the order—labor, machinery, and materials. A **bill of materials** is prepared *listing all parts and materials to be made or purchased:*

Make	Purchase
1,000 table tops	4,000 dowels (one to fasten each leg)
4,000 table legs	50 gallons of white paint

How much of these materials is already on hand? The production manager consults the perpetual inventory and discovers that enough wood and paint are on hand but that the company has only 2,000 dowels. So an order for an additional 2,000 is placed with a local supplier, who promises delivery in two days (well before they will be needed).

Routing

Routing, the second step in production control, is *the process whereby the production manager specifies the path through the plant that work will take and the sequence of operations.* The company has three departments. Each handles a different phase of the table's manufacture. Department 1 cuts wood into desired sizes and shapes. Department 2 does drilling and rough finishing. Department 3 assembles and finishes. In our example, the table tops and legs are routed from Department 1, where they are made, to Department 2 to have the dowel holes drilled, then to Department 3 for assembly, finishing, and painting. The dowels and paint are routed directly from inventory to Department 3, as shown in Figure 1.

Scheduling

Next the production manager must incorporate a time element into the routing plan. He or she sets up a schedule, which establishes a time for each operation on the route to begin and to end.

If Department 2 can drill 4,000 dowel holes in a day, then all 4,000 legs and 1,000 table tops should arrive on the same day. If Department 1 can make 1,000 table tops and 1,000 legs a week, it had better start producing the legs three weeks before starting to cut the tops, or all the parts won't be ready for Departments 2 and 3 at the same time. If the entire order is to be shipped at the same time as soon as possible, Department 3 should paint the first 500 tables as they are assembled and finished, so that the paint will be dry by the time the last 500 are completed. The schedule also tells management how much time will elapse before the job reaches Department 3, that is, how much time Department 3 has to work on other jobs before this one arrives.

Dispatching

Dispatching is *the issuing of work orders and routing papers to department heads and supervisors.* These dispatches specify the work to be done and the schedule for its completion.

In our example, the production manager would dispatch orders to the storeroom requesting delivery of the needed materials (wood, dowels, paint) to the appropriate departments and machines before the scheduled starting time.

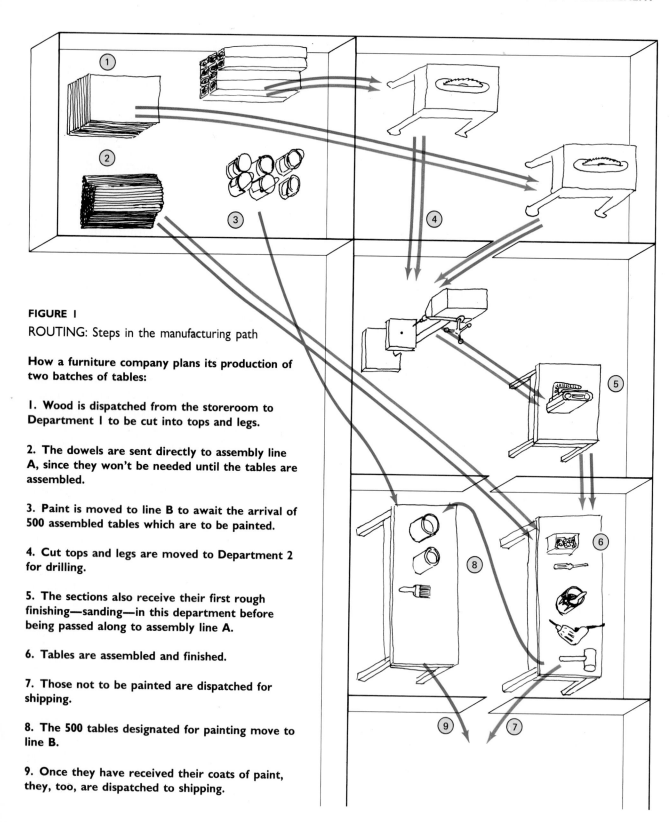

FIGURE I

ROUTING: Steps in the manufacturing path

How a furniture company plans its production of two batches of tables:

I. Wood is dispatched from the storeroom to Department I to be cut into tops and legs.

2. The dowels are sent directly to assembly line A, since they won't be needed until the tables are assembled.

3. Paint is moved to line B to await the arrival of 500 assembled tables which are to be painted.

4. Cut tops and legs are moved to Department 2 for drilling.

5. The sections also receive their first rough finishing—sanding—in this department before being passed along to assembly line A.

6. Tables are assembled and finished.

7. Those not to be painted are dispatched for shipping.

8. The 500 tables designated for painting move to line B.

9. Once they have received their coats of paint, they, too, are dispatched to shipping.

Follow-up and control

Once the schedule has been set up and the orders dispatched, production managers cannot, of course, just sit back and assume the work will automatically get done correctly and on time. Even the best scheduler can misjudge the time needed to complete an operation, and production can be delayed by accidents, mechanical breakdowns, or supplier failures. Thus the production manager must have a follow-up and control system to handle delays and prevent a minor disruption from growing into chaos. The system is based on good communication between the work stations and the production manager. In our example, suppose a machine breakdown causes Department 2 to lose half a day of drilling time. If the schedule is not altered to increase Department 3's time on other jobs, there will be an unnecessary half-day of idle waiting in Department 3. So, first of all, Department 2 must be sure to inform the production manager of its machine problem right away, and next the production manager must take time immediately to reschedule some fill-in work for Department 3.

In addition to this schedule follow-up system, production managers must set up a **quality control** system, through which *items are routinely checked and tested for quality as they are produced.* Some quality control systems provide for output to be checked and tested at random; some have every tenth item checked; some every hundredth; and so on. A report is prepared on all the "rejects," telling how many there were in a given time period and why they were thrown out or reworked. If the rejection rate is unusually high, the production manager must change the production process in some way to correct the problem at its source.

Coordinating production processes

The overall coordination of a project can become very complicated. If many steps must be taken to complete a project, production managers may have to use computers to help them with all the calculations. Making a chart of the project's different steps is often of great value to the production manager, just as seeing an actual painting is better than hearing a description of it. Earlier this century, Henry L. Gantt developed a technique that charts the steps to be taken and the time required (Figure 2, next page).

The Critical Path Method (CPM)

From Gantt's production-chart system grew another tool for production control, called the **Critical Path Method (CPM).** Basically, CPM *breaks down one large project into the many different steps necessary for its completion and analyzes the time requirements for each step.*

Take an example: the steps involved in making a record album, from the original idea to final distribution of the album in the stores. In our CPM chart (see Figure 3) we've shown six steps. (We've simplified the steps considerably for the purposes of this discussion.) If there is a delay in one of the steps—for example, it's taking longer than three weeks to record the songs—then the production manager looks at the CPM chart to see how this delay will change the overall schedule.

Notice that in the CPM figure the time needed for each step is given. Recording the songs will take three weeks and making the records themselves will take another four weeks—thus the albums will be ready for packing in seven weeks. This total seven-week sequence of operations is what is known as the **critical path:** *the specific sequence of operations whose prompt completion is essential to the prompt completion of the entire project.* Whether the design and production of the album cover are ahead of schedule or not (and the chart allows three weeks for steps 1-3-5), the complete album won't be ready until the records are. What the production manager has done is to estimate the *least possible amount of time in which the whole project can be completed,* basing this estimate on the projection of the time needed for completion of the critical path. Another method, **Program Evaluation and Review Technique (PERT),** is *similar to CPM, except that PERT involves using probabilities to estimate how likely it is that activities will require given amounts of time.*

MRP: materials requirement planning

A production management technique that is widely used to control inventory and schedule production steps is called **MRP (materials requirements plan-**

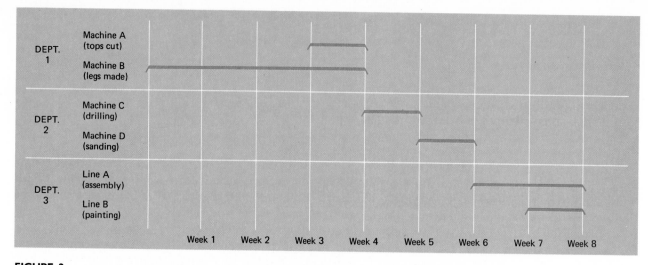

FIGURE 2

A GANTT CHART: Scheduling a complicated table
order

**A glance at a chart like this enables a production
manager to see immediately the dates on which
production steps must be started and completed if
goods are to be delivered on schedule. For example,
drilling must be done in the fifth week so that sanding
can be carried out in the sixth. Some steps can
overlap to save time. For instance, when Machine B
has been cutting legs for three weeks, Machine A
begins cutting table tops—so that both parts are
completed together and can move on together to the
next stage in the manufacturing process.**

ning). Its basic function is to *get the correct materials
where they are needed—and get them there on time—
without stockpiling unnecessary materials.* Using the
MRP approach, production managers set up a computer program designed to determine *when* certain
materials are needed, when the items should be ordered, and when they should be delivered so that
they will not arrive early and cost the company
money to store. The companies most likely to use
MRP are those whose products are complicated—
for example, an automobile manufacturer, whose
product is made up of many different parts.

To keep our discussion as simple as possible,
however, let's apply MRP to the table manufacturing example we used in the last section. In this case,
1,000 tables have to be completed by week seven. It
takes two weeks to assemble the tables. We need
1,000 tops and 4,000 legs. There are 500 tops in
inventory, and 2,500 legs. So the net requirements

for the job are 500 tops and 1,500 legs—and they're
needed by the fifth week of the production schedule. It takes three weeks to make the tops, so we
have to get cracking at the start of the second week.
It takes two weeks to make the legs, and we need two
weeks' lead time to buy the dowels for the legs, so
the dowels have to be ordered in the first week, or
the customer order will not be filled on time.

Compared with our tables, the manufacture of
more complex products—automobiles, for example—looks amazingly complex. There are many
more parts, and each must be in the right place at
the right time. What's more, there are many subassemblies—such as the motor and the steering mechanism—and they must all be completed on time. In
addition to coordinating the overall manufacture of
the car, the production manager has to break down
the elements of building the subassemblies. That's
where MRP becomes important. The computer program helps to coordinate the deadlines for each subassembly, the deadlines for various materials, and
the deadline for the whole project.

Advanced computerization and MRP

MRP and advanced methods that are related to it
have caused some dramatic shifts in certain levels of
corporate management. In the past, many managers
spent hours maintaining inventory records, some of
which were only 60 percent accurate.[5] Now, computerization has cut out some middle managers, and
freed others for planning, forecasting, and personnel management. The plant's rough-and-tumble

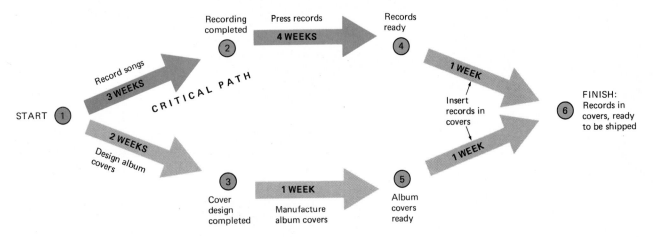

FIGURE 3

CPM (CRITICAL PATH METHOD) CHART: Production of a record album

The CPM chart shows the steps in producing the finished product, dividing them into separate paths. In this example, recording the music and pressing the records are the operations which are most crucial for the timing of the entire process. Therefore, they form the critical path (stages 1–2–4). Only three weeks are needed for the design and production of the album covers; but the entire operation will not be complete until the records are pressed and inserted into the covers.

foreman, a familiar figure in American manufacturing, now spends some of his time at the computer keyboard. These days he often has access to data that were once reserved for executives, such as inventory levels, back orders, and unpaid bills; thus, he is assuming a more managerial role.

He also tends to get along better with other department heads. In the old days, each department tended to maintain its own records of inventory, schedules, and planning. Each department worked toward its own ends, often at the expense of the others. Clashes were frequent, and when a snare occurred the buck passed feverishly from one manager to another. All this has changed thanks to computerized systems. Take, for example, the Littleton Industries plant in Florence, Kentucky; after this plant installed its computerized system, materials manager James Collins said, he began to mend fences with the plant manager—and 95 percent of his inventory emergencies simply disappeared.[6]

Because their financial return is so high, inventory systems are continually being improved. Already, advanced programs are available that will tie a company's operations system to its financial system. In this way, every department can work from the same data; moreover, the system will schedule each step of a job, and allow managers in different branches of the company to consult other managers' inventories, schedules, and plans. Still on the drawing board, but coming soon, is an even more advanced system, which would combine the inventory data base with computer-aided design, and automatically begin the process of ordering the parts and materials needed to complete a new product design.

PRODUCTIVITY AND QUALITY CONTROL

Recently, American business has turned back to better quality as a way to increase productivity. Over the years, management, convinced that a flood of advertising and gimmicks could sell anything, let quality levels in major industries slip drastically; it was during this time that Japan absorbed as much as one-third of the market share for American automobile sales. Experts in Detroit said that the average sticker price of an American car was inflated by as much as 25 percent to pay for costs directly related to low quality—such as the costs of surplus scrap,

JIT: THE "JUST IN TIME" APPROACH SOME U.S. MANUFACTURERS ARE ADOPTING FROM JAPAN

MRP, automation, and CAD/CAM have speeded up certain sectors of production through various applications of the computer. To bring human production into line with these faster systems, Japanese production experts have developed a new approach toward production called "just in time."

JIT, as it is known, is *a system in which materials and parts are delivered to each production step precisely when they are required for the production process.* The JIT approach stresses the fluidity of the production process: each stage in production is viewed as part of the whole, rather than an isolated step. JIT saves money by replacing America's jerky stop-and-go approach to production with a smooth movement, so that everything flows from the arrival of raw materials to subassembly, final completion, and shipment of finished products. JIT can save a lot of money: all along the line, costly inventory is reduced to nearly nothing (if the system is designed properly). Ironically, although JIT is a Japanese invention, it is really nothing more than the basic principle of Henry Ford's assembly line, expanded to embrace every aspect of production. It is another method of achieving the goal sought through MRP—having only the right amounts of materials arrive at precisely the times they are needed.

An example of a JIT ("just in time") delivery at the Nissan assembly plant in Nashville, Tennessee. Loads of truck seats arrive at the plant every $1\frac{1}{2}$ hours.

Naturally, working with a JIT system requires some serious preplanning. But even this preplanning has its own indirect benefits. Reducing stocks of materials and parts to zero requires managers to try to stabilize the production process: they are forced to make the process uniform, so that the flow of the production goes from beginning to end without any holdups. Managers must cut bottlenecks out of production. Workers know where the bottlenecks are, and therefore management must communicate with the workers in a friendly, cooperative way—which lowers tensions, improves morale, and increases productivity, both in the office and on the shop floor.

Companies that use JIT report enormous returns on their investment. When a company has low stocks

rejected parts, inspections, repairs, and warranties. Perhaps the most shocking inattention to quality occurred at one Motorola television factory, where workers and management produced 140 defective sets for every 100 good ones.[7] In recent years, however, some industries have improved their quality control; competitive results have been noticeable in American-made televisions and semiconductors.

THE INFLUENCE OF DEMING

Why are Japan's quality controls so highly developed and such an integral part of production? The answer lies in the long-underestimated work of consultant W. Edwards Deming. While Deming was ignored in his own country, the Japanese embraced his theories thirty years ago. In fact, to honor the

INTERNATIONAL BUSINESS TODAY

of materials and parts, it needs less storage space, less accounting, and less physical inventory; it saves more money; and it makes more money. A spirit of teamwork arises among workers: no one wants to be caught slowing the flow or standing out as the weak link in the chain. Quality control improves, too. In the old system of production, which depended on large volume, managers simply expected that a certain number of final products would be defective. But under JIT, production tends to be in smaller amounts and defects stand out. Floor managers can even apply preventive maintenance on the production line—a practice highly developed in Japan, but still scarcely known in the United States.

In Japan, Toyota uses a form of JIT known as the *kanban* system. This system has enabled Toyota to achieve a 150 percent increase in labor productivity, a 200 percent increase in the productivity of its materials-handling processes, a savings of 50 percent in factory space, and significant reductions in inventory, container requirements, and setup time. The Kawasaki U.S.A. plant in Lincoln, Nebraska, found great success in applying the Japanese concept with American workers and a traditional American management. John Deere's use of JIT at some of its Iowa plants has saved the company millions of dollars and cut inventory by 50 percent. Even two giants of America's old-school production philosophy—General Motors and Ford Motor Company—have applied JIT in a limited fashion. General Motors alone has reduced inventory by a fourth and saved several billion dollars.

SOURCE: John Holusha, "'Just-in-Time' System Cuts Japan's Auto Costs," *The New York Times*, March 25, 1983.

that crop up in industries like car manufacturing, where the production process is so complex that thousands of tests have to be conducted to ensure quality at all levels. Deming's system applies the same method that Gallup polls use to determine popular opinion: if you carefully select a handful of representative parts, you can figure out an approximate truth about the whole. By interviewing several thousand people, Gallup is able to project the opinions of millions; similarly, Deming was able to use 20 carefully selected quality tests to pinpoint flaws and weaknesses with almost the same accuracy that could be derived from 5,000 separate tests.

As with the JIT approach (see box), if a company can improve quality, other changes in productivity will follow. Inventories decline, work moves more smoothly, and costs drop. One electronics firm, for example, spent $250,000 to refine its process and to purchase better instruments. Not only was the end product finer, but the annual waste on one production line dropped from $3 million to $1 million. (To earn that $2 million the usual way, the sales department would have had to double their contracts.)[8]

A reputation goes up in smoke: this Grumman bus shows the importance of careful quality control during planning and production. Grumman sold a large, sleek-looking fleet to New York City, but mechanical problems caused endless headaches for the city's bus maintenance crews. Finally, this explosion and fire led to a decision to relieve the buses—and Grumman—of all further service in the metropolitan area.

American who taught them how to turn the words "Made in Japan" from a symbol of cheapness into one of quality, the Japanese regularly award the Deming Prize—the highest award in Japanese industry—to the company and person that contribute the most to raising quality levels.

Deming's system, called *statistical quality control*, was designed to solve the type of quality problems

Moreover, managers can also learn of other problems when they focus on quality. Deming himself recently began consulting with Pontiac managers on the quality of the product at its Engine Plant No. 18. He suggested that workers track the problems that were cropping up with some connecting-rod bolts; sure enough, they discovered that all the defects originated from one supplier, and that contract was immediately terminated. At that one plant, Deming's statistical quality control drove first-time acceptance by inspectors up from 60 percent to 96 percent. Scrap rates and inventories fell; and best of all, productivity skyrocketed by 27 percent.[9]

THE NEW AMERICAN DRIVE FOR QUALITY

Some American companies that have returned to a dedication to quality have created strong incentives for workers to help this commitment continue. Many firms now tie employees' bonuses and raises directly to quality improvements, and also link rewards to lower scrap piles and rework rates. Other firms are financing classes where managers and labor are taught to believe in the results of quality measures, and to take pride in their work.

The new dedication to quality at Ford—well publicized in its "Quality Is Job One" campaign—has raked in benefits: warranty costs and the number of defects per car have been cut in half. And Ford is looking for further suggestions to improve quality. At its Louisville, Kentucky, plant, Ford recently tacked up the latest car design (traditionally the sacred property of designers only) in the assembly area, and asked the line workers to give their opinions. One worker suggested turning some bolts around to face up instead of down. Previously, workers who worked on the bottom of the car had to tighten the bolts clumsily from beneath; now, workers could easily lean into the car and tighten the bolts from above.

Like this example, many of the suggestions Ford received were sensible—improvements that only a worker would know about. Of the 749 suggestions offered, Ford adopted an astonishing 542.

Morale improved at this plant, which had been known for its poor employee relations and attendance: absenteeism dropped all the way down to 1 percent from a high of more than 6 percent. Most important, though, Ford's drive for quality has positioned it well enough in some market segments to close in on foreign competition. In 1983, for example, the Toyota pickup truck was priced at $6,400; Ford's representative in the compact truck segment—the Ranger—was priced at only $6,000.[10]

One of the methods used at the Ford plant was a Japanese innovation, the **quality circle**—*a regularly scheduled meeting of about five to fifteen workers (who usually work in the same area), to identify and solve quality, safety, and production problems*. In Japan, quality circles not only improve the final product but also help create a sense of unity among all the employees of the company. That sense of unity, which Japanese managers compare to a feeling of belonging to a family, helps make the worker feel loyal and responsible to the company. Some American businesspeople have argued that quality circles work in Japan because of the Japanese cultural background, and that they would fail in American factories. Nonetheless, the Ford plant shows that quality circles can be employed with American-born labor and middle management with great success. (We discuss the psychological aspects of quality circles in Component Chapter C.)

Quality circles are also being used outside assembly-line industries. Many service businesses, such as banks, hospitals, and insurance companies, have introduced quality circles as part of employees' regular schedules. Hertz Rent-A-Car streamlined its car-reservation procedures using advice obtained in quality circles, and made its procedures easier for the customer and cheaper for the company. Citibank, which operates fifteen independent quality circles in its organization, claims one particularly happy result: the time a customer waits in line has been reduced. Often, a small suggestion from a quality circle yields a big savings. At InterFirst Service Corporation in Dallas, Texas, a quality-circle participant tipped off management to what seems like a simple problem—an inefficient copier. Replacing it, the company has said, will save $2,800 a year.[11]

CHAPTER REVIEW

The production or operations manager is responsible for coordinating the processes, raw materials, and personnel that are necessary for the creation of a product or service. In the United States, most industries operate on the principle of mass production, which has been made possible by mechanization, standardization, the assembly line, and automation. Adaptable, computer-controlled machines have been added to the production process; computers are also finding increasing use at the design stage. These new techniques, along with robot labor and computerized coordination, are being adapted for use in service industries.

Production managers make decisions about what, where, and how products are made. When the production manager plans a new site location, factors such as adequate labor and supplies, transportation and energy resources, and community attitude must be considered.

One of the most important decisions the production manager makes is how to produce the product. The two basic manufacturing processes are the analytic, which breaks down a raw material into one or more products, and the synthetic, which combines materials to form a product. Repetitive manufacturing—the production of individual items in large volume—minimizes setup costs.

Production control involves the coordination of the labor, materials, and machinery needed to ensure a smooth work flow. Production control consists of five basic steps: planning, routing, scheduling, dispatching, and following up and controlling the work. Among the tools available to the production-control manager are computers and the Gantt Chart.

The purchasing and inventory-control departments obtain materials for a firm and keep track of both raw materials and finished products. Inventory control is the process of maintaining a level of inventory high enough to meet production needs but low enough to keep costs down. PERT, CPM, and MRP are among the planning techniques being used. Questions to be solved are how much to spend (quality of materials) and whether to make or buy given components.

Under pressure from foreign competition, especially from Japan, American industry has found it essential to improve quality and productivity. Deming's system of statistical quality control and the JIT approach are helping to bring needed changes about. And the introduction of quality circles has led to many innovative and practical suggestions from assembly-line workers.

KEY WORDS

production (166)
mass production (166)
mechanization (166)
standardization (166)
assembly line (166)
automation (167)
hard automation (167)
flexible automation (soft automation) (167)
computer-aided design (CAD) (167)
computer-aided manufacture (CAM) (167)
CAD/CAM (167)
analytic process (171)
synthetic process (171)
repetitive manufacturing (171)
setup costs (172)
inventory (172)
inventory control (172)
materials inventory (172)
merchandise inventory (172)
hand-to-mouth buying (172)
forward buying (172)
lead time (172)
production control (172)
bill of materials (173)
routing (173)
dispatching (173)
quality control (175)
Critical Path Method (CPM) (175)
critical path (175)
Program Evaluation and Review Technique (PERT) (175)
MRP (materials requirements planning) (175–176)
JIT approach (178)
quality circle (180)

REVIEW QUESTIONS

1. What are the three major problems production managers must solve in the planning phase of their work?

2. Describe how the computer has revolutionized the factory (hard and soft automation, CAD/CAM). How does the greater flexibility offered by these new methods help industry?

3. What challenges are presented by the analytic production process? By the synthetic process?

4. What are the advantages and disadvantages of hand-to-mouth buying? Of forward buying?

5. Why would the engineering and purchasing departments be at odds over the quality of a needed material? How might this conflict be resolved?

6. Why is an efficient system of inventory control important to every manufacturer?

7. Explain and describe the JIT approach and outline its benefits.

8. Briefly outline the steps in production control.

9. Discuss the PERT, CPM, and MRP techniques and explain how they are used.

10. Why have quality and productivity become important issues for American manufacturers, and what is being done to improve them?

CASE 1

PRODUCTION PROBLEMS AT COMMODORE

In the fiercely competitive home computer market, Commodore International Ltd. seemed to have captured 40 percent of the market with a low-cost product, the Commodore 64. Commodore's rivals were not doing well, and executives predicted whopping sales for the Christmas 1983 season. But things didn't turn out that way. The Christmas season saw returns of 20–30 percent of Commodore's products by wholesalers and retail store owners, who claimed that the merchandise was defective. One computer buyer for a chain that was dropping the 64 remarked: "They've got the hottest product in that market—and they're ruining it."

How did such a successful company experience such a decline? First, demand soared when the retail price for the 64 dropped from $595, and then the wholesale price dropped in the summer of 1983. But facing the intense demand, Commodore had problems with quality control. Returns increased. When the Commodore 64 was first introduced to mass merchandisers in February 1983, only 5–7 percent of the machines were returned because retailers said they were defective. But by June and July, one distributor was returning 25 percent of everything he sold. Attempting to explain the decline in quality, another distributor remarked: "They make 'em quick."

A different assessment was offered by the president of a Tennessee electronics distributor: "A lot of returns aren't defective, they're based on . . . customer disillusionment." This disillusionment stemmed from a problem with supplies of the disk drive—a part that is as essential to a computer as a transmission is to a car. For two months, dealers received no shipments of disk drives: Commodore had underestimated the number of disk drives consumers would want. Worse, Commodore was having difficulties with its own supplier: in July 1983, Commodore's disk-drive supplier stopped making the part, and Commodore could not ship the part to wholesalers and retailers because it had none to ship. Even when production resumed, the disk-drive shortage remained: even though Commodore's factories could turn out 8,000 to 10,000 computers per day, it appeared that Commodore's supplier could only produce 50,000 disk drives per month. Problems also occurred with supplies of video-screen monitors, and with the functioning of the letter-quality printer.

Perhaps in an effort to cut costs, Commodore responded to its problem by firing its national sales representatives. The company subsequently hired an in-house sales staff, but fired them too. Summing up the situation, Commodore's former finance vice-president put it this way: "It's not a momentary problem. It's closer to a fundamental flaw in the way Commodore does business."[12]

1. As the former Commodore executive quoted above noted, there is a serious problem in the way the company does business. How would you describe the problem? Is it only a production problem? How would you solve the problem? Explain your answer.

2. How important is quality control to Commodore? What other production difficulties have surfaced?

3. Do you think it was wise of Commodore to fire its sales staff? Why or why not?

4. What production management systems might Commodore use to regain its place in the market?

5. How might Commodore solve its disk-drive supply problem?

CASE 2

CINCINNATI MILACRON: READY FOR THE REVOLUTION

James Geier presides over Cincinnati Milacron, a highly successful manufacturer of machine tools. In the fast-changing field of manufacturing, traditional machine tools are becoming as outmoded as the traditional assembly line. But Jim Geier is not pessimistic about his company's future. In fact, he is so optimistic that $9 million losses in the first half of 1983 did not discourage him.

Geier's confidence is based on a change at Milacron that may place the company in the forefront of the revolution in manufacturing. That change can be described in three words: the machining center. The machining center can build tremendous adaptability and economy into the manufacturing process. In a traditional factory, stationary machines perform a series of operations on an individual part, as that part moves along the assembly line. Step by step, the unfinished part is transformed into its final form. Milacron's newly developed machining center works just the opposite way. No longer do the parts move down the line to be worked on by a series of machines; instead, "a single machine, at the direction of a computer, performs the functions that six or more tools used to perform in sequences. In a machining center, *fixed* parts are cut and shaped by various moving tools."

When a few machining centers are grouped together, the manufacturing process becomes very flexible. A variety of similar and dissimilar parts can be manufactured in a range of sizes and shapes, and, according to Geier, it costs no more to purchase and set up the machining center than it does to buy the combination of individual machines needed to do the same job.

The real value of the machining-center approach for American industry lies in its effect on inventory. Managers can program the machining center to produce only the parts needed for the next day's production; this way, the costs of maintaining large inventories of parts will be considerably reduced. As Geier foresees it, "The cost structure will change." A manufacturer will be able to say, "I will make today only what I need to assemble tomorrow."[13]

1. With low setup costs, a manufacturer can afford to program a machine to make only a few units. How would this fit into the JIT approach?

2. If demand drops off, you can reprogram the machining center to make a different part. How does this affect productivity? How does flexibility differ from traditional manufacturing?

3. Milacron also manufactures the computerized robots that link the tooling centers and move materials from center to center. How will this affect its position in the machining industry?

4. Milacron is in the red now. Is it likely to do well in the future? Explain your answer.

MANAGEMENT AND UNIONS 7

Once, when a prominent labor leader was asked what labor wanted, he replied simply, "More." Today, that's no longer necessarily the case. Labor has, for example, granted some concessions to the troubled airline industry in the early 1980s: when American Airlines guaranteed existing salaries for already-hired workers, unions agreed to a two-tier contract that cut salaries for future hires, and when Eastern Airlines gave its employees 25 percent of the company's stock, labor granted one-year 18 percent wage concessions.

Are workers always this flexible, and do managements always come up with such creative solutions? In this chapter we'll look at labor-management relations—both cooperative and confrontational. As we'll see, labor and management sometimes have different goals; but ways can often be found to resolve their conflicts.

CHAPTER FOCUS

After reading the material in this chapter, you will be able to:

- trace the history of the labor movement in the United States from its formative period, through its expansive period, to the present leveling-off phase
- cite at least two reasons for the unions' decline
- enumerate at least three union strategies to regain strength and recruit new members
- state the substance of five major issues at stake in labor-management relations today
- describe the purpose of employee stock ownership plans
- list the major weapons of management and labor in dealing with one another
- describe the stages of collective bargaining
- cite four means of handling labor-management disputes
- discuss several trends in labor-management relations

In 1981, when Western Electric Company announced a pay cut for the engineers at its North Andover, Massachusetts, plant, the workers there decided to organize: they formed a chapter of the nonunion Association of Engineers and Associates. Then, further conflict arose. Management instituted changes in methods and performance evaluation systems that the workers thought were unfair—but management refused to discuss these changes. Result: in 1983 the nonunion group reorganized itself as a local of a national union, the Communications Workers of America. Now management would be obliged to talk to the workers whether they wished to or not—because now the workers were backed by the legal protection of the labor laws.[1]

In our economic system there are certain unavoidable differences of interest between workers and the people who pay them. On the one hand, owners of businesses have a right to use their resources as they see fit. But on the other hand, the workers know that owners depend on their labor, and they feel they should have some control over their working conditions and the rewards they receive. The potential for conflict is seldom far below the surface of labor-management relations. And it's because of this potential for conflict that workers join together to form **labor unions,** *organizations of workers formed to advance their members' interests.*

One thing workers have in common with management is that they have something to sell—their own labor, the services they can perform for the employer—and naturally they want to get the best price they can. And just as the price a company charges for a product is affected by forces of supply and demand, so is the price workers charge a company for their services. It is here that a labor union's power is felt, for it alters the basic supply-and-demand situation by representing most or all of the workers—the supply of labor—that the company needs. By using their bargaining strength as a whole, workers can put more pressure on management than they could as individuals. An individual worker can easily be replaced, but the whole group cannot.

What's important in disputes between management and labor is not deciding who's right or wrong but finding out whether the two sides can resolve their disagreement so they can continue to work together. In some cases, *unions and management go through a negotiation process* known as **collective bargaining.** But the two sides sometimes reach the point of hostile confrontation, resulting in a strike (a work stoppage) or lockout (in which management locks workers out of a plant), or any of a number of other forms of conflict. We'll discuss these patterns of cooperation and confrontation more fully later in this chapter. But first, let's take a brief look at the history of labor unions and see what their status is today.

The Knights of Labor began to grow strong in the early 1870s. But public opinion turned against them after the 1886 Haymarket Riot, in which a bomb killed several policemen.

UNIONS IN AMERICAN HISTORY

In 1792 a group of shoemakers held a meeting in Philadelphia to discuss matters of common interest. Without meaning to, they made history: the result of their modest assembly was the formation of the first known union in America. During the next several decades other unions appeared. They were chiefly local **craft unions,** *made up of skilled artisans belonging to a single profession or craft* and concerned only with trade-related matters.

THE DEVELOPMENT OF NATIONWIDE UNIONS

As improved transportation cut shipping costs, created a national market, and made workers more mobile, local craft unions banded together in the 1840s and 1850s into national craft unions. And in 1869 several national craft unions joined forces as the Knights of Labor. After the Knights won a strike in 1885 against the powerful Wabash Railroad, its membership multiplied sevenfold in just one year, topping 700,000. Their power proved to be short-lived, however. The Knights' leadership did not suit

In the early 1900s, the clothing industry was ripe for unionization: conditions were deplorable in factories like the "sweatshop" shown here. The 1909 "Uprising of the Twenty Thousand," a strike by New York City shirtwaist workers, laid the groundwork for the formation of the International Ladies Garment Workers Union.

Labor relations today: Important advances have been made, but scenes reminiscent of the past still occur. During a Greyhound Bus strike in 1983, for example, police clashed with demonstrators who wanted to prevent buses from rolling.

several of its member unions: the Knights' first priority was moral betterment, and only secondarily improvements in wages and working conditions. Furthermore, the 1886 Haymarket Riot—during which a bomb exploded among Chicago policemen trying to break up a labor rally—turned public opinion against the labor movement, of which the Knights were the most visible symbol.

By 1890 control of the trade union movement had passed to a rival group, the American Federation of Labor (AFL), founded in 1886. It survived to dominate labor for the next forty years.

THE EXPANSIVE PERIOD

During the 1930s labor took full advantage of President Franklin D. Roosevelt's sympathy and protective legislation to expand union membership enormously, especially among unskilled workers.

In 1935 an unofficial Committee for Industrial Organization was set up within the AFL. It was led by John L. Lewis, head of the United Mine Workers (UMW), an **industrial union** that *represents both skilled and unskilled workers from all phases of a particular industry.* The committee's drive to organize major industries took off with passage of the **National Labor Relations Act** of 1935, popularly called the **Wagner Act,** which *obliged an employer to recognize and negotiate with any union chosen by a majority vote of employees within the organizational unit.* The committee organized the auto and steel industries, boosting membership to over 4 million.

Three years later the AFL formally expelled the committee. Craft unionists who controlled the AFL viewed the committee's industrial unions as a threat to their own brand of unionism. Thus the committee became a fully independent federation of industrial unions and changed its name to the Congress of Industrial Organizations (CIO).

During World War II full employment helped unions grow, and labor won numerous benefits through the War Labor Board, set up in 1942 to foster negotiations between labor, management, and government. In exchange for a no-strike pledge, unions were able to win fringe benefits, including the right to set up "union shops"—that is, if the majority of the workers in a plant were represented by a single union, all workers in the plant could be required to join that union.

THE LEVELING-OFF PERIOD

After the war, labor's demands for wage increases erupted into a series of severe strikes. Proindustry legislators in Washington retaliated by enacting the **Taft-Hartley Labor-Management Relations Act** of 1947. This legislation *restricted some of the practices used by labor to force its demands on industry*—such as making union membership a condition of employment.

In 1955 the AFL and the CIO merged their 16 million members. From this point the unions' growth began to level off. Disclosures of corruption and links to organized crime in the late 1950s tarnished labor's image. To curb such abuses Congress passed the **Landrum-Griffin Act** in 1959, *imposing stiff new regulations on unions' internal affairs.*

THE LABOR MOVEMENT TODAY

Of the approximately 112 million men and women currently in the U.S. work force, only about 20 percent are union members.[2] This is the smallest proportion since 1953, when union membership peaked at 25.2 percent of the total labor force; even as recently as 1970, union members accounted for 24.7 percent of the workers in the United States, so today's drop represents a significant decline.[3]

Despite a general decrease in the number of unionized workers, however, in some areas union membership has increased sharply. Between 1968 and 1980, the number of unionized public employees rose from 3.9 million to 7 million.[4]

Why unions may be weakening

One reason for the overall decline in union membership is the massive change in American industry that's taking place as older, less efficient industries fall victim to more efficient, lower-cost foreign competitors. Coupled with this is the rise of high-tech and white-collar jobs that have resulted from the development and exploitation of the silicon chip. Some of the resulting new industries are much harder to unionize than were the traditional blue-collar "smokestack" industries where the unions were born and grew to maturity. An estimated 60 percent of the decline in union membership is due to changes in the kinds of workers that are needed in today's economy, and the kinds of jobs that are available in the marketplace.[5]

Figures compiled by the Bureau of Labor Statistics tell how membership in some unions dropped from the 1970s to 1980. Membership in the key United Auto Workers dropped 27 percent; the United Steelworkers of America saw its membership plunge 42 percent; the United Rubber Workers suffered a 31 percent slide in membership; and the International Ladies Garment Workers Union posted a drop of 17 percent.[6] All these unions are in industries that have been outdistanced by more efficient foreign competitors: some plants have closed (with mass layoffs), and other employers have been forced to trim their work forces and operate more efficiently to meet foreigners head-on.

Layoffs and tough economic times have forced many unions to make more concessions in their negotiations with employers. Significantly, 19 percent of the workers covered by union contracts negotiated during the first nine months of 1983 took wage cuts and another 19 percent got no wage increases. Only 32 percent were able to stay ahead of inflation with wage increases of 4 percent or better.[7] Not surprisingly, the union rank and file are not happy with the concessions their own leaders have been forced to grant. The 1982 United Auto Workers contract with General Motors just squeaked by, winning approval from a narrow 52 percent majority: the contract called for no wage increases, and even included some "give-backs" of paid holidays. Members were

Unions' role in American industry has shifted since they first gained strength in the early 1930s. Enrollments zoomed after 1935, when unions won the legal right to organize; but after peaking during the 1940s and 1950s, union membership gradually declined. Causes included economic problems, changes in the work force, and the growth of the hard-to-organize high-tech and service industries.

also dissatisfied when leaders allowed the automakers to make selective cuts in the work force to make some plants more efficient and profitable.[8]

New directions for unions

After a long period of prosperity and growth, the unions have come up against some of the hard facts of economic life. They are beginning to realize that

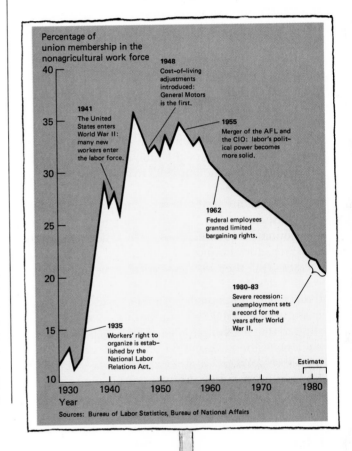

Percentage of union membership in the nonagricultural work force

1941
The United States enters World War II: many new workers enter the labor force.

1948
Cost-of-living adjustments introduced: General Motors is the first.

1955
Merger of the AFL and the CIO: labor's political power becomes more solid.

1962
Federal employees granted limited bargaining rights.

1980–83
Severe recession: unemployment sets a record for the years after World War II.

1935
Workers' right to organize is established by the National Labor Relations Act.

Estimate

Year

Sources: Bureau of Labor Statistics, Bureau of National Affairs

if they are to succeed in the current economic climate, they'll have to make some changes in their basic approach.

For one thing, they are focusing their organizing efforts on some new industries. Forecasts indicate that by 1993 the number of production workers in high-tech industries will jump 22 percent, to 1.8 million, and the number of engineers and technicians will soar by 32 percent, to 1.4 million[9] The unions are zeroing in on these key groups as they attempt to regain the ground they've lost during the past decade. In California, for example, a committee for forty local unions, which has organized a number of different industries, has launched at least three projects to organize workers in the growing high-tech industry. In the Boston area the United Auto Workers, the International Association of Machinists, the Communication Workers of America, and the International Union of Electrical Workers formed a coalition in 1983 to organize high-tech workers.[10]

The unions have not stopped pushing bread-and-butter issues: at high-tech companies caught in an economic squeeze, unions are making headway with workers who face layoffs and delays in pay increases. But they are also using new methods to reach workers. Hard facts may be more persuasive than rallies and pep talks: the Boston coalition commissioned a $100,000 study, for example, that showed that local employees of high-tech firms were paid between $.03 and $1.75 per hour less than high-tech workers in other parts of the country.[11] The unions are also seizing on new issues to recruit members. At one company where about half the workers were Hispanic, the union addressed an issue felt by many workers—that Hispanics were being passed over for raises and promotions. At a computer manufacturing company, the union addressed workers' health and safety concerns after their employer refused to tell them the names of the chemicals they were working with.[12]

BASIC LABOR ISSUES

Certain classic issues have always appeared on the bargaining table for labor and management to negotiate—union security and management rights, com-

KEY LEGISLATION RELATING TO UNIONS

THE NATIONAL LABOR RELATIONS ACT (WAGNER ACT) (1935)

Made it unlawful for employers to:

1. Interfere with the right of employees to form, join, or assist labor organizations.

2. Interfere with labor organizations by dominating them or make financial contributions to them.

3. Discourage membership in labor organizations by discriminating against members in employment or by requiring a promise not to join a union as a condition of employment.

4. Refuse to bargain collectively with a labor organization chosen by employees to represent them.

5. Discharge an employee because he or she has testified or filed charges against the employer under the act.

THE TAFT-HARTLEY ACT (1947)

Amended the Wagner Act to restrict unions. It:

1. Declared the closed shop illegal.

2. Required a sixty-day notice before a strike or lockout and empowered the government to issue injunctions to prevent strikes that would endanger the national interest.

3. Declared illegal: jurisdiction strikes, featherbedding, refusal to bargain in good faith, secondary boycotts.

4. Required union officers to certify that they were not Communists.

5. Required unions to submit financial reports to the Secretary of Labor.

6. Allowed unions to sue employers for contract violations.

7. Permitted employers to petition the National Labor Relations Board for elections in certain circumstances.

THE LANDRUM-GRIFFIN ACT (1959)

Motivated by discovery of corruption in unions and loopholes in the Taft-Hartley Act. Aimed largely at regulating the internal affairs of unions, the act:

1. Provided for controls to prevent bribing of union officials by employers.

2. Closed loopholes in the law forbidding secondary boycotts.

3. Prohibited hot-cargo clauses in employment contracts (recognition of the union's right not to handle goods of a company whose employees are on strike).

4. Required all unions to file constitutions and bylaws with the Secretary of Labor.

5. Required all unions to publish financial records open to inspection by their members.

6. Made union officials more personally responsible for the unions' financial responsibility. Made embezzlement of union funds a federal offense. Forbade unions to lend officers more than $2,000.

7. Denied convicted felons the right to hold union office for five years following their release from prison. (This provision applied also to Communist party members but the Supreme Court ruled this unconstitutional.)

8. Stated that every member of a union has equal rights: the right to vote on issues, to attend meetings, and to speak freely.

9. Stated that unions must follow specific procedures before raising dues: a majority of members must vote for the increase, and the vote must be carried out by secret ballot.

10. Stated that unions cannot stop members from suing them.

11. Stated that no member can be fired, expelled, or punished in any way until he or she has been formally charged and given a fair hearing and enough time to prepare.

(Items 8 through 11 are known as the Bill of Rights of Union Members.)

TITLE 7 OF THE CIVIL RIGHTS ACT OF 1964 (AMENDED IN 1972; NOW CALLED THE EQUAL EMPLOYMENT ACT)

Prohibits discrimination in employment based on race, religion, national origin, or sex:

1. Any employer with fifteen or more employees who engages in interstate commerce is covered by the law.

2. Discrimination covered includes evil intent, lack of equal treatment, and adverse impact unrelated to business necessity. When discrimination is charged, the burden of proof is on the employee, who must prove that discrimination has taken place.

3. The Equal Employment Opportunity Commission (EEOC) has authority to investigate discrimination complaints.

4. Either the EEOC or the wronged party can sue in federal court for damages resulting from discrimination.

UNION SECURITY AGREEMENTS

Ideally, the union would like to see all workers under their jurisdiction, but the **closed shop,** which *compelled workers to join the union as a condition of employment,* was outlawed by the 1947 Taft-Hartley Act.

The next best alternative for labor is the **union shop:** it *allows an employer to hire new people at will, but after a probationary period, usually thirty days, the worker must join the union.* Not all states permit unions to set up union shops. In opposition to compulsory membership certain states—mostly in the Sun-

belt—have passed **right-to-work laws,** which *give the employee the explicit right not to join a union.*

Another alternative is the **agency shop,** which *requires nonunion workers who benefit from any agreements the union has negotiated to pay dues to that union.* Last is the **open shop,** in which *nonunion workers pay no dues.*

Unions are more secure if there's some guarantee that they'll have continuing financial support. For this reason, a union may bargain for a **dues checkoff,** *an arrangement that authorizes management, with the employee's written approval, to deduct union dues from paychecks and pay them directly to the union.*

---

pensation, working time, grievance and arbitration procedures, and job security and promotion. And newer issues are appearing, including safety and health and quality of work life.

UNION SECURITY AND MANAGEMENT RIGHTS

A long history of opposition by management to organized labor has tended to sharpen union concerns about self-preservation. These concerns persist, and with good reason. Public sympathy with unions has been low in the 1980s—President Ronald Reagan's breaking of the Professional Air Traffic Controllers' Union, for example, seemed to echo public feeling that big labor was destructive, sometimes even corrupt. The AFL-CIO had campaigned unsuccessfully for labor law "reform"—new legislation that would have streamlined the National Labor Relations Board and slapped tougher penalties on companies that violated labor-relations laws.

Today, once a union has been established, the collective bargaining contracts it negotiates begin with a provision guaranteeing the security of the

union. And even before a union is established, while organizers are trying to rally workers, there may be strong opposition from management to the union drive. In 1981 the National Labor Relations Board (NLRB) found that 26,000 workers had been fired for engaging in union activities, and in the early 1980s companies were increasingly bringing in anti-union management strategists to defeat union organizing efforts.[13]

For example, after District 925 of the Service Employees International Union (SEIU) filed for an election at the ninety-three-person Syracuse, New York, office of Equitable Life Assurance Society, the big insurer brought in an outside consultant who specialized in defeating organizing efforts. At stake in this battle were not just the ninety-three employees in Syracuse but the 10,000 clerical workers Equitable employed nationwide. The consultant started spreading the word that joining a union would mean job losses and high dues. But District 925 won the election anyway. Equitable challenged it before the NLRB, and when the complaint failed, Equitable merely ignored the union, refusing to bargain in good faith. Outraged—but recognizing that it would be fruitless to stage a walkout against a company that had 300 offices nationwide—District 925 filed a complaint with the NLRB. Before that complaint could be decided, Equitable announced that it was closing the office as part of a consolidation of forty-seven offices. (The union, of course, claimed that the closing was intended only to keep it out.) At the time of this writing the battle is far from over: the AFL-CIO has started a boycott of Equitable, which manages more than $1 billion in union pension funds.[14]

COMPENSATION

Until recently, most new labor contracts won by the unions contained wage increases. But the recession of the early 1980s, coupled with tough foreign competition, led to a new pattern: many unions, recognizing the economic problems facing employers, have entered into "concessionary bargaining," giving employers financial leeway to try to work out their difficulties. Often, unions have agreed to contracts freezing wages at current levels. In the Chicago area, for example, unions representing carpenters, cement masons, bricklayers, and other construction workers agreed to a contract that held wages at the level set in the expiring contract. The only gain the unions won was a $.25 to $.40 per hour increase for each worker, which went to the unions to enable them to maintain health benefits at existing levels.[15] During the first quarter of 1983 the Bureau of Labor Statistics reported that the average wages negotiated during the first year of labor contracts declined by 1.4 percent. Over the life of the contract, wages increased only 2.2 percent, also a record low.

By mid-1983 the ailing economy was well on the way to recovery, and unions began to resist further concessions. Meanwhile, however, other complexities had entered union wage negotiations. Typical of these new negotiations was the three-year 1983 agreement between American Airlines and the 10,600-member Transport Workers Union. Although union members won a 21.4 percent pay increase over the life of the contract, costs to American would increase by only 2 percent a year. How was this possible? In return for the generous wage increase, the union agreed to a series of concessions.

Most important, new mechanics hired by American would earn 32 percent less than mechanics already on the job. But American would also be allowed to use up to 12.5 percent part-time employees, and it would be able to shift people between jobs, in some cases using lower-paid employees to do jobs previously reserved for higher-paid employees. As a result of these concessions, American Airlines expected to be able to cut its labor costs by $50 million a year by 1985.[16]

The profit-sharing alternative

Profit sharing is not a new idea; in the past, some companies used it to provide employees with deferred income that could be claimed upon retirement. Now, however, both management and labor are looking at profit sharing as a means of gaining noninflationary wage settlements, reducing unemployment during cyclical downturns, and increasing productivity. An estimated 10,000 companies now have profit-sharing or stock-option plans covering some 1 million workers.[17] By early 1983 corporations such as General Motors, Pan Am, Ford, Uniroyal, and International Harvester had joined the list of those offering profit sharing.[18]

Fringe benefits

Fringe benefits are also taking up more and more room in union contracts. A **fringe benefit** is a *financial benefit other than wages, salaries, and supplementary rewards;* it costs the company money without affecting basic wage rates. Now that pensions are regulated by federal law, employee-benefit costs are rising faster than wages. Unions have been stressing higher pensions in view of the trend toward early retirement and the increasing influence of retirees within their ranks. Employers are fighting hard against these demands because management has also had to absorb a large increase in Social Security taxes and unemployment compensation rates.

Recently, employers have also attempted to persuade unions to pay more of the $100 billion that medical insurance costs companies every year; as of mid-1983, unions at large companies such as AT&T and Boeing had resisted demands for health-care concessions, but others in the aluminum and glass industries had agreed to compromise on the issue.

JOB SECURITY AND PROMOTION

When managements won concessions from unions on wages and work rules in recent contract negotiations, the unions in turn asked for something from management. They demanded **lifetime security:** *arrangements that would give workers some protection against temporary layoffs due to economic slowdowns and would also protect them against permanent closing of outmoded plants.* These security provisions took several different forms. In 1982 the United Auto Workers (UAW), for example, won promises from General Motors and Ford that no plant would be closed due to the company's farming out of work it had previously done itself. The UAW also helped persuade GM to bring more work into one of its plants so that 800 workers would be added to the 7,000 already employed there.[19]

In addition, the UAW won agreement from GM to create a "guaranteed income stream," under which workers with at least fifteen years of seniority would be guaranteed between 50 percent and 75 percent of their last weekly paycheck until they reached retirement age. But by mid-1983 some workers had become disillusioned with this plan because it required laid-off workers to transfer to other GM plants at the option of GM. In fact, the giant automaker did exercise this option to move workers around: it recalled 700 laid-off workers from two closed California auto plants and assigned them to a plant in Oklahoma City where a second shift was being added. Some of the auto workers saw this as a plan by GM to eliminate workers from the guaranteed income stream program, since many workers were likely to refuse a transfer that would require them to uproot their families.[20]

A similar "guaranteed jobs" promise that the UAW obtained from Ford also led to some worker complaints. In exchange for promising not to lay off any workers during the life of the contract, Ford won from the union the right to change work rules in an effort to streamline operations. Ford was permitted to institute mandatory (required) Saturday overtime shifts, recall laid-off workers not according to seniority but according to their productivity records, broaden some job definitions, and toughen rules on absenteeism. These rules, especially the mandatory Saturday overtime, caused disagreements among the workers at the Ford plants and led them to reject the proposed contract containing these rule changes[21] (We discuss work rules in more detail later in this chapter.)

Meeting the automation threat

In the past, unions tended to react to automation after the fact: after management introduced new labor-saving equipment and techniques, the unions would fight against them to protect the jobs of their members. Now, unions are taking a new tack. They're meeting the challenge before it arises by demanding that management give them advance notice of any attempts to introduce new equipment that would cost their members jobs, and they're demanding that those workers already on the job not be laid off because of the introduction of automated equipment.

Two unions acutely aware of the potential of automation for reducing the number of jobs have been the Communication Workers of America (CWA) and the International Brotherhood of Electrical Workers (IBEW), who represent nearly 90 percent of the telephone work force. In 1980 both unions negotiated the creation of labor-management "technology committees," through which AT&T gave the unions six months' notice before introducing new equipment. More recently, however, the unions have complained that such notice is insufficient; they have been seeking the right to participate in the design and testing of new equipment—a proposal AT&T has been resisting.[22]

The CWA has also been seeking to create a "career development" program, under which AT&T would invest half the savings realized from the use of new, more efficient equipment in programs to retrain union members to use the new equipment. Meanwhile, the CWA itself is running classes in six cities, where members who are willing to pay their own tuition can learn high-tech skills ranging from computer programming to the repair of electronic equipment. The CWA has already had some success with another employer, GTE Corporation, winning from it detailed provisions for worker retraining, and as well as severance pay and health benefits for workers who lose their jobs due to automation.[23]

CHANGING WORK RULES FOR GREATER PRODUCTIVITY

For many years job titles and skills were narrowly defined. This approach, referred to as "Taylorism" (after industrial engineer Frederick W. Taylor, who preached the idea that jobs must be closely defined and minutely organized), was useful to management as a means of controlling work and the work force. But unions also seized on Taylorism as a means of preserving jobs. Under this system, if there was too much work for one carpenter, another had to be hired—even if an electrician already on the payroll was sitting by idly. Thus, certain jobs were created even if there was insufficient need for them. Even as times changed and the needs of management changed, the unions clung stubbornly to the idea that a worker must not work outside of his or her category.

The result of this dedication to Taylorism was that productivity suffered as union and management both adhered to time-encrusted work rules. But as competition from abroad increased and the economy got into difficulty in the late 1970s and early 1980s, management and unions both realized that there would have to be some fundamental changes.

After tough bargaining, sweeping changes in work rules have been made. For example, Chrysler Corporation, which was spending $51.5 million to produce auto seat covers at its Detroit Trim plant, found that it could have the seat covers produced by outside contractors for only $30.8 million, reducing its costs by 41.3 percent. But before Chrysler decided to close the Detroit Trim plant, officers of Local 212 of the United Auto Workers approached management in February 1983 to find out how the plant could be saved. After months of hard bargaining, labor and management worked out a plan under which the work force—union members and supervisors alike—would be cut, streamlined work rules would be instituted, and workers' production quotas would be increased. In all, the production

force was reduced by 21 percent, supervisors were reduced by 25 percent (a supervisor would now oversee thirty workers instead of twenty-one), and support staff was cut by 40 percent. "Taylorist" job definitions were changed. A welder who had been hired years ago and kept on the payroll to handle occasional welding jobs was dismissed and one of the maintenance workers was trained to handle the welding jobs. Under the old rules, only an electrician could unplug one of the plant's sewing machines; now anyone can do that. The result of the joint union-management effort was that the plant was kept open, production increased, and costs dropped by $6.4 million a year—even without automation.[24]

Labor and management in many plants are praising such changes as the wave of the future. But both sides agree that the only way to make work-rule changes a reality is for both labor and management to work together. If the management expects the unions to give up their hard-earned work rules, management will have to let labor in on the decision-making process that leads to these changes.

SAFETY AND HEALTH

Although the great majority of today's union contracts have provisions covering workers' safety and health, these provisions rarely do more than restate federal regulations already in force. But the combination of escalating health-care costs and greater awareness of environmental hazards has given rise to important new demands in labor negotiations. Union officials have become more aware than ever of the hazards facing their members on the job.

One area where there has been recent study is in **ergonomics,** *the science that seeks to adapt work to the capabilities of the human physique.* Even simple, repetitive tasks such as pulling, folding, pushing, and pounding can pose health problems. For example, workers who use their hands for tasks that involve constant bending at the wrist can fall victim to "carpal tunnel syndrome," one of many repetitive motion traumas, which can lead to numbness and tingling in the hands due to nerve damage caused when tendons and ligaments in the wrist pinch the nerves that control the fingers.[25] In one case Hanes

Signs like this one, put up by the United Auto Workers, are designed to help counter foreign imports. Though the UAW has traditionally opposed trade restrictions, it reversed its stance when foreign-made cars and parts threatened to cut 200,000 auto jobs by 1990. Now auto workers urge consumers to "buy American," and they're lobbying for new laws that would restrict competition from overseas.

Corporation agreed to pay a $100 fine, install adjustable chairs, spend more time training workers, and reduce T-shirt production quotas to help cut down excessive muscular stress.[26]

WHEN PLANT SHUTDOWN THREATENS

Increasingly, the closing of outmoded and inefficient plants has become a sign of the times. Complaining that a factory can't compete with newer, more efficient competitors, or that union wages make the plant unprofitable, management announces that the facility will close and that thousands will be out of work. Union response to such threats, as we have noted earlier, can take the form of concessions to keep the plant open. But all too often little can be done and the factory closes.

CLOSING PROBLEMS

A factory closing can cause a wide variety of problems. Some, such as unemployment and financial problems for the local area, are foreseeable. Others, such as alcoholism, drug abuse, depression, marital stress, and other psychological problems, are less obvious. Most plants close with little advance planning, and the workers bear the brunt of the problems.

But a plant closing doesn't have to take on tragic proportions. In Canada and in half a dozen European nations, employers are required by law to give advance notice of their intention to close a plant. They must then structure a program to help their employees make the transition to other jobs and, if necessary, retrain them in new, more marketable skills. There appears little likelihood that such laws will be passed in the United States, but some companies have voluntarily taken similar steps. Dana Corporation, for example, closed a plant in Wisconsin that employed 1,600 workers. Before closing, Dana located more than 3,000 jobs that its laid-off employees could fill, thus providing a safety net for them. Similarly, Brown & Williamson, required by its contract to notify the union eighteen months before closing its plant, instead gave three years' notice, transferred 350 of its 2,700 workers to a new plant, and arranged for vocational training, financial counseling, health insurance, and six months' severance pay for those it didn't transfer. The Tobacco Workers Union credits Brown & Williamson for working closely with the union to make the closing as painless as possible.[27]

Some employers are less interested in making a closing painless than they are in getting rid of a union or forcing a pay cut. In April 1983, for example, Wilson Foods filed for protection under Chapter 11 of the Bankruptcy Code, set aside its agreement with the union, and unilaterally cut wages by 40 percent to 50 percent. Wilson contended that it was losing $1 million a week, and that the wage-and-benefit package of $17 an hour that its workers were getting was substantially higher than what its competitors were paying their workers.

The union response to Wilson's move was to claim that the meatpacker was using the Bankruptcy Code illegally, and that its unilateral reduction in wages was an unfair labor practice. The union threatened to strike, but held off for fear of forcing Wilson to close for good. Meanwhile, union workers stayed on the job and took matters into their own hands: they slowed their production down by 40 percent to 50 percent, to reflect the pay cut that had been forced on them.[28]

Other employers have chosen to go the "alter ego" route, shutting a plant down and then selling it to another company—one that is supposedly independent but is actually under the control of the old employer. Esmark spun off its Swift & Company meatpacking operations to a new, independent firm called Swift Independent Packing Company, which took over the plants and reopened them using nonunion labor. The United Food & Commercial Workers Union, which represented the old Swift employees, filed a grievance with the NLRB but has been unsuccessful in pressing its claim. General Host (which owned Cudahy Company, a meatpacker) also tried this method, closing down its Denver packing plant and then selling Cudahy to its management. The company was rechristened Bar-S Foods Company, and eleven days after the plant had been closed, the company reopened it using nonunion workers who were earning $5 an hour less than the union workers they replaced.[29]

Other employers use a scheme called the "double-breasted employer." The parent company—which may be fully unionized—solicits work, but management then passes the work off to a nonunion entity controlled by the same employer.[30]

THE EMPLOYEE-OWNERSHIP SOLUTION

When all else fails, the employees of a plant threatened with shutdown may be able to buy the plant themselves, thus preserving their jobs, via an **employee stock ownership plan** (often called an **ESOP**). In 1984, about 6,000 firms in the United States had some form of plan for awarding employees shares of company stock. Some of these ESOPs are set up to motivate workers; some have been offered by management in return for bargaining concessions (Pan American did this in 1983); but in other cases, they offer a way to rescue a business that's failing. One of the more recent conversions to employee ownership was the Weirton steel mill in Weirton, West Virginia, once owned by National Steel Company. After being acquired by its employees in early 1983, Weirton Steel emerged as one of the ten largest steel mills in the United States, and with sales of nearly $1 billion a year, it also became one of the 400 largest companies in the United States.

The acquisition of the plant by its employees proved to be a good deal for both National Steel and for those who worked at the mill. National had announced plans to scale back operations and ultimately phase the plant out of operation. But closing the plant would have been expensive, since the steelmaker had pension liabilities of $400 million. Giving employees an opportunity to buy the mill solved this problem; moreover, it gave employees a chance to save their own jobs and help support the local economy. The mill was the largest employer in the state, with 7,000 employees (down from a peak of 12,000), and the economy of the entire region depended on the mill. Once they acquired the mill, the workers could do things that the management at National Steel couldn't do. ESOP-owned operations are eligible for certain tax benefits. Also, the workers voted to take a 32 percent pay cut, which would reduce operating costs by $128 million a year. (Before the pay cut, the typical Weirton Steel worker earned between $35,000 and $40,000 annually.) And favorable financing was possible. The Weirton ESOP issued stock in trust, which was then used as collateral for a loan to finance the purchase of the company.

The employee purchase of the mill in Weirton was met with enthusiasm, but some observers questioned whether it was fair to other steelmakers, who face many of the same problems, to give Weirton access to capital on favorable terms and to the tax breaks that go with ESOPs. Other observers also questioned whether the employee management (the board of directors is made up of two representatives each of labor and management, plus six outsiders) would be able to make tough decisions on layoffs, if it ever came to that. Nonetheless, the Weirton employees were excited about having saved their jobs and being their own "bosses."[31]

WHEN LABOR AND MANAGEMENT CONFRONT EACH OTHER

In the early days of unionism, when conflicts arose over basic issues such as money and working conditions, both sides used pressure tactics that are now illegal. To defy management, the unions used threats of force, property damage, violence against reluctant workers, and sabotage (attempts to hold up production processes). To try to prevent the spread of unionism, management used several weapons. One was the **yellow-dog contract**—*an agreement that forced workers, as a condition of employment, to promise not to join or remain in a union.* Another was the **blacklist**—*a secret list circulated among employers to keep union organizers from getting jobs.* These tactics were outlawed in the 1930s, but both sides still have a range of powerful weapons they can use when cooperation breaks down.

LABOR'S WEAPONS

The strike

The most powerful weapon organized labor can use is the **strike**, *a temporary work stoppage aimed at forcing management to accept union demands.* The basic idea behind the strike is that, in the long run, it costs management more in lost earnings to resist union demands than to give in. As unions began to resist management wage-concession pressures with the

strengthening of the economic recovery in 1983, strike activity started to rise, with bitter walkouts at AT&T, Continental Airlines, and other companies. Nationwide, work time lost in strikes involving 1,000 or more workers was running 10 percent higher than in the year before.[32] A strike as violent as those of unions' early days occurred at the Phelps Dodge copper mine in Arizona in August 1983.

An essential part of the strike is **picketing**: *union members* known as pickets *are positioned at entrances to company premises, where they march back and forth to try to persuade nonstriking workers and others not to do business with the company.* Picketing can help publicize the union's case to the general public: in most instances one union will honor another's picket line, so that even a relatively small union can shut down an employer by persuading other union members not to cross their picket line. Thus, striking department-store employees can close down a business if union truckers won't cross their picket line to make deliveries.

No matter how justified a union may feel its strike is, though, no one ever really wins a strike. Union members must do without their pay during the period of the strike, and management loses sales and profits that it will probably never be able to recover. In 1982 and 1983 a new trend seemed to be developing, whereby companies would prepare to continue operating throughout a strike, believing they must do so to survive. There seemed to be less respect for picket lines, and management's tough stance had a demoralizing effect on some unions. Yet if these new management tactics promised to strengthen companies in the short run, in the long run they threatened to bring more problems: some labor leaders claimed they would simply call more strikes, so the conflict could escalate in the future.[33]

Boycotting

A more indirect but equally powerful weapon is the **boycott**, in which *union members and sympathizers refuse to buy or handle the product or service produced by a target company.* Millions of union members form an enormous bloc of purchasing power, which can pressure management into making concessions.

Financial influence

Unions also have huge financial assets, including the $200 billion of assets in their members' pension funds, which they can use to exert influence. In an effort to persuade Mellon Bank of Pittsburgh to release a frozen bank account that contained $250,000 of its members' wages and health benefits, the United Steelworkers urged all of its members and sympathizers in mid-1983 to withdraw their funds from the bank. The union claimed that some $12 million was withdrawn from Mellon Bank, which has assets of nearly $12 billion.[34]

Political influence

Unions have significant political power, which they can obviously use by endorsing candidates and (theoretically, at least) delivering the votes of union members. But even more effective is the direct participation of union members in the electoral process. In 1980 some 500 union members were delegates to the Democratic presidential nominating convention. Labor unions can also be very active behind the scenes. They can raise funds for candidates; the Committee on Political Education (COPE) founded by the AFL-CIO in 1955, for example, solicits funds from union members for distribution to candidates favorable to labor's positions. In 1982 labor unions increased their political contributions by more than 40 percent over 1980, and 64.5 percent of the congressional and gubernatorial candidates labor endorsed were elected.[34]

Waging a publicity battle

One of the newer weapons labor has used is the publicity attack—mounting a concerted news and promotion campaign not only against the target company but against all companies affiliated with it. Thus, when J. P. Stevens, the textile giant, continued to resist direct efforts to unionize its workers, the Amalgamated Clothing and Textile Workers Union mounted an indirect attack with ads, letters, phone calls, and news releases, bringing pressure to bear on Stevens' lenders, major stockholders, and outside board members. Stevens had been famous— or notorious—as America's No. 1 labor-law violator.

In October 1983, it finally agreed to end its twenty-year battle with the union, with a $1 million payment to the union and $200,000 in back pay to employees it had dealt with unfairly. Similarly, faced with a situation where it felt it was being pressured by International Paper, the United Paperworkers Union moved to start a campaign to drive a wedge of publicity between the company and those it had to deal with. The Paperworkers retained Ray Rogers, who had planned the J. P. Stevens campaign, to create a similar effort aimed at International Paper. But before the campaign could get off the ground, International Paper and the union came to an agreement under which a high-level committee would be set up to resolve disagreements.[36]

MANAGEMENT'S WEAPONS

Using strikebreakers

When union members walk off their jobs, management has the right to replace them with **strikebreakers,** *people who cross the picket line to work.* (Union sympathizers call them "scabs," an uncomplimentary term.) But it is often difficult for companies to find qualified substitutes, since many of those with the necessary skills are union members themselves. In some cases, however, management has succeeded in diminishing the impact of a strike by substituting white-collar and supervisory personnel for the striking workers.

The lockout

The United States Supreme Court has upheld the use of the **lockout,** in which *management prevents workers from entering a struck business in order to pressure a union to accept management's last contract proposal.* A lockout is legal, however, only if unions and management have come to an impasse in negotiations.

The lockout enables managers to operate a plant themselves or shut it down. It is rarely used today in major industries, but some examples still occur: when newly militant representatives of the Major League Baseball Players Association were negotiating with team owners in 1976, several own-

THE HIGH-TECH HORIZON

HOW COMPANIES USE COMPUTERS TO SURVIVE STRIKES

In 1983, several very unusual strikes hit a number of U.S. industries. They included a nationwide strike against AT&T involving some 700,000 workers and 150 million customers; a strike in New York against the utility Consolidated Edison, again involving thousands of workers; a major strike against several oil refineries in various localities; and a strike at a jet engine plant in Ohio. What was so odd about these actions? Simply that despite their size, the strikes had very little effect on either management or the public. In certain industries, some large companies have found it possible to survive strikes simply by depending on their computers. In the words of Harley Shaiken of MIT, "Automation has shifted the whole balance of power in favor of management"—in industries where operations can be computerized on a large scale.

At AT&T, for example, 97 percent of all telephone calls go through automatically; human help is needed only where operator assistance is required. Similarly, at Consolidated Edison and the oil refineries, procedures are so highly automated that little human intervention is necessary. And at the Ohio engine plant, supervisors and secretaries—again thanks to automation—were able to take over the work of highly trained machinists.

A couple of other factors make it harder for strik-ers to drive their message home. One is the changing ratio of workers to supervisors that has been made possible by the computer in telecommunications-related industries. (At AT&T, the ratio has shifted from 5:1 to 2:1 over the past twenty years.) This lower ratio makes it easier for supervisors to take over. Another factor is the increasing use of electronic data transfer: a strikebound office can send its raw data by satellite to another office that is fully manned. As Shaiken says, "Once you have an operation tied into telecommunications, you can leapfrog the picket line."

Overall, computers have enhanced management's power in union-management relations in some high-tech industries, led numerous strikes to fail, and reduced the total number of strike actions. It's true that this type of victory comes at a price, since striking workers are likely to express their anger somehow. At AT&T, where more than 2,000 cases of vandalism were reported, workers took out their frustration on the new electronic "scabs." But management still seems to have come out ahead, since it has learned just how easily it can manage without labor, or with only skeleton staffs. That realization has led many bosses to wonder whether they weren't overstaffed to begin with, and this makes unions—the voice of labor—sound less persuasive than ever. Like high unemployment (which makes it easier to replace strikers) and the practice of stockpiling inventories, computerization has increased management's bargaining power.

SOURCE: "'Telescabbing': The New Union Buster," *Newsweek*, August 29, 1983, pp. 53, 54.

ers locked the players out of their spring training camp in Florida.

Injunctions

An **injunction** is *a court order, directing someone to do something or to refrain from doing it.* Management used this weapon without restrictions in the early days of unionism. Then, companies typically sought injunc-tions to order striking workers back to work on the grounds that they were interfering with business. Today, injunctions are legal only in certain cases. They are most often invoked by city governments against striking public employees in states where such strikes are illegal. The president also has the right, under the Taft-Hartley Act, to obtain a temporary injunction to halt a strike he deems harmful to the national interest.

Pacts and organizations

Business has copied the united-front strategy of the AFL-CIO; some industries have mutual assistance pacts in which they temporarily agree to abandon competition in order to assist a competitor singled out for a strike. Such agreements provide a form of strike insurance to help the company hold out against union demands.

Certain industries have also formed national organizations, such as the National Association of Manufacturers, to counterbalance the powerful national unions. These organizations try to coordinate industry-wide strategy and keep wage and benefit levels even between companies. They also lobby alongside company lobbyists for legislation to protect management against union demands.

COLLECTIVE BARGAINING

Having seen something of what both sides of a labor dispute can do to each other once they've reached the point of no return in their confrontation, let's take a look at some of the more peaceable alternatives. Fortunately, not every labor disagreement ends in a strike; the large majority of labor-management disagreements are defused before they explode into strikes. A number of techniques are used to resolve labor-management conflicts; the most widely used is collective bargaining.

The negotiating process is basically a guessing game. The union tries to guess how far management will go, and management tries to guess what the union's breaking point will be—the point at which it will call a strike. Since neither side really wants a strike, it is in the interest of both parties to bargain to a reasonable compromise.

PREPARATION

Before negotiations can begin, the union negotiating team must thoroughly understand the key demands of its members—since the rank and file must eventually **ratify** (*approve*) the contract by majority

vote. The management side, meanwhile, tries to anticipate the union's demands and calculates the point at which labor's proposals are likely to cost them more than a strike will. Of course, these realistic estimates are withheld from the other side at this stage, for each side is trying to outguess the other. Both may come to the bargaining table with extreme positions from which they can fall back during actual bargaining. Management may offer a contract with no wage gains, for instance, and the union may demand an outrageous pay increase. Neither expects these first demands to be met.

Before or during negotiations, the union may flex its muscle by calling a strike vote. This vote does not signal an actual strike. It is called merely to show management that the union members are standing solidly behind their negotiating team and to remind management that a strike *is* possible when the current contract expires.

MEETING

When the negotiating teams actually sit down together, management's chief negotiator may be the vice-president in charge of industrial relations or someone hired from the outside. The union's chief negotiator may be the local's executive director or a negotiator supplied by national headquarters, an alternative that is often preferable because people's nerves can be frayed in the grueling bargaining sessions. The meetings can last twelve to fifteen hours near the end of negotiations—and calm discussion may give way to personal insults, which don't help if a union negotiator has to go back to work later in a supervised job.

PRESENTING DEMANDS AND REACHING AN AGREEMENT

Once the negotiating teams have assembled, they state their demands and each side discusses them point by point. Labor usually wants additions to the current contract. Management counters with the changes it wants, including, at times, deletions from the contract. After many stages of bargaining, each party presents its package of terms. Any gaps be-

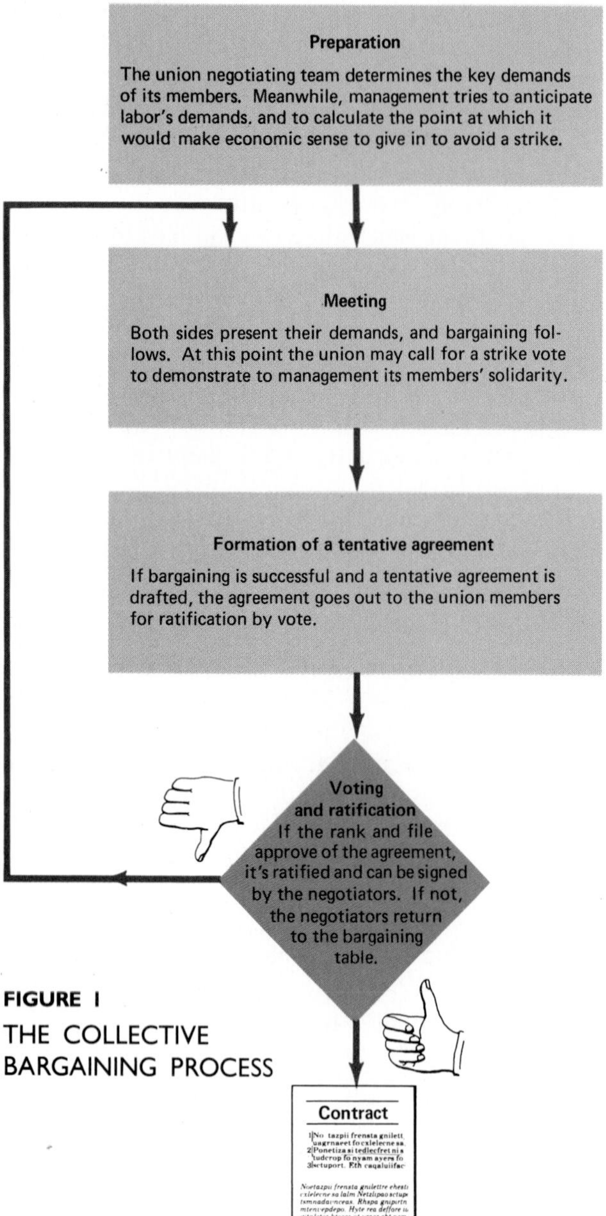

Preparation

The union negotiating team determines the key demands of its members. Meanwhile, management tries to anticipate labor's demands, and to calculate the point at which it would make economic sense to give in to avoid a strike.

Meeting

Both sides present their demands, and bargaining follows. At this point the union may call for a strike vote to demonstrate to management its members' solidarity.

Formation of a tentative agreement

If bargaining is successful and a tentative agreement is drafted, the agreement goes out to the union members for ratification by vote.

Voting and ratification

If the rank and file approve of the agreement, it's ratified and can be signed by the negotiators. If not, the negotiators return to the bargaining table.

FIGURE I

THE COLLECTIVE BARGAINING PROCESS

Contract

Obstacles to bargaining

If one side is unwilling to discuss a point, the other side is entitled to ask the National Labor Relations Board (NLRB) to rule on whether the topic must be discussed or may be omitted.

Failure to reach an agreement

If the negotiators seem unable to reach an agreement, a third party may be called in. The third party may be a conciliator, a mediator, or an arbitrator. (These terms are explained in the text.)

tween what labor wants and what management is willing to concede are then dealt with—sometimes in haste as the current contract's expiration date draws near.

If the bargaining process is successful and a tentative agreement is drafted, it goes to the rank and file for ratification. Finally, if the rank and file agree to the new contract, it is signed by the negotiators. Of course, at times the rank and file refuse to go along with the agreement their representatives have hammered out, and the negotiators must go back to the bargaining table.

What if one side or the other simply refuses to discuss a point? If one side is unwilling even to talk about a point, the other side can ask the National Labor Relations Board to rule on whether *the topic is one that can be omitted* (a **permissive subject**) or *one that must be discussed* (a **mandatory subject**).

THE GRIEVANCE PROCEDURE

The signing of a contract between labor and management doesn't mark the end of negotiations. Rather, it lays the groundwork for negotiations that will continue throughout the life of the contract to iron out details that were unspecified in the contract, and to deal with **grievances**, *disagreements that arise from changes in working conditions or from decisions made by lower-level managers.* Typically, grievances arise when a union member feels he or she has been passed over for promotion, isn't getting a fair share of overtime, or is being asked to work too much overtime.

Problems such as these are referred first to the **shop steward** (*a union member elected by the other union members*), who will discuss them with the employee's immediate supervisor. If these discussions fail, the problem may then be discussed by the chief steward and the department head. The next step in the negotiation process brings together the union grievance committee and the human resources (or personnel) manager. If they fail to solve the grievance, it is then up to the union **business agent** (*a full-time union staffer*) and the plant manager to try to resolve the issue.

In the final step of the process, the worker's complaint goes to an **arbitrator**, *whose powers are de-*

fined in the contract and whose ruling is, in most cases, final. Arbitration is generally considered a last resort, to be avoided if at all possible—if a grievance goes to arbitration both labor and management lose control of the situation.

Because the arbitration process can be complicated and expensive, there has been a shift to **grievance mediation**, where *a neutral third party meets with both sides and attempts to steer them toward a solution to the problem.* One study showed that the typical mediation meeting cost $250, as compared to $1,025 for arbitration, and that the average wait for a mediation session was only thirteen days as compared to twenty-five days for an arbitration session. The study also reported that thirty-two of the thirty-seven grievances mediated were resolved, and only five had to go to binding arbitration. Of those five cases, the arbitrator denied the grievances, as the mediator had predicted.[37]

NEW DIRECTIONS IN LABOR-MANAGEMENT RELATIONS

In the continuing battle between management and labor, management has found a new weapon: granting its nonunionized employees many of the same benefits enjoyed by union members. These benefits include salaries competitive with those earned by union members plus other attractive items, including liberal work rules, seniority privileges, and even formal grievance procedures. One study showed that 30 percent of all nonunion employers had for-

mal grievance procedures in place. These programs are designed to take the rough edges off employer-employee relations in nonunion companies and to make for a generally more harmonious workplace. Employers are recognizing that if they don't offer their workers these benefits, the unions will come in, organize the workers, and negotiate for them.[38]

Another factor in the changing balance of power between labor and management is the changing role of government. While past years saw much key legislation protecting the unions in their right to organize, no new legislation has been passed in this area in recent years, despite union efforts. But there has been legislation that directly guides and controls the actions of management, without unions' having to step in. There are now laws mandating health and safety standards on the job, as well as a variety of federal and local laws that prohibit discrimination on the basis of race, sex, or age. New legislation has also mandated employers' responsibility for pension plans, and the minimum wage law has been steadily expanded to include all workers. Unions once had to fight for these items; now the government regulates them.[39]

Faced with this basic change in the relationship between management and labor, the unions have started reconsidering their position and changing the way they operate. In addition to making organizing attempts in areas that they once avoided (such as clerical workers), the unions have also started calling attention to the benefits they can provide to *employers.* For one thing, unions can provide skilled workers who are less likely to quit; they offer a source of responsible labor.[40] Unions have also been stressing their ability to help train people and upgrade their skills.

CHAPTER REVIEW

Organizations formed by workers to advance their interests are called unions. Although some unions had appeared in the United States as early as 1792, the union

movement remained relatively weak even as late as 1886, when the AFL was founded. The great period of union growth began in 1932, when the government began to protect labor. The CIO took advantage of the situation to organize large numbers of unskilled workers into industrial un-

ions. Expansion was further spurred by full employment during World War II and continued until the Taft-Hartley Act was passed in 1947. Membership has leveled off since 1955, and the high-tech revolution—along with overseas competition—is posing new challenges. However, unions still play an important role.

Although unions have gained public-sector employees, they have lost membership elsewhere. The blue-collar sector is shrinking while the union-resistant white-collar sector grows. Also, hard times have forced unions to (1) moderate their demands and (2) cut back their own staffs. To regain strength, unions are now focusing their organizing efforts on workers in high-tech industries and on white-collar workers, using new techniques and issues to reach them.

The major issues that come up in union-management negotiation are union security and management rights, compensation, job security and promotion, work rules, and especially today, safety and health.

Unions put pressure on employers through strikes, picketing, boycotts, financial and political influence, lobbying or other political activities, and publicity campaigns. Although management has fought labor with yellow-dog contracts, blacklists, strikebreakers, lockouts, and injunctions, most disputes are now settled through collective bargaining. Skilled negotiators work to achieve an employment contract that will embody agreements on everything from union security to safety conditions. Its terms must be ratified by the union rank and file. Stalemates are resolved by arbitrators. Lately, unions have begun to settle for benefits other than wage increases.

Sometimes changes in work rules can improve productivity and prevent plant closings. Where a closing is unavoidable, the employer can often ease the blow or employees may be able to buy the plant and keep it in operation.

Some companies are able to forestall unionization by treating workers well without union pressure. Even if workers do unionize, however, conflict may not be inevitable; it is possible for unions and management to work together for higher productivity.

KEY WORDS

labor unions (186)

collective bargaining (186)

craft unions (187)

industrial union (188)

National Labor Relations Act (Wagner Act) (188)

Taft-Hartley Labor-Management Relations Act (188)

Landrum-Griffin Act (188)

Equal Employment Act (191)

closed shop (192)

union shop (192)

right-to-work laws (192)

agency shop (192)

open shop (192)

dues checkoff (192)

fringe benefit (193)

lifetime security (194)

ergonomics (195)

employee stock ownership plan (ESOP) (197)

yellow-dog contract (198)

blacklist (198)

strike (198)

picketing (198)

boycott (198)

strikebreakers (199)

lockout (199)

injunction (200)

ratify (201)

permissive subject (202)

mandatory subject (202)

grievances (202)

shop steward (202)

business agent (202)

arbitrator (202)

grievance mediation (203)

REVIEW QUESTIONS

1. Trace the history of the rise of the labor movement in the United States.

2. Discuss the factors that are contributing to the decline in the power of unions today.

3. What are the basic issues in labor-management relations?

4. What new groups of workers are unions trying to reach, and what strategies are they using?

5. Describe the weapons that labor and management use against one another.

6. Explain the three steps involved in collective bargaining.

7. How have recent economic trends affected labor-management relations, and what are the two sides doing by way of compromise?

CASE I

THE GREYHOUND BUS PACT: BIG GUNS VERSUS LITTLE GUYS

Until around October 1982, most economy-minded intercity travelers used to do as they were told in the slogan "Go Greyhound, and leave the driving to us." But then the transport industry was hit by deregulation, which allowed smaller intercity bus lines and even airlines to offer better fares than Greyhound. In 1983, for example, Greyhound lost $16 million during a price war with Trailways, and on some routes People Express was selling plane tickets at less than half of Greyhound's price. Still, the company continued to make a good profit—$76.2 million during the first nine months of 1983—and management got a healthy raise on the grounds that the competition had a more favorable executive wage scale.

One might not expect a historic "union-busting" confrontation to arise from a situation like this. Yet one did—the much-talked about Greyhound bus strike of 1983. According to Greyhound's chairman, John W. Teets, the company had lost its niche as the leading provider of low-cost ground transportation, was losing business, and was facing drastic cutbacks in routes. As Teets put it, "We have the highest-paid employees in the bus transportation business. We need—no, we must have—parity ['an equal wage level'] with other carriers." With this in mind, he outlined terms for a new contract to the Amalgamated Transit Union (ATU), which represents some 12,700 Greyhound employees: the workers would have to accept a 9.5 percent wage cut and a reduction in benefits, or the company would run the buses without them. He gave the workers two weeks to make up their minds.

In some observers' opinion, the two sides were unevenly matched. The union was relatively small, modestly financed, and unaggressive; it had long had a close, trusting relationship with Greyhound. Its last strike of any note against the company lay almost twenty years in the past. But well-heeled Greyhound, in presenting its demands, had prepared to pull out a lot of big guns, including the following:

- A multimillion-dollar national ad campaign explaining its position and promising to resume full service with nonunion personnel within ninety days of a strike
- A hiring and training program for 1,300 nonunion workers
- A half-price fare campaign to lure riders
- The resolve to hold out, regardless of cost, as long as it took to convince the union that the company wouldn't back down

That wasn't all. Greyhound geared up heavily for the anticipated strike. Again in Teet's words:

I learned long ago that you have to have plans, and backup plans. . . . The No. 1 assumption was that we'd have to operate during the strike. . . . Lawyers were designated in 150 cities to get temporary restraining orders or injunctions where necessary. . . . We dug holes in the ground so that rent-a-fences could be put up overnight around our buses. . . . We had hand-held video cameras at every terminal so that if anyone damaged the property we didn't get into arguments—"Yes, you did," "No, I didn't." It's a federal violation to interfere with a moving intercity bus, and we wanted hard evidence.

The strike began on November 3, Greyhound ran the buses and stuck by its demands, and the union stood firm. As the weeks wore on each side only became more stubborn. While the union hinted that the buses were unsafe in the hands of inexperienced drivers, the public tended to side with the Hound, partly thanks to the ad campaign. Although the ATU did fend off two "final offers," the negotiators, having no fallback positions, found themselves up against the wall. Finally, in early December, they opted to give in, reasoning "It's better to eat a little crow than get replaced." The deal they arranged (and which the workers later approved) was costly, since it included a 7.8 percent wage cut, a temporary freeze on cost-of-living adjustments, new or increased employee contributions to pension and health plans, and a "two-tier" program, whereby "second-tier"

workers (those hired after October 31, 1983) would start off with lower wages and benefits than their predecessors had enjoyed. The agreement did give the union a couple of small victories, allowing it to preserve current worker seniority and to protect the job security of its members (that is, no jobs were eliminated).

Back at headquarters, Teets said he was "delighted," saying, "Everything is about what we had planned. We made several concessions that were important to the union but . . . not as important to us." Although the bus runs were almost back to normal by Christmas, the strike ended up costing Greyhound over $25 million—not to mention the fact that it greatly solidified the union. In the long run, however, Greyhound will be able to cut operating expenses and expand services.[41]

1. What is your opinion of management's strategy and the union's strategy in the Greyhound strike?

2. How do the various points in the Greyhound pact reflect new trends in labor-management relations today?

3. Which points in the pact favor management? Which points favor the union? Do you think they balance out fairly? Do you think they will help each side reach its stated objectives (will the compromise prove workable for both sides)?

4. Are there any strategies that the union might have used but didn't?

5. In what ways might the Greyhound pact have set an example for other industries to follow?

UNIONIZATION AT DISNEY WORLD AND EPCOT CENTER

Yesterday central Florida had only some orange groves and communities of elderly people. Today, it's playing host to one of the biggest economic booms in the country. For example:

- An 814-room Hilton Hotel is going up.
- Also being built is a 750-room Hyatt Hotel—part of a $600 million project.
- MCA/Universal is building a Universal City/Florida studio tour park that will cost more than $170 million.
- Companies such as American Bell and Westinghouse are moving plants—and hundreds of workers—from the North to this area.

All together, there will be about $17 billion of new construction in central Florida by 1986, and some 90,000 new jobs will become available over the next few years. The city of Orlando, at the center of all this, is said to have "the expectant air . . . of Anchorage [Alaska] just before the [Alaskan oil] pipeline hit." What has attracted so much enterprise to this particular place? Actually, it's all due to Mickey Mouse, or rather to his spin-offs—Disney World and Epcot (the Experimental Prototype Community of Tomorrow). In addition to drawing tens of millions of tourists to central Florida, these attractions and others have stimulated the region's economy, bringing in—along with the entrepreneurs—thousands of workers, organized crime, and unions.

The appearance of the unions came as a jolt to the Disney management, which had tried to discourage unionization and continues to do so at Disneyland in Anaheim, California. In fact, the Disney managers' opposition to organized labor had sat well with the local citizens, who, like many southerners, had always tended to dislike unions. But the press had already made note of unhappiness among Mickey and his pals (low pay; hot, dirty costumes; obnoxious patrons), and management was eager to avoid more bad publicity. So management decided to let the unions in. Today, not only Mickey but also Minnie, Donald Duck, Goofy, and many of their colleagues are members of Teamsters Local 385 in Orlando, and sixteen other unions are also active at the Disney complex.

Apart from maintaining its pleasant image and continuing to collect good profits, the Disney management got another benefit from its acceptance of the unions: control of organized crime. During the construction of the Epcot Center, labor racketeers had moved in among the nonunionized workers. They had forced management to pay extortionate rates and had destroyed equipment when their demands were not met. By agreeing to use only union labor in future construction projects, the Disney people had ensured labor peace and forced the racketeers to do their dirty work elsewhere.

For the unions, these developments were on the plus side. But many projects are still being manned by nonunion labor, and many employers continue to hold out. How are the unions reacting? Some are making concessions, offering to lower their hourly rates of pay so as to win jobs away from unorganized labor. Others have become all the more militant, saying, "We're not going to put up with nonunion contractors."

Will the unions continue to make headway in this once hostile territory? Any gains are likely to be hard-won, mainly because Orlando's politics still remain conservative. Although unions may be tolerated, they are still disliked and strikes are discouraged. Besides, cheap nonunion labor is plentiful and the local law-enforcement officials willingly help contractors guard their nonunion work sites.[42]

1. Do you think that it was good strategy for the Disney management to let the unions come in? Why or why not?

2. Do you think it was a good idea for the unions to make wage concessions?

3. Apparently the majority of workers in the area are not interested in becoming unionized. Speculate on why this might be.

HUMAN RESOURCES MANAGEMENT

The booming economy of California's Silicon Valley has not been an unmixed blessing for the employees who work for the ultracompetitive high-technology firms there. Although some have enjoyed the dizzying pace, the stress of long work weeks has caused problems for others. Recently, some of the valley's employers have become concerned about the well-being of their workers. Hewlett-Packard and National Semiconductor have provided sports and recreational facilities; other firms offer help with drug, alcohol, financial, and marital problems.

In other parts of the country human resources managers have quite different concerns. In the upper Midwest thousands of workers in the steel, automobile, and rubber industries need retraining to work in other fields. And around the nation personnel departments are seeking ways to ensure that women and other minority workers are treated fairly by their companies. The field of human resources management, once concerned primarily with hiring, firing, and employee benefits, faces a number of new challenges today.

CHAPTER FOCUS

After reading this chapter, you will be able to:
- state the function of human resource managers
- define job analysis, and cite several means of conducting one
- distinguish a job description from a job specification
- name the stages in the worker selection process
- name three controversies surrounding equal opportunity in employment
- describe the changing role of women in American business
- list several means of training workers and managers
- name at least five methods of compensation
- discuss at least three options companies have to reduce their work force
- list at least three standard employee fringe benefits
- cite several ways of evaluating employees

In the early 1980s unemployment was front-page news as plants closed—often permanently—and workers by the thousands were laid off in the steel, rubber, and automobile industries. But even as the nation was considering the problems of the unemployed, managers in some industries began to worry about a coming *shortage* of workers. The job market in America is changing: though there are fewer jobs for factory workers in troubled "smokestack" industries, job opportunities are mushrooming in engineering, nursing, secretarial and paralegal work, and many other technical areas. Will there be enough people with skills in these areas to supply industries' needs? Business planners worry about reports that recent school graduates lack fundamental skills in reading and math. And they worry that the end of the baby boom will shrink the pool of new workers: by 1995, some experts believe the number of young people entering the labor market will have fallen by more than 10 percent.[1]

The coming shortage of technically trained workers is only one of the many concerns that are the responsibility of **human resources managers,** *the people in business organizations who forecast personnel needs, hire new workers, help train and educate personnel, and administer wages, salaries, and employee benefits and services.* Human resources management is becoming more and more complex and crucial as we reach the mid-1980s. Not only do we face snowballing technological change and a lack of workers with state-of-the-art skills, but economic and legal problems are looming ever larger. Human resources managers must figure out how to keep good workers when economic difficulties necessitate pay freezes; how to lay off workers equitably; how to retrain workers to enable them to cope with increasing automation and computerization; how to deal with increasingly complex (and expensive) employee benefits, such as pensions and health insurance; and how to cope with the challenge of equal opportunity in employment. Given the growing importance and complexity of human resources problems, it is scarcely surprising that all but the smallest businesses employ specialists to deal with them: for every 100 employees that a firm has, there is usually one human resources manager.

What exactly do human resources departments (sometimes known as personnel departments) do? While the specific duties assigned to them may vary quite a bit from one company to another, there are certain functions that every human resources staff must perform. In the pages that follow we shall consider these basic functions, beginning with human resources planning.

HUMAN RESOURCES PLANNING

Human resources planning is the first step in staffing business organizations. As one human resources staff director put it, it's not enough to have financial resources; a company *must* have "people on hand at the right time and in the right place to make a thing go."[2]

A miscalculation here could leave a company without enough staff to keep production up to the level of demand—with the result that business is lost as customers or clients go elsewhere. Yet, if a company expands its staff too rapidly, it may watch its profits disappear into payroll—or it may have to lay off the very people it just recruited and trained (at considerable expense). This situation confronted the Intel Corporation in early 1983, when an expected business upturn—which would be likely to speed up the demand for computer equipment—failed to materialize. Intel, anticipating greatly increased production, had hired 3,000 new workers the previous spring. But this misreading of economic conditions proved to be an awkward mistake. Orders for Intel's products, instead of setting new records, began to slump badly. However, rather than reduce its work force, Intel imposed a company-wide pay cut on its employees.[3]

JOB ANALYSIS

If you were the owner of a small business, you might be able to hire and evaluate your employees on an informal basis. You would be in a good position to know both the requirements of the jobs involved

Why do people leave their jobs? Some are fired, of course—but others choose to leave. Their reasons are various: some return to school, some take better jobs, some retire, some take time out for personal pursuits or family responsibilities, and some leave because of sexual harassment.

and how well your employees were meeting those requirements. In large organizations, however, management needs a more formal method of evaluating both jobs and employees' performance in them. To human resources specialists, *the process by which jobs are studied to determine the tasks and dynamics involved* is known as **job analysis.**

Several questions must be asked in job analysis. What tasks are involved in the job (what does the person do all day)? What qualifications and what skills are needed to do the job? (An architect, for example, must have a license; a secretary must be able to type.) What kind of setting does the job take place in? (Some jobs, such as sales, require extensive public contact; others, such as factory work, do not.) Is the job one in which there is much time pressure (such as newspaper reporting) or little time pressure (such as academic research)?

Any given job can thus be analyzed in a number of ways. If we consider one job—that of a college professor—we can see how job analysis works. A professor must have certain qualifications (usually a Ph.D. degree and teaching experience) in order to be hired. The professor's work could be broken down into a number of specific tasks: giving lectures, grading exams, leading seminars, supervising independent study, doing research, attending department meetings, and so on. The professor's job could be considered in terms of whether it requires

"people" skills as well as technical skills (it requires both). The professor's work could also be evaluated by its *results:* Are students learning anything in the professor's courses? Has he or she published any research, and if so, is it a major contribution to knowledge in the field?

You might wonder why all this analysis is necessary. But if you were the professor's superior, this breakdown would help you know whom to hire and whom to promote. It would also help you identify larger problems in the way duties are assigned. Perhaps no one is getting research done because teaching loads are too heavy. Or students' grades aren't being turned in on time because some professors have no teaching assistants to help them read hundreds of essay exams.

Job analysis can be carried out by a number of methods. In facilities such as factories, the duties of a job can be fairly easily defined. In such cases job analysis may make use of a *time-and-motion study,* analyzing jobs in terms of the physical movements they require. Another technique is *functional job analysis,* which focuses on the specific tasks (functions) of a job: Does the job require work with data, people, or things—or all three? What methods and techniques does it involve? What machines or other pieces of equipment are used? What products or services result? Functional job analysis is used by the U.S. Department of Labor to classify the many thousands of jobs that exist in our economy, and job planners often use similar scales to describe jobs.

Another job-analysis technique is the *Position Analysis Questionnaire (PAQ)*. The PAQ asks employees a number of questions about their work, focusing on the psychological processes the work requires (problem solving, combining information from several sources, and so on). The PAQ is oriented more to the worker than to the tasks of the job. It can often be helpful in counseling people about the kinds of jobs for which they are fitted. Yet another job-analysis technique, the *critical-incident method*, concerns itself with a few key demands of the job: for example, the employee may be required to meet a quota—so many letters typed or claims processed or boxes packed within an hour, for example. The critical-incident method is particularly helpful in evaluating employees' performance.

To obtain the information needed to do a job analysis, employers and human resources experts have several choices. They may simply ask employees for information, as in the PAQ. They may use *direct observation*—watching a factory worker, perhaps using a stopwatch or videotape to monitor his or her activities. In an *observation interview*, the employee is asked about the tasks involved in the job. Some employers have even asked employees to keep daily diaries describing exactly what they do during the work day.

Job analysis can be invaluable in large organizations, where management may need to keep tabs on hundreds or thousands of employees doing very different kinds of jobs. It can be expected to become still more important as managers seek ways to increase productivity. And because it is a relatively objective way of defining employee specifications, it also helps employers ensure fairness in recruiting and evaluating employees.

RECRUITING AND HIRING NEW WORKERS

After the job analysis has been completed, the human resources manager may develop a **job description** (see Figure 1), *a specific statement of the tasks*

```
                        JOB DESCRIPTION

Job Title _____  Job Number _____
Date Effective _____  Job Grade _____

Job Function:  Secretarial duties:  dictation, typing, routine correspondence and
               reports, record-keeping, distributing mail, scheduling appointments.
               Handle confidential information.

Duties and Responsibilities:  Transcribe letters, memos, reports from shorthand
               or dictating machine.  May include technical terminology.

        Take shorthand notes in meetings, transcribe into final form.

        Compose and type routine letters and memos.

        Read, distribute and follow up on incoming mail.

        Set up, maintain files of letters, reports, catalogs, manuals.

        Obtain information for supervisor.

        Answer telephone and take messages; monitor supervisor's incoming calls.

        Compose routine departmental reports.

        Set up and maintain records dealing with safety, output, employee time.

        Receive, disburse, keep records of petty cash funds.

        Receive visitors, schedule appointments.

        Order and maintain inventory of office supplies.

        Arrange travel reservations.

        Deal with confidential information.


Instruments, Equipment, or Machines:  Typewriter, dictating machine, xerographic
               copying machines.
```

FIGURE 1

JOB DESCRIPTION

A list of the tasks the job involves and the conditions under which the tasks are performed.

---

involved in the job and the conditions under which the holder of the job will work. The manager may also develop a **job specification,** *a statement describing the kind of person who would be best for the job—including the skills, education, and previous experience the job requires.*

The next step is to match up the job specification with an actual person, or a selection of people, from whom to choose. Where does the human resources department get these candidates? There are several avenues open to **recruiters,** that is, *the members of the human resources staff who are responsible for obtaining new workers.* Recruiters can promote employees within the company; they can use referrals made by employees; they can advertise in newspapers and work through public and private employment agencies; they can go to union hiring halls;

they can go to college campuses—they *may* resort to pirating key employees from other companies.

STAGES IN SELECTION

After going through at least one—but usually more—of the various recruitment channels, the human resources department may spend weeks and sometimes even months sifting through the many applications. Eventually, however, the choice is narrowed down, and the selection process begins. Exactly which method is used depends on the company, but there are certain basic processes which most companies go through.

First, a small number of qualified candidates are selected. A person may be chosen on the basis of a standard application that all candidates are required to fill out or on the basis of his or her **résumé**—*a summary of education, experience, interests, and other personal data compiled by the applicant*. Sometimes both sources of information are used. Next, each candidate is interviewed, and depending on the type of job at stake, the candidates may be asked to take a test or series of tests to gauge their abilities, aptitude, intelligence, interests, and sometimes even their personalities.

At some point in the selection process, often at the initial interview, the candidate is asked to fill out an application form, supplying certain personal and professional data. Typically, such forms include some questions about matters that are not strictly job-related (height, weight, marital status, number of dependents, arrest record, and so on). These questions are commonly included on application forms even in states where laws on the books forbid employers to ask such questions. Some companies who use such forms (often standard items ordered from a business stationer in another state) may unwittingly be violating the law.[4]

After the initial application and interview, there is usually another, more probing interview with the few most likely candidates, and following this, the candidates are interviewed by the person who will be the new worker's immediate supervisor. The supervisor and sometimes *his* or *her* supervisors pick the most suitable person, and the search is over—

provided that the candidate is all that he or she appears to be. This is made certain via reference checks and sometimes a physical examination.

ENSURING EQUAL OPPORTUNITY

As recently as twenty years ago, a job applicant's race, religion, sex, or national origin often determined whether he or she got any further than submitting a résumé. Since the passage of the Civil Rights Act of 1964, however, it has been against the law to discriminate against applicants—and personnel already employed—on these grounds. (A company can, however, discriminate on the basis of other characteristics that are also unrelated to skill or ability; it may, for example, routinely turn away homosexuals or candidates who wear unconventional clothes.) To help enforce the job provisions of the 1964 act and subsequent legislation, the federal government established the **Equal Employment Opportunity Commission (EEOC),** *a federal agency whose chief job is to handle discrimination complaints submitted to it*. It also issues guidelines for employers relating to human resources policies.

Since the passage of the Civil Rights Act, the number of complaints filed has been enormous. In the late 1970s over 5,000 employment discrimination cases were filed each year in federal district courts. The number of complaints filed with the EEOC has continued to increase. For the fiscal year 1981–82 the EEOC reported that 54,145 complaints were filed by individuals. In addition, state and local agencies that come under EEOC jurisdiction filed 38,255 complaints during the same period. While not all complaints filed with the EEOC are resolved through federal court action, the number of cases that are continues to rise. The backlog of unresolved complaints—which at one point had reached 130,000—had been reduced drastically to 7,700.[5]

Even as complaints of discrimination continued to come into the EEOC, the interpretation of the law was changing somewhat in the early 1980s. The Reagan administration, in keeping with its expressed opposition to "quotas" in hiring, told federal contractors in March 1983 not to set their goals for hiring women and minorities too high. Labor

AGE DISCRIMINATION IN EMPLOYMENT

Workers in middle age and beyond, many of them laid off or involuntarily retired after many years of faithful service to one company, have begun to seek relief in the courts. Although a federal law officially barring age discrimination in employment has been on the books since 1967, some employers have ignored it— and paid a hefty penalty. In 1982, for example, the Home Insurance Company was ordered to pay more than $6 million in back pay and pension benefits to former employees who had been forced to retire at sixty-two. In the same year the Consolidated Edison Company of New York agreed to pay $1.7 million to a group of 136 former managers who were discharged— apparently on the basis of age—in 1977.

More than 11,000 such cases are being filed with the EEOC each year, and this number is increasing annually. And the government continues to be sympathetic to the cause of older workers. In 1978 Congress raised the age of retirement (the age at which employees can be forced to resign) from sixty-five to seventy. In the same year those who complain of age discrimination were granted the right to a jury trial. This right (which those who complain of discrimination based on race or sex do not have) means that many more cases will probably be decided in the workers' favor, since juries are usually sympathetic to the problems of workers who have been asked to go because they are "too old."

The issue of age discrimination isn't likely to diminish in the near future. One reason is demographic: the aging baby-boom generation will be pushing hard for higher-level jobs held by older executives. Human resources planners are also alert to another trend— the tendency for older workers to stay on the job past the age of sixty-five or, if retired, to reenter the job market.

For many, extended employment has been made necessary by inflationary pressures that have eaten up fixed retirement incomes. For others, work is simply an alternative preferable to playing cards or knitting sweaters for the grandchildren.

SOURCE: Robert A. Snyder and Billie Brandon, "Riding the Third Wave: Staying on Top of ADEA Complaints," *Personnel Administrator*, February 1983, pp. 41–47; Arnold H. Lubasch, "U.S. Court Decides Cases on Age Bias," *New York Times*, December 16, 1982.

Department officials, through the Office of Federal Contract Compliance Programs, told companies, for example, that their yearly percentage goals for hiring blacks need not exceed the proportion of blacks in the population available to do a particular job.[6] Critics have suggested that such rule changes mean that efforts to ensure that women and minorities are hired will not be pursued. The revised interpretation of the law is further reflected in the policy changes of the reconstituted U.S. Commission on Civil Rights. In January 1984 the commission, with a new majority formed by members appointed by President Reagan, reversed the policy of the former commission, denounced the use of numerical quotas, and expressed its view that, in the future, the Supreme Court should forbid quotas that provide "preferential treatment" for women and minority groups.[7] In any case, the new interpretation of the law caused many companies to review their equal opportunity programs.

Nonetheless, the job-discrimination issue had by no means been put on the back burner during the early 1980s. A landmark agreement in 1983, the largest settlement to date of an EEOC complaint, required General Motors to spend $42.5 million over five years to increase the representation of women and minorities at all levels of the company. Significantly, the terms of the GM agreement included a new feature: GM was required to invest large sums in worker education and training, including $15 million for scholarships and college and university endowments for women and minorities and $8.9 million for in-house training to upgrade the skills of 1,250 workers.[8]

The entire subject of equal opportunity in employment is likely to remain controversial, with no solution likely to please either minorities and women, who complain of continuing discrimination, or white males, who complain of "quotas" or "reverse discrimination" that operates against their interest.

Testing

One much-debated aspect of the hiring process is *testing*—not just the actual tests that prospective employers give job applicants, but all devices they may use to categorize people in making personnel decisions. In the rush to make sure that tests were fair to women and to every minority, several government agencies imposed regulations and guidelines, and these regulations and guidelines often conflicted. In 1978 the EEOC, the departments of Justice and Labor, and the U.S. Civil Service issued some guidelines intended to clarify this situation.

The EEOC also changed its own emphasis. In the past it paid a good deal of attention to the *type* of tests that companies gave potential employees. But now it favors what it calls a "bottom line" approach: if a company has hired what the EEOC believes is a sufficient number of minorities and women, the EEOC will not take enforcement action against that company because of the type of tests it uses.

The handicapped

In recent years steps have been taken to guarantee equal job opportunities to the handicapped, a group that is not protected by the Civil Rights Act or the EEOC. According to one estimate, half of the handicapped who are capable of working are unemployed.[9] Since 1973, companies with government contracts for $2,500 or more have been required to make any "reasonable accommodation" necessary "to employ and advance in employment qualified handicapped individuals." The law's definition of "handicapped" covers both visible and nonvisible impairments. (Experts believe that handicapped job seekers facing the severest discrimination are not those conventionally regarded as disabled—the blind, deaf, or crippled—but instead those with diabetes, epilepsy, heart trouble, and cancer.)[10]

How effective has this law been? Little changed in the first six years after its enactment. A survey published in 1980 indicated that over 90 percent of the businesses affected by the 1973 law were not complying with it.[11] While there has been a marked improvement in the number of businesses complying with the law since then, the problems of equal job opportunities for the handicapped still exist. One major problem is satisfying the physical requirements of disabled workers—not only conditions on the job but also transportation to and from work. Another difficulty has been the attitude of employers, many of whom, despite massive evidence to the contrary, still believe that hiring the handicapped is a risky affair.[12]

On the other hand, some recent technological developments may make it easier for businesses to accommodate the needs of handicapped employees. One such device is the TDD, or telecommunications device for the deaf. This is a portable machine with a small keyboard and screen that, when plugged into a telephone, can transmit and receive messages. With such a device, a computer technician, for example, could go out to repair clients' machines, "calling" the office with the TDD for the next assignment. A device with a similar purpose is a pocket beeper that vibrates rather than beeps.[13]

WOMEN IN THE WORKPLACE

In 1960 women made up only 33.4 percent of the civilian labor force.[14] By 1983 this figure had climbed to 43.8 percent, and it is expected to reach 50 percent by 1990.[15] Obviously, an enormous number of American women are no longer full-time homemakers. But the median income for working women is about $10,000, while that for men is roughly $17,000. In other words, a woman's earnings are, on the average, only about 60 percent of a man's—a gap that has not narrowed in twenty years.[16]

One reason for the income gap is that the majority of women workers are doing the same kinds of work they have done for decades: as typists, secretaries, file clerks, salespeople, and waitresses. Inade-

MINORITIES AND WOMEN: WHERE ARE THEY TODAY?

Efforts to provide equal opportunity for minorities and women in the United States may be said to date from the Civil Rights Act of 1964, which made job discrimination illegal. In the years immediately following that law, a number of barriers fell as women and blacks began to enter the work force in more visible positions. Younger people, no longer satisfied with a vision of their future in a menial job, turned to college and professional training as a way of advancing themselves. Today, twenty years later, how much real progress have they made?

Women, on the whole, seem to have fared somewhat better than blacks as a group. Their participation in the labor force has grown steadily (to approximately 44 percent in 1983), and among highly educated and ambitious women, there have been some notable successes. For example, of the thirty-three women who earned MBAs at Harvard in 1973, only nine were making less than $50,000 in 1983. (The top earner among the women in that class was making more than $200,000, and four of her classmates

were making over $100,000.) On the other hand, the men in that same class were doing far better: more than one-third were making six-figure incomes.

Women with Harvard MBAs, of course, are hardly representative of women workers as a group. Even though more women are now working, and making more money than ever before, women workers as a group are still concentrated at the low end of the pay spectrum, where jobs lack prestige and offer little opportunity for advancement. Worse still, the Labor Department reported in 1982 that "the discrepancy between the average earnings of women and men hasn't lessened over the past two decades." In fact, compared with men, women earned proportionally *less* in 1981 than they did in 1955—ten years before "equal opportunity" came to be the law of the land.

For black workers, the deep economic recession of 1982–83 was yet another setback in what has been a difficult effort to increase their earnings. The situation for blacks has been similar to that for women: a few highly educated blacks have done well (but not as well as whites), while most black workers have remained in low-level, low-paying jobs. At the upper reaches of business, blacks, like women, are few. In 1981, for example, only about 4 percent of all corporate officials

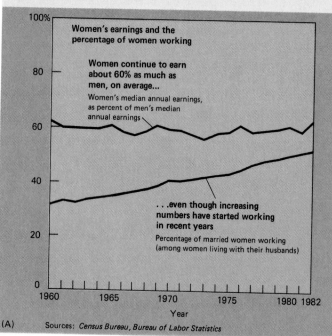

Women's earnings and the percentage of women working

Women continue to earn about 60% as much as men, on average...

Women's median annual earnings, as percent of men's median annual earnings

...even though increasing numbers have started working in recent years

Percentage of married women working (among women living with their husbands)

Year

(A)   Sources: *Census Bureau, Bureau of Labor Statistics*

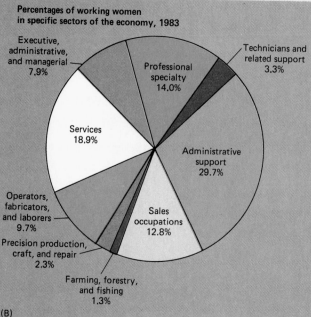

Percentages of working women in specific sectors of the economy, 1983

Executive, administrative, and managerial — 7.9%

Professional specialty 14.0%

Technicians and related support 3.3%

Services 18.9%

Administrative support 29.7%

Operators, fabricators, and laborers — 9.7%

Sales occupations 12.8%

Precision production, craft, and repair 2.3%

Farming, forestry, and fishing 1.3%

(B)

and managers in the United States were black. And of this select 4 percent, very few are top managers: none of America's thousand largest industrial companies is headed by a black. Even those blacks who have done very well generally earn less than whites with similar positions. (One civil rights attorney has estimated that black executives earn an average of $10,000 a year less than their white counterparts.)

Those few women and blacks who make it to the executive suite face common problems. Not only do they earn less, they also tend to "hit the ceiling" early: that is, they find themselves in jobs from which they cannot expect further advancement. (Some stuck in this position have quit to form their own companies—with good results.) Grappling with the long-held biases of many powerful white males in higher positions is also a common problem: blacks and women find that they are forced to prove themselves over and over, lest they be suspected of having gained their positions *because* they were black or female.

Most critical for some women executives and managers is the difficulty of combining a business career with marriage and child rearing. For those who earn enough, one solution is to hire housekeepers and baby-sitters (in effect, an extra "wife" to run the household and take care of the children). The typical business career—involving full-time work with no interruptions, long working hours, business travel, and the willingness to relocate if necessary—is very much a male pattern, one traditionally dependent on the presence of a wife with no outside employment. Women who have succeeded in business have done so by conforming to that pattern either by marrying a cooperative, self-sufficient man and hiring household help or by not marrying or not having children. Women executives, in fact, are far more likely to be single, divorced, or childless than are their male counterparts.

For both blacks and women, business achievement seems related to the same qualities as it does in white men: hard work, drive, confidence, and the willingness to take risks. These qualities, however, are not enough. An extra measure of talent, diplomacy, persistence, and sheer gumption—and the willingness to make personal sacrifices—may be needed to succeed.

SOURCE: Susan Dentzer and Renee Michael, "They Shall Overcome," *Newsweek*, May 23, 1983, pp. 60–62; Jennifer Bingham Hull, "Female Bosses Say Biggest Barriers Are Insecurity and 'Being a Woman,'" *The Wall Street Journal*, November 2, 1982; Roy Rowan, "How Harvard's MBAs Are Managing," *Fortune*, July 11, 1983; Bruce Serlen, "Mutterings from the Men's Room," *Working Woman*, May 1983, pp. 112–115.

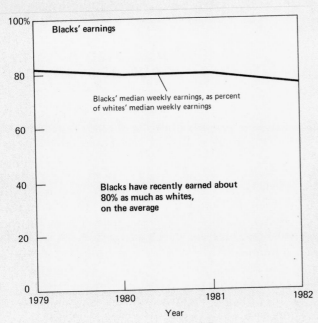

Blacks' earnings

Blacks' median weekly earnings, as percent of whites' median weekly earnings

Blacks have recently earned about 80% as much as whites, on the average

(C)   Sources: *Census Bureau, Bureau of Labor Statistics*

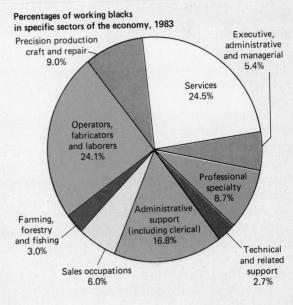

Percentages of working blacks in specific sectors of the economy, 1983

Precision production craft and repair 9.0%

Executive, administrative and managerial 5.4%

Services 24.5%

Operators, fabricators and laborers 24.1%

Professional specialty 8.7%

Farming, forestry and fishing 3.0%

Administrative support (including clerical) 16.8%

Technical and related support 2.7%

Sales occupations 6.0%

(D)

quate education has driven many women into low-paying jobs, as has lack of work experience. Discrimination is also a factor: many firms have been slow to hire and promote qualified women. And American business has a history of paying a woman less than a man receives for the same job. This practice was the target of the 1963 Equal Pay Act, which required firms to provide equal pay for men and women doing "substantially" equal work. The Equal Pay Act, together with the Civil Rights Act of 1964, has been the basis of a number of cases in which corporations have been charged with sex discrimination. Recently, there has also been debate over the concept of "comparable worth": equal pay scales for all workers whose jobs require equally demanding training and skills. (We discuss this and other issues related to discrimination against women and minorities in Chapter 1.)

Sexual harassment

One of the more sensitive issues concerning women in the workplace is **sexual harassment,** defined by the EEOC as *unwelcome sexual advances, requests for sexual favors, and other verbal and physical conduct of a sexual nature* that affects a person's job prospects or chances for promotion or that "unreasonably" interferes with work performance. EEOC guidelines issued in 1980 state that sexual harassment is illegal. Although either sex may be the victim, most of those who face harassment on the job are women.

Those most often the target of sexual harassment are women under thirty-five who are in entry-level positions. The harasser is typically an older man, either a co-worker or the woman's supervisor.[17] Incidents of sexual harassment are apparently not uncommon, and they can be costly to the company both in human terms (the woman may miss days at work, perform less efficiently, or quit) and financial terms (the woman may sue the company for damages).

Ideally, companies should deal with the problem of sexual harassment by establishing a clearly stated company policy against it. They should also set up a grievance procedure to deal with any harassment complaints. Finally, they should train supervisors in ways to avoid the problem (explaining to male supervisors, for example, that pats or pinches intended in a "friendly" way may not be received that way by their female co-workers).

TRAINING AND DEVELOPMENT

Since it bears a direct relationship to company profits, many companies rely heavily on worker training, either on the job or in classrooms. Often a training program simply teaches the nuts-and-bolts skills of a particular job. In an electronics plant, for example, workers may spend a few weeks becoming familiar with the components they'll be putting together, learning to attach components to a board, and so on. Increasingly, however, worker training efforts are going beyond the nuts-and-bolts approach. Since some new workers lack basic reading and math skills, employers today are often faced with the task of providing remedial education.

Retraining is also becoming more important. As technology overtakes workers' skills, companies may find themselves with an obsolete work force. Often, a company will cope with this problem by putting whole divisions of its work force through retraining courses on the job.

WAGE AND SALARY ADMINISTRATION

In these uncertain economic times issues of compensation are increasingly on the minds of both management and work force. (Ask a top executive who must make the hard choice between instituting pay cuts and laying off workers—or the worker who has to make ends meet with $20 or $50 less in her weekly pay envelope.) Because proper **compensation**—*the payment of employees for their work*—is crucial in keeping employees motivated, wage and salary administration is a prime concern of the human resources department. Because of the amount of paperwork and record keeping that is involved, it's also probably the department's most time-consuming task.

Japan's largest management school, near Mount Fuji, subjects trainees to a near-military discipline that spotlights their weaknesses and helps them understand themselves better. Long-distance marches teach students to control their bodies; positive-thinking techniques teach them to control their minds. Here, students learn to loosen their backs—essential for the traditional "lotus" sitting posture.

WAGES VERSUS SALARIES

For many blue-collar and some white-collar workers, the form of compensation consists of **wages,** *a payment based on a calculation of the number of hours the employee has worked or the number of units he or she has produced.* Wages provide a direct incentive to a worker: the more hours worked (or the more pieces completed), the higher the worker's pay.

What about paying workers whose work output is not always directly related to the number of hours they put in or the number of pieces produced? Most such workers are paid salaries. **Salaries,** like wages, *base compensation on time, but the unit of time is a week, a month, or a year instead of merely an hour.* Salaried workers normally receive no pay for the extra hours they are sometimes asked to put in; working overtime is simply part of their obligation. In return, they do get a certain amount of leeway in their working time. They are seldom penalized for time lost because of illness or personal problems, and they are always paid full salary for holidays.

BONUS PLANS

For both salaried and wage-earning workers, another method of compensation is the **bonus**—*a payment in addition to the regular wage or salary.* Some firms pay an annual bonus at Christmas (amounting to a certain percentage of each employee's earnings) as an incentive to reduce turnover during the year.

Another type of bonus arrangement, the **performance plan,** *pays employees extra money based on a company's growth statistics.* The statistics used vary, but they may include earnings per share of stock, return on assets, and increases in capital spending. One company, Honeywell, sets four-year performance goals, dividing "performance shares" among forty-one executives. In 1979 alone, it paid out $1.6 million through this program.[18]

Profit sharing, production sharing, and ESOPs

Employees can be rewarded for staying with a company and encouraged to work harder through **profit sharing**—*a system whereby employees receive a portion of the company's profits.* Depending on the company, profits may be distributed quarterly, semiannually, or annually. Or payment may be put off until the employee retires, is disabled, or leaves the company—provided that the employee worked the number of years called for in the plan. With deferred payments, the company pools and invests funds for the employees.

Production sharing is a plan similar to profit sharing, but with one significant difference. *The rewards to employees are tied not to overall profits but to cost savings resulting from increased output.* This plan is used as an incentive for operating-level workers rather than for managers, on the theory that workers can have a greater impact on production than their superiors can.

Another fringe-benefit program that rewards employees if the company does well is the **employee stock ownership plan,** or **ESOP.** In an ESOP, *a company places some of its stock in trust for all or part of its employees,* with each employee given a certain share. After the stock has remained in the trust for seven years, it may be sold by workers (or their heirs) if they leave the company, retire, or die. If the company does well, the ESOP can be a substantial employee benefit. It has the additional advantage of being free to the employee and nearly so to the employer, since it is financed by a federal tax credit. AT&T, which in 1976 set up an ESOP program covering more than 700,000 employees, reports that the only drawback to such a plan is the additional record keeping it requires.[19]

COMMISSIONS

Commissions are *payments based on sales made.* Used mainly for sales staff, they can be the sole compensation or can be an incentive payment in addition to a regular salary.

WHEN WORKERS MUST BE LET GO

A company invests time, effort, and money in each new employee it recruits and trains. This investment is lost when a reliable employee is laid off or fired. Many companies, faced with a downturn in business, prefer to reduce expenses rather than let employees go. They may cut administrative costs (curtailing travel, seminars, and other frills), freeze wages, postpone new hiring, or encourage early retirement. Sometimes, however, a company has no alternative but to reduce its work force, either by layoffs or by firings. These options inevitably present the organization with a number of problems.

FIGURE 2

THE BENEFITS PACKAGE: What goes into it?

LAYOFFS

Companies once were free to lay off whomever they pleased. Recently, however, some laid-off employees have sued, charging that they were unfairly singled out because of their age, sex, religion, or race. Even employers that have a supposedly discrimination-free system of layoffs based on seniority have found themselves in court. The reason? The so-called "last hired, first fired" (i.e., workers most recently hired are first to be laid off) means that women and minorities, usually hired in significant numbers only recently, are more likely to be laid off than are other workers.

One possible alternative is a "valuableness" system that evaluates each worker according to criteria (reliability, communication skills, and so on) picked by both workers and supervisors. Each worker accumulates a certain number of points under this system, and those with the fewest points are laid off. This method has been used in a number of large industrial companies, and to date it has not been successfully challenged in court.[20]

FIRINGS AND THE ISSUE OF "EMPLOYMENT AT WILL"

It has long been illegal for a company to fire an employee to get rid of a would-be union organizer, someone who has filed a job-safety complaint, or simply a person of undesirable race, religion, sex, or age. Beyond this, the courts have traditionally held that any employee not covered by a contract may be fired "at will." In other words, since the employee can quit whenever he or she pleases, the employer should be able to return the favor. Recently, however, a number of legal decisions have begun to alter this doctrine, holding that there may be in some cases an implied contract between employer and

Total Payroll $19,749: This is what the employee receives in his gross weekly paycheck.

Rest periods, etc. $523

Miscellaneous $444

| Overtime, premium pay and other payroll items $1,185 | Paid vacations, holidays, etc. $1,782 | Pensions, insurance, etc. $2,614 | Legally required payments $1,825 |

The weekly pay-check includes these benefits paid directly to the employee:

Benefits Payments: Inside Payroll

These benefits are paid after retirement, or when the employee needs medical care, etc.:

Benefits Payments: Outside Payroll

(Data from U.S. Chamber of Commerce, 1982)

Benefits paid by the average company to or on behalf of an employee who makes $19,749 a year.

employee that requires that any firing be done "fairly." Some commentators on the subject have called this notion "the right to a job."

How have employees won their suits against their former employers? Primarily by arguing that documents issued by the company (employee hand-books, for example) state that no employee may be fired without proper warnings, including opportu-nities to remedy whatever problems may exist. (Some fired workers have even argued that their being called "permanent" employees by the com-pany should protect them from firing—or at least unfair firing.) The question of fairness is difficult to pin down, of course, but most companies that lost court cases did so because they fired the employee with little notice, or fired the employee without hav-ing made it clear that his or her job was on the line and for what reasons.

To avoid lawsuits from disgruntled former employees, some companies are now inserting state-ments in their employment application forms or company handbooks that affirm the "we may fire at will" doctrine. It remains to be seen whether the courts will continue to hand down decisions that seem to support the "right to a job"; for the mo-ment, an official disclaimer would seem to protect a company's right to fire.

WORKER BUYOUTS

Another method a company may use to trim its work force is simply to offer its employees, or cer-tain groups of them (often those near retirement age), financial incentives to resign, such as enhanced pensions or cash payments. *The process of inducing workers to depart by offering, them financial incentives* is known as a **worker buyout.** In effect, the company pays certain people to leave. Although this method is obviously more expensive than firing or laying off

workers, it has several benefits. The morale of the remaining workers is preserved, since they feel less threatened about the security of their own jobs. Also, since those who participate in the buyout are usually senior staff members, younger employees who stay on see their chances for promotion in-crease. One company that chose the buyout route was Eastman Kodak, which in 1983 offered incen-tives to leave to nearly four-fifths of its 93,200 U.S. employees. Kodak's offer was one week's salary for every year worked up to twenty-five years, plus one additional week's pay.[21] Such a plan, like many buy-out proposals, is most attractive to employees who are already near retirement age.

EMPLOYEE BENEFITS AND SERVICES

Companies regularly provide their employees with certain **fringe benefits,** which are *financial benefits other than wages, salaries, and supplementary rewards.* They also provide services such as health and safety programs, which are very important even though their value can't be estimated in dollars and cents.

Actually, the term *fringe benefits*, though com-monly used, is somewhat misleading because the amount of money allotted for "fringes" is far from negligible. Fringe benefits make up a sizable per-centage of a worker's true earnings and an employ-er's costs (see Figure 2). According to Chamber of

Commerce statistics, the average company spent $6,627 on fringe benefits for each employee in 1981. The cost of these benefits amounted to an average of 37.3 percent of the payroll.[22] In other words, for every dollar spent on direct monetary compensation, employees spend another 37.3 cents on fringe benefits.

INSURANCE PLANS

Most businesses offer substantial protection for their employees in the form of life and health insurance. A company negotiates a group insurance plan for its employees and pays all or most of the premium costs. Firms offer this coverage not only because most union contracts require it, but also because it helps attract and keep employees. Although life and health plans are often administered by human resources managers, insurance is an important element of risk managment, so we'll discuss it in detail in Component Chapter E.

Unemployment benefits

The Social Security Act of 1935 provided for federal-state cooperation to insure workers against unemployment. The cost of this program is carried by employers, who must pay a set percentage of their total payroll into the federal and state funds. When a worker becomes unemployed for reasons not related to performance, the worker is entitled to collect benefits. The amount of the benefit is usually tied to the employee's total earnings during the previous year. Both the amount and the length of time it is available vary from state to state. Workers in certain industries, notably automobile, steel, rubber, and glass, receive additional benefits (called supplemental unemployment benefits, or SUB for short) from either their company or their union.

PENSION PLANS

Nearly everyone who works regularly is eligible for Social Security payments during retirement. This income is paid for by the Social Security tax, collected by the employer from employees' wages and matched by an equal contribution from the employer.

Social Security payments are barely enough to support a minimal standard of living, however: the average monthly payment to retired workers in July 1982 was only $406.[23] Therefore, private pension plans have been set up to provide additional retirement security (see Component Chapter F). Many of these pension plans are now under review as a result of a 1983 Supreme Court decision that held that employers could not pay women smaller monthly pensions than men. (Before this decision, retired women's payments were typically smaller than men's since actuarial tables show that women, on average, live longer than do men.)

OTHER FRINGE BENEFITS

This category includes paid holidays, sick pay, premium pay for working overtime or unusual hours, and paid vacations. Companies have various policies as to how many days of the year they consider legitimate holidays. A company with a liberal policy on holidays usually emphasizes this fact in its employment advertising. Sick days are usually limited in order to curb excessive absenteeism, but sick-day allowances also vary from company to company. To provide incentives for employee loyalty, most companies grant employees longer paid vacations if they have remained with the organization for a prescribed number of years.

"Cafeteria" benefits

Until recently, most fringe benefits came as a package with a particular job. Once hired, the employee got whatever insurance, paid holidays, pension plan, and other benefits the company had set up. But a newer approach to fringes allows employees to pick their benefits—up to a certain dollar amount—to meet their particular needs. A worker with a young family might want extra life or health insurance, for example, and feel no need for a pension plan. A single worker might choose to forgo life insurance for a tax-deferred retirement plan. Another worker might "buy" an extra week or two of vacation time, by giving up some other benefit. Although only a

TODAY'S SPECIALS
COMPANY CAR
STOCK OPTIONS
LIFE INSURANCE
MEDICAL INSURANCE
VACATION
PENSION PLAN
TUITION PROGRAMS
MATERNITY (PATERNITY)
FLEXIBLE WORK HOURS
DISABILITY INSURANCE
EMPLOYEE DISCOL

BENEFITS CAFETERIA

"Cafeteria" programs let employees tailor fringe benefits to their own individual needs. In 1984 the IRS proposed to restrict plans that reimbursed workers with cash for unused benefits; but "cafeteria" plans that lacked this feature would still be permitted.

few companies have taken this flexible "cafeteria" approach to fringe benefits, it would seem to be an idea that responds to employees' needs.

HEALTH AND SAFETY PROGRAMS

In 1982 about 105,600 people suffered an occupation-related illness. In addition, nearly 5 million workers were injured on the job. The cost of these illnesses and injuries? Over 36 million workdays were lost. An even more startling figure is the 4,090 work-related fatalities for 1982.[24] Not only are those figures appalling from a humanitarian point of view, they are also bad for business. What an employee health problem can do to a business is illustrated by the case of the Manville Corporation, makers of asbestos products. In the past fifteen years the company has been hit with more than 20,000 law-

suits from workers claiming that their cancers and lung diseases are directly related to the asbestos exposure they suffered on the job. The company, estimating that it might have to spend $5 billion to settle damage claims, entered bankruptcy proceedings in 1982 under "Chapter 11," which permits the company to continue operating while bankruptcy proceedings are carried out.[25] (We discuss the legal and ethical questions this action raises in Chapter 18.)

Health and safety programs are a means of reducing potential suffering and keeping health-related losses to a minimum. As such, they are, or should be, a major concern of every human resources manager. By educating employees in safety procedures, establishing and enforcing safety regulations, and redesigning work environments to minimize the potentials for death, injury, or illness, businesses have often succeeded in sharply cutting their health-related losses. And they also have happier, healthier, and usually more productive employees.

TRACKING HEALTH HAZARDS BY COMPUTER

The importance of employee health and safety has been brought home to business by a series of costly lawsuits—most notably, the thousands filed against the Manville Corporation. To companies that deal with hazardous substances—asbestos, petroleum, and chemicals, for example—this is an especially crucial concern. But the record keeping involved in monitoring employees' exposure to various substances (which workers were in contact with the dangerous materials, which materials, and for how long) has been a major problem.

Enter computerized monitoring of employees' health. With the computer, careful tabs can be kept on which hazardous substances are in use and who uses them for how long. Other data about employees' health (pre-existing medical conditions, results of physical exams, health-impairing habits such as smoking, records of diseases that run in the family) can be stored as well. All this information can be used to identify workers who may be at particular risk—so that the company can, for example, switch them to some other kind of work.

Not everyone is in favor of this innovation, however. Some workers fear that if they are identified as health risks, they will be fired. Others fear a loss of privacy, with so much confidential information available on a computer tape. Employers, on the other hand, worry about being sued by the very employees whom they have identified as at risk. Nevertheless, if properly used, this system could benefit both workers and their employers—by keeping workers healthy and enabling companies to avoid costly disability claims.

SOURCE: "Tracking Chemical Hazards on the Job," *Business Week*, March 21, 1983, pp. 14D–14F.

The Occupational Safety and Health Administration

In the late 1960s it was clear that the work hazards of modern industry were increasing, not lessening. Voluntary action by employers seemed inadequate to protect workers. The result was the **Occupational Safety and Health Act** of 1970, which *set up mandatory standards of safety and health and established the Occupational Safety and Health Administration (OSHA)* to enforce them.

OSHA is charged not only with preventing accidents but also with eliminating "silent killers": work-related diseases such as "black lung" among coal miners and "brown lung" among textile workers, and injury from the toxic effects of chemicals, asbestos, and other harmful substances. OSHA employees are instructed to inspect workplaces not only to investigate complaints but also on a random basis to check safety. Penalties for noncompliance include fines and imprisonment.

Although it was initially thought that the Reagan administration, with its antiregulatory philosophy, would approach the enforcement of OSHA rules with a gentler hand than its predecessors, this has not been precisely the case. Under its administrator, Thorne G. Auchter, the agency has gone ahead with rules that require extensive alterations in textile plants to reduce cotton dust—and similar strict rules governing exposure to asbestos, benzene, and lead. Although some business leaders have continued to protest these OSHA regulations, many major corporations prefer federal rules that are reasonable and consistent to a complex variety of state standards. In another far-reaching 1983 action, OSHA announced a new regulation that would require manufacturers to tell factory workers about any hazardous chemicals they might be handling. Though some labor spokespersons claimed that the "trade secrets" exception stated in the new regulation would render the rule toothless, other observers believed the new regulation was a major step toward better occupational health and safety.

EMPLOYEE VALUATION

At the Miami law firm of Arky, Freed, Stearns, Watson and Greer, an unusual system of employee evaluation is in place: a strict meritocracy. Twice a year, the firm's partners meet to decide who among them is doing the best work. The result is that sometimes the firm's junior partners earn more than the senior partners.[26]

Arky's approach might surprise some traditional businesses. It's an unorthodox way of solving an age-old problem: How do you evaluate an employee's performance? When should a worker be given a raise? When should an employee be promoted, demoted, or transferred? And under what circumstances should a worker be removed by **termination**—*let go* because of cutbacks or *fired* for poor performance?

Methods of evaluating workers' performance in many companies are now evolving into highly structured performance appraisal systems. Such systems offer several advantages: they are often fairer, in that their standards are usually closely job-related ("the employee turns in weekly reports on time") rather than being vague reactions to a worker's personality ("Ethel's always bustling around the office. She must be doing an efficient job"). Performance criteria, expressed in writing, become clear to both employee and supervisor, allowing both to determine whether the work being done is adequate. A formal system also usually requires regular evaluations of each employee's work—in writing—so that there is an actual record of the employee's performance. (This can protect the company in cases of disputes or threatened lawsuits.) Finally, many performance appraisal systems require that the employee be rated by several people (more than one supervisor, several co-workers, or even the employee himself or herself). Once again, this promotes fairness, since one person's biased appraisal cannot be taken as fact.

CHAPTER REVIEW

A major component of any business is its human resources, and planning for them is an important task. Among the factors planners must take into account are demographics, technological change, and legal requirements. Large firms have separate human resources departments to do this efficiently.

Managers plan their human resources needs. Then they determine corporate objectives and plan for the future. Different types of companies need different types of people in terms of talent, skills, and training.

Human resources specialists who recruit new workers make use of job analyses, descriptions, and specifications. Their sources may be the company itself, referrals, advertising, employment agencies, unions, and schools.

The selection process usually begins with a candidate's application and résumé. Companies pay particular attention to equal opportunity guidelines in hiring women, minorities, and the handicapped; they are also careful to avoid biased testing. Although the position of women in the workplace has improved, as a group they still do not receive equal pay for equal work and are not fairly represented at the managerial level. These issues, along with that of sexual harassment, remain important.

Training of employees is essential to a firm's smooth operation. Workers may learn company operations on the job, through job rotation, or in various classroom situations. Training methods for managers are similar and may also include the use of simulation and scenarios.

Compensation for workers consists not only of wages and salaries but also of supplementary rewards: bonuses, profit sharing, production sharing, ESOPs, and commissions. During the hard times of the early 1980s, some companies had to offer alternative, less costly rewards. Others had to freeze or cut salaries and to lay off or fire workers. Fired workers have, in some cases, won lawsuits against their former employers, and the latter have become more cautious about making promises, either explicit or implied. The worker buyout represents another way of trimming an overly large work force.

Employers also provide a wide range of services. Fringe benefits can include life and health insurance, unemployment compensation, and pension plans. Health and safety programs are monitored by OSHA.

Evaluating its employees is a crucial aspect of a firm's operation. Although "gut reactions" to employees are often used, more objective rating systems are favored, whether for judging a manufacturing worker's output or assessing a manager's behavior or accomplishments.

KEY WORDS

human resources managers (210)

job analysis (211)

job description (212)

job specification (212)

recruiters (212)

résumé (213)

Equal Employment Opportunity Commission (EEOC) (213)

sexual harassment (218)

compensation (218)

wages (219)

salaries (219)

bonus (219)

performance plan (219)

profit sharing (219)

production sharing (220)

employee stock ownership plan (ESOP) (220)

commissions (220)

worker buyout (221)

fringe benefits (221)

Occupational Safety and Health Act (OSHA) (224)

termination (225)

REVIEW QUESTIONS

1. How can accurate planning for human resources help a firm?

2. In what ways did the 1964 Civil Rights Act affect hiring? How are its provisions enforced?

3. How does the government seek to encourage hiring of the handicapped?

4. Compare the position of women in the workplace in 1960 with their situation today. What problems do they still face? Why?

5. Discuss some of the problems facing workers who are nearing retirement.

6. Describe three types of employee training programs.

7. List some approaches to employee evaluation and discuss the pros and cons of each. Also, list the advantages and disadvantages of the seniority system.

CASE 1

BULLYING BOSSES RISK LOSING BIG BUCKS

Having lost a costly lawsuit brought by a former employee, Bissell, Inc., maker of the Bissell sweeper and other home-care products, has recently revamped its personnel policies to forestall future replays. Other firms are making similar changes.

Bissell's employee—a manufacturing executive we'll simply call John Doe—had been with the company for twenty-three years and had risen to a level where a vice-presidency was the logical next step. The promotion failed to come, however, and Doe, discouraged, became careless about his work. Management let him know that his performance was poor, but Doe was neither given a chance to improve his performance nor clearly warned of dismissal before the ax fell. This enabled Doe to claim that Bissell had been negligent—that they should have told him exactly where he stood before they actually fired him. The trial judge, accepting this claim, awarded

$360,906 to Doe for lost wages, pension benefits, and mental distress, then reduced this sum to $61,354.02 because Doe's poor performance made him "largely responsible for his discharge."

The Doe case has led to important changes in Bissell's policies. Now the company emphasizes tough, honest work evaluations, so that its employees will know how they're doing. As one management lawyer has pointed out, supervisors may personally be found legally liable if they fail to exercise this responsibility. And before they can fire anyone, managers must ask themselves, at Bissell and elsewhere, "Has this worker been properly warned and notified? Have both the warning and grounds for dismissal been clearly noted in the worker's personnel record?"

Bissell's experience is part of a new wave of similar attacks on corporations, the most notorious probably being that of TV newscaster Christine Craft against Metromedia, Inc. (She claimed they had hired her under false pretenses—that they wanted a glamour girl, not a reporter.) Even when the employer wins—which seems to be difficult, since juries tend to sympathize with the "underdog"—the litigation costs money. Therefore, employers are doing their best to avoid it through approaches such as the following:

1. Policies like Bissell's of tough, honest performance evaluations as well as proper warning and notification.

2. More formal complaint procedures for nonunion workers. For example, General Electric, at a number of its plants, now uses a five-member panel (plant manager, human resources manager, and three hourly workers) to hear and judge the merits of employee complaints. Other companies go even further, resorting to outside arbitration. This speedier, more attentive approach to worker dissatisfaction has spawned the phrase "corporate due process."

3. Company-wide "peer review" procedures. This somewhat similar plan has been adopted by Control Data Corporation, which uses a computer to make its random choice of a review board (two peers of the complainant plus an executive from another division). A nonvoting human resources manager chairs the proceedings.

4. Careful rewording of the personnel manual. Blue Cross/Blue Shield of Michigan, for example, pulls no punches when it says that any employee "can be terminated at any time without reason." It avoids implied promises by referring to employees as "regular" or "full-time" rather than "permanent."

These new approaches are not trouble-free. They are felt to apply more to ordinary workers than to managers and professionals, leaving many dilemmas to be faced on those levels. Also, some bosses don't like to make tough evaluations, saying, "How can you expect a fellow to shape up after he's been told he's a loser?" Finally, supervisors tend to resent losing power to review boards; they claim that it undermines their authority and makes it tougher to keep subordinates in line.

Still another point of view is expressed by William Gould, a Stanford University law professor, who feels that corporations cannot be trusted to do right by their employees unless they are under outside pressure. Therefore, he is working toward a California law that will enable the state to review unjust dismissals.

As to lawsuits, Cliff Palefsky, a San Francisco attorney, says that they should not be undertaken rashly. In his opinion, "A good job is better than a good lawsuit. . . . The damage you can do to your reputation from suing your employer is irreparable."[27]

1. What do you think of Bissell's new approach to the management of its personnel? Would Bissell have been in a stronger position if it had had a company grievance procedure or a more bluntly worded company handbook? How and why?

2. Corporate decisions have been judged, found wanting, and penalized by outside individuals (juries). Is this right? Naturally, a jury made up mainly of working people and non-professionals will tend to be unsympathetic toward management. Is this proper? If not, how can it be helped?

3. Although we live in a democracy, the atmosphere in the workplace is sometimes highly authoritarian. Have you experienced this? Do *you* feel changes are needed? If you had a small manufacturing business, how would you go about managing your work force? Imagine some of the problems that might arise and how you would handle them.

CASE 2

A PROBLEM IN HIRING

Joe K. is a thirty-six-year-old man who lives in a small town in northern California where his family has lived for three generations. His wife, Phyllis, grew up in Denver, and she and Joe have two children in their teens. A year and a half ago Joe was a supervisor for a local lumber company. His firm had just installed a computerized data-processing system, and Joe completed a brief training course to learn how to use this system.

But like many other industries—notably automobiles and steel—the lumber industry was hard hit by the recession of the early 1980s. Joe, along with many of his co-workers, was laid off after seventeen years with the firm.

Joe was told that he would be rehired as soon as conditions improved, but months went by and Joe was still out of work. The K.'s survived on Phyllis's salary as an administrative assistant at a nearby community college, and Joe occasionally got a few short-term assignments doing freelance custom carpentry, mostly on vacation homes for affluent San Francisco residents.

Joe decided to take advantage of the tuition benefits he received from Phyllis's job, and he enrolled in computer programming and management classes at the community college. He did well in these courses, and the younger students were delighted to have Joe in their classes because of his insights gained from on-the-job experience. The K.'s began to consider a move to the Sacramento area, where white-collar opportunities in the computer field were more plentiful.

Joe began to mail résumés to computer firms in and around Sacramento, but none of them generated much interest. Finally, he was called for an interview at Data-Trax, a three-year-old company established by a former executive for a huge corporation who wanted to create a small, high-quality, more personal business. There was only one vacancy, and Joe was up against white-collar applicants who had far more on-the-job computer experience. But Data-Trax is a firm that sometimes takes calculated risks in hiring. The human resources director was impressed by Joe's supervisory experience and by the reference she received from his management professor. However, Joe would still need several months of training, while the other applicants would need two weeks at most.

Joe made a very favorable impression at the interview, but so did one of the white-collar applicants, whose paper qualifications were better. The human resources director found herself faced with a dilemma.

1. Think about Joe. He has been in a blue-collar industry all his working life. Is he making a mistake by trying to get into the computer field? Explain your answer.

2. Imagine you are the human resources director at Data-Trax. What specific steps could you take to determine how great a risk you would be taking by hiring Joe?

3. What skills could Joe bring to Data-Trax that more conventional applicants could not?

4. Why do you think Data-Trax called Joe for an interview in the first place? Be specific.

5. If Joe were hired, what specific steps could Data-Trax take to make someone with his background feel more "at home" in his new surroundings and work?

6. If you were the human resources director, would you hire Joe? Why? Be sure to base your answer on objective, not emotional, considerations.

HUMAN RELATIONS: MOTIVATION AND MORALE C

"I do my job because I love it—no one could pay me for the number of hours I put in." Those words, by a 37-year-old IBM computer designer, typify the values of a new breed of workers—people who aren't so interested in money and job title, the things that used to motivate people to work hard. Many of today's workers, especially the young and those with high-tech skills, look to their work for growth and personal satisfaction: they'd rather put in extra hours because they can learn something and gain recognition for their input than because they get time-and-a-half pay. According to pollster Daniel Yankelovich, perhaps 40 percent of the work force now falls into this category, and managing this new breed calls for creativity.

But at the same time, managers must recognize the needs of the other 60 percent of workers. In this chapter we'll look at the tried-and-true approaches to human relations on the job, and we'll also examine some of the newer methods.

CHAPTER FOCUS

After reading the material in this chapter, you will be able to:
- define human relations, and cite its three key ingredients
- describe the key elements in Frederick Taylor's theory of motivation
- indicate the significance of the Hawthorne studies
- list the five stages in Maslow's hierarchy of human needs, and explain the significance of the concept for worker motivation
- characterize Theory X, Theory Y, and Theory Z managers
- show how such methods as job redesign, teamwork, and work sharing help improve workers' morale
- cite three ways of preserving workers' jobs when layoffs threaten

Quick to scold an assembly-line worker for a rattling bolt or screw, the old-style foreman had all the tact and consideration of a charging bull. "A hard-nosed, loud-mouthed disciplinarian" is how Donald R. Hennion, a foreman at Ford's Edison, New Jersey, plant, describes himself in the old days. His job was to strut and bully, but never to analyze why the bolt or screw rattled, much less to ask workers for suggestions on how to fix the problem. In fact, he recalls, "If you didn't discipline an hourly worker, your manhood was challenged!" Now, however, Hennion trades smiles and jokes with his workers; he asks for their opinions on why parts aren't fitting correctly, carries out their ideas, and focuses on solving problems rather than dispensing harsh criticisms. Moreover, in an unprecedented change that would have horrified Henry Ford, he urges them to *actually stop the production line* whenever a defect interferes with their own task. Then, *he* has to quickly examine the problem and settle on a solution.

What happened? In mid-career, Hennion was asked by the "top brass" to change his pattern of dealing with subordinates. Ford's managers, spurred by economic pressure and foreign competition, are finding they must take a new approach to the way they treat people in their organization. They are finding they can boost productivity and quality if they pay more attention to their workers' opinions, and let them participate more in management decisions. They now encourage warmer informal relations, like Hennion's with his workers; they have also set up structured problem-solving groups, in which foremen meet regularly with assembly-line workers to discuss daily problems in plant productivity and quality control. (Indeed, many workers now know more about electronics and computers than their bosses do.) Although the outlook is not promising for the traditional gruff "boss man," the new foreman can look forward to a more satisfying position as the guiding member of a worker team. Hennion likes his new role. "You're more productive in the long run," he asserts. "People on the line seem happier. You still have the same boredom, but the attitude is changing. We're working as a team." [1]

THE SIGNIFICANCE OF HUMAN RELATIONS IN THE ORGANIZATION

What you've witnessed here is just one of a set of changes that are taking place at many levels of business in America. Nowadays we are seeing new trends in the ways people interact in business settings, from the assembly line to the office to the board room. These are, fundamentally, changes in organizational human relations. The term **human relations** refers to *the way two or more people behave toward each other in any situation;* in this book, of course, we're particularly concerned with the ways people interact within a business organization.

What are the ingredients of good organizational human relations? The first, perhaps, is *leadership* by the organization's managers. As we noted in Chapter 4, a leader can often get productivity and profits by inspiring enthusiasm and by working hard to help his or her people earn credit for what they do; this type of manager is more effective than the old-style boss who depends on authority and takes all the credit himself. A second ingredient is *communication.* Managers must show workers that they are valuable to the organization—through memos, policy manuals, written evaluations; through bonuses, training sessions, chats with subordinates; indeed, through every economic and managerial function of the company. Communication has to be clear. Even the best efforts to encourage good will and productivity will fail if managers communicate in one-syllable barks!

A third factor in good human relations is *motivation.* From management's point of view, we could simply define motivation as "getting people to do what you want them to do." But from the viewpoint of the worker as well as the manager, we could say that **motivation** is the *process of giving a person a reason for doing the things you want him or her to do.* Using the word this way, you might say, "Sheila felt that motivating the team to play for the joy of winning was her major function as captain." Managers must think about motivating their workers when they are trying to get the workers to accomplish the objectives of the organization. To begin with, an effective

If workers find their jobs tedious their productivity may decline.

manager must be aware of workers' individual needs, and must persuade workers that their needs can be satisfied within the framework of the organization. But that's not all: managers must also be sensitive to workers' morale. **Morale** is a broad concept: it is *the level of a person's cheerfulness and confidence,* and the level of enthusiasm with which he or she engages in activities. When managers try to boost the morale of their workers, they try to find ways to make them work more zestfully and to perform at their maximum capacity.

THE DEVELOPMENT OF MOTIVATION THEORY

Workers of the nineteenth century endured conditions that seem nothing less than barbaric today—twelve- to fourteen-hour workdays in cramped, unsafe factories, six or seven days a week, for wages that barely warded off starvation. Yet employers seldom had problems motivating the workers. Laborers had no legal protection, and poverty and unemployment were so severe that any job at all was something to feel grateful for.

One of the few exceptions to this dismal rule was provided by Robert Owen, a Scottish industrialist of the early nineteenth century. Pioneering such modern business practices as the merit system, Owen thought of his textile-mill employees as "vital machines"—in contrast to the factory's "inanimate machines"—and held that their well-being was as important as the upkeep of mechanical equipment. Owen's views were not widely shared, however, and it was not until the end of the nineteenth century that social pressures forced industrialists to begin to appreciate the wisdom of motivating workers.

THE CLASSICAL THEORY OF MOTIVATION

The **classical theory of motivation** can be stated simply: it holds that *money is the sole motivator in the workplace.* Humans are viewed as purely economic creatures who work only for money to pay for food, clothing, and shelter (and whatever luxuries they may be able to afford beyond that). To motivate workers, then, a manager has only to show them that they'll earn more money by doing things the company way.

The classical theory's chief spokesperson was Frederick W. Taylor (1856–1915), often called the father of scientific management. A firm believer in the division of labor, Taylor broke work into small units that were efficient and easy to measure. He then determined a reasonable level of productivity for each task and established a **quota,** or *minimum goal,* he expected the worker to reach. Under his **piecework system,** *workers who just met or fell short of the quota were paid a certain amount for each unit produced. However, those who surpassed the quota were paid at a higher rate for* all *units produced,* not just the number above the quota. Workers were thus given a very strong incentive to increase productivity.

Around 1900, Taylor's system was introduced at the Bethlehem Steel works, with impressive results: the average wage of steel handlers rose from $1.15 to $1.85 a day. At the same time, their productivity increased so sharply that the company's handling costs were cut by more than half—a profitable outcome for both sides.

Limitations of the classical theory

The classical theory of motivation worked well in the early part of this century for a good reason: most workers were very poor. Indeed, money still buys the essentials of life and many of its pleasures, and few people can claim that money has *nothing* to do with why they work. But the classical theory cannot explain why a woman whose husband already makes a good living goes out and finds a job, or why a Wall Street lawyer might take a hefty pay cut to serve in the government.

Clearly, money is not the only thing that can motivate people to work, and as more recent research into the subject revealed, workers are far more complex than even Taylor had imagined.

THE HAWTHORNE STUDIES

The Hawthorne studies, a landmark in motivation research, were conducted between 1927 and 1932 at Western Electric's Hawthorne plant near Chicago. The researchers, led by Elton Mayo of Harvard University, initially wanted to test the relationship between workers' physical surroundings and their productivity. They did find out something about this relationship—but not what they had expected. Altering the workers' environment did not affect their productivity nearly as much as the researchers had anticipated. Only extreme changes (such as reducing the light to moonlight level) had a notable effect. Otherwise, workers seemed to produce at the same pace, regardless of changes in their surroundings.[2]

How could this be? Perhaps there was something, some offsetting force, that made the workers either ignore the change, or if that was impossible, do their best to make up for the change. Further investigation revealed that there was indeed "something," a force even stronger than Taylor's wage incentive: this "something" was social pressure. Workers established their own standards of what the correct output should be, sneering at overproducers as "rate busters" and underproducers as "chiselers." And the pressure was effective: the workers were more interested in the approval of their peers than they were in earning higher wages.

As the Hawthorne studies revealed, the informal organization has tremendous power to motivate workers—more effectively in many cases than the formal organization can. And the Hawthorne studies also revealed, purely by accident, another phenomenon of great importance. By the time the project ended, the productivity of the workers involved had risen 30 percent—but not because of any change in work methods or new equipment. Simply participating in the research—being asked for opinions and ideas, being listened to—had given the workers a greater sense of involvement in their jobs, a sense of partnership with management in a common endeavor. In short, their morale had been raised, and their new-found enthusiasm and confidence in themselves provided a stronger incentive than any paycheck.

MASLOW'S LADDER

The next major study of human motivation was brought about by the need to increase worker productivity during World War II. In 1943, the psychologist Abraham Maslow published a theory of motivation in which he proposed that people's behavior is determined by a wide variety of needs. He organized these needs into the five categories illustrated in Figure 1. His theory of the "hierarchy of human needs," often called Maslow's ladder, is based on two simple premises: that people have many needs and that they act to fulfill the needs that have yet to be satisfied. A human being, according to Maslow, is a "perpetually wanting animal," and when needs on a lower level have been satisfied, at least in part, a person begins to strive for the next rung on the ladder.[3]

The steps in Maslow's hierarchy

PHYSIOLOGICAL NEEDS All the requirements for sustaining life—food, clothing, shelter, and the like—fall into this category. These basic needs have to be satisfied before the person can pursue other objectives.

SAFETY NEEDS When the bare essentials are taken

FIGURE I

MASLOW'S LADDER:
Needs people fill through work

Physiological needs

Safety needs

Social needs

Esteem needs

Self-realization needs

Why do people work? To fill emotional needs—as well as needs for safety and physiological satisfaction. The psychologist Abraham Maslow was one of the first human-relations theorists to point out this fact.

care of, the desire for future security, for a cushion against misfortune, becomes more important. In addition to saving for a rainy day, a worker's safety needs must be satisfied through such means as health insurance, pension plans, guaranteed job security, and Social Security benefits.

SOCIAL NEEDS Humans are social animals having a powerful need to associate with others, give and receive love, and feel a sense of belonging. This is the first level of needs that money cannot readily satisfy, and (as the Hawthorne studies showed) these needs can sometimes be more important to the worker than financial considerations.

ESTEEM NEEDS People need to feel self-esteem, an inherent sense of personal worth and integrity. They also need the respect of others, a respect based not on friendship (a social need) but on their competence and achievements. These needs are closely related to the idea of *status*—one's rank or importance in the eyes of others.

SELF-REALIZATION NEEDS Maslow defined the need for self-realization (also called self-actualization) as "the desire to become more what one is, to become everything one is capable of." This need is the high-

est and most difficult to fulfill of all those on the ladder; when a worker has reached this point, he or she works not simply to make money or to impress others, but also because the task is worthwhile and satisfying in itself.

Maslow's ladder in perspective

Maslow's ladder is a convenient way to classify human needs, but it would be a mistake to view it as a rigid one-step-at-a-time procedure. Each level of needs does not have to be completely satisfied (if that is even possible) before a person can be motivated by a higher need. Indeed, most people are motivated by a combination of needs, and the more needs that working satisfies for people at all levels of an organization, the better their work will be.

McGREGOR'S THEORY X AND THEORY Y

Douglas McGregor, a psychologist, accepted Maslow's ladder of needs. But he felt that management had failed to do so. Why? McGregor suggested, in an influential book called *The Human Side of Enterprise* (1960), that a certain set of assumptions under-

Theory X in action: New York Yankees owner George Steinbrenner offers manager Billy Martin some "advice."

lies most managers' thinking.[4] Labeling one set of assumptions "Theory X," he summed them up:

1. The average person dislikes work and will avoid it if possible.
2. Because of this dislike for work, the average person must be forced, controlled, directed, or threatened with punishment to motivate him or her to put forth enough effort to achieve the organization's objectives.
3. The average person prefers to be directed, wishes to avoid responsibility, has relatively little ambition, and wants security.

In other words, McGregor suggested, Theory X–oriented managers believe workers can be motivated only by fear—fear of losing their jobs—and/or by external rewards.

But, said McGregor, Theory X could not explain all of people's behavior in work situations. Theory X emphasized physiological and safety needs but tended to ignore the higher levels of needs on Maslow's ladder. So McGregor proposed another set of assumptions, which he thought man-

agers should concentrate on. These assumptions, which he termed "Theory Y," are as follows:

1. The average person does not dislike work. It is as natural as play or rest.
2. External control and the threat of punishment are not the only ways to motivate people to meet an organization's goals. The average person naturally works toward goals to which he or she is committed.
3. How deeply a person is committed to objectives depends on the rewards for achieving them.
4. Under proper conditions the average person learns not only to accept responsibility, but also to seek it.
5. Many people are capable of using a relatively high degree of imagination, cleverness, and creativity to solve problems that come up in an organization.
6. In modern industrial life the average person's intellectual potential is only partially realized.

In other words, Theory Y–oriented managers are those who feel workers can be motivated by being given an opportunity to be creative, or to work hard for a cause in which they believe, or to satisfy other needs beyond the basic need to pay the rent.

In summary, the assumptions behind Theory X emphasize authority; the assumptions behind Theory Y emphasize human growth and self-direction. It was McGregor's belief that workers would not continue working in organizational systems based on Theory X assumptions when they were ready to realize their social, esteem, and self-realization needs. Blocking them would only lead to antiorganizational behavior. Of course, Theory Y managers whose workers were Theory X would find the going as rough as Theory X managers whose workers were Theory Y.

THEORY Z

Today, as we noted in Chapter 4, a third "alphabet" theory has entered the management vocabulary: Theory Z, a perspective on human relations developed by UCLA professor William Ouchi. Theory Z was formulated to describe characteristics that are common to certain Japanese and American companies that have been notably successful because of their particular management style. Theory Z assumes that the best management involves workers at all levels. And it highlights the Japanese tradition of treating employees like family. In many Japanese companies, employment is guaranteed for life; no one is ever fired or laid off; everyone participates in decision making; and duties are rotated to avoid boredom, extreme specialization, and rigidity. Just as in the ideal family, everyone works harmoniously toward the same goal. (It should be noted that these principles are exercised only in connection with male employees. In Japan, only male employees are considered to be permanent employees; women are generally considered part-time workers.)

Theory Z satisfies lower-level needs by being parental—by looking after everyone's welfare. It also satisfies middle-level needs by working through the group process; and it satisfies higher-level needs by letting workers take responsibility and participate in decisions. Theory Z works effectively because it tries to satisfy needs on all levels.[5]

MOTIVATION THROUGH JOB REDESIGN: MOVING BEYOND TAYLORISM

Recently, some new trends in human relations have developed as a result of the technological changes that have swept American business. Just as foreign competition has altered motivational approaches in some American companies, social change, automation, and the tight economy have challenged the classical scientific management approaches we have inherited from Frederick Taylor. Taylor's extreme division of labor was successful with the uneducated workers of the early twentieth century, many of whom were immigrants. But such highly specialized jobs rarely satisfy today's better educated and more sophisticated workers, many of whom may know more about the latest high-tech advances than their supervisors do. Moreover, new machines may have taken over some of the specialized tasks previously done by human workers. Faced with these changes and the threat of new competition, companies have moved away from Taylorism in order to boost pro-

ductivity by reorganizing the way jobs are done. Such firms are challenging rigid work rules that dictate the number of hours worked, tasks workers must and must not do, and the rights of seniority; and they are even combining some jobs. Their aim is a more flexible distribution of tasks—a goal that has produced some resistance from organized labor (as we noted in Chapter 7), but may be essential to the survival of some American industries.

How do workers feel when their jobs are restructured to include new duties? Are they more highly motivated to do their jobs well? Some are not pleased; some welcome the change. Let's look at Kenneth E. Larned, a boilermaker with Gulf Oil for twenty-eight years, who now helps workers in other crafts after his union had to accept Gulf's demand for "total flexibility" in structuring work. Larned resents that change, as he does not take pride in performing unfamiliar tasks like pipefitting or welding. He believes that his new work is not "top-notch." Nor is it satisfying. "When you're not doing the thing you've been trained to do," he says, "it has to affect your identity."[6]

On the other hand, Christine Szczesniak, who spent seventeen years repeating one tedious step on a check-processing line at a Chicago bank, is excited by her new, less specialized job. Making use of recent advances in office automation, Szczesniak's bank assigned her to a computer terminal where she can perform most of the steps necessary to process and deposit checks. The new automated system is faster and more accurate, increasing productivity by 40 percent. "I like it," Szczesniak says, "because you see the package from beginning to end." The changes have not caused her a loss of identity, Szczesniak asserts: "It's better to be part of the whole thing. Everyone should have change in their life."[7]

A KEY CHALLENGE TO LEADERSHIP: GIVING GROUPS THE GO-AHEAD

One of the most notable departures from Taylorism is the recent effort to cut down on authoritarian management, and to help tough bosses like Donald Hennion to see themselves as members of a worker team. One of the major responsibilities of leaders is to accomplish objectives *through* the group they

OFFICE AUTOMATION: HOW DOES IT AFFECT WORKERS?

In the years ahead, the whirlwind of automation in office settings will cause major human relations problems for managers. Highly automated office systems are already transforming the tasks of file clerks, bookkeepers, secretaries, typists, bank tellers, and certain employees in the insurance industry; and changes in other office jobs are sure to come. Unfortunately, though these transformations get more pieces of paper processed per hour, they don't always make for happier office workers.

What exactly are the problems? For one thing, office automation sometimes insults workers' independence and intelligence. Up to now, office workers have generally been satisfied with their jobs; they've enjoyed the variety of work and friendships with co-workers. Most important, they've exercised control over how jobs get done, and made decisions about their work: they could decide how to format a report, whether to type certain letters in batches or one by one as they came in, and so on. Increased office automation often robs workers of these advantages. It may make the work more repetitive and dull, and it threatens the worker with a loss of control. Typists who become keyboard operators are given no chance to make fundamental decisions; often, they are not even expected to spot obvious mistakes in the material they are inputting, but are supposed to just perform just one task over and over. Expressing her frustration, one woman complains, "I feel like asking my boss, 'What do you think I am—an extension of this machine?'" It's ironic that these technological advances seem to take some industries back to extreme Taylorism, in which work becomes so specialized that it is degrading and meaningless.

Just as worrisome are the stress and loss of incentive that workers may feel as high-tech automation takes over their workplace. Fast-paced systems impose higher work quotas, but workers find that their increased productivity may actually lead to lower pay and little hope for promotion. A video-display-terminal (VDT) operator may earn less than a clerk-typist, even though typists' productivity increases 25–150 percent when they use a word-processor's VDT. And rarely do clerical workers advance to better-paying, more technically skilled jobs: in fact, automation has not lowered the percentage of low-level clerical jobs.

Additionally, workers may risk health hazards from the new office systems. People who stare at a display screen all day may suffer eyestrain and harmful effects from prolonged exposure to the low-level radiation in cathode ray tubes that are found in VDTs.

manage. Today, managers are quite serious when they invite workers to offer their opinions on why a product is not meeting quality standards. This new approach, in which workers and managers form groups to pool ideas, can release some of the tremendous potential for positive energy and high morale that can develop when people work together. For example, a Cadillac plant in Livonia, Michigan, relied on the power of groups to make dull jobs more productive. Managers set up "paid for knowledge" business teams, in which workers made more money for learning new skills, so that they were motivated to make their jobs less special-ized. In weekly meetings, these teams then used their expanded knowledge of factory work to make decisions in areas that had once been the sole responsibility of management, from safety precautions to housekeeping to redistributing tasks on the assembly line for greater efficiency.[8]

The group process

How does such group energy build up? Psychologists have noted that when groups of people work together, they may follow a developmental sequence known as the *group process*, which managers need to

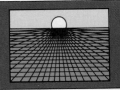

THE HIGH-TECH HORIZON

HOW CAN AUTOMATION WORK *FOR* EMPLOYEES?

Some experts have suggested practical ways to help counteract these problems.

Ask clerical workers to participate in the automation process

Studies show that workers who are given no control over the way their jobs evolve tend to suffer stress and become less productive, so it's well worth the dollars that may be needed to get reactions from those workers whose jobs will be directly influenced by new technology. World Bank discovered this, for example, when it invited employees to study the possible effects of coming automation, from eyestrain to radiation exposure: when the new system was finally implemented, managers and users greeted it enthusiastically.

Take steps to protect office workers' health

The World Bank, for example, limited users' time in front of the terminals to four hours a day. Other wise steps:

■ Use chairs whose height can be adjusted.

■ Make sure the surfaces of screens, keyboards, and surrounding decor are nonreflecting, to reduce glare.

■ Redesign the usual office lighting, and furnish subdued overhead lights with adjustable spotlights for keyboard inputting.

■ Provide good "high resolution" screens with easy-to-read character display to eliminate eyestrain.

Managers can also rotate jobs and allow breaks to reduce risks to workers' health from exposure to long-term low-level radiation associated with VDTs.

Involve workers in all steps of a job

Automation does not necessarily require that workers must sink to repeating one step endlessly: managers can restructure work so that employees perform jobs as they relate to others in the department, rather than as single, isolated tasks. For instance, clerks in an insurance company can do more than code one type of claim; they can offer complete services to claimants, so they eventually learn the various functions of their department and improve their chances for promotion.

SOURCE: Karen Nussbaum, "You Need People to Run Machines," *Working Woman*, May 1983, pp. 104–105.

---

understand in order to lead the group. When the people in the group first gather together, they may discover similar interests and gain a sense of mutual acceptance. Next, in their efforts to get things done and reach common goals, they may begin to make decisions together on ways to make their jobs run more smoothly. They may start to take pride in their project and become more efficient, more motivated, more excited by their group efforts. Eventually—though members of the group may not realize it—the group may start to develop **group norms** or *standards of behavior that all the group members accept.* Those members who live up to these norms feel

good about themselves, knowing that they've won the group's approval.

Managers are likely to see the effects of the strong group control that builds up—sometimes in a positive direction, sometimes a negative one. If the group's norms have developed in harmony with the goals of the company, managers will find that employees will work with energy and dedication—not simply from fear of the boss or from the need for money, but also from a desire to meet the group's standards. If an individual strays from the norms by doing sloppy work, the group may punish him or her harshly. But if managers try to get workers to perform contrary to firmly established group norms, their attempts will probably fail. In one case a manager stopped giving raises but demanded more work: his group of employees developed norms against hard work and the manager saw profits sink. Or look at what happened to dissatisfied employees at Continental Air, a luxury airline bought by smaller, economy-minded Texas International. The new management sliced salaries and benefits in an effort to make the airline profitable again. But many Continental employees resisted, feeling that top executives cared little about their interests. One pilot remarked about their new director, "He gets what he pays for from us, but nobody cares about doing a great job."[9]

Quality circles: a boon to morale

We noted in Chapter 6 that American companies are making increased use of quality circles, groups of workers who meet regularly to identify problems in productivity, to suggest solutions, and to put them into effect. As we saw, quality circles can boost productivity, and Ford is a good example: out of 749 proposals from hourly workers for practical ways to upgrade Ford's Ranger and Bronco II trucks, the company has already adopted 542, with impressive results. Many of the new methods are literally nuts-and-bolts changes that a designer could never anticipate.

But quality circles can bring psychological improvements as well as practical ones. Morale has risen dramatically, for example, at the Louisville plant where Ford now makes the Ranger and Bronco II. Workers used to call the Louisville plant a "war zone": it displayed the worst flaws of the auto industry, including harsh managers, hostile labor relations, filthy housekeeping, and low morale. Vehicles from the Louisville plant rated lowest on Ford's quality scale. After consultants analyzed the plant's atmosphere of alienation and anger, Ford enlisted the cooperation of managers, unions, and the rank and file to clear the air. Workers and managers talked together to solve problems, spurred by the threat of a permanent shutdown if quality didn't rise to an acceptable level. The result: a series of changes. To begin with, the plant was spruced up and remains spotless. Workers who once had to sit on spare parts to eat lunch now find picnic tables throughout the plant. Next, a new "employee involvement program," developed at Ford's headquarters, was tested at Louisville. In the program, top brass from the plant and the United Auto Workers union sponsor weekly quality circles that tackle a wide range of matters, from piping music into the

Managers in Japan often have no offices of their own. Instead, as in this Japanese office, they sit right alongside lower-level workers. The goal is to narrow the gap between management and labor, promoting teamwork and group consensus.

At Blue-Cross/Blue Shield of Durham, North Carolina, managers learn how quality circles can benefit their organization. After quality circle members have pinpointed a problem, they can "dry-run" a range of possible solutions.

paint shop to raising the quality of parts supplied by vendors. Ford also restructured old job categories by creating the new position of "quality upgrader"— without complaints from the union about violated work rules. For every thirty hourly workers there are now about three quality upgraders, who pay attention to problems such as loose bolts or poorly fitting parts while workers keep the assembly line running. Tony "Red Dog" Hamilton is a quality upgrader whose newfound dedication to his job reflects the considerable change at the former "war zone." Frequently absent in the old days and likely to develop an upset stomach while driving to work, Hamilton now likes his job and has rarely missed a day's work since the new program began.[10]

The auto makers aren't alone in using quality circles. Banks, hospitals, and other labor-intensive industries are also experimenting with this way of improving productivity and morale. The Cincinnati-based Kroger supermarket chain tested the concept for a year and now plans to introduce more quality circles in its stores. Kroger's managers found that the circles increased employees' commitment to their jobs and lowered the rate of spoiled goods.[11]

WHEN WORKERS' JOBS ARE THREATENED

At the same time that some companies have been dealing with human relations issues raised by technological growth and change, others have been faced with morale problems posed by the threat of plant closings and layoffs. In today's changing economy, some workers in certain industries, notably steel and other heavy manufacturing, have been threatened by the loss of a basic source of security— the jobs that help them feed their families. Workers who are worried about losing their jobs can cause productivity to slump even further, and they may suffer from increased family problems, alcoholism, mental disturbances, and other personal difficulties that ultimately affect their work. Managers have been forced to take practical steps to cope with these difficulties.

WORK SHARING

To relieve workers' anxiety about layoffs, and thereby improve morale, growing numbers of American companies are dividing the hardships of a downturn among their entire work force—if their workers agree to such a plan. One of these practices is called **work sharing**, in which *the total reduction in hours worked is accomplished not by laying off workers completely, but by slicing a few hours off everybody's workweek and pay*. Forced to cut production during the recent recession, Motorola, Inc., was able to save over 1,000 positions and avoid laying off experienced workers by using work sharing. When a company takes this measure, nearly everyone stands to gain, as Motorola discovered. Workers are less anxious about being unemployed; thus, they are willing to spend more money, helping the local merchants stay afloat. Since most employees keep their jobs and are not "bumped" from one job to another by more senior workers, quality remains high during the slump. When business surges forward again, companies that have instituted work sharing are better equipped to meet the stepped-up demand because they do not have to call back old workers or retrain new ones, a costly process. Additionally, workers are more willing to put in long hours when times get brighter for a company that helped them through a tough spell.

Though it isn't a complete cure for economic woes, work sharing can help companies that are experiencing a bleak season. It doesn't save the company as many dollars over the short run as a layoff does, but it can enable the company to avoid the devastating psychological damage of a layoff. After all, few managers like layoffs any more than workers do. One Motorola manager unhappily remembers the 1974–75 recession, when she had to walk through her plant with a yellow pad that listed the names of workers she would have to let go. She swears that she'll never carry a yellow pad through a production area again.[12]

This robot does a dangerous job in a Japanese factory. The Japanese believe robots should relieve humans of dirty and hazardous work, not deprive them of employment. They feel it would be short-sighted to pit robots against people for financial gain: new problems would probably result.

RETRAINING TO MEET AUTOMATION

Some companies are taking another approach to helping anxious workers threatened by economic change: company-sponsored courses that will teach workers to operate robots and other computerized equipment. Some of the workers who take these courses have already been laid off; some are still employed, but recognize that automation may soon take their jobs away. At GM's plant in Wentzville, Missouri, laid-off pipefitters, millwrights, and other tradespeople are studying to become robot technicians in one of the company's most innovative factories.[13] In even bolder programs, the United Auto Workers has joined forces with both Ford and GM to help workers find and prepare for high-tech jobs outside the auto industry.[14] Reactions to these programs vary. Though some workers feel that automation has made jobs more challenging, others fear that the fancy new hardware will in the long run create fewer opportunities for them. It's even tough for a robot technician to find a job; some experts predict a surplus of such technicians by 1990.

Blue-collar workers who seek to start new careers in the white-collar world sometimes suffer from "culture shock." When steelworker Frank LaRosa was laid off by National Steel Corporation in Weston, West Virginia, and retrained for a new white-collar job in computer programming, he found the change unsettling. He missed the joshing fraternity of his beer-drinking buddies at the steel mill; he found himself in the high-pressure white-collar business world where employees jockey aggressively for promotions, without the tightly knit, predictable social structure of a union-protected plant. Yet, as he saw, switching to white-collar work may have its advantages: a white-collar career is not tied down by strict union rules regarding seniority, so it may provide more chances for a motivated person to push ahead.[15]

BUYING THE COMPANY TO SAVE JOBS

Many recently boarded-up businesses are now reviving under new management—their own employees. As we noted in Chapter 8, businesses owned and operated by workers may sometimes be the best bet for people struggling to regain jobs, for human reasons as well as practical ones. The O&O supermarket in Roslyn, Pennsylvania, succeeded this way: a former A&P that was shut down, it is now profitably run by twenty-five worker-owners who share decisions, run separate departments, and pitch in at the cash registers when crowds jam the aisles. Though the O&O's new owners must cope with the usual managerial headaches, they have harvested personal as well as financial rewards; like other worker-owners, they've enjoyed the satisfaction of directly controlling how their company is run.[16]

CHAPTER REVIEW

At many levels of business today, people are learning to relate to one another in new and more effective ways, building good human relations. The vital factors in achieving this are (1) leadership, (2) communication, and (3) motivation, in which morale plays an important role.

Managers once thought that money was the only way to motivate workers. Taylor's experiences seemed to confirm this idea. But the Hawthorne studies found that social pressure was a more powerful incentive than wages. The research of Maslow demonstrates that many needs can motivate workers, and money can satisfy only some of those needs. Maslow's ladder of needs ascends from physiological needs to safety needs, social needs, esteem needs, and self-realization needs. Maslow felt that only unsatisfied needs strongly motivate work. McGregor, who agreed with him, advocated that managers discard the assumptions of what he called Theory X and work with the more productive Theory Y. A recent addition to this terminology is Theory Z, which refers to the more parental Japanese approach to motivation.

Social change, automation, and a tight economy are also bringing some innovations. For one thing, there is greater flexibility with regard to work rules, job descriptions, seniority rights, and so on. There is also more teamwork. For example, managers may ask workers for suggestions in solving problems, or people may work cooperatively in groups rather than individually. Quality circles in auto plants and other industries have helped boost both morale and productivity. Another innovation is work sharing, in which pay and workweeks are reduced for all workers to prevent layoffs of a few.

Because automation has displaced so many blue-collar workers, some companies are providing retraining designed to equip these people to find jobs in computer technology or technical white-collar fields.

KEY WORDS

human relations (232)

motivation (232)

morale (233)

classical theory of motivation (233)

quota (233)

piecework system (233)

group norms (239)

work sharing (241)

REVIEW QUESTIONS

1. Write a brief description of an old-time manager in operation and then show how a manager of today might handle the same situations. Which one would you rather work for? Why?

2. Define the classical theory of motivation. Who was its chief spokesperson? Why did it work well? What are its limitations today?

3. What did the Hawthorne studies reveal? What effect did they have on the productivity of the workers involved? Why?

4. What are the basic ideas behind Maslow's hierarchy of human needs? Name and describe the five rungs on the ladder.

5. List the assumptions on which McGregor's Theory X and Theory Y are based. Which set underlies most managers' thinking? Which did McGregor endorse? Why? What is Theory Z?

6. When blue-collar workers are retrained and move into white-collar settings, what adjustment problems may they face?

CASE 1

INNOVATIONS AT ALCOA

Mr A. (a real person, though we will not give his name) used to be successful as a manager partly because he was always on top of things—and people. Claiming that his interest lay only in getting the job done, he would say, "I'm not out to win any popularity contests." In fact, he prided himself on being a tough boss who didn't let his workers off lightly. Recently, however, he has enrolled in a management seminar aimed at making supervisors more flexible in their dealings with employees. He has studied his own behavior on videotape, and now he carries a list of reminders on a card in his wallet:

- Talk, don't bark.
- Avoid threatening words and gestures.
- Try to influence rather than control.
- *Show* people how to find their own answers; don't constantly *tell* them what to do.

Although the changes in Mr. A.'s attitude may seem dramatic, developments like this are not unusual among the numerous American companies that have adopted the modern, more humanistic approach to motivation. Many of these are companies oriented toward services and consumer products. But some of the smokestack companies have followed their example—among them, Aluminum Company of America (Alcoa). The demand for alumi-

num is no longer spiraling upward, and the company has had to think about streamlining its staff and increasing its productivity. Now, prodded by an upswing in the economy and the determination of its new chairman, Charles W. Parry, Alcoa is developing programs that challenge its traditional management structure and its "old-boy" network.

Among the most important innovations at Alcoa has been a gradual reduction in upper-level staff, eliminating a layer of management. As a result, "There's a lot less fat, which means you work harder, but there's also less formality." Other tightening-up measures include more frequent performance reviews for everyone, and closer observation of managers' strategies by the people at the top.

Alcoa's human resources department has brought in other changes too. The department has instituted programs designed to integrate women and minorities into the ranks of management. "Smokestack" companies have largely been managed by men—who often will, without meaning to be offensive, call a woman "Honey" or compliment her on her physical appearance. Some women object to such behavior, feeling that it is condescending or intended to "keep women in their place." The seminars at Alcoa are designed to make managers more aware of how their behavior may be interpreted. The aim is to improve communication and remove stereotypes: as Curtis Jackson,

Alcoa's manager of equal opportunity affairs, puts it, "We're saying in training that it's good business and exciting to work with different people."

Alcoa is also running seminars aimed at teaching supervisors to be better motivators and to appreciate the merits of teamwork. Moreover, it is offering assertiveness training, to promote open, more direct communication on all sides. The seminars get down into the nitty-gritty: one, for example, allows participants to study the problems of an imaginary organization and work at finding some practical solutions, and other seminars focus on the specific technical problems of Alcoa's various departments. Many of these workshops are attended by Parry himself, who says, "The goal is a more participatory style of management. . . . It isn't a matter of being altruistic [putting other people's welfare first] but of staying competitive." [17]

1. Point out changes in leadership, communication, and motivation that are affecting life at Alcoa.

2. How would you describe Mr. A.'s "old" managerial style? His "new" style? Also consider Charles Parry's ideas, especially with regard to teamwork. How do these various approaches relate to Theories X, Y, and Z?

3. What does Alcoa hope to gain from its more humanistic attitudes? Discuss this in terms of specific policies.

CASE 2

WHIPSAWING: A NEW WOE FOR AUTO WORKERS

When it comes to words that have to do with inflicting pain, the English language is rich in colorful terminology. You can, for example, *belt, boot, brain, cuff, paste, pummel, scalp, shaft, skewer, stomp, or throttle* someone, and that's only a small sample. An equally vivid expression is *whipsaw*, which means "to . . . victimize [someone] in two opposite ways at once." (The word also designates a large and fierce two-man crosscut saw.) Today, some observers think General Motors and Ford have been whipsawing members of the United Auto Workers (UAW) union.

The background is familiar. Since they were first organized in the 1930s, the auto workers have been among the aristocrats of American industry. Their union bargained so successfully that they came to enjoy wages often two or three times as high as those of line workers in other industries. Then came the Japanese imports, assembled by workers who enjoyed no special status among their kind, who were extraordinarily well disciplined and productive, and who also happened to live in a country that had lower living standards and lower wages across the board. The neat little cars the Japanese auto companies poured into the United States—just when the gas shortage was

creating a demand for them—hit the American auto industry hard. Then the recession cut sales still more, and American plants began to stand idle. The federal government had to bail Chrysler out with a huge loan, just to spare the country a disastrous bankruptcy.

Chrysler wasn't the only auto maker with excess plant capacity. GM has been threatened by idle plants too—and it was this problem that led them to adopt their "whipsawing" tactic. GM has six plants that make small items like door hinges and seat belts for its Fisher Body division. Because of high costs, two of these plants were to be closed; but when the UAW agreed to raise worker output by 20 percent, the plants were kept open. Then, GM demanded that the workers at the other four plants raise their productivity—even though no prior agreement had been made with the unions concerning these four plants. (It was these other four unions that ended up being "whipsawed.") Result: the assembly lines at all six plants moved faster, and GM saved money.

The auto companies have also put pressure directly on workers by raising tensions within the plants. For instance, the new "closer communications" between workers and supervisors, supposedly aimed at boosting morale, now sometimes serve to convey news of the competition and instill fear. The same is true of the "quality of worklife" meetings, which are supposed to promote teamwork but are actually sometimes turned into simple propaganda sessions. One worker says, "The company is giving us all sorts of information they never did before, but all they use it for is to tell us how badly we're doing against other plants." At a GM plant in Flint, Michigan, a weekly newsletter published by management tracks labor costs and performance, comparing local figures with data from similar shops elsewhere. The workers say that this makes them feel resentful toward their opposite numbers at the other plants, even though all of them are merely trying to hold on to their jobs.[18]

1. There is motivational theory and motivational practice. Compare the two in terms of the auto workers' experience. What are your opinions in this matter?

2. If plants had closed, what would have happened to workers' jobs?

3. In "whipsawing" the local unions, management is using the threat of plant closing to pit some locals in competition against other locals. But unions have used similar tactics: a number of years ago, the UAW used to gain benefits for an entire division by threatening to shut down a single crucial plant. Do you think that was a fair tactic then? Do you think GM management's tactics are fair now?

PERSPECTIVES ON SMALL BUSINESS MANAGEMENT ASPECTS

The basic management functions—planning, organizing, directing, controlling, and staffing—must be carried out by organizations, large or small. But the nature of these functions and how they are performed are vastly different in small business because the *resources* available to the small business are very limited. As one small-business owner noted, "When I go off to a meeting, so does my marketing, finance, research and development, personnel, and manufacturing management staff!" More than 50 percent of the businesses in existence today have only one or two employees.

When you compare a company with one or two employees with a large corporation of more than thirty thousand employees, it's not hard to see that the degree to which each function is emphasized will vary from business to business. It is also important to remember that for a small one-person company to grow into a large corporation, the developing management team must learn to gradually adopt the more complex functions of big business.

MANAGEMENT FUNCTIONS IN A SMALL BUSINESS

Planning

Planning is the crucial first step in a business of any size. If you don't know where you want to go, you're not very likely to get anywhere! Even more important, it is essential for every business to formulate a written business plan. Large corporations have long realized the value of such planning, and all small businesses should learn to follow their lead. This business plan must include all the details of where the business is going and how it will get there in the allotted time.

Let's say the goal is to expand your share of a given market. Having set that goal and the time desired to accomplish it, you must identify the factors that could help or block your efforts to reach that goal. Consider such factors as availability of materials, your business's capability for production and delivery, your need for money to finance growth, the demand for your company's products or services, the need for new products, the state of the economy in your region, and any trends you can identify among your competitors. All are important ingredients in the initial section of your plan.

When you have compiled all the above data, your next task is to write down all the steps that are necessary to reach your business goals. You must consider the following: what suppliers will be involved, how employees will be trained, how many new employees will be needed and in what departments, what machinery will be needed and how much it will cost to buy or lease, what machinery can be repaired, whether new marketing and advertising programs will be needed and, if so, what they will cost, whether the factory is adequate or needs to

be upgraded, whether the factory is automated sufficiently to compete, and similar questions that apply to your specific business. Another very important point to be considered is money. Where to find it—and exactly how much is needed—must be determined.

Once you have established the overall goals of your business and then listed all the specific tasks necessary to achieve these goals, you are ready to begin to set monthly, quarterly, and annual subgoals. At this point, you establish the specific steps that must be taken each month. Only by having this blueprint to follow can any business ever expect to progress. If you find that you fall behind in any given month or quarter, you'll know how much extra effort is required to get back on track again.

Marketing and organization

In the next Perspectives on Small Business the marketing aspects of small business are discussed in detail. The important point that we want to make here is that *customers write your paychecks*. This fact must be the focus of your organization and staffing plans. Your business must be organized so that all employees work together to get the job done. You may frequently hear the remark "That's not my job" from employees who do not realize that it takes a team effort to make your business a success.

Organizing means establishing the structure of a business—the role each employee should play and their interrelationships. Because there are so few employees in a small business, each employee must play multiple roles. This involves cross-training so each employee can perform several jobs. This team concept will take effect as each employee gains a better understanding of all of the jobs in the company.

Authority and delegation

Because a small business owner cannot be everywhere or do everything, he or she must delegate authority.

For example, if a salesperson has to call you every time a customer asks for a special deal of some sort, the effectiveness of your sales effort may be less than it could be. Many firms give salespeople a range of prices for goods and services and allow them to bargain and make decisions within those guidelines. In all cases, the individuals to whom you have delegated authority must be willing to be held accountable for what is done.

In order to delegate effectively, you must keep several things in mind:

1. You must clearly understand the tasks you are delegating, and the possible outcomes if they are done poorly.

2. Understand the limits or standards of performance that you expect.

3. You should write down the tasks in sequence, and the minimum acceptable standards.

4. Determine whether each person is willing to take on added responsibility. (Some employees may not wish to do so.)

5. Train your employees to do the tasks you want them to assume, or see that they know how to do them the way you want them done. If you ask someone, "Do you know how to do such and such?" the usual answer is "Yes." You won't learn anything by that answer, except that the employee is an adult and needs to avoid feeling foolish. Don't just ask—train your employees and watch them actually performing the tasks.

6. Communicate clearly the standards of performance and the limits you wish to impose, giving each employee a written copy for reference.

7. When you are sure that an employee understands the task, can do it, and accepts the limits you have detailed, step back and let him or her do the job. There is some risk in this approach, and you'll worry about it—but if you have designed your controls properly, you'll know what is happening soon enough. Bear in mind that you always retain the right to take back any authority you give away.

Staffing

Staffing includes recruiting, selection, training, performance evaluation, wage and salary administration, and health and safety management. Each of these functions is affected by all the others.

The importance of each function varies according to the size of the firm and the skill level of the jobs involved. The higher the skill level, the more carefully you must recruit and select; the lower the skill level, the more carefully you must train.

RECRUITING Small firms often have difficulty attracting job applicants, particularly those with specialized skills, since large firms usually offer more security, higher pay, and greater opportunity. Thus, many small firms choose to develop their own skilled employees, recruiting unskilled or semiskilled people and training them on the job. There are costs involved in this approach, but the benefits in loyalty and eventual job performance are often large enough to justify them.

SELECTION When selecting a new employee, it is important to ask yourself three questions: "Is he or she qualified to do the job?"; "Is this job an improvement over his or her last job?"; and "Will he or she be accepted into the 'team concept'?" You must address all three questions during the interviewing process. Work history is important to the first two questions, but you shouldn't rely on the applicant's past employers for accurate records. Legally they can't release much information, and they are often reluctant to give any details. Some firms will not allow you to talk to the applicant's former supervisors, and you will only be able to talk to the personnel department. Learn to be a good interviewer, and you'll locate better employees.

TRAINING The new employee is probably nervous about taking on a new job. Take the time to talk about the history of the company, the market it serves, and the products or services it offers. Follow this briefing with a tour of the facility. Introductions to other employees and to the supervisor are very important. In the well-run small firm the "team concept," which encourages everybody to work together, will solve many of the problems that come up when a new employee joins the firm. People will automatically pitch in to answer questions.

Nonetheless, you will still need to conduct some formal training. Acquaint yourself with this five-step method of training:

1. Write down the sequence of tasks that you are going to teach.

2. Find out how much the trainee knows about the job.

3. Teach the needed skills by demonstration, discussion, and example. Then let the trainee try the task under supervision.

4. As the trainee gains skill and confidence, let him or her carry out the task, checking less frequently as he or she improves.

5. Closely monitor the trainee for several weeks to be sure the job is being done correctly.

PERFORMANCE EVALUATION We all want to know how we're doing. While most small businesses have no formal evaluation system, many find that an annual or semiannual review of each employee can play an important part in keeping the organization healthy, especially if exceptional job performance can be rewarded.

To begin the process, you must develop a standard of performance for each job. The next step is to be sure that both the employee and the supervisor understand the job and the expected standard for it. Then, whether you use a rating scale, a measure of output, or simply a judgment of performance, all of you will know what is expected and how actual performance compares with

the desired levels. On that basis you can judge the performance of your employees, encourage their strengths, and help them to improve by identifying any areas of weakness.

WAGE AND SALARY ADMINISTRATION A very small business can never compete with the wages and benefits offered by large corporations. But, as sales and profits rise, the smart owner of a growing small business will share a portion of the growth with the employees who helped make it happen. Recruiting, selecting, and training are expensive, and it is far more efficient to return a reasonable percentage of profits to your employees than to lose your people to larger firms. An IRS-approved profit-sharing plan allows you to give employees of your corporation a tax-free bonus each year. This is just one of many very good ways to reward valuable employees.

Directing

Directing involves getting people to do the things that need to be done to move the firm toward its goals—by leading (showing employees how to do the job) and by motivating (giving the employees a reason to do the job and do it well).

If you're the owner, of course, you're willing to work hard—you'll benefit directly. But what about your employees? They're working for you because they choose to, not always because they have to. The "team concept" you have cultivated will allow you to motivate and direct them without threats. The use of fear will bring only some short-term success and much long-term resentment.

If you want your employees to give your firm a fair day's work, you have to give them a fair day's pay. But money alone is not enough. Many people choose to work in small businesses for reasons that have nothing to do with pay: personal contact with other people; a chance to do a whole job rather than a piece of one; a chance to do a number of tasks rather than just one; a chance to be recognized as individuals—and to gain respect because of the jobs they hold, not in spite of them. Be sure you are making these rewards available to your employees. (If that sounds like a lot to ask, consider why you went into business in the first place!)

The first step in deciding how to motivate your employees is to think of how you would behave if you were in their shoes. If you conclude that you yourself wouldn't want to work in their positions, perhaps you should think about what you could do to make them feel better about their jobs.

COMMUNICATION Communication is essential to all functions of management, especially directing.

One of the small firm's advantages over the large one is ease of communication. Even so, many managers fail to do one of the most important things they can do—keep employees informed about what's going on. It's important for your people to know where the firm is going and how fast, and whether new products or services are to be developed and when. In fact, they should know about *any* planned changes that will affect them directly. This does not mean that employees have to know everything that goes on in your mind or in your business. Some things are better kept to yourself. It's good business, though, to tell your employees good or bad news before they hear it somewhere else. Share your firm's goals and directions with them, but be careful about sharing your fears and your problems. You can't expect them to do their best if they're worried about something they can do nothing about.

Controlling

Once a plan has been made and organization completed, the action begins. This is the point at which the carefully made plan can collapse unless something is done to ensure that the firm is moving toward its goals. If it is not, there should be some way to recognize that fact soon, so that you can pinpoint the problem and correct it.

At the end of each month you will need to check the progress of each element of the business plan against actual work done. Without a monitoring system, progress will be non-existent. Most successful large and growing firms have a closely monitored and controlled plan.

We will be discussing some specific small business controls in the Perspectives sections titled Using Business Tools and Financial Aspects. But in the meantime, it is important to recognize that control is especially crucial to a small business because the margin to cover mistakes is so narrow. You just cannot afford to take the chances a large business can afford.

For example, with the high cost of money today, the need for inventory control is essential. If you don't have a system that tells you quickly and accurately how much material you're supposed to have on hand, how will you know whether there has been loss, waste—or worse, pilferage?

Controlling should not be done in a way that will suggest that you don't trust your people, even if in fact you don't.

PRODUCTION MANAGEMENT

The small business involved in the production of goods frequently operates less efficiently than a larger manufacturing company because of the way it grows. Often, a new process or machine is installed where space is available, rather than where it logically fits in the production process. Many small production operations could benefit from an analysis of the way materials flow in the plant, from raw inputs to final products. If the flow is erratic or congested, some reorganization may be helpful. In addition, because of tight cash-flow problems, many businesses tend to make do with obsolete or worn-out equipment in the mistaken belief that they're saving money. You should conduct a cost-benefit analysis to be sure that this is not the case. Sometimes the best way to save money is to spend some on a new machine.

Purchasing

The small business can waste a considerable amount of its limited funds when it purchases raw materials or finished products. You may be so eager to have a steady supply of goods that you stop looking for other suppliers when you've found one. You pay the price you're quoted and never push for a better price. Most suppliers sell at the highest price they can get. But if other suppliers are competing, you will often find them willing to bargain. Keep in contact with a number of suppliers.

Another important aspect of purchasing for the small business is value analysis. If you do a careful analysis of the goods you produce or the services you provide, you may find you can substitute a less expensive item for one you're now using. Popcorn Styrofoam packing, for instance, is far less expensive than molded Styrofoam and often serves just as well.

Once you've decided to place an order, you should find out whether the supplier offers a discount for prompt payment of bills. If you can save 1 or 2 percent by paying before the tenth of the month, your savings may be substantial by the end of the year.

WHAT DOES IT ALL ADD UP TO?

The small business owner carries out all or most of the management functions discussed in this section. They may be performed on a more limited scale than in a large corporation, but they are part of any business, whatever its size.

If these functions are not performed properly, the profitability and perhaps the survival of the business may be jeopardized. There is no room for neglect of details or for ignoring problems in the hope that they will go away. Small, independently owned businesses are fragile. They will survive only as long as their managers perform their functions well.

PART THREE

MARKETING

What do Tide, Pampers, Charmin, Ivory, Duncan Hines, and Crest have in common? They're all offspring of Procter & Gamble, the powerful consumer-products company that has dominated mass marketing for years. Today, for the first time, giant P&G and its products are under assault: no single company dares attack all product fronts, but a few are successfully taking potshots at single products, as with Kimberly-Clark's Huggies disposable diapers. P&G is fighting back fiercely. In 1984 it introduced a dozen new products, more than ever before. And at last it is moving away from the broad mass market: now it is targeting narrower segments—such as the fast-growing high-income households that are likely to buy such products as Liquid Tide.

But is P&G practicing what marketing theorists preach these days? The answer *might* mean success or disaster to the consumer-products leader. You'll learn all about marketing issues in Part 3.

☐ In Chapter 9, **An Introduction to Marketing,** you'll read about marketing's history and its current role.

☐ Chapter 10, **Product and Pricing Decisions,** looks at how marketers put together, package, and price their products.

☐ Chapter 11, **Promotion,** talks about selling products via advertising, personal selling, publicity, and sales promotion.

☐ Chapter 12, **Wholesaling, Retailing, and Distribution,** tells how goods are moved from manufacturer to consumer.

AN INTRODUCTION TO MARKETING

During the 1970s, businesspeople, worried about inflation, tried to increase productivity and cut costs. During the early 1980s, they worried about recession and used every possible strategy simply to stay in business. Now they're worried about keeping up with a changing business environment characterized by changing consumer values, deregulation, and fierce competition. As a result, they're knocking themselves out to win over the customer. By means of polls, interviews, and questionnaires, they are trying to say and do all that they can to elicit the magic "yes." They even use marketing consultants to complete the perfect match, saying, in effect, "Win the consumer for me and name your own price." Even such conservative industries as railroads and utilities are courting consumers, for as one marketing vice-president pointed out, "The customer is the most important product . . . because if he doesn't like what we have, he can go elsewhere."

What is the function known as marketing, and why has it become business's number one competitive weapon? In this chapter we'll find out.

CHAPTER FOCUS

After reading the material in this chapter, you will be able to:

- define marketing, and indicate its importance in our economy
- cite the eight major functions of marketing
- name the three stages in the evolution of marketing over the last century
- point out the population statistics and trends that are most important to marketers today
- describe several rational and emotional motives that affect people's buying habits
- name the characteristics that distinguish the industrial market from the consumer market
- specify the four basic components of the the marketing mix and how they should vary with the product and customer

 When quarterly losses at Atari Inc., the high-tech manufacturer of video games, began to exceed $50 million, its board of directors searched for a new chief executive. The man they hired wasn't an engineer or a computer specialist, but rather James J. Morgan, Philip Morris's crack marketer. Morgan is generally credited with keeping Marlboro, Merit, and Virginia Slims among the nation's best-selling cigarettes, and so he is partially responsible for Philip Morris's top-ranking $11.7 billion annual income.[1]

In a similar vein, the electronics division of Mattel, Inc., recently lured a marketing executive away from a beauty-aids company to serve as its president, and the new head of the burgeoning Apple Computer Inc. is John Sculley, who cut his teeth in marketing while he was president of Pepsi-Cola.[2] Why have so many young firms hired marketing specialists as chief executive officers? Many companies, especially new high-tech firms, are learning that quality products do not sell automatically on their own merits. If customers don't want what a firm sells, don't know a product exists, or can't afford something, they won't buy. Nor will they be able to buy if the product isn't distributed so that they can get it. It is up to marketers to come up with the products consumers want, put them into homes and businesses, and keep customers coming back for more.[3]

WHAT IS MARKETING?

Much of the nation's cheese is made in Wisconsin and much of its lettuce is grown in California, yet these foods are sold in most states, thanks to marketing. Folger's coffee and Charmin bathroom tissue, two standards on today's supermarket shelves, were lowly regional products before clever marketers got hold of them. Whether or not you have Wisconsin cheese or Folger's coffee in your kitchen, as a consumer you benefit from marketing, just as business does, because it gives you an option to use products and services you might not have access to otherwise.

Marketing, basically, is *finding out what buyers want or need and then getting it to them, to the profit or benefit of everyone involved in the transaction.* Marketing encompasses a wide range of functions, including *buying, selling, storing, financing, risk bearing, transporting, standardization and grading,* and *securing information.* Table 1 briefly describes each of these essential marketing functions.

Marketing is crucial for retail businesses, but it is equally important for other types of business too. Makers of materials, such as steel, must market their products to potential customers—auto makers, appliance manufacturers, builders, and others. Makers of high-tech products, including the most advanced robots, also must market to companies and individuals who can use them. Services, such as the Century 21 real estate company, have turned to marketing to increase the number of their customers. And marketing techniques have even been embraced by lawyers, who, in the face of an increasingly crowded field, have resorted to advertising and competitive pricing to capture new clients. Ideas, too, can be marketed by applying the same approaches that sell detergent.

In this chapter and the three that follow, we will examine marketing activities in some depth. We begin by asking, "What is a market?"

THE MARKET ITSELF

Christmas 1983 is likely to be remembered as the year of the Cabbage Patch Kids. It was a crazy time. Children all over America practically threatened to turn against Santa Claus if they did not receive one of the homely, soft dolls that were all the rage. Parents, in turn, assaulted salespeople and each other so their kids would not be disappointed on Christmas morning. One man reportedly flew to London from the Midwest to buy a $20 doll for $100. Why?

The story of the Cabbage Patch Kids is a marketing dream come true. At Coleco Industries, market research analysts found that adults and kids alike reacted enthusiastically to the prospect of being able to "adopt" a plain, one-of-a-kind "baby" doll. Based on the results of observation sessions,

---

TABLE I   Essential Marketing Functions

- **Buying:** Wholesale and retail operations must buy what they want to sell. Manufacturers must buy materials. All businesses buy the services of employees.

- **Selling:** Businesses sell products and services to other businesses and to individuals, using personal selling, advertising, sales promotion, and publicity to enhance sales prospects (see Chapter 11).

- **Transporting:** Shipping goods from their place of manufacture to their place of sale is a major expense for many businesses, but it increases their usefulness (see Chapter 12). For example, who in New Hampshire would buy gasoline if it were necessary to go to Houston to get it?

- **Storing:** Businesses store goods until customers are ready to buy them. Bookstores, for example, keep dictionaries and atlases in stock, rather than waiting for customers to request them before ordering them.

- **Financing:** Most businesses borrow against future sales to buy, promote, transport, and store their products.

- **Risk bearing:** Marketing carries the risk that people will not buy enough of a product to make it profitable to produce it.

- **Standardization and grading:** Quality and quantity control standards, many of which are set by the federal government, free buyers from having to check each unit. For example, eggs are graded so that if you buy a dozen grade A, large eggs you know you're getting high-quality eggs of uniform size.

- **Securing information:** Businesses gather information about their markets by using market research (see p. 257).

---

follow-up interviews, and psychological studies, Coleco began marketing the dolls in the summer of 1983. Their popularity skyrocketed, especially after the media picked up the story and reported that stores were unable to keep enough in stock to meet the demand. By the end of the year almost 3 million white and black Kids had been adopted, and Coleco geared up to add Asian and Hispanic Cabbage Patch Kids to the growing roster of adoptees.[4]

Cabbage Patch fever notwithstanding, dolls have long been a popular gift for children. Parents and grandparents the world over can always be counted on to buy dolls of one kind or another. These doll buyers constitute a **market,** that is, *a group of people who need or desire a specific product or service and have the money to buy it.*

The total market for goods and services consists of two large segments: the *consumer market* and the *business market.* The consumer market consists of individuals or households that purchase goods and services for personal use. The business market is made up of business enterprises that buy goods and services for resale or in order to continue their own operation. Often businesses try to distinguish certain groups from the overall market by age, sex, geographic location, income and spending patterns,

TYPES OF BUSINESS GOODS

Commercial goods: products, such as office supplies and equipment, used by business and industry in administering their affairs. *Examples:* word processor, duplicating machine.

Industrial goods: products used in manufacturing other products for either the consumer or the business market. *Examples:* sheet metal, earth mover.

population size, and mobility in order to market their product more successfully. Using these factors alone or in combination, they attempt to **segment the market,** that is, *to target marketing efforts toward a specific fraction of the total market.* The market for bubble gum, for example, is made up largely of kids, whereas adults comprise the market for breath-freshening chewing gum.

FIGURE 1 SOME SEGMENTS OF THE PAIN-RELIEVER MARKET

Consumer segment:

"High-tech" people   Traditionalists   People with digestive problems

Why they tend to prefer the product:

This group is forward-looking; they seek   These people prefer time-honored remedies,   These people want products containing
innovative solutions to problems   natural healing; they want to avoid   buffers against stomach acidity
                                             over-medicating themselves

Which brands they tend to prefer:

Excedrin Extra-Strength   Bayer aspirin   Bufferin
Anacin   Squibb aspirin   Ascriptin
Empirin

CHANGES IN MARKETING CONCEPTS

Marketing has changed dramatically in the last half-century, as rapid technological advances and increased competition for customers have forced many firms to be aggressive simply to stay in business. These days it takes more than the proverbial better mousetrap to get ahead of the competition and stay there.

PRODUCTION-ORIENTED MARKETING

Until the 1930s, many business executives viewed marketing simply as an offshoot of production. They concentrated on manufacturing and limited their marketing efforts to taking orders and shipping goods. Henry Ford, for example, focused on ways to produce his cars more quickly and cheaply, knowing that people would buy as many cars as he could manufacture.

Some modern companies still use production-oriented marketing, but it may be too limited for many of today's products. At least one highly successful Japanese company has learned this lesson the hard way. Sony, one of the most respected names in consumer electronics, began coasting in 1982. After opening up the video-recorder market with its Betamax, Sony did not improve or refine its product. Furthermore the company kept its prices high, believing Sony's name and reputation for quality would keep sales up despite competition. Competitors developed better video recorders, which they sold for less than Sony's. In the second quarter of 1983, Sony paid for its arrogance: profits crashed by a stunning 57 percent.[5]

SALES-ORIENTED MARKETING

As production capacity increased in the United States in the late 1920s, business leaders began to realize that they would have to persuade people to buy all the goods they could make, and so they expanded their marketing activities. To stimulate demand for their products they spent more on advertising. They also began to develop trained sales forces that could seek out and sell to the thousands of potential customers across the country.

The rapid growth of radio in the late 1920s and the 1930s boosted the shift in emphasis from production to sales. For the first time a manufacturer was able to get a sales message to millions of people at one time. The power of radio advertising transformed scores of brand names, such as Jell-O and Lipton Tea, into household words. Of course, the advent of television in the late 1940s provided the most potent advertising medium of all. TV made it possible—and, by now, commonplace—for a company to introduce a new product to the entire nation overnight.

THE TOTAL MARKETING CONCEPT

Since World War II, it has become important to serve the consumer, and marketing has come to be equated with an approach known as **total marketing.** Total marketing added to the traditional definition of marketing the concept of *giving the buyer a say in what goods or services the firm sells.* In other words, the efforts of all the firm's departments should be coordinated to produce what the consumer wants. Today this approach may be necessary for survival in many consumer markets, where the capacity to produce goods often outstrips consumer demand and an increasing number of businesses are vying for a limited number of customers.

As part of the growing trend toward total marketing, there has been an increasing emphasis on the marketing function of getting information through market research. Essentially, **market research** attempts to find out:

1. *what products or services the consumer wants;*
2. *what forms, colors, packaging, price ranges, and retail outlets the consumer prefers;* and
3. *what types of advertising, public relations, and selling practices are most likely to appeal to the consumer.*

This information helps manufacturers decide what to make and how to sell it.

TYPES OF CONSUMER GOODS

Convenience goods: products that are readily available, low-priced, and heavily advertised, and that consumers buy quickly and often. *Examples:* bread, razor blades, soft drinks.

Shopping goods: products for which a consumer spends a lot of time shopping, comparing prices, quality, and style. *Examples:* furniture, jewelry, appliances.

Specialty goods: products, usually brand items, that a consumer will make a particular effort to locate. *Examples:* perfume, high-fashion clothing.

PROFILING THE CONSUMER

Efficient total marketing begins, of course, with getting an accurate picture of the consumers who are being targeted. For example, many of the people who grew up eating frozen TV dinners now wouldn't go near what they consider junk food. They crave low-calorie gourmet fare instead, if sales volume is any indication. Stouffer's Lean Cuisine is so "hot" that factories churn out these 300-calorie-or-less delectables six days a week, but supermarkets can't stock them fast enough. The same goes for Campbell's Soup's Le Menu line of "Continental" classics, including chicken parmigiana with fettuccini Alfredo and green beans (500 calories).

Many of the consumers who want to dine on higher-quality prepared food are women in the work force (52 percent of adult females are employed outside the home). But according to a study of more than 13,000 supermarket consumers in Baltimore, Houston, Los Angeles and Minneapolis, nearly half of all shoppers today are men. And there's a swelling tide of singles who have more to spend on time-saving foods than their married counterparts and who want the convenience of

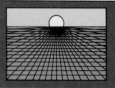
HIGH TECH AND TOTAL MARKETING

Few markets illustrate the importance of total marketing as clearly as the markets for high technology do. Bankruptcy has taught many high-tech companies this lesson the hard way. In the early days of computers, for example, most manufacturers followed a simple marketing scheme: they would produce a computer, put it on a shelf, and wait for it to sell—a classic example of production-oriented marketing. Before long most young firms realized they would have to teach their customers about the product, using sales-oriented marketing to inform customers why they should have the product. But recently, growing demand and technological advances have forced a shift to total marketing. More and more manufacturers now try to find out what customers' needs and specifications are, and respond to them directly. Computer firms that brought their marketing efforts to this stage quickly and efficiently are still in the business. The others are learning the details of bankruptcy law.

Robotics is a high-technology area that is only now making the transition from sales-oriented marketing to total marketing. U.S. robotics firms are still fighting an uphill battle in the sales-oriented marketing stage: many in both management and labor fear that robots will displace human labor, so the robotics firms are having to educate their customers about the potential of robots.

Meanwhile, as the benefits customers can reap from installing robots in their factories become more obvious, and as more capital-strong companies enter the market, robotics firms are starting to pay greater attention to customer preferences. General Electric, for example, assures customers that its intricate nationwide service system is equipped to cope with robotic ills. Cincinnati Milacron, another giant company that is entering robotics, is drawing customers by pointing to its longstanding reputation in the machine-tool industry. Smaller robotics firms, which are desperately trying to elbow their way into the market, offer even more satisfying advantages. Prab Robots has acquired new plants that will allow it to manufacture robots with a wide range of skills. Prab's approach is to assure buyers that they are getting a robot that does as much as needed—and no more. International Robomation/Intelligence, meanwhile, has managed to cut the typical $30,000–$50,000 price to less than $10,000. It may be the first robotics company to apply the ultimate concept of total marketing: selling a discount version.

SOURCE: Philip Maher, "Coming to Grips with the Robot Market," *Industrial Marketing,* January 1982, pp. 93–98.

cooking a single portion, plus a vast population of persons in the twenty-five–forty-five age range who earn $25,000 or more per year and have a special interest in low-calorie foods.[6] Even allowing for some overlap among these groups, the market for gourmet-style convenience foods is considerable.

The success of the new lines of frozen dinners might not have come about had the frozen-food packagers not asked some important questions about the changing needs of American consumers. The questions they asked were the same ones all marketers ask when they are trying to get their target consumers into sharp focus. First they want to know the facts about a given market. How many people might use a certain product? Where do they live? How old are they? How well educated are they?

How much do they earn, and how do they spend their money? Such facts are the subject of **demography**—*the study of population*—an area of research that is one of the marketing manager's basic sources of information.

The second kind of marketing information tells something about why consumers in a particular market behave the way they do. For example, why would a college professor and a crane operator who both make $25,000, live in the same city, and have the same size families tend to buy different kinds of motorcycles, cars, or types of food? To answer questions of this sort, marketing managers turn to **psychology**—*the study of individual behavior*—and **sociology**—*the study of group behavior.* From sociological research, marketing people acquire general information about ethnic, religious, cultural, social, and economic groups and the influences of these groups on people's behavior.

WHO ARE THE BIG SPENDERS?

Eighteen to thirty-four: the new breed

At present, the "hottest" consumer category is the eighteen- to thirty-four age group, the TV generation with money to spend. They are the young marrieds who buy houses, cars, appliances—all the goods needed to run a household and raise a family. They are also the young unmarrieds, a group that has grown steadily as an economic and social force.

Marketers view this generation, particularly the twenty-five- to thirty-four-year-olds, as a new breed of consumer, the most educated buying group in American history. Almost half have been to college,

and one-quarter possess degrees. With one-third of the purchasing power of all U.S. consumers and a combined annual income of $335 billion, they dominate the American economy.[7] The fact that many of the women in this group are in the work force contributes to their clout, creating new segments for products and services. Since young adults are enthusiastic TV viewers, they're particularly susceptible to automobile commercials. They are heavy consumers of time-saving devices, such as food processors, and items their parents viewed as luxuries, such as second cars, microwave ovens, color TVs and vacation packages. Sports figure importantly in their lives, as does physical fitness, a trend reflected in the emergence of such publications as *Jogging* magazine. Because they often buy on credit, their spending habits account for a 20 percent decline in the national savings rate and a rise in the total consumer debt.[8] Yet the materialism of this group is balanced by what some marketers refer to as "earth values" (simple,

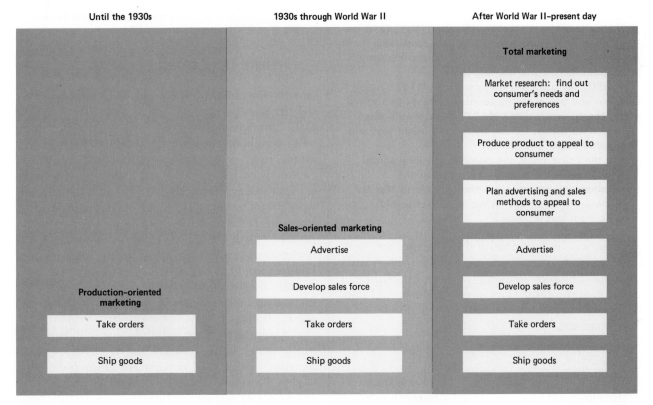

FIGURE 2

CHANGING CONCEPTS IN MARKETING

FIGURE 3

THE CHANGING AGE MIX OF AMERICANS: POPULATION CHANGES MEAN CHANGES IN MARKETS

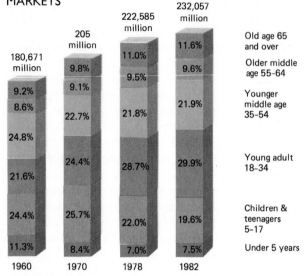

By comparing the proportion of each age group in the population in 1960 with the 1970, 1978, and 1982 proportions, you can trace the growth and decline of several important market segments.

In 1960, for instance, there were 20,415,823 young children and babies in the country. Twenty-two years later, there were only 17,404,275. What would this decline have meant for the baby-food, infant-toy, and disposable diaper industries?

On the other hand, the number of young adults swelled from 39,024,936 to 63,881,895, as the generation that started with the post-World War II baby boom came of age. What industries would benefit from this increase?

inexpensive, and durable) and "feather values" (self-indulgent, showy, sensual, and expensive)—values that may be a combination of the anti-Establishment outlook of this group's teen years and a more Establishment-oriented way of thinking that developed as they matured.[9]

Over sixty-five: the fastest-growing age group

In the early 1970s, marketers noticed that the over-sixty-five population was growing faster than other groups. Between 1970 and 1980, the membership of this group rose by 31.4 percent—from 20 million to

26.3 million people. Furthermore, the number of persons over the age of eighty-five increased 9.1 percent between 1980 and 1982, to 2.4 million. The American woman now has a life expectancy of eighty-four, the highest in human history.[10]

Another significant characteristic of this group is their rising income. Increasing numbers of Americans are choosing to continue working past the conventional retirement age of sixty-five, and there is some pressure on Congress to provide higher Social Security payments to people who work longer. If employer-mandated retirement at a fixed age were to be prohibited by law, as Senator Claude Pepper of Florida has advocated, many more people might continue working full time well beyond age sixty-five. These people no longer have children living at home, many have paid off their home mortgages, and Medicare pays a large part of their medical bills. Therefore, even though their income after retirement may be limited to Social Security and a pension, a greater portion of it is available for travel, and for health- and personal-care products.

WHERE DO CONSUMERS LIVE?

A company must consider geography when evaluating the sales potential of its goods and services, because climate and lifestyle have an impact upon what people buy. A clothing manufacturer, for example, needs to know if the market for heavy winter clothes is shrinking because people are moving to warmer areas. Similarly, a restaurant franchisor would want to sell more franchises in the flourishing states of Texas and the Southwest than in the depressed North Central states, whose population has declined in recent years. And an appliance manufacturer would be more likely to establish a new production facility in a region where the population is increasing, assuming other conditions (such as costs) are favorable.

Americans are among the most mobile people in the world. In 1980, according to the U.S. Census Bureau, about 17 percent of the population changed residence. This is down from 19 percent in 1970, and 21 percent in 1960, but it is still a significant number. Where are Americans moving? They are migrating to the Sunbelt—the area of the

United States that stretches from Virginia south to Florida and west to California (one out of every ten Americans now lives in California). And they are leaving the farms and large cities for small metropolitan areas.

Growth of the Sunbelt

The population of the Sunbelt states has increased by 20 percent for the past decade, a growth rate that is down from a peak of 25 percent for the 1970s. Nevertheless, this region is now growing about 2 percent a year—twice the national average.

Many of the new Sunbelt residents are from the North Central states. Minnesota, for example, lost 900,000 people to the Sunbelt between 1980 and 1982, as a record number of businesses decided to take advantage of lower taxes and better access to markets. Northeastern states have been somewhat more stable, having lost only 108,000 between 1980 and 1982, mostly from Pennsylvania and New York.[11]

Growth of small cities and towns

Industrialized societies such as ours characteristically experience population growth in large urban centers and a decline in the number of people living in rural areas. Yet, according to the 1980 census, the rural population of the United States grew as fast as urban areas between 1970 and 1980, despite the fact that fewer people still live on farms. In fact, many areas that were once considered to be rural are now classified as urban.[12]

What has happened is that people have forsaken the large metropolitan centers and gone to live in small towns and cities and in unincorporated areas near urban centers. The population of towns and unincorporated areas rose about 11 percent between 1970 and 1980, and cities having between 10,000 and 50,000 residents grew more than 30 percent.[13]

New urban patterns

One result of the migration to less crowded population centers has been the development of sprawling metropolitan areas without a clearly defined center.

As neighboring towns and small cities have expanded and people have taken up residence in between them, many of them have physically merged, and their combined population and density are great enough to warrant the area's designation as a metropolitan area. Houma-Thibodaux, Louisiana, is one such area. In 1983, Thibodaux had just 15,810 residents and Houma had 32,602, but the Census Bureau has classified the Houma-Thibodaux area, which includes people living in the area surrounding and between the two cities, as a metropolitan area because 176,876 people make their homes there.

In some cases, small cities have simply been overwhelmed by their suburbs as people, industry, and other institutions moved away from the center city. For example, Benton Harbor, Michigan (1983 population: 14,707), has been designated the center city of a new metropolitan area with a population of 171,276.[14]

What do these changes mean? For one thing, we probably will not see the development of any more center cities surrounded by suburbs whose residents depend on the city for jobs, entertainment, services, and the like. In addition, there is no longer a sharp distinction, statistically speaking, between what is rural and what is urban: we are becoming a more urban people living in a less urban environment.

OTHER CONSUMER CHARACTERISTICS: EDUCATION, INCOME, BUYING HABITS

Marketers are also interested in consumers' education levels: educated people tend to make more money, and they have a taste for certain types of goods such as foreign travel and hardcover books. Likewise, the incomes consumers earn are crucial to marketers' planning. Of particular interest is **disposable personal income,** the *personal income that a family is free to spend after taxes.* All families must spend a certain percentage of their disposable personal income on necessities such as food, clothing, and shelter. But the higher a family's income, the more **discretionary income** it has—*income that can be spent on nonessentials,* such as entertainment, vacation travel, weekend homes, and restaurant dining.

STUDYING CONSUMER BEHAVIOR

Think for a minute about some of the products you've seen advertised or come across in stores and supermarkets—Perrier water, Campbell's alphabet soup, mink vests, down parkas, and so on. Who were these items created for? What would make someone buy a mink vest? The answers to these questions are the concern of consumer-behavior researchers. They want to know how people decide to spend money, credit, and time; what products, services, and ideas attract people and why; when, where, and how consumers purchase and use goods; and who or what influences decisions. Companies that invest substantial sums of money to develop and market new products use this kind of information to reduce the risks involved and increase the chances of success. Market researchers classify the buying public into two groups. The first group consists of *ultimate consumers* (everybody), whose purchases fall into three categories: personal use—say, buying yourself a tennis racket; family use—for example, buying toothpaste the whole family will like; and someone else's use—buying men's cologne for Father's Day. The second category of buyers is collectively referred to as *organizational consumers*: businesses, professional offices, nonprofit institutions, schools, and government. Psychological and sociological factors affect the buying habits of both groups, as we shall see.

The psychology of buying

There are many theories about what induces people to buy products. This section will focus on the ones most widely used by marketers.

CONSUMER DECISIONS One way to look at the psychology of buying is in terms of how consumers make decisions. A simple formula sums up the decision-making process nearly everyone goes through when making a purchase:

Need + Ability to buy + Attitudes toward brand names under which product is sold

= Choice

Let's say you need a new car. Though a Chevrolet Malibu will satisfy the need, you opt for a costlier, more prestigious Mercedes-Benz, knowing that you can afford it, its quality will serve you well, and that the car will impress people because it's a widely accepted status symbol. Thus, your needs for quality and status as well as function have entered into your decision.

RATIONAL VS. EMOTIONAL MOTIVES Imagine that you are standing at a store counter buying a wool scarf. If someone approached and asked why you were buying it, you might say you want to keep your neck warm in cold weather. This would be a **rational motive,** *prompted by reason.* Rational motives relate to cost, dependability, and usefulness, elements marketers appeal to when selling goods.

- *Cost* invariably determines what consumers buy—if all other considerations, such as the quality of different brands and the consumer's ability to pay for any of these brands, are equal.
- *Dependability* is important to upper-middle-class consumers who will pay more for products that work better and last longer.
- *Usefulness* is important to consumers who buy products for functional purposes—the wool scarf, for example. By finding more uses for products, marketers can increase sales.

Emotional motives, on the other hand, *arise from feelings rather than reason.*

- *Sensory satisfaction*—pleasure for the senses of taste, touch, sight, and hearing—is a basic emotional drive. The food and beverage industries, for example, rely upon taste appeal to sell products.
- *Fear,* rooted in the instinct for self-preservation, motivates people to take care of themselves and to avoid unnecessary risks. Life, health, fire and theft insurance, health foods, and safety devices for cars are sold on the basis of fear.
- *Pride* in one's position, home, family, or appearance sells products that enhance the consumer's image.
- *Sociability,* the desire to be with other people, helps market soft drinks, restaurants, and resorts.
- *Emulation*—the desire to imitate others—is another motive marketers rely on. People like to identify with

Only in a Jeep.

Jeep ◢ CJ

TOOTH DECAY.

CAUGHT SOON ENOUGH, EARLY TOOTH DECAY CAN ACTUALLY BE REPAIRED BY COLGATE!

Now Colgate offers conclusive X-ray proof that Colgate does more than simply help prevent cavities. These special X-ray photos show—and the explanation beneath fully describes—how early tooth decay, when caught soon enough, can actually be repaired by Colgate—with the most clinically proven fluoride of any toothpaste.

NEW PROOF: CONCLUSIVE X-RAY EVIDENCE!

BEFORE | AFTER

EARLY TOOTH DECAY. Teeth are made of minerals. Tooth gain and loss minerals every day. But decay can rob and make minerals lose—using these mineral are replaced. Tooth decay starts.

AFTER 10 DAYS USING COLGATE! Colgate's mineral-rich MFP fluoride formula helps replace lost minerals to actually help repair early tooth decay.

*In extra-laboratory tests

COLGATE. THE MAXIMUM FLUORIDE PROTECTION IN ANY TOOTHPASTE.

THE RICOH XR-7. NO OTHER CAMERA GIVES YOU SUCH A COMPLETE PICTURE.

You are looking at what you look at through the viewfinder of the Ricoh XR-7. As you can see, the view encompasses everything.

Its viewfinder with liquid crystal display gives you all the facts. F-stop, shutter speed, exposure compensation and memory indicators. In short, it tells you everything you need to know, when you need to know it, without taking your eye off the subject. And without the distracting flashing LED's found in other less sophisticated viewfinders.

We call this wealth of information the Factfinder. And it is, in fact, just one reason to consider a Ricoh XR-7.

Other reasons include a three-way focusing system (a diagonal split image spot inside a microprism band and Fresnel field), shutter quartz-timed to sixteen seconds. An electronic LED self-timer. Manual and automatic operation. Multiple exposure capability. And a particularly impressive Ricoh attribute, a lightweight aluminum die-cast body for durability no plastic version can touch.

You can also get these advancements with the Ricoh XR-5. That's the remarkable Ricoh that draws its power from the sun.

All of this foresight is visible throughout the Ricoh line. Just tell your photo dealer you want to see something truly innovative. He'll direct your eye right to the Ricoh XR-7.

RICOH
We respond.

IF YOU CAN AFFORD A TELEVISION, NOW YOU CAN AFFORD A BETAMAX

Betamax

For years, ever since you first heard about home videocassette recorders, you've known which one you've wanted. The one VCR that set the standard since the beginning—the Sony Betamax. With Sony reliability. Sony engineering. Sony picture quality. You've heard all the wonders of the Sony Betamax. and you've been wondering when you could afford one.

Well, now you can. For less than the cost of a color television you can own a Sony Betamax SL-2300 video-cassette recorder—the lowest-priced Sony Betamax ever.

Not only is it an affordable VCR, it's an affordable Sony. So you get Sony quality and superb Sony features like BetaScan,™ high speed picture search, a low-profile, front-loading design, with convenient remote control and three-day programmability.

Like all Betamax VCR's, your SL-2300 lets you record one program while watching another. Or record your favorite shows when you're not at home. Or watch your favorite movies and concerts by buying or renting any of the thousands of pre-recorded tapes available in the Beta format. Or take advantage of our special toll-free number 1-800-221-9982 (1-800-522-5329 in New York) for up-to-the-second information about new releases and availabilities.

Most important, your SL-2300 will let you use the miraculous new Betamovie™—the world's first one-piece home video camera/recorder. Betamovie lets you tape up to 3 hours and 20 minutes on a standard L-830 Beta cassette without having to carry your SL-2300 along. So you can create your own movies, capture family memories, practice

your business presentation...open up a world of possibilities no other format can give you.

All that's available to you if you say "I want the Sony Betamax SL-2300." And it's available in your choice of Mandarin Red, Sapphire Blue or High Tech Silver finishes. Chances are, if you can afford a television, you can afford a Sony Betamax. And the only question is, why wait any longer?

Sony Betamax, Betamovie and BetaScan are trademarks of Sony Corporation. © 1984 Sony Corporation of America.

SONY
THE ONE AND ONLY

Advertisers try to capture buyers' attention by appealing to a variety of needs, interests, and feelings. How, in your opinion, does each of these ads attempt to motivate the buyer? Which ads have a rational appeal? Which appeal to the buyer's emotions?

movie stars, athletes, and other celebrities, such as the ones featured in many of the TV ads for the American Express Card.

Rational and emotional motives usually overlap because consumers have multiple motives for buying something. A wool scarf, for example, will keep you warm, but it might also appeal to your senses of sight and touch.

Psychographics: the lifestyle profile

Psychographics is a relatively new specialty that *characterizes consumers in terms of their behavior and attitudes.* A psychographic profile might draw hundreds of responses to statements about activities, interests, opinions, and social roles that help peg an individual's lifestyle. For example, a person who agrees with statements such as "I shop a lot for discounts," "I usually watch the advertisements for sales," and "A person can save a lot of money shopping around for bargains," would fall into the category of Price-Conscious Consumer. Heavy users of margarine and other forms of shortening might like housekeeping, be child-oriented, and fit into a Homebody category. Psychographic profiles identify market segments, target new products and reposition existing ones, develop media guidelines, and aid marketers in packaging design and product formulation.

BUSINESS BUYERS: A DIFFERENT BREED

Most of this chapter has been devoted to individual consumers because of their diverse characteristics and wide range of buying motives. But business buyers and markets are equally important to the economy. *Marketing to business,* or **industrial marketing,** has some unique characteristics. Look at the number of buyers, for example: whereas Procter & Gamble and Colgate-Palmolive compete to sell their products to millions of individual consumers, the most profitable market for the computers produced by IBM and Apple Computer Inc. is made up of a much smaller number of large businesses. Therefore industrial marketers will use somewhat different approaches from the ones used to market consumer goods.

Assume that Citibank, a major banking institution with branches throughout the New York metropolitan area, announced that it was going to overhaul its entire computer system. IBM and Apple both want to sell their systems to Citibank. What marketing methods will they use? What approaches will they take? In industrial marketing, products or services are generally sold for functional reasons rather than by brand name or attractiveness, because of their considerable cost and the need to tailor them to fit the customer's needs. The motivation for acquiring technical business equipment or services is usually rational, based on its usefulness to the buyer. Businesses try to avoid investing in unnecessary services or products, especially when costs may total many thousands, or even millions, of dollars. Emotional motives do not heavily influence business buyers.

The salesperson of a business service or product requires a technical background; he or she must be prepared to sell on the basis of cost and reliability. The customer is an employee of a business firm, government agency, or nonprofit institution, who is likely to be knowledgeable about the products or services being considered. The purchasing agent at Citibank, for example, will be capable of weighing the comparative advantages of one computer system over another. Moreover, the business buyer possesses negotiating skills that ordinary consumers lack. Because huge investments are involved, the business buyer will require assurance that the marketer understands the company's rational and technical needs. The marketer must provide this assurance. For instance, at Citibank, the marketer must guarantee the buyer that a computer system will be installed on schedule at the agreed price, and that service will be prompt and competent if anything goes wrong.

Impulse buying rarely occurs in business marketing, because the purchase time generally takes months, allowing for approvals, necessary modifications to the product, and delivery. Yet, even though buying services or equipment for business is a rational process, the personal relationship between buyer and seller can influence sales as surely as it influences the sale of consumer products. Creating and maintaining such relationships is part of the marketing person's job.

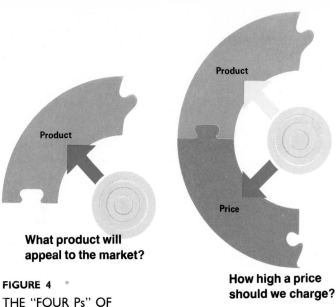

What product will
appeal to the market?

How high a price
should we charge?

What's the most
effective
promotion?

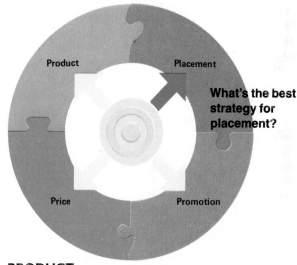

What's the best
strategy for
placement?

FIGURE 4

THE "FOUR Ps" OF
MARKETING: PRODUCT, PRICE,
PROMOTION, AND PLACEMENT

**Product, price, promotion and placement are four
aspects of marketing strategy which together make up
the *marketing mix*. Creating a marketing mix is like
solving a puzzle: the marketing manager must fit the
right product with the right price, and must find the
right promotional approach and the right methods of
placement (or distribution), to satisfy the needs and
preferences of the particular target market.**

**Looking at it another way, we may note that the
marketing manager's choice of product, price,
promotion, and placement is dictated by the target
market. We have emphasized this by showing arrows
pointing *from* the target market *to* the "Four Ps."**

**Marketers must study their target market carefully,
for the characteristics of the target market determine
the makeup of the marketing mix.**

THE MARKETING MIX: THE FOUR Ps

The variety of smaller market segments within the
consumer and business market is enormous, and
targeting the correct one is half the marketing battle. In any total marketing program the other half of
the battle is determining the **marketing mix,** *the
blend of product, price, promotion, and place (or distribution) that satisfies the demands of the chosen market segment.* The strategies that succeed generally blend *the
four Ps*—as the marketing mix is commonly called—
to develop the most lucrative market. Let's look at
each of the four Ps in turn.

PRODUCT

A businessperson's first marketing decision concerns the products or services that will attract customers in the target market. The key is to determine
consumers' needs and wants and translate them into
desirable products and services. Rising crime rates,
for example, have created a target market among
small businesses for a growing number of security
services. Similarly, the rapid increase in the number
of working women has inspired clothing manufacturers to include more high-priced women's suits in
their overall product mix: many women have discovered they need to "dress for success" just as men
do.

MARKETING WARFARE: competition among today's manufacturers is intense.

Marketers speak of "retrenchment," "frontal attacks," "guerrilla warfare," "flank defenses," and other strategies that smack more of the Pentagon than the executive suite.

Changing conditions require the continuous re-evaluation of product lines. Procter & Gamble, for example, is the largest consumer packaged-goods company in America. It sells Ivory soap, Tide detergent, Pampers disposable diapers, and Charmin toilet tissue, to name only a few of its successful products. But success can be dangerous. Many of the markets in which P&G products dominate are no longer growing, and some of their products are losing their market share in increasingly crowded markets. To ensure continued profit growth, P&G has expanded into new territories—soft drinks, fruit juices, and drugs.[15]

PRICE

Having made the basic decisions about the product line, the marketing manager must decide how the company should price its products. Sometimes low prices will maximize profits. Supermarkets have used this tactic successfully on two levels. Most offer unbranded, so-called *generic* products at the lowest price and offer their own brand, usually at a slightly higher price, in addition to the still-higher-price commercial brands. On the other hand, the desirability of some products depends on a high-quality image, which a high price helps to confer. The factors that enter into decisions about both product line and pricing will be discussed in Chapter 10.

PROMOTION

Very often the most important decision a marketing manager makes is how the manufacturer should inform prospective customers about its products. This involves promotion, which includes the sales approach. Some marketing strategists, like those at Avon Products, may decide to emphasize direct selling and spend most of their promotion dollars to train and pay salespeople. Others, like producers of soap and headache remedies, promote their products through advertising, primarily on television. Department stores also spend heavily on advertising, but they choose newspapers as the most effective medium. The alternatives are many and the choice may determine the success of a marketing effort. We'll discuss promotion in Chapter 11.

PLACE

The fourth element in the marketing mix is place (or distribution): how the manufacturer gets its products to the customers. Transportation is the major factor here, but place also entails decisions about distribution outlets. Tupperware, for example, distributes directly to the consumer through its party approach. Most clothing companies, on the other hand, sell to retailers, who resell to consumers. Some manufacturers employ multiple placement systems. Thus Whirlpool Corporation sells the Whirlpool brand of appliances to distributors for sale to dealers, and it also makes the Kenmore brand, which it ships directly to Sears Roebuck and Company. Sears itself sells through its stores and by catalogue. HARTMARX makes suits and sportswear for independent retailers, but also makes them available to consumers through its own retail stores, including Wallach's and Baskin. In short, there are many ways of distributing goods. We'll discuss them further in Chapter 12.

PUTTING IT ALL TOGETHER

The trick in marketing is to figure out a clever way to combine the four Ps in such a manner as to increase profits—and gain a larger share of the market. The right marketing mix is largely responsible for Noxell Corporation's stunning growth in the recession-ravaged cosmetics field in recent years.

While Revlon and other luxury cosmetic firms gasped for air in the late 1970s and early 1980s, Noxell's sales soared and so did its profits. Its secret was keen manipulation of the four Ps. Noxell was quick to notice that demand for inexpensive, no-nonsense cosmetics rose as more women entered the work force. It had been successfully selling Noxzema face creams to that market for years and had developed a line of low-priced cosmetics in the 1960s, so the decision was made to gear up promotion. Advertising now consumes some 20 percent of Noxell's sales, but who hasn't heard of its Cover Girl line? But no matter how heavily cosmetics are advertised, they, like other frequently purchased items, must be widely available. Knowing this, Noxell managed to place Cover Girl not only in drugstores but in supermarkets as well. The combination of good placement, low price, high recognition, and good product allowed Noxell to grow during a difficult period when many firms were merely seeking creative ways to cut losses.[16]

CHAPTER REVIEW

Many companies are learning that they need not only good products but also marketing skills in order to succeed. They must be able to identify consumer needs and to satisfy them in a mutually beneficial manner. Those people who want a given product and can buy it constitute its market.

The process of marketing includes all the activities by which goods and services move from the producer to the consumer. There are eight basic marketing functions: buying, selling, transporting, storing, financing, risk bearing, standardization and grading, and securing information.

Marketing has changed radically over the past half-century. At one time most firms were production oriented and restricted marketing activities primarily to taking orders and shipping goods. Then came sales-oriented marketing, which emphasized selling. Since World War II, however, most large firms have shifted to a consumer-oriented approach known as the total marketing concept, which has relied increasingly on market research. This approach is now also being used in industry.

Population statistics are a basic marketing tool. They can indicate with reasonable accuracy how many people there are, how old they are, what they earn, how they spend their money, and where they live.

The psychology of buying looks at consumer decision making in terms of rational and emotional motives. Rational factors include cost, dependability, and usefulness. Emotional factors are satisfaction of the senses, fear, pride, sociability, and emulation. Both types of motive often enter into the decision to buy a product or service.

Marketers use psychographics to uncover characteristics that demographic and sociological surveys can't isolate—to draw profiles of individual consumers and decide whether they're likely to want to use particular products.

Industrial buyers form a different market from individual consumers with respect to motivation, product, sales personnel, customer, and purchase time. Technical and rational considerations predominate with industrial buyers, but they need assurances from the marketer that the company will do the job it promises.

The marketing manager tries to develop a marketing mix that will have the greatest appeal to the target market. The marketing mix consists of four elements, the so-called four Ps: product, promotion, price, and placement.

KEY WORDS

marketing (254)

market (255)

market segment (255)

total marketing (257)

market research (257)

demography (258)

psychology (258)

sociology (258)

disposable personal income (261)

discretionary income (261)

rational motive (262)

emotional motive (262)

psychographics (264)

industrial marketing (264)

marketing mix (265)

REVIEW QUESTIONS

1. Define marketing and explain why it is important to the American economy.

2. How does the total marketing concept differ from the approaches that it replaces: product-oriented and sales-oriented marketing?

3. Why is it important for businesses to identify target markets for their products?

4. What is the fastest-growing age group in the nation today? Describe their overall consumer behavior.

5. What is the difference between disposable personal income and discretionary income?

6. List several rational motives and emotional motives for buying.

7. What have been the major geographic shifts of the past decade and what are their implications for marketing?

8. How does industrial buying differ from consumer buying?

9. What are the four Ps of marketing, which make up the marketing mix?

CASE I

CAN COCA-COLA MARKET MOVIES LIKE SOFT DRINKS?

The age of the corporate conglomerate has brought together some odd couples, and among the strangest is the Coca-Cola Company and Columbia Pictures. Coke bought the movie company in 1982 hoping to improve its 10-percent-per-year growth rate. With the burgeoning of cable TV and the video-cassette business, the market for movies was growing. By applying Coke's marketing expertise, Roberto C. Goizueta, Coke's chief executive, expected the acquisition to pay off handsomely.

Goizueta gave Peter S. Sealey the job of designing a marketing strategy for Columbia, which was well known for its haphazard approach. It would be a challenge for Sealey, who said, "I would put the movie business ten to fifteen years behind the consumer-package industry in marketing sophistication." To begin with, Sealey zeroed in on Columbia's number one marketing weakness: reckless spending on advertising. For example, the company's promotion of *Gandhi,* an Academy Award winner, cost tens of millions of dollars. Once the dust had settled, this left very little in the way of profits. Then Sealey conducted research to measure the payoffs from Columbia's ad campaigns.

Sealey also planned to test consumer reaction to ad *concepts* before launching expensive campaigns and—perhaps more important—to do similar research on movie ideas. If the results of these surveys match up with subsequent box-office data, the movie studio may well begin testing not only proposed scripts but also approaches to casting and production. Says Sealey, "If the basic premise is not going to be bought by the public, then great sensitivity and a great director may not be able to save it."

Pointing out that the kind of information long taken for granted in the soft-drink industry has never been available to the movie studios, Sealey tackled such questions as:

- *Who* are Columbia's customers?
- *Why* do they buy Columbia's products?
- *What* are they really looking for?

Armed with the answers to those questions, Columbia could explore new markets for movies (such as video cassettes and cable TV) and the extent to which these may overlap with the old-fashioned movie house and TV network audiences. This is important partly because there is a particular sequence in the marketing of movies, beginning at the movie houses and progressing, at intervals of six months to a year, through video cassettes, cable TV, network TV, and independent TV stations. If some of these markets do not overlap, Columbia may be able to speed up its revenue flow by releasing a picture to more than one market at a time.

In the meantime, Coke is gambling on TV, particularly on cable TV. It has, in fact, created a whole new studio called Tri-Star Pictures, whose releases, after their run in the movie theaters, will have guaranteed bookings on HBO before CBS airs them. At the very least, the arrangement is expected to cover Tri-Star's production costs.

The entertainment industry is changing rapidly, and Coke believes that marketing can determine who comes out on top. According to Coca-Cola president Donald R. Keough, "You used to live and die on how well a movie did at the Bijou in Racine"; now, however, film making "is a commodity business for the rest of the industry," supplying the needs of all the non–movie house markets. Coke is determined to learn what those needs are and to meet them.[17]

1. If you were designing a questionnaire to help profile the movie consumer, what key questions would you be sure to include?

2. Some "products" don't lend themselves to market research, and some "producers" can't work from formulas. Some of Coke's critics have pointed out that this is true of movies and movie makers—that film making is an art and therefore depends on intuition, not numbers. What do you think about this? *Can* successful popular entertainment be churned out according to formula? Consider other creative areas, such as fashion or interior design.

3. What is the point of "staging" the distribution of a movie? Under what circumstances might Columbia release one to the theaters and to cable TV simultaneously?

CASE 2

WHAT COLOR ARE YOUR SPARKPLUGS?

You have suddenly discovered that you can, after all, afford to buy a new car and are about to order a 1985 Chevrolet Citation. Having made that decision, you must consider the available options. First there's body style: two-door or four-door? Then there's the engine: four, six, or eight cyl-inders? Automatic or manual transmission? Power steering? Air conditioning? Central locking system? Tinted glass? Power windows? Defoggers? Defrosters? The list goes on and on. By the time you leave the showroom you will, in effect, have ruled out some 30,000 alternative versions of your particular vehicle. But you can take pleasure in the knowledge that the car will be truly *yours*—one of a kind. You may be less pleased to know that this "uniqueness" has added more than $1,000 to the car's price, because that's what it costs the manufacturer to build the required flexibility into assembly operations.

When Henry Ford started out, he simply built the best cars he could, and they were all pretty much alike. In fact, there was a saying that "You can have a Ford car in any color you want—as long as it's black." At that time Ford's buyers—who outnumbered the cars—were happy to snap them up as they rolled off the assembly line. Today's auto makers, however, offer an enormous variety, a result of the auto industry's greatly enlarged output, its apparent shortage of buyers, and its consequent determination to, in the words of a former GM chairman, build a car "for every purse and purpose." This is a logical approach to a buyers' market. That is, if there are many more cars than buyers, it makes sense to try to attract as many of those buyers as possible by finding out exactly what each one would like to have in a car, and then providing exactly that.

Now it's becoming obvious to many companies that this strategy does not always work. Apart from the fact that variety costs the manufacturers a great deal, they have found that it may not pay to focus on a very small market; the potential buyers may be so few that it will not be possible to recover the costs of design, manufacture, promotion, and distribution, let alone make a profit. Suppose, for example, that Chevrolet were to tool its line so that its Monte Carlo model could be offered with stripes or polka dots. Chances are that the number of interested buyers would be too small to justify the trouble and expense.

Rather than going the polka-dot route, Detroit is planning to follow the lead of the Japanese, who—with plants halfway around the world—have not been able to offer so many options. Instead, they have carefully researched the American market and broken it down into several large segments. By offering only twenty or thirty versions of a popular model, the Japanese are able to engineer and manufacture a higher-quality car, distribute it more efficiently, and sell it for less than the price of a comparable American car. It's a formula that has paid off nicely.

American auto makers would like to find a reasonable compromise between standardization and variety. As Thomas Staudt of GM says, "The challenge for all of us is to figure out what product differences the consumer is willing to pay for and which ones are spurious and too expensive."[18]

1. How do you think American consumers would react if Detroit started limiting options on cars? Explain your answer.

2. How could Detroit auto makers figure out what kinds of cars to produce?

3. If total marketing means catering to the consumer, then why have the standardized Japanese cars outsold the more customized American cars?

4. In Chapter 6, we read about new manufacturing techniques that can reduce the cost of doing small runs. These techniques might eventually make small runs cheaper than mass production. How might this change Detroit's marketing strategy? Explain your answer.

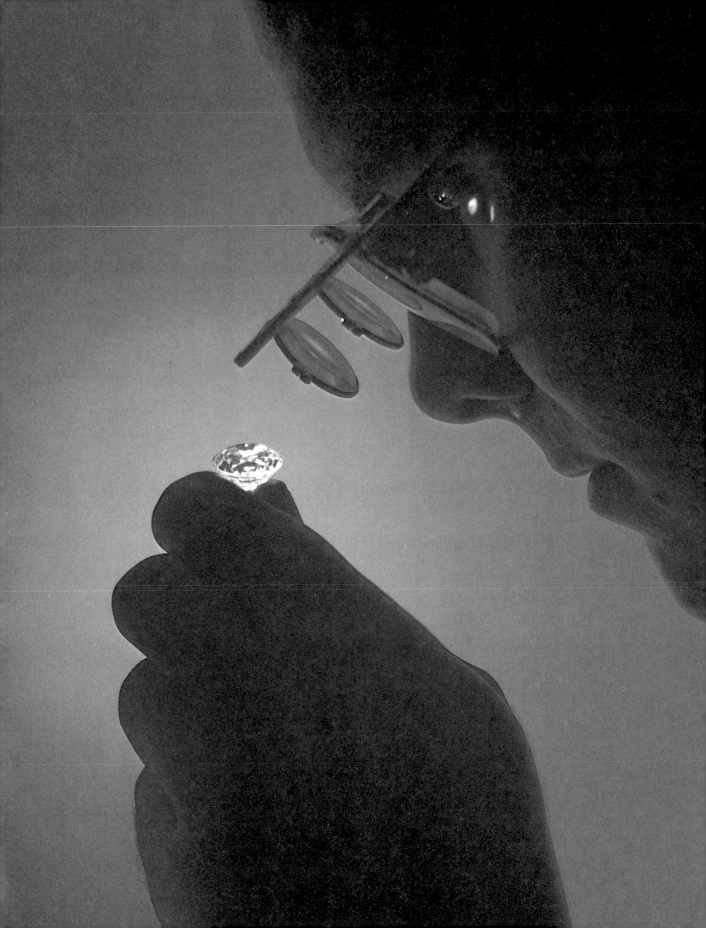

PRODUCT AND PRICING DECISIONS 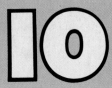 10

In 1977 General Foods' marketing people discovered that Jell-O brand puddings and gelatins, family favorites for many years, were no longer selling well. Why? Time-pressed consumers had no patience with desserts they had to make for themselves. Moreover, the burgeoning health and fitness movement had fostered greater interest in low-calorie foods. In response to these shifts in market needs, General Foods created a new type of no-fuss treat: frozen pudding on a stick. Called Jell-O Pudding Pops to take advantage of the well-known Jell-O brand name, the new product was heavily promoted with ads proclaiming that Pudding Pops are just as quick and easy to eat as ice cream bars, but they are also considerably lower in calories. The introduction of Pudding Pops caught the competition napping. No one had a comparable product. Today Pudding Pops sales exceed $100 million annually, and General Foods is considering a whole line of new frozen dessert products. Of course, by now a horde of late-coming competitors have galloped into the frozen pudding field, all trying to follow in Pudding Pops' tracks.

CHAPTER FOCUS

After reading the material in this chapter, you will be able to:

- name one advantage and one disadvantage of offering a broad product mix
- specify the stages in the life cycle of a product
- describe the seven stages of new product development
- cite the advantages and possible disadvantages of establishing a brand name
- name two alternatives to establishing a brand name, and indicate the value of each
- discuss the functions of packaging and the possible environmental threat it poses
- cite several laws affecting product labeling
- specify three traditional pricing policies and the forces that currently affect those policies
- describe two options for pricing new products
- distinguish several techniques of pricing, including markups and discounts

Jell-O Pudding Pops are an example of a product that succeeds because it is innovative; it carves out a new market *niche*, or product category. Such products are the exception rather than the rule. Generally, a product is designed specifically to do battle in an already crowded market. This has been the case in the fiercely competitive, $20 billion domestic soft-drink industry, where the big three in carbonated beverages—Coca-Cola Company, PepsiCo, and Philip Morris's Seven-Up—have been launching salvos of new sodas in what has come to be known as the "cola wars."

In the early 1970s the soft-drink industry was growing at a healthy 10 percent, but by 1982 the growth rate had shrunk to 2 percent.[1] One reason for the decline had to do with demographics: the soda-loving baby-boom generation had gotten older and had turned to more sophisticated beverages, such as mineral water and white wine. Another factor was the health and fitness boom. Many health-conscious consumers were avoiding sugary, caffeinated cola drinks like Coke and Pepsi, which are the industry's traditional leaders.[2]

Seven-Up struck the first blow in the cola wars with a nationwide ad campaign proclaiming that its popular lemon-lime product, Seven-Up, contains no caffeine. Then, in 1982 Seven-Up introduced two new caffeine-free colas—Like and Sugar Free Like. (Actually, Royal Crown Companies had pioneered the caffeine-free field with *RC100* two years before, but lacked the size and marketing strength to capitalize on its innovation.) PepsiCo quickly countered Seven-Up's initiative with two decaffeinated colas of its own, Pepsi Free and Sugar Free Pepsi Free. Smash hits, the new Pepsis quickly grabbed 50 percent of the growing caffeine-free market. Next Coca-Cola entered the fray with diet Coke, which, along with long-established Tab, made Coca-Cola a powerful contender in the sugarless cola market. In the spring of 1983 Coca-Cola entered the decaffeinated market with a vengeance, introducing Caffeine Free Coke, Caffeine Free diet Coke, and Caffeine Free Tab.

In less than a year's time, the number of big-brand cola products grew from ten to eighteen, and the struggle for cola shelf space at the supermarket and other retail outlets became intense. New brands

FIGURE I

ASPECTS OF THE MARKETING MIX: PRODUCT

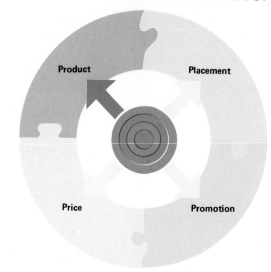

When deciding what product to produce, the marketing manager considers the needs and wants of the target market.

that did not demonstrate immediate customer appeal were quickly replaced. To persuade retailers to stock their products, the cola makers offered discount prices and other money-back promotions. Discounting can lead to other problems, however; it may attract new customers and perhaps build market share, but it also drains short-term profits. Only a firm like Coca-Cola, which has many different revenue sources and almost inexhaustible cash reserves, can successfully weather a prolonged price war. Smaller competitors, such as Dr. Pepper, have been forced from the field, and even PepsiCo has found continuous discounting burdensome.

The story of the cola wars highlights just a few aspects of the complex, challenging process of creating and pricing a product. In this chapter we'll examine the various factors that go into product and pricing decisions and look at what can happen when these decisions are carried out.

THE PRODUCT MIX

When the soda manufacturers launched their new caffeine-free colas, they were trying to fill a new niche in the vast soft-drink market. The soda makers, like most companies, continually reevaluate

FIGURE 2
THE PRODUCT MIX

A company may choose one of the following approaches in developing its product mix:

The single product approach:
Many companies begin by manufacturing one product or performing one service for their customers. The Ford Motor Company, for example, began its automotive life by building one type of passenger car, the famous Model T.

Developing one basic product line:
Shoe manufacturers do not generally make only one type of shoe. They try to capture a year-round market by turning out dressy shoes, casual shoes, sandals, bedroom slippers and so on. This is an example of a basic product line.

Developing diversified product lines:
Most large companies go beyond one basic product line to several lines. If, for instance, your shoe factory were a great success, you might expand by acquiring an appliance company, with its own product line consisting of toasters, blenders, and irons. Diversifying further, you might buy a publishing company, with a product line of gothic novels, reference works, and children's books.

their markets and add or drop products as needed to meet changing consumer demands. In this way they develop their **product mix,** which is *the list of all products offered by a manufacturer.*

The simplest product mix consists of a single product, such as a cola beverage. The Coca-Cola Company originally marketed only Coca-Cola, but it has since added Sprite, Tab, diet Coke, and several other sodas to create a **product line,** which can be defined as *a group of products that are physically similar or are intended for similar markets.* A product line may be narrow; for example, a beverage manufacturer may restrict its output to a regular cola, a diet cola, and a caffeine-free version. Or it may include a broad range of similar products, such as fruit juices, party snacks, and iced tea. A third alternative is an expanded mix made up of any number of widely diversified product lines. (We show all these possibilities in Figure 2.)

Before deciding whether to stay with a single product, to produce a line of related products, or to develop several product lines, a company must con-

FIGURE 3

STAGES IN THE PRODUCT LIFE CYCLE

"Typical" sales curve—and sales of an actual product

Smart strategy: riding the life-cycle roller coaster

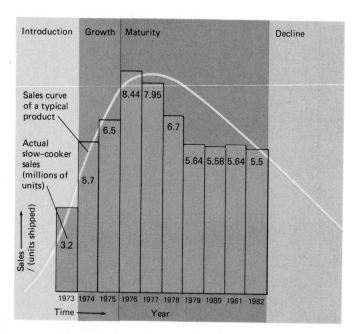

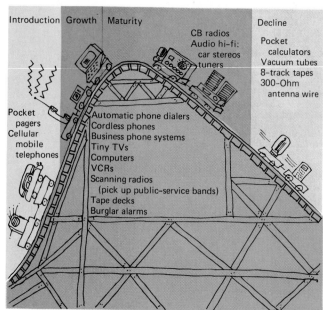

Almost every product has a "life cycle": sales grow, peak, and then level off (or sometimes decline). This typical life-cycle pattern is shown by the curve in this diagram. The bar graph shows how an *actual* product, electric slow-cookers, performed in recent years.

A business must introduce new products periodically to balance sales losses as older products decline. Shown here, product categories for Tandy Corp., a leading distributor of a wide range of consumer electronics. In 1983–1984, telephone products were hot; tiny TVs were still growing; and CB radios and audio hi-fi equipment were in the maturity stage. Pocket calculators and eight-track tapes were going downhill.

sider the risks and benefits of each approach. Some companies opt for limited product offerings because this method is economical: by keeping production costs per unit down and also limiting selling expenses to a single sales force, they expect to maximize their profit. Other companies, by contrast, follow the philosophy that a broad product mix is insurance against shifts in technology, taste, or economic conditions.

THE PRODUCT LIFE CYCLE

Every product—be it mood rings or microcomputers—goes through a **product life cycle,** or *stages of growth and decline in sales and earnings* (see Figure 3). The length of the product life cycle varies greatly, from a couple of months for a fad item to several years for a staple. But the stages of the life cycle are fairly standard and can be identified as follows.

The first stage in the product life cycle is the *introductory stage*, during which the initial manufacturer tries to inform the public that the product exists and tries to stimulate demand for it. Typically, this stage involves an expensive advertising and promotional campaign, plus research and development costs, so the manufacturer isn't likely to make a great deal of profit during this phase. Still, these costs are a necessary investment if a product is to succeed.

Next comes the *growth stage*, marked by a very rapid jump in sales—and, usually, in the number of competitors—as the introductory effort starts paying off. A classic example is smoke detectors. In 1978 they were a big item, with sales of 8.5 million units—a very sharp increase from the 50,000 units sold in 1971, their first year on the market. In fact, sales were so good in 1978 that two dozen manufacturers started producing smoke detectors, flooding the market with them and forcing the average price per unit down from the original $50 price tag to about $15.

Once the product reached the *maturity stage*—when sales continue to rise for a time but eventually level off—all but four manufacturers dropped out of the smoke detector market. During this stage of the product life cycle, the number of potential new customers drops. In 1979, sales of smoke detectors fell[3]. By 1982 they were holding steady at about 8 million per year.[4]

Finally, during the *decline stage*, the continuing drop in profits leads competing firms to make one last effort to undersell each other and clear out their inventories before the market fades away entirely. The decline can be accelerated by the arrival of new and more desirable products. In the case of smoke detectors, a line of home burglar alarms that also detect smoke offers better protection for safety-conscious households. Sometimes a product's decline simply reflects a change in public taste or perception. So it was in the early part of the 1970s when the natural look in men's hair styles replaced the slicked-down cuts and condemned Brylcreem and other once-popular hair creams to the product graveyard.

Most products have a four-stage life cycle. But the amount of time that elapses during any one of the stages depends on consumer needs and prefer-ences, economic conditions, the nature of the product itself, and the manufacturer's marketing strategy, among other factors. A basic product that serves a real need is likely to show steady growth for quite a few years before leveling off. In contrast, such fads as video games and electric hot-dog cookers may sell well initially, but their cycles peak quickly when the market becomes saturated.

It is important to note that when we talk about the product life cycle, we are referring to the product as a class, and not to an individual brand. (We will talk more about brands later in this chapter.) The automobile, for example, is a product that is now in its maturity stage. True, many imported brands are currently enjoying record sales, but their gains are balanced by the losses suffered by American car manufacturers, and so the automobile market overall is no longer in the growth stage.

NEW PRODUCTS

The lure of new products is obvious. To consumers, new products offer something different—an escape from the routine. To manufacturers, they offer the hope that their new mousetrap, snack food, automobile, or computer will be a big winner, with sales and profits that will set the standard for years to come.

Manufacturers today are turning out new products at a much faster rate than ever before. *New Product News*, a newsletter devoted to this field, reported that in 1982 more than 1,500 new foods and health and beauty aids were introduced—and 1982 was a recession year![5] Another study estimated that between 1970 and 1979, 6,695 new food products entered the market. But only 93 of these new foods—or about 1.4 percent—attained annual sales of $15 million or more. The majority disappeared, only to be replaced by other new products.[6]

STAGES OF PRODUCT DEVELOPMENT

Between the time a product idea is born and the time the finished products actually arrive in the marketplace, the concept may undergo many changes. The end result reflects decisions made during several stages of **product development.**

The first stage is the *generation of ideas.* A manufacturer may get new product ideas from its own people or from outside consultants. It may buy the rights to someone else's invention. Or it may simply adapt a competitor's idea.

New product ideas are subject to *screening,* which separates plainly unworkable concepts from those worthy of further development. Marketing consultants and advertising agencies are often called in to help evaluate new ideas. (In fact, there is a growing new-products industry, made up of consultants who are contracted by manufacturers to handle all aspects of product development.)

One widely used evaluative method is *concept testing,* whereby potential customers are asked what they think of a new product idea. Traditionally, this type of testing has been done with survey questionnaires or with focus groups, in which volunteers from the target market are carefully questioned about their specific likes and dislikes. Lately, however, some marketing specialists are trying out less formal approaches. For example, Gerald Schoenfeld and his agency have used what he refers to as "unfocus groups." Through game playing and other imaginative techniques, Schoenfeld encourages volunteers to be creative and brainstorm about products. Sometimes this method is productive: some years ago, Schoenfeld discovered that consumers liked to keep an open box of baking soda in their refrigerators to freshen them. This preference had been overlooked by a traditional survey conducted by the makers of Arm & Hammer baking soda. Schoenfeld's discovery led to a major advertising campaign and, ultimately, to a huge sales boost.[7]

A product idea that survives the evaluation stage is subjected to a *business analysis.* At this point the question raised is, can the company make enough money on the product to justify the investment? This analysis can be assisted by special computer programs that assimilate information about the proposed product, its potential market, consumer reactions, and other factors, and then recommend whether to go ahead or to kill the product. The reliability of these computer models is the subject of much controversy, however, and most companies still prefer to base their decisions on past experience and human judgment.

The next step may be *prototype development,* in which a few samples, or prototypes, of the product are created and performance-tested. During this stage a company generally evaluates the feasibility of large-scale production.

In the *product testing* stage a small group of consumers actually uses the new product, often in comparison tests with existing brands. If the results are good, the next step is *test marketing,* introducing the product in selected areas of the country and monitoring consumers' reactions. If the results of product tests are extremely favorable, test marketing is sometimes skipped, since it is an expensive, time-consuming process.

The final stage of development is *commercialization.* After a decision has been made to go ahead with a new product, production and marketing programs must be set in motion at once, because competitors (spared the need to conduct their own pretesting) will be likely to rush into the market with a similar product.

PRODUCT ANALYSIS

A great many things can go wrong with a new product. As we have seen, it can suffer from lack of preproduction planning and testing and thus be out of touch with market needs. It can also be too similar to existing products or too different to compete effectively. Sales can be hurt by introducing a new product at the wrong time, by underestimating (or overestimating) demand, or by plain bad luck. For these reasons and many more, introducing new products is considered to be the most uncertain aspect of marketing.

When a new product fails to live up to expectations or when an old one loses market share, a company must make hard strategic decisions. Do you invest more money in the hope that a renewed marketing and promotional effort will turn sales around? Do you swallow your losses and kill the product to avoid further cash drain? Or do you hold to your course and wait for market conditions to change? To help answer these questions, manufacturers and their consultants have devised special methods for analyzing product performance and developing future strategies. Most large companies utilize some form of *portfolio analysis,* which examines the comparative strengths and weaknesses of various product lines. The most widely used portfolio analysis technique is the four-cell matrix developed by the Boston Consulting Group. (See chart.) This procedure takes into account two basic indicators of product success: growth in sales and market share (compared to the leading competitor). Products are categorized as follows:

■ *Stars* are products in the growth stage of the life cycle that have already captured a dominant share of the market. It is generally understood that high growth requires a large investment, so much of a star's profits are reinvested to promote further growth.

■ *Cash cows* are often stars that have reached the maturity stage. Their large market share makes them quite profitable, but they have limited growth potential, so their income can be used to support other ventures. Hence their name: cash cows are "milked" to nourish other products.

■ *Problem children* have high growth potential, usually because the market itself is expanding for that product, and yet their share of the market is disappointing. This may be because they have been targeted to the wrong segment of

that market or perhaps because the product itself is not competitive.

■ *Dogs* have neither growth potential nor a strong market share. They are often good candidates for elimination or replacement with a new product line. However, if their investment requirements are low enough, some dogs may still generate a modest income.[8]

Other, more complicated portfolio analysis systems include the General Electric–McKinsey and Company nine-cell matrix, which employs slightly different criteria to measure product strength and provides an "average" rating in addition to "low" and "high." But whatever method of analysis the company uses, when that analysis shows that a leading product line has reached maturity, it may be time for the company to seek new stars.

PRODUCT BRANDS AND TRADEMARKS

When Coca-Cola developed a second diet cola, the company made a point of giving its new product the "Coke" name, probably the best-known brand name in the world. Not since Coca-Cola itself was introduced about a century ago has the fabled trademark appeared on another product. To emphasize the relationship, the "d" in diet Coke is not capitalized.

What exactly is a **brand?** It is any *name, term, symbol, sign, design, or combination of these used to identify the products of a firm and differentiate them from those of competitors.* Tide, Oldsmobile, and Bic are *brand names.* McDonald's golden arches, the Jolly Green Giant, and the Pillsbury doughboy are *brand symbols.*

Not all products are marketed under brands owned by their manufacturers. Brand names may also be owned by middlemen or retailers. Sears buys appliances from many manufacturers and sells them under the Kenmore brand. A&P purchases canned fruits, jellies, rice, household cleaning products, and frozen foods from hundreds of different suppliers and offers them under Jane Parker, A&P, and Ann Page brand names. *Brands owned by national manufacturers* are called **national brands.** *Brands owned by middlemen,* such as Sears and A&P, are **private brands.**

Portfolio analysis matrix: a two-by-two diagram that lets marketing managers plan their product strategy.

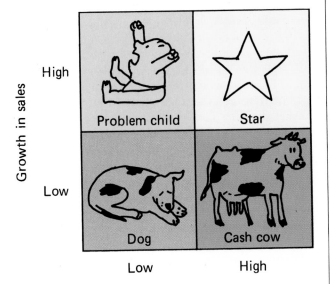

Growth in sales — High / Low

Problem child | Star

Dog | Cash cow

Market share
(compared to leading competitor) — Low / High

Brand names and brand symbols can be registered with the United States Patent and Trademark Office as trademarks. A **trademark,** then, is *a brand that has been given legal protection so that its owner has exclusive rights to its use.* Coca-Cola and Coke are both registered trademarks.

A well-known and respected brand name offers several marketing advantages. It provides immediate identification for the product, and suggests a certain level of quality that the consumer has come to expect and is willing to pay more for.

Establishing a brand name can be worthwhile, but it can also be very expensive, for it takes a huge promotion campaign to gain widespread recognition. The cost of such a campaign may drive up the price of the product and make it possible for other manufacturers to sell unbranded or lesser-known brand products at a substantially lower price.

Manufacturers must sometimes go to extreme lengths to protect a popular trademark. In 1982, a federal court held that the name "Monopoly," a trademark for the Parker Brothers board game, had so completely passed into common usage that it has become a generic name, no longer protected by law. This decision was then invoked in another court case a year later, in which Nestlé's "Toll House cookie" was also declared to be a generic name.[9]

The threat posed by these decisions is that other companies can now market products bearing variations on the Monopoly and Toll House titles, and not a penny of their profits will accrue to Parker Brothers or Nestlé's. If these decisions are left standing in future years, marketers face a problem: a product may become so successful that its brand name becomes a household word and the manufacturer then could lose its trademark rights.

ALTERNATIVES TO THE BRAND-NAME APPROACH

"Licensed" labels

Recently, a number of companies have taken a new approach to establishing brand names. Instead of spending the time and money needed to build a new product's identity from scratch, they are buying the rights to specific names and symbols that are already well known and using these licensed labels to help sell their products. This practice is quite common among manufacturers of children's products, who license popular cartoon or movie characters or best-selling video-game titles and affix them to everything from toys to clothing to presweetened breakfast cereals. General Mills is backing its new Pac-Man cereal with a $20 million promotional budget and Ralston Purina's Donkey Kong cereal is selling as fast as the company can produce it.[10]

Generic products

Many supermarket chains have given over precious shelf space in recent years to unbranded **generic products,** *products packaged in plain black-and-white boxes, bags, or cans bearing only the name of the product.* These products are most often "standard quality" rather than first quality. They cost less than brand-name products because of their lower quality and plain labels. They are not individually advertised, another fact that helps cut prices; note, however, that brand-name advertising (by Planter's Peanuts, for instance) may also stimulate the demand for a generic product (canned peanuts, in general).

Generic goods have found a definite market niche, as a look at your local supermarket shelves will demonstrate. Virtually all major supermarket chains offer full lines of generic products—Jewel Company has over 250—including paper goods, cleansers, canned goods, pet foods, and staples such as sugar and flour. Some supermarkets even carry generic beer and cigarettes. Recent marketing studies indicate that brand loyalty among consumers has declined markedly in recent years, which means that many people are no longer willing to spend more just to have their favorite brand product. Nevertheless, generic products have not captured a major market share to date. Consumers who try them out frequently go back to their old brands, complaining that the quality of the generics is inconsistent. To them, the assurance of quality that a brand name provides is more important than a lower price.

PACKAGING

Seventy-five years ago the concept of packaging was rather primitive. Many consumer goods were sold out of a barrel, in plain bags, or in an old newspaper

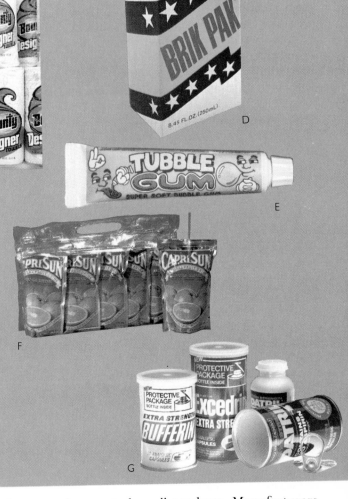

Packaging sells: often, the covering is as important as the content in making goods attractive and easy to use. Some recent innovations: **A)** a distinctive dispenser, with nozzle, for liquid soap; **B)** a new squeezable bottle whose unique multilayer design protects oxygen-sensitive foods formerly packaged only in glass or metal; **C)** generic packaging that offers simply economy; **D)** aseptic cartons for juices and milk (they're light, they take up minimal space, and—once filled with their sterile contents—they require no refrigeration); **E)** a new multilayer tube that protects (like this soft bubble gum) and allows for eye-catching graphics; **F)** a hot-fill multilayer stand-up pouch, that keeps its sterile contents fresh without refrigeration or preservatives; **G)** all-metal safety cans for pharmaceuticals (developed in the wake of the Tylenol disaster, these are virtually impossible to open and reclose without leaving obvious signs of tampering, yet they are easy for even arthritic fingers to deal with).

wrapping. Today products come in a wide assortment of packages—everything from the ubiquitous tin can to the new aseptic, or airtight, box. Packaging has itself become a major industry; with over $52 billion in annual sales, it is larger than both the steel and the textile industries in America.

THE NEED FOR PACKAGING

Packaging serves several important purposes. It protects products from damage (as in the case of egg cartons) and from tampering (particularly food and drugs), makes products easier for the retailer to display, attracts customers' attention, and reduces the temptation to steal small products. Manufacturers also strive to make packaging as convenient as possible. For example, more and more frozen foods are being packaged in cardboard rather than aluminum for use in microwave ovens. In addition, some manufacturers market their wares in reusable containers. Distilleries that bottle their liquor in cut-glass decanters and margarine makers that package their product in handy little plastic bowls believe that it gives them a competitive advantage. In many cases, packaging is an essential part of the product itself. Think of the number of products in the supermarket that come in dispenser packages, for example. Dispenser packaging makes products such as toilet tissue and liquid detergent easier to use and to store.

Innovative package design can be a powerful marketing tool. A recent example is the aseptic box, an easily transportable container that can keep liquids fresh for months at a time. Aseptics are composed of layers of polyethylene, paper, and foil that provide an airtight seal for their contents. They also stay chilled for relatively long periods of time and fit nicely into brown bags and lunch pails. Quite popular in Europe and Asia, aseptics did not look too promising for the American market until an easy-to-use version (with a straw attached) was approved in 1981. Now, U.S. packagers are gearing up their production lines for a flood of aseptics, which is expected to reach 4 billion units by 1987.[11] Another new development in packaging is the "retort pouch," a flexible bag made of various synthetic materials, which can preserve foods as long as cans and jars do without refrigeration; you simply drop it in boiling water to produce hot food in five minutes. The "TetraPak," a new package from Scandinavia, makes it possible to store milk and other dairy products without refrigeration. Finally, plastic bottles made of flexible plastic and resins may replace glass bottles as containers for many domestic foods and beverages.[12]

PACKAGING FOR SAFETY

Safety is an important factor in packaging, especially in the over-the-counter pharmaceuticals field. Since the fall of 1982, when seven people died after taking cyanide-laced Extra-Strength Tylenol capsules, pharmaceutical companies and food packagers have redesigned or reinforced their packages to discourage tampering. The Tylenol incident was perpetrated by someone who removed the pain reliever from the shelf at the retail level, replaced the contents of the capsules with cyanide, and restored the packages to the shelf, from which they were plucked by unsuspecting consumers. Tylenol's parent company, Johnson & Johnson, immediately withdrew and destroyed over 30 million bottles of the pain reliever. And marketers at Johnson & Johnson were faced with the tough decision of whether or not to reinstate the tainted Tylenol brand name. They chose to bring it back to the market as soon as possible in a new tamper-resistant package and to make an advertising point of the improved safety features. Close to a dozen different manufacturing and packaging companies were involved in producing and attaching the new inner seal, "shrink" neckband, and glued box that now protect all Tylenol products. The repackaging was carried out at unprecedented speed, and Johnson & Johnson was shipping Tylenol within a few weeks of the incident.

Meanwhile, the Food and Drug Administration had responded to the Tylenol tragedies by announcing a new set of packaging guidelines for all drug manufacturers. One immediate result was a sudden boom for packagers like Paco Pharmaceutical Services, of Lakewood, New Jersey, whose stock skyrocketed. Another outcome was the emergence of an entirely new concept in drug packaging: the fiber canister, engineered by Bristol-Myers Company for its Excedrin, Bufferin, and Datril products. The canisters are expensive, costing about five cents per unit to produce, which will be reflected in the products' prices. But Bristol-Myers is counting on convincing customers that the new package is the safest that money can buy.[13]

PACKAGING AND POLLUTION

The argument against packaging is that it is a source of litter and waste. Environmentalists are especially concerned about the growing use of plastic packaging, because plastics cannot be recycled or easily destroyed. Some, like polyvinyl chloride (PVC), emit dangerous gases when burned. Antipollution legislation has attempted to promote more and better recycling efforts, but most of this packaging stills ends up as trash.

As far as environmentalists are concerned, one of the most offensive forms of packaging is the disposable beverage container. It is estimated that 91 percent of all beer containers and 90 percent of all soft-drink containers are nonreturnable.[14] The volume of discarded glass could be measured in millions of tons. Nonreturnable cans add millions of tons of steel and aluminum to the nation's garbage dumps and roadside litter. In an effort to curtail this type of pollution, nine states have passed laws requiring a nickel deposit on every beer and soft-drink container purchased in the state. The idea is to encourage the return and recycling of these containers, and thereby to help protect the environment.

Not surprisingly, the bottling industry opposes the so-called bottle bills. Glass bottle makers have the most to lose by the legislation. Compared to aluminum cans, their products are expensive to store, clumsy to transport, and difficult to recycle. Retailers will thus be tempted to remove glass-bottled products from their shelves, and customers will prefer to have the beverages in more easily returnable cans. Therefore, in 1983 the Glass Packaging Institute began a costly advertising campaign promoting glass as a quality packaging material with a longer shelf life than aluminum or plastic. Several big bottle makers have also stepped up their glass recycling programs, hoping to build a better public perception of glass as an environmentally sound investment and at the same time to lower product costs with the reusable materials. Nevertheless, the process of glass recycling is still a long way from matching either the efficiency or the profitability of recycling aluminum cans.[15]

LABELING

As we mentioned earlier, marketing is much more than creating a product. A company must also develop a suitable label—and the label must meet government regulations. A label is either a separate item attached to a package, or a part of the container that holds the product. Generally it serves to identify a brand. Sometimes it also gives grading information about the contents, as discussed in Chapter 9.

More and more food product labels specify when the item's shelf life expires. Another growing trend is toward computer-coded labels that provide pricing and inventory data when scanned by the new electronic checkout devices at many supermarkets and other large retail stores. A label may also include promotional information to help sell the product.

GOVERNMENT REGULATIONS AND LABELING

Because labeling is used for promotional purposes, it is regulated by the government. The labeling of foods, drugs, many health products, and cosmetics is regulated under the federal Food, Drug, and Cosmetic Act (1938). This act gives the Food and Drug Administration (FDA) the authority to monitor the accuracy of the list of ingredients on labels. For example, a fruit drink cannot be labeled and sold as a fruit *juice* unless it contains an established minimum fruit content. Chicken cannot be named first in the list of ingredients for a frozen chicken pot pie unless chicken is the primary ingredient in the product.

Furthermore, the FDA requires labels of all products to which a nutrient has been added and all products that make a nutritional claim to list nutritional content. Another FDA regulation requires that labels on bubble bath carry a warning that prolonged use could cause skin rash and urinary tract infection, and labels on hair dyes containing certain chemicals must inform consumers that those chemicals have been identified as cancer-causing substances in lab tests with animals. Similar regulations apply not just to foods that contain the artificial sweetener saccharin—which the FDA would like to limit to prescription use—but even to the *stores* that sell them.

All these restrictions form part of the growing body of regulations designed to safeguard consumers' health. The first of these safeguards was the Fair Packaging and Labeling Act (1966), which mandates that every label must carry the product name as well as the name and address of the manufacturer or distributor and must show the net quantity conspicuously. The law also requires that labels on cosmetics list the ingredients—a provision that greatly dismayed an industry that has traditionally guarded its product formulas like state secrets.

SETTING PRICES

A manufacturer must make decisions not only about the development of products but also about how to price them. Setting prices is an extremely complicated process because prices are affected both by the external economic environment and by the company's internal policies, and there are no hard-and-fast rules to use in setting them.

PRICING AND BUSINESS POLICIES

Almost every business follows a general approach to pricing that might be called its pricing policy. A major factor in the company's pricing decisions is its overall profit goals. A company may be aiming at a certain **return on investment (ROI)**, which means that it wants to earn *profits equal to a certain percentage of its capital investment*. General Motors, for example, which pioneered this concept in the 1920s, traditionally set an ROI goal of 20 percent per year. Once a projected ROI figure has been established, a complex marketing formula (and a degree of guesswork) is then applied to come up with appropriate product pricing.

In addition to its general pricing policy, a com-

FIGURE 4

ASPECTS OF THE MARKETING MIX: PRICE

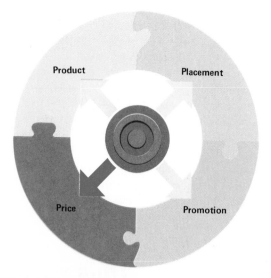

What should you charge for your product? To determine the best price, you must consider the product's life-cycle stage and the prices that are charged by competitors. But even more important, you must consider how strong demand is in the target market.

pany may also have specific objectives for individual products. Does it want high returns on each unit sold? Or broader sales that will translate to a larger market share? These decisions will help determine whether the product is priced above, below, or with the market.

Some firms follow a policy of **pricing above the market,** or *charging prices that are higher than those of competitors*. These may be firms selling low-volume luxury goods—Rolls-Royces, say, or Joy perfume—to high-income groups that want prestige. On the other hand, some manufacturers price higher than the competition because they want consumers to perceive a *price-quality relationship*. They want to persuade customers that their product is better than the competition (hence the higher price), but they don't necessarily want to limit their sales to any one segment of the market.

Other firms follow the practice of **pricing below the market,** *charging prices that are below those of competitors*. Sometimes this policy is adopted by a company coming into a market in which competitors are well established. Foreign car manufacturers initially priced their automobiles in this manner. Some firms rely totally on lower prices to attract customers. Discount stores use this approach. Pricing below the market is a particularly effective way to capture a larger share of the market.

A third alternative is **pricing with the market,** or *charging prices that match those of competitors*. Generally this means following the pricing policy of *a major producer in the industry*. This producer is known as the **price leader.** In the steel industry, for example, U.S. Steel has been considered the price leader. By pricing with the market, producers avoid the tremendous effort required to find out what the consumer would actually pay. Instead, they assume that the price leader has done this research and has established the right price. In this way, they also avoid the unpleasantness of price competition. Companies almost always prefer to compete through brand differentiation rather than through pricing wars.

CURRENT PRICING PROBLEMS

The practice of product pricing has changed dramatically in recent years. In general, prices are much less stable than they were just a decade ago, and pricing decisions are made more frequently and under greater time pressures.

Fast-breaking technology

One important reason for these changes is the rapid pace of new technological development. In such fields as computers, audio and visual recording, electronic games, and many others, it only takes a few months—or at most a year or two—for engineering breakthroughs to become new products. As the new generations of products emerge, the older models are considered less valuable to retailers and their prices are discounted. The profitable life expectancy of new products has diminished from two to three years to just a little more than one year today. As a result, the initial pricing decisions that a company makes on a new product have become much more critical. If the introductory price is not competitive, the product may not have time enough to recover before it is replaced by the next generation models.

This is what happened when Mattel Inc., the toy manufacturer, entered the low-priced home computer field in early 1983. Mattel began test-marketing its new model, the Aquarius, at $150 just when its chief competitors, Commodore and Texas Instruments, lowered their prices to $100 and below. Mattel quickly responded by cutting its price to $105. But the Aquarius' slow start, combined with the fact that it seemed to offer no special performance advantages over the competition, may well have been too much to overcome. At this writing, Mattel was preparing a second-generation model, to be introduced in 1984.[16]

Additional pressures on pricing

Other important factors influencing current pricing strategies are foreign competition and changes in the legal environment. One marketing text describes these changes as follows:

FOREIGN COMPETITION Thanks to reduced trade barriers, the loss of American superiority in productivity, and the emergence of aggressive new industrialized powers with cheaper labor, foreign competitors have undercut American prices, and often with products of better quality. This is apparent in our television and automobile industries, both of which are now responding to Japanese products and pricing.

CHANGES IN THE LEGAL ENVIRONMENT Popular concern over product costs, quality, and safety has led to greater regulation of business from local, state, and federal governments. This has resulted, to some degree, in regulated prices. But compliance with government regulation has added to the cost of doing business, which necessitates price increases. Also, the rash of lawsuits in recent years over product liability and quality has meant additional legal costs which are typically passed on to consumers via higher prices.[17]

PRICING NEW PRODUCTS

Special pricing options exist when manufacturers introduce a new product. The most popular approach is called **skimming:** *the manufacturer charges a high price during the introductory stage and later reduces it when the product is no longer a novelty and competition heats up.* Companies that adopt a skimming policy try to recover their development costs as quickly as possible through high initial prices. Skim pricing was used by Polaroid when they introduced their original picture-in-a-minute camera. As time went on, they lowered the price and also added less expensive models that attracted different market segments. Skimming is also widely practiced in the movie industry. A new picture often premieres in a "showcase" theater for a dollar or two above what will be charged when it reaches neighborhood theaters.

Another approach to the pricing of a new product is **penetration pricing:** *a manufacturer introduces the product at a low price and plans to get back the initial investment through large sales volume.* Texas Instruments practiced this strategy in selling pocket calculators and so has the manufacturer of Timex watches. Penetration pricing offers two potential advantages, in addition to rapid sales to a large market. It may discourage competitors from entering the field because the low price means only a small profit per unit. And it may be economical because producing large quantities saves money.

PRICING TECHNIQUES

Let's assume that a company has established a general pricing policy and decided how it will sell a new product. How will the company actually set the price? It will undoubtedly take into account several factors. Among these factors are markup and geographic considerations.

MARKUP

As usually defined, **markup** *is the difference between the cost of an item and its selling price.* In modern merchandising, *firms generally express this difference in terms of percentage,* the **markup percentage.** If an item costs a firm $50 and is sold for $75, the markup is $25; the markup percentage is 33⅓ on the selling price. The markup percentage has two purposes. It must cover all the expenses of the firm, including not only the cost of the item but also the cost of selling it. And it must contain an allowance for a planned profit.

Most businesses today carry a large number of items. (Macy's department stores, for example, reportedly handle over 100,000 different items.) It would be extremely difficult to calculate the markup percentage for each one. For this reason, many businesses tend to use an **average markup** in setting prices; that is, *the same markup percentage is used for each item in a given product line.*

Markups vary by type of store. Take, for example, an item costing 50 cents in various types of retail outlets: the markup for this item might range from a low of 22 percent for a supermarket to a high of 55 percent for a florist, and the retail price might thus vary from a low of 61 cents to a high of $1.11. Florists have a high markup percentage because they deal in extremely perishable goods sold to a relatively small market. Another factor in the wide range of markup percentages is **turnover,** *the number of times average inventory is sold during a given period.* If a firm's average inventory is $1,000 and sales for a month (or some other specific time period) amount to $3,000, the turnover is 3. Therefore, a gift shop with a turnover of three times a year must make more profit on each item than a liquor store with a turnover of thirty times a year.

OTHER PRICING STRATEGIES

Many companies follow a policy called **price-lining,** *offering their merchandise at a limited number of set prices.* Record companies may offer a $3.95 line, a $4.95 line, and a $6.95 line. Price-lining is justified in two ways: it simplifies the selling job for the storekeeper, and it makes choice easier for the consumer by limiting the number of alternatives.

In many industries, *price lines tend to end in numbers slightly below the next dollar figure,* such as $3.95, $4.98, or $7.99. This method is known as **psychological pricing.** The assumption here is that a customer sees a $3.98 price as significantly lower than $4.00, so that the store will sell more at 2 cents less. Another rationale for this kind of pricing is that customers set price limits for themselves, defining how much they will pay for a given product. For example, a man may decide that $25.00 is the maximum that he will spend on a dress shirt. According to this reasoning, a price tag of $24.99 will appear to be safely within his range, while one of $25.00 may give him pause. Few studies have been made to test the effectiveness of such pricing. Those that have been done suggest that customers are more rational than psychological pricing assumes. Also, customers are usually aware that sales taxes, where they exist, raise the price of an item. Yet another theory of why so many prices fall just below the next full-dollar figure is based on more practical considerations. It is certainly more likely that a person will pay for a $1.98 item with two dollar bills than with the exact change. The store clerk, having to make change, must use the cash register, which records the sale of the item. This record of sales guarantees the store manager an accurate account of business.

1. Charting the costs of the business

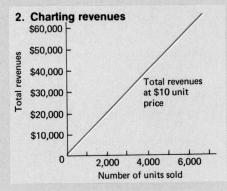

Costs

- Total costs (fixed costs + variable costs)
- Fixed costs ($30,000 per year)
- Variable costs ($2.50 per unit)

$50,000 / $40,000 / $30,000 / $20,000 / $10,000 / 0

2,000   4,000   6,000
Number of units produced

2. Charting revenues

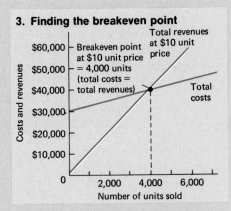

Total revenues

Total revenues at $10 unit price

$60,000 / $50,000 / $40,000 / $30,000 / $20,000 / $10,000 / 0

2,000   4,000   6,000
Number of units sold

3. Finding the breakeven point

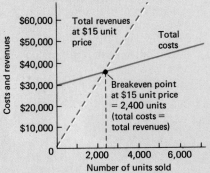

Costs and revenues

- Total revenues at $10 unit price
- Breakeven point at $10 unit price = 4,000 units (total costs = total revenues)
- Total costs

$60,000 / $50,000 / $40,000 / $30,000 / $20,000 / $10,000 / 0

2,000   4,000   6,000
Number of units sold

4. Finding the breakeven point at a second price

Costs and revenues

- Total revenues at $15 unit price
- Total costs
- Breakeven point at $15 unit price = 2,400 units (total costs = total revenues)

$60,000 / $50,000 / $40,000 / $30,000 / $20,000 / $10,000 / 0

2,000   4,000   6,000
Number of units sold

BREAKEVEN ANALYSIS

One of the basic questions all businesspeople need to answer is, "How many units of my product (or service) will I have to sell in order to break even—that is, to cover costs?" And of course the question that goes along with this one is, "How many units will I have to sell in order to make a reasonable profit?" If you don't have a basic estimate of these two figures, you may be out of business before you know it.

The best way to attack these questions is through a method known as breakeven analysis. Here's how it's done.

1. Charting the costs of the business When a marketing manager considers the costs involved in operating a business he or she generally has to look at two different kinds of costs.

Fixed costs are those that *must be covered no matter how many units of the product or service the business produces;* they include items such as rent, insurance, and office salaries. For a small beauty salon, for example, fixed costs might amount to $30,000 a year.

Variable costs include items such as raw materials and labor, which *increase with the number of units of the product or service the business produces.* In a beauty salon, for example, labor and shampoo for one haircut (with wash and set) might be $2.50—so ten units would cost $25.00, twenty units would cost $50.00, and so on.

To figure out the total costs of operating the business, simply add the variable costs to the fixed costs. Total costs increase with the number of units produced.

2. Charting revenues The next step is to chart the revenues, or payments, the company will receive as it sells more and more units at the price the manager plans to charge. If the beauty salon charges $10 per haircut, its revenues are $1,000 for 100 units, $2,000 for 200 units, and so on.

3. Finding the breakeven point Next, we put the two graphs together, to show costs *and* revenues. Notice that there is a point at which the line representing revenues crosses and goes over the line representing costs. This point is the **breakeven** point—*the point at which revenues will just cover costs.* Now, to find the number of units the business must sell to reach the breakeven point, just look along the "number of units produced" line at the bottom. Any additional units sold will produce profit for your business.

4. Finding the breakeven point at a second price What if you charge a higher price for your product or service? You will break even after selling a smaller number of units. To find out exactly how many units you will have to sell to break even at your second price, simply repeat steps 2 and 3 using the second price. Here, we have charted revenues and breakeven point at a unit price of $15.

Making a final decision on a price Clearly, each of the two prices offers you certain advantages. The higher price, which allows you to break even after selling fewer units, may be attractive if you suspect that the market for your product or service is limited in your geographic area. At the lower price you will have to sell more units, but your price may bring in more customers. Which price do you decide on? Here you have to make an "educated guess" about *your* customers and *your* product.

Some manufacturers of consumer goods advertise their merchandise at **suggested retail prices.** They may even stamp such a price on a product at the factory. Retailers have the choice of selling the goods at the suggested price or of selling for less and creating the impression that they are offering a bargain.

Finally, companies offer different types of *discounts,* depending on the type of customer and the type of item being offered.

CHAPTER REVIEW

Deciding on the product mix, or list of products, that a manufacturer will sell is one of the marketing manager's main responsibilities. The product mix may consist of a single product line, a group of products with similar physical characteristics or uses, or several product lines. Having a single product line is economical and efficient; however, having several product lines may let a company adapt to changing business conditions more easily.

Because all products go through a life cycle that includes a final period of decline in sales, new products are essential to a company's success—and today new products are being turned out at a much faster rate than ever before. New or improved products can help keep sales high. The process of developing new products falls into several stages—generation of ideas, screening, concept testing, business analysis, prototype development, product testing, test marketing, and commercialization. (One or more of these stages may be omitted.) Another crucial consideration is timing. Product analysis helps to determine exactly where a product stands as well as to diagnose possible problems that it may be facing.

A company may decide to sell its goods under a brand name, with or without a brand symbol. The brand name may be one established by a national manufacturer (national brand) or it may belong to a middleman (private brand). Generic brands are products that have been labeled as to contents only; they carry no special names. A licensed label involves a known name that is applied to a new, often unrelated product.

Packaging is also a marketing concern. Many people believe that packaging is often overdone in America, but it does serve several significant functions, including promotion, convenience, and protection of the product.

The label is an important part of the package. For many common supermarket and textile goods, government regulations specify what must be stated on the label.

Pricing policy is another key marketing decision. A company may choose to price above the market, below the market, or with the market, although rampant inflation, dramatic changes in demand, increased shortages of natural resources, and fast-breaking technological innovations have tended to upset traditional pricing strategies. Foreign competition and changes in the legal environment are complicating matters still more. The introduction of a new product requires a special pricing approach, and companies often use the method of skimming or of penetration pricing. An important pricing concept is the markup, which varies depending on the type of merchandise and the turnover rate. Other pricing considerations include discount policies and selling policies such as price-lining, psychological pricing, and suggested retail prices.

REVIEW QUESTIONS

1. What are the three basic kinds of product mixes? What factors does a company consider in selecting its product mix?

2. Discuss the four life-cycle stages most products go through.

3. List the stages of product development and discuss both product timing and product analysis.

4. Why do businesses continually introduce new products, given the risks and high rate of failure of new products?

5. What is the significance of allowing businesses to maintain exclusive use of a trademark?

6. What is a licensed label? Why would a marketer want to use one?

7. Explain the advantages of generically labeled products.

8. Why is packaging considered a problem? What are some of the remedies that have been proposed and tried?

9. What are the three general pricing policies? Discuss some of the recent patterns in pricing and the factors that have complicated this process.

KEY WORDS

product mix (275)
product line (275)
product life cycle (276)
product development (278)
brand (279)
national brands (279)
private brands (279)
trademark (280)
generic products (280)
return on investment (ROI) (284)
pricing above the market (284)
pricing below the market (284)
pricing with the market (284)
price leader (284)
skimming (285)
penetration pricing (285)
markup (286)
markup percentage (286)
average markup (286)
turnover (286)
price-lining (286)
psychological pricing (286)
breakeven (287)
suggested retail prices (288)

CASE I

WINDHAM HILL RECORDS: THEY WILL MAKE YOU CRY

Is this your kind of music? It's been described as "an amalgam of improvisational folk and classical influences," "California mellow music," and music for those who are "too old for rock and too young for Mantovani." Its producer, Will Ackerman, founder and head of Windham Hill Records, has a simple standard for the material he chooses: "Do I cry when I first hear it?"

The stuff Ackerman picks *is* somewhat out of the ordinary, lacking the heavy beat and super-amplification that buyers of popular music generally take for granted today. Instead, it concentrates mainly on unelectrified acoustic instruments—pianos and guitars—for a "warmer, fuller, richer sound." Whether or not it makes you cry, it's been making good money for Ackerman.

Between 1980 and 1984, while other record producers were gasping to stay alive, Windham Hill realized gains in annual sales ranging from 181 to 597 percent, and its total sales in 1983 approached $8 million—pretty good for an outfit that started as a one-man business only seven years earlier. An editor of *Rolling Stone* says, "They have found a market that wasn't being served. There's nothing else like Windham Hill. Their popularity is due to a reaction against loud music."

Ackerman's success may be due at least in part to his unorthodox ways of doing business. Although he does not skimp on the quality of his recordings, he sells them for considerably less than one would expect to pay. He spends very little on promotion (less than 0.5 percent of net revenue, as opposed to 20 percent or more of gross income among major companies), depending instead on brand loyalty among his customers. For example, by occasionally issuing a "sampler" album that includes a variety of artists, Ackerman encourages the public to associate a particular "sound" with

his label. Also, many sales stem from radio plays and word-of-mouth advertising. His outlets, too, are unusual—in order to attract new customers, they include florists and health-food shops.

Until early 1982 Ackerman depended on independent operators and on Pick Wick International, a subsidiary of American Can Company, to distribute his records. But then Pick Wick, which had covered Windham Hill's five largest markets, announced that it was pulling out—a heavy blow. It led Ackerman to sign a distribution agreement with A&M Records, a major company, and to raise the price of his albums by 60 cents. Retailers and the independent distributors are not especially happy about the changes, but Ackerman justifies the A&M agreement by pointing out that it will open up new markets, including some outside the United States. He says, "There's a wall you reach in independent distri-

bution. We would have run into that wall in a year. To maintain our sales momentum, we needed a dramatic shift." To those who suggest that pressure from A&M may force him to compromise on musical quality, Ackerman replies that since A&M is artist-owned, he is not worried about that.

Stephen Traiman, of the Recording Industry Association of America, says, "What Windham Hill has done is amazing." Ackerman, of course, hopes that this judgment will still apply a few years from now.[18]

1. How do you explain Windham Hill's success despite its low budget for promotion? What is the company's main asset in gaining loyal customers?

2. How important is it to retain retailer support and loyalty?

3. Windham Hill's retailers are griping about its 60-cent price increase. How important is price with this product?

CASE 2

PROCTER & GAMBLE'S NEW PRODUCTS

Suppose that you're the president of Procter & Gamble, maker of such well-known brands as Ivory soap, Tide detergent, Crest toothpaste, and Pampers disposable diapers. You are faced with a critical dilemma, which you outline over lunch to Jones, your close aide, adviser, and second in command.

You: Jones, we're in trouble. The competition is crowding us in soaps and toothpaste, and there simply aren't that many more little bottoms to be diapered. If we want to stay big, we'll have to expand into new areas and launch some new products. Got any ideas?

Jones: Well, boss, juice is a coming thing, what with all the hype about health. Maybe orange juice. And then maybe cookies. Really nice cookies that are soft in the middle and crunchy outside. Of course, tea is also tasty. We could sell teabags. And in line with our reputation for cleaning things, we could clean toilet bowls. Maybe a nice automatic toilet-bowl cleaner.

At this point, you might very well be tempted to tell Jones that you are not exactly thrilled with his ideas and that he might, indeed, be happier offering them to another employer. But you'd be *wrong.* Because the fact is that P&G's real president, facing exactly the same dilemma, is pushing all these ideas and more besides.

P&G is first and foremost a nationwide marketer, producing, promoting, and distributing whatever the public seems willing to buy. (P&G apparently limits itself to supermarket products, but within that constraint, almost anything goes.) Therefore, when P&G realized several years ago that it had to expand, it was willing to consider a broad range of possibilities and to spend big money developing them. In 1983 P&G tested a total of twenty-two new products, including additions to an already established product line, some new ones, and others in areas it had tried but failed to exploit in earlier efforts. Among the leading contenders in this heterogeneous array were Duncan Hines cookies, Citrus Hill orange juice, and Brigade toilet-bowl cleaner.

The cookies were the golden hope. All six varieties are made according to a patented baking process that, it is claimed, ensures a soft center and a crunchy exterior. With a little help from a heavy ad campaign, cents-off coupons, and free samples, the cookies grabbed 25 percent of the Kansas City test market within weeks of their introduction.[19]

Citrus Hill, the orange juice entry, is interesting in terms of numbers alone. It must compete in a $2.5 billion market, and P&G plans to spend up to $100 million on advertising and promotion just during the first year (an all-time high for a single new product). Yet the juice does not differ markedly from the other leading brands, none of which have been vigorously promoted, although it will cost more. Although Citrus Hill won 15 percent of the Indiana test market, critics say that this in the result of heavy advertising and a "buy one, get one free" promotion.

Brigade seems to be doing at least as well as the cookies, but the market for toilet-bowl cleaners is rather small. Apparently, Americans don't take great interest in their toilet bowls—but P&G plans to change that.

1. P&G has clearly opted to diversify its product mix. What do you see as the possible advantages and disadvantages of this strategy?

2. Do you think that consumers might balk at buying orange juice or cookies from a company widely identified with soap? What can P&G do to prevent this?

3. Why do you suppose P&G has decided to tackle the orange juice market?

PROMOTION

The phone rings. You answer it and hear: "Hi, I'm a computer. Please don't hang up; computers have feelings too, you know." Or: "Hello, my name is AD-2001; I'm a cousin to R2D2. My boss Bill Cady, at Servisoft Water Conditioning Company, wants me to ask three short questions. Do you have a minute?"

If you have not already received such a call, be prepared, for the day of computer-controlled telephone selling is at hand. Once "programmed," an automatic dialer can complete more than a call a minute, but that's the least of its virtues. It never forgets a name or number, never gets tired, doesn't take breaks, and can't lose its temper (as the humans at the receiving end occasionally do). In fact, it's shown itself to be so handy that schools, politicians, and religious institutions, as well as businesses, are using it.

Futuristic as they sound, these machines are the latest in the endless variety of methods companies use to promote their products and services. In this chapter, we'll learn about telemarketing and about the more familiar ways in which businesses try to attract customers.

CHAPTER FOCUS

After reading the material in this chapter you will be able to:
- define promotion and distinguish four basic categories of promotion
- distinguish between "push" and "pull" promotional strategies
- distinguish the three main types of advertising
- list the advantages and disadvantages of advertising in each of the media
- describe the steps in the development of creative and media strategies
- describe how an advertising agency functions
- distinguish between business selling and retail selling
- specify the role of publicity in marketing
- name at least five types of sales promotion
- cite two federal agencies that regulate advertising and three professional or industry bodies that do so

 What do popular musicians Rod Stewart and Hall & Oates have in common with Sony and Canada Dry? They are joining forces to boost the sales of their respective products. Advertisers have found that rock music gives them an effective way to communicate with twelve- to twenty-four-year-old consumers. To build a new image for ginger ale, Canada Dry dressed up six-packs with $1-off coupons for Hall & Oates albums; it sponsored a concert tour for the group, mobilizing local bottlers to award free tickets in local contests; and it distributed free posters featuring Hall & Oates holding the drink. Other promoters have used everything from emblazoned beach balls to electronic scoreboards—and even the musicians' shoes—to project a product's image during a rock concert.[1]

Promotion can be defined as *persuasive communication designed to sell products, services, ideas, persons, or organizations to potential customers* (target markets).

Most businesspeople would agree that effective promotion can be the most important of the four Ps of marketing (see Chapter 9). Promotions include four basic activities: advertising, personal selling, publicity, and sales promotion. These four activities, usually referred to together as the *promotional mix,* are valuable tools for a company's marketing manager.

Using well-known personalities and tie-ins that associate different products, such as record albums and soft drinks, is a common promotional strategy. A promotional strategy begins with a choice between two distinct approaches, "push" and "pull." By appealing directly to the end customer (through advertising, direct mail, and so on), manufacturers can "pull" a product through the distribution channel: consumers learn of the product from the manufacturer's promotion and request the product from retailers, who respond by asking their wholesalers for it or by going directly to the manufacturer. Or the manufacturer can "push" the product to the end user by persuading wholesale and retail vendors to

Michael Jackson (here receiving the second of his eight Grammy awards) and the New York Yankees both have millions of devoted fans. But what else do they have in common? They're in the same business: not music or baseball but promotion. Jackson has earned $10 million pushing Pepsi-Cola, and scores of advertisers fight for air time on Yankee baseball TV broadcasts.

FIGURE I

ASPECTS OF THE MARKETING MIX: PROMOTION

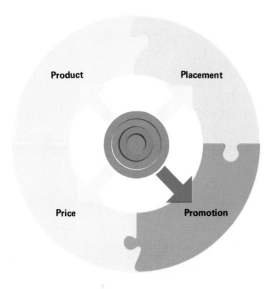

Developing an effective promotional approach is a tough challenge for the marketer. The right promotional approach depends on the needs and interests of the target market—as do all other aspects of the marketing mix.

carry it. The manufacturer promotes the product to wholesalers and retailers via strategies such as trade discounts and personal selling, and the retailers finally promote it to the end users.

Although a business may use both push and pull approaches, consumer goods tend to rely on pull strategies, whereas industrial goods are often pushed. However, the "push-pull" decision often depends on the strengths of the product, its particular market, and the organization behind it. Hershey Candy Company traditionally relied on push, for example, because it could count on its strong sales force to get the product displayed at cash registers. Nestlé, its competitor, was heavily oriented toward the pull of advertising, and its success with this technique forced Hershey to include advertising in its approach or risk losing its market share.

Having made these preliminary observations, let's look at promotional techniques in detail.

ADVERTISING

Advertising is defined as *any paid form of nonpersonal presentation made by an identified sponsor through a mass communication medium on behalf of goods, services, or ideas.* Advertising is distinguished from other forms of promotion in many ways. First, it is paid for—in contrast to publicity, which seeks to attract attention in the news media and elsewhere without making any direct payment. Advertising also is "nonpersonal" in that it is done through television, newspapers, and other media, in contrast to the face-to-face contact that takes place in personal selling. What advertising has in common with other forms of promotion is that it can be used not only to sell goods like soap or automobiles but also to promote services such as banking and insurance. It can even be used to sell ideas that may not be concerned with profit at all—drug-abuse prevention, for instance, or population control.

Advertising is used to communicate both with consumers and with other businesses. Trade and industrial advertising is important if businesses are the ultimate consumer of a product or if other businesses play an important role in getting the product to the consumer. For example, retailers such as supermarkets and bookstores have limited shelf space on which to display the flood of new product offerings. Thus, these retailers are important targets for the advertising messages of food companies and publishers.

The great advantage of advertising over other types of promotion is its ability to reach mass audiences quickly at a low cost per person reached. It is also the form of promotion over which the company has the greatest control. For example, when a publicity release is distributed to the media, it may be edited, rewritten, or even ignored. In an advertisement, however, the company can say whatever it chooses to say, so long as it stays within the boundaries of the law and conforms to the moral and ethical standards of the advertising medium and trade associations. For this reason many companies, including United Technologies and Mobil Oil, use advertising to communicate their positions on current issues to the public.

Advertising is an effective means of introducing

a new product nationwide and generating sales leads. In addition, it can rekindle interest in a product whose sales have grown sluggish, as illustrated by the memorable ad campaign in which young children told how Colgate-Palmolive's Curad bandages "help boo-boos heal fast." Begun in 1978, the series of television commercials had boosted the product's market share to 25 percent by mid-1980.[2]

Little wonder, then, that businesses of all kinds allocate large sums of money for advertising; in 1983, American companies spent $75.1 billion on advertising.[3] The percentage of income a company spends on advertising varies according to the product and the market. A cosmetics company, for example, may spend 30 percent or more of its total sales dollars to promote its products in a highly competitive market. Yet a company that manufactures heavy industrial machinery may spend less than 1 percent.

TYPES OF ADVERTISING

Advertising is classified as *primary-demand, or generic, advertising; selective, or brand, advertising;* and *institutional advertising.* These three categories reflect different promotional goals.

Primary-demand, or **generic, advertising** *tries to increase the total demand for products without distinguishing between brands.* The American Dairy Association has sought to remind the public that milk is a healthful alternative to other beverages. Similarly, the Citrus Growers' Association uses generic advertising to suggest, "'Orange' you smart for drinking orange juice?" Trade associations are the most common source of this type of advertising, but industry-wide unions also occasionally sponsor promotional appeals. For example, in 1983 the International Ladies' Garment Workers' Union sponsored ads to encourage people to give American-made goods for Christmas. "Make it an American Christmas," the ads read, "and maybe next year we'll all have something to celebrate."[4]

Selective, or **brand, advertising** *aims at getting purchasers to use a particular brand of product,* such as Sunsweet prunes or Head skis. By far the most common type of advertising, it accounts for the major

share of all money spent on advertising. Brand advertising for products targeted at the consumer market turns up on TV and radio, on billboards and buses, and in newspapers and magazines; industrial advertisers rely heavily on trade shows, mailing brochures, and trade magazines to promote brand-name merchandise.

Advertising is a powerful tool for distinguishing a brand from its competitors. Sometimes it turns a trademark into a familiar logo. The Morton umbrella girl did more than introduce the idea that Morton salt flows freely despite humidity—she created a lasting image for Morton salt. Likewise, the koala bear has become a familiar mascot for Qantas Airlines. But the phenomenal success of some brand advertising has also caused some monumental headaches for a few major advertisers. Coke, Kleenex, Jell-O, and Xerox, for example, are all registered trademarks and vigorously promoted brands that have become virtually synonymous with cola, tissues, gelatin dessert, and photocopying, respectively. As we noted in Chapter 10, the owners of familiar trademarks like these have had to take legal action to try to stop the use of their trade names in conjunction with other brands. Thus, there are complex legal considerations involved in the planning of brand advertising campaigns.

Institutional advertising is *designed to create goodwill and build a desired image for a company rather than sell specific goods.* Also known as *corporate advertising,* it is often used by corporations to address immediate threats to the product image. (Following an avalanche of bad publicity generated by the crash of one of its DC-10 jumbo jets a few years ago, McDonnell Douglas, for example, ran a series of ads to inform the public about the company's excellent track record.) Corporate advertising has an important political role, particularly in highly regulated industries such as utilities. When private utilities want to get permission to raise rates or build a nuclear reactor, they often use institutional ads to build a public-spirited image.

When institutional ads are *used to address hotly debated public issues,* they fall into the realm of **advocacy** or **controversy advertising.** Atlantic Richfield Company, a major oil producer, chose this strategy to rebut environmentalists who were blocking mineral exploration on public lands. Motorola and United Technologies have used institutional ads to express their views on America's productivity and technology in the face of foreign competition.

Cooperative advertising

An increasingly common method of advertising is **cooperative advertising,** whereby *makers of nationally sold products and local merchants share the cost of local advertising.* An estimated $8 billion a year is available for cooperative newspaper advertising alone.[5] Depending on the industry, the manufacturer may provide from 50 percent to 100 percent of the retailer's cost of advertising. Manufacturers support co-op advertising because it helps to sell more of their goods, not only by promoting them but also by telling consumers where they can purchase them. For example, when Estée Lauder and the New York store B. Altman purchase co-op advertising for a new line of Estée Lauder makeup, the cosmetics company assures consumers that the product is locally available and obtains the benefit of Altman's fashionable image.

ADVERTISING MEDIA

As used in promotion, **media** are *all the different means by which advertising reaches its audience.* Newspapers attract the largest share of advertising dollars, as Figure 2 shows. Magazines, radio, television, and direct mail account for most of the remaining outlays.

Newspapers

Newspapers offer several *advantages.* Most important is their great flexibility. An advertiser can change a local newspaper ad overnight, so that if there's a blizzard in the afternoon, the local department store can feature snow shovels and boots in the next day's ad. Newspapers also offer advertisers an opportunity to zero in on the specific groups most likely to want the products or services. Zoned editions of newspapers reach shoppers who live in the neighborhood of particular stores. Sports and auto-

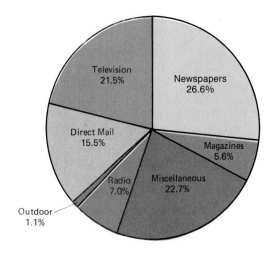

(Data from *Statistical Abstract of the United States,* 104th ed., 1984, p. 567)

FIGURE 2

THIS MESSAGE IS BROUGHT TO YOU BY . . .
Advertising expenditures, by media

motive pages let advertisers place ads in context and thus appeal directly to sports fans and car buffs. Special-interest newspapers reach narrow segments of the population: a major Spanish-language daily, like *El Diario La Prensa,* is ideal for promoting an English language school, and *The Wall Street Journal* is an appropriate place to advertise a brokerage firm.

But newspapers also entail a number of *disadvantages.* Most newspapers are regional or local, so mounting a nationwide ad campaign by newspaper is a cumbersome process. Color and reproduction quality are poor, and pictures of the product may not be very attractive. Furthermore, newspapers appeal only to the sense of sight and thus are not as "gripping" as media that have both visual and audio appeal.

Radio

Radio advertising has recently experienced a great boost from the renaissance of network radio. Fully half of U.S. radio stations have affiliated with one or more of the twenty radio networks, hoping to improve their programming while lowering production costs.[6] Though network TV audiences have fallen recently, network radio audiences have increased in the last decade; yet the cost of network radio advertising has grown only half as fast as that of advertising on network TV.[7] Network radio's burgeoning nationwide coverage, combined with its cost advantage over other media, is expected to bring a resurgence of interest in radio advertising from major national advertisers.

One of the important *advantages* radio offers to advertisers is access to the greatest number of people: there are more than 470 million radio sets in the United States, about 5.8 per household.[8] Radio advertising is also relatively low in cost, especially on small, local stations. Local stations offer considerable flexibility as well, enabling advertisers quick access to the listening audience.

In addition, radio offers a high degree of market segmentation. Increased competition among the ever-growing number of stations has led to more specialized radio programming. Many stations now devote the major part of their day to one type of broadcasting (news, rock music, sports, talk shows, or ethnic programs) in order to attract a certain kind of audience. Therefore advertisers can select those stations and times that will assure them that their messages will be heard by the audience they want to reach.

Radio advertising is not without *disadvantages,* of course. Listeners can easily switch from one station to another to avoid listening to commercials. Thus, advertisers regard radio primarily as a reminder medium to suggest at appropriate times the use of already familiar products like a fast food. It is considered less effective for introducing new products, unless combined with a medium that can carry more information, such as print or TV. A final important limitation of radio is that it appeals only to one sense: hearing. This provides a certain personal impact; the listener has the illusion that someone on the radio is talking directly to him. But it also prevents radio from selling, say, decorative pillows and costume jewelry.

PAY RADIO In the future, one of the most dynamic segments of radio broadcasting may be "pay radio." Like pay TV, pay radio provides specialized programming for people who are willing to pay a subscription rate. Furnished with the equipment needed to unscramble the signal, subscribers can tune in informative or entertaining broadcasts. Although the audience may not be broad enough for full commercial support, the fact that listeners subsidize pay radio doesn't rule out the sale of air time for advertising. Pay radio is too new for its impact on advertising to be fully evaluated, but as new services become available, advertisers might be able to use it efficiently to reach a larger, relatively affluent audience.[9]

Magazines

Despite increased competition from other media, magazines still have important *advantages* for some advertisers. Unlike newspapers, which are usually thrown out after a day, magazines may remain around the house for weeks, so the ads they carry have a better chance of being read and remembered. Magazines also provide a good medium for effective photography and artwork, an important factor for advertisers who want to show their products accurately or to create a quality image with visually attractive ads.

Realizing that they cannot hope to compete with television as a medium for mass advertising, many magazine publishers have changed their approach: they publish a range of **geographic and demographic editions** *aimed at narrower audiences on the basis of region and occupation,* instead of a single national edition. Printing innovations have enabled *Time* magazine, for example, to publish 357 different editions worldwide, including special editions for doctors, educators, and college students. Advertisers can thus buy space only in those editions that suit their purposes, reaching a more receptive audience and saving money at the same time.

There has also been a surge of growth among **special-interest magazines,** established ones and newcomers alike. These magazines offer advertisers even greater market selectivity because they *are designed to appeal to distinct reader groups.* For example, *Diversion* is aimed at doctors who travel, *Microkids* at kids who program, and the increasingly popular regional business magazines such as *Crain's Chicago Business* are aimed at firms located in one geographic area.

Television ads reach millions of people almost overnight. No sooner had this Wendy's commercial started running than "Where's the beef?" became part of our slang across the country. Wendy's burger sales increased, too.

Television

The most significant *advantage* of television advertising, which now accounts for more than 20 percent of the nation's total expenditure on advertising, is the combination of sight and sound that enables advertisers to present promotional material in a lively and compelling manner. Furthermore, 98 percent of American homes have TVs, and Americans watch them an average of about 29 hours a week.[10]

Television also offers advertisers flexibility in terms of geographic coverage. An advertiser who markets products nationally can buy **network time,** *which guarantees broadcasts of a message by hundreds of local stations.* A local firm, on the other hand, can buy **local time** *on a single station to reach a limited geographic area.* Television also enables advertisers to target their messages. A toy company might advertise on the Saturday morning children's shows, whereas a razor-blade manufacturer might choose Sunday afternoon football, and a household products manufacturer might opt for air time during a daytime soap opera. Furthermore, advertisers have

the choice of sponsoring an entire program, either alone or with others, or of buying **spot time,** *which consists of ten-, twenty-, thirty-, or sixty-second announcements during or between programs.* Spots may be purchased on either network or local TV.

The "one-time" nature of television advertising is one of its *disadvantages*—when the purchased broadcast seconds have elapsed, the message is lost and the viewer can never go back for another look. Also, an advertisement may lose some of its impact when it is sandwiched in among a large clutter of commercial messages. But the most important disadvantage of television advertising is its high cost. The great size of TV audiences brings down the actual cost per person reached, but the total cost of a

Though TV ads reach the most people fastest, they are also costly. Broadcasters price their commercial spots in terms of expected audience size, which is based on closely monitored ratings. Thus, costs can vary widely even for the same show: when M*A*S*H was first aired in 1972, a thirty-second commercial drew $62,100, but in its final season (1983) that spot cost $96,900, while similar commercials on syndicated M*A*S*H reruns were going for an average of $3,500. The show's final two-hour special, which drew a record-breaking audience of some 60 to 70 million, commanded $400,000 for a thirty-second spot.[11]

Why is TV time so expensive? Because of supply and demand. Supply is limited (there are only a few networks and relatively few prime-time minutes), while demand—spurred by the boom in new products (such as video games and purchasable telephone sets)— is constantly growing. Advertisers compete to be associated with important public events, and the demand for time on a big draw like the Olympic Games can be spectacular: ABC had no trouble selling out its ad minutes at the 1984 Olympics at $500,000 *each*. (A regular prime-time minute sells for "only" $180,000.)

network TV ad campaign can be enormous. Over the past decade the price of TV air time has skyrocketed; in 1984 advertisers expected to pay 44 percent more than they did in 1980 for network advertising.

Major advertisers, who still regard TV as the most effective promotional medium for mass-market products, are searching out cheaper alternatives. The trend-setting advertiser Procter & Gamble shifted its spending on network commercials from 68 percent of its 1982 ad budget to 56 percent of its 1983 ad budget, with the difference going to unaffiliated local stations and cable.[12] Better advertising values are also slowly pushing more advertisers to local TV stations, whose new prosperity means better programming. Better programming draws larger audiences, which in turn means still more value for the local TV advertising dollar.

CABLE TV An even more striking new outlet for TV advertising is provided by the fledgling cable industry. Cable TV has had a rather slow gestation period since it became technically feasible. Hopeful cable entrepreneurs had to wait for FCC deregulation, a decline in satellite transmission costs, and financial backing. But cable has finally reached a take-off threshold, with over 40 percent of all TV households subscribing, over 50 percent having access, and almost no major population center without

service that is either established or in the works.[13]

Nevertheless, cable programming has so far failed to attract large-scale interest from advertisers. Even the wildly popular twenty-four-hour music-video channel, MTV, has had difficulty finding advertisers, despite low rates. The short rock-music films that MTV broadcasts were received by at least 14 million homes in 1983, but because they appeal mostly to the under-thirty-five age group, major TV advertisers have been reluctant to buy time to sell packaged foods and other consumer products. So far, MTV has had to rely mostly on video-game makers, car companies, and beverage makers for advertising.[14] The lack of a broad-based audience has also plagued other advertiser-supported cable TV services, some of which have disappeared as a result. Ironically, although they were intended to serve special-interest segments of the TV audience, cable services must attract a broad range of advertisers in order to be successful, and to do so they may first have to broaden their viewer base.

Other advertising media

Although newspapers, magazines, radio, and television account for the lion's share of all advertising dollars spent, other media are also very effective in reaching certain kinds of customers. The ways of bringing advertising messages to the public are limited only by the imagination, and many promotion professionals have let their imaginations run wild. Today, free movie magazines are distributed in theater lobbies, commercial airlines carry in-flight advertising, and supermarkets flash ads on TV monitors to captive audiences in the aisles and checkout lines. Each of these media is reaching a key promotional target, be it frequent moviegoers, frequent fliers, or the grocery buyer just an arm's reach from the shelf.

PUBLIC DISPLAYS A popular advertising category, public displays include skywriting, neon signs, electronic scoreboards at sports stadiums, and even hot-air balloons and blimps, which Goodyear so successfully used to build its image. The most widely used forms of public displays, however, are billboards, and posters mounted on benches, trash cans, and bus-stop shelters. Billboards are ideal for advertisers who do business in a restricted geographic area, such as stores and cable television operators, and want to reach only that market segment. Used in combination with TV, billboard advertising effectively reinforces the broadcast message.

DIRECT MAIL One of the fastest growing types of advertising in the "other media" category is *direct mail,* which includes not only catalogue sales (which we discuss in Chapter 12), but also sales of single items. As far as audience selectivity goes, **direct mail,** which *uses mailing lists to reach a business's most likely customers,* is the most effective medium. Once thought of as "junk mail," direct mail has become an increasingly valuable supplement to personal sales. According to one estimate, the average cost of a personal sales call rose 10.3 percent in 1983.[15] By calling only on those who have responded to a direct mail pitch, the sales staff can use their time most effectively to generate business.

The use of computers to assemble specialized mailing lists makes it possible and inexpensive to vary the contents of a mailing according to the very precise characteristics of individuals. With computers, it's a routine data-processing job to store, update, compare, sort, and sell entries from a great number of mailing lists. The more specific the mailing list, the more effective it's likely to be. One lead-

ing direct-mail marketer, Direct Mail Corporation of America, which sends out over 140 million pieces of mail per year for a large number of top corporations, has access to 50,000 specialized lists, including commercial and private pilots, purchasers of gold coins, managers of computer departments, and physicians between the ages of thirty-five and fifty-five.[16] Computers also sort mailings by zip code, which not only improves geographical targeting, but also cuts postage rates. And computers speed order fulfillment, boosting consumers' satisfaction with shopping by mail.

TELEPHONE MARKETING The marketing and microprocessing minds that brought us beyond direct mail addressed to "occupant" are now bringing us "automatic telephone dialing": you answer the phone and hear a prerecorded voice informing you that a local burger joint is offering free french fries or that your favorite store is running an unadvertised special. These technological advances have brought the telephone into the realm of advertising media. The degree of automation in this method can vary, as does the degree of irritation this marketing approach provokes in some consumers. In some cases, a human operator intervenes after the automatic equipment selects a phone number from the data bank, dials it, and records it; the operator will then obtain the consent of the person who is on the line to play the recorded message. This human touch is legally required in California and Michigan, where consumer hostility toward automatic dialing has been particularly fierce. Obviously, an angry consumer is unlikely to be responsive to a sales pitch.

Automatic dialing is sometimes used merely to deliver sales-related messages rather than solicit orders. For this purpose, some businesses find the technology extremely efficient: it does the work of four to six operators, it's as polite at the end of the day as at the beginning, and it doesn't get depressed when people hang up. New uses of automatic telephone dialing are being energetically explored by consulting firms that have sprung up to deliver this service. Some retailers have found that consumers will sign up to receive the calls if they're invited to do so!

THE ADVERTISING PLAN

Advertising campaigns are planned with careful consideration of the following questions:

- What objectives does the company want to achieve with its advertising?
- What is the target audience?
- How much can the company afford to spend on advertising this product?
- What creative theme or appeal shall be used?
- Which medium is best for delivering the message?

Let's explore the ways in which promotion specialists use the answers to these questions to develop creative and media strategies.

Creative strategy

The creative strategy is designed to achieve the advertiser's promotional objectives. It is usually set down in the form of simple statements, both to clarify the thinking of the advertiser and to guide the advertising agency. The first statement positions the product, that is, establishes the image it should have, determines the target market, and details the product's strengths with regard to the competition. For example, promoters of science-fiction movies try to carve out a special niche for each film. They may want their ad messages to stress the film's special effects or 3-D; or, they may build a position for their movie based on a popular TV show, a fictional character, or a previous film in a sequence.[17]

Next, the creative strategy requires a **copy platform,** *a simple statement of the benefits the consumer can expect to obtain from the product and the specific features that provide these benefits.* The copy platform also indicates the general theme and tone of the message. "There's more for your life at Sears" is an example of a copy platform. Finally, advertisers specify the objectives the promotional message is expected to achieve in terms of its "level of response." What reaction do we want from the audience—increased awareness of the product? creation of a brand preference? stimulation of inquiries from qualified prospects? With this final element of creative strategy,

the ad agency knows not only how the target customer should see the product, but what the customer should do about it (become aware of it, send in an order for it, and so on).

Media planning

The media plan, usually set up by the firm's advertising agency, translates the advertiser's objectives, message, and creative theme into explicit decisions about how much to spend on advertising, how to divide the budget among alternative media, and exactly when to schedule the purchased time or space. The goal of the media plan is to make the most effective use of the firm's advertising dollar.

THE MEDIA MIX The critical task of the media planner is to select a **media mix,** that is, *a combination of print, broadcast, and other media for the advertising campaign.* Step one is to determine the characteristics of the target audience and to determine which types of media will reach the greatest number of target consumers at the lowest cost. The choice is also based on what the medium is expected to do (show the product in use, list numerous sale items and prices, and so on). Once the media mix has been established the media planner chooses specific vehicles in each of the chosen media categories, such as individual magazines (*Time, People, Sports Illustrated*) or individual radio stations (a rock station, a classical station), using the directories published by the Standard Rate and Data Service (SRDS). An increasingly popular approach to creating the media mix is the "concentration" strategy—channeling most of the budget into one media type, such as full-page newspaper ads or a heavy spot TV schedule. This strategy allows the advertiser's message to dominate a particular medium in its particular product class, and may help the advertiser obtain better price deals from the medium selected.

MEDIA BUYING Media buying, the choice of specific media vehicles and schedules, relies on four important pieces of information. The first is **cost per thousand,** a standardized ratio that converts the nominal cost of the ad space in question to the more meaningful *cost of reaching a thousand people with the ad.* Cost per thousand is especially useful for comparing

$$\text{COST PER } 1000 = .27$$

$$M_{xy} = \int_0^1 dx \int_0^{1-x} dy \int_0^{4-x}$$

$$E = MC^2$$

$$Q = \sum_{L=1}^{n} n^2 + 3 \qquad \text{REACH} = 150,000$$

$$2\pi \gamma \cdot \frac{\delta x^2 y^2}{\delta 3 x^3 + 4}$$

$$\text{FREQUENCY} = 24$$

$$\rho z \delta 2 = \frac{95}{36} \rho \qquad \text{CONTINUITY} = 12.5$$

As the old joke puts it, "Half of any advertising budget is wasted. The question is, which half?" Our media planner here is trying to figure out how to make the best use of the firm's advertising dollar.

the cost of different vehicles that reach similar audiences. The next two decision tools are reach and frequency, which conceptually represent the tradeoff between breadth and depth of communication for the advertising dollar. **Reach** refers to the *total number of households that will be exposed to a given message at least once in a given time period*. It is usually expressed as a percentage of the total number of households in a particular population. **Frequency** expresses *the average number of times each household in the population is exposed to the message*. It is calculated by dividing the total number of exposures by the total number of households reached.

The last scheduling concept is **continuity,** which refers to *the amount of time the media schedule spans and how the ad messages are timed*—evenly spread over the schedule or heavily concentrated in some periods. Obviously, within a fixed budget, the plan cannot maximize all of these factors; if you want to reach a high percentage of your target group with significant frequency, it would be very expensive to do so on a continuous basis. Media planners often resort to the strategy of airing their messages in

"waves" or "flights"—short periods of high reach and frequency that sacrifice continuity between high- and low-wave periods. This strategy is common in the travel industry, which crowds much of its annual media spending into the peak vacation seasons.

ADVERTISING AGENCIES

In 1983 there were about 850 advertising agencies in the United States. Together they billed their clients for $31.1 billion.[18] The complex problems involved in creating the advertising campaign have made advertising agencies a key element in the nation's marketing system. Advertising agents were originally hired by the media themselves to sell space to marketers. The ad agency evolved when the agents found that marketers didn't know how to advertise, and that supplemental services were required. Although ad agencies are now independent and work for the client, many of the larger agencies are still paid, in effect, by the advertising media. Under this arrangement, the medium gives a 15 percent discount on the cost of media space to an agency, which then charges the client for the full amount, keeping 15 percent as its commission. In other words, the agency could buy $100,000 of media space for $85,000 and bill the client for $100,000. The $15,000 commission would cover the research, artwork, copywriting, and other services that went into producing the campaign. If the client had chosen to create the campaign, it would have cost $100,000 just to buy the media space.

PERSONAL SELLING

According to the latest available statistics, over 6 percent of the work force is involved in some form of personal selling.[19] The cost of this promotional activity is a major item for many companies. It includes the salaries and commissions paid to salespeople; the expenses involved in hiring, training, and supervising a sales force; and the money spent for travel and entertainment. Taken together, these activities involve increasingly huge amounts of

THE AIRLINE BORN TO SERVE BUSINESS TO ATLANTA AND MEMPHIS IS HERE.

To the hassled business flyer tired of being overlooked and underserved, we dedicate Air Atlanta.

With no overbooking. Streamlined check-in. A roll-on valet for hanging bags. 727 jets redesigned for bigger seats with more legroom. Gourmet snacks and a choice of fresh, delicious entrees. All at current coach fares.

If you're travelling on business, it's the only way to fly.

The only business hour nonstops from New York's JFK to Atlanta. And the only direct service from New York's JFK to Memphis. Call your travel agent, 212-517-8216 or 1-800-241-5408.

AIR ATLANTA
BORN TO SERVE BUSINESS

Get a Canon PocketPrinter for tax season and find a better way to tax your mind.

Forget about worrying about taxes this year. Get a Canon PocketPrinter instead.

A Canon PocketPrinter can take the heat of tax time simply by helping you to calculate quickly and accurately.

And because Canon PocketPrinters leave a clear record of all your calculations, you don't have to sweat out the figures so much. So you can relax.

They print out on thermal paper too. So they're very, very quiet.

They even run on penlite batteries. And easily fit into your pocket. So you can start figuring your taxes on the train, or on the bus, or even at the bus stop if you like. Take one everywhere.

Use it everyday too. Start keeping track of receipts and other little taxes you pay throughout the year. Organize yourself not only for this tax season, but for others to come.

So get a Canon PocketPrinter. There are two to choose from. The reasonably priced TP-8 with fluorescent display. And the even more affordable TP-7 with liquid crystal display.

You'll find either a very small price to pay for so much peace of mind. So go find something better to worry about. Like whether "they're biting or not."

Where quality is the constant factor.

Canon Pocket Printer
ELECTRONIC

Canon U.S.A., Inc., One Canon Plaza, Lake Success, NY 11042.

With Lucite Wall Paint you won't be seeing red for long.

Parents don't get quite as angry at wall "art" when their walls are painted with Lucite* Wall Paint. Its exclusive formula actually resists dirt penetration. Smudge marks, finger marks, even crayon marks wash off easily. So Lucite helps walls look freshly painted for a long time.

LUCITE
THE PAINT THAT LASTS AND LASTS.

LUCITE Wall Paint

FOUR QUESTIONS TO ASK IN EVALUATING A LAYOUT

How do you know if an ad will really sell? Here are four key questions to ask:

1. Does the ad "send the massage" fast and clear? (Even a complex layout should be organized to communicate as directly as possible.)

2. Does the ad have an arresting focal point? (Some one element, either verbal or visual, should grab the eye—making the viewer stop to read the entire ad more closely.)

3. Do the art and the copy work hand in hand, or are they at cross purposes? (The aim of the design is to guide the reader through the copy, and crucial factors include the type's style and size as well as the integration of the type with the pictorial elements. It is not enough for an ad to "look good," if it goes unread.)

4. Does the ad reflect the correct "image"? (A conservative advertiser—a bank, say—might want to make one sort of impression, while a rock band might want to make quite another. The style of the ad sends a message that may attract or repel the viewer.)

269 shades for your lips.

143 shades for your fingertips.

Color with shine. Color with soul.

Have we got the Revlon color for you.

REVLONCOLOR

Shoes that fit your moods

Set sail for summertime fun and adventure in our cool 'n breezy leather sandals. From $18.99.

BUTLERS SHOES
MALINGS SHOES

With over 500 stores nationwide.

LAWRY'S MAKES STEAKS.

No matter how juicy the steak. How fresh the fish. How crispy the salad. Anything you make, you'll make even better with Lawry's Seasoned Salt.

It's a delicate blend of twelve herbs and spices, balanced to perfection to give ordinary steak extraordinary Lawry's flavor.

Lawry's Seasoned Salt. And your next meal. They were made for each other.

LAWRY'S SEASONED SALT

STEPS TO AN EFFECTIVE SALES PRESENTATION

In personal selling, the sales representative has an opportunity to build a face-to-face rapport with the prospect—a sense of psychological connection. The skillful salesperson constantly uses two-way feedback: he or she uses body language and verbal directions to get a message to the prospect, and responds to body language and verbal directions *from* the prospect.

Here are some hints on how it's done.

ESTABLISHING A BOND

Prospects are much more inclined to buy from people who make them feel good, and with whom they have developed a personal bond.

■ *Try to make yourself seem compatible with the prospect.* Be similar (or seem so) in dress, speaking patterns, and interests.

■ *Be sure to set aside a preliminary period to build a feeling of agreement.* Don't lunge into the presentation immediately.

■ *Pace your statements and gestures to mirror the customer's observations, experience, or behavior.* "It's been awfully hot these last few days, hasn't it?" . . . "You said you were going to graduate in June."

■ *Use a "probing" period to draw out information and identify the prospect's real needs and problems.* A consumer may want status from a car as much as performance; the industrial buyer wants to avoid looking bad to management. Good salespeople are excellent listeners at the probing stage.

DESCRIBING AND DEMONSTRATING THE PRODUCT

Once the prospect's needs are identified, you should concentrate on relating product features to benefits that can meet the buyer's needs or solve a problem.

■ *Focus on benefits.* "This drill will help you make holes faster and more cheaply" is better than a statement about product features ("This drill engine delivers *x* foot-pounds of torque").

■ *Use product demonstrations that the prospect can easily see and comprehend.* For example, let's say you have won an appointment with Ms. McCormick to discuss your company's cash management account. You could show Ms. McCormick a sample statement of the type she would receive every month, outlining the activity of an imaginary account and showing how the client's money will be kept busy earning interest.

THE TRIAL CLOSE

Your purpose is ultimately to close the sale by obtaining an order by securing the prospect's signature on an order book or getting some other commitment.

■ *You may try using a "yes" technique.* Use a series of questions or statements that get the prospect to nod or say "yes" over and over; by the time you finally ask for the order, the prospect may be in the mood to say "yes" just one more time.

TRYING A TRIAL CLOSE

Experienced salespeople know that most prospects won't be entirely satisfied until they've asked questions or posed objections to the sales points. To deal with this, you may want to launch a trial balloon known as the *trial close*—a manueuver that may not get the order then and there, but will draw out whatever may be standing between the prospect and the sale. A typical trial close would be:

Salesperson: Would you agree that your money works harder to earn you interest in a cash management account than in the money market fund you're using now?

Customer: I suppose it does.

Salesperson: Then we can open an account for you this week with as little as $1,000 . . . and I can sign you up today with your signature on this acceptance . . .

Customer: Yes, but what about getting at my money when I need it in an emergency? I don't want to tie up my funds or pay a penalty for taking them out.

Now you have an bona fide objection on the table, and you know where the buyer's resistance lies.

HANDLING OBJECTIONS

The way to answer objections is *not* to argue with the customer. If you do, you may prove how smart you are by winning the argument, but you will probably lose the sale. Instead, you should:

Recognize the nature of the objection.

■ The buyer may not see how the product meets his needs or ability to buy: "I won't be able to get that purchase approved without a one-year warranty."

■ Or, the prospect may be stalling because he or she doesn't want to confirm the decision for some reason: "I'll have to ask my wife," or "I'll take it up with the finance committee when we have our budget meeting next month."

■ Or, the prospect may just need more information: "I'm not sure that your service will be as reliable as the service I get from our current supplier."

■ Some objections are *rational* and product-oriented. Others are *psychological*: they have more to do with the buyer's "hidden agenda" of needs. For instance, the prospect may be afraid of trying something new, or may dislike the salesperson.

Register agreement.

No matter what the buyer says, the skillful salesperson usually agrees courteously, and then shifts the derailed prospect back on the right track. Instead of

blurting out, "Oh no, our service is better than you'd get from your supplier," it's smarter to begin, "I can understand why you're concerned about service. These days, you have to be. That's why we offer a seven-point service contract . . . " In other words, answer with a statement that *proves* your service is better.

Probe with a new trial close.

Once the objection is handled, you can use another trial close to extract new objections. You handle these objections one by one, and eventually, you exhaust the buyer's doubts and problems, so that you can go to a final close. For instance:

Salesperson: I can appreciate your need for 24-hour access to your cash without paying a penalty. That's why we give you this special American Express Gold Card [pulls the card out of portfolio] that lets you get cash from any participating bank whenever you need it . . .

THE FINAL CLOSE

The most striking characteristic of the great salesperson is the ability to close the sale and walk away with the prospect's signature on an order blank. For some salespeople, the final close is a frightening or embarrassing moment: it always entails the risk of rejection. Some salespeople just don't stop talking: they effectively sell the product and then buy it back. So be sure that when you end the presentation stage and go for the final close, you are able to keep quiet while the customer orders. Here are some useful closing techniques:

■ *Summarize the presentation.* Use a simple anecdotal statement that clearly positions the need for the product in the buyer's mind.

■ *Make the offer available only for a limited time.* This approach often gets immediate action.

■ *Ask for a small "trial" order.* You can reduce the customer's risk this way.

■ *Turn the buyer's last objection into a close.* Say, "Then you'd order if I could guarantee a one-year warranty in writing?" This way, you leave the buyer in the position of having run out of *valid* objections.

money. In 1983, for example, the average cost of one sales call by a traveling salesperson was nearly $90.[20] Needless to say, a company would hardly part with so much money if it wasn't considered a worthwhile investment.

The great advantage of personal selling over other forms of promotion, the quality that makes it so essential, is its *flexibility*. Salespeople can tailor their presentations to fit different situations, responding to questions, handling objections, and foreseeing a customer's particular needs and problems. They can also develop a personal rapport with the customer, building a feeling of trust and making it known that they are acting on the customer's behalf as well as their employer's. They can demonstrate the special features of their products, and finally, they can complete a sale on the spot.

In recent years, the nature of personal selling has changed radically. Today's salespeople are better trained than before; they must draw on an intimate knowledge of the product and a strategic understanding of the buyer, rather than using "pushiness" to make the sale. Salespeople are no longer expected to be simply order takers; now, they are required to mediate problems between customer and plant, gather intelligence about competitors, find out about any new needs the customer may have, and help work out the arrangements for financing the order. For this they are more highly compensated than ever. The opportunity for independence and high rewards has attracted a large number of women and minorities to the profession of personal selling, particularly selling to businesses, where the 1980 census shows a more than doubling of their numbers since 1970.

Personal selling can be divided into two categories—Business selling and retail selling.

BUSINESS SELLING

Business selling (also known as *industrial selling*) involves the *selling of products or services to businesses, nonprofit institutions, and government agencies*. It is considered the most challenging kind of selling because the products or services are bought for resale or business use, not for personal use, and the buying is done on a far more professional and knowledgeable

basis than is consumer buying. To sell a computer to General Motors, to the Social Security Administration, or to a large hospital, the salesperson must have detailed knowledge not only of the product but also of the buyer's needs.

There are three main *problems* in business selling. First, the salesperson can have difficulties getting in to the right prospect. The salesperson must carefully select the firms that could have use for the product, and then determine the appropriate individuals to approach within those organizations. Good pre-approach information is essential for effective use of the salesperson's time, because the universe of potential buyers for many industrial products is very limited and because a number of people in the buyer's organization are likely to be involved in industrial purchase decisions.

The second problem in business selling involves selling against competition. The sales effort may take some time, and meanwhile the prospect is evaluating other companies' sales efforts as well. The skillful salesperson pinpoints the prospect's needs early in order to know which of the product's advantages to stress and to keep up forward momentum in the sales effort.

The third business selling problem is assuring the customer of prompt delivery. The buyer often has a tight schedule to meet and also may require customized attention from the seller's own production department. In addition, industrial products often require special installation, operator training, maintenance, and other services that are as important as the actual product.

RETAIL SELLING

Retail selling is *direct, face-to-face selling of goods and services to the people who will use them*. Most retail selling takes place in stores. Selling automobiles, fur coats, and fine jewelry requires patient, expert work, but in general the status of personal selling jobs is quite low. Most customers are presumed to have been presold by need or advertising, so that salespeople serve primarily as order takers. Retail selling has been further downgraded due to the growth of self-service stores and catalogue showrooms, where a customer's only contact with store personnel is at the checkout counter.

A special kind of retail selling is the **in-store demonstration,** in which *sales representatives show how to use their company's products.* While less common than in the past, this method is still used successfully by some retailers. A southern chain of drug stores, for instance, has between one and three cosmeticians in each of its stores. Kept up to date through periodic classes offered by manufacturers and meetings at company headquarters, they demonstrate new products and offer personalized advice to their customers. Another type of in-store demonstration involves a videocassette player. Placed where it will draw a maximum amount of customer attention, the videocassette shows how products work and how clothing looks on models at less cost than live demonstrations.

Another development in retail selling has been the attempt by some companies to expand and improve sales positions. The job of insurance salespeople used to be to sell as much insurance as possible. Training was limited to insurance. Today, however, many insurance companies have trained their salespeople to be financial planners who can plan a client's whole estate. Of course, the object is still to sell insurance; in the process, though, the planner may also advise on mutual funds, trusts, and stock portfolios. Frequently these salespeople write more policies and earn more money than those with less training.

Another kind of retail selling is **door-to-door selling,** in which *a salesperson goes from one house or apartment to another to sell goods.* Some firms, such as Avon, have used this method with astonishing success; they deliver a product that is essentially a blend of tangible goods and personalized attention. But this approach faces some problems today. With the dramatic rise in two-career households, the salesperson is less likely to find people at home during the day. Moreover, many people, both sales personnel and customers, dislike door-to-door selling because of the high-pressure sales methods that sometimes accompany them. Federal regulations require door-to-door salespeople to give customers a seventy-two-hour cooling-off period, during which time buyers can change their minds and cancel an order, even if a contract has been signed. People who sell from door to door must also clearly announce when they ring someone's doorbell that they are doing so for the purpose of selling something. The regulations, plus the growing reluctance of people to admit strangers to their homes, have made door-to-door selling increasingly difficult.

Selling at the home of the salesperson rather than the customer is becoming popular with a number of products. Party-plan sales, which began with Tupperware in the 1940s, have grown tremendously in the past twenty years into a $9-billion-a-year business.[21] Home Interiors & Gifts Inc., founded in 1957, today sells $400 million worth of decorative accessories annually through home parties. The success of Home Interiors is built on an inspirational approach to training the sales force (now numbering 40,000, including managers).[22]

PUBLICITY

On the fiftieth anniversary of the filming of "King Kong," a giant plastic ape was shipped from its place of manufacturer in Southern California and placed atop the Empire State Building in New York City. This was not the work of some clever nostalgia buff, but of a clever manufacturer of giant cold-air-inflatable advertising displays that licensed the trademark from Universal City Studios Inc. King Kong cost the firm of Robert Keith & Company Inc. $100,000, but he attracted valuable publicity for the promotional use of giant balloon replicas of products ranging from soda cans to cigarette packs. Within six months of his debut, Kong had brought his investors more than $100,000 in new business.[23]

Publicity includes *any information relating to a manufacturer or its products that appears in any medium on a nonpaid basis.* Companies seek favorable publicity in newspapers and magazines—reports about boat and auto shows, for example, or recipes using new food products or stories about charitable deeds—to create interest in their products. One such article can generate more sales than pages of paid advertising.

Of course, publicity can be negative as well as positive. A striking example is the uproar that accompanied the poisoning deaths in 1982 of seven

INFORMATION TECHNOLOGY MANAGEMENT: SALES TOOL OF THE FUTURE

As fast as engineers can design new technologies, sales managers are discovering ways to use technology to increase the productivity of their sales force. Take, for example, the critical task of identifying "qualified prospects," so that the firm can concentrate its sales effort on those targets whose size, past purchasing policy, or creditworthiness indicate that a sale is possible. A factory fire-insurance salesperson, for instance, must determine from sources of published data where manufacturing plants are situated, whether they're in a high-fire-risk industry, and what recent trends indicate a possible change in each factory's need for insurance protection. This job used to be time-consuming and laborious; now, using a computer, the salesperson can sift qualified prospects from a data base in just a few minutes. With a computer, it's easy to vary the qualifying criteria and the data base of potential accounts to turn up sales opportunities.

Or consider the problem of how to make the best use of travel time. Here too the salesperson can rely on a number of new information technologies. A mobile telephone can relay messages to the salesperson while he or she is in transit, so it's easy to rearrange appointments quickly. So-called *speech mail,* which delivers recorded messages by phone, permits a salesperson to continue essential communications when out of town, recording those messages before departure or while traveling. If the salesperson wants to know the most efficient travel route to reach a set of destinations, computer programs are available to analyze geographic problems. Computers can also coordinate the schedules of a large staff; sales managers will rely on them increasingly to monitor travel plans, record past contacts, and schedule convenient meeting times for a busy sales staff.

The new videodisc demonstration kits, futuristic audio-visual support devices, can lend punch to a sales call. The information recorded on a videodisc need not be accessed sequentially: rather than playing a "canned" presentation, the salesperson can skip to any part of the presentation in response to the prospect's questions, saving time for both the salesperson and the customer. Another great gadget is the portable microcomputer—an outstanding tool for the information-intensive sales call. When a product requires complex calculations involving price, delivery schedule, or production configuration, the salesperson can simply make a telephone connection between the portable terminal and the firm's data-processing support, type in the essential data, and get back a cost estimate, a delivery date, or a determination of the feasibility of the customer's product specifications—right in the customer's office. Newer models even feature two-way radio capability that lets them communicate with other computers without a phone.

Finally, technology can help the salesperson reduce the amount of time he or she spends checking in with the field office. Working at home with a computer terminal, the salesperson can receive and send electronic mail and transmit correspondence and proposals to the office staff for printing and distribution. Or office staff can generate documents for the salesperson, who can electronically receive, review, and approve them for distribution without a visit to the office. And the

people who had taken Tylenol from packages that had been tampered with. As we noted in Chapter 10, Johnson & Johnson immediately removed all of the product from retail shelves nationwide while it devised tamper-resistant packaging. The product was rereleased with a massive advertising campaign, which successfully countered the fears instilled by the negative publicity.[24]

THE HIGH-TECH HORIZON

travel and expense report no longer looms as horrid drudgery; if the salesperson gets into the habit of routinely entering schedules and expenses into the terminal as they occur, the T&E report will write itself according to a preprogrammed format.

TELEMARKETING

Sales representatives have traditionally been big users of the telephone for scheduling and following up sales calls. Now they are finding that the phone can be an excellent tool for making first-time sales calls. As the cost of long-distance calls drops and the cost of traveling continues to rise, many companies are turning increasingly to what American Bell calls "telemarketing." Telephone selling can be ideal for reaching new prospects at the outer limits of the sales rep's territory, for example, and it's a good way to reach reluctant prospects who are willing to entertain a short verbal presentation but don't want intrusions into their office routine. Some firms are making effective use of toll-free 800-number service lines to capture and channel targets reached by advertising and of conference calls to bring together the many parties to a sale.

Of course, telemarketing is not appropriate in all situations. Some products must be seen to be appreciated and some require lengthy explanation, which is difficult to give by phone. It may be difficult, too, for the sales rep to convey enthusiasm over the phone, and a phone prospect can easily terminate the sales call at any moment. As videophones become increasingly widespread, the salesperson's ability to convey technical and emotional messages by phone should increase.

SALES PROMOTION

The fourth promotion technique is **sales promotion,** defined by the American Marketing Association as *"those marketing activities, other than personal selling, advertising, and publicity, that stimulate consumer purchasing and dealer effectiveness."* This is a very broad definition, emphasizing the fact that sales promotion covers a wide variety of activities. They extend from arranging plant tours and trade show exhibits to distributing free samples, setting up speakers' bureaus, and publishing promotional booklets.

Some sales promotion efforts are aimed at dealers: for example, General Motors holds training sessions for the salespeople who work for its franchised dealers. Other sales promotion programs are directed at the customer but channeled through the dealer: a cosmetics manufacturer may sponsor a skin-care clinic for teenagers at a department store. Some firms aim promotions directly at the consumer, and reach their target very effectively. Manufacturers Hanover Trust, a major New York bank, sponsors marathon races all over the country. Sixty percent of the entrants it draws are professionals and thirty percent are middle and senior managers—the bank's key clientele. The bank's marketing director says that at $30,000 a race, "it is the biggest bang for our buck in our whole marketing effort."[25]

Another effective sales promotion device is the **point-of-purchase display (POP),** *a device by which a product is displayed in such a way as to stimulate immediate sales.* This can be a fairly simple affair, such as the stacks of recipe-book coupons found in many retail outlets or the racks offering Tic-Tac mints at supermarket checkout counters. It can also be quite elaborate. The almost overnight success of Hanes' L'eggs pantyhose was due to the unique seven-foot egg-shaped display unit on which the pantyhose were displayed and sold in supermarkets and drugstores.

COUPONING **Couponing** is *a sales promotion technique that aims to spur sales by offering a discount through redeemable coupons.* Coupons are distributed in a number of ways. Newspapers and magazines, free-standing newspaper inserts, and direct mailings are among the most common means of circulation. But by far the most effective method is to print a coupon on the product package.

Couponing has been very successful in recent years; between 1979 and 1983, manufacturers increased the number of coupons they issued by 65 percent. This successful promotional strategy is threatened, however, by the soaring costs of printing, processing, misredemption, and a rising tide of organized coupon fraud.[26]

REFUND OFFERS Manufacturers have been experimenting with higher-value refund offers that require multiple proofs of purchase. Some companies make money-back offers of $1 to $24 and more to get people to try a variety of their products, or to encourage repeated use of a product. For example, Kimberly-Clark offered a choice of a $2 cash refund or $4 worth of $.25 store coupons for nine proofs of purchase, and a number of manufacturers have offered rebates of $5 to upwards of $1,000 on high-ticket items such as home appliances.

GAMES AND SWEEPSTAKES Sweepstakes and games have become an increasingly important promotional tool. An estimated 1,000 sweepstakes are nationally advertised each year (triple the number in 1975), and they are cropping up in such unconventional markets as banking, airlines, and industrial products. The games are designed with great care to meet the firm's advertising objectives. The prize must be chosen for its appeal to the product's target market—would they be enticed by a Rolls-Royce or something more practical? And some connection between the prize and the product image is also sought. A hot-air balloon trip with in-flight French cuisine was the bait when General Mills ran a sweepstakes for its Yoplait, "the yogurt of France"; and Union Carbide chose a battery-powered car for an Eveready battery sweepstakes.

PREMIUMS AND GIVEAWAYS Giving things away is a tried and true method of promotion that has been making a comeback as a means of boosting sluggish sales. Giveaways may be simply samples of the merchandise that a company wants to sell, such as cigarettes distributed on street corners, shampoos distributed through the mail, or Mr. Turkey franks served up by a product representative in a supermarket. Or they may be items unrelated to the firm's product, given away merely as a reminder of the firm's name and address, such as the ever-familiar giveaway calendars, pens, ashtrays, matches, and key rings. **Premiums** are a type of *giveaway offered as a bonus only to people who use a specific product or service.* Banks haven't yet adopted the practice of handing

out money on street corners, but they are heavy users of premiums. Depending on the size of the initial deposit, new bank customers have carted away all kinds of loot, including microwave ovens and color television sets. Some banks have also begun to offer customers discounted merchandise through their own catalogues.

REGULATION OF ADVERTISING

Of the four methods of promotion directed at consumers, people are most likely to be aware of advertising because it is so visible and widespread. Over the century, advertisers have had to respond to an array of public criticism. Does advertising raise costs? Is it wasteful? Does it perpetrate false racial and sexual stereotypes? Does it manipulate the consumer on a subconscious level and deepen his or her feelings of insecurity? Is it truthful in general?

Public concern about potential misuses of advertising is responsible in part for the growth of government regulation of advertising: several federal agencies and state governments strive to guarantee "truth in advertising." Advertisers themselves, their agencies, the media, and many trade and professional associations also set guidelines to protect the public from unscrupulous pitches. But the efforts of these regulators to protect the consumer interest have been immensely complicated by the recent debate over just what is in the consumer's interest. One view holds that too much regulation can be as harmful and costly to the public as not enough. Some advertising regulations are under fire from consumer groups who believe they are anticompetitive. There are even some regulations that advertisers like and are fighting to maintain.

THE FEDERAL TRADE COMMISSION (FTC)

The federal government's advertising watchdog is the Federal Trade Commission (FTC). This agency dates back to 1914, when the Federal Trade Commission Act was passed by Congress. The Commission's role was expanded in 1938 by the Wheeler-Lea Act, which gives the FTC specific authority to control false or misleading ads by most food, drug, health, and cosmetic companies.

The FTC has developed ground rules for advertisers. One is that *all statements of fact must be supported by evidence.* This includes words ("Bounty soaks up more than the next leading brand") and demonstrations. Thus, advertisers cannot use whipped cream in a shaving cream commercial to create an impression of a firm, heavy lather. Furthermore, *advertisers not only must avoid specific language that is untrue, but they also must not create an overall impression that is incorrect.* In other words, they cannot claim that doctors recommend a product if they do not; nor can they present an actor who delivers the message dressed in a doctor's white jacket.

The current FTC chairman, James Miller III, has taken the position that ad substantiation is an extremely costly process, and that consumers would be better served if these rules were eliminated: consumers could exercise their own good judgment, and they might pay less for products because advertising costs might decline. Although there has been no formal change in FTC regulation, lately the FTC seems to favor a loose interpretation of appropriate evidence for advertising claims.

In one recent policy change, the FTC abolished a ban on comparative advertising—ads that identify the competition by name, a technique that makes ads more informative to the consumer and encourages competition. That FTC action and the apparent effectiveness of brand-name comparisons have led to a steady increase in their use. An estimated one of every ten TV commercials now involves competitive product demonstrations. A comparative ad campaign mounted by Burger King in 1982 claiming broad public preference for their "Whoppers" drew a lawsuit from McDonald's alleging "false and misleading" assertions. As it turned out, Burger King sales benefited even more from the publicity generated by the suit, which went as far as having a Waldorf-Astoria chef perform a taste test.[27] Some advertising people have complained that the practice of comparative advertising damages the industry as a whole, but overall its success seems to have created more converts than critics.

OTHER GOVERNMENT CONTROLS

THE FOOD AND DRUG ADMINISTRATION The Food, Drug, and Cosmetic Act (1938) gives the U.S. Food and Drug Administration (FDA) authority to regulate the labeling and branding of foods, drugs, and many health products and cosmetics. The FDA monitors the accuracy of ingredient lists on the labels and the form of the labels themselves. One area in which the FDA has not been active is prescription-drug advertising to consumers. Although there are regulations for pharmaceutical ads directed to doctors, pharmacists, and other professionals, there is no FDA policy on consumer advertising, primarily because drug companies have not pitched to consumers in the past. The situation is changing, however. In 1983, the FDA approved the first prescription-drug commercial, allowing Boots Pharmaceutical to promote its antiarthritis drug, Rufen, exclusively on the basis of price comparison rather than any claims about arthritis relief. The FDA does not prohibit prescription-drug advertising to consumers, but because manufacturers have been reluctant to embark on consumer ad campaigns without FDA approval, the agency may develop guidelines in the near future.

THE U.S. POSTAL SERVICE The Postal Service plays an important role in regulating any advertising that travels through the mail.[28] Much of its activity is geared toward preventing obscenity in advertising and stopping promotional fraud. In 1982 the Postal Service took a more aggressive enforcement stance with its own advertising, encouraging victims of mail fraud to bring forth information to the postmaster to help end such activities.

STATE REGULATION OF ADVERTISING Advertising is regulated by forty-four states that have passed the Printer's Ink Model Statute, drawn up in 1911 by the trade newspaper of the advertising industry. The statute provides punishment for "untrue, deceptive or misleading" advertising. Most states also regulate advertising practices by individual industries such as liquor stores, stock brokerages, employment agencies, and small loan companies.

SELF-REGULATION

Professional associations, such as state bar associations and the American Medical Association, have long regulated advertising by their members and successfully pressured many state legislatures to enact their standards into laws. In the past few years such restrictions have come under attack by consumer groups as well as by professionals who claim that they restrain competition, keeping the cost of their services high and denying consumers the right to make an informed choice. Moreover, in 1977 the Supreme Court invalidated state and bar association restrictions against advertising legal services. In a similar action in 1978 the FTC lifted state and private bans on advertising for eyeglasses, contact lenses, and eye examinations, and mandated that eye doctors must provide consumers with copies of their prescriptions so that they can shop comparatively for glasses. FTC efforts to prohibit the American Medical Association from barring advertising by member doctors have been appealed.

Self-regulation by advertisers provides still another vehicle for the restraint of false and misleading ads. The National Advertising Review Board, whose members include advertisers, agencies, and the general public, has a full-time professional staff whose job is to investigate complaints of deceptive advertising. If the complaint appears justified, the board will try to get the offending company to stop, using both its moral power and the threat of referral to governmental agencies. Many individual advertisers and agencies also practice self-regulation.

Finally, the media themselves exercise control over the advertising they carry. Newspapers often require proof before they will accept an advertisement claiming that a given product is "the lowest priced." Magazines are particularly sensitive on the matter of taste. *Ms.* magazine, for instance, turns down ads it believes are offensive to women. The National Association of Broadcasters, a trade organization for TV and radio stations, has established voluntary codes that regulate the kind of advertising that may be accepted. For example, advertisements for hard liquor are forbidden. Even beer and wine ads on television may not show people actually drinking the product.

CHAPTER REVIEW

The promotion activities of the marketing mix include four methods: advertising, personal selling, publicity, and sales promotion.

A promotional strategy may involve either a "push" or a "pull" approach. The latter depends on consumer demand to "pull" a product through the distribution channel, while the former begins with the producer, who "pushes" an item through to the consumer. Consumer goods are more likely to rely on pull strategies, while industrial goods are more often pushed.

Most promotional expenditures are devoted to advertising, which can be subdivided into three categories. Primary-demand, or generic, advertising tries to increase total demand for a product without distinguishing among brands. Selective, or brand, advertising aims at getting customers to buy a particular brand. Institutional advertising is designed to create goodwill for a company or cause (as in advocacy advertising) rather than to sell specific products. Of the total media budget, the largest percentage goes to newspapers.

Most of the rest goes to radio, magazines, and television. Other media include outdoor advertising, direct mail, and telephone marketing.

The advertising campaign first establishes the company's objectives for its advertising, then devises an appropriate media plan—the ideas that shape the actual advertising message. It determines how a firm's advertising dollars are to be spent; the specific media mix will depend on the goals for a given product and on the audience to be reached.

A very large part of all advertising expenditures are made through advertising agencies, which are usually paid on a commission basis.

Personal selling involves both selling to business and retail selling, in stores or door to door. Business selling often requires knowledge of a customer's needs as well as familiarity with the product.

Publicity is information about a company or its products that is reported as news. Companies try to get favorable publicity both in trade publications and in consumer-oriented media; they sometimes spend a great deal of money in the process.

Sales promotion, aimed at stimulating dealer effectiveness and consumer purchasing, can encompass anything from plant tours to training sessions and from point-of-purchase displays to discount coupons, refund offers, games and sweepstakes, and, finally, premiums and giveaways.

In recent years the public has been critical of advertising's cost, informational value, social utility, and honesty. In response to these attacks, government regulation has increased. In addition, the media exert considerable control over advertising, and the advertisers themselves try to enforce standards of truthfulness and taste.

KEY WORDS

promotion (294)

advertising (295)

primary-demand (generic) advertising (296)

selective (brand) advertising (296)

institutional advertising (296)

advocacy (controversy) advertising (296)

cooperative advertising (297)

media (297)

geographic and demographic editions (298)

special-interest magazines (298)

network time (299)

local time (299)

spot time (299)

direct mail (301)

copy platform (302)

media mix (302)

cost per thousand (302)

reach (303)

frequency (303)

continuity (303)

business selling (308)

retail selling (308)

in-store demonstration (309)

door-to-door selling (309)

publicity (309)

sales promotion (311)

point-of-purchase display (POP) (311)

couponing (311)

premiums (312)

REVIEW QUESTIONS

1. Define advertising. Give examples of the three types of advertising.

2. Discuss the advantages and disadvantages of the major advertising media.

3. Make a list of several real or imaginary products and/or services, then draw up a media plan for each one. Be sure to explain the reasons for your decisions.

4. What is the great advantage of personal selling over other forms of promotion? Discuss the two categories of personal selling and recent trends in each.

5. What is publicity? How and why do companies seek publicity?

6. Define sales promotion and give three examples of sales-promotion devices.

7. Discuss the roles of government, the media, and advertisers in the regulation of advertising.

PROMOTIONAL RAZZLE-DAZZLE FROM DU PONT

(Setting: Neiman-Marcus's carpet department)

Salesman: May I help you?

Shopper: Yes. I want to buy a really classy carpet for my California condo. What would you suggest?

Salesman: You can't do better than this one made of nylon from Du Pont.

Shopper: Oh? Why?

Salesman: Simply because with every purchase you get a home computer.

Computers and carpets? A strange combination for a promotion campaign, perhaps, but the Du Pont Company did in fact give away 50,000 home computers to buyers of carpet made with its nylon as part of an effort to increase its share of a $12-billion-a-year retail business. The company has also used honeymoon trips (to Acapulco) to promote suitcases made of Du Pont fibers and a tennis tournament (at Hilton Head Island, South Carolina) to attract attention to its new apparel fibers. It has even given away a new home (with new carpeting) in a sweepstakes.

In the past Du Pont would never have dreamed of resorting to such tactics, for it has long been known as first in the field of synthetic fibers, both as a developer (nylon, Dacron polyester) and as a producer. The company has coasted along primarily on its reputation, without the need for promotional gimmicks. But fearing that today's consumers are less aware of Du Pont brands and that competition from within the industry and from overseas threatens to reduce its market share, Du Pont has decided to start promoting its wares.

The pressure from competitors is intense. Monsanto Company has published a slick, eighty-page magazine for carpet salespeople, designed to sell them Monsanto products; Celanese Corporation hired *Dynasty*'s fashion designer to publicize its brand of polyester; and Allied Corporation is offering free advertising to stores selling its Anso IV brand of carpeting. At the same time, natural fibers (wool and cotton) are getting a strong push from their producers, including TV ads designed to attract high-income consumers.

Du Pont is particularly eager to crack cotton's corner on the denim jeans business, a tough proposition. But Celanese, maker of Fortrel E.S.P. polyester stretch yarn, seems to have gotten a head start in this endeavor. (Celanese claims to have already captured more than 10 percent of the indigo denim market and to be selling to both Lee and Levi.) Although Du Pont has spent over $1 million for TV ads promoting its Denimotion stretch polyester/cotton blend, it may have moved too late. Says Richard S. Roberts of Celanese, "Du Pont has been fairly well asleep in this market. . . . They've had a real good product (using Lycra with denim) but in effect blew it. I don't envy them trying to get off the ground at this late date."

Consumers buy Du Pont fibers only after they have been woven into other products; however, the company hopes that, by improving brand loyalty, it can strengthen its position in some very large markets. In the words of Du Pont's C. L. Henry, "A lot of our products are maturing, and we have to be better marketers."[29]

1. A competitor thinks Du Pont was wrong to go for gimmicks rather than explaining product advantages. What "message" do you think Du Pont was trying to get across, especially with the computer giveaway?

2. Do you agree with Du Pont's approach, or do you think that the company should have focused more on advertising?

3. How would you advise Du Pont to promote its Denimotion fabric for jeans? What should the "copy platform" be?

4. Pick a product that you think might compete with one of Du Pont's. Develop a promotion for it, including promotions aimed at end consumers, salespeople, and store managers.

CASE 2

SPINNAKER'S MEDIA MIX FOR EDUCATIONAL SOFTWARE

The personal computer business has been booming in recent years, and although the big profits for computer manufacturers have more or less gone, the number of sales is continuing to increase. Today these devices are finding their way into more and more households, where they are used to do many things besides balance the checkbook. Parents have become interested in the educational software now available that, they hope, will give their offspring an edge in school.

Spinnaker Software is a young company that's making a place for itself in this burgeoning field. Only a couple of years after it began, Spinnaker had five of the ten leading educational programs and anticipated sales of about $70 million for 1984. In an area where market researchers predict over $1 billion in annual sales by 1987, that's still only a toehold. But if moving up from there means knowing what to do next, Spinnaker's founders—William Bowman and David Seuss—seem well on their way.

Bowman and Seuss differ from others in their field in that they stress promotion. In 1983, while some of the competition was still scratching hard just to pay for equipment, Spinnaker put $3.5 million into advertising; it will probably raise that to $18 million in 1984, when it plans to move into regional TV. Says Bowman,

explaining his company's no-frills style, "Around here . . . we spend it trying to grab shelf space. What we really are is a marketing organization."

Knowing exactly where to advertise is a large part of Spinnaker's secret. You can have the best, most exciting educational program imaginable, but if you tout it in small type in the back pages of computer magazines—which, according to Spinnaker's research, are read mainly by business and professional men—you won't make many sales. Bowman and Seuss, realizing that their potential market was made up mainly of mothers, bought space in *Good Housekeeping, Better Homes & Gardens, Newsweek,* and *Money,* as well as *Popular Science* and *Science Digest.* Says Seuss, "Eighty percent of the parents with home computers will see our ads three times."

In its ads, Spinnaker stresses the company name as much as individual programs in the hope that the name will be firmly established by the time the real heavyweights—Atari, CBS Software, Coleco, and others—move in on the market. These competitors will pose a serious threat because they outrank Spinnaker in just about every category: size, money, distribution, trade con-

tacts, and retail experience. All Spinnaker has is its head start and its growing expertise in developing programs. (With this in mind, it began placing greater emphasis on product development in 1983.)

Seuss sums up Spinnaker's approach as follows:

> At first, we thought we might even form a minicomputer company, but we selected educational software because we thought an opportunity existed. It wasn't the largest area, or the fastest growing. But there was no clear leader, and we thought good marketing could give that position to us.
>
> Our early strategy has been to build brand awareness by spending a lot on marketing. That awareness builds greater sales, which allows us to spend even more to make ourselves known and, if everything works, eventually it will be too expensive for any newcomer to attack our position.[30]

1. What is Spinnaker's target market? Who will be the users of Spinnaker software? With all this emphasis on brand awareness, will product quality make any difference to consumers?

2. Spinnaker is planning to advertise on regional TV. How, in your opinion, should these ads differ from those in the print media?

3. Would advertising in each of the following magazines be a good idea? Why or why not?

Magazine	Readership	Value of this choice
Personal Computing		
BYTE—The Small Systems Journal		
Newsweek		
Psychology Today		

WHOLESALING, RETAILING, AND DISTRIBUTION 12

In old-time, small-town America, circus proprietor P. T. Barnum used to pull folks toward his tent by giving them a taste of the show—a circus parade—before they actually had to plunk down their cash. Today, retailers too increasingly turn to theatrics to draw in the crowds. At the big new Kids "Я" Us store in Paramus, New Jersey, for example, colorful carpets, bright neon signs, clown-costumed salespeople, and amusing novelties create a carnival atmosphere. But that's only the "parade." The real show is the merchandise: first-quality, in-season, brand-name children's apparel at bargain prices. It's a new entry in the booming discount-store field, and it looks like a hit. When one competing retailer walked in, he reportedly turned pale. Kids "Я" Us is a real threat to traditional, nondiscount stores.

Discount or no discount, retailing can be a ferocious business. So, too, can operating at other levels of the distribution channel—the route by which goods move from the producer to the consumer. In this chapter, we will discuss not only retailing, but also wholesaling and physical distribution. We'll learn about the tactics used to make all these operations profitable.

CHAPTER FOCUS

After reading the material in this chapter, you will be able to:

- name the main types of channels of distribution along which goods travel
- cite six functions wholesalers serve for manufacturers and for retailers
- discuss the major trends affecting department stores, discount stores, supermarkets, and convenience stores
- name three other types of retail stores
- give reasons for flare-ups of channel conflicts
- define physical distribution, and specify the three activities it includes
- list the pros and cons of the basic modes of transporting goods

Once upon a time, if you wanted to see a movie, you *went* to the movies. Gigantic studios with names like 20th Century–Fox and Paramount produced feature films and then distributed them to local theaters for a share of the box-office take. Now all that has changed. The largest moviemaker in America isn't an old-style Hollywood studio, it's Time Inc.'s Home Box Office. As its name implies, HBO usually sends its films directly to the viewer's home via cable TV, bypassing the silver screen. Sometimes HBO acts just like the old studios by financing and then distributing its films to theaters before playing them for home audiences. But even then, HBO's main concern is feeding the giant movie appetite of its twenty-four-hour cable schedule.

Recently, warfare between HBO and the studios for Hollywood's glitter has been tearing the film industry apart. Salaries for top stars skyrocket as studios and their rivals compete to sign up talent. Films flash through local theaters, which serve only as way stations on a movie's journey to such newer, and more financially rewarding, showcases as home video and cable TV. Stakes are high in the struggle for control of the multibillion-dollar movie industry: the studios get 45 cents of every theater box-office dollar, but only 25 cents from HBO showings. When HBO controls the film from script to screen, of course, the studios get nothing.[1]

Despite the glitter, this competition between HBO and the studios actually reflects a perfectly ordinary business process: distribution. A product has to travel from the original manufacturer to the ultimate consumer, along a route called a *channel of distribution*. Product distribution channels are extremely important: when a new middleman muscles in to change a channel, as HBO did in the movie business, the resulting changes in an industry can be dramatic.

In this chapter we'll look at the practical question of how a manufacturer actually gets its products into the hands of a consumer or buyer. We shall look first at the different channels of distribution, the marketing routes between producer and buyer. We'll then examine the functions of the two types of middlemen, wholesalers and retailers, involved in the distribution of most products. Finally, we'll consider the physical distribution of products, discussing the advantages and drawbacks of each major mode of transportation.

DISTRIBUTION CHANNELS

Quite simply, a **channel of distribution** (also known as a **trade channel** or **marketing channel**) *is the sequence of marketing agencies (such as wholesalers and retailers) through which a product passes on its way from the producer to the final user.* Let's look at some of the channels.

THE MOST DIRECT CHANNEL: MANUFACTURER TO CONSUMER

The most direct way to market a product, of course, is for the manufacturer to sell directly to the consumer. Artisans who sell their leather goods or jew-

FIGURE I

ASPECTS OF THE MARKETING MIX: PLACEMENT

Part of the marketer's job is to choose the most effective channels of distribution for a product or service.

FIGURE 2

Distribution channels for consumer goods

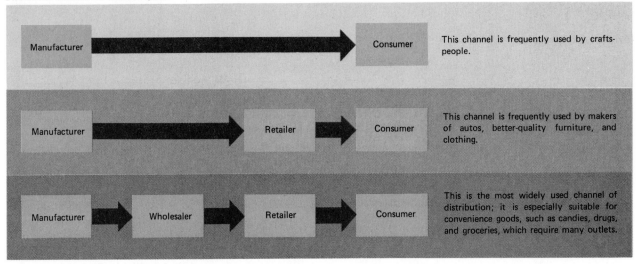

Manufacturer	→		Consumer	This channel is frequently used by crafts-people.

| Manufacturer | → | Retailer | → | Consumer | This channel is frequently used by makers of autos, better-quality furniture, and clothing. |

| Manufacturer | → | Wholesaler | → | Retailer | → | Consumer | This is the most widely used channel of distribution; it is especially suitable for convenience goods, such as candies, drugs, and groceries, which require many outlets. |

Distribution channels for industrial products

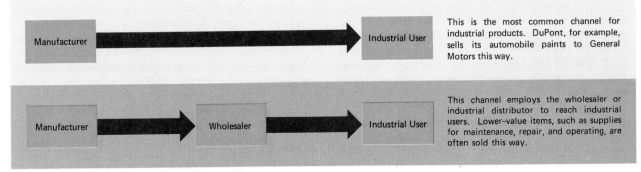

| Manufacturer | → | Industrial User | This is the most common channel for industrial products. DuPont, for example, sells its automobile paints to General Motors this way. |

| Manufacturer | → | Wholesaler | → | Industrial User | This channel employs the wholesaler or industrial distributor to reach industrial users. Lower-value items, such as supplies for maintenance, repair, and operating, are often sold this way. |

elry at crafts fairs or on the street are using this simple distribution channel. Charles Chips and various other firms also sell directly to the consumer. Some manufacturers have their own retail outlets; an example is Goodyear Tire and Rubber Company. Pepperidge Farm markets day-old bread in this way. There is a trend, too, for manufacturers to open their own discount outlets in order to take advantage of consumers' increased bargain consciousness.

The problem with this direct form of distribution is that it forces a manufacturer to assume a lot of nonmanufacturing, marketing functions. Hiring a marketing and sales staff, setting up a marketing budget, and distributing goods can be quite costly, so most producers rely on outside agents, or middlemen, to channel their products to customers.

THE ALTERNATIVE: CHANNELING GOODS AND SERVICES THROUGH MIDDLEMEN

Middlemen fall into two general categories—wholesalers and retailers. The **wholesaler** *sells products to others who buy them either for resale or for industrial use.* The **retailer** *sells directly to the public.*

The number of middlemen involved in the channel of distribution depends on the kind of product and the marketing practices of a particular industry. There are also important differences between the channels of distribution for consumer goods and those for industrial products. The basic types of marketing channels are illustrated in Figure 2.

INTERNATIONAL TRADING HOUSES: AMERICANS MOVE IN AMONG THEM

The name Mitsubishi is familiar to many Americans these days. Less familiar, but also important, are Mitsui, Marubeni, Nissho-Iwai, C. Itoh, and others—the nine *sogo shosha* of Japan, general trading companies that do business around the world. The *sogo shosha* are giants in their field, accounting for some 9 percent of total merchandise exports in the United States alone and roughly half of all imports and exports in Japan.

These companies, which developed in the seventeenth century, eventually became the driving force behind Japan's phenomenal post–World War II growth as an industrial power. They have handled everything from Chinese noodles to nuclear power plants, sometimes even serving as middlemen between non-Japanese principals. (In 1975, for example, they mediated the sale of a $7.3 million U.S. factory to the Soviet Union.) Such "offshore" deals, as they've come to be known, have since become relatively commonplace, representing the latest stage in the evolution of these trading companies.

The strength of the *sogo shosha* rests on vast international networks of employees who search out business opportunities, rarely taking possession of the goods they buy and sell. Since these agents handle both imports and exports, they have access to enormous stores of information; this information enables them to operate efficiently and to minimize the currency-exchange risks that foreign trade involves.

Quite naturally, the success of the *sogo shosha* has aroused much envy on this side of the Pacific. Until recently, antitrust laws prevented the growth of similar ventures here. So did laws passed shortly after the crash of 1929, prohibiting banks, which have access to the needed capital, from creating trading companies. But there was certainly a need for U.S. trading companies. Though many smaller American companies produced goods for which there were markets overseas, there were no middlemen to bring makers and buyers together. Worse, the U.S. balance of trade was in poor shape, generating economic problems both at home and abroad. (A look at the numbers emphasizes this point: while the United States was exporting less than 8 percent of its gross national product, such nations as Canada, West Germany, and Great Britain could point to percentages roughly three times as large.) Experts were suggesting that changes in the law could enable the United States to boost its exports by 30 percent within three to five years.

These considerations finally caused the removal of some of the barriers preventing the formation of Japanese-style trading companies in the United States. The

HOW WHOLESALERS HELP MANUFACTURERS

Wholesalers serve a number of important functions for manufacturers.

1. *Providing a sales force.* Many manufacturers find it expensive and inefficient to employ their own salespeople to visit the many retailers who carry their products. Instead, they rely on wholesalers to perform this function. For example, a stationery wholesaler will send its own salespeople to visit dozens of small stores, selling notebooks, pencils, rulers, and typewriter ribbons from a variety of manufacturers.

2. *Carrying stock.* Most wholesalers maintain an inventory of merchandise, which they buy from a manufacturer in the hope of eventually selling it to retailers or industrial customers. Without the wholesaler, a manufacturer would have to provide storage space until goods were ordered, and would have to wait for payment until then. For example, Christmas-card manufacturers ship their goods to wholesalers in late spring, even

INTERNATIONAL BUSINESS TODAY

upshot was the Export Trading Act of 1982, which lightens the prohibitions on banks and eases the antitrust laws restricting the ties between traders and suppliers.

This new freedom has led an odd assortment of businesses throughout the United States—including manufacturers, retailers, and banks—to create new companies or divisions that focus on export. Such familiar names as BankAmerica, Sears, Roebuck & Company, K mart Corporation, and Citicorp are among them; many hope to pool resources, including the banks' credit and foreign-exchange services and the retailers' purchasing power and merchandising expertise. Smaller companies, too, have been moving in since June 1983, when the U.S. Commerce Department authorized companies in related industries, export specialists, and banks to organize export associations.

Here are some examples of the new ventures:

■ *In manufacturing:* Peabody International Corporation (a maker of energy and environmental equipment) and General Electric Company have both set up general trading companies that deal in all the parent organizations' products, and can make use of the parents' international offices and communications systems.

■ *In retailing:* Sears, K mart, and J. C. Penney are try-ing to push U.S. exports through their links with overseas retail chains. (Since these companies also make huge purchases outside the United States in order to keep their home stores supplied, they have enormous business leverage overseas.)

■ *In banking:* As we have already noted, the banks have both the needed capital and worldwide information networks to build on. But two of the leaders in these new efforts—BankAmerica and Security Pacific—are proceeding slowly and cautiously.

■ *In combinations:* First National Bank of Chicago plans to work with Sears World Trade Inc. in a joint venture, with the bank acting as a holding company in Sears's export business.

It's a whole new world for American business, and it could pay off in a big way. In the words of Suzanne Stafford, a consultant for BankAmerica World Trade Corporation in San Francisco, "We're sitting on a lot of deals—this is going to be bigger than we dared hope."

SOURCE: Ann M. Reilly, "In Search of an American-Style Mitsui," *Dun's Review,* November 1980, pp. 107–112; Masayoshi Kanabayashi, "Japan's Big and Evolving Trading Forms: Can the U.S. Use Something Like Them?" *The Wall Street Journal,* December 17, 1980, p. 56; "Here Come the New Yankee Traders," *Business Week,* May 30, 1983, p. 50.

---

though the retail stores do not want delivery of the cards until September or October. Card manufacturers then can use the storage space for their Valentine's and Mother's Day lines. And, if these manufacturers sold directly to retailers, they would not receive payment for Christmas cards until October or November. By dealing through wholesalers, they are paid months earlier.

3. *Assuming risks.* By dealing with a few wholesalers rather than many small stores, the manufacturer reduces chances of bad-debt losses. The manufacturer can also save time and effort by running credit checks on a few large wholesalers instead of on hundreds of small retail accounts. In addition, by moving goods down the channel to wholesalers, the manufacturer can avoid the risks associated with damage, theft, product perishability, and products' becoming out of date.

4. *Providing market information.* Wholesalers deal with hundreds of retailers, selling dozens of competing or complementary lines. Thus they are in an ideal position to tell the manufacturers which products are currently popular, and give them other useful marketing information.

5. *Providing promotional support.* Wholesalers often help a manufacturer promote its products by advertising certain product lines to boost their own sales to retailers. Wholesalers also design and distribute eye-catching store displays and other promotional devices for a manufacturer's product.

6. *Transporting.* Wholesalers make deliveries to retail stores, saving the manufacturer the trouble of arranging transportation of its goods to widely scattered outlets. Since many retailers take delivery in smaller quantities than manufacturers can conveniently supply, wholesalers also help by breaking down shipments into smaller lots.

7. *Providing financing.* Sometimes the wholesaler is much larger than the manufacturers it represents; it may provide them with loans.

When hard times hit wholesalers, manufacturers quickly realize how important wholesalers are to them. In the recent recession, many wholesalers nearly went out of business because they couldn't sell all the goods they had ordered. Manufacturers had to step in, often reluctantly, to take over the wholesalers' functions and keep the distribution pipeline open. For example, in 1983, RCA was forced to purchase the troubled New York–area distributor of its television sets and other electronic products. The move kept RCA's goods on the market, but the company had to take on responsibility for many of the important services—such as carrying stock, promoting sales, and assuming risks—that a wholesaler typically provides.[2]

HOW WHOLESALERS HELP RETAILERS AND INDUSTRIAL CUSTOMERS

Wholesalers also provide services to retailers or industrial customers on the receiving end of the distribution channel.

1. *Predicting needs.* The wholesaler's ability to forecast future consumer demand can be very valuable to retailers. Christmas-card wholesalers must decide fairly early in the year whether to stock up more heavily on religious or on humorous cards. Unless wholesalers correctly predict which product mix retailers will require, they will be unable to supply customers' needs.

2. *Shipping convenient units.* Wholesalers help the many low-volume retailers by breaking large shipments from manufacturers into more convenient units. An appliance wholesaler may order a truckload of TV sets, and then deliver half a dozen to a single appliance dealer. In many cases the wholesaler can pass on to customers part of its quantity discounts and transportation-cost savings.

3. *Delivery.* Prompt and reliable delivery is important to retailers. A service station may need same-day delivery of a starter motor to complete a repair job. Only a nearby wholesaler can provide what is needed. On occasion, a wholesaler may even deliver the goods directly to the retailer's customer, who may have seen a sample in the retailer's store.

4. *Offering credit.* The credit terms wholesalers offer their customers are often better or more readily obtainable than those offered by the manufacturer. Wholesalers sometimes allow retail or industrial customers several months to pay. Small new firms might well be unable to obtain credit on any terms from manufacturers.

5. *Buying.* Wholesalers who call on retail stores are relieving retailers of part of the buying responsibility: they save retailers the trouble and expense of going out and finding sources of supply.

6. *Providing marketing information.* With their numerous contacts with manufacturers and other retailers, wholesalers can keep retail customers up to date on the latest technical and marketing developments. They may suggest better methods of inventory control, or report on trends in window and interior display or store hours.

The activities of Super Valu Stores Inc., the nation's largest grocery wholesaler, illustrate some of the ways retailers can benefit by dealing with a wholesaler. Super Valu helps independent supermarkets become more profitable—and become better customers for its goods—by offering what it calls "retail support." To help its customers compete with the large supermarket chains, Super Valu gives sophisticated advice on store location and shelf display. A Super Valu computer-aided design system offers more than 100 different floor plans for a supermarket that wants to remodel. Super Valu also trains the store's employees, from the butcher to the checkout clerk, and sends out experts to assist grocers with special problems. Super Valu's greatest strength, however, lies in its sixteen computerized grocery warehouses. The company's engineers have developed a computer-controlled system of "slot positions" that stores goods as efficiently as possible, yet still lets them be retrieved quickly to fill orders. The computerized system cuts Super Valu's warehouse costs, so that it can pass on some of the savings to its retailer customers; since these independent groceries thus have access to lower-priced goods, they can match the prices of the large supermarket chains. Without this program, Super Valu's customers would have trouble surviving.[3]

RETAIL OUTLETS

Retail outlets can be divided into various categories. The most important are department stores, supermarkets, discount stores, and convenience stores. Others include specialty shops, variety stores, catalogue showrooms, and mail-order firms.

These categories are not as clear-cut as they used to be. Warehouse showrooms and home centers for the "do-it-yourselfer" have recently gained popularity. Economic pressures have also led many kinds of outlets to increase their profits via **scrambled merchandising**—*changing the merchandise mix by*

Retail stores are the testing ground where the manufacturer's marketing program must prove itself.

stocking goods that are generally handled by another type of retailer. Thus, supermarkets may sell clocks, and many department stores sell food items.

DEPARTMENT STORES

Department stores are *large retail establishments that bring together a vast variety of merchandise under one roof*, and departmentalize both their merchandising activities and their operating functions. Department stores have long been dominant in general merchandise retailing because they are uniquely equipped to serve the needs of middle- and upper-class women, who do most of the consumer buying in the United States. Department stores enjoy a reputation for quality, fashion, and service. And a large measure of their popularity also stems from hometown pride. Until about thirty years ago, most department stores were located only in downtown shopping areas, and many of them helped to put their home cities on the map. Hess's in Allentown, Pennsylvania, for example, is as much a landmark as a department store. Every year at Christmas, Marshall Field decorates its dozens of street-level windows with elaborate Christmas scenes, attracting customers from all over the Chicago area. Similar traditions include Macy's Thanksgiving Day parade in New York City, and the Christmas catalogue from Dallas's Neiman-Marcus, which always sprinkles several odd items—such as Lasma Arabian horses that cost $5,000 and up—among its regular merchandise.[4]

Strategies for department store profitability

In the early 1980s, increased competition from other types of retailers—plus consumers' tendency to spend more cautiously—has forced department stores to find new ways to attract and keep customers. Selling merchandise not available anywhere else is one way to appeal to consumers; in many cities, department stores are also the fashion leaders. They are usually the first retailers to carry a variety of the newest merchandise, and some, like Bloomingdale's and Neiman-Marcus, offer unusual and one-of-a-kind items, as well as goods bearing their own labels.

Another approach is to maximize the profit that

the store makes per square foot of selling space, by focusing sales efforts in the areas where they will be most successful. Some department stores have eliminated major appliances and furniture from their inventories, concentrating instead on fashionable goods and services—including car rental services, travel bureaus, interior decorating advice, and wardrobe consultation—for upper-middle- and high-income groups. In some cases these new departments are actually "leased departments," operated by other companies that simply rent the space from the store.

Department stores are also sprucing up their selling floors. Bloomingdale's rich, elaborate displays, for instance, seem to create a sort of chic that customers want to be associated with. J. C. Penney, likewise, is spending more than $1 billion to shed its lowbrow image, replacing vinyl floors with wood parquet, adorning stark display cases with live plants, and brightening the selling floor with mirrors and spotlights. Penney's new look also includes partitioned-off specialty departments that resemble boutiques—a recent trend in department store layout that permits more flexible use of floor space and creates the feeling of many elegant shops under one roof.[5]

Mergers and conglomerates

To protect themselves against shrinking profits, many department stores also have added new branches, diversified, or merged with larger organizations. The list of conglomerate-owned stores now includes most of the big names: for example, Federated Department Stores, one of the largest chains, owns such well-known stores as Rich's (Atlanta), Bloomingdale's (New York), Bullock's (California), and Filene's (Boston). Some stores are trying even more aggressive tactics: Sears, for example, is bringing its finance businesses—including Allstate Insurance, the Dean Witter Reynolds securities brokerage, and Coldwell, Banker & Company, a real estate broker—right into its retail stores. "Financial centers" in thirty-three Sears stores now permit shoppers to buy stocks where they buy socks. Sears also recently launched an international export trading company called Sears World Trade.[6]

TABLE 1 Retailing's Top Ten: Department Stores with Largest Sales in 1983

COMPANY	VOLUME*
1. Macy's, New York	$975
2. Bamberger's, Newark, New Jersey (*tie*)	975
3. Macy's, San Francisco, California	825
4. Broadway, Los Angeles, California	735
5. Dillard's, Little Rock, Arkansas	711.3
6. Hudson's, Detroit, Michigan	683.8
7. Bloomingdale's, New York	680.5
8. May Co., Los Angeles, California	654.5
9. Abraham & Straus, Brooklyn	650.5
10. Marshall Field & Co., Chicago	650

*In millions of dollars

SOURCE: *Stores*, July 1984, p. 24.

DISCOUNT AND OFF-PRICE STORES

Discount stores, which developed after World War II, *sell a variety of goods below traditional market prices.* Many discount stores carry broad lines of both nationally advertised and private-brand goods. Discounting is now a crowded field: the success of such chains as King and Zayre has encouraged conventional retailers to enter the discount business too.

As economic recession hit consumers in the early 1980s, off-price stores, an offshoot of the discounting concept, emerged as the hottest new idea in retailing. **Off-price stores** *sell top-quality, name-brand merchandise, usually designer-label clothing, at prices 20 to 60 percent below those in department stores.* Unlike the true discounter, off-price retailers buy their goods at below-wholesale prices. They either buy through "diverters" who buy a manufacturer's excess stock, or they may be able to buy directly from the manufacturer if they promise not to "debase" (lower the value of) the brand name by advertising discount prices. An off-price store—such as T. J. Max or Burlington Coat Factory—features the same merchandise that is typically found in more luxurious department stores. Though shopping in an off-price outlet is not relaxing—it has been likened to visiting an air-raid shelter—consumers don't seem to mind; they spent $7 billion, or 6 percent of all retail clothing sales in

A

B

C

Which product is real and which is a knockoff? In looking for "a piece of the action," counterfeiters often duplicate brand-name products and flood the market with them. In offering "bargain" prices, these sellers make it difficult for legitimate retailers to stay afloat. Shown here are (A) a real "Must de Cartier" wristwatch and a copy; (B) two similar sweaters, only one of which is a genuine Christian Dior; (C) two almost identical jars of petroleum jelly, one of which is falsely labeled "Vaseline": and (D) counterfeit and authentic Sony tape cassettes.

D

1982, at off-price outlets.[7] The boom is so rapid that experts predict almost one-fourth of all retail clothing sales will be made in off-price stores by 1990.[8]

Off-pricers and the clothing business

The off-price phenomenon poses dilemmas for businesses in many parts of the clothing industry. Manufacturers enjoy increased sales through the popular new off-price outlets, but some fear their carefully nurtured brand-name image will be ruined by its association with a discounter. Some have threatened to cut off diverters who supply off-price stores. Phillips–Van Heusen Corporation, a maker of men's and women's clothing, warned off-price retailers with full-page ads in a trade magazine that read, "If you cheapen our brand, we won't sell to you."[9] Meanwhile, department stores, which have been losing business to the off-price competition, have threatened to stop buying from manufacturers that sell to off-price outlets. Some lawyers contend

that these measures may violate antitrust laws if they are aimed at keeping retail prices high. Yet even as they try to isolate the off-pricers from their suppliers, department stores themselves are entering the off-price game. For example, Dayton Hudson Corporation has added a new chain, Plums, which it calls "the elegant discounter," while keeping its showy downtown department stores.

Computers and off-price retailing

The controversy over off-price retailing isn't limited to clothing manufacturers. Many popular personal computer brands make their way through a "gray market" to discounters who undercut prices charged by authorized dealers. Unlike a black market, which operates illegally, the gray market relies on dealers who unload their excess stock quickly to raise cash. *Some dealers purposely supply the gray market, ordering far more of the product than they need to obtain the manufacturer's volume discount and selling the excess to discounters.* (This process is known as **trans-ship-**

ping. It is a problem that has been particularly serious in international retailing, where currency differentials may make trans-shipping quite profitable.) Like the brand-name clothing manufacturers, computer makers are threatening to cut off dealers who trans-ship to discounters. They claim that discounters give the computer brand a bad name because they don't service the machines they sell. Manufacturers also say dealers are cutting their own throats by supplying the off-price outlets to which their customers flock. Some dealers, on the other hand, complain that the manufacturers are to blame because their volume discount policies encourage the trans-shipping merry-go-round.

SUPERMARKETS

The *large departmentalized food stores* known as **supermarkets** vary in size from those with annual sales of less than half a million dollars to giant block-long stores with annual sales of several million dollars. They carry nationally branded merchandise, private brands, and generic products packaged in plain wrappers that carry only a description of what they contain. Self-service is an important characteristic; but there is also a trend toward separate delicatessen or bakery departments employing salespeople.

In recent years competitive pressures have forced supermarkets to adopt many changes. The "superstore" takes one new approach: it offers the customer a wide variety of nonfood items, ranging from children's pajamas to small TV sets. New stores in the Kroger Company supermarket chain are giving nonfood items up to 50 percent of their selling space.[10] The reason is simple: *Supermarket News* estimates that an average supermarket makes a net profit of about 15–16 percent, of which a scant 1.5 percent is the pretax profit on food sales. Some of Kroger's "superstores" now feature financial service centers, beauty salons, and restaurants—all designed to capture higher-profit business.

CONVENIENCE STORES

Convenience stores, such as the 7–Eleven chain, in a sense represent the rebirth of the traditional Mom-and-Pop store. As the name implies, these are *food stores whose chief stock in trade is time and place convenience.* They are typically open twenty-four hours a day, seven days a week. They can operate in a fringe location that does not have an adequate population base for a supermarket. In return, they control expenses by carrying only a limited selection of brands and sizes, and charging higher prices to their customers—who may be too late to get to the supermarket or may simply want to pick up some cigarettes, soft drinks, or beer without standing in a long checkout line.

After years of stable profits, the convenience-store industry now faces stiff competition from the increasing number of all-night supermarkets, and from the new gas-station convenience outlets that several oil companies have opened. One chain, the Houston-based Stop N Go stores, is fighting back by creating the "convenience superstore." Stop N Go has doubled the the size of some stores, expanded the fast-food section, and even added an old-fashioned drugstore lunch counter. These superstores are designed to overcome a common customer perception that many convenience stores are dirty and unsafe.[11] This approach also turns the convenience store into much more than a miniature grocery. If the idea catches on, it suggests that convenience stores can continue to grow by taking away business from other outlets—such as fast-food and drugstore chains—that also promise time convenience.

OTHER TYPES OF RETAIL STORES

Three other types of retail stores are important in terms of their familiarity and number.

SPECIALTY STORES **Specialty stores,** so called because they *carry only particular types of goods,* are among the most common small businesses. The basic merchandising strategy of a specialty store is to offer a limited number of product lines—but an extensive selection of brands, styles, sizes, models, colors, materials, and prices within each line that is stocked. Recent entries in this category include stores that rent or sell videocassettes of popular movies for home viewing. Similarly, computer manufacturers like Digital Equipment Corporation have opened

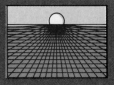

THE HIGH-TECH HORIZON

LASER SCANNERS: HIGH TECH COMES TO THE CHECKOUT COUNTER

At about 8,000 supermarket checkout counters across America, laser scanners add up your purchases by "reading" those little black-and-white-striped bar codes on the packages. But the scanners aren't just feeding prices into the cash register. They also support a $25 million industry that puts together sophisticated research on consumer buying habits. Manufacturers can use data collected by checkout scanners to decide what new products to sell, when to bring them to market, how much to charge, and even which label design to use. Store owners earn as much as $30,000 annually by selling this information to companies that analyze it for use by manufacturers.

Companies used other methods to monitor purchases before the scanners came into fashion in the early 1980s. But those methods were far slower and less accurate than computer-paced scanner research, which can be nearly immediate. As each item moves past the checkout scanner, computers record information encoded on the package. Some scanner-research firms use test panels of purchasers, who present an identification card to the cashier, so the computer can monitor their buying habits. In old-style research, panelists merely kept written diaries of their purchases.

Scanner research helped Johnson & Johnson decide whether to reintroduce Tylenol capsules after the poison scare in 1982 in which seven people died. As we noted in Chapter 10, Tylenol sales nationwide fell 80 percent in three weeks, even though the product itself was shown to be safe. Many marketing experts thought the Tylenol brand couldn't be resurrected, but Johnson & Johnson's scanner research showed otherwise. In thirty-two supermarkets in four test cities equipped with scanning systems, previous Tylenol users quickly started to buy the capsules again when they reappeared on shelves with tamper-resistant packaging. The results helped persuade the drug maker to retain its well-known Tylenol brand name.

Scanners can help manufacturers in less dramatic ways, too. A company can run different advertisements in different test markets, then monitor purchases to see which ads work better. It can calculate how frequently coupons are used to buy products. As more scanners come into use, companies will find more uses for the data they collect. One of the leading scanner-research firms, Nielsen's Scantrack, predicts that half of all grocery sales will be made in scanner-equipped stores by 1986.

---

retail outlets specifically to sell their small, low-cost computers to small businesses.

VARIETY STORES **Variety stores,** the old-fashioned five-and-tens, *sell a wide array of small items at low prices.* These have long been a familiar part of American life. Gradual changes in retail merchandising and consumer buying habits, however, have made it increasingly difficult for them to operate. In 1975 W. T. Grant went out of business after a long decline, leaving Woolworth in the uncertain position of being the last national variety-store chain.

MAIL-ORDER FIRMS **Mail-order firms** *provide customers with a wide variety of goods ordered from catalogues and shipped by mail.* Some major firms, such as Spiegel, sell only through the mail. Other familiar mail-order names are Sears, Montgomery Ward, and J. C. Penney, which also run department stores. Like variety stores, the mail-order business is a type of retailer that has been around a long time.

Some mail-order firms are applying advanced computer technology. With annual catalogue sales now estimated at $35–$40 billion, this industry has been growing for the last several years at an annual rate of 12–15 percent, double that of the leading

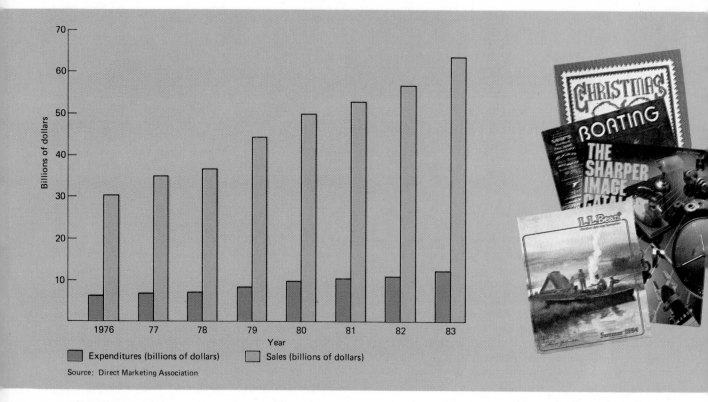

THE DIRECT-MAIL BOOM: Growth of the mail-order industry, 1976–1983

Consumers' shopping habits and lifestyles have changed. As more women go to work, they have less time to shop. High gasoline costs and tight money are keeping some people away from shopping centers, so they buy by mail. Elderly consumers find mail-order shopping more physically convenient.

Source: Direct Marketing Association

mass merchandisers.[12] A remarkable example is L. L. Bean, a producer of clothing and camping and fishing equipment that has one small store in Free-port, Maine, and does the rest of its business through the mail. On the strength of a boom in out-door recreation, along with a solid reputation for quality and an efficient, computerized merchandis-ing system, Bean increased its sales from $3 million in 1967 to more than $224 million in 1982.[13]

Bean's success rests in large part on its image as specialists in "preppie" clothing and well-made out-door recreation gear. Even general mail-order com-panies with fat catalogues crammed with diverse merchandise are finding that specialization pays off. Though Sears, Roebuck & Company still issues its five-pound general catalogue, the company recently launched a series of twenty-one "specialogs," or mini-catalogues, featuring such items as cookware or infant clothing. A computer monitors customer orders to give Sears a targeted audience for each "specialog." Targeting reduced Sears' costs.[14]

FRANCHISES Another important kind of retail activity, franchises, are discussed in Component Chapter B.

CHANNEL CONFLICTS

In an ideal world, one would think, merchandise would move smoothly through the various distribu-tion channels: after all, success in each phase of the

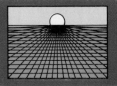

THE HIGH-TECH HORIZON

TELESHOPPING: WILL IT SUCCEED?

Since the days of the first printing press, sellers of goods and services have tried to use advances in communications technology to reach their customers more effectively. Today's big leap in communications is the capability of computers to talk to each other. This technology is being harnessed for "teleshopping" systems, designed to let consumers purchase a wide variety of goods and services at the push of a button, without leaving home.

Marketers are experimenting with many different ways of electronically presenting the merchandise and taking the order. The most ambitious is "videotex," in which the consumer's home computer and telephone or two-way cable (an *interactive* or *coaxial* cable) are hooked up. He or she calls up the teleshopping service and punches in a password on the computer. The data bank at the other end puts a "menu" on the shopper's screen; the shopper, pushing more buttons, can gather detailed information on many available products—and can of course find out how to transmit an order. "Teletext," by contrast, does not require a personal computer, but simply a small control box with a microchip that turns your TV into a teleshopping terminal. The shopper can only select from the information that is being transmitted by the teletext TV station, and cannot transmit an order back that is not on the screen. But the technology enabling any TV station to transmit a fat "electronic catalogue" is fairly simple.

Major companies in retailing (Sears, J. C. Penney, B. Dalton) and in communications (Knight Ridder, AT&T, CBS, Time Inc.) are rushing to get their feet wet in this area, and are conducting numerous studies and pilot projects. To their alarm, they are uncovering some difficulties: not everyone has a computer—and furthermore, many people don't want to do their weekly shopping at a computer terminal. Some management consultants see retail stores, with their high fixed assets, inventory, and labor costs, as a thing of the past, but critics seriously doubt that consumers are going to be willing to pay installation fees and monthly charges to use teleshopping services.

Thus, before electronic shopping can become fully commercial, marketers will have to find the ingredients necessary to spark consumer enthusiasm. Some think the answer will be improved graphics. Today's technology is limited to mosaic images (similar to video games), and thus cannot deliver an enticing picture of the product. ("You can't sell a dress that looks as if it were made of Lego blocks," claim many in the field.) Others think the consumer will be lured to videotex by the related services it carries—home banking, news, travel-reservation services, video games, and even schedules for local movie theaters and reviews of neighboring restaurants. Bargain hunting is another prospective appeal of teleshopping. A computerized barter network is already available to subscribers of the Compuserve consumer data base, and other services use the electronic equipment's easy information handling to let shoppers compare features of high-ticket items such as home appliances. Flash price cuts for electronic shoppers are also possible, as the transmitted data can be changed instantly; vendors can benefit from this outlet for slow-moving inventory.

But spiffing up the technology alone may not be enough to bring us all to the "electronic mall." Much time may be needed to develop the right format for the right market. If the future of teleshopping can be judged by the outpouring of corporate interest in delivering the service, then eventual success appears very likely.

SOURCE: Bill Abrams, "Electronic Shopping Awaiting Consumer, Corporate Support," *The Wall Street Journal*, June 16, 1983

process depends on success in the phase before. A retailer can't make money unless it gets a steady supply of merchandise from wholesalers, and the wholesalers, in turn rely on manufacturers to deliver goods for resale. But the business world doesn't always operate so simply. When one participant in the distribution process is stronger than another, conflicts often flare up.

A prime example is the market for sunglasses. Most sunglasses sell for under $10, and nearly all are alike; thus, the retailers have the upper hand, because they can choose freely among sunglass brands. Manufacturers are forced to offer attractive deals to get retailers to display and sell their glasses. Some of the retailers insist that glasses be delivered to the store, not a warehouse; some demand a manufacturer-supplied display case; some simply delay payment until the end of the summer sales season. No manufacturers dare to object, for fear of being frozen out of the market.[15]

In other businesses, manufacturers have all the power. Take, for example, the movie industry, whose product is popular films—a short-lived product that distributors control and theater owners are hungry for. A large theater chain can make a deal with a movie company to obtain hot new films because the large theater chain can distribute the films widely. A small theater owner, however, often finds itself last on the movie company's list. Brian Fox, a solo movie house owner in Connecticut, often finds that distributors won't offer him popular new films. Once he signed up a 3-D movie, but when 3-D films became popular, the distributor broke its contract. Mr. Fox had little choice but to go along. If he fought the film company, he'd probably never get a good film again.[16]

Channel conflicts can arise unexpectedly. Pan Am, expecting a travel boom in the summer of 1982, decided to save some money by reducing certain bonuses that it paid travel agents. But the move backfired: business didn't pick up as expected, and travel agents, not surprisingly, booked their customers on competing airlines that had kept the bonuses. Pan Am's marketing vice-president had to personally woo the travel agents back to the fold—after Pan Am re-established the bonuses. Pan Am's quick reversal wasn't surprising, given the power that travel agents have over the airline industry. According to some airline executives, the event that finally tipped Braniff International into bankruptcy in May 1982 was a decision by travel agents. Believing that Braniff's financial status was so shaky that passengers might be left holding worthless tickets for future flights, the agents stopped booking Braniff flights. The airline lost business, and bankruptcy became inevitable.[17]

PHYSICAL DISTRIBUTION

Whatever channel a manufacturer chooses, there is still a decision to be made about how to actually distribute the goods physically. In order for that new computer or that three-speed hair dryer to reach the customer, the distributor (or the manufacturer—or sometimes the buyer, too) must resolve the practical, sometimes difficult question of how to get it there. For a producer with goods to move, there is a great deal more involved than loading cartons onto a truck and waving goodbye.

Technically, **physical distribution** encompasses *all the activities required to move finished products efficiently from the producer to the consumer.* In addition to transportation, physical distribution includes warehousing, materials handling, packaging, inventory control, order processing, and customer service (see Figure 3).

WAREHOUSING

Often, a customer will not be able to take immediate delivery, or the firm may want to hold its merchandise until market conditions improve. It's helpful for the company to control the timing of the final distribution of the goods. Under these circumstances, the company needs a warehouse.

If the firm needs to keep tight control over its products—either because the goods require special handling, or because the company wants flexibility in moving them—the best choice may be a **private warehouse,** *a storage facility owned or leased by the company storing its goods there.* Businesses that frequently move large quantities of goods into and out of storage generally use private warehouses.

Alternatively, the company may simply rent space in a **public warehouse,** *a storage facility operated by others.* Companies that don't have expertise in materials storage can escape the burden of day-to-day warehouse operations by using a public warehouse. Firms may also wish to use public warehouses when they need widely dispersed storage locations for products with uncertain or seasonal demand.

A newer type of warehouse, the **distribution center,** *resembles a private warehouse, but also serves as a command post for moving products to customers.* The

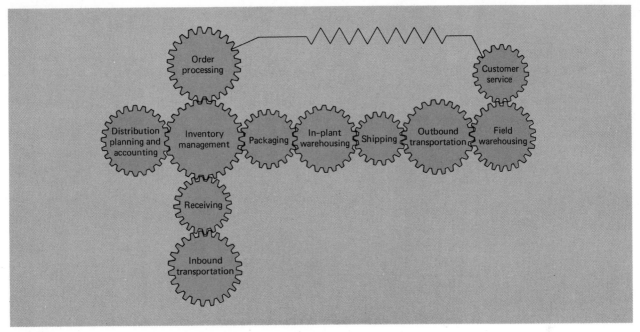

FIGURE 3

ACTIVITY COGS IN A PHYSICAL DISTRIBUTION SYSTEM:
HOW THE FUNCTIONS SHOULD WORK TOGETHER

The activities in a physical distribution system should mesh as smoothly as cogs in a machine. Streamlined inventory management—the central cog—can mean lower costs in other parts of the system; denser packages, more consolidated field warehouses, and other measures can help too. Meanwhile, the order-processing department should communicate frequently with Customer Service (see top of diagram).

company maintains its inventory records right there at the distribution center; it arranges transportation at the center too, and controls the flow of shipping orders. Levi Strauss & Company, which ships jeans and other casual clothing all over the country, operates such a distribution center in Little Rock, Arkansas. Some public warehouses now offer similar services to their customers.

MATERIALS HANDLING

Materials handling, *the movement of goods within and between physical distribution facilities,* is an important part of the distribution process. Materials handling involves deciding on a storage method—individual packages, large boxes, or sealed containers ready for shipment. The choice of storage method depends on how the product will be shipped, in what quanti-

ties, and to which location: a firm that typically sends small quantities to widely scattered customers, for example, probably wouldn't want to store its goods in large containers. Materials handling also involves keeping track of inventory, so that the company knows where in the distribution process its goods are located and when they need to be moved.

Recently, there have been improvements in materials handling techniques that permit companies to move goods more cheaply and efficiently. For example, there is the method called **containerization:** *large standard-sized sealed containers for shipping merchandise are packed and sealed at the factory, loaded on trucks, and then reloaded on railroad flat cars, ships, or planes without disturbing the contents.* This approach has several advantages: it eliminates theft and loss of small individual items, it reduces time and effort in shifting goods from one form of transport to another, and it saves money and energy.

TRANSPORTATION

For any business, the cost of transportation is normally the largest single item in the overall cost of physical distribution. It doesn't necessarily follow, though, that a manufacturer should simply pick the cheapest available form of transportation. Many companies today use the **total physical distribution concept,** an approach that involves *maximizing the efficiency of physical distribution activities while minimizing their cost.* Often, this means that the company will make cost tradeoffs between the various physical distribution activities. For instance, air freight may be much more expensive than rail transport, but a national manufacturer might use air freight to ship everything from a single warehouse and thus avoid the greater expense of maintaining several warehouses.

When a firm chooses a type of transportation, it has to bear in mind its other marketing concerns—storage, financing, sales, inventory size, and the like. Transportation, in fact, can be an especially important sales tool. If the firm can supply its customers' needs more quickly and reliably than its competitors do, it will have a vital advantage: so it may be more profitable in the long run to pay higher transportation costs, rather than risk the loss of future sales. In addition, speedy delivery is crucial in some industries. A mail-order distributor sending fruit from Oregon to Pennsylvania needs the promptness of air freight. On the other hand, a manufacturer shipping lingerie from New York to Massachusetts may be perfectly satisfied with slower (and cheaper) truck or rail transport.

The pros and cons of different forms of transportation

Let us take a closer look at the major types of transportation available to the shipper—namely, trucks, rail, air, sea, pipeline, and various combinations of these.

TRUCKS Trucks rank high in meeting the needs of most manufacturers. They are the most frequently used form of transportation, for two reasons: (1) they offer door-to-door delivery from the manufacturer to the customer without intermediate unloading; and (2) they operate on public highways that do not require an expensive terminal or right-of-way, as airlines and railroads do. The main drawback of trucks is that they cannot carry all types of cargo. Federal regulations limit weight loads and truck dimensions, so trucks cannot cost-effectively haul heavy, bulky commodities like steel or coal.

Trucks can now carry larger loads on interstate highways, thanks to a 1983 law permitting the use of tandem trailers—two trailers hooked together and pulled by a single cab. Some states are fighting in court to keep tandems off their highways because they claim the extra-heavy loads cause excessive road damage. Even with this change in federal rules, however, certain types of cargoes, such as gases, are difficult to handle by truck.

RAILROADS Railroads carry a larger amount of goods than any other mode of transportation: they can carry heavier and more diversified cargoes. But they have one major disadvantage: they can seldom deliver directly to the customer, but must usually rely on trucking companies to make the final delivery from the station.

PLANES Although air transportation is the fastest form of transportation, it has numerous disadvantages. Many areas of the country are still not served by conveniently located airports. Planes can carry only certain types of cargo because of size and shape limitations. Furthermore, planes are the least dependable and most expensive form of transportation. Weather can cause flight cancellations, and even minor repairs can lead to serious delays.

But despite its limitations, air transport has become absolutely essential in certain industries. Speedy shipment by air sometimes saves overall distribution costs by reducing the need for storage and insurance. Without air service, perishable items like California-grown strawberries, for example, could not be marketed in Boston or Philadelphia. Companies like Federal Express, which promises "absolutely, positively overnight" package delivery, must rely on airplanes for service between distant cities.

SHIPS Shipment by water is the cheapest form of transportation. Thus, it is widely used for such low-cost bulk items as oil, coal, ore, cotton, and lumber.

FIGURE 4

COMPARING THE FIVE BASIC FORMS OF TRANSPORTATION:

What's the best way to deliver the goods?

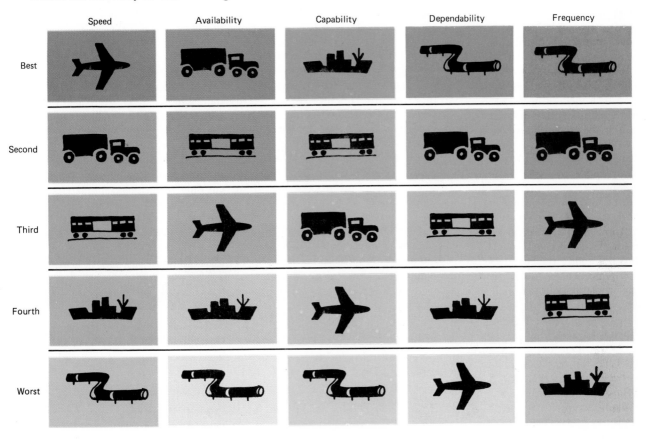

But the disadvantages of shipping make it unsuitable for most businesses. Ships are slow, and service to any given location is infrequent. If goods miss the boat that sails this week from New York City to France, there may not be another boat for two weeks. Furthermore, another form of transportation is usually needed to complete delivery: reloading may add substantial cost because of theft, extra handling, and spoilage caused by weather.

PIPELINES Pipelines are used almost exclusively to ship liquids and gases, and are of little use to manufacturers of most other types of goods. Pipelines do provide dependable, continuous delivery for oil and natural gas (though in some cases it costs less to ship oil by water). For this reason, a pipeline was selected as the means of bringing the vast oil deposits of Alaska to other parts of the United States.

CHAPTER REVIEW

The process by which goods make their way from producer to consumer is known as distribution. The system of distribution consists of three enterprises: wholesaling, retailing, and physical distribution, which includes transportation. A manufacturer must first consider the channels of distribution—the various routes a product may take to reach the consumer. There are three channels for consumer goods: from manufacturer to consumer, from manufacturer to retailer to consumer, and from manufacturer to wholesaler to retailer to consumer. For industrial goods, the channel is from manufacturer to one or more wholesalers to the final user.

Wholesalers are middlemen who operate between the manufacturer and either the retailer or the industrial customer. Wholesalers perform four main functions for the manufacturer: they provide a sales force, carry stock, assume credit risks, and provide market information. The wholesaler serves the retailer or industrial customer by anticipating needs, shipping convenient units, delivering, offering credit, buying, and providing marketing information. Many different kinds of wholesale operations have developed in response to the special needs of various industries.

Retail stores can be divided into a number of categories—department stores, discount and off-price stores, catalogue showrooms, supermarkets, convenience stores, specialty stores, variety stores, and mail-order firms. The differences among these categories are becoming blurred as several different types of retail outlets may actually sell the same goods. Channel conflicts arise when one participant in the distribution process is stronger than another—for example, when retailers bypass a certain supplier, or a manufacturer does not provide the wanted goods.

Physical distribution of goods encompasses not only transportation, but also warehousing, materials handling, packaging, inventory control, order processing, and customer service. The total physical distribution concept takes the entire process—not only the cost of transportation—into account in order to arrive at the most cost-effective solutions.

Businesses have a wide choice of forms of transportation to move their goods; trucks, railroads, planes, ships, and pipelines are the most popular. Each has advantages and disadvantages, and a business must select the mode that best suits its products and customers. Various combinations—or coordinated systems of transportation—have been developed to utilize the advantages of each.

KEY WORDS

channel of distribution (trade channel, marketing channel) (320)
wholesaler (321)
retailer (321)
scrambled merchandising (325)
department stores (325)
discount stores (326)
off-price stores (326)
trans-shipping (327–8)
supermarkets (328)

REVIEW QUESTIONS

I. What are the basic channels that manufacturers use to distribute consumer goods and industrial goods?

2. List and briefly discuss four functions that wholesalers perform for the manufacturer.

3. Wholesalers provide a number of services for retailers and industrial customers. List and briefly discuss some of these.

4. Discuss some of the ways in which a large grocery wholesaler can help independent supermarkets to succeed.

5. What are the advantages offered by off-price stores, and how do these businesses function? Why do other retailers sometimes object to them?

6. What are some of the strategies that department stores have begun using to keep and attract customers?

7. Describe the nature of mail-order retailing, and outline some of the reasons for its recent growth.

8. What are the factors a manufacturer must consider when selecting a form of transportation? Select one type of transportation discussed in the chapter, and describe the advantages and disadvantages of each.

CASE I

STORE WARS

Today, bringing home the bacon can turn out to be pretty complicated: on your way to the smoked meats, you may have to pass displays of imported cheeses, exotic fruits and vegetables, homemade pasta, fresh and even live fish, "natural" meats, freshly baked breads and pastries, gourmet salads, and delicatessen—not to mention cosmetics, perfumes, and other nonfood items. Many of the newer supermarkets even include pharmacies, restaurants, beauty salons, appliance departments, and florists. But not Winn-Dixie Food Stores, which "haven't changed much since the Studebaker" and "offer three kinds of catfish as a seafood department."

Familiar throughout the Sunbelt, Winn-Dixie stores have all the glamour of the Great Depression, when they were born. Their total predictability may not appeal to you, but other supermarket executives love it, regarding Winn-Dixie as "good competition" because "you can pretty much count on them doing things their way." And until fairly recently, their way wasn't bad. In fiscal 1983, for instance, Winn-Dixie's sales were more than $7 billion and earnings reached $116 million. The company's net profit on sales was 50 percent above the industry average.

With figures like that, how could Winn-Dixie be in trouble? Well, the fact is that while the numbers look good, the trends don't. For example, fourth-quarter sales for 1983 were 5 percent below those for the same quarter in 1982, and the operating margin has declined more than 36 percent since 1978. Store openings, too, have dropped, from eighty-nine in 1980 to twenty-nine in 1983. It's been said that "some of the company's numbers are wilting under the heat of new competition like fatback in the Florida sun." To understand these developments, you have to look at the supermarket business as a whole.

Basically, the supermarket industry is in flux because it is adjusting to massive social, economic, and population changes such as these:

- Stabilizing levels of food consumption
- Fewer large families
- More working women
- More one-stop shopping
- Greater interest in health and nutrition
- More discretionary spending on food

The result? More upscale merchandising. At the same time, however, there are still plenty of customers who are out of work or in economic trouble; they want value for every last penny. To cater to these groups as well as others in between, there has been extensive segmentation in the food industry.

For example, the number of upscale supermarkets with 30,000 or more square feet of selling space has just about tripled since 1978, and the number of combination stores (food stores whose volume is at least one-third general merchandise) has increased sixfold—as has the number of cut-rate, warehouse-type outlets. In short, the growth has been greatest at the extremes, hurting stores in the middle, such as Winn-Dixie.

Winn-Dixie's management faces a two-pronged battle: they will somehow have to compete effectively with the upscale stores and, at the same time, outmaneuver the warehouse contingent. In trying to catch up with the luxury trade, the company did open bigger stores, but those stores still lacked pizzazz. Said consultant Herb Ross, "I told them they were building brand-new old stores to compete with themselves."

Now, the company is building its first store designed to "catapult Winn-Dixie into the 1990s"—one that will keep customers shopping longer and buying more. Twice as large as the average Winn-Dixie, this superstore boasts such features as merchandising boutiques, varied ceiling heights, and dramatic lighting.

The company is also taking a new approach to the products it sells. In the past, Winn-Dixie depended heavily on it own labels (on which it sometimes got wholesale and producer's profits as well as retail profits), and these house brands were used as loss leaders. For national brands and the other unadvertised items on the shelves, however, the company generally charged more than the going rate. Winn-Dixie's new superstore will stress national brands, as the competition does, and will offer greater variety.

At last, Winn-Dixie is in a position to win back some of its higher-income customers. But it also plans to hold on to its regulars—modest blue-collar families in small towns throughout the South, many of whom have remained faithful all along. And Winn-Dixie's management is prepared to fight the warehouse stores with price wars, if need be.

Thus, the future for Winn-Dixie looks brighter than last year's figures might suggest. Even though Winn-Dixie got a late start in the superstore wars, it may come out

ahead for one simple reason: its stores are profitable because their costs are low.[18]

1. Should Winn-Dixie go all-out for modernization, or should it leave some of its stores as they are? (Consider that a typical Winn-Dixie store can be run by a staff of four while a superstore requires at least twelve.)

2. What can Winn-Dixie do to compete with wholesalers who have warehouse stores and help independent grocers keep prices down? What has Winn-Dixie got that these rivals haven't?

3. One supermarket executive has said, "There is very definitely a market out there for upscale, but we think that market is very limited." Do you agree? Why or why not?

4. What, in your opinion, would be some good ways to cater to the changing needs of supermarket shoppers? What strategies would you propose if you headed a chain such as Winn-Dixie?

CASE 2

CAR BUYERS AND PRICES—A NEW KIND OF DEALER

Howard Van Bortel ultimately decided to change his way of selling cars, saying:

> I finally got tired of trying to rob every customer who came in the door. I did some polls showing that 70 percent of the people don't like the way car dealers do business. When that many people don't like the way you do business, it's time to change.

Van Bortel, like many who have changed their lives, is now busy spreading his ideas far and wide, trying to sell other car dealers on his $49-over-factory-invoice concept.

It all began in 1977, after Van Bortel had spent some twenty-four years selling Chevrolets and Oldsmobiles in a small upstate New York community. Having made his big discovery about people's feelings toward car dealers, he decided to rearrange his whole way of doing business. First, he cut overhead down to the bare bones by dismissing his sales force (who had received a share of his profits) and disposing of his new-car inventory. Then he let it be known that he was prepared to sell cars at exactly $49 above the figure on the factory invoice; no "deals," no bargaining. As a result, his sales increased tenfold within two years—and GM canceled his franchise. The reasons for this are unclear, though Van Bortel claims that GM was trying to protect other dealers nearby who were losing business to him. In any case, GM's action fueled his anger with the auto maker and his wish to get other dealers to imitate him; he receives a small commission from these dealers on each car they sell.

One of Van Bortel's disciples is John Peterson, who, until Van Bortel came along, was running a failing dealership in Lake City, Minnesota. (Van Bortel says, "I don't appeal to dealers who aren't failing. They're too greedy.") Peterson offers his customers any GM model, with any options they choose, at "the cheapest price on

earth"—exactly $49 above invoice. It took *him* only seven months to increase his sales tenfold. Peterson says:

> People are intelligent. They can buy a copy of a consumer magazine and find out exactly what I pay GM for a car. You insult their intelligence when you play sticker-price games and jack them around.

Of course, his customers have to wait at least six to eight weeks for the factory to deliver, but they report that Peterson's prices are as much as $700 below those quoted by conventional dealers in nearby Minneapolis (who also, incidentally, try to talk their customers into buying a car off the lot rather than ordering one from Detroit).

How can Peterson make a living this way? Certainly not on the $49 above invoice. The chief source of his revenue is the so-called holdback, or 3 percent of the car's invoiced cost, which GM keeps only temporarily to make sure that the dealer's accounts with the auto company remain clear. Since the holdback (for example, $150 on a $5,000 car) is eventually returned to the dealer, it is actually part of his or her profit.

So things look good to Peterson, but he, too, is running into trouble with GM. GM can't seem to deliver its cars as fast as he sells them. GM says that although

other dealers tend to complain about Peterson and his kind, it makes no effort to penalize anyone. GM's Donald W. Hudler says that since Peterson "has elected not to stock any cars . . . he's putting the burden on us to make cars available when he needs them." In fact, Hudler asserts that Peterson is already getting many more cars than he would typically be entitled to according to GM's allocation system.

Despite his problems with GM and the extended waiting periods these sometimes impose on his customers, Peterson plans to continue doing business just as he has been. He says, "We're operating on the Robin Hood theory . . . stealing a little business from the rich dealers in Minneapolis and bringing it to poor little Lake City."[19]

1. Do you agree with GM's decision to try to freeze Van Bortel out? Why or why not?

2. One GM manager claims that Peterson's problems are of his own making. Do you agree?

3. Is a dealer like Peterson a threat to the other dealers? Why or why not?

4. Identify the aspects of the "middleman" role that a dealer like Peterson performs; identify other aspects that he does *not* perform. Does he make money on anything besides the $49 above invoice and the holdback? (Hint: Consider his inventory policy.)

5. In what way or ways might Van Bortel be helping dealers? In what ways does a dealer like Peterson really help consumers? Overall, do you think this system is a good one? Explain your answer.

PERSPECTIVES ON SMALL BUSINESS MARKETING ASPECTS

While the function of marketing in any business is to create and satisfy customer demand, a significant difference exists between marketing in the smaller firm and in the large corporation.

Part of that difference is due to money. Limited funds require immediate profitability, so each marketing program in a small business must be cost-effective—that is, every outgoing dollar must be spent in the most effective way possible for success. In the following pages, we will discuss some major areas of marketing that can help any small firm to maximize sales.

STUDYING THE MARKETPLACE

For a small business, success depends on developing a growing group of customers. The Small Business Administration has identified four key marketing areas for your small business. The first, market research, will determine the needs of the customer. The second, market strategy, will identify customer groups that your small business can serve better than the competition.

A third important area for the small business is market segmentation, or grouping your marketing efforts: a market can be grouped according to geography, product line, or similarity of customers. The final area is the market mix. You will now determine how the needs of your customers can be satisfied with your products or services.

Once you have identified the key areas of the market, you must determine the potential acceptability of your product or service to the consumer or end user, via the product life cycle concept.

The product life cycle concept

The product life cycle is the multiphase sequence of growth and decline in sales and earnings that most products go through. Effective use of this concept hinges on the entrepreneur's ability to perceive where in the cycle a particular product might be located. An error in judgment at this point could easily make the difference between success or failure. Let's take a closer look at this idea.

THE INTRODUCTORY PHASE The primary achievement of small business has always been the introduction of new ideas and new products, and the creation of entire new industries; thus, a small business's product is likely to be in the introductory phase of the life cycle. While this phase offers maximum return on initial investment, the risks are high, and success is not guaranteed.

How can you increase the odds in your favor? Here are some rules:

1. Test your market. You can sample your potential customers on the phone or by personal visit. Develop a short series of questions to provide feedback on your new venture and seek the opinion of fifty to a hundred well-chosen people. Your main cost will be time.

2. Seek advice. Small-business consultants, seminars, fellow business associates, bankers, accountants, local political figures, and librarians can provide advice and counsel to help reduce your risks.

3. Update your educational skills. Seminars, trade journals, college classes, and special books and magazines geared to new business ideas can increase your awareness of potential new marketplaces and business trends.

THE GROWTH PHASE If your product is in the second, or growth, phase of the cycle, you may have a good chance for success since high risks will no longer be a factor. But good management is especially important for a growth-phase product, since you must now compete with others for your share of the product's growing market.

MATURITY In this phase, as demand for the product continues to grow, more and more competitors will be entering the market. Large corporations will be beginning to show interest, and the profit squeeze will begin.

This concept holds true not only for products and services, but also for geographic areas. For example, let's look at a typical medium-sized town in suburbia (population 30,000), 40 to 50 miles from a major metropolitan area. The vast majority of retail stores in the area will have developed with the growth of the town, and distance, coupled with the high cost of gas, will have caused the average consumer to purchase locally. Now, as this somewhat isolated area develops, each new growth spurt entices the large chains to re-evaluate the area's potential. Finally, a major chain like Sears or K mart opens a large store, and its variety, selection, convenience, and lower prices attract many new customers. At this point the profit and sales squeeze is a reality.

What to do? You can lessen the impact of this phase through long-term planning and product specialization. Large chains are geared to the mass market; they generally do not cater to the unique and special needs of the consumer. Thus, if you have a local shoe store, for example, offering an excellent selection of extra-wide and extra-narrow shoes, you may be able to develop a loyal clientele that the mass merchandisers can't penetrate.

DECLINE Unless you have a penchant for failure, you should avoid the final phase of obsolescence and dropout. And avoiding it is tricky: spotting the end of a product's usefulness requires experience, good advice, and common sense. A sense of timing is critical at this point.

Frequently, business failures are the result of a failure to recognize this phase of the product life cycle. Each year, hundreds of thousands of small businesses fail or quit; many have ignored the natural product life cycle in their day-to-day decision making.

APPROACHES TO PRICING

Effective small-business marketing should begin with careful consideration of the selling price of each product or service the business offers for sale. There are several things to think about when you establish prices:

1. What is the competition charging?

2. Do you offer features or benefits that the competition does not provide, and that would allow you to charge a higher price or earn a greater profit margin?

3. Is your major competitor well entrenched and a recognized price leader in the market? If the answer to this question is "yes," the upper limits of your price range may already be established. Even if your product is better, you may still be forced to sell for less, or at the same price. It is best to look for ways you can be unique—ways that make you look different.

4. How close are you to major urban centers? Geographic isolation may allow you to charge a higher price without complaints from customers. The key question here is how much more inconvenient and expensive it would be for the customer to buy from a more distant competitor.

5. Who pays the cost of shipping? The cost of shipping represents a percentage equal to about 2 to 5 percent of the selling price.

6. How much profit will you need to make? You will need sufficient profit margin to cover overhead, plus an adequate return on your investment.

Let's consider various pricing concepts that are important in retail and wholesale, plus some ideas on handling costs in a service business.

Retail markup

THE BASIC MARKUP While there will be minor variations throughout the United States, a markup of 40 to 50 percent (depending on the industry and who pays the shipping costs) is considered essential for success in a retail business. For example, consider a product for which the wholesaler charges the retailer $6. Most experts say that the retailer should figure that about 40 percent of the final price will pay for rent, utilities, insurance, taxes, employee salaries, and the costs of inventory and advertising, and provide some profit. So the final price is $10: the retailer added $4, or 40 percent of the $10 selling price, to the wholesaler's price.

Here's another key question: will your price cover the cost of shipping, or will you be able to pass that cost on to the buyer? In the book business, for example, some publishers offer a discount of 40 percent to bookstores and don't charge for shipping; others offer their books to retail outlets at a 45 percent discount but add a charge for shipping. Both methods are considered normal and acceptable in the industry; they merely reflect different approaches to the same pricing problem.

Certain types of business (television and appliance sales, and office equipment, for example) must maintain service departments to perform warranty work. For such a business, it is essential that the retail markup be large enough to cover the extra costs involved in maintaining the service function. A minimum of 5 percent extra markup is recommended to prevent an unnecessary profit squeeze in a business of this kind.

Finally, especially large margins must be planned if the business sells products that go in and out of fashion; the large margins serve as a hedge against style and seasonal changes. Prices must cover the costs of the large inventories required to satisfy varied customer tastes, and must allow for the large customer discounts that will be used in selling out-of-season and out-of-style goods. Typically, the margin in these fields is 50 to 60 percent, and as high as 80 percent for jewelry.

One word of caution, however: the size of the potential profit is meaningless unless the product sells! So before you worry about your pricing, think about what you're purchasing; poor judgment in purchasing can bankrupt a small store.

High-volume retailing

An entirely different set of pricing considerations is involved if your business sells in high volume. The aim here is to lower your prices in the hope of attracting more customers. But before you do this, be sure to consider:

1. Will the lower price increase sales enough to compensate for the profit loss? Don't automatically assume that lower prices will increase sales over the long run. Temporary hoarding is often the result, especially on essential items. Then you'll have less business in a few months, while the customers use up the goods they've hoarded.

2. What is your competitor's pricing policy? If your local competitor is already a discounter, do you really want to start a price war? Someone will lose, and it may be you.

If you still think you should lower your prices, proceed with caution and check all the numbers carefully. You must be sure you are right. A faulty judgment here could ruin your business.

Wholesale markup

The wholesaler is the middleman between the retailer and the manufacturer. The wholesaler's job is to provide storage facilities, a sales force, and feedback to the manufacturer on new trends and popular products, and to assume the credit risks on all sales made to the retailer.

The typical wholesaler requires an additional discount over and above the one granted to a retailer. Usually, the discount is 20 percent. Here's how the wholesale and retail markups relate to the price charged by the manufacturer for an item priced at $10 in the retail outlet:

Suggested retail selling price	$10.00
40% retailer discount or markup (40% of $10)	−4.00
20% wholesaler discount or markup (20% of $10)	−2.00
Price charged by manufacturer (40% of $10)	$ 4.00

Incidentally, it should be noted that specialized wholesaling offers good small-business opportunities. For example, a small wholesale distributor catering to stationery stores might choose to market only felt-tip pens, offering the retailer a wide selection and faster delivery of felt-tip pens than larger general-purpose distributors do.

Uniform pricing

The Robertson-Patman Act states that you can't make a price concession to one buyer without giving all other buyers in the same industry the same concession. For example, you can't sell one product to General Motors for $55 and the same product to AA Auto Repair for $110. This is inconsistent, and if you are a flagrant violator, it could invite a lawsuit. It is especially important to carefully watch your written price sheets. Make sure they are consistent within an industry. Don't offer the large chains more attractive terms than low-volume orders. This is a sure way to invite trouble.

Service-business pricing

If yours is a service business, your prices will depend on your competition, the quality of your service, and any special or unique service you offer. If your service is office machine or computer maintenance, you'll find that prices are established by industry price leaders such as IBM, Xerox, Monroe, Burroughs, and other major office-equipment manufacturers, and you will not be able to increase profits by raising prices; the growth of your service business will depend on the quality of your service. On the other hand, if you are a well-regarded artist, designer, or consultant, you will be able to command an hourly rate that's in direct relationship to your value to your clients, without concern for the current going rate.

THE SELLING PHASE

The only reason any business exists is to sell its products or services. All other business functions are secondary. Selling techniques can be broken down into four categories: advertising, sales promotion, publicity, and personal sales.

Advertising

Small businesses use five main forms of advertising: newspapers, magazines, radio, direct mail, and telephone directories. There are some basic rules which apply to all these areas:

1. Work within a budget to control expenses. Your budget should be set at an affordable figure, with allowances for the other costs of operating the business.

2. One-shot advertising is a waste of money. You need a *series* of ads or exposures to get the best results.

3. The greater the frequency of exposure in a variety of media, the greater the success. For example, it's a good idea to run radio, newspaper, and magazine ads simultaneously.

4. It's important to keep your advertising format consistent, so that potential customers will begin to recognize your company. Each ad you run will become more powerful.

5. Quality advertising will tend to indicate a quality product or service, and poor advertising will indicate a poor product or service.

NEWSPAPERS Newspaper advertising offers the small-business owner several advantages. First, a newspaper is distributed to a specific geographic area—frequently the very area covered by the small entrepreneur. Secondly, newspapers have a high degree of readership, since they supply all the local news. This is especially true of local newspapers published outside the larger metropolitan areas.

By advertising in a newspaper, local businesspeople can contact a large percentage of their potential customers. Naturally, the rates (or costs) are geared to the circulation of the paper (number of paid readers) and the size of the ad.

The success of your newspaper ad will depend on several factors:

1. Size: the larger the ad, the more likely it is to be seen. The smaller the ad, the more times you will have to run it to get attention.

2. Uniqueness: if your ad looks like the rest of the paper, people will not pay attention to it. Eye appeal is important. Use catchy lead-in captions such as "Lowest Price Ever," "20% discount," "$10 off," "Only Six Days Left," "First Time Ever."

3. Repetition: it may take three or four exposures of the same ad, or slightly different ads, to reach your potential customers. Consumers of any type need prodding to change their typical buying habits.

MAGAZINES Magazine ads offer unique advantages to small businesses that are specialized in nature. A firm that produces booklets for the savings and loan industry could reach that market via trade magazines that are read by savings and loan personnel. Likewise, real estate professionals can easily be contacted through publications geared to their field. For about $1,500, a firm could display a full-page ad in *California Real Estate Magazine* and have its product exposed to 150,000 real estate people. No other form of advertising media could directly contact that many interested realtors, over such a large area as California, at so low a cost. Truly cost-effective!

Magazine advertising is cost-effective for any specialized small business whose potential customers are not necessarily local but are related by occupations (such as banking), hobbies (such as sailing), politics, and so on. Most special-interest groups maintain at least one newsletter and/or magazine that makes these consumers readily accessible at a low cost per person.

RADIO "Lowest cost per person reached"—that's the claim of the radio industry. The reason is simple: radio audiences have recently increased. And the cost for the preparation of simple commercials is normally included in the price of air time. In short, radio is very cost-effective when the area served by the radio station is the area covered by your business.

But remember one point: because radio only appeals to the customer's hearing, you need to repeat your ads frequently. Directing a customer to go to a retail store or call a number is the best application of radio. Since the lack of visual appeal limits the use of this medium, plan for a long campaign to achieve maximum impact.

DIRECT MAIL This form of selling may actually complete a sale for you. The mailing must include all the ingredients for purchase: order form, complete descriptive literature, a reply envelope, and the all-important letter.

How does direct mail work? You may purchase or rent mail lists, or develop them using membership files, phone directories, and industrial journals. We should note here that there's one problem you'll face with all lists: high addressee mobility causes 15 to 20 percent of mailers to reach the wastebasket. You must constantly update your lists, removing the names that the post office returns.

Like magazines, direct mail is a form of advertising that suits the specialized nature of small firms. Many specialized markets have easily identifiable potential customers. For example, if your business is geared to banks, you can obtain the several catalogues that list every bank in the United States (including all the bank officers), and prepare your mailing list from these sources. The key is to send out a *carefully selected* mailing, not a mass mailing.

For maximum success, think about careful use of both direct mail and magazine (or newspaper) advertising. One form will reinforce the other. Delphi Information Sciences Corporation, a producer of premium items (commonly called "sales incentives"), increased the success of their direct-mail program 500 percent by combining it with a magazine ad. Both media hit the potential customers at the same time.

Expected response to any given mailer will vary between 0 and 3 percent of the total number of people who receive the mailer. (In rare instances, it can go higher.) For safety, figure your potential profit at a response rate of 1 percent before you begin the campaign, and remember that the campaign's profitability will depend on the profits generated from each sale. If you can't justify the mailer at a 1-percent response rate, you should realize you may have a loser.

And one more point: because of the overabundance of businesses that use direct mail, you can expect lower customer-response figures in today's market. Unless your ad and your products are quite unique, 1 percent may be the best you can achieve. If your profit per sale is small (less than $20), direct mail is not for you.

TELEPHONE DIRECTORIES Both local directories and the Yellow Pages are excellent forms of advertising for a new business. Buyers frequently use these directories when they are ready to purchase a product or use a service. No matter what other advertising you do, you ought to be in these directories.

Special sales approaches

Another excellent selling method in any type of small business is to send special mailings to current and past customers. Advance sale announcements, special sales, and new products can be offered to these people via well-timed mailings. This is a low-cost way to stimulate new sales.

Lists of past and current customers are easy to compile. Use one or more of these methods:

1. Place a sign-in guest book at the cash register.

2. Hold free gift-certificate raffles. The raffle tickets become an ideal source of customers' names and addresses.

3. Make out handwritten customer sales receipts.

4. Collect business cards from people you meet at business shows.

5. Refer to past invoices.

Sales promotion

This more subtle approach is not a direct attempt to sell: it's an attempt to provide a service that may ultimately lead to a sale. For example, a model and hobby shop could sponsor a model-airplane contest, which would attract hobbyists who usually deal with large chains or other competitors. This way, the old habit patterns of these potential customers might be broken, and sales might follow. Another promotional device is a handsome window display of new products, which will increase foot traffic.

For manufacturers, special vacation promotions are often used ("Sell 1,000 Plymouths and win a trip to Alaska"). Cosmetics manufacturers often offer customers free items for buying their product. Also, in-store product displays help stimulate sales.

Publicity

This nonpaid form of promotion relies on articles in newspapers or newsletters, and promotions on talk shows. Local interest, and/or the uniqueness of the product, sometimes prompts free coverage in the papers, and editors and program directors are constantly seeking newsworthy events that will generate audience interest. The tremendous growth of radio and TV talk shows in recent years offers a ready market for your innovative ideas.

Another important aspect of publicity for the small business is the new-product release. Most magazines devote a section to introducing new products to their readers. Each product insert includes a small picture of the product and some descriptive information, along with the name and address of the company. To have your product included in any publication, simply send a picture and description (no more than a single page, double-spaced) of the product to the publications of your choice. This is probably one of the most important marketing tools available to a small company, and it's free.

Personal sales

The small retailer must have informed, helpful, and courteous salespeople to compete successfully with the lower prices and greater selections of the larger chains. Frequently, a small business's main appeal is the specialized expertise of its salespeople. A salesperson in a small hardware store, for example, can help the customer understand wiring designs, plumbing requirements, and other similar information—a service that's not usually available from salespeople in the large, more impersonal chains.

Personal sales is by far the most expensive form of selling a product or service, but it can be the most effective. Only a well-informed and properly trained salesperson can personally contact potential customers, assess their needs, match the product benefits to the customers' needs, make the sale, and collect a check. There is no other way to sell as effectively. It even works on the phone.

If you can't afford your own sales force, you should be able to hire independent sales representatives who work for many manufacturers. Although their attention is divided, they are an excellent way to start. You can find good independent representatives by asking your customers for recommendations or by advertising in trade journals.

PART FOUR

FINANCE

Many businesses believe in the philosophy "Grow or die"—and among them is Vicorp Restaurants, a corporation that is trying to transform itself from a small local operator of pancake houses to a nationwide restaurant chain. Vicorp is growing as fast as an adolescent basketball player: in just eight months it has acquired 147 restaurants from ailing or bankrupt firms. But it's also paying the price—a whopping $95 million in long-term debt. Vicorp's management is confident about taking this risk, though, because of the company's impressive track record: the corporation's stockholders have gotten an average yearly return of 37 percent on their investment. And Vicorp expects to be able to pay off about a quarter of its long-term loans soon by selling $25 million in new stock.

Vicorp's management has been facing the classic issues that confront all financial managers, as they plan for the future in-

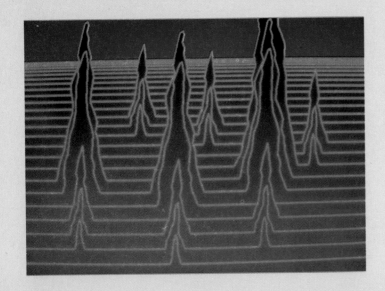

flow and outflow of funds. As you'll see in Part 4, sound financing requires a knowledge of many areas.

□ In Chapter 13, **Short-Term Finance,** you'll learn how businesses manage funds that are obtained and spent within a one-year period.

□ Chapter 14, **Long-Term Finance,** deals with stocks, bonds, and other means of obtaining funds for long-term use.

□ Chapter 15, **The Stock Market,** explores the fascinating role of securities markets in the American economy.

□ Component Chapter D, **The Money and Banking System,** focuses on the Federal Reserve System and on private banks and other financial institutions.

□ Component Chapter E, **Risk Management and Insurance,** discusses the risks businesses face and ways to minimize them.

SHORT-TERM FINANCE 13

In 1981, Ned Steinberger launched his business dream: a small company to manufacture the new bass guitar he'd designed. The guitar, with a distinctive look and a top-of-the-line price tag, quickly caught the fancy of a number of famous rock musicians. Steinberger Sound Corp. produced ten guitars a month, then fifty, then over a hundred.

Like many business managers with a promising future, Steinberger is faced with the challenge of short-term finance: how to obtain and manage the money he needs to pay obligations owed within a year. His company needs funds to buy materials, pay workers, and ship its products—even before any money comes in from sales. And now that his business needs to expand, his need for money, and skilled money management, will grow.

In this chapter, we'll consider aspects of short-term finance: what short-term assets and liabilities are, how a company judges its needs for short-term funds and obtains these funds, what forms of short-term credit are available. As we shall see, good short-term financial management is important to all businesses—firms as small as Steinberger Sound and as large as the multinational giants.

CHAPTER FOCUS

After reading the material in this chapter, you will be able to:
- name the activities involved in financial planning and financial control
- distinguish short-term from long-term finance
- distinguish assets from liabilities, and cite several examples of each
- discuss how financial managers put short-term excess cash to use
- define trade credit, and specify three principal sources of such credit
- distinguish secured from unsecured loans, and name three types of collateral used for secured loans
- describe the function of commercial paper
- discuss the role of finance companies
- name three factors that affect interest rates

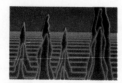 When Peter Fuller and David Leggett decided to start a new foreign-car remanufacturing business, Automotive Import Recycling, they thought they had the only ingredient they would need to make their business work—a steady flow of satisfied customers. They suspected that there would be a healthy market of loyal Volvo and BMW drivers interested in having their old models disassembled for complete part-by-part evaluation, overhaul, and rustproofing. With enough orders, they reasoned, their new firm would soon be off and running.

But it wasn't long before they discovered that they needed financing as well. Since they began their remanufacturing business, their revenues have doubled every year, and they have built up an order backlog of eight weeks. But they do not have enough cash to run the business effectively. Customers do not pay until they drive away with their finished autos; meanwhile, during the five to eight weeks it takes to rebuild a car, cash must be paid out for wages to thirty-six employees, for parts, and for rent on the company's too-cramped quarters. The company needs a way of obtaining this money to pay its operating expenses.

Furthermore, Leggett and Fuller desperately need more capital to expand their business. Right now, they are operating on such a small scale that they have to put up with many inefficiencies that cut their profits. They don't have enough money to buy parts wholesale: they have to buy them through middlemen, at a cost 30 to 50 percent above wholesale. They can't afford to buy advertising—they must be content with word of mouth. And they're forced to pass up bargains on used autos if these vehicles are going to be put into inventory rather than an actual customer order.

In sum, their lack of adequate financing is keeping their business small: they have a good business *idea,* but they don't yet have a good business.[1] Now, Fuller and Leggett are trying to solve their financial problems.

FINANCE: BASIC CONCEPTS

In general, any business tends to have two kinds of expenditures. First, there are the frequent, rela-tively small expenditures, such as wages, raw materials, and utilities. Second, there are expenditures that occur less often but require major cash outflows, such as the cost of buying production equipment and the cost of building manufacturing plants. Sometimes, managers can control the timing of expenditures: instead of buying an inventory of parts in frequent small amounts, for example, they may be able to buy periodically in large quantities. But no matter how a business's cash outflows occur, these expenditures are likely to have their own timing pattern, a pattern that probably will *not* match the inflow of cash from customers. Thus, the business must have adequate financing in order to carry on its operations. And as we've seen in the case of Automotive Import Recycling, the size of the operation is limited by the level of the firm's financing.

Where can a firm like Automotive Import Recycling obtain the money it needs for its various business expenditures? One major source of money is the firm's **revenues,** *cash inflows a company receives from sales, rentals of its property, and so on.* Some of the money the company needs may be borrowed. Some may come from the sale of **common stock**—*shares of ownership*—in the company. And in some instances, the company can simply get **credit** from its outside suppliers—that is, it can make *arrangements to put off paying them for a time.*

But whatever method or combination of methods the company employs, management must make sure the money is obtained and used as efficiently as possible. This area of management, **finance**—or *the management function of effectively obtaining and using money*—is a tremendously complex area. In all but the smallest businesses, there is at least one person, and sometimes even a whole department, whose sole responsibility is to keep tabs on the flow of funds and to plan the best way to get and use them.

THE FUNCTIONS OF FINANCIAL MANAGEMENT

Financial managers in business firms have major responsibility for decisions about the inflow and outflow of money. They must direct financial operations and measure the results of monetary transactions. They must be equally skilled in *planning* and *control,* two basic functions of financial management.

Financial planning and related functions

Financial managers must find ways to obtain operating funds at the lowest possible cost and to invest wisely any surplus funds the company may have. The financial managers are also responsible for maintaining the company's financial reputation among shareholders and the investment community—bankers, Wall Street analysts, and stockbrokers. How are these responsibilities met? Following are some key functions:

- *Financial planning* is crucial; financial managers must try to predict the need for funds and plan the best way to get them.

- They must concern themselves with *tax management:* they must keep the company's tax costs as low as possible, and evaluate the tax consequences of actions the company is considering.

- They must maintain the company's *financial relations* with creditors and investors.

- They must keep physical *custody of the company's funds,* and they are responsible for *credit and collection*—collecting overdue payments and keeping bad-debt losses down to a minimum.

- They must also make sure the company has enough *insurance* to protect itself against a variety of risks.

Financial control

Equally important, financial managers must set up firm controls: they must maintain records and prepare reports that meet corporate legal and tax requirements, they must measure the results of the company's operations, and they must provide detailed, conscientious accounting services.

Many activities are involved in financial control.

- One is *general accounting,* keeping formal records of the company's assets and liabilities. Its subactivity, *cost accounting,* is keeping records of the company's expenses for labor, equipment, and supplies.

- Another key component of control is the *planning and budgeting* of revenues, costs, and profitability of company operations.

- Financial managers are responsible for *internal audits* of their firm's accounting records. (An **audit** is *an official examination of accounts and records,* especially of financial accounts.)

- They must also have *systems and procedures* that will keep all these functions working.

ASSETS AND LIABILITIES: TWO BASIC CONCEPTS IN FINANCE

Managing a company's finances means thinking in terms of two opposite categories: assets and liabilities. **Assets** are the *items of value the company owns* (including money itself). **Liabilities** are *debts, the sums the company owes to other businesses or individuals.* If a company subtracts its liabilities from its assets, it knows exactly where it stands financially: the remainder is what belongs to the owners of the business. This remainder is often called **owners' equity** or **shareholders' equity,** *the portion of a company's assets that belongs to the owners after obligations to all other creditors have been filled.* For example, one company's records might show the following:

Assets — Liabilities = Owners' Equity
$100,000 − $30,000 = $70,000

In most corporations, shareholders' equity (ownership) consists of **common stock** *(shares of ownership of a business)* sold to thousands of individual investors through a public stock exchange, plus **retained earnings**—*the total net income a company has earned over its life, minus funds returned to shareholders or owners in dividends.* (**Dividends** are *sums of money paid to shareholders of the corporation out of earnings.*)

We will see that there are different kinds of assets and liabilities, each with its own advantages and disadvantages. One company may have the same dollar amount of assets and liabilities as another company, yet be in better shape to face the future because of the *nature* of its holdings and its debts. For example, it may own a piece of undeveloped real estate that would skyrocket in value if buildings were put up on it. Or it may have the greater part of its debts in long-term loans that can be paid back over a ten-year period, rather than in short-term loans that must be paid by the next year.

In this chapter and the chapter that follows, we're going to take a look at some of the details of business finance. As you might imagine, the financial manager's problems are different when he or she is looking for money to take care of next month's payroll than when he or she is thinking of developing a uranium mine that will be open in five years' time. For this reason, we'll look at finance in terms of two different time periods. This chapter

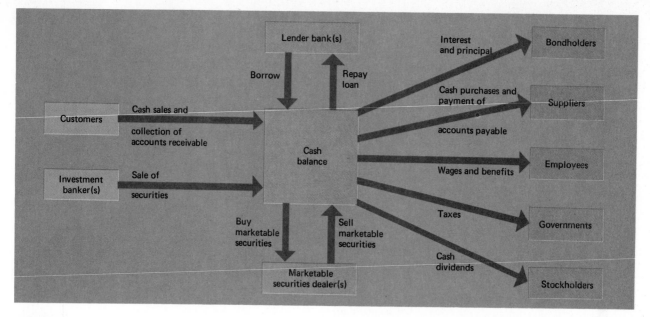

FIGURE 1

CASH FLOW:

The capital that keeps a business running

This diagram shows you how cash flows in a typical firm. Payments must be remitted on a regular basis to investors, suppliers, employees, the government—and if the company can't raise enough cash to do so, trouble may ensue.

will focus on **short-term finance,** *finance involving a time span of one year or less.* The chapter that follows will discuss **long-term finance,** *finance involving time spans of more than a year.* (Some experts in finance use "intermediate-term" to describe financing that relates to periods between one and ten years, but we will use "long-term" for this category.)

A CLOSE LOOK AT SHORT-TERM FINANCE

As we saw in the story of Automotive Import Recycling, one big problem in short-term finance is that a company's revenues don't always come in at exactly the same rate that bills have to be paid. This is true for every business, and it is why the financial manager must carefully monitor **cash flow,** *the total amount of capital, both acquired and spent, that is needed to keep a business running* (see Figure 1).

Gaps between incoming and outgoing cash *can* be dealt with. But the financial manager must have

an effective strategy for figuring out which kinds of short-term assets and which kinds of short-term liabilities are going to offer the company the greatest advantages.

THE NATURE OF SHORT-TERM ASSETS AND LIABILITIES

What kinds of assets and liabilities are categorized as "short-term"? **Short-term assets,** often termed **current assets,** are defined as *those resources that can be turned back into cash within one year.* A bin of raw materials like steel, cotton, or flax, or a warehouse full of jeans ready to be shipped to stores across the country, is a type of short-term asset generally referred to as **inventory,** that is, *goods held on hand for the production process or for sales to final customers.* Cash itself is a short-term asset. So are **time deposits—** *savings accounts at financial institutions and U.S. government bonds.* Other short-term assets include a company's **accounts receivable,** *the money that is owed to the company for items or services it has sold.* (A factory, on the other hand, is not an easy item to convert into cash and so isn't included in any list of short-term assets.) Short-term assets are generally highly **liquid assets—***assets that are relatively easy to turn into cash.* The faster any asset can be converted into cash, the higher its liquidity. Cash, of course, is the most liquid asset.

Borrowed money that must be paid back within one year is a prime example of a **short-term liability,** or *short-term debt.* Other short-term liabilities in-

How much is that short-term asset in the window—the one with the waggly tail? This pet shop's inventory will be exchanged for cash well within the year.

clude rent, salaries, insurance premiums, and unpaid bills for short-term assets such as raw materials.

COMMON PROBLEMS IN SHORT-TERM FINANCING

Short-term finance calls for balancing cash flow to get the most out of the business dollar. The task is not a simple one. It involves a variety of difficult financial policy questions.

For instance, how liberal should a business be in extending credit to other companies and individuals? How big should its accounts receivable be? On the one hand, liberal credit policies may attract more customers. On the other, a company may risk not having enough ready cash to cover its immediate expenses.

Or take another problem: how large an inventory of finished goods should a company stockpile? Will the large cash investment in this inventory be offset by a high demand for the goods? These are

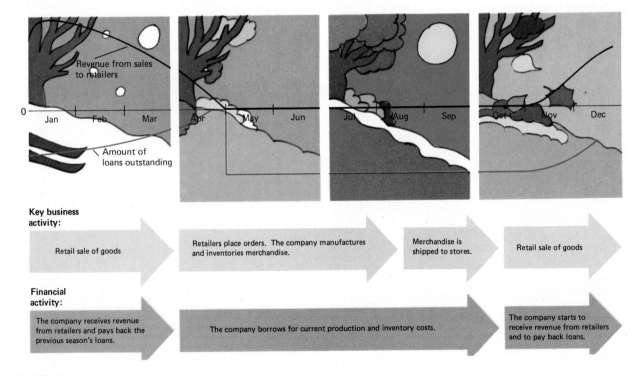

FIGURE 2
THE YEARLY FINANCING CYCLE IN THE SKIWEAR INDUSTRY

What relationships do you see between short-term debts and revenues as the year progresses?

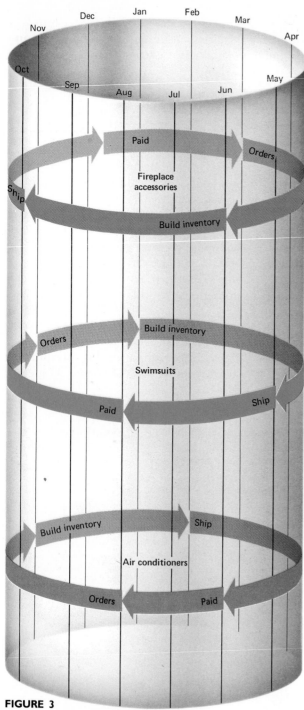

FIGURE 3

SHORT-TERM FINANCING CYCLES
IN THREE SEASONAL INDUSTRIES

In each of these industries, how many months elapse between the time orders are received for the merchandise and the time the company receives payment?

just a few of the short-term financing questions facing the financial manager.

How much short-term capital should a business borrow?

Just how much a business should borrow to meet its short-term needs and for how long depends, first, on the nature of the business. Tobacco farmers borrow short-term capital to pay bills for seed, fertilizer, and labor during the time between planting and harvesting. This period can be six months. Restaurants and other businesses that operate on shorter time cycles may have only a short lag—a month, perhaps—between the time they acquire their inventory and the time they sell it. Figure 3 shows how long the manufacturers of three types of seasonal products must wait for payment for their goods.

The second factor that determines short-term needs is the size of the business. IBM doesn't depend on short-term loans as much as the little clock-repair shop on the corner.

These two factors—the nature of the business and its size—are crucial in determining which of the numerous different *sources* of short-term financing is best to use. We'll look more closely at these different sources in a later section of this chapter.

Ongoing short-term needs

For some businesses, short-term finance is more than a stopgap measure, it's a regular way of doing business. In fact, entire industries are often dependent on the concept of short-term financing. The ski-equipment industry is a case in point. A ski-equipment company such as Salomon/North America, which holds about 40 percent of the market for retail ski bindings, usually encourages retailers to place large orders early in the first quarter by offering discounts of 15 percent or more. Deliveries are made in late summer or early fall—but payment is not received until December. In the meantime, to pay for the raw materials, labor, and office expenses incurred while producing its line of ski equipment, Salomon must borrow short-term capital.[2] (Note that when we're discussing financing, the term **capital** simply means *money*.) The company will then repay this short-term capital when the stores that have purchased the line pay the company.

Is such dependence on borrowing poor business practice? Hardly. There was a time perhaps when it was considered unwise for businesses to owe large sums, but those times are long gone. Today it's a common and well-respected business practice to borrow money in order to make money.

Uses for short-term excess cash

A financial manager with a tight grasp on the firm's cash flow sometimes observes that the firm temporarily has more cash on hand than it needs. In a seasonal business there may be a quiet period between the time customers' bills are collected from the last busy season and the time suppliers' bills are due for the next busy season. Department stores, for example, may have excess cash during a few weeks in January and February—after they collect on their Christmas bills but before they have to pay their Easter bills. A firm may also have excess cash if it is holding funds aside to meet a large commitment in the near future: it may be about to reach the next stage in the construction of a new plant, or it may be waiting for a special bargain on inventory. Finally, every firm keeps some surplus cash on hand as a cushion in case its cash needs are higher than expected—just as we do with our checking accounts.

Part of the financial manager's job is to make sure that this cash is not just lying there doing nothing, but is invested so that it earns interest. The task is to find a good "parking place" for the funds— some sort of investment that will yield the highest possible return, but will create no problem if the firm needs to liquidate the investment for instant cash. There are a number of types of **short-term investments,** called *marketable securities,* that meet these needs. These securities are said to be easily "marketable" because they are relatively low in risk and standardized into familiar forms.

When a firm buys marketable securities with its excess cash, it is essentially lending its cash to an organization (the government or another business) that needs to borrow it. But thanks to our nation's highly organized securities market, the firm with the excess cash does not actually have to go out and look around for a borrower. Instead, it merely goes to an organization known as a *financial intermediary* (the word *intermediary* simply means middleman). It hands over its cash to this organization in exchange for some of the formal commitments to borrow that the intermediary already has in its inventory. And

the company can just as easily reverse the transaction, getting its cash back by selling those formal commitments to some other company that is looking to park excess cash. Marketable securities maturing (coming due) in a year or less are bought and sold on the *money market.* Securities maturing in more than one year are traded on the *capital market.*

The financial manager has many varieties of marketable securities to choose from. We can distinguish among the various kinds according to the type of organization that will ultimately receive the loan— a bank, the government, or another corporation. Frequently, when corporations wish to buy marketable securities, they select the large-denomination **certificates of deposit (CDs)** that banks use to raise funds—*short-term securities issued by a bank based on the time deposits at that bank.* Or, they may choose the securities issued by the federal government itself, called **treasury bills**—*short-term debt instruments issued by the federal government that mature in less than one year,* sold at auction on a regular basis. Many federal agencies also borrow in the money market to finance housing and student loans; they issue securities known to financial managers by names such as "Fannie Maes," "Freddie Macs," "Ginnie Maes," and "Sally Maes" (all abbreviations of the lengthy agency names; see Table 1). Alternatively, the financial manager may choose to buy securities issued by other corporations, which are called *commercial paper.* (We describe commercial paper in more detail later in this chapter.) Foreign banks, governments, and corporations also issue short-term securities, and these play an important role in the placement of excess cash for firms with global operations.

TABLE I Examples of Securities Issued by Major Federal Agencies

FAMILIAR ABBREVIATION	ISSUING AGENCY
"Fannie Maes"	Federal National Mortgage Association (FNMA)
"Freddie Macs"	Federal Home Mortgage Corporation (FHMC)
"Ginnie Maes"	Government National Mortgage Association (GNMA)
"Sally Maes"	Student Loan Marketing Association (SLMA)

INTERNATIONAL BUSINESS TODAY

CASH MANAGEMENT, MULTINATIONAL STYLE

Cash management is a challenge to any business. But to a multinational corporation like Fiat, which handles more than $50 billion per year and has 421 companies in 55 countries, sophisticated financial management is an absolute necessity. It was creative cash management, in fact, that saw Fiat through several years of losses in the late 1970s and early 1980s.

What is Fiat's approach? First of all, extreme centralization. A central financial management team in the corporation's headquarters in Turin sets policy for the company and manages the implementation of that policy. Fiat has had great success with its centralized strategy. For example, by applying for one large loan to cover the cash needs of several of its businesses, the company can wield enough negotiating clout to obtain favorable interest rates. In Italy in 1983, for example, the company was able to borrow $1.5 billion at one point below the prime rate. As Gian Luigi Garrino, the company's director of corporate finance, puts it, "We operate as a central bank, and we think it works."

Another key to Fiat's cash management success has been a meticulous reporting system. Via telex and computer, managers in the head office check the financial status of each subsidiary company every ten days. This careful checking makes possible a four-month forecast of each company's income and outflow, which is continuously updated. When surpluses are expected, the company can move quickly to invest them. When shortfalls occur, arrangements can be made to cushion the blow.

Finally, Fiat takes financial advantage of its multinational status. Since Italy's currency, the lira, is weak, it is extremely important that the company guard against foreign-exchange losses. To do this, Fiat bills all exports in the customer's currency—dollars, marks, or whatever. The company also encourages its subsidiary businesses to obtain certain funds in local currencies, so no foreign-exchange risk occurs. The home office managers in Turin communicate weekly with all companies in Italy, issuing strict guidelines for transactions involving the lira during the week.

All these efforts have paid off for Fiat. The company is currently making new investments at the rate of nearly $1 billion a year, and it has reduced its debt by $1.5 billion since 1980. In today's multinational market, the successful corporation must not only be able to make money, but to manage it as well.

SOURCE: "Clever Cash Management Revs Fiat's Finances," *Business Week*, April 30, 1984, p. 60.

OBTAINING SHORT-TERM FINANCING: WHERE TO TURN?

When we see a new product on the shelf, most of us don't stop to wonder how its manufacturer found the short-term financing to get it there. For that matter, many a new entrepreneur makes plans to bring us a new product without giving too much thought to the financing it will require. Take, for example, Ellen Wessel, who founded a business called Moving Comfort Inc. with the aim of producing better women's running shorts than she could find on the market. When Wessel quit her job and began to build her business, she made a number of good moves. She created a new, comfortable design with the aid of a dissatisfied customer who also happened to be a tailor, and she sent out precut shorts kits to home sewers. Before long her company began to flourish. But the bustle of activity only made Wessel's lack of financial management skills more obvious. Wessel was able to live off her savings for a year, but soon her company was swamped by cash-flow problems.[3]

Quite often a business finds that it needs more cash than it has flowing in. One course open to it is to sell off part of its portfolio of marketable securities. But it has many other options for raising short-term money. To meet their needs for short-term finance, businesses ranging from little Moving Comfort to giant IBM rely on three broad types of sources:

1. They can get trade credit—credit from their suppliers.
2. They can borrow from a commercial bank or some other type of short-term lending institution.
3. If they are among a few large companies, they can borrow from outside investors or other businesses.

Table 2 gives an overview of all three sources. Let's examine them in some detail, and see which ones Wessel was able to take advantage of.

TRADE CREDIT

On one rather shabby block of West Forty-seventh Street in midtown Manhattan, it's estimated that half of the world's supply of diamonds can be found at one time or another. This is a remarkable fact in itself. But more remarkable still is the way in which these stones are bought and sold. So close a commercial community is the New York diamond market that, more often than not, stones worth the ransom of a whole gathering of kings are sold on credit. No more than a handshake and mumbled good wishes seal the deal. That's an example of trade credit at its most breathtakingly simple.

Though rarely transacted on so grand a scale, **trade credit** is the most widespread source of short-term financing for business. It means that rather than borrowing money to pay for goods or supplies, the *purchaser gets credit directly from the supplier*. The degree of formality in such arrangements can range

TABLE 2 Major Sources of Short-Term Financing

ARRANGEMENT	EXAMPLE
TRADE CREDIT	
Open-book account	Smith's grocery store buys display racks from Jones to be paid in full in 30 days or with a discount in 10 days.
Promissory note	Smith signs a note promising payment in 30 days.
Trade acceptance	Jones orders Smith to pay either in 30 days or immediately.
LOANS FROM FINANCIAL INSTITUTIONS	
Unsecured bank loan	Smith borrows from First National Bank on his good name and repays with interest.
Secured loan	
Pledge of accounts receivable	Smith borrows from First National on the bills owed him and repays with interest.
Pledge of inventory	Smith borrows from First National on his marketable groceries and repays with interest.
Pledge of other property	Smith borrows from First National on his delivery truck and repays with interest.
Sales of accounts receivable	Smith sells what is owed him for less than the amount owed.
LOANS FROM INVESTORS	
Commercial paper	Smith, Inc., becomes so large that it can borrow money from First National and Jones, Inc., at a lower interest rate solely on the promise to repay.

from the diamond-district handshake to relatively iron-clad written agreements. However, most trade credit falls within one of three categories: open-book credit, promissory notes, and trade acceptances.

OPEN-BOOK CREDIT

A majority of all business transactions involving merchandise are financed through **open-book credit,** sometimes referred to as "open accounts": *informal arrangements whereby purchasers may obtain goods from suppliers and pay for them later.* Open-book credit, one of the oldest of credit systems, dates back to those primitive days before credit cards when store owners usually knew their customers well enough to allow purchases "on the book." It still exists in this form today, for example, in many a corner grocery store. You can see it if you go into one of New York's *bodegas,* or Puerto Rican grocery stores. When a customer (who is probably a neighbor) needs a quart of milk but doesn't have the cash, the shopkeeper simply lets him or her have the milk and adds it to the bill. To keep track of such transactions, the shopkeeper records in a ledger, or book, the amounts owed by credit customers.

How available was open-book credit to Ellen Wessel's business? Eventually, Wessel was able to persuade fabric wholesalers to extend open-book credit to her on their usual sixty-day terms. But this arrangement was far from automatic—it only became possible once Wessel's firm had gained some strength. At first, fabric wholesalers refused to even accept Wessel's tiny orders, forcing her to buy at retail prices. When she placed her first quantity order, she was shocked when a semitrailer arrived and dumped a thousand yards of cloth at the apartment where she worked! In the early days these suppliers required her to pay in advance or by certified check.[4]

Open-book credit plays an important role for many businesses. Without this means of financing their inventories, many small firms would find it impossible to start a business or keep it going. Most of them are not overly supplied with cash from their own resources. Relatively stiff bank requirements, plus today's high interest rates, mean that such customers often have nowhere to turn for credit except open-book arrangements.

HOW IT'S ACTUALLY DONE

OPEN-BOOK CREDIT

Companies using the open-book credit system indicate credit or repayment terms to the customer on the invoice that accompanies delivery. The terms vary with the industry. In the paperboard-box industry, for instance, open-book credit is usually extended for thirty days. Customers are expected to pay their bills by the end of this period. However, many businesses try to pay before the end of the credit period because suppliers, in order to encourage speedy repayments, offer special discounts for early payments. In the box industry, terms are 1/10, net 30, which means that bills are payable either with a 1 percent discount in ten days or in full in thirty days. A customer who is billed for $10,000 worth of boxes on June 15 is not required to pay for them until July 15. But if the firm pays the bill by June 25 (ten days after the date of the invoice), it can subtract 1 percent, or $100, from the amount owed to the manufacturer.

This is not to say, however, that by allowing open-book credit a supplier can be regarded as an easy mark for any fly-by-night operation. Most sellers investigate the credit rating of any new customer before extending credit. A supplier can check a potential customer's credit by asking the customer to show a financial statement and by contacting the customer's bank for information. Or, if necessary or more convenient, a supplier may use the services of a **credit-rating agency** such as Dun and Bradstreet, which *maintains its own staff of investigators and keeps records of the paying abilities of tens of thousands of firms.*

In addition to being of use to the customer, open-book credit is important to suppliers themselves. Liberal credit policies serve as an attraction to customers. A printer, for example, may offer retail customers sixty days to pay their bills. Although the general industry practice is to require payment in full in thirty days, a sixty-day policy may bring in more business.

PROMISSORY NOTES

Not all businesspeople or, for that matter, all industries are always comfortable with the relative informality of open-book credit. They prefer the security of a written agreement to repay, signed in advance by the customer they're supplying. One such agreement is a **promissory note,** *an unconditional written commitment drawn up by the borrower, who promises to pay the creditor a fixed sum of money on a specified future date in return for immediate credit.* (See Figure 4, below.) Often there is an interest rate on promissory notes, indicated on the note itself.

Promissory notes provide a means of extending

HOW IT'S ACTUALLY DONE

PROMISSORY NOTES

The mechanics of a promissory note are simple. The *borrower who draws up the note, signs it, and so promises to pay* is called the **maker** of the note. The **payee** is the *person or firm who receives the money at the designated time in the future.* Shown below is a promissory note for $5,000 signed by John Simpson, the maker of the note, to the Gray Manufacturing Company, the payee.

What if the creditor needs the money before the due date on the note? In this event, the money can be obtained in advance without breaking the written terms of the agreement. The creditor, or payee, need only *sign the note on the back (endorse it) and take it to the bank. The bank then pays the maturity value of the note, minus a fee for this service.* This procedure is

called **discounting** a promissory note. The bank will collect the full amount on the note for itself when the note falls due.

For example, the $5,000 note shown in Figure 4 matures on September 1. If Gray Manufacturing Company discounts the note at its bank on July 1, the bank may give Gray $4,957.64. The $84.03 discount is the bank's interest charge to Gray for advancing funds to the company. In effect, the bank has advanced Gray the money for the two months between July 1 and September 1, using Simpson's promise to pay as the basis for the loan. The dollar amount of the discount depends on the rate of interest the bank is currently charging. In this example, a 10 percent discount rate is assumed; 10 percent of $5,041.67 is $504.17 per year, or $84.03 for two months (one-sixth of a year). The dollar amount of the discount would have been different, of course, if the bank had used a different discount rate.

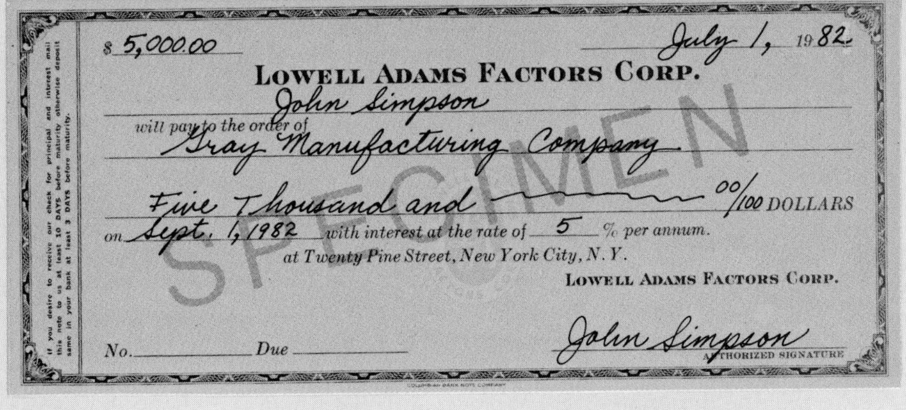

An example of a promissory note

$ 5,000.00   July 1, 1982

LOWELL ADAMS FACTORS CORP.

John Simpson

will pay to the order of

Gray Manufacturing Company

Five Thousand and   00/100 DOLLARS

on *Sept. 1, 1982* with interest at the rate of 5 % per annum.

at Twenty Pine Street, New York City, N.Y.

LOWELL ADAMS FACTORS CORP.

John Simpson
AUTHORIZED SIGNATURE

No. _____ Due _____

FIGURE 4

credit to customers who might otherwise not qualify for it because of the extraordinarily high value of the goods received (furs, for instance), or to customers who have poor credit ratings or a history of having fallen behind in paying open-book accounts. A promissory note from a customer provides the supplier with relative peace of mind about the payment of the bill. This holds true particularly when, as in most cases, the supplier's bank "takes up" the note when payment is due—that is, the bank serves as its client's collector. The persuasive power of a bank is generally more powerful than that of the business's own credit department. Bank-held promissory notes are often repaid without any problems whatsoever. It should be noted that this type of credit arrangement is not restricted to transactions between customers and suppliers; it can be used for any specified purpose.

TRADE DRAFTS AND ACCEPTANCES

The third category of trade credit is drafts and acceptances. Drafts and acceptances give the supplier a way of combining the attractions of open-book credit with the relative security of payment that promissory notes afford. Drafts and acceptances can be particularly useful when the merchant is dealing with poor or unknown credit ratings or with foreign customers whose credit positions are difficult to check.

A commercial draft, or trade draft, is like a promissory note in that it is a piece of paper exchanged between the supplier and the customer and binds the customer to pay for goods or services. But whereas a promissory note is initiated by the customer—the maker of the note—a draft is initiated by the supplier. A **trade draft** is *an order to pay a stated amount of money within a certain number of days, as drawn up by the creditor* (the **drawer**). When the Acme Refrigeration Company, for instance, sends a shipment of refrigerators to a customer, Ace Appliances, it attaches a trade draft to the *shipping document* (the **bill of lading**). This draft is an order for Ace (the **drawee**) to pay the stated amount within a certain number of days. Ace must sign, or "accept," the draft in order to receive the merchandise. By signing the draft, Ace agrees to pay the designated

sum for the refrigerators. The *signed trade draft,* which is now a **trade acceptance,** is returned to Acme. Figure 5 shows a draft for $5,000 drawn up by the Acme Refrigeration Company and duly signed, or accepted, by Ace Appliances.

LOANS FROM BANKS AND OTHER FINANCIAL INSTITUTIONS

As important as trade credit may be to the operation (and often to the survival) of a business, there may come a time when the business has needs that trade credit cannot fill. Perhaps the business finds itself unable to pay its own debts because the customers haven't yet paid theirs. Or the managers of the business may want to make a purchase for which they have to pay cash. At this point, the business may turn to a bank or other financial institution for short-term credit.

A company's financial manager must choose from three principal sources of short-term loans: commercial bank loans, commercial paper, and finance companies. In this section we will review the different lending arrangements that are typical of these three sources of credit.

COMMERCIAL BANK LOANS

Commercial bank loans account for 20 percent of all short-term financing. Approximately two-thirds of commercial bank loans mature in a year or less; these loans are guaranteed by promissory notes, which specify repayment terms.[5] The interest rate charged on short-term loans varies; banks charge higher rates when they think a higher risk is involved.

Loans were an important part of the financing package for Ellen Wessel's business. In its earliest stages Moving Comfort was considered so risky that it could not even obtain a commercial bank loan. It was forced to rely on a commercial finance company (a type of organization we will discuss later in this chapter), and pay 6 percent above the **prime rate,**

HOW IT'S ACTUALLY DONE

TRADE DRAFTS

There are two kinds of drafts: sight drafts and time drafts. A sight draft *is payable on demand (or on sight).* The customer must pay the sight draft as soon as the drawer presents it for payment. (The draft in Figure 5, for example, is a sight draft drawn up by Acme Refrigeration Company on July 1 and payable by Ace Appliances on demand.) A time draft *specifies a particular date in the future on which the draft must be paid.*

What happens after a customer has accepted a draft? Once a sight draft is back in the hands of its drawer, it can be presented for immediate payment. With a time draft, the drawer has the option of holding the draft until the designated payment date. More commonly, the supplier gets money for the draft at once by discounting the time draft at a bank in much the same way that a promissory note is discounted.

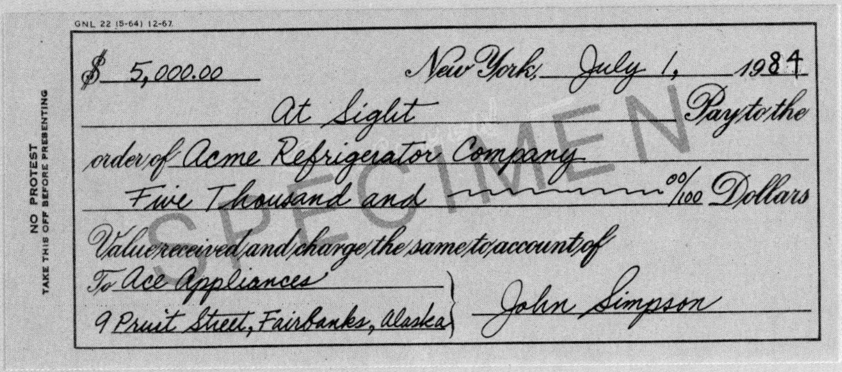
GNL 22 (5-64) 12-67
NO PROTEST
TAKE THIS OFF BEFORE PRESENTING
$ 5,000.00 New York, July 1, 1984
At Sight Pay to the
order of Acme Refrigerator Company
Five Thousand and 00/100 Dollars
Value received and charge the same to account of
To Ace Appliances
9 Pruit Street, Fairbanks, Alaska
John Simpson
SPECIMEN

An example of a trade draft

FIGURE 5

the rate major banks charge their best and strongest customers. (The prime rate serves as a benchmark for many other interest rates throughout the lending industry.) But eventually, by improving her company's financial controls, Wessel was able not only to sharply pare down the total credit she needed to finance her operations but to obtain a $450,000 line of credit at a commercial bank. The bank saw that she had a well-run operation: she got cash in quickly by getting her invoices out as soon as her orders were shipped, and she made a practice of minimizing the cash she had tied up in inventory by keeping her inventory at low but precisely recorded levels.

The loans businesses arrange with banks are of two types—secured loans and unsecured loans.

Secured bank loans

Secured loans are *loans backed by a pledge of some specific valuable item or items,* known as **collateral,** *which can be seized by the lender should the borrower fail to repay the loan.* The three main types of collateral for bank loans are accounts receivable, inventories, and other property.

PLEDGING ACCOUNTS RECEIVABLE One way of obtaining a secured loan is by pledging **accounts receivable,** which are *the amounts due the business from customers with open-book accounts.* The procedure is this: suppose the Global Gadget Company has sold $100,000 worth of corkscrews to various customers on open-book credit. Global can then go to a bank or commercial finance company and borrow about $75,000 against the promise that the lender will get all the payments received from these customers until Global pays off the loan. This sort of arrangement is usually handled on a **nonnotification plan,** meaning that Global's *customers are not told that their accounts have been pledged.* They continue to send their checks directly to the manufacturer of their corkscrews, and Global then forwards them to the bank or finance company.

FACTORING ACCOUNTS RECEIVABLE A less attractive alternative, for most businesses, is the *actual selling of accounts receivable to a financial institution.* This procedure is known as **factoring accounts receivable.** It leads to a **notification plan** whereby *customers are informed of the situation and directed to pay their bills directly to the financial institution.* Such an arrangement means that a business's financial weakness will probably become apparent to customers and others in the field.

Raising money by either pledging or selling accounts receivable to a financial institution is an expensive proposition. It is almost always more costly than obtaining an ordinary unsecured bank loan. In many cases, the financial institution charges a commission of 2 percent for each open-book account handled, plus an interest rate considerably higher than the charge for a straight loan. As a result, the practice of pledging or factoring accounts receivable can significantly increase a business's interest costs compared to other sources of short-term financing.

PLEDGING INVENTORIES What's in store for that field of golden corn rustling in the breeze? More often than not, a few months after it's harvested it will be in some warehouse—cooked, canned, and looked on as collateral by its packer and by the bank or lending institution that has advanced the packing company a short-term loan.

In some businesses it's common to borrow by pledging inventories, generally finished-goods rather than raw-materials inventories, as the security for a loan. If a firm has an excellent credit rating and valuable inventories, then its bank or finance company may simply accept the firm's signed statement that the inventories are pledged to the lender in the event of nonpayment. It's more usual,

though, for the lender to insist that the borrower place the inventory in a warehouse, as we implied in predicting what might happen to a field of corn.

PLEDGING OTHER PROPERTY Other forms of collateral against which loans are made vary widely. If something has value, chances are some bank or finance institution will lend on it. The most common loans are those made against movable property, including automobiles, trucks, and agricultural machines. In fact, the loans are most often taken out to buy such items. When a loan is made for that purpose, the bank or finance company will sometimes require that the borrower sign a **chattel mortgage** agreement in addition to a loan agreement. Under the terms of the chattel mortgage *the movable property, along with the risk of loss, belongs to the borrower.* However, *the lender has a legal right to take possession of the property if payments are not made as specified in the loan agreement.*

Unsecured bank loans

An **unsecured loan** is one that *requires no collateral, or security.* In this type of loan the bank relies on the general credit record and the earning power of the borrower. To increase their returns on such loans, as well as to obtain some protection in case of default, most banks insist that the borrower maintain some minimum amount of money at the bank while the loan is outstanding. Such a deposit—called a **compensating balance**—means that while a borrower pays interest on the full amount of a loan, *a substantial portion of that loan is kept on deposit in the bank.*

For example, if the Hibernian National Bank requires a 20 percent compensating balance and Ed Vogel borrows $10,000, no less than $2,000 of that amount must be kept on deposit in Vogel's account at Hibernian. In other words, although Vogel has borrowed $10,000 and is being charged interest on that amount, he has only $8,000 to actually use. More important from the bank's point of view, it has only $8,000 actually at risk. The compensating balance also has the effect of raising the real interest rate Vogel is obliged to pay. On paper, a loan of $10,000 that requires an interest payment of $1,200 carries an interest rate of 12 percent, but Vogel is paying $1,200 for the use of only $8,000. That means he's really paying 15 percent annual interest. This true interest rate is equal to the dollar amount of the interest paid divided by the amount of funds available for the loan. Moreover, the bank retains use of the $2,000 that Vogel has on deposit. Hibernian is thus eating its cake and having it too. Of course, should Hibernian or any other bank take too big a bite in compensating balance requirements, it would run the risk of dropping out of competition with other institutions. If Vogel could get his money for a lower interest rate and a smaller compensating balance, Hibernian might lose a customer.

Another important type of unsecured loan is the line of credit, which eliminates the need to negotiate with the bank each time a business needs to borrow. The **line of credit** agreed upon by the bank and a business is the *maximum amount of money that the bank is willing to lend the business during a specific period of time*—usually a year. Once a line of credit has been established, the business can automatically obtain unsecured loans for any amount up to that limit.

COMMERCIAL PAPER

When it comes to raising money, many businesses—particularly large corporations—have other options besides borrowing from their own suppliers, banks, and lending institutions. As we've mentioned above, other businesses may have spare money that they are willing to lend on a temporary basis; relatively large businesses can borrow large amounts of short-term capital from other businesses by selling commercial paper. **Commercial paper** is *a company's promise to pay back a stated amount of money on a stated date within 3 to 270 days from the time it is issued.* Commercial paper is unsecured; behind it stands only the good credit of the business itself. For this reason, it is a source of financing available only to large corporations with top credit ratings.

For example, a $1 million offering of Exxon commercial paper is a promise by Exxon to repay $1 million to the holder of the paper ninety days from the date of the loan. The buyer would pay a price somewhat less than $1 million, perhaps $970,000. The difference between the purchase price and $1 million is the interest earned by the holder during the ninety days, since commercial paper is sold on a discount basis. Figure 6 shows an example of this form of corporate IOU.

Why doesn't Exxon go to a bank for the money? Its managers may prefer not to if the interest rate other companies are charging for commercial paper happens to be lower than the rate banks are charging for unsecured loans at the time Exxon wants to borrow. Using commercial paper also saves the corporation from having to maintain a compensating balance, which, as we saw, raises the effective interest rate the banks charge. At the time of this writing, for instance, the prime lending rate at large New York banks was 11.5 percent, compared to commercial-paper interest rates that are hovering between 10 and 10.5 percent. The exact rate depends on the issuer and the maturity date of the paper. Commercial paper is generally sold in units of $100,000 or

FIGURE 6

COMMERCIAL CREDIT COMPANY

A CORPORATION OF THE STATE OF DELAWARE

For Value Received

$4,000,000.   Nº 15N

will pay to bearer on   *the sum of*

FOUR MILLION ($4,000,000.) DOLLARS

at the office of
Baltimore, Md.   COMMERCIAL CREDIT COMPANY

SPECIMEN

AUTHORIZED SIGNATURE   AUTHORIZED SIGNATURE

An example of commercial paper

more (although occasionally it is available in lots as small as $15,000), so these fraction-of-a-percent differences in the interest rate are of great significance to the borrower.

In the 1970s many corporations deserted U.S. banks in favor of commercial paper because it offered far lower interest rates. Since then the "spread" (the difference between the two sets of interest rates) has narrowed, of course. But by and large, corporate borrowers are still sticking with commercial paper and short-term loans instead of choosing long-term financing options, which carry higher rates. This strategy is not without its risks, however. When credit was squeezed in the late 1970s, these firms found they no longer had a friendly banker to turn to, and when interest rates repeatedly zoomed and crashed in the early 1980s, they suffered the full effect because they had not locked in longer-term rates.

All in all, commercial paper is a convenient and thrifty vehicle for raising money. But there are definite legal limitations to its use. According to government regulations, for instance, commercial paper cannot be used to finance long-term projects. The reason behind such a rule is obvious: if a corporation attempted to use commercial paper to finance anything other than current transactions—to build a new plant, for example—it could soon find itself issuing paper to cover the repayment of previous papers. Then it might issue newer papers still to cover those until, eventually, the whole shaky paper structure could be blown away in one puff by a recession.

Purchasers must be wary, too, of commercial paper issued by corporations that are not as stable as they may seem. Investors in the commercial paper issued by the Penn Central Railroad still look back on the transaction with a shudder. Given the size and importance of the corporation, commercial-paper investment had seemed a sure thing. Then, in 1974, Penn Central unexpectedly started bankruptcy proceedings in one of the largest such cases in history. As a result of its bankruptcy Penn Central defaulted on its outstanding paper. Several banks that had, as third parties, guaranteed the paper might have collapsed along with the railroad if the government had not stepped in.[6]

FINANCE COMPANIES

Just as the commercial-paper market exists outside of the banks to provide a source of *unsecured* loans, finance companies operate outside of banks as a source of *secured* loans. In the legal sense finance companies are different from banks because they do not get their money from deposits. (For this reason, they escape the regulation to which banks are subject.) They get their money by borrowing in the money and capital markets, but in larger chunks than their customers can—and thus at lower rates. In the practical sense, finance companies differ from banks by serving the riskier end of the business—their customers are small- and medium-size companies rather than corporate giants. As a result, finance companies tend to be an expensive source of funds, but they also tend to have more specialized expertise (skills) in evaluating the potential of a small business—weeding out the strong from the weak. Finance companies' lending is "asset-based": to minimize risk, most of the loans these companies make are secured against accounts receivable, inventory, or other assets.

INTEREST RATES: THE COST OF BORROWING

Financial managers are constantly concerned with interest rates, and the most important word in the vocabulary of a financial manager should be *timing*. The financial manager's job is to shop around among the many sources of finance for the best interest rates available, and interest rates depend on timing in several important ways.

INTEREST RATES AND THE ECONOMY

First, as we frequently read in the newspaper, interest rates can increase or decrease due to changes in underlying economic factors. The lone financial manager can't do much about the economy. But he or she should attempt to predict the impact of economic factors on interest rates so as to time the company's borrowing and lending most profitably. For example, if it seems likely that interest rates will soon fall, the smart financial manager will delay borrowing as much as possible to take advantage of the lower rates that will probably be available in the near future. If, on the other hand, interest rates seem to be on the rise, speeding up planned borrowing will save the company money.

CASH FLOW AND INTEREST RATES

Past experience shows that experts do not always have overwhelming success in forecasting interest rates; thus, it is important for financial managers to have other tricks up their sleeve. One way the financial manager can exert some control over his or her company's borrowing costs is by watching the timing of the company's cash flow.

The level of risk

As we have seen, there are many different types of short-term lending arrangements. The price of the loan—that is, the interest rates charged—varies with the type of arrangement and the firm, but most significantly with the riskiness of the loan.

How do creditors judge this risk? They evaluate the timing of the borrower's cash flow to find out how soon the firm's collection of assets can be expected to be turned into cash. How soon, they ask, is this firm likely to use these funds to buy inventory, process it into goods, distribute and sell the goods, and send out and collect on invoices for those sales? Creditors are interested in being repaid with cash, and they want to know how soon the company will be able to pay them.

Some types of businesses require longer cash flow cycles, and thus usually have to pay higher interest rates. But in any business skillful financial managers constantly search for ways to shave the timing to a minimum for their industry, so as to attract financing at lower rates than their competitors.

The matching concept

When the financial manager looks for the best combination of liabilities, he looks at timing factors in the firm's combination of assets. To a large extent creditors make this decision for the manager, by their efforts to "match" liabilities to assets.

Suppose that, on the average, the firm's inventories are on the shelf for three months, its accounts receivable are on the books for thirty days, while its marketable securities can be turned into cash virtually immediately. (The lender can find these things out by reading the prospective borrower's financial statement.) Loans that roughly match these assets, both in their amount and in the time frame of their scheduled repayment, are relatively safe. The wider the mismatch between the timing of assets and liabilities, the riskier the loan, and the higher the interest rate that will be charged.

Smart financial managers know that their creditors price their loans (or extend credit) using terms that are dictated by this matching concept. If they present their firms to creditors in the best possible light, they can pay more favorable interest rates.

THE LENGTH OF THE LOAN

When we buy toothpaste, we expect the large size to cost less per ounce than the small size, but we will see that this does not hold true for financing. In general, interest rates are lower for short-term loans than for long-term loans—the further a loan extends into the future, the greater the risk.

Why then don't financial managers load up on short-term credit to finance all their assets, and entirely shun long-term debt and equity? The answer has to do with the matching concept we have discussed above. Some of a firm's assets, like a new blast furnace or a new computer, are long-term in nature and generate cash over an extended, unknown period of time. Thus the timing of repayment must be matched accordingly. Financial managers also have to be concerned about changing interest rates on short-term debt. These rates change more frequently and more drastically than long-term rates; this could present problems when the firm has to refinance its short-term borrowings.

DIPPING INTO FLUID CASH

What if a company can't—or doesn't want to—borrow on a short-term basis? There is another source of cash to which more and more companies are turning as the cost of credit soars. These firms get funds by tapping **fluid cash,** *the money that companies temporarily gather in the course of their business.* It is an attractively cheap alternative to short-term financing. Some ways of using it are perfectly legal; some are in a "gray area," ethically speaking; and some are both illegal and unethical.

■ These tactics are legal:

Take possession of cash as quickly as you can.

This is the chief principle of the fluid-cash concept. To get their money as soon as they're entitled to it, many corporations have established a good network of so-called **lockboxes,** which are simply *post-office boxes in strategically selected locales with good mail deliveries.* Companies instruct customers to mail their remittances to these addresses and then arrange with a local bank to pick up and deposit those checks to the corporation's credit. In this way companies can make immediate use of cash that might otherwise have taken days of "mail-float" time to arrive at headquarters. One major midwestern metals company established six lockboxes across the country. Its available cash was thereby increased by $2.5 million, which the company used to pay off some short-term debts.

Put off paying bills as long as possible.

This is simply the converse of the first principle of fluid-cash management. Just as a corporation can take advantage of good mail service, it can also rely on the shortcomings of the postal service in certain areas to make certain that outgoing checks go out as slowly as they possibly can. On the premise that what's not yet anyone else's is still your own, corporations have hunted out the most inaccessible of banks on which to draw checks for paying bills and debts. One West Coast food company has increased its available cash by some $7 million by using a bank in Richmond, Virginia—a city with "horrendous" airline schedules, which delay the dispatch of mail.

Of course, the simplest way to increase available cash is to pay bills only at the very last minute. According to harried credit managers, that's just what more and more businesses are doing. The money game has reached the point at which bills **in arrears** *(late in payment)* for sixty days are becoming the rule rather than the exception.

Use controlled disbursement accounts.

A company can both write its checks on a remote bank and not cover them with funds until they are

The corporation uses a check to pay the vendor (the company to which it owes money). The check is drawn on a remote bank, the "disbursement" bank.

The vendor deposits this check in its own bank.

The vendor's bank sends the check to be processed via the Federal Reserve System (the government agency that oversees the private banking system—see Component Chapter D). Processing may take several days; meanwhile, the corporation can put its cash to work elsewhere.

actually presented for collection, if it chooses a bank offering controlled disbursement accounts. Every morning before 11:00 A.M. the bank will tell the firm exactly which checks will clear that day, leaving the firm enough time to transfer sufficient funds from other accounts or borrow them on the money market. Controlled disbursement accounts are often called "zero balance accounts," for ideally there is never any idle, uninvested cash left in them at the end of the day. The bank is only able to provide this service if it is situated relatively close to its regional branch of the Federal Reserve, so that it receives its morning check delivery early enough to complete such a round of tallying and phoning with its customer. But the bank must still be far enough away not to receive two Fed deliveries a day! The Fed is doing all it can to cut down on this practice, as it winds up absorbing much of the float costs created by remote accounts.

■ These tactics are unethical and in some cases illegal:

"Kite" a check.

Even when bills are paid, there's a way some companies still manage to cling to the cash for just a bit longer. By **kiting checks**—*writing drafts on nonexistent funds and then covering them with deposits drawn on other overdrawn accounts*—some companies are able to float massive short-term loans before bringing

their accounts back to earth with a cash infusion. There are, however, serious drawbacks to check kiting. For instance, TI Corporation, the nation's largest title insurer, was charged some years ago with mail and wire fraud after it had generated fictitious balances of more than $100 million. What went wrong? A courier took an unexpected day off, so one of TI's overdrawn checks didn't arrive in time to cover another overdraft and the whole scheme collapsed.

Use the "cheapest money in town."

A common, but absolutely illegal and inadvisable, business ploy is to withhold from the U.S. government the income tax and Social Security money deducted from employees' paychecks. By hanging on to and using that cash until the last possible moment when it must be turned over to the government (sometimes up to four or five months after the deductions are made), a business has the use of a considerable sum without paying any interest on it at all. To repeat, however, it *is* illegal, and the number of fraud convictions for this practice is increasing.

SOURCE: Lockbox discussion is based on "Companies Gain Funds by Speeding Intakes and Slowing Outgoes," *Wall Street Journal*, July 31, 1974, p. 1; TI example is based on "Top U.S. Title Insurer, TI Corp., Indicted for Fraud in Huge Check-Kiting Scheme," *Wall Street Journal*, January 15, 1976, p. 6; controlled disbursement discussion is based on Irwin Ross, "The Race Is to the Slow Payer," *Fortune*, April 18, 1983, pp. 75–80.

The Fed eventually sends the check back to the corporation's own disbursement bank, along with other checks that have been drawn on that account.

The disbursement bank lets the corporation know the total of that day's checks. The corporation then transfers funds into the disbursement account, in the amount of that day's total (only).

CHAPTER REVIEW

Finance is the management function of effectively obtaining and using money. Two basic concepts in financing are assets and liabilities. Assets are the items of value that the company owns. Short-term assets, sometimes called current assets, are resources that a company can turn into cash within a year. Short-terms assets include raw materials, money that is owed by other firms, time deposits, accounts receivable, and cash on hand. The faster an asset can be converted into cash, the higher its liquidity. Liabilities are debts that the company owes to other businesses or to individuals. Short-term liabilities include unpaid bills for short-term assets, such as raw materials, as well as rent, salaries, and insurance premiums.

Financial managers are responsible for shareholders' equity, or the claim the owners or stockholders have on a company's assets after its obligations to all other creditors have been fulfilled. They must also monitor cash flow, or the amount spent and the amount received from customers. Because there may be gaps in the flow, companies must often seek short-term financing. At other times, they may have excess cash on hand for short periods. This must be placed in short-term investments.

Trade credit given by one business to another is the most important source of short-term capital. Most of this credit is extended on an open-book credit basis, but some is procured through promissory notes and trade drafts.

Short-term capital can also be obtained through banks and other financial institutions. Banks make unsecured loans to many customers, usually on the basis of a pre-arranged line of credit. In addition, banks and commercial lending companies lend money on a secured basis against accounts receivable (which may be pledged or sold), inventories, or other property.

Some large companies raise short-term capital through the sale of commercial paper. This may be a good investment for businesses with a temporary excess of funds.

Finance companies operate outside of banks as a source of secured loans. They offer asset-based lending.

The financial manager must be informed about interest rates as well as the overall economy in order to time borrowing to the best advantage. Managing the company's cash flow cycle (a shorter cycle carries less risk) and short-term assets effectively is another way of obtaining favorable terms. In general, the longer and/or riskier the loan, the higher the interest rate.

KEY WORDS

revenues (350)

common stock (350)

credit (350)

finance (350)

audit (351)

assets (351)

liabilities (351)

owners' (or shareholders') equity (351)

common stock (351)

retained earnings (351)

dividends (351)

short-term finance (352)

long-term finance (352)

cash flow (352)

short-term (or current) assets (352)

inventory (352)

time deposits (352)

accounts receivable (352)

liquid assets (352)

REVIEW QUESTIONS

1. What is financing? What are some of the major sources of business financing?

2. Discuss the problems involved in short-term financing. What are the three primary sources of short-term financing?

3. Under what conditions would a supplier require a promissory note or a trade acceptance?

4. When might you expect banks to look favorably on the idea of providing short-term financing for businesses?

5. Explain the differences between a secured and an unsecured bank loan. What are some of the assets a business can pledge as collateral for a loan?

6. Why might a business purchase commercial paper rather than getting short-term financing from a bank?

7. What factors must a financial manager consider when seeking sources of short-term capital? What are the advantages of the various options available? How will fluctuations in interest rates affect the manager's decisions?

8. How would a company's cash flow cycle affect its ability to borrow? Under what circumstances might the higher cost of a long-term loan be justified?

CASE 1

SHORT-TERM FINANCIAL PROBLEMS IN A SKIWEAR COMPANY

What kind of work is a person suited for after he has set a world speed record in skiing? C. B. Vaughan's athletic achievements left him with many ideas for designing ski clothing. He founded CB Sports in 1969, and since then he has built it into one of the hottest skiwear makers in the world.

Time and determination have helped Vaughan overcome many obstacles—especially his lack of knowledge about making wearing apparel. Vaughan keeps his fingers busy in every facet of the business. For the first few years he cut the cloth for every garment himself, and after fifteen years in business he still does most of the designing. He has not always been able to count on the assistance of others—once he brought a new product to a contractor for sewing, and several weeks later he found the same product for sale at a trade show under the contractor's own name. But Vaughan has learned to encourage cooperation from those around him, notably by offering opportunities for incentive pay to his 300-person work force.

One of CB's biggest problems has been the need for financing. Vaughan had only $5,000 of his own money to meet start-up expenses. Happily, he was able to win thirty-six retail accounts for his "Super Pants" in the first year. But while his reputation as a skiing champion helped win the enthusiasm of customers, it counted little with bankers, and Vaughan had trouble finding the working capital he needed to fill his retail accounts' orders. Banks would not make unsecured loans to an unproven company. Vaughan had to borrow by using his order book as collateral, at the hefty rate of 3 percent over prime.

CB Sports earned a profit of about $650,000 in fiscal 1983, thirteen times its 1976 level, on sales thirty-four times greater than 1976 sales. But two factors beyond Vaughan's control pose tough challenges to his business: snowfall and interest rates. Skiwear sells slowly when snow falls sparsely—something that happened on the East Coast for two out of the past three winters.

And climbing interest rates have taken a large bite out of sales revenues. Vaughan's entire workforce is in the United States, and all of his materials, from zippers to insulation, are premium. This means that a lot of his money is tied up before goods are shipped and paid for—and that money must be borrowed at high cost.

To offset the riskiness of the skiwear business, Vaughan is prospecting for new customers: other sportsmen, perhaps wind surfers and ocean sailors, who require high-performance, high-technology outfitting.[7]

1. Vaughan has hired you as his chief financial officer and has charged you with developing some lower-cost sources of short-term finance for CB Sports. What alternatives might you try? How could you get bankers to have enough confidence in you to give you unsecured loans rather than making you take out loans against your order book?

2. The skiwear market is a risky business, due to its dependence on snow. How might CB Sports lessen its dependence on this market?

3. In creating the business, Vaughan's athletic reputation was an important asset (considered by accountants to be a form of "goodwill"). How might CB Sports continue to build on this asset as it expands into new lines?

COLECO: LOOKING FOR SHORT-TERM FINANCING IN THE CABBAGE PATCH

During the 1983 Christmas shopping season, the thoughts of many parents and store managers focused on one problem: how to lay their hands on Coleco's Cabbage Patch Kids dolls. The thoughts of Coleco managers, on the other hand, were not concentrated on the profits rolling in from this astonishingly successful doll. They had a problem of their own: repaying debt.

Since that spring, Coleco had drawn over $100 million on a line of credit negotiated with Chase Manhattan. The terms of the credit line included a "clean-up period"—a thirty-day period every year during which no loans could be outstanding. This type of arrangement is fairly common practice. By requiring the borrower to be fully paid up for one small part of the year, bankers assure that their short-term lending is indeed used for short-term purposes. Unsecured short-term loans are meant to finance a firm's working capital only: for its major investments, firms should obtain secured long-term financing instead.

The working capital cycle of companies in the toy business is well known to bankers—borrowing expands as the toy companies purchase materials to fill Christmas orders, and borrowing shrinks as the companies collect their accounts receivable. By January 31, 1984, Coleco should have collected from wholesalers, who would have collected from retailers, who would have collected from their customers. And that's why Chase Manhattan chose this date as the beginning of Coleco's thirty-day clean-up period.

But despite the $25 million 1983 profits it made from the Cabbage Patch dolls alone, Coleco suspected that it would not have enough cash on hand to "clean up" its credit line. Much of the borrowed money had gone to finance the firm's other hot new item—the Adam computer. Adam provides complete word-processing capability for the home computing novice for about $600. Adam was expected to make a strong showing during the 1983 Christmas season, but it was held up by production problems. By the time defects were eliminated and production was brought up to speed, it was too late for Coleco to make the computer sales it had been counting on to repay its debt.

Coleco's financial worries did not go unnoticed by its stockholders. Share prices fell sharply in December despite the Cabbage Patch euphoria. Twenty percent of Coleco's stock was involved in "short selling"—the selling of shares borrowed from a broker, in the expectation that the share price will decline before the stock must be purchased to repay the loan. The stock market seemed as grim a place to turn for capital as did the banks.

Coleco's chief financial officer held talks with the firm's investment bankers about tapping new sources of long-term capital. The firm wanted to wait as long as possible, however; once the market potential of Adam was established, Coleco's managers felt, potential investors would feel more confident and require a lower return on their capital.

During the final days of 1983, Coleco was short on cash, but long on potential. The Adam was receiving favorable reviews from computer experts, and the Cabbage Patch Kids were still getting rave reviews from little boys and girls. If the company defaulted on its loans, it might never have the chance to realize its potential.[8]

1. If you were Coleco's banker, would you enforce the "clean-up" provision of the loan this year? If not, how would you explain your decision to your boss, who feels strongly that anything but short-term working capital loans are too risky for this bank?

2. If you chose not to require repayment by January 31, what other assurances might you write into your loan agreement with Coleco to make it more secure? How might you avoid facing the same problem next year?

3. If you were Coleco's treasurer, how might you persuade your bankers to waive the clean-up provision?

4. Is Coleco's problem one of short-term or long-term finance? Should short-term loans have been used to finance the Adam's manufacturing and development? Can you cite reasons why top financial managers at Coleco might have chosen to use short-term financing?

LONG-TERM FINANCE 14

One of the most striking developments in industry in recent years has been the development of robots to perform highly skilled tasks. In just one ingenious application, robots have taken over the job of installing and servicing oil rigs hundreds of feet beneath the ocean—an effort that used to cost several lives each year when it was the task of human divers. By the end of this decade, the diving robots are expected to have taken over most of this treacherous work.

But one question remains: where will companies get the money to pay for these robots? Such highly sophisticated new technology costs a great deal of money: a single diving robot, for example, may cost as much as $3 million. Solving this problem requires long-term financial management—the management of assets and liabilities over periods of time that are longer than a year (usually, many years). All companies need long-term financing to pay for big-ticket projects and purchases—not only exotic items like undersea robots, but also everyday needs like a new factory.

CHAPTER FOCUS

After reading the material in this chapter, you will be able to:
- describe the major features of a bond, and distinguish between secured and unsecured bonds
- indicate how bonds are priced and what types of new bonds were issued because of recent market upheavals
- discuss several ways to pay back the debt that bonds incur
- name three types of tax-free bonds
- distinguish stocks from bonds, and describe recent trends contributing to the popularity of stocks
- distinguish between preferred and common stock
- cite at least three other means of long-term financing besides stocks and bonds
- name at least three considerations in making long-term financial choices

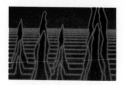

When a company that has financial needs on a large scale decides to undertake a big new project, it must plan for long-term financing.

■ Today, the average major motion picture costs $10 million to produce and another $6 million to market. How does MGM raise this much money for each of the seventeen or so films it produces a year?

■ In 1981 U.S. Steel bought Marathon Oil Company for $6.6 billion—a bargain if you figure the value of the oil Marathon had in the ground at today's cost of finding such reserves. How could a huge but troubled corporation like U.S. Steel get hold of such a sum?

■ In the auto industry, today's manufacturers must continually devote huge sums to engineering and design to keep up with foreign competition, government regulation, and consumer preferences. How can a company like American Motors finance all this and pay for its huge annual operating loss?

We'll look at some possible solutions to these and similar problems in this chapter.

OPTIONS FOR LONG-TERM FINANCING

To some extent, it may be possible to obtain long-term financing internally. True, such financing is not usually available directly from sales revenues; though large corporations take in large amounts of cash from their revenues, most of that money has to be set aside to cover production costs. Surplus revenue funds are rarely on hand waiting for new projects to come along. But other company funds may sometimes be tapped for long-term financing. A company may distribute some of its profits to shareholders immediately. But it may also keep back certain sums categorized as **retained earnings** or **undistributed profits;** these are *profits retained by the firm for investment in new projects,* which may ultimately generate future profits for shareholders.

But internal sources may not always be sufficient to fill all a company's long-term financing needs. For additional funds, companies have two other major alternatives. They may raise **debt capital** (*funds obtained by borrowing*) by selling bonds, which are essentially "corporate IOUs," to private investors. A bond is a long-term loan that gives the investor the legal right to repayment with interest. Or, they may raise **equity capital**—*funds obtained by selling investors stock, or shares of ownership in the company.* Stock gives the investor a share in the risk as well as the profits: the company is legally obligated only to make "good faith" efforts to earn profits.

To undertake new projects and pursue their objectives, many companies use various combinations of these three sources of long-term finance—debt, equity, and internal funds.

■ In 1981, for example, MGM took the debt route when it purchased United Artists from Transamerica Corporation; it borrowed almost the entire $380 million that it needed. Its bankers were so unhappy about this severe debt load that they pulled in the reins on the new movie budgets they would agree to finance. By 1984 MGM was desperate for blockbuster movies: it was counting on large undistributed profits from hoped-for hits in order to work off its debt, although it would have less to spend on actors and sets.[1]

■ U.S. Steel also favored the debt option not long ago. It succeeded in pulling off the second largest acquisition in history, the Marathon Oil deal, by assembling a financing package that included about $3 billion in fixed-rate debt and $3 billion in variable-rate debt. (We will discuss fixed- and variable-rate bonds later in this chapter.) As a result the company's debt rose to 60 percent of its total capital, and its interest expense to $1 billion a year. This heavy debt burden was necessary because U.S. Steel has been quite unpopular in the stock market.[2]

■ American Motors, on the other hand, was able to use the equity alternative recently. Stock market investors' hopefulness about American Motors' future rose in 1983, and the company was able to raise $99 million by issuing 15 million new shares. Combined with its $230 million in new long-term loans, AMC felt it had the cash to implement its "survival plan."[3]

Long-term financing is a major part of the U.S. economy. In this chapter we'll look at some of the most important aspects of long-term financing, including debt and equity capital and the way each is obtained. We'll discuss the pros and cons of each, and the factors that financial managers must consider when it becomes necessary to raise capital for their companies' long-term needs.

THE BASICS OF BONDS

A **bond** is *a certificate indicating that its issuer has borrowed a sum of money from the bondholder.* When a corporation raises money by issuing bonds, it usually sells parts of the issue—individual bonds—to many different buyers. For instance, a $300 million issue of AT&T bonds may consist of thousands of individual bonds. Each of these bonds has a **denomination,** *the amount of the loan represented by one bond.* Bonds sold by corporations are usually available in $1,000 denominations, but they also come in denominations of $5,000, $10,000, $50,000, and $100,000.

A bond usually shows the date when *the full amount of the bond,* the **principal,** must be repaid. That date is called the **maturity date.** A bond is typically issued for ten years or more. Many large corporations sell bonds whose maturity dates are thirty-five or forty years after the date of issue.

A bond provides for **interest,** *payment that the issuer makes to the bondholder in return for the use of the borrowed money.* Thus, the holder of a $1,000 denomination 8 percent bond that pays interest on January 15 and July 15 would expect to receive $40 on each of these dates. The owner of the bond collects the interest by presenting one of the coupons issued with the bond. (A **coupon** is *a statement of due interest that can be cut from a bond when the interest is payable and is presented for payment.*) Long-term debt tends to be issued on a *coupon basis,* as opposed to the *discount basis* we encountered when we looked at common methods of short-term financing.

An example of a bond

SECURED AND UNSECURED BOND ISSUES

If you want to borrow money from a local bank, your banker will require **collateral** for the loan—*a valuable item or items that can be seized if you fail to repay the loan.* The car you purchase with a loan is the collateral for the typical automobile loan. If you do not make the payments as they are due, the bank will repossess the car. Occasionally, however, banks make personal loans to individuals with good credit standings without specific collateral, merely on their signatures.

Similar arrangements exist for issuing bonds. Some issues, called **secured bonds,** *offer bondholders specific backing for their bonds.* This backing, or security, consists of property of one kind or another that will pass to the bondholders if the issuer does not live up to the terms of the agreement. The security can be a mortgage on a piece of real estate or a claim to other assets, such as freight cars, airplanes, or plant equipment owned by a company. **Unsecured bonds,** also called **debentures,** are *backed not by collateral but by the general good name of the issuing company.* If the bond-issuing company fails, the bondholders have a claim on the assets, but only after creditors with specific collateral have been paid. Examples of secured and unsecured bonds are shown in Table 1.

At first glance, unsecured bonds appear to be riskier than secured bonds. However, unsecured bonds are issued by many of the best-known borrowers. Their **credit rating,** or *ability to get loans on the basis of their past financial record,* is so good that they need not offer security to get investors to buy their bonds. Dow Chemical, U.S. Steel, and other major U.S. corporations issue only debentures.

BOND INTEREST RATES

A look at the financial section of any newspaper will show that some corporations are selling new bonds at an interest rate of two or three percentage points higher than other companies. Yet the terms of the bonds seem similar. In 1983 most high-quality corporate bonds of industrial companies were yielding between 11 and 14 percent interest. Municipal bonds—on which income from the interest earned is untaxed—were yielding over 10 percent.

What accounts for the different interest rates? What determines bond interest rates in the first place? Basically, the bonds of a borrower (the issuing company) that is in a strong financial position represent less risk to the investor (the buyer of the bond) than those of a weak company. As a result, a

TABLE I   Types of Secured and Unsecured Bonds

TYPE	BACKING	EXAMPLE
SECURED		
First mortgage	Real estate	$25 million Iowa Electric Light and Power Company first mortgage bonds due December 1, 2007. Proceeds used to repay outstanding commercial paper used primarily for construction. Rated "A."
Equipment trust	Capital equipment	$40 million Union Tank Car Company equipment trust certificates due December 1, 1987. Certificates secured by equipment costing $53.3 million. Proceeds used to retire $33.2 million of indebtedness and to buy 267 rail cars. Rated "A."
Mortgage-backed	First mortgages on residential real estate	$100 million Home Savings and Loan Association mortgage-backed bonds. Due November 15, 1983. Secured by mortgage notes, which must be secured by mortgages constituting first liens on one-to-four residential dwelling units. Rated "AAA."
UNSECURED		
Debenture	Faith and credit of borrower	Leading corporations such as AT&T, Dow Chemical, and U.S. Steel.

corporation with excellent prospects of earning enough money in future years to pay both the interest on the bonds and the principal at maturity can afford to offer bonds at a relatively low interest rate. A less secure borrower has to offer a higher interest rate in order to attract buyers.

The theory of bond pricing

Once a company issues a bond at a certain interest rate, that rate remains fixed permanently. (*The fixed interest rate of a bond* is known as its **coupon rate.**) However, we know that in the economy, interest rates are moving up and down all the time. And though the bond's **face value** (*the dollar amount indicated on the face of the bond*) does not change, the investor may eventually sell the bond for more or less than the face value.

What happens if an investor buys a $1,000 bond with a coupon rate of 8 percent and wants to sell it to get the money back two years later when interest rates have risen to 10 percent? Obviously, the investor cannot get $1,000 for the bond, since new bonds selling for $1,000 are now paying $100 in annual interest, while the old bond pays only $80. In order to sell the bond, the investor will have to lower the price to the point where it can match the *yield* that the market is currently paying. (The **yield** is *the income produced by a financial investment,* usually expressed as a percentage of the cost of that investment.) In other words, the investor will have to lower the price of the bond to the point where $80 represents a 10 percent return. This price would be $800, and thus the bond would have lost $200 in value. The new bond owner would have paid $800 for the right to receive the $80 annual payments, and would thus be earning 10 percent interest even though the corporation has not changed the terms of its bond. (Note that when the new bond owner holds the bond until the maturity date, he or she will still receive $1,000, not the $800 he or she paid for it—with the results we'll discuss further on in this chapter.)

The opposite can happen as well. If interest rates fall below 8 percent, investors will be willing to pay more than the $1,000 face value for bonds with an 8 percent coupon rate, thus creating a profit for the original owner of the bond. In fact, interest rates move up and down every day, and so do the prices at which bonds are traded—but in the opposite direction. These ups and downs in bond prices have been found to serve as an excellent way of predicting what will happen to the economy in general.

UPHEAVALS AND TRENDS IN THE BOND MARKET

We can easily imagine that investors are not too happy when a rise in interest rates causes a loss in the value of their bonds. For this reason, when interest rates are expected to climb in the future (for reasons we will explore in Component Chapter D), corporations must pay somewhat higher rates in the present in order to attract debt capital (sell bonds). In the late 1970s and early 1980s, however, interest rates rose much higher and faster than anyone had anticipated, and investors found themselves taking huge losses year after year. Eventually, the bond market "dried up." No one wanted to lend money at a fixed rate for many years into the highly unpredictable future, and with rates so steep, companies themselves were not anxious to commit to such huge interest payments for the long term.

Floating-rate and index bonds

One attempt to deal with the problem of fast-rising interest rates was the introduction of the floating- or adjustable-rate bond. With **floating-rate debt,** the lender is not committed to one interest rate for the life of the loan. *The lender earns a rate that is periodically adjusted according to terms arranged with the borrower*—such as weekly or monthly changes based on changes in the prime rate or the treasury bill rate. But even with the option of using floating-rate bonds, firms that wanted to finance new projects during the high-interest-rate period relied to a large extent on bank loans rather than the bond market, and on short rather than long maturities.

Happily, interest rates stabilized at lower rates by 1982, and more fixed-rate long-term debt capital became available. But unhappily, by that time a great number of corporations had saddled themselves with huge amounts of short-term debt that they urgently needed to refinance. (As you recall, short-term debt obligates the borrower to pay back the principal in the near future, whereas with long-term financing the borrower need only come up with interest payments for the present.) The result was a staggering level of new bond and equity (stock) issues in late 1982 and early 1983, with the funds being used to reduce short-term debt. However, because long-term interest rates were expected to fall even further, many firms tried to postpone new bond issues even longer; they issued new stock instead, taking advantage of the sudden strength that had developed in the stock market around that time.

During the same period, with long-term credit still tight, borrowers and lenders became more flexible and began to experiment with many new types of lending arrangements. By the time the debt market had improved, the usefulness of many of these innovations had already been proven, and thus new types of long-term credit arrangements became a permanent part of the scene. To date, floating rates are still considered an excellent way of absorbing risk in a highly volatile or unstable economic environment. An alternative method of adjusting rates is the **index bond,** which is *a bond tied to an economic indicator such as the Consumer Price Index* rather than to a particular short-term interest rate. The indexing arrangement assures the investor that the **real return** (or *inflation-adjusted return*) will not fall; that is, if the investor is guaranteed a real interest rate of, say, 6 percent, and the Consumer Price Index jumps from 5 percent to 8 percent, the bond yield will rise from 11 percent (6 + 5) to 14 percent (6 + 8). Index bonds were first introduced in high-inflation countries such as Israel and Brazil.

Deep-discount and zero-coupon bonds

After adjustable rates, the second key "creative financing" strategy was to fit new financial instruments to loopholes in the tax laws, effectively relying on Uncle Sam to subsidize higher interest rates.

Earlier, we encountered the idea that bondholders can earn income in two different ways—from straight interest or from a combination of interest plus the bonus that comes from buying for $800 a bond that can be cashed in for $1,000 when it matures. Our tax laws draw a sharp distinction between these two kinds of earnings. When bondhold-

ers receive their regular coupon interest payments, they are taxed at their personal income tax rate, which may be as high as 50 percent. But when a bondholder earns $200 by collecting $1,000 for a mature bond that was bought at $800, he or she receives a **capital gain,** *a sum of money representing the difference between the sales price of an asset and its original cost (assuming that the sales price is higher).* This capital gain is taxed at the capital gains rate, which can be no more than 20 percent, regardless of the investor's income tax bracket.

Investors are quite aware of the tax advantages of capital gains, and thus a new bond yielding 10 percent is less attractive than an old 8 percent bond discounted to yield 10 percent. Financial strategists thought: Why not take this one step further? Why not just issue new bonds with a coupon rate of, say, 2 percent? With today's high interest rates, we could only sell them at a lot less than face value—say, $300 instead of $1,000. Although investors will only earn $20 a year at the coupon rate (taxed at their high income tax rates), they will receive a $700 profit on maturity, and this profit will be taxed at the lower capital gains rate. Hence, the **deep-discount bond**— *a bond sold at a sizable discount from face value*—was born. When this approach worked, creative financiers, never inclined to sleep on the job, thought: Why not take it even further and offer not a 2 percent but a zero coupon interest rate? And so the **zero-coupon bond**—*a bond with no interest rate at all*— entered the financial scene.

"Junk" bonds

A final trend on the postrecovery bond market horizon is the increased interest in "junk" bonds. Just the reverse of discount or low-coupon bonds, junk bonds were issued during the recession with very high coupon yields, reflecting the very high risk associated with their issuers (either young, unproven ventures, or old, established money-losers). Many individual and institutional investors maintain a strict policy of staying away from high-risk borrowers. But as the economy began to recover, many of these companies shaped up better than expected, and now the extra-high fixed yields of their bonds more than compensate the investor for the extra risk.

PAYING BACK THE PRINCIPAL: CALLING AND CONVERTING

As we've indicated, a corporation that sells bonds must repay its bondholders, and normally the simplest arrangement for doing so is to repay the bonds at maturity date. Some issues consist of **term bonds,** in which *all the bonds mature at the same time.* The $100 million Southwest Bell Telephone 4¾ percent bonds of 1992 will all come due in 1992. Another type of issue consists of **serial bonds,** which *mature at different times.* In 1974, for example, the Philadelphia Parking Authority issued $5.6 million worth of serial bonds to help finance construction of an airport parking facility. Of these bonds, $175,000 matured in 1978, $190,000 in 1979, $200,000 in 1980, and additional amounts will mature each year through 1994.

Serial bonds provide issuers with a convenient schedule of repayment that relieves them of the need to pay off an entire issue in any one year. Another way of accomplishing this objective is through a **sinking fund.** When a corporation issues a bond payable by a sinking fund, it must *set aside a certain sum of money each year to "sink," or pay off, the debt.* Either this money is used to buy in and retire a few bonds each year from investors or it is set aside to accumulate until the issue matures.

Callable bonds

With some bond issues *a corporation retains the right to pay off the bonds before maturity.* Bonds containing this condition are known as **callable,** or **redeemable, bonds.** Why would a business want to pay off its debts before it must? The answer is, to save money. If a corporation issues bonds when interest rates are high and then interest rates fall, it may want to call in its high-interest bonds and pay them off by selling a new issue at a lower interest rate. However, this feature, which is of course attractive from the company's point of view, carries with it a price tag— investors must be offered a higher interest rate to encourage them to buy callable bonds. In addition, there is usually a "call premium" that the company must pay over the market price of the bond at the time that the bond is called by the company. For

example, the agreement between the company and the bondholders might state that if the company called the bonds at a given point in time, it would pay 102 percent of the then current market price of those bonds.

For example, ITT Financial Corporation recently sold a $100 million issue of bonds at 8½ percent, maturing in 2001. The bonds are callable after 1987. If interest rates were to decline to 5½ percent by 1987, ITT could call in the issue. To obtain the funds to repay the bondholders, it could sell a new issue of bonds at 5½ percent. Thus ITT would save three percentage points each year on the interest on $100 million, or $3 million a year. For the fifteen years from 1987 to 2002 the total savings would be $45 million.[4]

Convertible bonds

Another way for a corporation to pay off bonds is to repay them with stock rather than with money. *Bonds that may be paid off with stock* are called **convertible bonds.** The actual decision to accept stock or money is left up to the bondholder. For example, several years ago Philip Morris sold an issue of $1,000 denomination bonds with a coupon rate of 6 percent and a maturity date of 1994. A purchaser would receive $60 a year and get back the original $1,000 loan in 1994. The bonds were convertible, so that the bondholder could exchange each bond for approximately seventy-two shares of common stock in Philip Morris, the equivalent of just under $14 a share. When the bonds were first issued, the common stock was selling at about $12 per share, giving a *conversion premium* of about $2, or just under 17 percent. The price of the stock went up to $50 per share in a few years. At that point, a bondholder might well have decided to convert a bond into seventy-two shares, which could then be sold for $3,600. Because convertibles offer investors a bet on the company's future as well as a firm debt arrangement, they are often called debt with an "equity kicker." These issues become extremely popular when debt markets sag and require a kicker (as in 1980) or when investors want a steady stream of income but are attracted by an upswing in the stock market (as in 1983).

TAX-FREE BONDS

Another category of bonds, known as **tax-free bonds,** *enables an investor to earn an income that is legally exempt from federal income taxes;* some issues are also free from state and local taxes. This feature is an extremely attractive one: for federal income tax purposes, a tax-free yield of 6 percent is the equivalent of a 12 percent yield from a regular corporate bond, if the investor is in the 50 percent personal tax bracket.

The traditional source of tax-free investment income has been the **municipal bond,** *issued by a town, city, state, port authority, territory, or the like, and used to finance new public services such as housing, schools, roads, hospitals, or power plants.* Municipal bonds' most important characteristic is that the interest they earn is exempt from federal income taxes—something *not* true of federal bonds, or (as of this writing) of savings certificates. Nationwide, new municipal bond issues totaled over $7.5 billion in 1983.[5]

Risks of municipal bonds

Municipal bonds are not without risks of their own. When interest rates fall sharply, borrowers are likely to call in their municipal bonds for early redemption, in order to re-fund their debt at a lower cost. Investors who expected to collect high tax-free yields for thirty years may find their principal returned to them in five.

A more serious risk, however, is the prospect of **default**—a bond issuer's *inability to make the agreed-upon payments.* Default is a possibility whether the municipal is a **general obligation bond,** *a bond backed up by the municipality's taxing power* (as with New York City or Cleveland), or a **revenue bond,** *a bond that guarantees repayment only on the strength of the revenues generated by the project being financed.*

The municipal bond market was rocked, for example, by the 1983 default of the Washington Public Power Supply System—known as WPPSS (pronounced "whoops"). The WPPSS bonds had been issued to fund two nuclear reactors, and sales of electricity were expected to generate revenues for repayment. When the plants were only 15 percent completed, however, it became apparent that con-struction costs were mounting much higher than planned funding and that demand for the electricity from the project had vanished, due to the impact of recession on the industries of the Northwest. The project was called to a halt, leaving no source of wealth to repay the bonds other than many cubic feet of concrete in the ground and commitments signed by regional utilities (which then backed out of the agreements). When WPPSS defaulted, investors who had purchased bonds for $5,000 in early 1981 found them worth only $700.[6]

Other tax-free bonds

An interesting variation on the municipal-bond theme is **industrial-revenue bonds.** These bonds are something of a cross between corporation bonds and those issued for purely municipal purposes; they are *sold by cities and states to finance private industrial development in their own localities.* There are no federal taxes on these bonds, and interest on them is often 3 percent lower than the going rate on corporate bonds.

A newer investment alternative is a category of tax-free bonds actually issued by corporations themselves—**pollution-control bonds,** *authorized by Congress in 1968 to help companies keep up to date in environmental technology.*

THE BASICS OF STOCKS

Stocks are, simply, *shares of ownership in a company.* Thus a *purchaser of stock* (or **stockholder**) is also a **shareholder**—in other words, a *part-owner of the business.* The **stock certificate** that a shareholder receives is *evidence of ownership.* Each certificate shows the name of the shareholder, the number of shares of stock owned, and the special characteristics of the stock.

The number of shares of stock that a corporation can sell is based on the amount of equity capital (capital obtained through the sale of stock) the corporation will require and on the price of each share that it sells. One of the largest initial public stock offerings in recent history was the 1983 issue of 8.8

A certificate of common stock

million shares at $19 a share by Gulfstream Aerospace.

The *maximum number of shares into which a business can be divided* is called the **authorized stock.** In theory, all of these shares may be sold at once. What often happens, however, is that the corporation will sell only part of its authorized stock. *The part sold and held by stockholders* is called **issued stock;** *as yet unsold stock* is referred to as **unissued stock.**

Many stock certificates bear a face value, or **par value,** *an arbitrary dollar amount that is usually less than the stock's estimated market value.* As we'll see, the par value may be used as the basis for figuring dividends. Stock that *does not carry a printed dollar amount on the certificate* is called **no-par-value stock.**

Many companies *distribute part of their profits to their shareholders* in the form of **dividends.** Dividends may be paid in cash, but growth-oriented corporations often issue dividends in the form of stock. This conserves the firm's cash for capital investment, research and development, and similar types of cash expenditure.

ECONOMIC FACTORS AND THE STOCK MARKET

Stocks are bought and sold in secondary markets known as **stock exchanges**—*organized systems that allow investors to buy stock from and sell stock to one another.* Most stocks are purchased from other investors, at prices that are determined by the ups and downs of investors' enthusiasm for the stocks, as expressed through the workings of the stock exchange. The value of a stock goes up if investors are willing to pay more for it, and this gain in value goes into the pocket of the present owner of the stock—not the company in which it is a share. (This return on investment falls into the category of **capital appreciation**—*growth in the value of an investment over time*.) Investors base their valuation of a stock on the amount of dividends it pays: by watching changes in dividends, they can make assumptions about the profits the company is making, for it is out of those profits that the company pays dividends. If investors foresee that a company's earnings are likely to increase tomorrow, they will try to acquire shares in that company today, thus bidding up the price of the company's stock.

The coming of the 1982–83 bull market

One of the most important factors in investors' expectations about a firm's future earnings is the expected future economic environment. During the 1970s inflation and tax policy were the major economic problems affecting stocks: these combined to lower the dividends companies could pay, and thus they lowered the value of the stocks themselves. A second set of economic problems, high interest rates and recession, loomed in the early 1980s: these combined to dampen companies' profits and keep their stock values trading low. However, by August 1982, economic indicators had begun to signal a turnaround: inflation had dropped and was now hovering at around 5 percent, and interest rates had taken a sharp dip, with prominent forecasters expecting them to go lower. These factors ignited a major **bull market**—*a sustained rise in stock prices*. Some analysts believed the bull market would last through the decade, as it did in the 1960s; but at the time of this writing the outcome seemed uncertain.

How lower interest rates contributed to the bull market

What exact role did the lower interest rates play in bringing about this change? Lower interest rates make investors expect future profits for many reasons. First, investors are constantly comparing the returns they can earn in the stock market to the returns they can earn through long- and short-term debt instruments. When interest rates fall, bonds and money-market funds become less attractive as alternatives: in comparison with them, the dividends earned in the stock market start to look more attractive. Second, when interest rates fall, consumers are more likely to borrow money to purchase automobiles and houses, and this increase in consumer borrowing sets off a wave of new sales and profits among firms in many related businesses, such as home appliances, furniture, auto-parts suppliers, and the steel, plastics, and services that go into them. Finally, when interest rates fall, corporations spend less money on their interest payments, so that more earnings are left over to be distributed as dividends. Above, we saw how the fall in interest rates led many companies to refinance their short-term debt on a long-term basis. In so doing, these companies provided a double bonus to stock investors: they not only raised their potential profits, but they also lowered the riskiness of their businesses.

New issues

When a company issues new stock, it is offering more slices of the same profit pie, and the amount of money a company can raise for each new slice depends on what the market expects the size of the total earnings pie to be. Not surprisingly, corporations often react to a rise in their share prices on stock exchanges by deciding to issue new stock.

The bull market provoked a flood of new issues—corporations floated $8.7 billion of new stock in the first quarter of 1983, up 378 percent from the levels of the preceding year.[7] Current stock market giants stepped in in a giant way: in late 1982, AT&T's underwriters sold an entire new issue of 8 million shares, valued at just under $500 million, between 4 P.M. one afternoon and 10 A.M. the following morning![8] More important, the mood of the bull market enticed flocks of new ventures to make initial public offerings (that is, to offer their stock to the public), in some cases for very substantial amounts. This trend was quite pronounced, for example, among firms selling software for personal computers. Since the software industry was viewed as being on the verge of a boom, and since it was populated primarily by small privately held firms, investors were anxious to grab any opportunity to participate. In May 1983, Schuchardt Software Systems, a firm with eleven employees still lacking sales or products, was able to raise $1.5 million by issuing shares to the public, and owner Fred Schuchardt watched those shares go on to climb 60 percent in value.[9]

The excitement of the bull market made raising money via stocks a tempting alternative for many companies. Yet it meant an extremely complex decision for those companies—as it does at any time. If a company is considering this option, the company's treasurer must compare the advantages of a new equity issue (assuming, let's say, that the stock market is strong) with the advantages of a new debt issue (say, assuming low interest rates at present, with the prospect of higher rates in the future). Then he or she must decide precisely when to act, trying to determine whether an improvement in either market is merely temporary (a "window"), thus calling for immediate action, or whether it will be a continuing trend, making it advisable to wait while the trend becomes even stronger.

PREFERRED STOCK

A corporation may issue two types of stock. *Preferred stock,* as the name implies, refers to a class of stock that gives its holders certain preferences or special privileges that holders of *common stock* do not have. Preferences vary from one corporation to another. In general, all **preferred stocks** *have preference over common stock in at least two areas:*

1. *They are preferred as to dividends.* Dividends on preferred stocks must be paid before any dividends are paid on common stocks.
2. *They are preferred as to assets.* If a corporation fails, preferred stockholders have the right to receive their share of whatever assets are left (after the corporation's debts have been paid) before common stockholders receive anything.

Some companies issue **convertible preferred stock,** which *gives the shareholder the option to convert preferred into common stock of the corporation.* From the shareholder's point of view, conversion would be desirable if the value of the common stock rose above the value of the preferred. Inclusion of a convertibility clause therefore makes a preferred issue more attractive to prospective buyers. Some companies issue *participating preferred stock,* which allows the preferred stockholders to share with the common shareholders in dividends beyond the fixed dividend rate that is stated on the preferred stock.

How are dividends paid?

The amount of the dividend on a preferred stock is shown on the stock certificate. It can be expressed either as a percentage of the par value or as a dollar amount. For example, Koppers Company has a $100 par value 4 percent preferred stock. Thus, each share of this stock pays a dividend of 4 percent of $100, $4 a year. On the other hand, General Motors $5 preferred pays an annual dividend of $5 a share.

Most preferred stock is **cumulative preferred.** This means that *if a corporation does not pay the designated dividend in one period, the unpaid dividends accumulate.* The company must pay this accumulation before it can pay any dividends on its common stock. For example, the General Motors $5 preferred is cumulative. Let us assume that GM decided not to pay the $5 dividend in 1983 and 1984. The company would not be able to pay any common stock dividends in those two years. It also could not pay any common stock dividends in 1985 until it had paid $15 in dividends on preferred stock ($10 accumulation plus $5 current).

What are the voting rights of shareholders?

Generally it is the common shareholders who participate in company affairs by voting rights on company proposals, as we discussed in Chapter 2. The degree of participation permitted to preferred stockholders is much smaller. In some companies, preferred shareholders have no voting power at all. More commonly, they receive limited voting privileges, usually on matters that directly concern their rights, such as a decision to sell off a major part of the company or to change a provision of the charter that involves the preferred stock.

INTERNATIONAL SUPERGALACTIC LIQUIDATION

BOND HOLDERS LINE STARTS HERE

PREFERRED STOCKHOLDERS LINE STARTS HERE

COMMON STOCKHOLDERS LINE STARTS HERE

Common shareholders can vote on company affairs—they're generally the only investors allowed to do so. But if the corporation goes bust, they're at a disadvantage. They stand in line *after* bondholders and preferred stockholders to receive whatever funds are left after prior claims have been settled.

COMMON STOCK

Like preferred stock, common stock represents equity in, or ownership of, a corporation. Unlike preferred shareholders, however, common stockholders enjoy no special privileges as far as dividends or assets are concerned. The opportunities they offer for financial gain, however, make common stocks attractive to many investors. Owners of **common stock** have *last claim on distributed profits.* Common stockholders also have only a **residual right,** or *last claim on the assets of a corporation if liquidation occurs;* that is, they stand in line after bondholders and preferred stockholders to receive any funds that may remain after settlement of prior claims. This priority order is depicted in the accompanying cartoon.

In general, common stockholders have two sources of return on their investment: dividends and capital appreciation on their investment. A risk of owning common stock is that, because of the residual right, market prices vary much more than prices of bonds and preferred stock. Also, common stock never carries a stated dividend, nor are its dividends cumulative.

Common stock dividends

Fundamentally, the board of directors in charge of the company determines whether or not to give dividends and how much they should be. There is nothing in any law that requires a corporation to distribute to its shareholders any percentage at all of its cash on hand during the normal course of business. Even so, over the years, shareholders in many companies with growing earnings have seen the dividends on their stock soar—and have seen the market value of the stocks grow tremendously as well.

Companies often have legitimate reasons for failing to declare a dividend or keeping the size of dividends at a minimum. In the case of a small, young company, for instance, it's only natural to put all the profits back into the business. By so doing, the company can build and grow while keeping expensive outside financing as low as possible.

Companies are often forced to cut or omit quarterly dividends when a quarter shows sharply reduced profits or even a loss. This happens on a wide scale during recessions, and it is also common when a particular industry has been weakened. In the third quarter of 1983 Mattel Inc.'s board of directors voted to omit the regular quarterly dividend of $7\frac{1}{2}$ cents a share, after the company reported a $156 million loss. The loss was due almost entirely to a decline in sales of the company's video games, which only a year before had been responsible for generating very high earnings and dividends. The firm's stock fell $12\frac{1}{2}$ cents on the stock exchange. The drop was understandable in light of the fact that dividends on common stock are not cumulative; a missed dividend is income permanently lost to the shareholder.[10]

It's usually not until a company is fairly well established that it will declare any dividends at all. As a young company, Control Data Corporation, for example, decided to use its impressive earnings to finance expansion. In the late 1970s it declared a dividend of $.15 a share, which it raised in 1979 to $.40 a share for common stock and $4.50 for preferred. The results of the company's growth strategy were gratifying: sales in 1979 were $3.2 billion.[11] Clearly, caution in the paying out of profits can do much to build up a company. And many investors are willing to forgo current dividends in order to achieve greater returns as the price of their common stock appreciates.

Stock splits

A dividend is not the only benefit a corporation can offer its shareholders. An increasingly popular alternative is a **stock split,** a procedure whereby the *company doubles (or triples, or whatever) each share in the business that each stock certificate represents.* For instance, in 1979 stockholders of IBM approved a four-for-one stock split, authorizing an increase in the number of shares from 162.5 million with a par value of $5 each, to 650 million, with a par value of $1.25 each.[12] In cases like this, if the market price of one new, split share increases, the investor could realize a handsome profit by selling some or all of the split shares.

Investors in Walgreen Company fared well in February 1982: after the company declared a two-for-one stock split that reduced its share value to $23, the stock steadily rose to over $50.[13] Why

should a stock split boost the market price of a firm's stock this way? Indeed, why should investors care whether they own 100 shares at $46 apiece, or 200 shares at $23 each? The reason is that stocks generally trade in "round lots" of 100 shares. Buyers of fewer than 100 shares pay a significantly higher commission. To buy 100 shares at the presplit price costs $4,600—perhaps more than many investors wish to put into one company at a time. If the firm lowers the share price to $23, however, it can put round lots of its shares within the reach of a broader segment of investors. At the same time, management signals its expectation of excellent future prospects: they wouldn't have bothered with the split if they thought the firm's trading price was going to fall on its own. Stock splits are common during bull markets, when firms see their share values drift upward.

A stock split is different from a stock dividend in that a stock dividend is paid in existing stock whereas a stock split involves the authorization of new stock. Splits benefit the companies as well as the shareholders because the more shares a company has outstanding, the less affected it is by the ups and downs of the market. Splits, too, have the advantage of making undesirable power plays or mergers that much more difficult. The more shares outstanding, the tougher it is for any one individual or group to accumulate a controlling interest in the company.

The attraction of common stock for investors

If a company's earnings decline, dividends on common stock may be reduced or eliminated entirely, and the price of the common stock will probably fall. In such cases, the common shareholders suffer the greatest losses. For example, consider the unfortunate situation of an investor who started 1977 as the owner of $10,000 worth of shares in Eastman Kodak, when the stock was selling at almost $87 per share. Although the company had done well over a long period of time, 1977 was not an especially good year for the camera maker and film processor. It was being challenged by low-priced competing products, both American and Japanese, and it was also being sued for violations of antitrust regula-

STOCKS AND BONDS COMPARED

Stocks differ from bonds in several important ways. The differences may be explained as follows:

1. *Stocks show ownership; bonds show debt.* A stockholder buys part ownership in the company, whereas a bondholder lends money to the company.

2. *No principal is repaid with stocks; principal is repaid upon maturity with bonds.* Stock represents ownership, which continues indefinitely. When a company sells stock, it does not have to refund money to the shareholder at any future time. Bonds, however, have a date of maturity, at which time the company is required to return funds to the bondholder.

3. *Shareholders may receive dividends; bondholders must receive interest.* A shareholder is not legally entitled to any regular payments. It is true that many companies distribute part of their profits as dividends to their shareholders. The board of directors of the company decides whether dividend payments will be made. Generally the board cannot be sued if it does not pay a dividend, but it can if it misses an interest payment on a bond. Because bonds represent debt, a company has a legal obligation to pay the stated interest on them at regular intervals.

4. *Dividends are paid, if at all, after taxes; interest on bonds is paid out before taxes.* Under the present tax laws of the United States, the money that a company pays out in stock dividends is treated quite differently from the interest payments on its bonds. Say a corporation earns $2 million in a year. Given a corporate federal income tax rate of 46 percent of net earnings over $100,000, the corporation would have only about $1 million available for dividend payments. Interest on bonds, however, is paid out before a corporation pays its income tax. A corporation earning $2 million a year would have this entire amount available for interest payments.

5. *Stockholders have a say in running the company; bondholders do not.* Under most circumstances, as long as bond interest and other requirements are being met, bondholders have no management rights. They do not participate in the election of boards of directors. In contrast, participation in the management of a corporation is the right of stockholders. They exercise this right by voting for the board of directors.

---

tions. Investors' confidence in the company decreased, the demand for its stock fell off, and stock prices fell as well—to a low of just under $49. By the year's end the worth of the block of shares had fallen about 40 percent; an investment originally worth $10,000 had shrunk to a value of $6,000.[14]

While spectacular losses are always possible with common stock, so are spectacular gains. And it's for this reason that many investors are drawn to common shares rather than preferred shares. They are also attracted because owning common stock guarantees the investors at least some voice in company affairs. Investors can participate in the selection of the company's management personnel at the annual stockholders' meeting, for example. Occasionally, they speak out on more dramatic issues, as we mentioned in Chapter 2.

OTHER APPROACHES TO LONG-TERM FINANCING

Although most firms rely on stocks and bonds for the majority of their long-term financing, other sources of long-term capital are available. One of these, leasing, has grown so popular over the past decade that it now represents a considerable proportion of all the financing that companies use for acquiring new equipment.

As an alternative to borrowing and buying, a firm wishing to obtain the use of a major piece of equipment can enter into a **lease,** *a legal agreement between the owner of the equipment or asset (the lessor) and the individual using the equipment or asset (the lessee).* Under a **financial lease** *(a long-term, noncancelable lease),* the lessor (usually a bank or a finance company such as General Electric Credit Corporation) makes the purchase for the company that needs the equipment (the lessee), and provides the use of that equipment in exchange for monthly payments over an agreed number of years. At the end of the lease period, the equipment usually belongs to the lessee. Under an **operating lease,** *a short-term lease agreement that is cancelable under certain restrictions,* the lessor provides much more than just financing. IBM uses operating leases as one of its primary sales tools— the company supplies its customers with training and maintenance for their IBM computers, and it also gives the customers a way to easily dispose of their old models when the next generation of gadgetry becomes available.

Why would a firm prefer to lease rather than borrow and buy? If a company buys a piece of equipment, it will be allowed an investment tax credit: it can make a deduction from its profits before those profits are taxed. Suppose, however, a company is not having a good year, and it has no profits. In this situation, an investment tax credit would do it no good because it has no taxable profits. Instead, it leases the piece of equipment; the lessor (bank or finance company), being a profitable company, can as legal owner of the equipment take the credit against its own income tax, and pass some of those savings along to the lessee in the form of lower lease payments.

Leasing may also be a good alternative for a company that is a bad credit risk and has difficulty obtaining loans. Creditors are more willing to provide a lease than a loan because, should the company fail, the lessor need not worry about a default on loan payments; it can simply repossess the equipment that it legally owns. Some firms use leases to finance up to 35 percent of their total assets, particularly in industries such as airlines where assets are composed primarily of large pieces of equipment.

LEVERAGED BUYOUTS

Another special-purpose arrangement for long-term financing is the **leveraged buyout,** a financing setup in which *the original owners of the business (the equity owners) are bought out by a new group of owners using large amounts of borrowed capital.* Leveraged buyouts are used by individuals and companies

seeking to purchase an ongoing business from its existing owners. The financer, often a company that specializes in leveraged buyouts, advances funds against the assets of the new company. As the recession-battered profits of the 1980s force many companies to reconsider the overzealous acquisitions of ill-fitting business lines that they made in the 1970s, leveraged buyouts have become increasingly popular as a way companies can sell off their "nonperforming" divisions. Often the buyer is not another company, but a group of current managers of the operations, who put their own funds at risk as well.

Today's entrepreneurial managers are actively browsing for leveraged buyout candidates. William Flaherty, a former executive vice-president of Gulf & Western's Natural Resources Group, anticipated that his firm would want to divest itself of its subsidiary, New Jersey Zinc. He lined up a group of private investors (including five New Jersey Zinc managers) and a finance company, and won approval of his offer from Gulf & Western management. As often happens, the new entrepreneurial owners ran a tighter ship than the corporate owners, and the firm was able to operate on less working capital. The firm was soon in the black, and paid off its loans ahead of schedule. If, for any reason, the firm had fallen into financial disarray, the terms of the leveraged buyout agreement stated that the lender would have had recourse to the firm's assets—valuable zinc deposits in the ground.[15]

LIMITED PARTNERSHIPS

The limited partnership is another example of a long-term capital arrangement that is highly attractive under specific circumstances and that relies on details in the tax laws to bring down the cost of funds. The **limited partners** *provide equity capital to a firm, but* (unlike full or general partners) they *are not personally liable for the firm's losses beyond their equity contribution.* They can, however, show their share of the firm's losses in their personal income tax calculations, thus lowering their taxable income, which makes this a very attractive way to invest their savings. The limited partnership arrangement is sometimes used where the venture being financed is highly risky (oil drilling, movie making, real estate development)—where success could mean enormous returns, but large losses are not unusual.

There's something unusual about this person—Dustin Hoffman made up as Tootsie, the main character in Hoffman's funny and thought-provoking film about an out-of-work actor who lands a (female) part on a soap opera. *Tootsie* was a classic example of the limited partnership: a good but risky idea (Hoffman's) was teamed up with money from many partners, each of whom had limited liability and put in no more than he or she was willing to lose. Though most of *Tootsie* was owned by Columbia Pictures, 35 percent of it belonged to the Delphi I group, a $60 million limited partnership with many members investing as little as $5,000 each. Such ventures, particularly in movieland, often yield only tax-shelter advantages to hopeful investors. But *Tootsie* made nice profits too: it brought in $160 million in six months.

CHOOSING AMONG FINANCING OPTIONS

As we have seen, a corporation seeking long-term finance has three major options—using internal funds, selling debt securities, or selling equity securities—and a number of minor options. Often, the costs of the various financing alternatives differ sub-

stantially from each other, and so a company must weigh the choices carefully. Of course, these alternatives are not mutually exclusive. For instance, when American Motors needed money to retool, it chose to sell common stock *and* borrow long-term *and* sell off some assets.

BONDS: PROS AND CONS

Given a choice, many managers would prefer to raise money through the sale of bonds. Bonds have a number of advantages. First, they represent the cheapest type of financing. Because bond interest comes out of pretax dollars, the company does not have to earn nearly as much to pay interest on bonds as it would to pay the same amount in dividends on stock. Second, because bondholders do not have any voice in management, there is no loss of control. And finally, the sale of bonds has no effect on stockholders' rights to residual earnings. Once the interest on the bonds has been paid, common stockholders do not have to share company earnings with bondholders.

Against these advantages, the company must weigh the one major disadvantage of bonds: their high risk factor. A company that sells stock to obtain financing can survive a few bad years simply by omitting dividends. But the company that can't meet bond-interest payments could be forced into bankruptcy by its bondholders.

STOCK: PROS AND CONS

The sale of preferred stock is an attractive way of getting financing. It generally leaves control in the hands of the common shareholders and preserves their residual rights. It is also much less risky than the sale of bonds. Dividend payments to preferred shareholders are not legal obligations, and unlike bondholders, preferred stockholders do not have to be repaid at some future date. However, preferred stock is a relatively expensive way of raising money because dividends are paid with dollars that remain after the company has paid its federal income taxes.

What about financing through common stock? This method carries some of the same advantages and disadvantages as financing through preferreds. On the one hand, it is riskless; on the other hand, it is expensive. There are two additional disadvantages to raising new money through the sale of common stock. When new common stock is sold, the original stockholders are forced to share both their control of the company and their rights to future residual earnings with the new stockholders. This is referred to as dilution of control and dilution of earnings.

THE IMPACT OF MARKET CONDITIONS ON FINANCING CHOICES

At any given time, the choices available to a company seeking long-term capital are limited by the state of the stock and bond market and the general economic climate, including the federal government's *fiscal policy*—its choices of action with regard to spending and funding.

For example, in 1981, President Reagan's Eco-

FIGURE I

STOCKS VERSUS BONDS: HOW TWO TANDY INVESTORS FARED
Annual returns of a Tandy Company stock investment and a Tandy bond investment (in percent), 1977–1983

Here's how two investors in Tandy would have fared—one investing in bonds, the safer but usually somewhat less profitable course, and the other investing in stocks, the riskier but potentially very profitable course. As you can see, Tandy stock was up every year except 1977. The peaks in 1978 and 1980 were due to investors' response to exceptionally successful operating results; due to investors' enthusiasm, the stock split in both these years. Bonds did not do as well as stocks overall, although they outperformed stocks in 1977 and 1982, when interest rates fell.

How do you figure the annual return of an investment vehicle? You take whatever gain in price the vehicle has experienced during the year (if you sell at the end of the year, this gain is part of your profit), and you add whatever dividends the vehicle has paid during the year (these dividends are "gravy" for you too). You express this total—price gain plus dividends—as a percentage of the price you paid for the stock at the beginning of the year. Say, for example, you had bought Laughco at $100 in January and sold it the next year for $115, and it had paid a dividend of $3. The price gain ($15) plus the dividend ($3) would equal $18, which would be 18 percent of your initial investment (before taxes); so the annual return would be 18 percent.

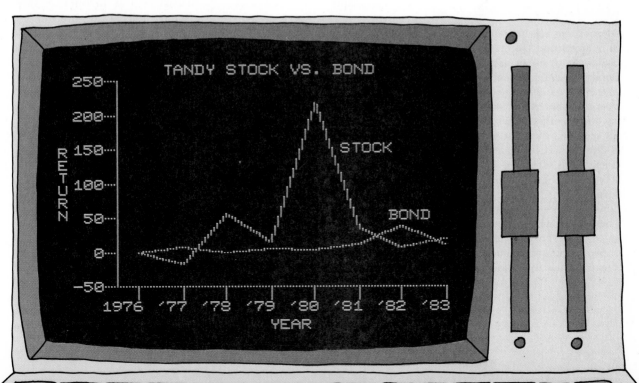

nomic Recovery Tax Act sought to increase the supply of savings and investment by taxing it less (this policy reflected part of Reagan's "supply side economics" philosophy). In addition to making an across-the-board cut in individual income tax rates, the Economic Recovery Act significantly lowered taxes on capital gains, on savings for individuals' retirement, and on many types of savings and investment done directly by companies. These changes in fiscal policy were designed to give individuals more incentives to keep their money in banks and in stocks and bonds, thus assuring a plentiful supply of capital to business. What is plentiful becomes less expensive, and thus this fiscal policy was expected to lower interest rates.

GOVERNMENT BORROWING The other side of the tax-cut picture, however, is that the government will have less money to spend, and if it doesn't cut its spending plans an equal amount, it may be forced to borrow. The government can borrow in capital markets somewhat the same way a corporation does: it issues financial vehicles of various maturities and sells them to investors. Because the government's "credit rating" is very high, investors find government securities (treasury bills, notes, and bonds) a very attractive investment, and thus the government can acquire funds at a somewhat lower interest rate than other borrowers. The problem is that when the government's borrowing needs increase (because tax collections have fallen, for example, or because spending has risen due to recession or war), it must offer a higher interest rate in order to attract more funds. This will lead businesses and consumers to compete with the government for loans, by raising the interest rates *they* offer to investors. (Consumers may find, for example, that banks are offering them higher interest rates for time deposits of various maturities.) Everyone pays higher interest rates, but this may not be sufficient incentive for people to save more. If the amount of savings in the economy remains relatively fixed, then as government borrowing increases, less capital is left over for loans to private borrowers. As economists say, government borrowing "crowds out" private borrowing.

CHAPTER REVIEW

Corporations raise long-term capital from outside sources. Such capital can be either debt capital (bonds) or equity capital (stock). In the early 1980s high interest rates contributed to a slump in the bond market, which traditionally has been the most secure way to finance. Floating-rate and index bonds offered a way out; other expedients—including deep-discount, zero-coupon, and "junk" bonds—came into use. The stock market remained very active, however, particularly with respect to new companies formed to exploit new technology.

In 1982 the decline of interest rates brought a flood of new bond and equity issues as well as many new stocks. The 1982–83 bull market also greatly increased the demand for and ownership of these instruments.

A bond is evidence of a debt. The corporation issuing the bond has borrowed money from the bondholder. Corporations also sell stocks, which represent ownership in the corporation.

Preferred shareholders have precedence over common shareholders in the payment of dividends and the liquidation of the firm's assets if the firm goes out of business. The voting power of preferred shareholders is generally limited. Common shareholders normally participate in the management of the company by electing the board of directors. Their right to the residual income of the corporation offers potential for high earnings, either through future dividends or through appreciation in the market value of the stock.

Other approaches to long-term financing include leasing, leveraged buyouts, and limited partnerships.

REVIEW QUESTIONS

1. Define *debt capital* and *equity*.

2. What is a bond? Explain the difference between secured bonds and unsecured bonds (debentures).

3. What have been the effects on business financing of upheavals in the bond market during recent years? Of government fiscal policy?

4. Define stocks and dividends. What advantages does preferred stock offer an investor over common stock?

5. Define and explain leveraged buyouts, limited partnerships, and leasing.

6. What is a stock split?

7. What is the attraction of common stock for investors?

8. Suppose a corporation wants to raise a large sum of money to finance the purchase of equipment. What factors should enter into the choice of a method of long-term financing for this use?

9. Explain the advantages of deep-discount, zero-coupon, and "junk" bonds.

CASE 1

OFF-PRICE RETAILERS GO PUBLIC

Off-price retailing is a new and booming phenomenon, as we noted in Chapter 12. Many off-price merchandising chains blossomed overnight from family-owned outlets. And in mid-1983, three family firms cashed in on their companies' astronomical market values by going public. The Jaffe family received $17 million for their 66-unit "Dress Barn"; one short month later, the 31-unit Burlington Coat Factory Warehouse Corporation brought in $66 million for the Milstein family; and then Sy Syms Merns raised $44 million, in exchange for 3 million newly issued shares of stock in the Syms Corporation.

It is no coincidence that these and other off-pricers chose this time to cash in on the value they had amassed. The off-price industry is "hurtling toward maturity at a record pace," according to the National Retailing Merchants Association. In 1983 off-pricers accounted for 6 percent of the clothing sold in the U.S., but off-pricing was growing faster than any other segment of the retailing business. One analyst of retail investments predicts that off-pricing will grow by about 15 percent a year during the next five years, tripling in value to $20 billion by the end of the decade.

Some manufacturers still call off-price retailers "undertakers" because of the particular role off-pricers play. Manufacturers routinely work 18 months ahead, ordering fabrics according to their expectations of demand. Sometimes, however, the manufacturers then find they are not receiving enough orders from traditional retailers to sell their merchandise at full value. When this happens, the manufacturers are faced with a choice: they can either shut their factories and sell the fabric at a great loss, or produce garments and sell them to off-pricers at cost. The off-pricers thus gain a significant cost advantage. They do not order in advance; instead, they take what's left after full-price orders are handled.

But what happens to the off-pricers if times are good for the manufacturers and there's no excess output waiting for the off-pricers to "undertake"? Off-pricers faced considerable risk as the recession of the early 1980s ended. Perhaps that is why the stock of these newly public firms has remained flat since they went public. Sy Syms Merns, pioneer off-pricer who began discounting in 1959, has two solutions to the problem. First, he is counting on the longevity of his relationships with manufacturers: he hopes they'll continue supplying him when it's his turn to be on the short end of the economic stick. Second, he's hedging his bets. Syms has given new meaning to the word "diversification," by purchasing a chain of super-luxury apparel stores, A. Sulka & Company, a 90-year-old London haberdasher. Sulka sells high-margin, high-overhead items such as $2,500 silk-lined cashmere dressing gowns.

What will these successful retailing families do with their stock-market bonanzas? Some are using the new funds to expand their businesses further. They maintain control over day-to-day operations by retaining large shares of the company stock themselves. Others are using public stock sales to wind down their financial and operational role in the company—perhaps to move to an island in the Caribbean.[16]

1. What do you think will happen to the stock of the off-pricers in the future?

2. Would you have advised another off-price retailer to go public a year later, in the spring of 1984? If not, what other methods of obtaining long-term financing would you suggest to a person in this business?

3. Do you think these families will be able to retain control of their companies? Why or why not?

CASE 2

LEVERAGED BUYOUTS IN GLAMORLAND

A group of executives at Metromedia, Inc. got together to borrow $1.3 billion and buy a company. They weren't planning to change jobs, however; they bought the company they already worked for. After this record-sized "leveraged buyout," Metromedia's top management will report to themselves instead of to shareholders.

Managers buy out their companies for all sorts of reasons. They may want to buy control from the retiring founder; or they may want to take advantage of gains from tax quirks. Often they are spun off from a large conglomerate that is no longer interested in handling the smaller unit's product line or supporting its losses. But almost universally, it seems, companies earn more money after they are owned by their managers, even though the cast of characters hasn't changed. Some speculate that Chairman Kluge took Metromedia private because he tired of watching the company's stock go up and down: in 1983, the stock bounced between $20 and $57 per share. (Kluge offered $40 per share for it.)

It wasn't difficult for Metromedia's managers to come up with financing for the deal. Leveraged buyouts are becoming increasingly popular. Institutions such as insurance companies and pension funds have been lured by reports of returns exceeding 50 percent. Prudential, the biggest player in deals of this kind, has invested $2 billion in the stocks of more than 100 companies that have been bought with huge leverages. New funds are even being organized to help investors find leveraged-buyout opportunities. Even traditionally cautious bankers have been providing "10-year money"—loans with much longer terms than the loans banks usually make for investment purposes. The bankers' confidence has been sparked by observing the couple of hundred leveraged-buyout deals that worked during 1982–83. Nevertheless, these leveraged-buyout companies have yet to prove themselves five or ten years down the line, and appraisals of their market value once they are public are purely speculation.

There are a number of dangers in leveraged buyouts. Some observers fear that the rush of enthusiasm will bid up prices for the limited number of management buyouts, and will allow these companies to take on more debt than they can handle. Typically, the companies that are bought out in these transactions wind up with long-term debt that accounts for nearly 90 percent of their total capital. This is about three times the proportion of debt that most corporations would consider prudent, and in a sense, leveraged buyouts seem to go against the rules of economic sanity. Such a load of debt puts a huge strain on a company's cash flow. It *must* generate enough revenue each month to repay the interest that has been agreed upon. It loses the privilege of simply cutting dividends in bad times, as public companies do.

How will Metromedia come up with the cash to pay the mortgage? It is counting—some say gambling—on its bid to become a part-time fourth network, as well as a major force in the new cellular-radio (car-telephone) business. But achieving these goals will not be easy. Programming costs will be expensive if Metromedia is to woo audiences from the established networks. And in the cellular-radio market, Metromedia faces intense competition, as well as the heavy up-front development costs that confront any new product. Thus, Metromedia is defying a cardinal rule of leveraged buyouts: avoid businesses with heavy cash-flow needs. The company's future cash flow is all that creditors have to count on

for loan repayment. Though the creditors may have formal liens on the company's assets, what will investors be able to do with a roomfull of used TV cameras? And does Metromedia really possess $1.3 billion worth of such equipment?

Metromedia shareholders have agreed that they will accept part of their stock dividends in cash, and part in an IOU that will not pay interest for the first five years. After that, this debt instrument will pay 16 percent interest. With this creative financing proposal, Chairman Kluge is getting the new company off to a healthy start, and giving it a good chance to make it.[17]

1. If you were a manager at Metromedia, would you want to be one of the buyers of the new company? Remember: since there will be so few owners to divide up the profits, the returns may be enormous.

2. On the other hand, though Metromedia's equity is only a small slice of the company's total capital, and your share is a mere sliver of that capital, your share may represent your life savings. What are your chances of losing it?

THE STOCK MARKET 15

Back when Wall Street got its name, it was a narrow path along which a barrier had been erected as a defense against the Indians who were native to Manhattan. Today, Wall Street represents the very core of the capitalist system: Wall Street is the home of the New York Stock Exchange (NYSE), the busiest and most important marketplace for the securities of the world's leading companies. Amid the littered floors and noisy calls of the floor traders, in excess of 159 million shares were traded on January 4, 1984. Average volume for the first quarter of 1984 was about 105 million shares, but trading volumes in excess of 110 million shares per day are not uncommon.

Securities markets such as the NYSE perform a number of helpful services for American businesses. They provide investors with a place where stocks can easily be bought and sold; they supply an investment outlet for private and corporate funds; they provide a means for industry to obtain some of the capital it needs to expand, to create additional jobs, and to supply new products and services. We'll study the inner workings of securities markets in this chapter and talk about how they have changed in recent years.

CHAPTER FOCUS

After reading the material in this chapter, you will be able to:
- distinguish stock exchanges from over-the-counter markets
- describe how automation is affecting securities markets
- discuss how a stock purchase is made
- distinguish margin trading, short selling, and options trading
- name at least three techniques for predicting trends in the stock market
- use the newspaper to gain statistical knowledge about stocks and bonds
- define mutual funds, and describe several types of such funds
- describe the role of commodities markets and financial futures
- cite the major regulations affecting securities trading

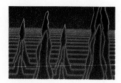 In August 1982 the Dow Jones Industrial Average (a stock market composite measure based on the stocks of thirty major industrial firms) stood in the 700s. By the following June it had risen to a record-breaking 1,248—a 61 percent increase. On November 3, 1982, the market scored its biggest one-day gain ever (up 43 points), and also broke the all-time record for the index (1,051) set a decade earlier. Record volumes for a single day's trading were set day after day in January 1983 (just under 150 million shares).[1] Individual Americans, who had shied away from investing in the stock market since the 1960s, returned in droves. Twenty-five percent more Americans now own stock than in the mid-1970s; and three-quarters of this gain is accounted for by investors under thirty-four years old. The 32 million Americans who own stock saw the total value of their investments jump by $1.5 billion over this period.[2]

The bull market was in part a symptom of the nation's recovery from the recession it had been struggling with in 1981–82. Stocks had become a more attractive investment as investors became more confident that inflation was under control, corporate profits were rising, and unemployment was falling. Stocks looked particularly good in comparison with long-term debt (bonds) and short-term debt (money market funds), as the interest rates investors could earn by investing in these other securities fell from their early-1980s peak. The stock market also gained energy in late 1983 and early 1984 from the breakup of AT&T, the phone company.

Some of these overall trends had begun to change by mid-1984, and it was not clear where the bull was headed: dampening factors such as continued unemployment and the looming $200 billion federal deficit *could* turn the energetic bull into a bear.[3] Yet the market was still very attractive to corporations scurrying to raise new equity capital while their share prices were still high: 1982 had seen an all-time record of $63.0 billion in new equity offerings made by U.S. corporations, and the record was topped in 1983, with $97.3 billion in new offerings.[4] All these companies were still eager to take advantage of the convenience and efficiency of today's securities markets.

SECURITIES MARKETS: STOCK EXCHANGES AND THE OTC MARKET

Securities markets are *the marketplace wherein investors can conveniently invest in stocks and bonds.* They provide investors with a convenient means of disposing of their stocks and bonds as well as purchasing new ones. They operate amazingly fast—the New York Stock Exchange boasts that once the order to sell has been placed, it can take less than one minute to dispose of a stock such as IBM. Contrast this with an investment in real estate—which can take months or years to dispose of—and the usefulness of securities markets is readily apparent.

The most important marketplaces for the stocks of the largest corporations in the United States are the stock exchanges. A **stock exchange** is an *organization whose members join together and provide a trading room where members can meet to buy and sell securities for their customers.* Stock exchanges provide a key service: they organize all the information that exists, at any one moment, about the prices at which investors are currently willing to buy and sell particular stocks. Thus, the stock exchanges save investors and their brokers the trouble of shopping around. (It should be noted that stock exchanges do not hold an inventory of stocks for sale; they are merely a place for matching a buyer with a seller.)

But there is also another very important kind of marketplace for stocks and other securities—the **over-the-counter (OTC) market.** In this market there is no single trading floor where transactions occur. Instead, the market consists of *a network of about 250,000 registered stock and bond representatives scattered across the country, who trade with each other by telephone or teletype.* They provide stocks to their customers by holding stocks in inventory. They also stand ready to purchase stock from their customers (at a price of the dealers' choosing), and thus they are said to "make a market" in that stock.

AMERICAN AND FOREIGN EXCHANGES

The New York Stock Exchange (NYSE) is the largest of the nine stock exchanges now operating in the United States. It accounts for about 81 percent of

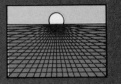

THE HIGH-TECH HORIZON

HOME BROKERAGE SERVICES

To woo the small investor, stock brokerage firms have been making intensive efforts to deliver services that appeal to every taste. E. F. Hutton, the nation's second largest brokerage firm, has probably gone furthest in appealing to the gadget fan, as well as to the person who has an insatiable need for details about his or her portfolio. Hutton is now offering a home brokerage service that enables home computer owners or videotex subscribers to log on to their brokerage accounts, find out how their investments have done today, and calculate their worth at this very minute. Also available are dividend information, a listing of every transaction in the account in the previous thirty days, and data on checks and deposits cleared through the customer's E. F. Hutton cash management account.

Furthermore, for $17 a month, "Huttonline" customers enjoy use of an electronic mailbox, which they can use to type in messages asking their broker's advice, or to communicate instructions to buy, sell, or transfer funds between accounts. (Orders cannot be transmitted directly to the market, however.) This electronic mailbox service could allow investors who have insomnia or work the night shift to do all their money management at 3 A.M. Investors can also use the electronic mailbox to receive messages from their brokers—a great boon to brain surgeons and airline pilots who can't be phoned at work, but still want to be informed of investment opportunities that appear throughout the day.

Is "Huttonline" a step toward replacing the broker with a machine? No, say the system's planners; a better informed investor is likely to invest more often. Hutton will be letting Hutton-employed machines do what machines do best (namely, transmit information efficiently), thus leaving Hutton-employed humans more time to do what *they* do best—here, enhancing the broker-client relationship. Brokers will waste less time on routine phone calls, and customers will be happier and more active—all of which adds up to higher profits for Hutton. Hutton's advantage is not expected to last for much longer than a year, however. Soon, other financial giants such as Merrill Lynch, American Express, and even Sears are expected to enter the fray with their own home brokerage services. Home brokerage is particularly attractive for discount brokerages, which earn their living only by putting through transactions quickly, not by giving out advice.

All this competition will probably mean that more services will be made available to customers. Firms may offer bill-paying arrangements, telecommunicated securities research, and lower usage fees; ultimately, they may even offer electronic links that hook up the customer directly to the market, bypassing brokers altogether.

SOURCE: "Hutton's Head Start in 'Home Brokerage,'" *Business Week,* June 13, 1983, p. 38.

the trading on all the exchanges. The American Stock Exchange, or Amex, also located in New York City, is the next largest, handling roughly 7 percent.[5] These two exchanges—NYSE and Amex—are sometimes referred to as the **national exchanges.** This is because they *trade primarily in stocks of companies that operate throughout the nation.*

Besides these two national exchanges, there are the regional exchanges. These include the Midwest (in Chicago), Cincinnati, Boston, Pacific Coast (in San Francisco), and Philadelphia exchanges. **Regional exchanges** tend to *trade the stock of companies that do business only in their areas.* For example, the stock of Hollymatic, which makes restaurant equipment, trades on the Midwest Exchange; Pacific Gas Transmission trades on the Pacific Coast Exchange. Some stocks are traded on a national exchange and on several regional exchanges as well. U.S. Steel stock, for example, is traded primarily on the New York Stock Exchange, but it's also available on all the regional exchanges.

There are stock exchanges in all major cities of the world, including London, Paris, Hamburg, Tokyo, and Toronto. The world's oldest exchange, founded in 1611 when the Dutch East India Company sold its shares to the public, is in Amsterdam. Each of these exchanges specializes in the securities of its national companies. However, some U.S. companies that do substantial business abroad now trade on these foreign exchanges (IBM, for example, trades in both London and Tokyo), and some foreign companies (Sony of Japan and Holland's Royal Dutch/Shell) trade on U.S. exchanges.

AUTOMATION AND THE EXCHANGES

How can traders in the over-the-counter, or OTC, market get an up-to-the-minute feeling for the market value of their stock without being in touch with an exchange? The OTC dealers have a nationwide network by which they communicate among themselves the prices at which they transact sales. Originally this record keeping was done by circulating mimeographed price sheets—they were left each morning on dealers' doorsteps. In 1971 this function was automated, and in 1982 the computers of the major OTC dealers were linked into *a nationwide electronic network that communicates OTC trades* 90 seconds after they take place. This electronic trading floor includes not only the price at which the stock was traded, but information on highs, lows, and volume to help traders analyze trends. The system, called the **National Association of Securities Dealers Automated Quotation system,** or **NASDAQ,** may well revolutionize stock trading.

Traditionally, the over-the-counter market has served smaller companies. Today, however, thousands of corporations large enough to be traded on the New York or American Stock Exchange are choosing to remain with NASDAQ. For one thing, a computerized exchange is more in keeping with the philosophy of firms such as Apple, MCI, and Intel. Too, there is the problem that stock trading is like an auction, and being listed on one of the major exchanges puts the firm's shares at the mercy of a single auctioneer. Firms such as Apple, MCI, and Intel prefer the multiple market-makers who work through NASDAQ. NASDAQ's growing importance is reflected in the growth of its total volume: trading volume has ballooned 208 percent over the past five years, compared to 128 percent for the "Big Board," or New York Stock Exchange, and 35 percent for the American Exchange.[6] Most financial publications now report the most active NASDAQ quotes, along with their regular coverage of the major exchanges.

The electronic revolution has also come to the major stock exchanges: in 1982, for example, the New York Stock Exchange's computerized system made it possible to process a record 16.4 billion shares, with the number of trades in a single day soaring as high as 149 million.[7] Yet despite computerization, the stock market is still basically patterned after the old sidewalk exchange that began back in the 1790s, in which salaried clerks had to physically move from place to place, generating a blizzard of paperwork. Many observers believe that such a system is outdated and should be replaced entirely by a sort of "black box"—a huge computer that would be fed all the "bid" and "offer" prices and would spit out trades. This view became popular during the late 1960s, when a large spurt in trading volume caused a flood of errors in processing stock trades. Although today's semiautomated market can handle many times the volume of trades it did in the late 1960s, critics still argue that as volume continues to grow, the system will break down under its burden of paperwork.[8]

The New York Stock Exchange undertook a major automation program in order to address such fears, and in order to respond to the competitive challenge posed as more highly automated exchanges such as NASDAQ, the Cincinnati Exchange, and the private trading rooms of financial institutions lured away the NYSE's business. In the early 1980s, $70 million went into the Big Board to improve efficiency. Trading posts haven't been eliminated, but now computer terminals have replaced the old handwritten ledger book jammed with "buy" and "sell" orders. Electronics now facilitate the matching process, the reporting of floor trades to brokers, and the completion of posttrade paperwork—the stock market's equivalent of check clearing. These improvements are designed to ready the Big Board for 250-million-share days by late 1984, without changing the essential "organized confusion" of the exchange, which has always served it well.[9]

INVESTORS AND INVESTING

The old Monopoly-game image of the "fat cat" investor—a wealthy old man in a frock coat smoking a cigar—no longer holds true. Today, the **institutional investors**—that is, *companies that invest money entrusted to them by others*—are a very important force in the stock market, accounting for almost 65 percent of the daily trading volume on the NYSE.[10] Institutions such as pension funds, mutual funds, and insurance companies employ professional money managers who make stock market decisions for the countless individuals whose money is handled by these large institutions. Because institutions trade such large blocks of shares, their investment outlook has a major impact on market swings and trends. It was the renewed optimism of institutional investors, in fact, that set off the bull market in 1982.[11]

However, the continued strength of that market was sustained by the small investor, who surged back into the stock market in record numbers in early 1983. Today, fully 18 percent of our population owns stock, either individually or through mutual funds, compared to 12 percent of the population in 1975. A survey conducted by the NYSE found that 5 million adults who had never owned shares entered the market in the period from July 1982 to June 1983. The new investor, on average, is female (57 percent), college-educated, in her thirties, living in a city, with a family income just over $30,000. Eighty percent of the new investors put up less than $5,000, and the size of the typical stock portfolio fell from $10,000 in 1975 to $5,000 in 1983.[12] In the first half of 1983, these new investors were not following institutions into the old familiar Big Board stocks; instead, they were seeking out exciting opportunities with the newly issued stock of high-tech firms. Names such as Glaxo Holdings, maker of an anti-ulcer drug, Minicomp, a computer servicing company, and the Merrill Lynch Sci/Tech

Holdings fund attracted eager seekers of high yields. The strength of this trend was reflected in the fact that in 1982 and 1983, the daily volume of trades soared 77 percent on the NASDAQ system and 63 percent on the Amex. This contrasts with a modest 33 percent growth on the NYSE, where institutional investors tend to concentrate their money.[13] (The stocks traded over the counter and on the Amex are typically less established issues that are often too small or too risky to meet institutional investors' objectives.)

HOW INVESTING ACTUALLY WORKS

The first step an investor takes is to select a brokerage house. Next, the investor chooses, or is assigned, an account executive, known as a **stockbroker,** or **registered representative (RR).** The stockbroker is *an expert who has studied extensively in the area of investment practices and has passed a series of examinations on the buying and selling of securities.* The most important stockbrokers are registered with many exchanges—sometimes all nine.

Placing an order

If you wanted to buy or sell a stock on the New York Stock Exchange you would give your stockbroker specific instructions. You could place a **market order.** This means that *the broker will instruct the member on the floor to make the trade almost immediately at the best price that can be negotiated at the moment.* Or you could place a **limit order.** This means *specifying the highest price you're willing to pay if you're buying the stock or the lowest price you will accept if you're selling.* For example, if you enter a limit order to buy 100 shares of AT&T at 54, the member on the floor is not permitted to pay more than $54 a share. If the stock is selling at 54¼ ($54.25 per share) when you place your order, he or she will be unable to buy it for you. It is possible, however, that the stock may later become available at the lower price. At that time your broker will execute your order.

Unless otherwise specified, limit orders are entered for one day only. The brokerage house will try to buy the stock for you at your limit price during that particular day, but your order will expire at the end of the day. If you wish, you can enter an **open order,** which *instructs your stockbroker to leave your order in on subsequent days until you cancel it.*

A customer with special confidence in a stockbroker's ability to judge the trend of market prices may place a **discretionary order,** which *gives the stockbroker the right to judge whether to have the order executed at once or whether to wait for a better price.* In some cases, discretionary orders save the customer money. If the stockbroker's judgment proves wrong, however, and the customer ends up paying more for a purchase or getting less on a sale, he or she can't hold the broker responsible.

For completing a customer's order, the stockbroker gets a commission (which varies with the size of the trade). The **transaction costs** consist of the *commission plus taxes.*

The role of the specialist

The key person in a transaction on the NYSE or the Amex is the **stock specialist,** *an intermediary exclusively assigned to facilitate trading in particular stocks.* Stock specialists keep the market functioning smoothly by buying and selling specific stocks for their own inventory, with their own capital, to smooth out gaps in supply or demand—during periods when sell orders are piling up, but no one is willing to buy without a considerable drop in price; or during times when buy orders outnumber sell orders, but a hefty rise in price is needed to make a sale possible. When the market for a particular stock is smooth, the specialist acts as an auctioneer, helping to match offers to buy at a specific price with offers to sell at a specific price.

SPECIAL KINDS OF STOCK TRANSACTIONS

The basic stock market transaction is a simple buy or sell order, but there are also special variations of these trades.

Margin trading

In **margin trading,** customers do not pay for the stock in full; instead the customers *borrow money from*

MAKING A STOCK PURCHASE

Suppose that Nancy Richards, who lives in Chattanooga, wants to buy some shares of Eli Lilly common stock because she believes that growth prospects for drug companies are good. She has read the listing of New York Stock Exchange transactions that appears daily in her Chattanooga newspaper and knows that Lilly is selling at around $57 a share. She calls her local stock-brokerage firm, Jones & Company, and talks to her broker. Ms. Richards enters a market order to buy 100 shares of Lilly.

The order is telephoned to the Jones & Company clerk on the floor of the New York Stock Exchange. The clerk hands it to the New York Stock Exchange member who is a partner in Jones & Company. This member goes to the Lilly **trading post,** *the specific location on the floor where a particular stock is traded,* and calls out, "How's Lilly?" A specialist in Lilly stock answers, "57 to a quarter." This means that someone is currently bidding $57 a share for 100 shares (or more) of the stock, and that someone else is willing to

The broker receives a call from the customer, who requests that a market order be entered.

HOW IT'S ACTUALLY DONE

Brokers trading with each other.

unlisted stock. Her stockbroker would work through the over-the-counter department of the brokerage. A clerk there would check to see which brokers trade in this stock. Then calls would be placed to several of them, and the clerk would buy the shares at the lowest price quoted. Once the transaction was completed, Richards would be billed for this price, plus commission.

In addition to commissions, there are small costs involved in buying or selling **odd lots,** deals that involve *fewer than 100 shares of stock.* The odd-lot buyer pays 1/8 of a point (or 12.5 cents) more for each share of stock bought. The odd-lot seller receives 1/8 of a point less for each share sold below $55 on the New York Stock Exchange. (The fee goes up to 1/4 of a point for each share selling above $55.) Thus if you were buying ten shares of Lilly at the same time the Richards/Andrews transaction occurred, you would pay $57.25 per share for the stock. The customer selling forty-four shares at that moment would receive only $57 per share.

sell at $57.25. The Jones & Company member could buy the stock immediately for Nancy Richards at $57.25 a share, because hers was a market order. More likely, however, the member will bid 57⅛ for a few minutes, hoping to save a little money.

Meanwhile Doug Andrews, in Palo Alto, California, has decided to sell his 100 shares of Lilly in order to pay his son's college bills for the year. He has phoned his broker, giving him an order to sell 100 Lilly at 57⅛. The Exchange member representing Andrew's brokerage firm reaches the trading post in time to hear the interchange between the Lilly specialist and the Jones & Company member. He hears the Jones member bid 57⅛ for the stock and shouts out, "Sold at 57⅛." The two members initial each other's order slips. *A stock exchange employee called a* **reporter** *makes a note of the trade.* Within minutes the transaction is reported back to the brokerage houses and to the two customers.

The transactions just described involve listed securities. If Nancy Richards wanted to buy over-the-counter stocks, the procedure would differ. Say she wanted to buy 100 shares of American Greetings, an

A clerk calls in an order to a member firm as a broker (left) checks on incoming orders and an ITS operator (right) receives incoming orders from the Intermarket Trading System.

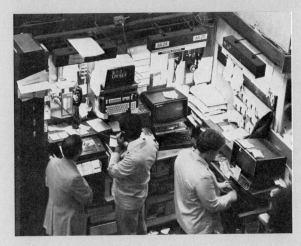

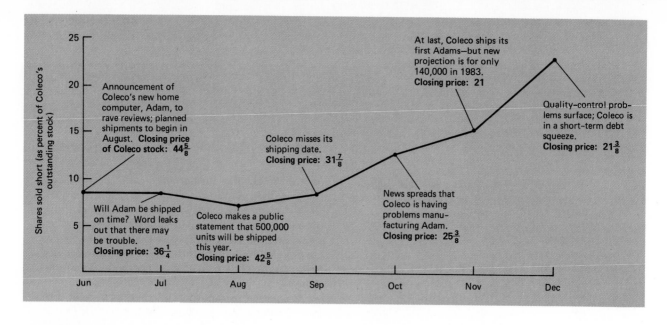

Chart annotations:

Announcement of Coleco's new home computer, Adam, to rave reviews; planned shipments to begin in August. Closing price of Coleco stock: 44 5/8

Will Adam be shipped on time? Word leaks out that there may be trouble. Closing price: 36 1/4

Coleco makes a public statement that 500,000 units will be shipped this year. Closing price: 42 5/8

Coleco misses its shipping date. Closing price: 31 7/8

News spreads that Coleco is having problems manufacturing Adam. Closing price: 25 3/8

At last, Coleco ships its first Adams—but new projection is for only 140,000 in 1983. Closing price: 21

Quality-control problems surface; Coleco is in a short-term debt squeeze. Closing price: 21 3/8

Y-axis: Shares sold short (as percent of Coleco's outstanding stock) — 5, 10, 15, 20, 25

X-axis: Jun, Jul, Aug, Sep, Oct, Nov, Dec

INVESTORS CAN PROFIT FROM COMPANY TROUBLES:
Short-selling in Coleco, 1983

"Sell now, buy later": that's the short-selling philosophy. If investors think a company is in trouble and its stock price is going to drop, they may borrow stock and sell it while the price is high, paying for it later after the price drops. Coleco hit some bumps in 1983 with its new Adam home computer, and as the price of Coleco stock dropped, investors "shorted" more and more shares.

their stockbrokers, paying interest on the borrowed money and leaving the stock with the broker as collateral. Margin requirements (the percentage of the purchase price of the stock that the customer must place on deposit with the broker) are set by the Federal Reserve Board and are periodically changed. Buying on margin enables an investor to use leverage. (**Leverage** is *the use of borrowed funds to finance a portion of an investment.*) For example, an investor with $1,000 could buy only 100 shares of a stock selling at $10 a share. But if the margin requirement were 40 percent, an investor could control $2,500 worth of stock with his $1,000 ($2,500 × 40% = $1,000). Therefore, the investor could buy 250 shares of this $10 stock if he or she were willing to buy on margin. Note that margin trading increases the profit potential because a greater number of shares are owned with the same amount of capital. However, an investor's risk is also increased, since he or she is using borrowed funds to finance a portion of the investment.

Short selling

Short selling involves *selling stock that the customer doesn't own in hopes of buying it back later at a lower price.* Selling a stock short is something an investor who is pessimistic (or, in Wall Street jargon, "bearish") does. Thus, in 1981 an investor who felt that General Motors (then selling at $58) would be hard hit by the recession and would suffer an earnings drop due to its difficulty in selling cars would have sold GM stock he didn't own. By early 1982, GM was down to $34 per share—at which time the investor could have purchased stock on the open market, covering his short position and making $24 a share profit—minus transaction costs, of course.

Selling short is not without its risks. The question to be addressed by an investor who sells short is when to purchase back the stock. If the individual cited above had not covered his short position at $34 a share, but instead had held out in hopes of seeing GM go even lower, he would have been disappointed. In 1982 the economy started to rebound from the recession. By early 1983, GM was selling for over $65 per share. If our investor decided to cover his short position at this point, he would have sustained a $7 loss per share plus transaction costs.

It should be pointed out that someone selling short (selling stock he doesn't own) isn't breaking any laws—he's merely "borrowing" the stock from his broker. At some point he'll have to return it by actually buying the stock.

Options trading

A **stock option** is the *purchased right to buy a specified number of shares (often 100) of a stock at a predetermined price during a specified period of time.* Here we'll discuss two kinds of options.

A **call option** works this way: *the option buyer,* placing money on what's known as a call, *is betting that the price of the stock will rise during the option period.* If it does, then the owner of the option can either buy the shares (which are thus obtained at a bargain price) or sell the option to someone else at a profit.

A **put option** works the opposite way: it *gives its purchaser the right to sell to (or "put to") another investor a block of shares at a fixed price within a specified period of time.* The purchaser of the option is betting that the value of the shares will fall below the specified amount during the option period. If it does, the right of sale can be exercised, allowing the purchaser of the option to get rid of the shares at a price higher than their market value.

TRYING TO BEAT THE ODDS: TECHNIQUES FOR STOCK MARKET PREDICTIONS

A variety of techniques are used for making predictions about the stock market.

Analyzing fundamentals

One tried-and-true method is **fundamental analysis,** *an approach to stock selection that involves careful examination of a company's history, current financial position, and prospects for the future.* Analyzing a company's fundamentals requires careful evaluation of the firm's balance sheet and income statement, making comparisons with benchmarks established by that company in earlier years and by other firms in the industry. It also means digging energetically for clues about the future prospects for the firm's industry and the quality of the firm's management, so that the investor can take advantage of opportuni-

ties that come up. The fundamental analysis method emerged shortly after the stock market crash of 1929, when the most common means of stock selection could have been called the "grapevine method."

Technical analysis

In the 1960s emerging computer technology increased the popularity of **technical analysis,** *an approach to stock selection that searches for patterns in the movement of stock prices.* Followers of this method ignore a company's fundamentals; instead, they try to identify stocks that are about to increase in value by looking at "technical" factors in the way the stock market has behaved—factors that are partly statistical, partly psychological. To do this, they plot a chart of the stock's price at consecutive points in time, and look for patterns such as "support levels" and "resistance points." The analyst will probably recommend purchase of a stock that is currently near the beginning of the upswing portion of a pattern, or has just broken through a resistance point. He or she will probably recommend selling a stock that has just broken through a support level, or is showing signs of a downswing pattern.

Many technical market analysts (sometimes called *chartists*) grew prominent after making large sums of money in the market. But other researchers, particularly academics such as professors of finance, have strongly challenged this approach. Some challengers have shown that if you made a graph of the tosses of a pair of dice, you would get the same sort of patterns that chartists use for predictions. They assert that the technical approach is no more valid than selecting stocks by throwing darts at the financial pages, or having a monkey thumb through them.

The "random walk" theory

Some of these critics point to studies that show that in the past there has been no consistent association at all between firms' earnings and the stock prices of those firms. Stock prices do not follow a predictable pattern: they simply take a "random walk." These critics believe in the **efficient market hypothesis,** the theory *that investors make the stock market highly efficient by rationally assessing all information as soon as it* *is available.* In an "efficient market," they say, investors will bid up the price of a stock to its proper value minutes after good news about the company comes over the wires. So don't run and buy a stock because you hear something exciting about it in a weekly magazine: if you act on stale news, you will always be paying more than a stock is worth. "Random walkers" believe that a "killing" in the market is only made by accident, not for the long run; in their view, the only rational investment strategy is to "buy and hold."

Ways to minimize stock market risk

For the more careful investor, systems have been developed to soften up—if not actually beat—the odds against the investor. The only highly favored method, *hedging,* involves limiting the dollar amount at risk to a given figure. It works like this: Suppose an investor thinks the price of a given stock is going to go down. He sells some of the stock short to make a profit when it falls; but at the same time, to protect himself ("hedge") against the possibility that the stock may go up in price instead, he will buy a call option on some shares of the same stock.

Another approach is to watch for **volatile stocks**—*stocks whose prices have tended to fluctuate drastically*—and avoid buying them. A third investment system is based on the tendency of stock prices to fluctuate in a fairly regular pattern. Called **dollar averaging,** it *involves investing a fixed amount of money in a stock at regular intervals, regardless of the current selling price per share.* Finally, there's the **indexing approach,** in which *the investor studies Standard & Poor's Index* (see p. 406), *notes the proportion in which various stocks are represented, and then tries to accumulate a portfolio in exactly these proportions.*

UNDERSTANDING THE FINANCIAL NEWS

A great deal of investment information is readily available. The media are full of financial news. General, though often scanty, information is available on television news programs. More information is

carried by *The Wall Street Journal,* a financial newspaper published every business day and on sale throughout the country. Weekly magazines such as *Barron's* and *Business Week* can provide valuable insights into the state of the market. In addition, economic, industrial, and company surveys are available from leading banks, from financial service companies such as Moody's, Standard & Poor's, and Value Line, and from individual brokerage houses.

Today, the information source many professional investors rely on most is the computer terminal. At the push of a button, electronic data services such as Quotron, Reuters Monitor, and Telerate can provide the investor with up-to-the-minute data, both on market prices and on world events that can affect investment markets. The price of gold responds instantly to a new outbreak of war; the price of wheat responds seconds after the Department of Agriculture issues a new long-term weather forecast; the price of bonds fluctuates with every straw vote of a congressional tax committee. If markets are indeed efficient today, it may be because instant communications bring such news items to the attention of professional investors immediately.

For the average investor, however, the most convenient source of financial information is probably the local newspaper. It provides statistics of various kinds, including stock quotations and prices of bonds and other commodities. Securities listed are both those sold on the national exchanges and those of local interest. The information, which looks forbidding in condensed form, is not difficult to read once you know how.

STATISTICAL DATA IN NEWSPAPERS

Stocks traded on a stock exchange

Following the day's activities, a listing of trading is prepared by each stock exchange. Most newspapers carry the New York and American stock exchange reports. Many papers also provide a report from a regional exchange.

A sample from a daily newspaper listing and an explanation of how to read it is shown in Figure 1. For any given stock, the information begins with the high and low prices for the last fifty-two weeks, pro-

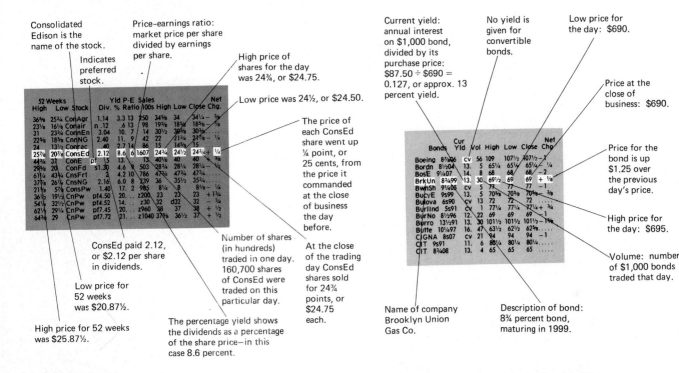

FIGURE I

HOW TO READ A NEWSPAPER STOCK QUOTATION

FIGURE 2

HOW TO READ A NEWSPAPER BOND QUOTATION

ceeds through the number of shares traded, and ends with the net change from the closing price of the day before.

One item of information included is the **price-earnings ratio,** or **p/e** (also known as the **price-earnings multiple**). This is *the relationship between a stock's market price and its earnings per share.* It is computed by dividing a stock's market price by its earnings per share. Say that Acme stock sold for $20 a share last year and earned $2 per share. The price-earnings ratio would be 10:

$$\frac{\$20 \text{ market price}}{\$2 \text{ earnings per share}} = 10$$

If Central stock cost $20 but earned $4 per share, the price-earnings ratio would be 5:

$$\frac{\$20 \text{ market price}}{\$4 \text{ earnings per share}} = 5$$

Central would seem to be a better investment than Acme, since Central's stock costs the same but has higher earnings. However, the price-earnings ratio alone is not a foolproof guide to the best investment. Central's p/e may reflect a lack of investor confidence in the company's prospects. And if the Acme company can be expected to do very well in the future, it may be the better buy despite its current higher multiple. The problem, of course, is that the investor cannot know for certain whether Acme's performance will come up to his or her expectations.

Bond prices

Many newspapers also carry a report of trading that occurred in bonds listed on the major exchanges, as shown in Figure 2. In reading bond prices, remember that the prices bid and asked are given as a percentage of the bond's face value. For example, a

$1,000 bond shown as closing at 65 actually sold at $650.

Prices for over-the-counter stocks

Prices in the over-the-counter markets are determined somewhat differently from prices for securities listed on a stock exchange. Prior to 1971, it was difficult to keep track of the exact prices at which the most active shares were trading because of the number of dealers scattered throughout the country. With the activation of NASDAQ, however, it became possible to call up opening and closing quotations on a screen merely by pressing a button.

The newspapers print the daily **bid price,** *the price at which dealers were willing to buy the stock,* and the **offer price,** *the price at which dealers were willing to sell.* This information appears under the headings "bid" and "asked," as shown in Figure 3. There is a difference between the price information for stocks listed on an exchange and that for over-the-counter stocks. The former represents actual trades, while the latter is merely the price bid and asked at one particular moment.

Stock averages

For a quick summary of the general stock market trends, investors often use **stock averages,** which *describe the overall action of stock market prices.* For example, the Dow Jones Industrial Average reached a record high of 1,287.20 on November 29, 1983. This was an indication that stock prices in general were high and investors were optimistic. Averages are derived by adding the closing prices of selected stocks and dividing by the Dow Jones divisor, a number that is adjusted to reflect stock splits and stock dividends among the stocks in the average.

THE DOW JONES AVERAGES The oldest of the averages are the four prepared by Dow Jones (which also owns *The Wall Street Journal*). The best known is the Dow Jones Industrial, an average of thirty leading industrial stocks, including U.S. Steel, General Electric, Eastman Kodak, and Du Pont. There is also a Dow Jones Utility, an average of fifteen utility stocks; a Dow Jones Transportation, an average of twenty transportation stocks; and a Dow Jones Com-

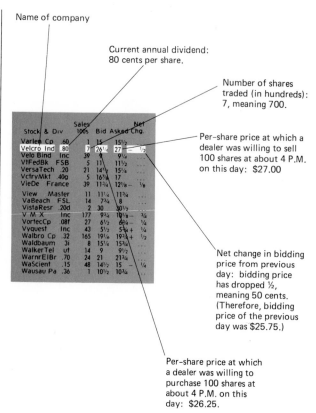

FIGURE 3

HOW TO READ OVER-THE-COUNTER QUOTATIONS IN THE NEWSPAPER

posite, an average of the sixty-five stocks in the other three averages.

OTHER AVERAGES Many people prefer to use two other averages, which include more stocks. These are the Standard & Poor's 500 Stock Average (S & P 500) and the New York Stock Exchange Index, which covers the more than 2,500 common and preferred stocks listed on the exchange.

When the stock market is rising, as it began to do in mid-1982, we speak of a **bull market.** *When it is declining,* as it was in late 1981, we speak of a **bear market.** (The origin of these terms is uncertain, but you can remember which is which by recalling that a bull tosses an attacker upward with his horns while a bear wrestles his downward to the ground.) The various averages do not always move together. In the current bull market, the Dow Jones Industrial Average was up 61 percent, while Standard & Poor's was up 69 percent.

Mutual funds

After a decade-long period of decline, mutual funds have made a tremendous comeback in the 1980s. An estimated $70 billion found its way into the funds in the year following the onset of the bull market—a 61 percent rise. A **mutual fund** (or investment company) is *a company in which many investors pool their money to buy securities*. Each investor owns shares in the fund (just as he or she would own shares in any company), and the fund uses the pooled money to buy stocks or bonds of publicly held companies.

Mutual funds are particularly suited to small investors who don't have the time or experience to search out investment opportunities. They also offer small investors more clout than they would have as individuals in a market dominated by huge institutional trades. Mutual funds offer *diversification*: they provide a broader selection of stocks than the small investor could have bought on his or her own, thus reducing the risk that any one or two may go sour. And they offer *liquidity*: you can turn shares of a mutual fund into cash without paying a broker's commission and without worrying about short-term market conditions that may push down a particular stock just when you need to sell it.

The share price of a mutual fund is its **net asset value,** which is *determined by adding up the value of all of the securities the fund holds and dividing by the number of shares outstanding.* **Load funds,** usually sold by stockbrokers, *require that a sales charge (load) be added to the net asset value.* **No-load funds,** which don't employ salespeople, *have no additional sales charges.* Daily prices for the larger mutual funds are printed in the newspapers, along with any charges the investor would have to pay to buy shares in each fund.

One reason for the rise of mutual funds is the variety of funds tailored to particular objectives. For example, there are tax-exempt mutual funds that buy only tax-exempt bonds; there are high-growth funds that invest only in speculative emerging technology ventures; and there are utility funds that purchase only utility stocks and bonds, offering the individual the security and income of utility securities plus the diversification and liquidity of a fund.

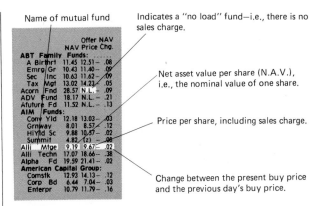

FIGURE 4

HOW TO READ A NEWSPAPER MUTUAL-FUND QUOTATION

Some mutual funds *invest only in short-term securities rather than stocks and bonds,* and are thus known as "money market mutual funds," or more commonly, **money market funds.** These have been the most innovative of all mutual funds, and their spectacular boom in popularity in the early 1980s probably paved the way for the resurgence of the other varieties of funds. (You will read the story of the growth of money market funds, to a peak of $250 billion in assets in 1982, in Chapter D.)

In 1982, when interest rates fell and the stock market rebounded, investors, now accustomed to money market mutual funds, shifted their dollars to stock mutual funds. The excellent performance of these stock funds was a strong selling card: between 1982 and 1983 they rose 77 percent, while the Dow Jones Industrial Average rose only 61 percent.

Commodities

Many businesspeople are interested in the prices of the raw materials they use to produce finished goods. A manufacturer of pots and pans, for example, would closely follow swings in the price of copper; a maker of breakfast cereals must keep track of price trends in wheat, rye, oats, and sugar. These *raw materials,* which are known as **commodities,** are traded on commodity exchanges. (Figure 5 shows a report of spot prices for a partial list of traded commodities.) The commodity exchanges operate just as stock exchanges do—members meet on a floor to trade contracts calling for the delivery of a set

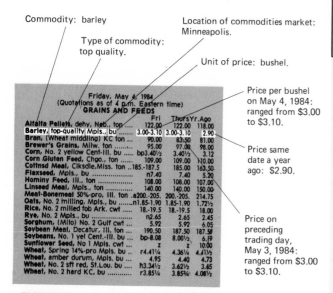

Commodity: barley

Type of commodity: top quality.

Location of commodities market: Minneapolis.

Unit of price: bushel.

Price per bushel on May 4, 1984: ranged from $3.00 to $3.10.

Price same date a year ago: $2.90.

Price on preceding trading day, May 3, 1984: ranged from $3.00 to $3.10.

Friday, May 4, 1984
(Quotations as of 4 p.m. Eastern time)
GRAINS AND FEEDS

	Fri	Thurs	Yr. Ago
Alfalfa Pellets, dehy, Neb., ton	122.00	122.00	118.00
Barley, top-quality Mpls., bu	3.00-3.10	3.00-3.10	2.90
Bran, (Wheat middling) KC ton	90.00	83.50	81.00
Brewer's Grains, Milw. ton	95.00	97.00	98.00
Corn, No. 2 yellow Cent.-Ill. bu	bp3.40½	3.40½	3.12
Corn Gluten Feed, Chgo., ton	109.00	109.00	110.00
Cottnsd Meal, Clksdle,Miss. ton	185.-187.5	185.00	163.50
Flaxseed, Mpls., bu	n7.40	7.40	5.20
Hominy Feed, Ill., ton	108.00	108.00	107.00
Linseed Meal, Mpls., ton	140.00	140.00	150.00
Meat-Bonemeal 50%-pro, Ill. ton	a200.-205.	200.-205.	214.75
Oats, No. 2 milling, Mpls., bu	n1.85-1.90	1.85-1.90	1.72½
Rice, No. 2 milled fob Ark. cwt	18.-19.5	18.-19.5	18.00
Rye, No. 2 Mpls., bu	n2.65	2.65	2.45
Sorghum, (Milo) No. 2 Gulf cwt	5.92	5.92	6.05
Soybean Meal, Decatur, Ill. ton	190.50	187.50	187.50
Soybeans, No. 1 yel Cent.-Ill. bu	bp-8.08	8.00½	6.19
Sunflower Seed, No 1 Mpls. cwt	z	z	10.00
Wheat, Spring 14%-pro Mpls. bu	r4.41¼	4.36¼	4.41½
Wheat, amber durum, Mpls. bu	4.95	4.40	4.73
Wheat, No. 2 sft red, St.Lou. bu	h3.34½	3.62½	3.45
Wheat, No. 2 hard KC, bu	r3.85¼	3.85¾	4.08½

FIGURE 5

NEWSPAPER LISTING OF CASH-TRADING PRICES ON THE COMMODITY MARKET

amount of a commodity at a given time. The Chicago Board of Trade and the New York Mercantile Exchange are two such exchanges.

Some of the trading on the commodity exchanges is *trading for immediate delivery* and is called **spot trading,** or **cash trading,** but most of the trading is *done for future delivery,* often at dates a year or more distant; this is called **futures trading.** While a great many commodity traders are speculators (that is, they neither produce nor consume the commodity they're trading), the original purpose of commodity trading was to allow producers and consumers of commodities to hedge their positions (protect themselves against violent price swings). Thus, a farmer might sell a futures contract calling for delivery of some of the wheat he expects to have grown by harvest time to a baker who expects to use the flour milled from that wheat to bake bread. By selling before the crop is in, the farmer gets operating capital—as well as the assurance that he'll get a certain fixed price for his crop, even if prices collapse later on. The baker, on the other hand, can buy a certain percentage of the supplies he expects to use and be assured that no matter how bad the crop is or how high the price goes, he'll have enough wheat to stay in business.

HOW SECURITIES TRADING IS REGULATED

Since the early days of stock trading, regulation by the various states has had a strong influence on the way stocks have been bought and sold. The first state law was passed by Kansas in 1911, and today almost every state has its own *laws governing securities trading,* often known as **blue-sky laws.** (The name refers to a remark by a Kansas legislator that unless his state passed some effective legislation, promoters would even try to sell unsuspecting investors shares of stock in the blue sky.) State regulations vary. Some require that all securities dealers or salespeople register with the state. Others provide that all new issues of securities must be registered with the state. Almost all include penalties for fraudulent statements or actions in connection with the sale of stocks or bonds.

In recent years, however, the federal government has gradually come to take the leading role in investment regulation. From the depths of the Great Depression to the years of recession at the beginning of the 1970s, Washington has taken a series of steps to make the world of securities more secure.

WHO REGULATES THE STOCK EXCHANGES?

The federal government, through a five-member, presidentially appointed body called the Securities and Exchange Commission (SEC), has primary responsibility for all securities traded in the United States and for every exchange in which they're traded. Established by the Securities Exchange Act of 1934, the SEC is required to receive a detailed annual financial report from all corporations listed on any American stock exchange. The SEC also acts as something of an enforcement agency to make certain that the provisions of the Securities Act, passed in 1933, are upheld.

WHO REGULATES OVER-THE-COUNTER TRADING?

The government has decided to leave over-the-counter traders to their own devices—up to a point.

In 1938 the Maloney Amendments to the Securities Exchange Act established a private trade organization, the National Association of Security Dealers, which is responsible for establishing self-regulated rules and practices. The SEC, however, retains final authority over the over-the-counter traders. Furthermore, 1964 amendments to the Securities Exchange Act require that all over-the-counter companies with assets of more than $1 million and at least 500 shareholders must file comprehensive annual financial reports with the SEC, just as listed companies must do.

WHAT IF A BROKERAGE HOUSE FAILS?

It's been known to happen. In fact, during the late 1960s several major brokerage firms were forced out of business because of financial trouble. The NYSE was obliged to step in to prevent as far as possible any losses to the customers of those troubled firms. Clearly, steps needed to be taken to retain the faith of the nation's investors. To cope with such collapses in the future, Congress passed in 1970 the Securities Investor Protection Act. This act established the Securities Investor Protection Corporation (SIPC), which provides up to $500,000 worth of insurance for each investor who buys and leaves securities for safekeeping with a brokerage house and up to $100,000 of insurance for cash left with a brokerage house. SIPC does not, of course, protect investors against losses from declines in the price of their securities. That would take all the fun out of the game. It merely insures them against losses resulting from fraud or bankruptcy in the brokerage house itself.

HOW CAN AN INVESTOR BE SURE THAT SPECULATIVE INFORMATION IS ACCURATE?

Can the SEC handle the kind of frenzy that occurs in a bull market, when many formerly private companies leap in to sell shares to the public while prices are high? In 1983 just this type of situation developed: a lot of companies wanted to go public, and they generated a flood of registration statements for SEC lawyers and accountants to review and investigate. The problem is, that while we all want the government to guard us against stock fraud, we also tend to favor cutting civil service staffs to a minimum. In the past twenty years, the number of corporate filings received by the SEC almost quadrupled, but its staff actually shrank—and the Reagan budget portends further cuts. The resulting strain has been visible mostly in the increased waiting time the SEC imposes on companies planning an initial public offering. But the regulatory crunch may mean also that some fraudulent issues will inevitably slip by.

Meanwhile, there are other types of potential fraud that keep SEC staffers busy. Among them, insider trading is highest on the list of Reagan-appointed SEC Commissioner John Shad. Any firm's top employees *could* use their insider knowledge of the firm's condition to reap gains in the public market that exists for the company's stock. The law prohibits their doing this. But it is not always easy to track down or even define violations of this law. One significant case involves a former chairman of Atari. Atari's parent company, Warner Communications, announced in December 1982 that there would a sharp decline in expected earnings. Only twenty-three minutes before this announcement—which was about to send the stock plummeting—Atari's former chairman sold 5,000 shares of his stock! He was forced to resign, but the charges against him were ultimately settled by his paying back the $81,875 he allegedly earned, without either admitting or denying that he had done anything wrong.

Somewhat different is the case filed against bankrupt Osborne Computer by nineteen of its shareholders and two of its creditors, most of them influential institutional investors. The plaintiffs are angry because Osborne lost $1 million in 1982, after forecasting a profit of $9 million. (The SEC only recently began to allow, and even encourage, companies to provide forecasts to their investors.) The suit charges that top Osborne managers made a host of illegal efforts to hide the bad news from stockholders while protecting themselves. The case has yet to be resolved, and it is further complicated by the fact that the bankruptcy laws may provide Osborne with a certain amount of protection.

Step right up, folks: the commodities markets are featuring some exciting new attractions. Investors are crowding into the tent to buy and trade financial futures—contracts in debt instruments, stock indexes, even foreign currencies. Options in these futures are also hot.

Financial futures

Besides the traditional commodities—gold, copper, wheat, coffee, pork bellies, and so on—some exchanges also trade futures in financial instruments, including treasury bonds, foreign currency, and loans. Traders in these areas agree to deliver, or accept delivery of, a set amount of bonds, loans, or foreign currency on a set date at a set price. As in the case of actual physical commodities, investors in "financial futures" are betting that the spot price of a financial instrument will either rise or fall. Trading in financial futures began in 1975 when treasury bond contracts began to be sold at the Chicago Board of Trade; quickly, futures trading spread to new types of instruments and new exchanges. The financial futures market is beginning to overshadow trading in agricultural commodity futures: the dollar volume of financial futures trading tripled between 1980 and 1982, while commodities futures trading grew by only 25 percent.

STOCK INDEX FUTURES One of the newest types of financial futures has also become one of the most popular: *stock market index futures*. With this financial instrument, essentially a mythical "market basket" of the stocks that are included in a particular stock market index, you can be assured of doing no worse than the average for the market as a whole. This is good news for investors such as a small school in Lake Forest, Illinois, which turned to index futures after its professional money managers underperformed the market average for two years straight.[14] The Kansas City Board of Trade began selling futures on the Value Line Index in February 1982, and soon other exchanges got into the act with futures on the S&P 500 and the NYSE Composite Index. Trading in stock futures grew so rapidly that it has edged out pork bellies in annual volume on the Chicago Mercantile Exchange, and on some days volume in this "shadow market" exceeds volume on the Big Board.

STOCK INDEX OPTIONS As if investing in financial futures weren't complicated enough, in 1983 many stock exchanges introduced another wrinkle: *options on stock market indexes*—the right to buy or sell a hypothetical portfolio of stocks on a particular index, at a particular price and time. Stock index options instantly became the fastest-growing investment in the country. Through these options, a small initial cash outlays buys command over a sum many times larger, and thus the options provide a quick, cheap path to stock market speculation. But because quite small changes in an index can easily produce dollar losses greatly exceeding the investor's available cash, stock index options are considered a highly risky investment. They are attracting the attention of regulatory bodies, but at this point there is disagreement over whether the index options fall within the jurisdiction of stock market regulators or commodity regulators.

CHAPTER REVIEW

Securities markets provide a means whereby investors can buy and sell stocks. The two kinds of securities markets are stock exchanges and over-the-counter markets. The New York Stock Exchange (NYSE) and the American Stock Exchange (Amex) are the two national exchanges. There are also regional exchanges and foreign exchanges. The National Securities Dealers Automated Quotation system (NASDAQ) is a computerized nationwide OTC network of growing importance. Computerization is also being adopted by the NYSE.

A customer who wants to buy or sell stock can indicate the price basis for the transaction by entering—through a stockbroker—a market, limit, open, or discretionary order. In addition to simple orders for buying and selling stock, there are special kinds of trading—margin trading, short selling, and options trading—each of which involves certain risks.

Reports of daily trading in specific stocks and bonds appear in most newspapers, along with various stock averages. Astute businesspeople and investors also carefully follow other news that may have a bearing on the market, including broad social trends and the state of the national and international economies. A customer may also invest through a mutual fund, a company in which many investors pool their money to buy stock. Money market funds, another type of mutual fund, buy corporate and government short-term, high-interest-bearing commercial paper. These funds are particularly attractive to the small investor because they require a relatively small initial investment that can be withdrawn at any time without penalty.

Exchanges that trade in commodities—basic raw materials—operate like stock exchanges. Commodities trading is riskier and far less closely regulated than stock trading. Trade in financial futures—including stock market index futures and options—has been increasing in importance.

REVIEW QUESTIONS

1. How does trading on the over-the-counter market differ from trading on a stock exchange?

2. What are the arguments for creating a centralized electronic stock exchange?

3. List the basic steps involved in investing in stock.

4. When might an investor sell stock short? What risks are involved in selling short?

5. Discuss some of the methods an investor might use to improve his odds on the stock market.

6. What factors account for the renewed interest in mutual funds?

7. Why is trading in commodities riskier than trading in stocks?

KEY WORDS

securities markets (396)

stock exchange (396)

over-the-counter (OTC) market (396)

national exchanges (397)

regional exchanges (397)

National Association of Securities Dealers Automated Quotation system (NASDAQ) (398)

institutional investors (399)

stockbroker, or registered representative (RR) (399)

market order (399)

limit order (399)

open order (400)

discretionary order (400)

transaction costs (400)

stock specialist (400)

margin trading (400)

trading post (400)

reporter (401)

odd lots (401)

leverage (402)

short selling (402)

stock option (403)

call option (403)

put option (403)

CASE 1

WILL AMEX REMAIN BRAND X?

We tend to think of stock exchanges merely as the places where shares of businesses are traded. But stock exchanges are businesses themselves—and they are expected to turn a profit for their owners. The owner/investors in a stock exchange are the specialists and the brokers who have bought "seats" on that exchange. Exchanges promote their wares, compete for markets, and sometimes lose out to the competition—just the way other businesses do.

Essentially, a stock exchange's goal is to get companies to list their securities on that particular exchange. Companies tend to choose exchanges on the basis of the services the exchanges offer: they look for services that will attract investors to their stock and are useful to management.

Traditionally, young, fast-growing but solid companies have listed their stocks on the American Stock Exchange (Amex). The Amex was the scene of the stock market's hottest action in the mid-1960s, and again during the energy stock craze of the late 1970s. But lately, Amex's chief rivals, the New York Stock Exchange and the over-the-counter market, have been redefining their turf. The NYSE has been courting growth companies, and the NASDAQ has been pioneering sophisticated nationwide electronic trading systems that are increasingly popular among all sorts of public companies. The Amex has been left wondering what it has to offer. The traditional path for firms going public was to sell shares over the counter first; then list on the American Exchange; and then to move to the Big Board, where listing requirements are most rigorous. But today, some firms are choosing to stay with the OTC system after they've grown up, and others are listing with the NYSE immediately upon going public.

As a result, since 1978 the Amex has seen its number of listed companies dwindle by 18 percent, while NYSE listings slipped only 3 percent, and OTC listings rose a dramatic 42 percent. The Amex has also fallen behind the other exchanges in volume, dropping from 14 percent of the Big Board's volume in 1978 to 10 percent in 1983; and from 36 percent of the OTC system's 1978 volume to 14 percent in 1983.

How can the Amex preserve a market niche? Companies listing with the Amex are currently offered free use of the Exchange's well-appointed board room; a visit by an Exchange official to their annual stockholders' meeting; and eighteen attractive club facilities around the world, where listed companies can hold meetings to promote their stock to local brokers. The Amex, like the NYSE, also has specialists who smooth out trading when there is an excess of buy or sell orders. And in recent years, the Amex has made enough profit to invest in sophisticated systems to computerize its transactions. Companies that list on the Amex say they do so, in part, because of these services. They also desire the status of listing on a major exchange, but can't meet the NYSE's size and profit standards.

Under the energetic and innovative leadership of Arthur Levitt, the Amex has been thinking hard about other steps it can take to assure a role for itself in our nation's securities trading. It is seeking to create an image as *the* exchange for quality companies, and as an essential public relations arm for its listed companies. It is also diversifying in a big way. It started trading options in 1975, and is now the number-two institution for options trading. Options now contribute 15 percent to the Amex's revenues (though somewhat less to its profits). Other attempts at diversification have had mixed results. Financial futures trading failed to take off, and activity in stock index options has been weak.

Recently, the Amex started up an exciting new line of products known as "narrow index options"—

stock indexes that only track a specific, narrow segment of the market. For example, an investor can buy options on an index of thirty computer-technology stocks, or thirty oil and gas stocks. This concept is consistent with what the Amex does best—offering the investing public a share in America's dynamic younger firms.

But these innovations are not meant to take the place of trading in equities, which Levitt calls the Amex's "bread and butter business." Levitt thinks that closing the American Stock Exchange would be a "national tragedy": he feels there's no other home for "our kinds of companies." According to Amex President Robert Birnbaum, questioning the existence of the Amex is like saying, "Do you need Commodore and Apple when you have IBM?"[15]

1. One Amex executive, getting defensive, said, "If we weren't needed, why is anyone here?" Why do you think the Amex is still here?

2. Do you think the Amex should get out of equities entirely and concentrate on options trading?

3. What other alternatives are available to the American Stock Exchange?

4. If you were president of a small but rapidly growing laser dental equipment maker, do you think you'd list your firm on the Amex? the NYSE? Or would you stay over-the-counter? Why?

CASE 2

MONDAY-MORNING QUARTERBACKING

It was the best of times, it was the worst of times for stocks in 1983. It was a great year for stocks in general, and extraordinarily good for a few stocks—but for several others it was unspeakably bad. For all stocks, listed and unlisted, the biggest percentage gainer in 1983 was Dento-Med, an over-the-counter company that has developed a new type of false teeth. Dento-Med's stock rose twenty-five-fold. Among the Dow Jones Industrials, the biggest gainer was International Harvester. A year earlier, people had written International Harvester off as bankrupt, but in 1983 it rose from $11.50 to $45.50.

One company that *was* forced to file for bankrupcy was Baldwin-United: its stock lost 91 percent of its value. This piano-maker-turned-insurance-giant was the biggest loser on the NYSE. Following close behind was Mattel Inc., whose stock collapsed 70 percent due to an unforeseen decline in the video-game fad.

Were there any investment lessons to be learned from 1983's stock performance record? Professional and amateur stock market analysts are fond of searching out generalizations as a guide to future investment strategy. The year 1983 produced general observations such as these:

- There were many hot plays in high technology—the perennial glamor stocks.
- Some companies lost heavily from cutbacks in consumer spending on nonessentials during the recession.
- There were some tremendous performances in ordinary, non-glamor industries that benefited from the economic recovery.
- Big gains were experienced by some very small firms that only a few lucky investors had heard about before the stock climb.
- As oil prices fell, drilling dropped off and hurt oil exploration and its suppliers.
- Many small firms in intensely competitive high technologies got squeezed.
- Utilities with troubled nuclear projects tumbled.

Monday-morning quarterbacking is also a popular pastime among stock market watchers. For some reason, immeasurably higher profits are chalked up in "might-have-been" sessions than in the real ones that take place in cold cash on the exchange floor. Once a stock booms, everyone seems to have been "about to" buy it; when it falls, everyone was "about to" sell it.[16]

1. Can you add any of your own observations to the general observations about the stock market provided in the chapter?

2. Why not try your hand at calling some stocks? Based on the above generalizations about the 1983 stock market, pick the gainers and the losers in the list below.

- *Hindelang-Tucker Corporation*: a contract oil and gas driller.
- *DesignTek*: a maker of computer-aided design systems.
- *Gotham Lighting Co.*: a major suburban utility, nearing the final stages of constructing a nuclear generating facility.
- *QRS Corporation*: a manufacturer of tissue and plastic products, listed on the NYSE.
- *Thin Today*: runs a nationwide chain of weight-control centers.
- *Matrix Graphic*: a microcomputer firm. Many observers thought it would move to the NYSE.
- *Tommaso Foods*: an Italian food chain.

WHAT WOULD YOU LIKE TO DO:

1 GET CASH

2 MAKE A DEPOSIT OR PAYMENT

3 TRANSFER MONEY TO ANOTHER ACCOUNT

4 SEE BALANCES OR OTHER INFORMATION

5 EXAMINE STATUS OF INVESTMENTS

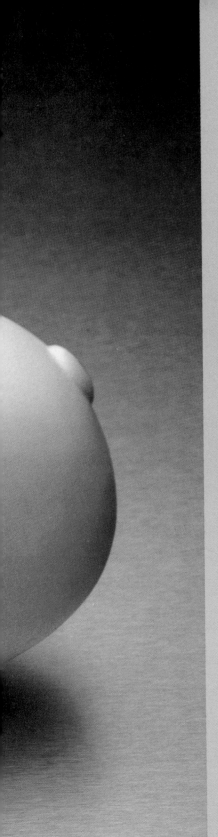

THE MONEY AND BANKING SYSTEM

Banks are not what they used to be. With the coming of deregulation in the early 1980s, banks said good-by to their pin-striped past and became competitive businesses. Advertising aggressively, offering new services (such as twenty-four-hour automated tellers, or "money machines"), and expanding into new activities, banks entered a new era.

Some banks, like New York's Citibank, have thrived on their new enterprises. Others, like California's Crocker Bank, have taken risks to expand their business and have had bad luck. In Crocker's case, high interest rates and a downturn in California's overheated housing market caused millions of dollars of its real-estate loans to be classed as "nonperforming." Crocker found itself the reluctant owner of hundreds of unsold luxury condominiums and townhouses—and with a huge dent in its corporate balance sheet.

Crocker Bank has sought to solve its problems by calling in a new management team. As they develop solutions to Crocker's predicament, they'll be operating in a whole new banking environment—one that is freer and more competitive than ever. In this chapter we'll learn about these new developments in banking, and some of the challenges they offer to bankers and business.

CHAPTER FOCUS

After reading the material in this chapter, you will be able to:

- distinguish M1 from the total money supply
- define demand deposits, and indicate how they are created and how the cash reserve requirement protects them
- describe the basic workings of the Federal Reserve System
- cite the four basic ways the Federal Reserve regulates the money supply
- indicate how the deregulation of interest rates has affected banking
- cite examples of "nonbanks," and outline their advantages over banks
- list several ways that banks are changing in response to the challenge of nonbanks

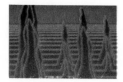As we noted in Chapter 3, our economic system can be thought of as circular flow of money with no beginning or end. Money goes round and round: as individuals receive it in salaries and wages, they spend it for goods and services. In this chapter we will examine the institutions and practices that play important roles in the flow of money through the economy. These government and business institutions have money-handling concerns much like your own: How much is there? How safe is it? How can it be invested to yield the best return? Recently, some of the answers to these questions have changed in interesting ways.

WHAT IS MONEY, AND HOW DO BANKS HANDLE IT?

Money *is anything that is generally accepted as a means of paying for goods and services.* Any objects can be used as money—but some objects serve better than others, of course. Some societies have used cattle, but they had problems with purchases costing one-half a cow and with savings wiped out by hoof-and-mouth disease. Salt served well for the Romans (the word *salary* comes from the Latin for "salt") because it was hard to come by with the technology of the times. Most societies have tended to choose substances that are fairly durable and relatively easy to divide and to carry around. In addition, most societies have designed and produced their currency so that it's hard to copy or counterfeit: one of the reasons money is valuable is that it's scarce (it would lose value if people could fabricate more of it whenever they wanted), and making it hard to counterfeit helps to assure the currency's legitimacy. Finally, of course, any society's money has the characteristic of **liquidity:** *it can be converted into other forms of wealth relatively quickly.*

Currency—*bills and coins*—makes up only a small part of the spending money that is used in the United States today. Think about how much of your income leaves through your checkbook rather than your wallet. You probably use checks to pay your rent, your phone and utility bills, your payments on car loans and charge cards, and perhaps your tuition. Indeed, only about 28 percent of the nation's *money supply* is made up of the stuff that crackles and jingles; the rest consists of many different kinds of bookkeeping entries at financial institutions.[1] The noncurrency part of the money supply resides in checking accounts, savings accounts, and the many other arrangements available to us for storing our money.

MEASURING THE MONEY SUPPLY

Not too long ago, only economists in government and business were interested in the money supply, but today the nation's barrooms and coffee breaks resound with heated debates on the subject. Everyone is affected by economic problems such as inflation and high interest rates, and some experts think these problems are partly related to how much money is in circulation.

"M1" and other measurements

Economists often make the front page in the news when they become alarmed about changes in the nation's total supply of spending money. To gauge this quantity, economists once assumed if people intended to spend certain sums, they would put that money in checking accounts; the money they didn't plan to spend, they would put in savings accounts. (Of course, money that's saved is eventually spent, but it circulates much more slowly, and it is often transferred from savings to checking accounts first.)

The term **M1** is used to designate *those components of the money supply that indicate the intention of spending*—currency, travelers' checks, and checking accounts. (The checking account category includes accounts held at banks or credit unions, accounts that can be disbursed from a written draft or via automatic teller machine, and interest-bearing and non-interest-bearing accounts.) The size of M1 is measured weekly; on April 16, 1984, it totaled $535.9 billion.[2] Economists also keep close watch on the money that people temporarily take out of circulation and put into savings. They break this money

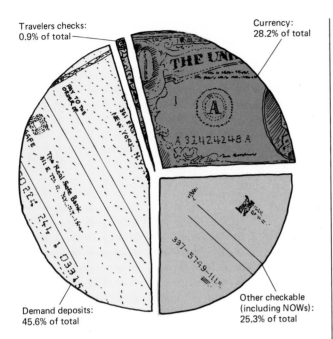

Travelers checks: 0.9% of total

Currency: 28.2% of total

Demand deposits: 45.6% of total

Other checkable (including NOWs): 25.3% of total

FIGURE I

THE MONEY SUPPLY DEFINED AS M-I: TYPES OF MONEY IN CIRCULATION (1984)

down into categories known as M2, M3, and L, according to the money's time characteristics (for example, passbook accounts versus two-year certificates of deposit).

Recent problems in measuring the money supply

Back when interest rates were low, it wasn't too difficult to put people's spending intentions into neat little categories. But recent banking deregulation and new banking products have made things more complicated. It is now possible and attractive for people to keep money they *don't* intend to spend in certain accounts that resemble checking accounts— NOW and SuperNOW accounts, which we will discuss later in this chapter. And it is possible for them to keep money they *do* intend to spend in savings-type accounts, such as money market funds that can be drawn on for large regular expenses such as rent or car payments.

In this kind of world, economists can agree nei-

ther on what M1 means nor on how to change it. So when the annual rate of growth of M1 spurts, as it did in mid-1983 from 4 to 8 percent all the way up to 14 percent, there is a good deal of public debate over whether this reflects inflation to come, just a change in regulation, or merely a random "blip."

DEMAND DEPOSITS

It would be difficult to imagine the business environment without the convenience of checks as a substitute for the clumsiness of cash. The checking account is an agreement by which a customer deposits money in an account and is given a book of checks to be drawn against that account. Each **check** the customer writes and signs is, in effect, *an order to the bank to release the amount of money specified on the check* to the **payee**, *the business or person indicated.* (Of course, the bank may not honor the check if the account is overdrawn—that is, if the customer's account lacks sufficient funds.)

In addition to customer's checks, banks also sell cashier's checks, money orders, and traveler's checks. They can be purchased from a bank for their face value plus, usually, a small additional fee. The main difference between these checks and a customer's checks is that checks purchased from a bank are payable from the funds of the bank itself rather than from an individual's account. As such they are usually acceptable as a form of payment in situations in which the individual isn't personally known.

Checks are essentially orders on paper that direct a bank to pay you, or someone else, specific amounts of bills and coins on demand. Thus the origin of the term "demand deposit": *when a bank establishes a checking account for you, it sets aside a sum of money called a* **demand deposit,** and those to whom you write checks can demand money from your account.

How demand deposits are created

How do demand deposits originate? The most familiar way to create a demand deposit is literally to hand over money to a bank. It's understood in the transaction that the bank will hold your money for safekeeping until you issue a demand—in the form of a check—for some or all of the money you have on deposit.

But there's another way of creating a demand deposit that might not immediately occur to you. A demand deposit can also be created with a bank loan. Say you apply to your bank for a $1,000 loan. If the bank grants you the loan, it does so essentially by permitting you to write $1,000 in checks, on an account into which you *haven't* made any deposits. This $1,000 account is a new loan obligation. But it is also, in a sense, "new" money, created by the bank. The government allows banks to create money in this fashion, as long as they observe the cash reserve requirement.

The cash reserve requirement

Let's backtrack for a minute and look at demand deposits that are created by the depositors' actually handing over money. If banks kept 100 percent of the money deposited on hand to meet the arrival of checks demanding payment, they would not be able to make loans with those funds. The fact is, however, that at any one time people are spending only *part* of the funds they store in banks. Thus, the banks can safely lend out part of their customer deposits (though obviously not 100 percent). The smaller the percentage of its total deposits a bank keeps on "reserve," the more new loan obligations it can create, while the less cash remains to meet these obligations.

What level of reserves is safe? Obviously, that depends on how many people decide to draw on their accounts at the same time. If a bank's depositors lost confidence in the bank and all rushed to withdraw cash at the same time, the bank would not be able to meet the demand. Just such a situation occurred on a massive scale during the Great Depression. Seeing the banks forced to close their doors, President Franklin D. Roosevelt euphemistically called the crisis a "bank holiday." To safeguard the nation's banking system against a recurrence of this kind of catastrophe, the government now imposes a "reserve requirement" on the banks, under which banks are required to hold a specified portion of their deposits in cash or in deposits at a Federal

Reserve Bank. The reserve requirement for demand deposits varies from 7 percent to 16.25 percent, depending on the total amount of demand deposits that a particular bank has on deposit from its customers. The reserve requirement is adjusted from time to time, for reasons we will discuss later in this chapter.

The impact of the reserve requirement is more far-reaching than meets the eye. Just for the purpose of argument, imagine a desert island with only one bank, having only one $100 deposit on its books, and a 20 percent reserve requirement. The bank could make a loan of $80 from that deposit, and in the process would create for the borrower an $80 checking account. The bank would be required to reserve 20 percent, or $16, out of that new deposit, but could then loan out the other $64 by opening up an account in that amount. Once again, 80 percent, or $51.20, out of that could be loaned out. When the bank finally reached the limit of allowable loans against its original $100 deposit, it would have lent out a total of five times that amount. (We are assuming, of course, that no more than one of the five borrowers is likely to return to the bank to demand his total loan in cash.) Our own economy works in fundamentally the same way. Our *fractional reserve system* puts a limit on the total amount of money banks can create while still allowing a substantial degree of money expansion.

HOW BANKS HANDLE MONEY

In the Middle Ages gold was the only widely accepted form of currency. Because traveling merchants found gold bulky and dangerous to carry, banks emerged: they provided the service of issuing documents that would be honored abroad, against a gold deposit that would remain at home.

Today, people require a variety of money-handling services, and banks provide these services in exchange for specific fees.

■ *Trust services* provide a way to safeguard and invest funds in the name of a person unable to do so directly (such as a child or a mentally retarded person).

■ *Checking services* allow us to transfer any portion of our money to anyone else without picking up or delivering it;

businesses enjoy this service on a larger scale in the form of *payroll services*, which save both employer and employee the inconvenience of handling large amounts of cash.

■ *International services* include travelers' checks, facilities for wiring funds around the globe, and facilities that allow customers to buy or sell foreign currency without leaving the country.

When it comes to holding our savings, however, banks don't charge us a fee—in fact, they generally pay us. Banks earn sizable amounts by finding borrowers willing to pay interest for the temporary use of *our* savings deposits. As long as the bank collects a higher interest rate from the borrower than it pays to the saver, it assures itself revenues from which to pay salaries and overhead—and perhaps make a profit as well.

Banks are important to business because, as lenders, banks are a source of much of the money that businesses need to operate. They are also important to households, because they handle households' regular payments and offer various accounts for savings.

THE FEDERAL RESERVE SYSTEM

Since banks are a crucial element of the country's economy, they must at all times be carefully regulated. The federal and state governments all keep a watchful regulatory eye on the nation's banks, but by far the most powerful watchdog is the **Federal Reserve System.** The **Fed,** as it is commonly known, is *an agency that governs the country's banking system; the Fed sets monetary policy.*

One of the Fed's goals is to make certain that enough money and credit are available to allow the economy to expand—thus giving the country an ever-increasing supply of goods, services, and jobs. But the system is also designed to ensure that there is never too much money and credit available at any one time. If too much money and credit *were* available, people would spend more; suppliers would respond to the surge in spending by charging increasingly high prices for their goods, and so every dollar would purchase less. When a dollar purchases less, it's worth less; that's the essence of inflation. In

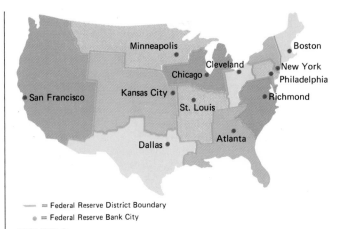

= Federal Reserve District Boundary
● = Federal Reserve Bank City

FIGURE 2

THE FEDERAL RESERVE DISTRICTS

sum, the Federal Reserve System is supposed to act as a safeguard to keep just the right amount of money available in the country.

The Federal Reserve System encompasses all federally chartered banks and many state chartered banks. The Federal Reserve Board oversees operations of the almost 6,000 member banks. The Federal Reserve System is so named because it governs the amount of reserves banks are required to keep on deposit when they create various types of deposits. Figure 2 shows the Federal Reserve Districts.

THE CHECK-CLEARING FUNCTION OF THE FED

A major objective of federal banking regulation is to ensure that the mechanics of the entire banking system function smoothly. One way the twelve Federal Reserve banks carry out this responsibility is by acting as clearing houses for checks. In 1982 the Federal Reserve System cleared about 14 billion checks, involving interbank transactions of about $9.4 trillion.[3]

How the check-clearing mechanism works

Banks may use the Fed's check-clearing service to clear checks drawn on banks outside their Federal Reserve districts. For example, a check written

FIGURE 3

HOW A CHECK MOVES THROUGH THE FEDERAL RESERVE SYSTEM

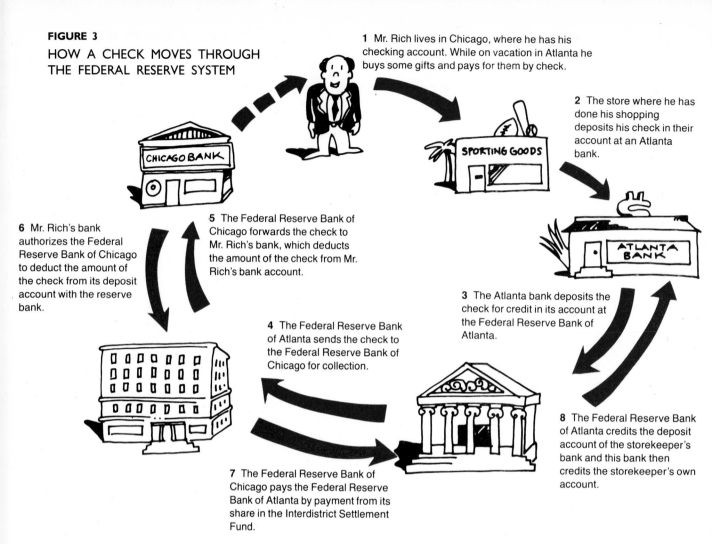

1 Mr. Rich lives in Chicago, where he has his checking account. While on vacation in Atlanta he buys some gifts and pays for them by check.

2 The store where he has done his shopping deposits his check in their account at an Atlanta bank.

3 The Atlanta bank deposits the check for credit in its account at the Federal Reserve Bank of Atlanta.

4 The Federal Reserve Bank of Atlanta sends the check to the Federal Reserve Bank of Chicago for collection.

5 The Federal Reserve Bank of Chicago forwards the check to Mr. Rich's bank, which deducts the amount of the check from Mr. Rich's bank account.

6 Mr. Rich's bank authorizes the Federal Reserve Bank of Chicago to deduct the amount of the check from its deposit account with the reserve bank.

7 The Federal Reserve Bank of Chicago pays the Federal Reserve Bank of Atlanta by payment from its share in the Interdistrict Settlement Fund.

8 The Federal Reserve Bank of Atlanta credits the deposit account of the storekeeper's bank and this bank then credits the storekeeper's own account.

against an account in a Chicago bank may be deposited in a bank in Atlanta. The Atlanta bank forwards the check to the Federal Reserve bank in Atlanta, which collects the funds from the Chicago Reserve bank and credits the account of the local bank accordingly (see Figure 3). For a high-value check, the Atlanta bank may do a "direct send"—it may forward the check to the Federal Reserve bank in Chicago.

Handling transactions in quantity

Not all checks are sent to the Federal Reserve for clearance. Many rural banks simply pay larger banks to perform this service for them. And transactions among banks in the same area are handled locally and then reported to the Federal Reserve, which charges and credits their accounts accordingly.

Let's look at an example involving the Sixth District Federal Reserve Bank in Atlanta. On a given day, customers of the Tallahassee National Bank may have written checks on their accounts for a total of $550, checks that have been deposited by recipients in accounts at the First Miami Bank. At the same time, the Sixth District Bank notes that depositors of First Miami have written $400 worth of checks, which have been deposited at Tallahassee. The reserve bank will balance out the difference, crediting the Miami bank's account with $150 and subtracting the same amount from Tallahassee's account. Of course, the checks written by the customers of Tallahassee National and First Miami are actually deposited in banks all over the district during the normal course of business. In actuality, *all* the debits and credits from all the banks in the district have to be added up before the proper amounts can be added to or subtracted from Tallahassee National's and First Miami's accounts with the district bank.

THE FDIC AND THE FSLIC

All nationally chartered banks, and state banks belonging to the Federal Reserve, must participate in the Federal Deposit Insurance Corporation (FDIC). The FDIC insures depositors for up to $100,000 per account if their bank should fail. If a member bank is on the brink of closing, the FDIC may arrange a merger with another bank. The FDIC sets guidelines for safe bank policies and sees that those guidelines are followed.

Where does the money come from to fund these FDIC functions? Each of the member banks pays the FDIC a percentage of its deposits. If for some reason—say, the closing of too many banks—the fees of FDIC members do not cover the expenses of paying insurance, the FDIC can borrow on the United States Treasury.

And what agency protects depositors in federal savings and loan institutions? The Federal Savings and Loan Insurance Corporation (FSLIC) provides the same services for its members as the FDIC provides for banks that fall under its protection.

SUPPLYING CURRENCY

The individual Federal Reserve banks are also responsible for providing member banks with adequate amounts of currency. The demand for coins and paper money is a seasonal one. For instance, as you might expect, many people withdraw some of their savings from the banks in the form of cash during the Christmas shopping season. The Federal Reserve has to supply the currency that banks need at such times.

REGULATING THE MONEY SUPPLY

The Fed has specific methods of controlling the money supply, which it uses to try to stimulate growth and employment while keeping down inflation. These efforts, known as *monetary policy*, involve many complicated problems. For example, we have

already seen that when the money supply increases, there is more money to go around, and banks can charge lower interest to borrowers. But an increased money supply can lead to more spending and thus more inflation. During inflationary periods, the dollars that borrowers repay to lenders have less purchasing power than they had when the loan was made. To offset this loss of purchasing power, lenders must add a certain percentage—corresponding to the rate of inflation—to the interest rates they would otherwise charge. So a growth in the money supply—*if* it fans inflation—can actually lead to higher interest rates.

The Fed has an additional responsibility: it is the official banker of the federal government, specifically the U.S. Department of the Treasury. When the Federal budget is in deficit, the Treasury must raise money to fill the gap by selling bonds. If the Treasury borrows from the public, it competes with consumer and business borrowing, which can push up interest rates. To avoid this, the Federal Reserve might choose to buy up the Treasury's bonds. But there is a problem: the cash (or demand deposits) that the Fed supplies to the Treasury in exchange for these bonds is new money pumped into the economy. This increase in the money supply may lead to inflation and may conflict with other aspects of the Fed's monetary policy.

Up till 1979, the Fed sought to achieve its monetary policy goals by determining an ideal level of interest rates for the economy. But at times the Fed found it had chosen an interest-rate level that did not equal the equilibrium rate to which the market automatically tended. As a result, an alternative approach, consistent with the trend toward deregulation, gained favor. This "monetarist" view suggests that rather than attempting to control interest rates, the government should simply try to assure that the money supply increases in a slow, steady fashion. The monetarist approach has not been unanimously acclaimed a success. If the Fed sticks to a low rate of money-supply growth, it is accused of causing a recession; if it speeds up money growth, it is accused of igniting inflation; and if it frequently adjusts the money supply up and down to keep on target, it is accused of causing instability and never giving the monetarist concept of *steady* money-supply growth a chance to work.

To implement its monetary policy, the Fed wields four basic tools: it can *change reserve requirements*, it can *buy and sell government bonds on the open market*, it can *change the interest rate that member banks must pay to borrow from it*, and it can *exercise selective credit controls*. The Fed's regulatory authority was strengthened recently by the Depository Institutions Deregulation and Monetary Control Act—the Monetary Control Act, for short—that was passed by Congress in 1980. Among other things, the Monetary Control Act extended some of the Fed's regulatory powers to cover nonmember banks, savings banks, and savings and loan associations. Often, the Fed can persuade banks to follow its credit policies simply by "jawboning," or threatening to use these tools. We'll discuss them in some detail.

Changing reserve requirements

We noted earlier that the Fed requires all member banks and financial institutions to set aside **reserves**—*sums of money equal to a certain percentage of their deposits*. (*The percentage of their deposits banks must keep on hand* is called the **reserve requirement.**) The reserve requirement is one of the Fed's ways of controlling the money supply. The Monetary Control Act specified a reduction in reserves for member banks, and tightened the Fed's grip by authorizing it to gradually extend the reserve requirement to nonmember institutions over an eight-year period.

If the Fed believes that consumers and businesses are buying too much and that inflation is threatening, it will increase reserve requirements. When that happens, banks cannot lend as much to their customers, which means they create a smaller amount of demand deposits, and thus there is less spending in the economy. Conversely, if the Fed's economists feel that the country would benefit if business were stimulated, it will reduce reserve requirements. Then, in theory, banks will make more loans to businesses and consumers so that they, in turn, will buy more. The desired result is more sales for business and more jobs for everyone. Changing the reserve requirement is a very powerful tool that is used for occasional gross adjustments rather than for the Fed's more frequent "fine-tuning" of the money supply.

Some banks invariably find they have more on deposit at the Fed than they need for the short term, while others find that their reserves are insufficient for the short term and that they must make up the difference. If a bank with a surplus wishes to lend its excess reserves to a bank with a deficit, the Federal Reserve very conveniently makes the bookkeeping entries for the two banks so that the funds never actually need to be moved around. *The rate banks charge each other for overnight loans* is called the **Fed funds rate.**

Changing the discount rate

One way for banks to obtain extra funds to lend to their customers is to borrow from their Federal Reserve Bank, which, in a sense, is banker to the banks. Often, when banks borrow from the Fed, they use government securities or other securities as collateral. *The rate that the Fed charges banks for loans* is called the **discount rate.** Discounting may be attractive to commercial banks if they can charge their customers a substantially higher rate for loans than they themselves must pay the Fed. But is has disadvantages too: when a bank borrows from the Fed, the Fed typically imposes conditions on the bank's operations.

Here again is a way in which the Fed can control the economy. If the Fed wishes to encourage member banks to make loans to customers, it will lower the discount rate. And if the Fed wants to discourage loans, it will raise the discount rate. This may have an indirect effect on the **prime interest rate**—*the lowest rate at which banks will make loans to their most credit-worthy business customers*. The prime interest rate is more directly affected by supply and demand for loans.

Open-market operations

The tool the Fed uses most frequently to carry out monetary policy is its power to *buy and sell government bonds on the open market*, in what are known as **open-market operations.** If the Fed is concerned about inflation and wants to reduce the amount of money available, it will sell government bonds to the public and to banks: the bonds are attractive purchases since lending to the government is considered a risk-free way of earning interest. When the public and the banks pay for the bonds, the money paid immediately goes out of circulation. Conversely, when the Fed wants to get the economy moving again, the government will buy back its bonds, thus putting additional cash back into the economy.

Selective credit controls

The Fed has the *power to set credit terms on various kinds of loans.* By exercising this power, known as **selective credit controls,** it can exert a great deal of influence on business activity. For example, it sets **margin requirements** that *limit the amounts of money stockbrokers and banks can lend customers for the purpose of buying stocks.* When the government's economists feel that there is too much stock market speculation for the economy's good, the Fed simply sets margin requirements at a high enough level to prevent financial institutions from lending very much money for stock purchases. (It should be noted, of course, that changes in margin requirements apply only to subsequent loans; they don't affect loans that are outstanding when the change occurs.)

TODAY'S BANKING ENVIRONMENT: THE DEREGULATION OF INTEREST RATES

Banks have two ways of attracting depositors. First, they can offer interest. Second, they can offer services such as convenient local branches, free or low-cost checking, long hours, and gifts for new accounts. Banks' operating costs, then, include two types of expenditures: the interest they pay to depositors, and the rent, salaries, and other overhead costs of running their establishments. A bank with nineteen branches and long hours will of course have higher operating costs than one with three branches, if both are offering the same interest to depositors.

In the past, in the hopes of keeping banks' costs low and encouraging lending to consumers, the government kept limits on the interest rates that banks offered to savings account depositors. The ceilings were 5¼ percent, or 5½ percent for institutions that concentrated on home-mortgage lending (these institutions are known as "thrifts"). Since banks could not compete with each other on interest rates, they competed by trying to offer conveniently located branches, low service charges, and gifts such as alarm clocks and toasters. But all this changed in the late 1970s, when inflation began to dramatically erode the value of the depositor's dollar.

MONEY MARKET MUTUAL FUNDS ENTER THE PICTURE

When inflation passed 5¼ to 5½ percent, depositors soon realized that their savings were actually losing value rather than growing each year. Though they were eager to borrow—hoping to eventually repay their loans in cheaper dollars—they quite rationally began to deposit less of their money in banks. Instead, they began to turn to "nonbank" institutions, which could offer highly attractive services that had been legally forbidden to banks. Prominent among these services were the money market mutual funds, which grew phenomenally from close to zero in 1975 to a peak of over $200 billion in assets in 1983.[4] (Newly legal competition from banks then began to whittle the money market funds down—a story we will tell in the next section.)

Money market funds were the logical response to the fact that the only unregulated accounts banks could offer were their high-yielding certificates of deposit (CDs), which were issued in denominations of $100,000 or more. How could the small saver earn more than 5½ percent on money? Smart entrepreneurs saw that they could put together, let's say, fifty people with $2,000 in savings each. Using the fund thus created, they could let all these people tap into the highest yields available in the inflationary market. Result: the money market fund.

As the funds grew in size and sophistication, they allowed the saver to invest and withdraw funds with almost the convenience of a checking account. Unlike banks, brokerage firms were not prohibited from selling money market mutual funds, and they rushed in to fill the need. Some of the earliest and most successful firms in this business, such as T. Rowe Price, operated entirely by using toll-free phone numbers and the U.S. mail. They were able to operate without retail premises for customers—a surprising marketing lesson that taught the industry how flexible consumers can be when the price is right.

THE BANKS PRESS FOR REGULATORY RELIEF

Deserted by many of their depositors, banks began to feel the need for relief from the regulatory ceilings on the interest rates they could offer. Also, many thrift institutions were near bankruptcy, and desperately needed authority to offer competitive deposit accounts; the thrifts also needed to broaden their lending authority beyond home mortgages. In response to pleas from these institutions, the government began to lift interest-rate ceilings.

The deregulation of CDs

The first deregulatory step toward putting the banks on a more competitive footing came in November 1978, when commercial banks and thrifts were allowed to offer CDs in small denominations (say, $2,500). This permission came with many restrictions: yields were limited to ¼ percent above the Treasury bill rate for CDs maturing in less than 30 months, and a minimum deposit of $10,000 was required for six-month certificates. (The maximum deposit for these certificates was $99,999.) But the new smaller CDs were the banks' first means of offering market-level rates on insured deposits. Then in October 1983 the rules limiting both yields and maturities (over thirty days) were eliminated, and the penalty for early redemption of CDs was reduced from three months' to one month's interest.

NOW and SuperNOW accounts; MMDAs

By this time, however, consumers were already enjoying new higher-yielding accounts that didn't lock them into fixed denominations and fixed maturities—new accounts that could accept deposits of any size over the legal minimum and could be drawn on at any time interval. In January 1981 banks were authorized to pay interest, although limited interest, on checking accounts carrying a minimum balance of $500. (These so-called NOW accounts got their name from the negotiable orders of withdrawal that some states allowed banks to substitute for checks during the days when interest on checking accounts was still illegal.) Then, unlimited interest rates on checking accounts with $2,500 minimum balances

were approved for January 1983; these accounts were called SuperNOW accounts.

But the reserve requirements on SuperNOWs made this source of funds more costly for banks than a similar new product, the money market deposit account (MMDA). Perhaps the biggest hit in new banking services, these MMDAs allowed banks as of December 1982 to pay unlimited interest on accounts with $2,500 minimums and limited monthly withdrawal privileges. MMDAs drew an overwhelming $310 billion in their first three months of existence; of this sum, almost $40 billion had been lured away from nonbank money market funds.[5] Like any bank deposit, MMDAs are federally insured, a feature that consumers see as an important advantage over the nonbank funds.

The struggle of the thrifts

The Depository Institutions Deregulation Committee (created by the Monetary Control Act of 1980) is required to take its final step, complete elimination of all interest ceilings, by 1986. By that time, however, many of the differences between the thrifts and the commercial banks will have vanished. Swifter deregulatory action for the thrifts was compelled by the thrift industry's dire financial condition in the early 1980s.

The source of the thrifts' financial instability was simple: thrifts could not charge market rates for loans when market rates for deposits rose because, unlike commercial banks, where ninety-day or one-year terms are common, most loans at thrifts are mortgages carrying fixed rates for twenty to thirty years. Seven percent mortgages may have made sense when they were made from 5½ percent deposits, but what happens when those depositors pull their money out and offer it back at 9 percent? In an effort to shore up the thrifts, lawmakers allowed the thrifts to enter the formerly prohibited territories of commercial and credit-card lending, as well as including them in on all the new accounts mentioned above.

However, medicine is more important to a sick person than permission to go out and play: these efforts in many cases were not enough. The FDIC had to rescue some thrifts from their financial jeopardy by arranging, and subsidizing, mergers with other financial institutions. (The FSLIC arranged

Who's up?

High-balance depositors: Higher interest rates bring them big rewards.

Buyers of financial services: They can shop around among competing institutions.

Convenience seekers: They can often do all their financial shopping at one "store."

Bank employees: Automation is creating some more challenging and interesting jobs.

Travelers: As more states permit regional interstate banking, a customer from one state may be able to bank in another.

Who's down?

Small businesses: Loans cost more, since banks pay higher interest on deposits.

Low-balance depositors: New fees for bank services may be large in proportion to deposits.

Poor people: High service charges hit them, proportionately, the worst.

Home buyers: Fixed-rate mortgages are harder to get; only floating-rate loans may be available.

Aggressive banks: Banks may make riskier loans to earn higher returns.

Old-line institutions: Stock brokerages may be hurt by competition from banks.

Bank employees: Costs may force banks to streamline staffs.

FIGURE 4

THE DEREGULATION OF BANKING: WHO LOSES, WHO GAINS?
Deregulation's positive and negative impact

Banking deregulation has changed the financial scoreboard. "Big spenders" (of borrowed money) are now out of luck; savers have the interest-rate advantage.

---

some mergers across state lines.) Thrifts are very slowly finding ways to earn more on mortgages, pay less for funds, and gather the financial strength they need to put ammunition in their new weapons.

THE BANKS VERSUS THE "NONBANKS"

Until the late 1970s money-handling functions were divided among many different types of depository institutions. This meant the customer had to go to a different type of institution for different types of services. But each type of institution was virtually assured a certain "turf" that it could count on to pay the rent. *Commercial banks* offered checking services and lent these deposits primarily to businesses. *Thrifts* (also known as savings and loan associations and savings banks) primarily offered savings accounts and lent these funds largely for home mortgages. *Investment banks* were not really banks at all—that is, they did not take deposits; they served businesses that wanted to raise funds from selling new stock (a service called *underwriting*), and they bought and sold existing stock for individuals and businesses (a service called *brokerage*). Finally, other services related to money handling, such as insurance and real estate, were provided by firms that weren't banks at all.

This segmented approach to delivering financial services was dictated by laws that recognized the importance of a sound money-handling system to our nation's economy. The legislative tradition springs mainly from the Glass-Steagall Act, passed in 1933 in the depths of the Great Depression. It was designed to remedy some of the flaws and abuses in banking practices of the period. Legislators at that time felt banks should not be tempted to "push" the stock of a firm whose ability to repay its loans was in doubt. Thus, under the Glass-Steagall Act, no bank that was engaged in underwriting stock was permitted to make commercial loans. All banks were forced to choose between commercial banking and investment banking, or to split in two. The law also protected working people from having their savings lost by banks' buying and selling in the stock market.

By the 1960s and 1970s these laws had already addressed the needs for which they were intended. But they had not evolved to meet the new needs that were being created by high inflation and high-speed electronic transfer of funds. Despite pressure for change, the system was set in a rigid legal mold that resisted change. But recently we have seen an interesting struggle to adapt old institutions to new realities and to reflect these realities in new legislation. Today the lines between different kinds of banks, and between banks and "nonbanks," are blurred. This evolution is expected to lead to what has been called "one-stop financial shopping," or "stocks-to-socks" marketing. The changes have spread from the prime contenders in these financial wars to a whole range of related financial institutions that are groping for new ways to make a profit now that their traditional "bread-and-butter" businesses have been invaded.

THE INVASION OF THE "NONBANKS"

There have always been firms offering financial services outside the traditional banking functions—insurance companies, stockbrokers, real estate brokers, consumer debt specialists. And, as we have noted, money market mutual funds have been active since the mid-1970s. But today there are giant firms offering *all* these services, and these firms have nothing in common but their readiness to leap into as many different financial markets as the law will allow. Sears, Roebuck is one leader in this trend toward catering to all the customer's financial needs. Sears took the route of expanding its involvement in consumer finance (from its already strong base of credit card holders): it bought up existing financial giants, including Allstate Insurance, Dean Witter

(brokerage), and Coldwell Banker (real estate). Other nonbank heavyweights include Prudential Insurance, which scooped up Bache Securities, and American Express, which compounded its already huge credit card and travelers' check business with purchases such as Fireman's Fund Insurance Company and the major brokerage firm Shearson Loeb Rhodes. Whether these financial conglomerates will reap great profits from the "synergies" in these overlapping businesses and whether customers will indeed flock to the institutions that provide the largest selection of financial services remains to be seen.

Two recent consumer trends—a willingness to hold savings in a money market fund, and a tendency to purchase a variety of financial services from the same firm—converged in the cash management account, pioneered by Merrill Lynch in 1977. This innovation combines a money market fund, a stock and bond account, and a line of credit on a major credit card. The customer's money works harder when it is in one place: for example, a dividend paid on one of your stocks will go directly into your money fund and immediately start earning high interest. Merrill Lynch took an unmistakable lead in the financial supermarket race by introducing such new services rather than merely merging with existing firms.

THE BANKING EMPIRE STRIKES BACK

As savers found better ways to invest and businesses found better ways to borrow, banks saw that much of their traditional business was being eroded. At the same time, interest-rate deregulation was forcing banks to shift from "service competition" towards "price competition." Banks responded to these pressures by offering new products and seeking new revenue sources, and by trying to cut their operating costs. The banks that could not make these adjustments either failed or were acquired by other banks.

The banks move onto the nonbanks' turf

The banks' ability to respond competitively has been highly constrained by the fact that banks are heavily

INTERNATIONAL BANKING: DEBT SWAPPING

One of the important functions of banks is to link savers with borrowers, and in international banking it's no different: Western European and American banks played this role internationally in the 1970s by loaning out the deposits of oil-rich OPEC countries to oil-poor undeveloped countries. But unfortunately for the banks, some of the profits from those loans have never materialized, because some of those loans have not been repaid. In fact in many cases default is a real possibility. Complicating the situation, some banks have tied up a substantial part of their assets in loans to just one nation. Now, the United States government is pressuring banks to inform their shareholders when they have lent 1 percent or more of their assets to one country.

What can the banks—afraid of shareholder reaction—do to free themselves from such potentially disastrous ties? Some banks have come up with an ingenious plan. Basically, it involves swapping the very risky loans of one country for the less risky ones of other countries. Though the bank gives up more secure loans for loans that might be defaulted on, the deal is usually sweetened by the addition of cash or other favorable terms. Take the case of a swap involving Brazil's Banco Real and the U.S. Bankers Trust. The Brazilian bank was short of cash, so it agreed to give Bankers Trust $190 million in more secure loans in exchange for $100 million of a very risky loan to Brazil plus $90 million in cash. Bankers Trust eliminated the need to explain a potentially embarrassing loan to its stockholders, and arranged things so that its risk was no longer concentrated in one country.

In certain deals, the sweetener is not cash but a big discount on the loan, and the swapping partners are not banks but banks and multinationals. Some multinationals have been able to pull off some very clever exchanges by buying back loans made to their subsidiaries at rates cheaper than the face value of the loans. For example, one American multinational recently bought back a $50 million loan made to its Brazilian subsidiary for a 19 percent discount—a saving to the corporation of $9.5 billion.

American banks and multinationals seem to be the big winners in these swaps, but appearances may be deceptive. Many of the swaps American banks have made involve the exchange of one Latin American country's loans for the loans of several other countries in that region. Bankers Trust's future profits may no longer be tied to the fate of a single country, Brazil, but they still depend on the prosperity of other countries in Latin America. Western European banks, less willing to gamble on the future of one region, are instead swapping their Latin American loans for Eastern European and African debts. In the long run, it may turn out that U.S. banks have not spread their risks widely enough to withstand the aftershocks of world-shaking defaults.

SOURCE: "A Hot New Market in Swapping High-Risk Debt," *Business Week*, December 5, 1983, p. 144.

---

regulated, whereas nonbanks are more loosely regulated. Therefore, the banks have been running to their regulators and legislators crying "foul": they want to be free to compete with the nonbanks on the nonbanks' ground. The banks are in a precarious position, for the same deregulatory trend that will free them to compete with the nonbanks could also free the nonbanks to invade even more of the banker's traditional territory. Nevertheless, in an effort to regain lost ground, banks are aggressively competing with each other and with nonbanks to develop new services and spur further changes in the laws.

The banks' new assertiveness has, in fact, taken on the proportions of a stampede in their efforts to offer discount-brokerage services. Bank of America began the trend with its late-1981 attempt to buy the number one discount broker Charles Schwab and Company—a move that took a full year to be approved by the Fed, which had traditionally viewed the entire brokerage business as off-limits to commercial banks. The Glass-Steagall Act explicitly excludes banks from underwriting stocks and from giving customers advice on stocks; but discount brokers do neither of these (a main reason why they are able to put through customer trades at 40 percent reductions on the fee charged by "full-service" brokers like Merrill Lynch), and so banks could legally offer discount-brokerage services. By February 1983 six hundred banks and thrifts had entered or planned to enter the market opened up by this reinterpretation of the law, and by 1984 the number of banks and thrifts in the brokerage business had grown to approximately 1,200.[6] In that same year the authority of bank holding companies to offer discount-brokerage services was before the Supreme Court.

Cutting costs and raising revenues

Banking is a very people-intensive business—Bank of America has more branches in California than does the U.S. Post Office. Combine this with an explosive shift from service competition to price competition, and you are likely to get out-of-control costs. Combine it with an explosion in the cost of loanable funds, and you are likely to get a very quick reexamination of these costs. Banks are trying new ways to hold down costs: hiring more part-timers so as to staff more appropriately for peak loads; closing slow branches; limiting services offered at most branches and concentrating expensive services at just a few. Recently, some banks have even installed more camera surveillance to cut down on the number of lobby guards.

One of the most promising but controversial cost-cutting tools is the automated teller machine. The ATM can handle 2,000 transactions a day and costs about $22,000 a year to run, as opposed to the human teller, who handles only 200 transactions a day and costs $9,000 to $20,000 a year plus fringe benefits.[7] New York's Citibank has done most to ignite the automation controversy: it installed over 500 twenty-four-hour ATMs in New York, and in the process raised its share of the New York banking market significantly. But Citibank went much further: it required low-balance customers to use the machine rather than dealing with the humans behind the counter during peak hours at high-traffic branches. This brought Citi some bad publicity, and Citi soon dropped the requirement that low-balance customers use the ATMs.[8] Studies show, however, that only a small percentage of the population objects to doing their business with ATMs, and in the future ATMs may carry a larger proportion of consumers' routine banking transactions.

Many banks are taking a more direct approach to earning more from each customer: they are avidly courting the affluent, using a carrot or a stick. The carrots range from practical inducements such as reduced waiting time for routine transactions and special approvals to imaginative ones such as vault space for customer furs, discounts on opera seats, and cocktail parties offering the opportunity to rub shoulders not only with a bank officer who isn't "too busy," but with other "select" customers like yourself. The stick covers all those ways that banks communicate their lack of enthusiasm for small accounts: some take the direct approach of requiring high minimum balances, some impose hefty fees on lower balances, some allegedly use the subtler approach of providing less convenient or pleasant service for low-balance customers.

For many banks, charging higher fees for the whole range of traditional services is not just a weeding-out tactic; it has become an essential measure for continued profits. Every service must be carefully priced at what it costs the bank to deliver. The new charges are causing many unhappy faces among people who open their statements to find they are socked with higher fees for basic checking accounts, for "bouncing" checks (insufficient funds), for credit cards, and even for their low-balance passbook accounts.

One more source of revenue for banks, controversial but important, has been the "float"—the interest they earn on your money between the time they actually collect it and the time they give you access to it. Banks assert that check-clearing delays are necessary to protect them from the risk of bad checks; a bad check requires the bank to return funds it has already collected from the Fed's clearing house. However, an officer at one major bank estimated that his institution only loses $3 million a year on bad checks, while it earns over $3 million a *day* off the float.[9] Until now, regulation in most states has not covered the banks' ability to put a "hold" on deposited funds. But customers, with their increasingly sophisticated understanding of the lightning speed of electronic check processing, are getting angrier at this practice. Even if some states continue to allow the practice, this source of revenue may shrink; some banks are using shorter holds as a competitive tool, and others may be forced to follow suit or lose business.

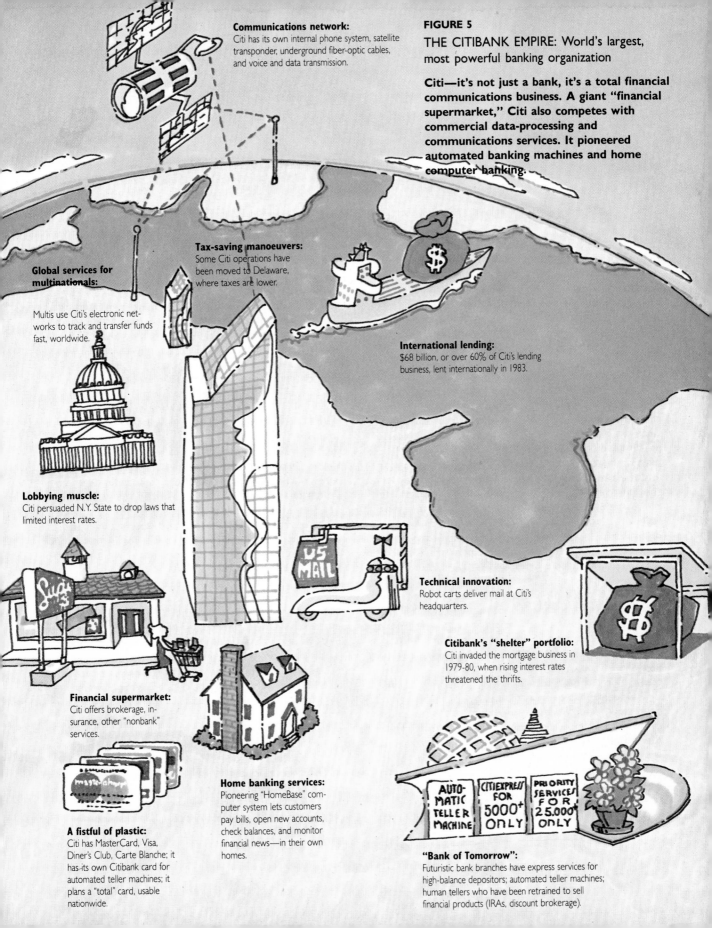

Communications network:
Citi has its own internal phone system, satellite transponder, underground fiber-optic cables, and voice and data transmission.

FIGURE 5

THE CITIBANK EMPIRE: World's largest, most powerful banking organization

Citi—it's not just a bank, it's a total financial communications business. A giant "financial supermarket," Citi also competes with commercial data-processing and communications services. It pioneered automated banking machines and home computer banking.

Global services for multinationals:
Multis use Citi's electronic networks to track and transfer funds fast, worldwide.

Tax-saving manoeuvers:
Some Citi operations have been moved to Delaware, where taxes are lower.

International lending:
$68 billion, or over 60% of Citi's lending business, lent internationally in 1983.

Lobbying muscle:
Citi persuaded N.Y. State to drop laws that limited interest rates.

Technical innovation:
Robot carts deliver mail at Citi's headquarters.

Citibank's "shelter" portfolio:
Citi invaded the mortgage business in 1979-80, when rising interest rates threatened the thrifts.

Financial supermarket:
Citi offers brokerage, insurance, other "nonbank" services.

Home banking services:
Pioneering "HomeBase" computer system lets customers pay bills, open new accounts, check balances, and monitor financial news—in their own homes.

A fistful of plastic:
Citi has MasterCard, Visa, Diner's Club, Carte Blanche; it has its own Citibank card for automated teller machines; it plans a "total" card, usable nationwide.

"Bank of Tomorrow":
Futuristic bank branches have express services for high-balance depositors; automated teller machines; human tellers who have been retrained to sell financial products (IRAs, discount brokerage).

ELECTRONIC BANKING

Behind all the economic issues that are shaping the flow of money are the humdrum functions that banks perform: processing payments, keeping records, and protecting against fraud. In the coming decade, most of the excitement and innovation in the banking world will probably come from these functions, as more of them come to be performed electronically.

There are many ways to get money from the person who wants to spend to the person who wants to sell. One is the credit card, which revolutionized funds transfer in the 1970s by freeing spenders from carrying cash. But credit cards have disadvantages: between the time you walk off with your purchase and the time the merchant receives payment, many pieces of paper have to be processed by many pairs of wage-earning hands. Between the time you leave the store and the time the money leaves your checking account, the bank and the merchant bear the expense of the "float." Moreover, credit cards are subject to a high level of fraud and abuse. All these added costs of doing business are built into the prices we pay.

Eventually, technology may help to provide better ways. With *electronic funds transfer (EFT),* for instance, computers can immediately communicate your purchase to the bank and transfer money from your account to the merchant's account. The transfer is initiated from a *point-of-sale terminal* at your merchant's checkout counter, which is electronically linked to the computer at your bank. By presenting your *debit card,* you enable the merchant to gain access to your account. For the past decade, the technology to make EFT a reality has been available, but progress has been slow. The two most important obstacles appear to be the risk of customers' not accepting EFT and the initial start-up cost (including hardware costs, software costs, training costs, and costs of removing obsolete equipment). But EFT is finally on the verge of becoming part of our daily lives, thanks to a wide variety of systems for introducing it.

The first widespread use of EFT will probably be at your neighborhood gasoline pump, an institution that has already proved that we can change our habits. Self-service gasoline pumps were virtually unknown just a few years ago, but they now provide 60 percent of all the gasoline sold. Why not continue to lower costs and speed service with terminals that allow gasoline buyers to process their own payments? These "automated fuel systems" accept credit cards, debit cards, and/or cash. Although they are just emerging from the experimental stage, one-third of all gas stations are expected to automate payment by 1986. The oil companies are anxious to smooth the introduction of this innovation as a means of competing in a declining market. They estimate that the equipment will pay for itself in one year by cutting labor costs and theft.

If we can adjust to paying for gas this way, why not for groceries and airline tickets? Delivering this service will require a vast effort to coordinate the linkup of so many merchants with so many purchasers, but whoever succeeds will have grabbed a huge piece of transactions-processing business away from the banks. One front-running contender in this effort is Visa International, which says that it will be able to use debit cards to quadruple its transactions volume between 1983 and 1988. The first step is a planned network linking 8,000 automatic teller machines around the world. More than 100 different networks already link the ATMs of unrelated banks; six of these networks have national rather than regional coverage. Visa's network will surpass these by including 400 new machines to be installed at airports, railway terminals, and tourist attractions worldwide, giving travelers access to home bank accounts. Terminals at major supermarket and department store chains are planned next.

Visa's system will rely on the familiar magnetic strips on the back of its debit cards. But an intriguing alternative approach to EFT is the "smart card," which actually has a tiny computer chip embedded in it, giving it microprocessing and memory capacity. You begin by electronically recording the transfer of

THE HIGH-TECH HORIZON

any amount of money from your bank account to your card; then with each purchase the appropriate amount is deducted from the balance on the card. Any time you wish, you can get a printout or a screen readout of all your purchases. The merchant's terminal electronically stores the details of each transaction, and at the end of the day the terminal wires that data to the bank in order to effect payment. Although most experimental uses of the smart card in the United States are in the government (in the military and in welfare systems), many EFT uses are planned in Europe, where the cards originated.

Finally, the banks have put in their own bid for the lead role in EFT with the concept of home banking. Bank-at-home services allow customers to monitor checks as they clear their accounts; transfer funds between accounts; make payments to participating merchants, utilities, and landlords (or arrange to have regular payments made automatically); and call up stock and bond quotes and data on the latest interest rates being offered. Generally, there is a monthly fee for the service, and the customer must purchase some sort of home computer equipment. Banks have done a tremendous amount of experimenting to attack the obstacles of cost and customer acceptance.

How enthusiastic will people be about all this button pushing? What portion of the population will have the home gadgetry necessary to make it work? And how can the customer be persuaded to pay for these services? Some innovative approaches have been tried, with promising results. Some systems minimize the subscriber's need for equipment by relying on television or on telephone or cable TV lines. Many are teaming up with larger videotex services (described in Chapter 12) to offer news bulletins and services for travel and entertainment reservations along with the banking service. And some are motivating consumers by homing in on special needs. The best example of successful targeting is "FirstHand," a home banking service being tested by First Bank System Inc. of Minneapolis. The system serves 200 North Dakota farmers, giving them essential up-to-the minute data on commodity prices and weather and saving them the long trip to the bank.

Once home banking becomes widespread, banks should enjoy considerable savings in their cost of processing the transfer of funds. Gone will be all those pieces of paper, and better yet, the hands expediting the transfer will be the paying hands of customers rather than the salaried hands of bank employees. Meanwhile, some employees may be given work in other phases of the banks' operations. But at present, banks are wary of the huge initial cost of developing and delivering these services. Again, some interesting approaches are in the works. Chemical Bank, the nation's sixth largest, has spent $20 million developing its "Pronto" home banking service, but plans to reap great profits licensing the software to smaller banks wishing to jump into the electronic age. While others, such as Citibank, Merrill Lynch, and American Express, are also going it alone, a group of banks nationwide has teamed up to form VideoFinancial Services. They're developing home banking services to be marketed through Viewtron, the advanced videotex joint venture of AT&T and Knight-Ridder Newspapers. Other banks are teaming up with existing data communications services such as Compuserve, Tymshare, and Automatic Data Processing.

Although we may have to wait until children raised with their fingers on keyboards are wielding their own checking accounts, it seems inevitable that banking will no longer be thought of as something that requires a big stone building.

SOURCE: Maria T. Padilla, "Home-Banking Tests Begin in a Few Places, but the New Systems May Be Slow to Spread," *The Wall Street Journal,* January 17, 1983; "Home Banking by Computer," *The New York Times,* March 29, 1983; Martin Mayer, "Here Comes the Smart Card," *Fortune,* August 8, 1983, pp. 74–82; Ruth Stroud, "Visa Charges Ahead with Teller Machines," *Advertising Age,* April 18, 1983; Thomas J. Lueck, "Technology: Automating Gas Stations," *The New York Times,* June 9, 1983; "Automated Billing Arrives at the Gas Pump," *Business Week,* May 30, 1983, pp. 90F–90H.

CHAPTER REVIEW

Money is anything generally accepted as a means of payment for goods and services. The total money supply comprises currency, checking accounts, savings accounts, and many other arrangements that facilitate financial transactions. M1 is that part of the money supply that is slated to be spent fairly soon. It is closely watched as an indicator of inflation and interest rates but—because of banking deregulation and new types of accounts—has become more difficult to define. Banks that are members of the Federal Reserve must protect demand deposits by keeping a certain percentage of them in reserve. This reserve may be stored in the bank's own vaults and in government banks.

Banking is regulated by the Federal Reserve System (the Fed), which monitors all federally chartered and many state chartered banks. In overseeing the mechanics of banking, the Fed facilitates the clearing of checks, insures the safety of bank deposits, and supplies banks with the currency they require to conduct business. In its regulatory capacity, the Fed uses monetary policy to make sure enough money and credit is available and to guard against inflation. The Fed regulates the money supply through four basic procedures: changing reserve requirements, changing the discount rate, carrying out open-market operations, and setting selective credit controls.

As a result of recent legislation, many of the distinctions among different types of financial institutions are disappearing. At one time, for example, savings and loan associations and savings banks were not allowed to offer many of the services provided by commercial banks, such as short-term business and personal loans. But because of new needs, many such barriers have now fallen.

Today both banks and nonbanks are evolving toward "one-stop financial shopping," and they are also selling new products. However, the nonbanks have still enjoyed a decided edge in being able to offer services—such as money market mutual funds—that are legally forbidden to banks and in having developed new services to make them more competitive. Furthermore, the nonbanks don't have to worry about reserve requirements. The banks, which found themselves being left behind, reacted by demanding a freer rein, and they have been getting it through the deregulation of CDs; through NOW, SuperNOW, and MMDA accounts; and with other innovations, such as new rules for the thrifts. Banks are also trying to shore themselves up by seeking new ways to cut costs and obtain revenue. Even so, some banks have been unable to keep up and have failed. The long-term implications of the current deregulatory trend are still at issue.

KEY WORDS

money (416)
liquidity (416)
currency (416)
MI (416)
check (417)
payee (417)
demand deposit (417)
Federal Reserve System (the Fed) (419)
reserves (422)
reserve requirement (422)
Fed funds rate (422)
discount rate (422)
prime interest rate (422)
open-market operations (422)
selective credit controls (423)
margin requirements (423)

REVIEW QUESTIONS

1. Explain the difference between the total money supply and M1. Why do economists keep a close watch on the latter?

2. How are demand deposits created? Explain how the federal government regulates them.

3. What is the main objective of the Federal Reserve System? Discuss in detail the four tools the Fed uses to achieve this objective.

4. Discuss the role of the twelve Federal Reserve banks in clearing checks drawn on commercial banks.

5. In what ways have banks been adversely affected during times of high inflation?

6. Give some examples of "nonbanks" and outline the advantages over banks that they have enjoyed.

7. Describe the ways in which banks and their offerings have changed to serve new needs and to compete more successfully.

CASE 1

THE BANKS BACK OFF FROM A RATE WAR

U.S. banks are just learning to live with intense competition. For many years, regulation imposed ceilings on the interest rates they could offer to customers. Banks competed by offering 5 percent

plus a toaster, not 8 percent. As we learned in this chapter, Congress decided to gradually deregulate the banks, perhaps prodded by the fact that many depositors were taking their money out of banks and putting it into unregulated money market funds.

Banks said they could bid competitively for the consumer's savings, if only given a chance. The banks were given many chances—the first one back in 1978 when regulators created the so-called Suicide Sixes. These certificates of deposit allowed banks to offer rates that tracked the six-month treasury bill rate. Overnight, the implications of the new game hit home: old mortgages weren't earning a bank any more money, but new deposit sources sure were costing it more. Trouble loomed.

The worst of the rate wars was brought on by the 1982 deregulation of money market deposit accounts (MMDAs). At one point, the bidding for deposits had banks paying savers up to 21 percent. Each bank thought that if it could only build up deposits (at any price), cash flow would get back on its feet—but there was a limit to the amount of deposits to be had. Fortunately, the rate wars did not last long: once a certain number of consumers had chosen to place their funds in the MMDAs, the banks reduced their rates again.

The perils of unhealthy competition loomed again in 1983 when one- to thirty-month certificates of deposit were deregulated. Since rates on a CD are fixed, a bank offering a 21 percent return cannot cut the rate a week later, as it could on a money market account; it must pay that rate until the agreed maturity of the certificate. What's worse, if a bank's existing money market customers decide to buy high-yielding CDs from the bank, then for all the bank's effort it is merely paying more for the same money. The stakes were higher in this new game, and banks seemed to develop a new sense of caution: they backed off. Nationwide, rates rose only slightly above preregulation levels, except for a small competitive flare-up in the New York City market.

Banks are searching out new ways to attract deposits without bidding up the price they'll pay for the saver's dollar. They want to build a stable base of customers, rather than trying to lure the bargain shopper. Many are trying to offer convenience, such as flexibility in maturities and complimentary services. For example, at Empire Savings Bank, a minimum CD of $2,500 earns you a free interest-bearing checking account and a free VISA debit card. At Bank of America, a $500 deposit locked in for five years would yield 10 percent, while a $100,000 deposit for the same term would earn you an interest rate of 11.5 percent. A competitor down the street might give you a higher rate on your $500 but require you to lock it in for ten years.

We have seen in this chapter that banks have to live on their spreads—the difference between what they pay for money and what they receive for lending it. When fewer companies and consumers want to borrow, banks can't charge as much for the privilege of borrowing. When fewer consumers and companies want to save, banks must pay more to lure in their share of deposits. Banks today are learning to live with smaller spreads than ever before. It is expected that some won't make it, but the rest will be healthier than ever. However, they will always have to live with the fact when it comes to banking, people have learned to shop around.[10]

1. What choices do banks have in the ways they can raise deposit money? What are the advantages and disadvantages of each alternative?

2. In a competitive situation, what happens when one bank tries to increase its market share? How does it affect spreads and profits for all banks? What effect does it have on the consumer's pocketbook?

3. Does a bank expose itself to long-run risks by paying consumers too well for their deposits? By granting loans at cheap rates? By providing fancy services in plush surroundings?

4. A cabbage farmer can try to increase profits by earning a higher margin on each cabbage he sells. Or he can settle for the same "spread" per cabbage, and try to increase his profits by selling more cabbages. How is banking essentially similar?

CASE 2

BANKAMERICA IN SEARCH OF ITSELF

BankAmerica, holding company for the San Francisco-based Bank of America, was once unchallenged as the nation's biggest banking organization. At its peak, it had more branches in California than the U.S. Post Office— 1,077 of them. In days gone by, it was a highly profitable enterprise. But earnings have been down or flat since 1980. In the third quarter of 1983, per-share earnings fell a disastrous 45 percent from the year before, and the bank's president confessed that he didn't expect a turnaround soon. Where was that old magic?

Some of the old magic, it seemed, had rubbed off on New York's Citibank, perennial rival for the top banking honors. Thanks to aggressive growth policies, Citicorp's assets topped Bank of America's for the first time in 1983, and by a healthy margin. Citibank was also generating profits at a fast clip, enabling it to spend lavishly on campaigns to enter new markets—notably B of A's turf in California.

The bad times Bank of America was now facing, it seemed, were partly the result of the good times the bank had enjoyed earlier. Bank of America had thrived in a regulated environment. California's relatively relaxed banking laws allowed banks to branch statewide. Before deregulation, banks could not compete by offering savers a higher return, so they competed with convenience. With a branch at every crossroads, B of A was able to attract 40 percent of the California deposit market— a source of high earnings when the legal maximum payable to depositors was so much lower than the maximum chargeable to borrowers.

The progressive deregulation of banking forced Bank of America to fight for its customers by offering them competitive rates. But how could this mammoth bureaucracy, with its expensive administrative overhead, offer rates as attractive as its leaner competitors? Pruning the establishment was foremost in the minds of B of A policymakers. But cutbacks have proceeded very slowly. Although the bank is planning to consolidate by offering full services only in key branches, so far only fourteen branches have been closed. And though long-term staff cutbacks have been announced, a mere 2,000 of the bank's 83,000 employees were laid off in 1983. By relying on attrition for almost all staff cutbacks, the bank has tied its own hands. Wholesale layoffs, it seems, would not fit the traditions of the organization. And they would intensify the morale problems that already threaten a no-growth institution.

Bank of America is suffering from its past successes in other ways, too. During the 1975 recession, it hardly had to "pull up its socks," in the imagery of its new chairman, Sam Armacost. It was heavy with loans to foreign governments, farmers, and single-family homeowners. These sectors traditionally hold strong in good times and bad. But by 1983 hardship had hit from all sides, producing a mountain of bad debt. Home mortgages were devastated by towering interest rates and risky "creative financing." Unprecedented declines in the value of California farmland took the security out from under agricultural credits. Worst of all, B of A's great success in lending to foreign governments came back to haunt it when those nations began to stall on repayment of their huge loans. All in all, B of A was looking at a whopping $215 million in losses for the third quarter of 1983, almost double the loss for the comparable period of 1982. And 3.5 percent of its total loans were not accruing interest.

What can Bank of America do to regain the strength that it has lost due to low revenues and bad debt losses? Mr. Armacost has two ideas—clarifying the bank's goals, and grasping opportunities more aggressively. Some of the opportunities B of A has grasped have stunned the banking community. It acquired the money-losing Seafirst bank of Seattle. It made an unprecedented bid to purchase a securities brokerage, the discount house of Charles Schwab, thus sending other banks scrambling to catch up. This acquisition thrust Bank of America strategically into the finances of relatively affluent consumers in forty-eight states. Finally, B of A fought fiercely, with high rates and expensive advertising, for a large slice of the deregulated deposit pie. Its aggressiveness may have driven up the cost of money market accounts for all banks in the area, but it was a keystone in the bank's drive to regain market share lost in the 1970s. Balances in B of A's money market accounts grew from zero to 10 percent of the bank's total liabilities.

Do these moves add up to a new mission for the bank? If not, what is its corporate objective? The answer hasn't been easy for top management to pinpoint. They say they do not want to be all things to all people. Yet, they can't really decide which people they don't want to be all things to. What they really want to do is serve the same markets— consumer, corporate, and foreign— but at a lower cost.

Can this be done by an aging bureaucracy whose management may lack the experience and the will for the "lean and mean" approach? By an organization that got into automated teller machines at a snail's pace and still clears checks the old-fashioned way? By one that is hiring outside consultants to diagnose its corporate culture? B of A may need a boost from the spirit of A. P. Giannini, the bank's immigrant founder who financed the rebuilding of San Francisco after the 1906 earthquake.[11]

1. Which of Bank of America's strategies do you think has been the most appropriate? Which has been the least appropriate? Where do the bank managers seem to have been dragging their feet?

2. Do you agree with the bank chairman's claim that in this situation gradual changes are better than sudden, fundamental changes?

3. If you were thinking of investing in Bank of America, would you take the plunge?

4. If you were president of a competing California bank, how would you position yourself to compete with Bank of America? What lessons would you learn from B of A's past?

RISK MANAGEMENT AND INSURANCE E

At a conference in Westchester County, New York, several key executives of a small electronics company have died in a tragic flash fire. Are the company and its stockholders protected against the loss of their expertise?

Hit from behind, a Ford Pinto explodes into flames. What is Ford's liability for the driver's injuries?

Risks like these are inescapable in business. Every business venture is something of a gamble, because the possibility of loss is as real as the prospects for profit. And even though managers do everything possible to minimize the risk of loss on a company's business transactions, a host of other risks are more difficult to guard against. They include bad weather and natural disasters, strikes, lawsuits, freak accidents, and so on.

In this chapter we'll examine these risks and the means that have been developed to deal with them. Insurance plays a major role in this process, so we will analyze the types of insurance available to protect both businesses and their employees against some risks.

CHAPTER FOCUS

After reading the material in this chapter, you will be able to:

- cite the difference between pure risk and speculative risk
- name four approaches to risk management
- distinguish uninsurable risks, insurable risks, and absorbable risks
- name four types of business risks and several types of protection against each
- describe four types of insurance that businesses provide employees

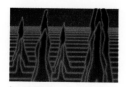 Business disasters take many forms, and no business is immune—certainly not the Baltimore Orioles baseball team, which saw profits washed away in 1983 after seven rainouts dampened ticket and concession sales to the tune of $50,000 to $250,000 per game. Never again, vowed the 1979 American League pennant winners: they bought a Lloyd's of London policy protecting them from inclement weather, power failures, bomb threats, kidnapping, and injuries.[1] For General Electric Corporation, however, there is no insurance bailout from the $30 million in damages they must pay to New York State for allegedly dumping 450 tons of toxic wastes in Saratoga County. The most any insurer will cover under these circumstances is $10 million per single occurrence.[2] And who could ever anticipate that Dow Chemical Company would be confronted with a $750,000 verdict in 1983 and forced to halt production of Bendectin, an antinausea product deemed safe by the Food and Drug Administration and used in 33 million pregnancies for seventeen years? After Dow was held liable for a birth defect attributable to Bendectin, negative publicity, litigation costs, and escalating insurance premiums made the company decide to stop producing the drug.[3]

Events like these represent one kind of risk that no business can predict or escape. Known as **pure risk,** it is defined as *the threat of a loss without the possibility of gain.* In other words, a disaster such as a fire is costly for the business it strikes, but the fact that *no* fire occurs contributes nothing to a firm's profit. This is different from the type of risk that offers the prospect of making a profit and prompts people to go into business in the first place. Every business accepts the *possibility of losing money in order to make money.* This kind of risk is known as **speculative risk.** To see the difference between pure risk and speculative risk, think about the following situation. A record company takes a speculative risk in recording and marketing an album by a new group. It may prove to be a gold record or a dud. But the company takes a pure risk when it ships 10,000 copies of the album from its factory by truck. If the truck crashes and burns, reducing the albums to blobs of plastic, the loss will amount to many thousands of dollars.

PROTECTION AGAINST RISK

How can a company protect itself against events that it can't control? Buying insurance from a company that agrees to cover a particular type of loss is one answer. But that's not the only alternative in **risk management,** *the process of reducing the threat of loss due to uncontrollable events.* In general, there are four approaches to risk management: (1) avoid risk, (2) minimize losses through good management techniques, (3) absorb losses, and (4) purchase insurance to pay for losses.

Going back to the record-company example, we can see how good risk management works. For instance, the company could protect itself from losses due to truck accidents by choosing a trucking firm with a good accident record. It might decide to own its trucks itself; that way it could control the maintenance of the trucks, the caliber of the drivers, and the routes chosen. It could not, of course, rule out *all* possibility of risk: as a well-managed company it should also protect itself by buying insurance coverage and should back this coverage with some sort of self-insurance plan, possibly a risk retention fund to cover any losses that are disallowed in the policies it has purchased.

INSURABLE AND UNINSURABLE RISKS

A useful distinction to make in risk management is that between insurable and uninsurable risks. Let's look at uninsurable risks first.

UNINSURABLE RISKS

Not every business risk can be covered by some form of insurance. **Uninsurable risks** *are those that few, if any, insurance companies will agree to cover.* For example, businesses must cope with unforeseen changes in the physical environment. It is possible to pur-

Part of the risk manager's job is to identify sources of potential danger before mishaps occur. The result: a reduction in overall risk.

chase disaster insurance against such calamities as floods, hurricanes, tornadoes, and earthquakes. But there is no way to buy insurance against more prolonged disruptions, such as the drought that scorched much of the Midwest and South in 1983, devastating crops and crippling many farm-related businesses. Because "heat" was not a named peril on most private insurance policies in the region, farmers had to seek federal assistance.

Other risks that insurers are reluctant or unwilling to consider include potential government actions and general economic conditions. Such uncertainties as changes in the law and economic fluctuations are beyond the realm of insurance.

Can a business reduce its uninsurable risks?

The answer to this question is yes. A business that keeps close watch on governmental, social, and economic trends is unlikely to be caught unprepared. For example, when Time Inc. discontinued publication of TV-Cable Week in 1983, with a subsequent $8.5 million loss, the corporation could still report an overall rise in revenues of 12.4 percent from its video operations, book divisions, and forest-products businesses.[4] As the TV-Cable Week case suggests, diversification is one of the best hedges against failure of a product line.

More directly, a company can try to cut its uninsurable risks by constant loss-prevention efforts, such as equipment maintenance, fire drills, and safety and health education. Well-managed companies employ risk managers who are trained to identify and analyze potential losses of all kinds. For example, Ronald Cooke, a loss-prevention director at the Maryland-based Giant Food supermarket chain, sold his company on the advantages of electronically sensitized gates that set off alarms when shoplifters leave the stores with stolen goods. His company reports an 80 percent reduction in security costs and an increased profit margin because of fewer thefts.[5]

Changes in uninsurable risks

Sometimes uninsurable risks become insurable when enough data become available to permit estimation of the actual risks. Insurers were reluctant to cover passengers on airplanes in the early years of this century. But decades of experience have made these risks accurately predictable. Similarly, companies can now buy insurance against the prospect that a foreign country will seize their factories, mines, or offices.

But as insurers iron out one set of complexities, others arise. Now, the insurance industry is beginning to address new risks related to computers, such as electronic theft, destruction and distortion of data, and illegal shutdowns. Insurance covering computer disasters is now the most sought-after type of crime coverage, though devising formulas to cover computer fraud still presents difficulties to the insurance industry. Several companies offer computer fraud insurance, but at staggering premiums, ranging from $25,000 to $100,000 per year for many businesses to as much as $1 million or more annually for a large bank.

Robots, too, are elbowing their way into insurance policies. While the mechanical arms of assembly-line robots are now insurable as "machinery," the computers that control them are not, despite their intricacy. One single power surge could cause $20,000 worth of damage in terms of replacement, labor, and lost production. Companies' increasing reliance upon such equipment has produced a demand for full insurance coverage.[6]

INSURABLE RISKS

Some risks are far easier to foresee than others. It is more likely that a fire will sweep through a crowded hotel casino than that a meteor will plunge into your room while you're reading this chapter. Therefore, it is far more reasonable to worry about fire—and it is also easier to insure, or buy protection, against it. This means that you or someone in business (the *insured*) pays a company (the *insurer*) for protection against damage by fire. Should a fire occur within the scope of the coverage provided in your *insurance agreement* (the **insurance policy**), the insurer would be obliged to **reimburse** you *(pay you back)* for the losses caused by the fire.

Of course, an insurance company cannot count on making a profit on any particular insurance policy. Rather, a pool of insured parties is required, most of whom will never collect damages. The insurance company can't pay for sizable damages out of

the **premium** *(the fee that the insured pays to the insurer for coverage)* it has received from any one insured. But it *can* pay for the damages by drawing some money out of the pool of premiums it has received from *all* its insureds.

The risk of fire is a good example of what is known as an **insurable risk**—*a risk for which it is possible to buy insurance from some insurance company*. Insurance companies offer insurance against fire because they have statistics telling them how frequently fires occur, under what conditions, and how much the damages generally cost. Using this information, the company can calculate how much it must charge each policyholder in order to be able to pay for fire damages and still make a profit (assuming that the company also knows approximately how many policyholders it will have). Other types of insurable risks are theft, auto collisions, and—of course—death. It should be noted, however, that many insurance policies carry riders that disallow certain claims. In some areas where floods are a common occurrence, for example, you cannot get insurance against damage caused by a flooded basement.

What kinds of risks do insurance companies cover?

An insurable risk generally meets the following requirements:

1. *The peril insured against must not be under the control of the insured.* This means, of course, that policies do not pay losses that are intentionally caused by an insured, or caused at the insured's direction, or caused with the insured's collusion. For example, a fire insurance policy excludes loss caused by the insured's own arson. It does not, however, exclude loss caused by an employee's arson.

2. *There must be a large number of similar cases subject to the same peril.* For example, fire is a common danger that threatens virtually all buildings. Most insurance is based on the law of averages; that is, as the number of *potential* risks in a category increases, the numbers of *actual* losses in that category move closer to the *predicted* risk figures, which were based on prior experience. However, the law of averages cannot be applied to unusual risks—those that threaten only a small number of subjects. For example, the possibility that John McEnroe will fracture

his serving arm and miss several lucrative tennis matches is an unusual risk because there is only one John McEnroe. Thus, most insurance companies would not consider this an acceptable risk. A famous exception is Lloyd's of London, which is not actually an insurance company, but an association through which members buy and sell insurance risks. Lloyd's has drawn worldwide attention by insuring such show business folk as Elizabeth Taylor, whose legendary illnesses classify her as a poor risk in terms of turning up for the entire run of a Broadway show. Lloyd's of London also arranges coverage for a host of other risky businesses—television networks, for instance. Lloyd's paid out a hefty $78.3 million to NBC when a political boycott of the 1980 Summer Olympics in Moscow forced the network to cancel its coverage.[7]

Lloyd's of London: founded in the seventeenth century, this organization is famous for taking on unusual risks. Lloyd's members paid out $100 million in claims for buildings destroyed by the 1905 San Francisco earthquake and $5 million after an iceberg sank the Titanic. The bell at Lloyd's headquarters has traditionally been rung when a ship insured by the company has been reported lost at sea.

3. *Losses must be calculable, and the cost of insuring must be economically feasible.* Insurance companies must have data on the frequency of losses caused by a given peril. This information should cover a long period of time and be based on a large number of cases. The insurance company can usually predict quite accurately how many losses will occur in the future with this information. For example, the number of people who will die each year in the United States has been calculated with great precision, and insurance companies use this information to set policyholders' payments.

4. *The peril must be unlikely to affect all insured simultaneously.* An insurance company should spread its coverage over large geographic areas. Otherwise, a single fire or natural disaster might force an insurance company to pay out on all its policies at once.

5. *The possible loss must be financially serious.* An insurance company could not afford the paperwork involved in handling numerous small claims of a few dollars each. As a result, many policies have a **deductible clause** that *specifies that the insurance company will pay only that part of a loss which is greater than an amount (the deductible) stated in the policy.* The deductible represents small losses which the insured has agreed to absorb. Your health insurer, for example, may require you to pay up to $100 of your physician's fees, and the company that insures your car may require you to pay the first $100 (or $500) of any needed repairs.

Absorbing insurable risks

Within the realm of insurable risks, there are many that may be absorbable. **Absorbable risks** *can be covered by insurance, but for one reason or another they're assumed, or absorbed, by a business itself.* In effect, such a company is *arranging to insure itself, rather than buying insurance from another company.* With this form of protection, called *risk retention* or *self-insurance,* the company plans for some means of absorbing losses due to accidents or disasters. Companies can either rely on their own self-insurance protection or combine it with conventional coverage.

For example, a huge corporation with a hundred factories might put aside a certain amount of money each year to cover possible fire losses. During the years in which there were no losses, the self-

FIGURE 1

INSURABLE AND
UNINSURABLE RISKS:
Do you see why each
of these was accepted
or rejected?

NAME:
Clark Kent

TYPE OF INSURANCE
REQUESTED:

Kryptonite Insurance

REJECTED
REASON No. **2**

NAME:
Mick Jagger

TYPE OF INSURANCE
REQUESTED:

Broken Guitar String Insurance

REJECTED
REASON No. **5**

NAME:
Carl Sagan

TYPE OF INSURANCE
REQUESTED:

Being-hit-by-a-meteor-Insurance

REJECTED
REASON No. **3**

NAME:
Noah

TYPE OF INSURANCE
REQUESTED:

Universal Deluge Insurance

REJECTED
REASON No. **4**

NAME:
Little Orphan Annie

TYPE OF INSURANCE
REQUESTED:

Dogbite Insurance

ACCEPTED

NAME:
Lizzie Borden

TYPE OF INSURANCE
REQUESTED:

Life Insurance on Parents

REJECTED
REASON No. **1**

NAME:
Methuselah

TYPE OF INSURANCE
REQUESTED:

Life

ACCEPTED
ACCEPTED
ACCEPTED

To be insurable, the risk must satisfy five requirements:

1. **The peril must not be under the control of the insured person or corporation.**

2. **The peril must be one that threatens many similar cases.**

3. **The losses must be of a type that can be calculated; the cost of insuring must be economically feasible.**

4. **The peril must *not* be likely to affect all insured persons or corporations at the same time.**

5. **The possible loss must be financially serious.**

insurance fund would grow. If a factory should burn down, the company would have enough money on hand either to rebuild or to replace it. Since it's unlikely that more than one factory would be totally destroyed by fire in any given year, the company should always have a fund large enough to meet that contingency. Setting aside money on a regular basis could very well be cheaper than purchasing insurance on each of a hundred factories.

Moreover, the company could earn interest on the reserved cash. For those companies that can afford it, self-insurance is becoming an increasingly popular alternative to buying protection from outside firms. Self-insurance in the area of medical costs and health benefits represents another important trend, as soaring medical premiums jolt businesses and state and local governments into seeking alternate routes for providing medical benefits.

PROTECTING A BUSINESS WITH INSURANCE

To protect itself from loss, a business has to insure its property against damage. Furthermore, it needs to protect assets such as cash and securities from loss due to natural or human causes.

LOSS OF PROPERTY

When a cannery in California ships jars of pizza sauce by truck to New York, the goods face unavoidable risks in transit. One wrong turn could cover a whole hillside with broken glass and sauce, and cost the manufacturer plenty. Furthermore, the canning factory itself is vulnerable to fire, flood, and, especially in California, earthquake. To protect against such losses, the company buys property insurance. **Property insurance** *covers the insured for physical damage to or destruction of property* and also its wrongful taking or theft. This insurance comes in three varieties: fire insurance, natural disaster insurance, and marine insurance. (Marine insurance, despite its name, covers losses related to transportation on water and on land.)

TABLE I Business Risks and Protection

RISK	PROTECTION
Loss of property	Fire insurance
	Disaster insurance
	Marine insurance
Loss from legal liability	Liability insurance
	Worker's compensation
Loss of earning power	Business interruption insurance
	Extra expense insurance
	Contingent business interruption insurance
	Small business and key-executive life insurance
Loss from dishonesty or nonperformance	Burglary, robbery, and theft insurance
	Fidelity bonding
	Surety bonding
	Credit life insurance

LIABILITY INSURANCE

As every licensed driver is aware, he or she can be held liable for substantial damages for causing an auto accident. Similarly, businesses are liable for any injury they cause to a person or to the property of others. **Liability insurance** *covers the insured for losses arising from injury, including death, to an individual and damage to the property of others.*

Sources of liability

What sorts of accidents or corporate practices might make a company liable for damages? The types of accidents that most commonly result in legal action are injuries received on the company's property, injuries caused by the company's products, and injuries from professional malpractice. Injuries received on the company's property may affect employees and/or outsiders; for instance, an elevator accident may involve both, whereas injury resulting from the collapse of metal shelving in a warehouse is likely to affect employees only. Malpractice includes bodily injury arising from treatment by doctors and dentists and loss of assets due to mishandling by lawyers and accountants. Examples of injuries caused by a company's products are food poisoning and choking on a loose toy part.

New trends in liability

In recent years, the scope of liability has been greatly extended to include even indirect involvement in loss, injury, or death. Some court decisions have held that businesses that distribute goods, like the companies that make them, are liable for any damages they cause. Other court rulings have held that a manufacturer not only must protect employees from diseases and injuries sustained during the manufacture of a product with dangerous elements, such as asbestos-lined heat chambers, but also has a "duty to warn" customers of those dangers. A company that provides services rather than products also may be sued for injury or damages.

Changes in the law have also made it easier to sue. Therefore, more and more workers and consumers are taking companies to court for injuries suffered on the job or while using the company's

THE INSURANCE POLICY

Assume that a business faces an insurable risk and wants to buy insurance. What actually happens? *One party, the* **insurer,** *agrees to pay another party, the* **insured,** for losses specified in a *written contract,* the **insurance policy.** The insured agrees to pay the insurer a fee called the *premium,* the amount of which is also specified in the policy. The premium is payable annually—first when the policy is issued, and then at each anniversary. The policy states the amount of money the insurer will pay if the insured suffers financial loss that falls within the scope of the policy's coverage. The amount the insured seeks to recover from the insurer is the *claim.* The *recovery* is the amount actually paid, often after some negotiation between the insurer and the insured. If the policy is a liability policy, the *recovery* is an amount determined by a court or negotiated between insurance company lawyers representing the insured and the plaintiff's or claimant's attorneys.

The amount of the premium is based mainly on the probability of loss in insuring a specific type of risk. For example, since fire is a greater risk for wooden buildings than for brick ones, insurance premiums tend to be higher for wooden structures. The insurance company must collect enough money in premiums to pay the claims of policyholders and also enough to cover its own expenses and operate at a profit.

Persons employed by an insurance company to compute expected losses and calculate the cost of premiums are called **actuaries.** An actuary considers three basic factors in setting premiums. One is the estimated loss rate—how much the insurance company expects to pay out in claims. A second is company expenses, such as taxes and salaries. In life insurance, a third factor is interest rates. Because reserve funds are invested to earn income for an insurance company, falling interest rates may force it to raise premiums.

products. For example, a series of cases was brought against makers of football helmets filed by young players injured while using them.[8] Hooker Plastics and Chemical Company faces what some experts regard as a legal "time bomb" in the form of liability suits. Hooker dumped toxic waste in Love Canal, near Niagara Falls, New York, from the early 1940s until 1953. Residents of the area, some of whom have suffered from serious illnesses believed to be caused by the dumped chemicals, have since sued Hooker for a total of no less than $12 *billion* in damages.[9]

Worker's compensation insurance

Worker's compensation insurance *pays the medical bills of employees who are hurt or become ill as a result of their work.* It covers loss of income by occupationally injured or diseased workers plus rehabilitation expenses for these workers, and it provides death benefits to the survivors of any employee killed on the job. In most cases it covers both full- and part-time employees.

If an injury is serious enough to disable an employee temporarily, he or she receives weekly benefits, usually after a waiting period of a few days to two weeks, depending on the state. If the injury is fatal, dependents receive weekly payments for a specified period (frequently eight years). This insurance protects businesses from loss of assets due to compensation claims, even if the injured employee wins a lawsuit for damages greater than those provided for in the policy.

LEGAL HANDLING OF WORKER'S COMPENSATION What's unique about worker's compensation insurance as a form of liability protection is that negligence need not be shown. Instead, negligent or not, an employer is obligated to reimburse—usually through an insurance company—the financial losses of employees whose health is impaired because of their work. Over the years the courts have interpreted worker's compensation laws broadly—holding companies liable for injuries related even indirectly to an employee's work. In one recent case, a worker in Rhode Island got angry and punched a coffee machine—and permanently damaged an arm. The worker was awarded $7,500 because the injury was "deemed to have met the requirements for a compensable situation—arising out of and in the course of employment."[10]

COSTS OF WORKER'S COMPENSATION Today all fifty states require almost every employer to carry worker's compensation insurance or to set aside enough money for self-insurance. In nearly all states the weekly benefit ceilings for an injured worker are two-thirds the average weekly wage.[11] But the cost of insurance to the employer varies from state to state, depending on the hazards in particular lines of work—and these costs have been rising, largely because of the steady climb in medical-care expenses.

Worker's compensation premiums have more than doubled in recent years, for a variety of reasons: higher benefits are being paid as wages and living costs rise; the courts have expanded the definition of "work-related injuries," as we have seen; and lawsuits have opened up whole new areas of coverage. Work-related illness, especially lung ailments from chemicals and fibers encountered on the job, is an area in which worker's compensation claims seem certain to grow.

To find less expensive alternatives, many businesses are turning to self-insurance programs. Another way to avoid paying high premiums is to cut down on the number of employee claims by reducing injuries and job-related illnesses. With that aim in mind, many companies are examining their safety programs more closely.

LOSS OF EARNING POWER

A fire in a supermarket chain's warehouse would, obviously, result in property loss, but that's only part of the story. Fires also disrupt the business, often costing the company more than repairs or replacement of damaged stock. Expenses continue—salaries, interest payments, rent—but no new revenues are coming in. Disruption also results in new expenses—leasing temporary space, paying overtime to meet work schedules with a reduced capacity, buying additional advertising to assure the public that the business still exists.[12] A prolonged interruption of business could even cause bankruptcy.

Tennis is much more than a game for stars like Martina Navratilova—a fact that's reflected in the costly and comprehensive insurance coverage major sports figures are obliged to carry.

For this reason many companies carry insurance protection over and above coverage for mere loss of property. Available coverage includes **business interruption insurance,** which *protects the insured when a fire or other disaster causes a company to temporarily shut down;* **extra expense insurance,** which *pays the additional costs of maintaining operations in temporary quarters;* and **contingent business interruption insurance,** which *protects against loss of business due to an interruption in the delivery of essential supplies.*

LOSS DUE TO DISHONESTY OR NONPERFORMANCE

Dishonest employees and criminals outside the company pose yet another threat to business property and assets. There are various ways of dealing with

FIGURE 2

The special multiperil policy (SMP) is a comprehensive policy that includes mandatory property and liability coverage plus optional coverage for theft and other perils.

this problem. A business owner can obtain a **fidelity bond,** which *protects the insured against dishonest acts—* such as embezzlement, forgery, and theft— *committed by employees.* And he or she can obtain a **surety bond—***a three-party contract in which one party agrees to be responsible to a second party for the obligations of a third party.* For example, in public construction projects, the law requires that surety bonds guarantee the performance of every contract. The insurance company would pay damages for any uncompleted or incompetent work of its insured—a construction company, let's say, that had been awarded a contract by a municipality. Similar bonds are required for contracts for garbage collecting and snow removal, as well as for elected officials, who must be insured against untrustworthiness while in

office. Surety bonds are also commonly used in the private sector. Railroads, for example, permit shippers to defer payment of freight charges upon the filing of a bond; corporations reissue lost or destroyed securities if there is a satisfactory bond indemnity.[13]

Another form of insurance against loss due to nonperformance is **credit life insurance,** which *guarantees repayment of the amount due on a loan or an installment contract if the borrower dies.* Yet another is **crime insurance,** which *covers loss from theft of any kind,* whether it is burglary (forcible entry into the premises) or robbery (taking property from another person by violence or the threat of violence).

EMPLOYEE INSURANCE

Besides insuring its property and assets, every business buys coverage for risks to its employees. Disease and disability, whether work-related or not, can cost employees huge sums of money unless they are insured. In addition, death carries the threat of financial hardship for an employee's family. Unemployment caused by a slowdown in business threatens even model workers with loss of income. And all workers must prepare to meet the cost of retirement.

For each of these risks there is a corresponding type of insurance available through employers. Federal law already requires employers to pay half the cost of employees' Social Security taxes. Most states also require companies to help finance state unemployment insurance funds, and as we have seen, all fifty states mandate worker's compensation. A few states even require employers to provide disability income insurance. But beyond these mandatory programs, most businesses also provide employees with substantial additional coverage.

Generally, companies are interested in three kinds of employee protection: health insurance, life insurance, and pension plans. These are usually provided through group policies, which are sold to the company by the insurer. In some cases, the employer pays for the insurance in full; in other cases, employees pay part or all of the cost through a payroll deduction plan.

HEALTH INSURANCE

Today, employee health insurance is more complete than it was ten or fifteen years ago. There have been traditionally two main types of insurance—one covering medical expenses, the other guaranteeing income in the event of a disabling illness or injury. That framework still exists, but today there tends to be more coverage for "ordinary" care as well as for serious medical problems. Dental coverage, for example, is more widespread—more than 80 million people now have some form of dental insurance, compared with 18 million a decade ago.[14] As for group disability protection, benefits now last longer and payments are higher. In 1982, 60 percent of disabled workers received $900 or more per month; in 1977 only 16 percent received this much. Waiting periods are longer, though: many policies do not begin paying benefits until six months after the disability has occurred, a pattern that was far less pervasive in 1977.

Americans received more than $100 billion in private health benefits in 1983. Just over $26 billion of that was provided by insurance companies, and most of the rest—over $24 billion—was paid by Blue Cross–Blue Shield, a well-known nonprofit health insurance program.[15]

Medical insurance

Medical insurance covers a variety of expenses. Although the types of coverage available have increased in the last few years, the vast majority of programs fall into five general areas.

HOSPITALIZATION INSURANCE **Hospitalization insurance** *pays for the major portion of a hospital stay.* Coverage varies, but most policies pay all or part of the cost of a semiprivate room and the total cost of drugs and services while the insured is in a hospital. Blue Cross is the best-known hospitalization plan.

SURGICAL AND MEDICAL INSURANCE *The costs of surgery and of physicians' in-hospital care are paid for by* **surgical and medical insurance.** Policies usually specify a maximum for each surgical procedure covered. Blue Shield is the best-known plan.

MAJOR MEDICAL INSURANCE *Medical expenses that fall outside the coverage limits of the two basic plans just discussed are covered by* **major medical insurance.** Benefits are usually limited to a percentage (often 80 percent) of medical expenses, and frequently the insured must pay at least $100 per year. A typical major medical policy may pay 80 percent of all medical expenses up to $250,000, and after the employee's own contribution in a given year has passed $1,500, most plans pick up 100 percent of the rest.[16]

DENTAL AND VISION INSURANCE These programs are becoming increasingly widespread. Like other medical plans, **dental and vision insurance** *covers a fixed percentage of an employee's expenses for eyeglasses, medically prescribed contact lenses, and various forms of dental work.* The best dental plans, however, have a "stop-loss" cutoff of about $1,000, after which the insurance pays the whole tab.[17]

MENTAL HEALTH COVERAGE Some companies also provide **mental health insurance** for *psychiatric care or psychological counseling.* But such plans generally require the insured to shoulder more than half of these expenses. After satisfying the deductible required by the policy, an employee with a mental or nervous disorder is usually eligible for mental health benefits ranging from 50 to 80 percent of the cost of treatment. However, relatively few companies offer mental health insurance.[18]

Covering the increasing costs of medical care

As medical technology becomes more sophisticated, the cost of medical care increases. To help employees cope with costs above and beyond the scope of traditional health insurance policies, some employers have either included new types of policies in their insurance packages or offered their workers the option of paying for extra coverage through payroll deductions.

Indeed, as medical expenses climb, businesses are less inclined to finance employee illness. In 1983, for example, there was a 20 percent jump in health care expenditures—four times the current rate of inflation as measured by the Consumer Price Index.[19] Cost containment is becoming essential;

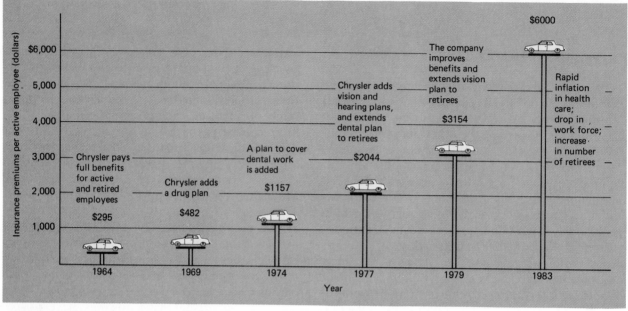

FIGURE 3

JACKING UP HEALTH CARE COSTS AT CHRYSLER: THE STEEP RISE IN EMPLOYEE INSURANCE PREMIUMS

Chrysler has much larger medical costs than most other companies. Its medical insurance plan is unusually generous. Ironically, too, cost-saving cuts in personnel have meant cost increases in insurance: Chrysler pays medical bills for long rolls of retirees.

thus, more and more companies now have worksite disease-prevention programs, referred to as "wellness programs" or "wellcare." Keeping employees healthy reduces absenteeism and lowers health costs. Johnson & Johnson's version of a wellness program is "Live for Life"—employees volunteer for physical checkups to identify health risks, after which they participate in free, professionally run workshops on smoking cessation, weight control, nutrition, stress reduction, and physical fitness. Other companies reward employees for staying well with cash incentives.

For a few years, **health maintenance organizations (HMOs)** looked like the answer to the business world's prayer for big savings in health insurance. **HMOs** are *comprehensive, prepaid group-practice medical plans in which consumers pay a set fee and in return receive all their health care at little or no additional cost.* Companies would cut expenses by enrolling employees in HMOs. Unlike hospitals and doctors in

private practice, who charge on a fee-for-service basis, HMOs charge a fixed annual fee from which they must cover all their expenses. Forced to operate within each year's "subscription income," they have a strong incentive to limit treatment and to avoid costly hospitalization. Yet a recent government-funded national survey indicates that while cost escalation has been less among HMOs than for conventional plans, savings offered by HMOs are slight. Moreover, administrative costs go up when companies offer HMO coverage in addition to conventional medical insurance. In 1982, only 10.8 million people were covered by this type of health plan, and there were only 277 of them around the country.[20]

Displacing HMOs, to an extent, in this quest for lower medical costs are **preferred provider organizations (PPOs)**—*health care providers that contract with employers, insurance companies, or other third-party payers to deliver health care services to an employee group at a reduced fee.* Employees are not required to use preferred providers, but they are often offered incentives to do so—reduced deductibles, lower copayments, or wellcare. PPOs not only save the employer money, they allow employers to control the quality and appropriateness of services provided. But critics point out that because of lack of cost-control incentives, PPOs may be tempted to make up in quantity of services what they lose in reduced fees. Other disadvantages cited are restrictions placed on employees' choice of hospitals and doctors, and the possibility that employers may be enjoined with hospitals and doctors in malpractice actions.[21]

Disability income insurance

The worker is protected from loss of income while disabled or partially disabled because of illness or accident by **disability income insurance.** The insured receives monthly payments while disabled, usually after a specified waiting period. Benefits normally depend on the extent of disability: whether it is partial or total, temporary or permanent. Disabled workers generally receive 50 to 60 percent of salary until retirement, offset by disability payments from Social Security. Some policies even provide partial payments if an employee is able to return to work but unable to maintain the same pace of career advancement or hours of labor per week.[22]

LIFE INSURANCE

Businesses generally insure the lives of their employees. Of the roughly $4.5 *trillion* of life insurance in force in the United States in 1982, over $2.2 *trillion* was bought on an individual basis to cover individuals. (Some of that individual coverage, though, was purchased by companies to insure key executives' lives). Another $2.1 *trillion* was invested in group policies by employers for their employees. Typically, these policies guarantee payment of twice or three times an employee's annual salary to his or her beneficiaries in case of death. Many plans also provide for "double indemnity" in case of accidental death or death while on the job. Most of the remaining $194 billion in life insurance is made up of credit life insurance, required by many lending institutions of borrowers of large sums of money in case the borrower were to die before paying off a mortgage or other large loan.[23]

PENSION PLANS

Few working people are able to save enough money in the course of their working years to be financially independent when they retire. Although nearly all workers are covered by Social Security, they can hardly rely on it to support more than a minimal standard of living once they've retired. The average monthly Social Security payment to retired workers in December 1983 was $430; the average monthly payment to couples was $742. However, most retirees collected the maximum monthly benefit: about $710 for a single worker, $1,240 for a family.

Pension plans have grown rapidly over the past decades as a way of providing retirement security. In 1940 only slightly more than 4 million people were covered by pension plans; by 1982 the figure had increased to over 50 million, and enrollment is still growing.[24]

Employers are not required by law to provide pensions for their employees. Many choose to do so, however, as an incentive to attract and keep good workers. Under some company pension plans, retired employees are paid out of the business's current income. More often pension plans are *funded*; that is, money is set aside on a regular basis to provide retirement benefits.

Pension guarantees

Despite their pensions, retirees are often in fairly tight economic circumstances. If their pensions were suddenly cut off—if their former employer went out of business or declared bankruptcy or if the pension fund simply ran out of money—many of these people would be destitute. Recognizing this fact, Congress passed the **Employee Retirement Income Security Act of 1974 (ERISA),** which *established the Pension Benefit Guaranty Corporation to insure the assets of pension plans.* (Not all provisions of the act became effective immediately; they were staggered to take effect between January 1, 1974, and January 1, 1981.) This act guarantees that, with some exceptions and limitations, retirement benefits will be paid no matter what happens to the company or the plan itself. It also sets standards for managing pension funds and requires public disclosure of a plan's operations.

While this law has meant a new degree of security for retirees, it's also potential trouble for companies with pension plans. Salary rates are increasing, and people are living longer than ever after retirement. As a result, many companies are finding that their pensions claims for the foreseeable future have grown nearly as large as their total assets.

Current pension issues

In the uncertain economic climate of the 1980s, companies have become more creative about substituting other assets in lieu of cash. Despite ERISA rulings that companies must pay at least 75 percent of pension funds in cash as liabilities occur when pensions are paid out, companies frequently ignore these requirements without fear of reprisal from ERISA or the Department of Labor. Some employees are being offered the option to choose stocks and bonds over cash contributions to pension plans: college teachers and administrators—members of the Teacher's Insurance and Annuity Association/College Retirement Equities Fund, for example—can opt for 50 percent stocks and 50 percent bonds, if they like, or any other ratio. Many companies meet pensions with specially created issues of preferred stock, real property, and royalty interest. U.S. Steel, for example, has been meeting pension plan obligations with unregistered preferred stock that can't be sold, thereby upping its cash equity by $333 million—a ploy that puts corporate officers in the driver's seat for pension plan strategy, linking pension plans to the corporation's future success in a way that threatens the arm's-length relationship companies are supposed to have with their retirement funds.[25]

As companies scramble to keep pension funds from drying up, *unisex legislation* threatens to strain pension programs further. In 1983 the Supreme Court ruled against companies that provide different levels of annuity benefits to men and women, paying women smaller monthly amounts than men on the assumption they live longer.[26] Legislators and women's groups argued that treating women as members of a class was a violation of their civil rights; they said it was not unlike discrimination suffered by blacks, who at one time were charged 50 percent more than whites for life insurance because they died at a younger age.[27]

What would happen if a pension plan collapsed? The first to feel the crunch would be the shareholders of the company involved. Before any profits could be taken from the company, it's likely that pension obligations would be honored. If there were still a gap between what was in the company's pension fund and what was demanded of it, the "plan termination insurance" policy set up by the ERISA legislation would go into effect. Whatever guaranteed benefits were left uncovered would be picked up by all the other companies in the government-established insurance scheme.

UNEMPLOYMENT INSURANCE

Business's responsibility to an employee doesn't end when the job is over. According to laws in all fifty states—and based on a federal mandate—employers finance special **unemployment insurance** *to benefit workers who are laid off and, to a lesser extent, those who quit their jobs.* The tax paid by each employer is related to the number of people from the business who have been on the unemployment rolls previously.

In the prolonged unemployment of the early 1980s, many people used up their unemployment benefits, including extended payments added to the usual twenty-six-week benefit period in most states. These additional funds were borrowed from the federal government, though a number of states now seek "forgiveness" of these loans.

CHAPTER REVIEW

Businesses confront speculative risk (the chance that their products may not be profitable) and pure risk (a definite loss); protecting against pure risk is the function of risk management. Risk management options include good management, risk avoidance, risk absorption, and insurance. An uninsurable risk is one for which insurance generally is not available—for example, losses due to economic and environmental conditions, poor management, and changes in government regulations. An insurable risk is a relatively calculable one that an insurance company is willing to cover. An absorbable risk is one that a business chooses to cover without going to an outside insurance company.

The two most important insurable risks are loss of property and loss due to liability. Property insurance includes fire insurance, natural disaster insurance, and marine insurance (which covers transportation on both land and sea). Liability insurance covers personal injuries, death, and property damage for which the insured is held responsible. Its scope has expanded greatly in recent years. One important type of liability insurance is worker's compensation. Loss of earning power and loss due to dishonesty or nonperformance are other categories of risks that business insurance covers.

Businesses also buy insurance to cover risks to their employees. Health insurance, life insurance, pension plans, and unemployment insurance are the major types of employee insurance. The primary categories of health insurance are medical and disability coverage. Some companies have dealt with the rising cost of employee health insurance by using health maintenance organizations (HMOs), which provide services in exchange for a regular contribution from employer and employees. Today HMOs are being displaced by preferred provider organizations (PPOs), health care providers that contract with employers and third-party payers to deliver health care to an employee group at a reduced rate.

Group life insurance is another benefit provided by many companies. Some also take out individual life insurance policies on key executives.

Company-funded pension plans provide a measure of financial security for retirees, but because of escalating costs, many businesses have accumulated pension claims that almost equal their total assets and are in danger of failing. The Employee Retirement Income Security Act (ERISA) of 1974 provides some guarantees that pensioners will not lose all of their benefits if their former employer fails to meet pension commitments.

By law, employers also finance unemployment insurance, which benefits workers who are laid off and, to a lesser extent, those who quit their jobs.

KEY WORDS

pure risk (438)
speculative risk (438)
risk management (438)
uninsurable risks (438)
insurance policy (440)
reimburse (440)
premium (440)
insurable risk (440)
deductible clause (441)
absorbable risks (441)
property insurance (443)
liability insurance (443)
insurer (444)
insured (444)
insurance policy (444)
actuaries (444)
worker's compensation insurance (444)
business interruption insurance (445)
extra expense insurance (445)
contingent business interruption insurance (445)
fidelity bond (446)
surety bond (446)
credit life insurance (446)
crime insurance (446)
hospitalization insurance (447)
surgical and medical insurance (447)
major medical insurance (447)
dental and vision insurance (447)
mental health insurance (447)
health maintenance organizations (HMOs) (448)
preferred provider organizations (PPOs) (448)
disability income insurance (449)
Employee Retirement Income Security Act of 1974 (ERISA) (449)
unemployment insurance (450)

REVIEW QUESTIONS

1. What is the difference between speculative risk and pure risk? How can risk management protect a company against pure risk?

2. Define absorbable risk and self-insurance. Why is self-insurance becoming increasingly popular among large corporations?

3. Define and give examples of an uninsurable risk. What steps can a business take to avoid such risks?

4. What is an insurable risk? What are the five requirements that characterize an insurable risk?

5. Discuss the importance of liability insurance to a business. Why has the cost of liability insurance risen dramatically in recent years?

6. What is worker's compensation insurance?

7. What are the five major forms of medical health insurance? Explain how an HMO works. Do the same for a PPO.

CASE 1

COPING WITH MEDICAL COSTS

Auto makers are up in arms about paying out a whopping $3 billion a year for employee medical benefits. The Big Three—Chrysler, Ford, and GM—report that benefits cost $3,000 per year per worker, plus an extra $2,000 per retiree. Benefits include up to 363 days of hospitalization, emergency-room care, visits to psychiatric clinics, and teeth cleanings, plus partial costs of prescription drugs, eye examinations, and glasses. Auto makers also foot the bill for 50 to 90 percent of dental work, including up to $800 worth of orthodonture.

Predictably, these expenses drive up the price of cars—as much as $400 to $600 per auto. The extra costs are a sore point with U.S. car makers, who are competing with Japanese companies. The Japanese produce autos that cost less, thanks to nonunionized workers who pay for part of their own medical coverage. Nissan, for instance, a U.S.-based Japanese company, pays one-third less for medical insurance. Nissan pays about $1,000 per worker, with employees responsible for 12 percent of their coverage. Retirees receive no medical benefits whatever. Not surprisingly, the Big Three are demanding quotas and restrictions on imported cars.

Auto makers are also pushing for cost sharing of medical insurance, claiming that workers would use benefits more sparingly if they

had to pick up part of the tab. But health care experts theorize that paying an extra $500 to $1,000 per year wouldn't necessarily convert workers into more discriminating consumers of medical care, and that unions might retaliate by seeking higher wage settlements—inevitably resulting in zero savings.

In the meantime, union officials firmly resist cost-sharing proposals: they take the position that burdening employees with such expenses will do nothing to slow the accelerating costs of medical care. Yet Ford Motor Company has made some changes along these lines, requiring nonunionized office personnel to pay $250 deductibles and $750 in other yearly health expenses they never had to pay before.

The Big Three cite overuse of insurance and outright fraud as reasons for asking workers to shoulder their share of soaring medical costs. The auto makers say that violations occur among doctors who order batteries of unnecessary tests to protect themselves from lawsuits; meanwhile, they declare, workers pop in and out of emergency rooms and hospitals without real need. Chrysler, for example, had to crack down on abuses at its Michigan plant, where so many foot surgery claims were filed that podiatry

had become a multimillion-dollar business. Under the United Autoworkers' contractual provision for medical insurance, workers get a week off with disability pay while podiatrists net fat fees for even minor surgery. Chrysler has since established a policy that requires employees to get prior Blue Cross approval for 111 different types of foot surgery—a measure that netted Chrysler $1 million a year in savings and brought an antitrust action by the Michigan State Podiatry Association. And an enterprising Detroit chiropractor is now serving five years in prison, having cost Ford, GM, Chrysler, and their insurers $4.6 million in 18 months by paying workers $20 a crack to visit him. Nearly 1,900 "patients" were "treated," costing auto makers $1.5 million in sick pay and $1.9 million to replace the "injured" workers.[28]

1. What nonmedical factors figure into excessive use of medical insurance by auto workers? What human needs of the workers are perhaps not being met that, if corrected, would alleviate this situation?

2. Since some auto workers may have misused medical benefits to get time off, what could auto makers offer in terms of alternative vacation arrangements and holidays that might reduce these abuses?

3. Devise an incentive program not mentioned in this chapter that would reward employees for minimal use of medical insurance.

4. What is your opinion of labor's resistance to cost-sharing plans for its members? Would workers be better off copaying medical costs and receiving higher wages that they could use at their discretion?

RISK MANAGEMENT AT A HOSPITAL

You have been assigned the job of managing risk for Sheltering Arms Hospital, a 400-bed general hospital located in a midwestern metropolitan area, and you are trying to analyze the various kinds of losses to which the hospital is exposed. Here are some of the major features of the situation:

The physical plant: The hospital's main building is a ten-story, fire-resistive building adjacent to the intersection of the two major expressways in the downtown area of the city (replacement cost $15 million). Steam to heat the hospital buildings and for other uses is furnished by the hospital power plant, a fire-resistive building located approximately 250 feet from the main building: the power plant (whose replacement cost is $340,000) contains four large steam boilers, any three of which can supply all the steam needed for the hospital, and the power plant is connected to the nearby steam plant of the local public utility. The hospital laundry, less than a year old, is located in a fire-resistive building adjacent to the power plant. An additional building owned by Sheltering Arms is a three-story nurses' home of ordinary masonry construction. The cost to rebuild it in its present form would be $300,000, but if this building

should suffer damage to the extent of 50 percent or more of its value, it would be necessary to demolish it and replace it with a fire-resistive structure to comply with present building codes (cost $400,000).

The facilities: Sheltering Arms has the usual facilities of a general hospital. There are operating rooms, dietary facilities, laboratories, and a pharmacy. There is a complete radiology laboratory where radioactive cobalt is used. The hospital operates two cafeterias in the main building. It also owns three parking lots; two of these are used for employee parking, and the third is leased to a private operator and is open to the general public.

Records and computer equipment: The medical histories of all patients—about 200,000 files—are stored on open filing shelves in a large room on the second floor of the main building. All billing records, payroll records, and purchase records are maintained by computer, using equipment leased from the manufacturer; computer tapes are stored in a room adjacent to the computer room on the first floor of the main hospital building.

Sheltering Arms' financial picture: The hospital's total annual income is $10 million. About $800,000 per year is required to pay interest and principal on the hospital's long-term debt; the hospital has 600 full-time employees.[29]

1. First, analyze Sheltering Arms' position in terms of potential property losses. What property losses might be very serious financially? What losses might be somewhat less serious? Can you identify some losses that should definitely be insured, and some that the hospital might consider absorbing? (Bear in mind the hospital's overall financial picture.)

2. Do the same for potential liability losses. What liability losses might be the most serious?

PERSPECTIVES ON SMALL BUSINESS FINANCIAL ASPECTS

APPROACHES TO FINANCING

Since the failure rate among small proprietorships, partnerships, and even corporations is high during the first five years of operation, and especially deadly during the first two years, financial institutions are wary of making small-business loans. In fact, it's fair to say *any* small business will have difficulty obtaining funds for any purpose unless there is sufficient collateral (property or equipment with a recognized resale value used as security) to protect the lending institution against losses.

Nevertheless, there are numerous ways small entrepreneurs can borrow funds for daily operations and other necessary expenses. Financing approaches open to the entrepreneur include:

1. Trade credit

2. Short-term bank loans

3. Leasing

4. Outside investors

5. Home-mortgage equity financing

6. Accounts-receivable financing

7. Lines of credit

8. The Small Business Administration (SBA)—the lender of last resort.

Below, we'll take a closer look at all these categories, except the SBA. (For information on the SBA, see the Perspectives on Small Business Section at the end of Part 6.)

Trade credit

To obtain trade credit, the owner of a business must establish a credit standing with vendors—the manufacturers or wholesalers who offer the goods needed to operate the business. Then, once the firm's credit has been established, the suppliers, rather than requiring cash on delivery, will allow the firm to delay payments on goods received.

It is difficult for new firms to obtain trade credit. Few vendors are willing to risk selling their products to a brand-new small business. Any firm without a track record of paying its bills is considered too high a risk. All large firms rely on prompt payment of their invoices—in fact, any large corporation will have a credit department whose sole function is to reduce credit risks. In a medium-size to large corporation, all incoming funds are immediately invested, and this interest income can be a healthy source of profits. So trade credit is not easy to obtain, and it must be respected once granted.

How, then, does the small operator effectively establish a credit relationship? Here are some steps you may wish to follow.

1. If you lack start-up funds, it's a good idea to negotiate a special arrangement with a few of your new customers. Ask if you can ship the goods they've ordered COD, in exchange for a reduced price. This way you'll obtain some cash from your customers early on, and you can use this cash to obtain goods from your own vendors. In this manner, you can begin to establish a relationship with several vendors that could lead to the granting of credit.

Once you have demonstrated your ability to pay bills and remain in business for three to six months, most vendors will begin to issue you a small line of credit, which will state a maximum dollar amount they'll allow you to purchase on a minimum of thirty days' credit. By the end of one year—with proper money management—your firm will have developed a good enough track record to qualify for more credit.

2. Some manufacturers who are aggressively trying to expand their markets or who have weaker products and/or product lines may offer more liberal terms. Ninety-day credit without interest is often available. This arrangement is especially useful to retailers who need a large inventory to display available product lines effectively, and to seasonal businesses such as toy stores, which must have most of their sales inventory available for only a brief portion of the year.

3. Another common method of providing products to sell for a new small business is flooring. Under this program, the manufacturer arranges with a bank or finance company to provide the funds for the small business to purchase inventory. The interest is paid by either the manufacturer or the business, or a combination of the two. Most new cars are handled in this fashion, along with hundreds of other high-ticket items like computers. Usually the product floored has a serial number and is tightly controlled. However, in all cases the flooring is arranged, guaranteed, and secured by a manufacturer who can command a top credit rating. A small business with limited funds could not establish flooring on its own.

4. Your small business will benefit greatly if you pay all vendors' bills promptly. You should make a concerted effort—even sacrifice, if necessary—to pay bills when they come due or earlier. Avoid past due notices! Aside from the obvious advantage of maintaining a good credit rating, you'll increase your leverage with your vendors. Occasionally, you'll want to be able to offer your customers special services when they have special problems. If you can help them when they need it most, you'll develop loyalty. And if you pay your vendors' invoices promptly, you'll be able to ask them to do favors for your customers. You may need a speedy delivery of a certain order—or an extended warranty period to cover a persistent maintenance problem.

If a small firm is slow in paying bills, vendors won't want to do special favors. In fact, the overall quality of the service you get in every area may drop. A large firm that is slow to pay may still ask for favors because its large purchases are important to any vendor. The small operator lacks this advantage.

Short-term bank loans

Banks, it is often said, are happy to lend you money if you can prove you don't need it. But does that mean you, the small operator, will never get a loan from a bank? No. Under the right conditions, banks are excellent sources of money.

The first point to remember is: always begin your borrowing when your need is small. That way you can easily repay on time, and you are more likely to receive the next loan. If you try when you are desperate, forget it.

Next, be aware that in dealing with small firms, banks generally like to limit their lending to loans that are completely repaid in less than a year. These loans are called short-term loans. (Small businesses are not considered solid risks for long-term loans unless they have collateral that's greater in value than the amount of the loan. Loans that are not repaid will go against the bank manager's record, so few will accept even moderate risks.)

Typically, short-term loans fit into the small-business situation quite well, since small businesses frequently have short-term needs—such as financing seasonal inventory, meeting an unusually large payroll in order to complete a contract, purchasing inventory to fill an order from a large firm that's usually slow to pay, or making a bulk purchase of goods at a reduced price. If your business is in need of short-term money, these approaches are likely to be effective with the bank:

1. Maintain a healthy bank balance. The money a bank lends comes from funds kept in checking and savings accounts. You must have a balance in the bank before it will consider your loan application. (Incidentally, you should always have at least two checking accounts. The second account will give you a safety factor.)

2. Always contact the manager first. His or her approval is essential, so why not start there?

3. Apply at two banks simultaneously for the same loan. As long as you don't attempt to borrow twice on the same collateral, this procedure is neither illegal nor unethical. If one bank denies your loan you'll need a second option, and it would be more difficult to go to the second bank after being refused by the first. It's also possible that each bank may grant you a portion of the loan only. You may even want to let both banks know they are competing for your business; this tactic could enhance your position.

4. Dress is important. Banking is a very conservative business, and you will improve your chances of success if you dress accordingly.

5. Present a sound business reason for wanting the money. Have detailed facts and figures ready. Be sure to stress that the loan is for the improvement of the firm, not for its survival.

6. Submit complete financial statements to the bank. This establishes the financial stability of your company, and indicates that your business is receiving professional accounting supervision.

Leasing

Leasing is not only another form of financing, but also an excellent way to acquire the capital equipment you will need. With leasing, you pay for the use of the equipment during the term of the lease, and when the time expires you can either return the equipment to the leasing company or renew the lease at a greatly reduced rate.

Leasing has a number of very important advantages over other forms of business financing:

1. The term of the loan payback is usually in equal monthly payments for terms from twelve to as high as sixty months.

2. One of the prime advantages of a lease is the low initial cash investment. If you purchased a $10,000 piece of equipment through a bank loan, you would need a down payment of at least 25–35 percent. For a standard twenty-four-month lease, in contrast, the only cash you'll need is the first and last month's rent. Some leases require only the first month's rent to start the lease. This gives you tremendous leverage. You pay for the equipment as you use it, just like you pay for other services in your company—employees, rent, and so on.

3. On a standard lease, the investment tax credit is kept by the leasing company. However, you can get most leasing companies to pass the investment tax credit on to you simply by asking. The leasing company will raise the monthly rent, but the right to use this tax credit should be well worth the extra cost. Entrepreneurs forget to ask for this right all too often.

4. The only real disadvantages of a lease are the high cost of the money—at least 24 percent—and the fact that you don't even own the equipment at the end of the lease. But is the cost really high? You must remember the low down payment and the investment tax credit.

A lease is excellent from a cash-flow standpoint, and should be strongly considered when the equipment leased will benefit your business's growth and you lack the cash to purchase the equipment or make a down payment on it.

5. Some leases offer buy-out agreements, but remember that any such lease will be questioned by the IRS. The special tax status of a lease allows the entire monthly rental to be deducted from profits as a regular monthly business expense. Outright purchase at the end of the lease period can affect the tax treatment of these lease payments. Purchasing leased equipment is a very touchy subject; it will require attention from your accountant.

Outside investors

Another way for a small business to raise capital is by attracting individuals who will invest in the firm. Their investment will buy either an ownership position in the business, or an opportunity to share in the business's profits.

You must first decide what legal form of business you will adopt. In the Perspectives on Small Business at the end of Part 1, we outlined five of the most common forms of business: sole proprietorship, partnership, limited partnership, the regular corporation, and the Subchapter S Corporation. Remember to consider the implications of liability and investor participation, and to analyze the options with your financial and legal consultants.

Next, you'll need to explore all the possibilities of attracting people willing to invest money. The first and most obvious place to look for investors is among your employees. This doesn't mean you should offer ownership in the business to all employees. Doing so could represent a threat to your control: any employee who becomes a part-owner might want to participate in management decisions. But you might offer key employees an opportunity to invest in the company. You'll also want to talk to your CPA, lawyer, business associates, or a recognized consultant. They may know people who are interested in investing in a small firm. Try every possibility; you never know what door will lead to an investor until you knock.

Newspapers, trade journals, and newsletters can be good places to advertise for potential investors. If you choose this method, remember these rules:

1. Give as many details as possible without revealing the identity of your company. Be very careful and conservative when you indicate anticipated investment returns, and always mention the risk factor involved in the investment. Even if the risk is high, many investors will be interested if returns in excess of 25 percent per year are available. Also, be sure you do your homework on all the financial mathematics involved. Your figures must be right.

2. Receive all leads and information at the newspaper, or at a location that's not traceable to your company. You don't want to be bothered by salespeople, money brokers, or other opportunists. Furthermore, you can't afford to waste your time with endless and unproductive meetings. Your only contact should be with investors, not with agents who represent them.

3. Once you have arranged a meeting with a potential investor, make sure that your financial statements are neatly and professionally prepared for presentation, and that a clear statement of your financial needs is arranged in logical steps. An investor will want to see a concrete program of action.

4. Don't expect an investor to fund executive salaries, or luxuries such as company cars or plush furniture.

5. Reduce any possible areas of doubt. Allow the investor to bail out at any time. You're not trying to trap anyone; you want someone who will be willing to help your business grow, in exchange for a better-than-average return on the investment.

6. Don't deal with anyone who needs the income from this investment for living expenses. The risk is too great for this type of investor, and in the event of any problems, are more likely to sue.

7. Expect to have several meetings before any serious commitments are made. Don't rush investors. Let them rush you. A reluctant person who is pushed into a deal can cause you endless problems—including a lawsuit.

8. Impress the investor with your knowledge of the industry or marketplace. Give details. Who are your competitors? What are their strengths and weaknesses? Indicate the relative size of each competing firm. A display of knowledge of this sort will create an atmosphere of trust, and enhance your chances of success.

Home-mortgage equity financing

One of the means small-business owners use most frequently to obtain funds is to borrow money against the equity of their homes. Your equity—the difference between your home's market value and the amount of money you owe on the existing mortgage—can be turned into cash for any worthwhile purpose. With the rapidly appreciating values of real estate, equity in a home is an excellent source of funds. As a homeowner, you have two options:

1. You can refinance your first home loan and obtain a new, larger loan; the cash gain is tax free, and the interest is tax deductible. This approach is often unattractive because the interest rate on the new loan is usually higher than the rate on the old loan. This means a lot of extra interest, since first loans usually have long terms. In some states, though, this is the only type of real estate loan available to the homeowner.

2. Many states, including California and Florida, allow a homeowner to obtain a second mortgage on a home without refinancing the first one. This will be a better option if the interest rate on the existing mortgage is lower than the interest rate on a refinanced first mortgage. The savings in interest will be substantial.

Since owning a home is generally a family venture, it is advisable for both husband and wife to agree to borrow against the equity of the home. The risk of losing the home if the business fails is a very serious disadvantage of this approach.

Accounts-receivable financing

Many of the small-business owner's larger customers are likely to pay their bills slowly. Large corporations' elaborate accounting procedures require forty-five to sixty days before a check can be issued. Yet the small entrepreneur requires both prompt payments and the business of the larger firms. What solutions are available?

The first option is to sell your accounts receivable to a firm that specializes in the purchase of such ac-counts at a discount. Your small firm will receive immediate cash, and the firm purchasing the bills will keep the cash it collects. Usually, this service is available only when the firms that owe you money have high Dun and Bradstreet ratings.

You can also borrow money at the bank to cover late bills, either occasionally or on a regular basis. You might consider increasing prices to those companies that are usually slow to pay, in order to cover the cost of the interest you have to pay for the loan. (If you charge interest, be sure you don't violate state laws for maximum interest rates.) You should also print a statement on all your invoices that the customer is responsible for all legal fees necessary to collect unpaid bills. This will give you some added leverage.

Lines of credit

Every small business should consider establishing a line of credit with several banks. By doing so you determine the maximum amount of money your business can borrow at any given time. Knowing the limits of your credit is essential for your long- and short-term planning.

INSURANCE

As we noted in Component Chapter E, insurance is necessary in any business regardless of its size, because it helps offset the adverse effects of property and personal losses. Frequently, small-business owners feel they can't afford to insure themselves and their businesses fully—but this type of cost cutting can be disastrous.

Health insurance

Low-cost medical and dental insurance is a major problem for most small entrepreneurs and their employees. It costs insurance companies more to service small businesses than large ones, so medical coverage for a small owner is expensive. Some insurance organizations have formed trusts that are available to small firms. The rates are high, but the coverage is adequate. The risk of excessive medical expenses is greatly reduced.

Life insurance

One area of insurance that offers some unique advantages and opportunities to small business is life insurance. Because it creates instant money upon the death of an insured owner, life insurance has helped solve many sticky business problems.

The first of these problems is, of course, the death of the owner—one of the most serious problems that can befall a sole proprietorship. Usually, when the owner dies the business dies too—along with the careers of its employees and the income of family members who survive the owner. But life insurance can solve this problem.

If one or more of the employees wishes to buy the business at the owner's death, they can (before the owner's death) purchase an insurance policy on the life of the owner in the amount equal to the value of the business. The employees who wish to buy the business pay the premiums on the policy. When the owner dies, the face value of the policy is paid to the owner's heirs or estate, and the business is transferred to the policyholders. The insurance money has provided the funds for the transfer of ownership. (An attorney must provide the legal documents necessary for the transfer at death.)

Next is the problem of the firm's key employees. All small businesses have one or two people who are critical to the firm's survival. Their lives can be insured. In the event of the death of one of these key people, the face value of the policy becomes available to hire a replacement. The company will still go through a difficult period, but the insurance money should enable it to survive.

Furthermore, as mentioned earlier, life insurance can be used as a means of funding buy/sell agreements for partnerships and corporations. Few small firms have enough capital to pay a dead owner's heirs the full dollar value of their share of the inherited business and pay inheritance taxes. Life insurance provides that needed money.

And finally, life insurance can be used to provide a death benefit in a company retirement plan. The death of one of the members of the plan, especially in the early stages, could easily bankrupt the program. The immediate money from life insurance can solve this problem.

PART FIVE

TOOLS OF BUSINESS

At Giant Foods, a major supermarket chain, computers have become almost as universally useful as the old-fashioned clipboard and pencil. In Giant's checkout lanes, for example, computerized scanners whizz over cans of soup, loaves of bread, and other purchases, adding up what customers owe and updating shelf inventory as the goods move out of the store. In the pharmacy departments, computers record customers' prescription histories, supply current price information, and print out drug labels. Behind the scenes, other computers monitor employee clock-ins, the temperatures of freezer cases, and meat-cutting and deli operations. Meanwhile—perhaps most important—computers are at work in the accounting department, helping managers keep track of revenues, accounts payable, and all the other transactions and money flows that take place in the business.

Computers, of course, are only the newest development in business managers' age-old effort to stay in touch with "the

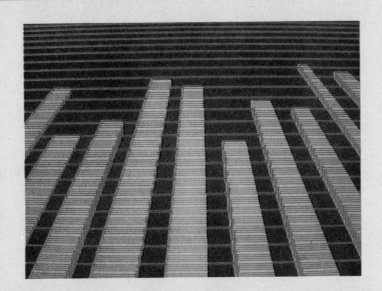

numbers"—all the vital numerical information that tells them what their costs are, how their goods are moving, and, in general, how healthy their business is. In Part 5, you'll read all about "the numbers," and how businesses use computers to keep track of them.

☐ We start with accounting, the most important topic, in Chapter 16, **Basic Accounting Principles.** Here you'll learn how accountants set up two basic accounting documents, the balance sheet and the income statement.

☐ Chapter 17, **How Computers Are Used in Business,** tells how companies use computers to keep track of accounting records and other crucial functions.

☐ Component Chapter F, **How Computers Work,** talks about computer hardware, the parts of a computer system, and the codes used to represent data inside the computer.

BASIC ACCOUNTING PRINCIPLES

Once each year, *Forbes* magazine publishes a list of what it calls "Up & Comers"—small companies with an excellent track record. These firms, in every line of business from fast food to high tech, are those that *Forbes* thinks have a good chance of becoming tomorrow's corporate giants. *Forbes'* 1983 class of Up & Comers included innovative Tandon Computer, which has stayed on top of the personal-computer market via better and cheaper disk drives; Dreyer's Grand Ice Cream, which increased its prices to expand into a twenty-state chain; and Timeplex, a manufacturer of data-communications equipment, which has aggressively recruited skilled employees. But *Forbes* didn't pick these companies just because it liked their looks or their policies. It picked them on the basis of their numbers. To be an Up & Comer, a company must show an average increase in earnings per share of at least 15 percent or more over the past five years, and it must also have an average return on equity of at least 15 percent over the same time period—with debt not exceeding equity.

Does all this sound a little mysterious? It may, if you're not familiar with the language of accounting—those all-important numbers that tell you how a business is doing. But take heart: accounting is not an impenetrable jungle of detail. It involves some intriguingly logical procedures, which you'll learn about in this chapter.

CHAPTER FOCUS

After reading the material in this chapter, you will be able to:
- define accounting, and describe its importance to managers, investors, and creditors
- distinguish between public and nonpublic accountants
- state the substance of the two basic accounting principles
- distinguish between a balance sheet and an income statement, and cite the effects of inflation on each
- define ratios, and state how to calculate six common ones
- cite the purpose of a budget, and list three types of subbudgets

When is a basketball player interested in accounting? You might not think such a sober subject would excite the magicians of the hoop. But when a union agreement ties their salaries to the total revenues the basketball league takes in, players are vitally interested in accounting, especially the branch of that field known as revenue accounting. Starting with the 1983–84 season, for example, the National Basketball Association put into effect an agreement to distribute 53 percent of all the league's gross revenues for players' salaries. And the way the league accounts for these revenues involves a whole set of policies for deciding *how much* of *which* money belongs to *which* categories, and *when*. Because there are so many possible ways of calculating revenues, these accounting policies are matters of vital concern to the basketball players.[1]

When is an ex-football player interested in accounting? When he's totaling up the amount he has invested in the 200 franchises of his fast-food chain. Doug Sheley left football for the fast-food business, and not long after, he could tell you the cost of a frozen yogurt machine or a warehouseful of whole-wheat burger buns. Often, business managers like Doug need to place a dollar amount on things that change in value over time, and accountants help them to make such determinations in a standardized way. Doug's keen eye for accounting details has nurtured "D'Lites," his nutrition-conscious fast-food chain, from start to success.[2]

Traditionally, the accountant has been responsible for giving management the financial information and the means of control that it needs to run its business profitably. And even in those cases in which profit doesn't enter the picture, the accountant must still insure that the organization is efficiently run.

THE NATURE OF ACCOUNTING

We've met some accounting concepts—assets and liabilities—in our discussion of short-term and long-term finance (Chapters 13 and 14). In this chapter we'll talk about accounting methods and some of the problems today's accountants are facing. **Accounting** is a *system of principles and techniques that permits bookkeepers or computers to record, classify, and accumulate sales, purchases, and other transactions.* In addition to providing ways of recording data, accounting *provides ways to present and interpret this information so that a company's past performance, present condition, and future planning can be clearly and efficiently evaluated.*

Such information is crucial for business management; it is the basis for all important decisions affecting a company's future. **Accounting statements**—*summaries of a business's operations during a given time period and its financial position at the end of that period*—are produced by the accounting systems that trace the flow of resources through the business. Through these statements, accountants help managers see that customers are billed for sales of goods and services; that **receivables**—*money owed to the business*—are collected; and that cash is put to work. Likewise, accounting helps management keep track of wages, taxes, and other **payables,** or *money the business owes.* And in addition to keeping management informed, accountants have traditionally kept others (stockholders, investors, creditors, and the government) aware of the company's financial position and the results of its operations.

Today none of that has changed. What has changed, however, is the depth in which the accountant performs these tasks and the power he or she exercises in doing so. Some accountants rise to the position of controller in their firms, keeping a firm financial hand on virtually every phase of a company's operations. The controller of a medium-to-large corporation monitors and cross-checks every aspect of financial data, usually with the help of a computer, to pinpoint the company's financial health at any given point in the past, present, or future. More than that, however, the controller is charged with making certain that a company uses all of its assets to the fullest, and that it acquires new assets that will increase the company's earning power even further.

WHAT ARE THE MAJOR TYPES OF ACCOUNTANTS?

Considering the diversity of opportunity that accountancy offers, it's not surprising that there is a range of types of accountants. Accountants can be divided into two basic groups: public accountants and nonpublic, or corporate, accountants.

Public accountants

Public accountants *operate in a service capacity; they are independent of the businesses and other organizations they serve.* Their position of detachment permits them to submit honest and, when necessary, critical reports on the financial statements of a business. They are of value to anyone who must have an accurate picture of the financial workings of a particular business; their clients include creditors, stockholders, investors, and even government agencies. Objectivity is a public accountant's stock in trade, and he or she can be sued for issuing financial information that doesn't accurately reveal a business's condition and income.

Public accounting firms have been in the news lately as a result of the increasing number of business failures. Certain accounting firms have given unqualified approval to the accounting statements of companies later found to be on the brink of bankruptcy: the result, of course, has been embarrassment to the accounting firms. The financial statements of the banks involved in the major bank failures of our decade, Franklin National, Penn Square, and United American Bank (the bank that financed the 1982 Knoxville World's Fair), had all been given a clean bill of health by their auditors (the public accounting firms assigned to report on them) just before the Federal Deposit Insurance Corporation declared the banks bankrupt. Next came investigations, warnings, and sometimes legal proceedings against the auditors. Clearly, if an accounting firm wants to avoid such situations, its officers must be willing to insist on disclosure of financial difficulties in a company it is auditing—even if that company isn't happy to hear the bad news and may take action in response. It can be quite a challenge for accountants to maintain objectivity, knowing that their client may fire them for shedding light on sensitive areas. And there is evidence that an increasing number of auditors are indeed getting fired for just these reasons—a sign of a job well done, from the public's point of view.[3]

Public accountants fall into several categories. Those who *meet a state's requirements for education and experience and pass an examination prepared by the American Institute of Certified Public Accountants* become **certified public accountants (CPAs).** It's estimated that every year another 10,000 accountants are certified. In 1982 there were approximately 1.2 million accountants in the country, or one for every two lawyers, but of these only about 250,000 were CPAs.[4]

About half of the CPAs in the United States are in private practice, working in no fewer than 29,000 accounting firms. Approximately 2 percent of those firms are large, having about fifty partners each and hundreds of lesser, salaried accountants. There are twenty-one giant nationwide and multinational firms with more than fifty partners each. And finally, there are those eight firms at the top, universally known as the Big Eight of accounting: Arthur Andersen & Co.; Arthur Young & Co.; Coopers & Lybrand; Deloitte Haskins & Sells; Ernst & Whinney; Peat, Marwick, Mitchell & Co.; Price Waterhouse & Co.; and Touche Ross & Co.

Nonpublic accountants

Nonpublic, or corporate, accountants are *those in the employ of one business or individual,* supervising the accounting system and the bookkeeping staff. They're responsible for both the flow of financial reports and their interpretation. They usually specialize in one of the areas listed in Table 1.

TABLE I   Areas of Specialization for Nonpublic Accountants

AREA	JOB RESPONSIBILITIES
General accounting	Records all business transactions and prepares reports and financial statements
Controlling (management) accounting	Uses reported data to help managers plan operations, price new products, select alternative methods of financing, and make other decisions
Internal auditing	Checks the accuracy of company's records and accounting methods; polices errors and possible larceny of employees
Cost accounting	Controls the cost of manufactured products and their distribution; helps management estimate future costs
Accounting systems installation	Designs systems for recording and reporting financial data that include cross-checks on the record keeping

KEY ACCOUNTING CONCEPTS

In this section we will see how accountants go about their work. To begin, let's examine the important accounting equation and the double-entry bookkeeping system.

THE ACCOUNTING EQUATION

For thousands of years businesses and governments have kept records of their **assets**—*valuable things they owned*, like gold and wheat—and of their **liabilities**—*what they owed*, like loans. When it was said of ancient princes that they were as "rich as Croesus" (a wealthy king of Lydia), it was not just because they had stored away much gold and grain. It was because they owned these treasures almost outright and had few debts or creditors' claims on their assets.

The wealth of a person or a business is not measured by assets alone. It is what remains after you deduct liabilities from the assets. And that remainder is called **owners' equity,** which is the *owners' claim on the assets.*

Assets	$100,000
Liabilities	−30,000
Owners' Equity	$ 70,000

This rather ordinary observation is the basis for the all-important **accounting equation**:

$$\textbf{Assets} = \textbf{Liabilities} + \textbf{Owners' Equity}$$
$$\$100,000 = \$30,000 + \$70,000$$

The liabilities are placed before the owners' equity because creditors have first claim on the assets. After liabilities are paid, anything left over belongs to the owners or, in the case of a corporation, the stockholders. However, if you want to emphasize the amount of owners' equity, you might write the same equation as:

$$\textbf{Assets} - \textbf{Liabilities} = \textbf{Owners' Equity}$$
$$\$100,000 - \$30,000 = \$70,000$$

Whichever form you use, the relationship between assets, liabilities, and owners' equity remains in balance; in other words, one side of the equation equals the other side.

DOUBLE-ENTRY BOOKKEEPING

Like many other useful discoveries, double-entry bookkeeping surfaced here and there for centuries before anyone took a careful look at it. It was not until Columbus landed in America that a practical Italian monk named Fra Luca Pacioli wrote the first clear, systematic description of double-entry bookkeeping. His system immediately caught the attention of the merchants and princes of his day.

Pacioli explained that every transaction—a sale, a payment, a collection—had two sides or two monetary effects. Every transaction led to changes in parts of the accounting equation. But no matter what kinds of transactions were made, the accounting equation remained in balance if the transactions were properly recorded. **Double-entry bookkeeping** *requires a two-part, "give and get" entry for every transaction.* The accounting equation is kept in balance by offsetting any change in one part of the equation with a change in another part.

Double-entry transactions

Let's say you decide to open a video cassette rental shop. You need to stock 1,000 titles, costing you $30 each, so you'll have to raise $30,000 in capital. You have $20,000 of your own to invest, so your accounting equation would show:

$$\textbf{Assets} = \textbf{Liabilities} + \textbf{Owners' Equity}$$
$$(cash)\ \$20,000 = 0 + \$20,000$$

In other words, $20,000 in cash is equal to your owners' equity of $20,000. As yet, your business has no liabilities.

Next, let's say that you do three things:

■ You borrow $10,000 from the bank. The same amount ($10,000) is added both to your cash account under "assets" and to your bank-loan account under "liabilities." Thus your accounting equation is kept in balance.

■ You go video cassette shopping and buy the $30,000 of inventory that you need.

■ In the first month, you rent out 500 films, charging $4 per rental, for total revenue of $2,000. You find that it costs you $1,500 to run your store, including salaries, rent, and $400 of wear and tear on your video cassettes. The $500 excess (rental revenues minus costs), which is your profit, becomes a part of the owners' equity and is called *retained earnings*.

These three transactions might be recorded as shown in Table 2.

The meaning of double-entry transactions

Each of the transactions of your business was recorded to show the dual effect of what happened in dollar terms. Your initial investment in the business increased cash by $20,000. At the same time it increased owners' equity (stock) by the same amount, showing that the owner had a claim on the business equal to the full amount of the assets (cash).

If you had recorded the second transaction (the bank loan) merely by increasing your cash account by the $10,000 borrowed, your records would be out of balance. More important, the other part of the transaction (the liability created by the $10,000 bank loan) would have caught you by surprise when the loan came due. One of the beauties of the double-entry system is that errors of omission (such as neglecting to record half a transaction) throw the accounting equation out of balance. This imbalance gives warning that an error has been made.

The third transaction demonstrates how one asset can be exchanged for another. The $30,000 in cash is exchanged for $30,000 in inventory. Cash is decreased by $30,000 while inventory is increased by the same amount. Subtraction and addition of the same amount on the "assets" side keep the accounting equation in balance.

The fourth transaction illustrates how revenue activities provide asset inflows (the $2,000 increase in cash), consume assets ($1,000 cash outflow for salaries and rent and the $400 wear and tear on cassettes), and increase the owners' equity by the amount of the profit ($500).

Obviously, after a few months, the transactions recorded by a bookkeeper can pile up. Management would need weeks to sort through all of them for the information it needed. To save time, accountants prepare summary reports. Let's take a look now at the two most common reports: the balance sheet and the income statement.

THE BALANCE SHEET

In 1982 Apple Computer was a company ready for the future. It had pioneered the personal microcomputer, starting in a garage in 1977. In 1980 its stock had become a favorite of investors, with the popular Apple II holding promise of spectacular

TABLE 2 An Example of Double-Entry Bookkeeping

| TRANSACTION | ASSETS | | = LIABILITIES + OWNERS' EQUITY | | |
	CASH	INVENTORY (CASSETTES)	BANK LOAN	STOCK	PROFIT (RETAINED EARNINGS)
Investment	+20,000	—	—	+20,000	—
Loan	+10,000	—	+10,000	—	—
	30,000	—	= 10,000	20,000	—
Inventory purchase	−30,000	+30,000	—	—	—
	—	30,000	= 10,000	20,000	—
Rental revenue	+ 2,000	—	—	—	+2,000
Expenses	− 1,100	− 400	—	—	− 1,500
	+900	+29,600	= +10,000	+20,000	+500

earnings, and many models on the drawing board. Shortly thereafter, IBM introduced its contender in the personal computer field, and it became apparent that the road to microcomputer megabucks would not be without bumps. But Apple was ready to fight: it had significantly enlarged its production facilities, and at that point in time it had relatively little debt, thanks to the popularity of its stock. (Apple had been able to finance much of its investment in new production facilities from profits.) Soon, however, Apple would have to start paying out more of those earnings as dividends, or it would lose favor with its shareholders and would need to turn heavily to banks to finance its growth plans.

The kind of information we're talking about here is something we can derive by looking at a company's balance sheet or statement of financial position—a kind of "snapshot" of where the company is, financially speaking, at one moment in time. The **balance sheet** *includes all of the elements in the accounting equation.*

Figure 1 shows the balance sheet of Apple Computer, Inc. It reveals the kind and amounts of assets, liabilities, and owners' equity at a specific moment in time. (For example, note the difference between Apple's "property, plant, and equipment" in 1982 and the same category in 1983; and note the large increase in Apple's "retained earnings" from 1982 to 1983.) Using the information on this statement, potential creditors can determine whether a company is likely to be able to cover its present and future debts.

Of course, no business can hold still for someone who is examining its financial condition. Even during a holiday, office fixtures grow older and interest on a savings account accumulates. Yet the accountant must set up a balance sheet to show the condition of a business *at one moment in time.*

At least once a year, every company prepares its balance sheet. This is most often done at the end of the year. The year is most often the **calendar year,** *January 1 to December 31.* However, many business and government bodies use a **fiscal year,** which may be *any twelve consecutive months.* For example, a business may choose a fiscal year from June 1 to May 31 because its peak selling season is over in May. Such a fiscal year would then include its full manufacturing, selling, and collection cycle.

Some companies prepare a balance sheet more often than once a year, for example at the end of each month or quarter. Thus every balance sheet is dated to tell you when the financial "snapshot" was taken.

Most detailed balance sheets use categories similar to those shown in Figure 1 to classify assets, liabilities, and equities. A closer look at these categories will help you understand other balance sheets you may come across.

ASSETS

Most often, the asset section of the balance sheet is divided into three groups—current, fixed, and intangible—listed in order of the ease with which the assets can be turned into cash.

Current assets

These assets are always listed first. Included in this group are cash and other items that will or can become cash within the following year.

The term **cash** includes *cash on hand, in checking accounts, and in savings accounts.* Not included are funds in special deposits or in any other form not readily available for use.

Marketable securities (temporary cash investments) are *stocks, bonds, and other investments that can be quickly turned into cash when needed.* Such investments are temporary and not important to the business as a means of long-term control over the company in which it invested.

"Accounts receivable" and "notes receivable" are accounting terms for the short-term financial instruments you learned about in Chapter 13. *Amounts due from customers* are known as **accounts receivable.** Often accountants deduct from accounts receivable an allowance for bad debts (doubtful accounts). This deduction notifies creditors and stockholders that not all of the receivables are considered collectible. **Notes receivable** differ from accounts receivable in that they *are written and signed promises to pay a definite sum, plus interest, usually on a certain date and at a certain place.* As noted in Chapter 13, they are generally collected routinely through the customers' banks.

FIGURE 1

Consolidated Balance Sheets of
Apple Computer, Inc., 1982 and 1983

September 30, 1983 and September 24, 1982 (Dollars in thousands)	1983	1982
Assets		
Current assets:		
Cash and temporary cash investments	$143,284	$153,056
Accounts receivable, net of allowance for doubtful accounts of $5,124 ($3,606 in 1982)	136,420	71,478
Inventories	142,457	75,368
Prepaid income taxes	27,949	2,089
Other current assets	18,883	9,223
Total current assets	468,993	311,214
Property, plant and equipment:		
Land and buildings	19,993	7,220
Machinery and equipment	51,445	26,136
Office furniture and equipment	22,628	13,423
Leasehold improvements	15,894	10,515
	109,960	57,294
Accumulated depreciation and amortization	(42,910)	(22,811)
Net property, plant and equipment	67,050	34,483
Other assets	20,536	12,090
	$556,579	$357,787
Liabilities and Shareholders' Equity		
Current liabilities:		
Notes payable to banks	$ —	$ 4,185
Accounts payable	52,701	25,125
Accrued compensation and employee benefits	15,770	11,774
Income taxes payable	—	15,307
Accrued marketing and distribution	21,551	12,575
Other current liabilities	38,764	16,790
Total current liabilities	128,786	85,756
Non-current obligations under capital leases	1,308	2,052
Deferred taxes on income	48,584	12,887
Shareholders' equity:		
Common stock, no par value, 160,000,000 shares authorized, 59,198,397 shares issued and outstanding	183,715	141,070
Retained earnings	195,046	118,332
	378,761	259,402
Notes receivable from shareholders	(860)	(2,310)
Total shareholders' equity	377,901	257,092
	$556,579	$357,787

TWO IMPORTANT INVENTORY ACCOUNTING METHODS: PERIODIC AND PERPETUAL

Picture two calendars. One is the monthly wall calendar variety, with each sheet representing an entire month. The other is a daily desk calendar, with individual sheets representing individual days. Each of the calendars might roughly be compared to one of the two basic systems of inventory accounting—periodic and perpetual.

Periodic inventory accounting doesn't lose sight of individual items, but it records only the amount of the sales—as if we were crossing off the days on the monthly sheet. With periodic accounting, the profits and losses are recorded and balanced on some regular (periodic) basis, as one tears off the sheet of the calendar each month.

The perpetual inventory system, on the other hand, accounts for every inventory change in detail. The inventory records are constantly being adjusted; each new inventory item acquired is added to the appropriate account, and inventory is reduced for each sale. Much like the daily desk calendar, which has the remaining number of days in the year and the number of days elapsed recorded at the bottom of the page, a perpetual inventory record always shows where the inventory level stands at any given time. It is also more difficult to keep.

Both are valid inventory accounting methods, and the choice between them is a choice between apples and aardvarks. That is, if there are lots of apples or nuts and bolts in inventory, periodic accounting is adequate to keep track. But rare or large items, whether they are aardvarks or yachts, have lower sales volume, so they're easier to account for on an up-to-the-minute basis. Thus, a trailer-load of laundry soap is likely to be on periodic inventory accounting, while the dealer selling trailers is likely to use perpetual accounting.

In either case, a physical inventory—an actual count of the items in stock—should be taken at least once a year. It confirms the status of perpetual accounting and provides actual inventories for a business that uses the periodic system.

Inventories are usually *merchandise on hand.* Manufacturing companies, however, may have inventories of *raw materials, goods in process, and finished goods ready for sale* as well.

Supplies on hand and services paid for but not yet used are known as **prepaid expenses.** An example is prepaid insurance, the unexpired portion of insurance purchased by a business. It is classified as a current asset because it can be turned into cash if canceled, or because it will be used and thus reduce cash outlay in the next year.

Fixed assets

Fixed assets, sometimes called **property, plant, and equipment,** are *permanent investments in buildings, equipment, furniture and fixtures, transportation equipment, land, and any other tangible property used in running a business.* They have a useful life of more than one year and are not expected to be converted into cash.

A long-lived asset such as a machine or a truck slowly wears out day by day through age, obsolescence, or use. This wear may not be noticeable, but it occurs nevertheless, like the gradual deterioration of a favorite record album played every day on the stereo. At some point, the asset will have to be replaced, and this will cost money. How do we account for this cost? Through a procedure known as **depreciation**—*the allocation of the cost of a long-lived asset to the periods in which it is used to produce revenue.* In the ordinary course of business, no transaction is recorded to show this depreciation. At the time the balance sheet is prepared, however, the accountant will record the depreciation for the period. Depreciating a fixed asset has the effect of spreading the cost of that asset over a number of years. (Note that of the various kinds of fixed assets, only land does not depreciate.)

Intangible assets

Intangible assets include *patents on a process or invention, copyrights to written or reproducible material, and trademarks.* Even though they are not solid, physical properties like a chair or a desk, they can be valuable because they can be licensed or sold outright to others.

Least tangible of all but no less valuable an asset is goodwill. **Goodwill** is a resource that consists mainly of a *company's reputation, especially in its relations with its customers.* Goodwill is not entered as an asset in a company's books unless the business is purchased. In that case, there are specific guidelines used in determining the amount of goodwill to be recorded, and its value may be put at anything from one dollar to several millions.

LIABILITIES

Liabilities, the debts a business owes, represent claims against the assets and come next on the balance sheet. Liabilities may be current or long-term, and they are listed in the order in which they will come due.

Current liabilities

Debts that will have to be paid within a year of the date of the balance sheet are known as **current liabilities.**

Because they are generally *due in thirty days or less*, **accounts payable** are sometimes listed first. Generally they result from buying goods or services on credit.

Notes payable, like the notes receivable mentioned in the assets section, are *written and signed promises to pay a certain sum, plus interest, at a definite time and place.* In this case, however, it is money owed rather than money coming. These notes may come due after a much longer time than accounts payable.

When the balance sheet is prepared, certain expenses, such as purchases, may have been *incurred for which bills have not yet been received and recorded.* Labor, interest, and taxes may also be payable in the near future. Such payable—but unrecorded—items are known as **accrued expenses.** If such expenses and their associated liabilities were not recorded, the financial statements of the business would be both incorrect and misleading.

Long-term liabilities

Debts that fall due a year or more after the date of the balance sheet are categorized as **long-term liabilities.** They are similar to owners' equity in that they are claims on the business that may remain unpaid for a long time. Usually, however, the claims of the long-term creditors are paid before those of the owners when a company goes out of business.

Other items that may fall in the long-term category are many types of long-term **leases,** *agreements that enable their holders to use assets without legally owning them,* and **mortgages,** *agreements conveying land, buildings, machines, or other property owned by a business to creditors as security.*

THE DEBATE OVER PENSION LIABILITIES In most cases, part of the money the corporation owes consists of the pensions it must pay to its employees when they retire. Pensions are unlike other liabilities in that a precise total cannot be recorded for this commitment, since no one is sure how much money a retired employee will actually draw in his or her life span. Nevertheless, many people feel that if balance-sheet readers are to get a true and total picture of the firm's financial position, it is important to include **unfunded pension liabilities**—*the difference between how much a company estimates that its pension obligations will be in the future, and how much it has put aside today to meet that expense.* Currently, pension liabilities are disclosed in a relatively obscure footnote, but the Financial Accounting Standards Board (FASB) has proposed more conservative rules. If these rules are implemented, many corporate giants will be forced to display unfunded pension liabilities in the liability section of their balance sheets.

Of course, adding unfunded pension liabilities to the liability section will require adding something on the asset side to keep the accounting equation in

THE DEFEASANCE CAPER

Toward the end of 1983, some of Wall Street's top international investment specialists hit on a creative new technique of debt management. The method, called defeasance, had been practiced for some time in the United States. It permitted a company to remove a debt (one of its bond issues, for example) from its balance sheet—*if* it could match the interest it would owe on that debt with income it would be receiving from government securities. (To be allowed to remove or "defease" the debt, the company had to place those government securities in an irrevocable trust, guaranteeing that the interest and principal on the debt would be paid.) Defeasance was quite legal and acceptable here; only when it was extended into international financial markets did it become a subject of controversy.

The defeasance technique became popular in the international field when some U.S. companies discovered that they could get a higher yield on some European bonds than they would have to *pay* to borrow money in Europe. How does defeasance work in the international market? Suppose you are a U.S. company and you have borrowed 500 million German marks at 7.75 percent—a debt you want to remove from your corporate balance sheet. You use *most* of

those 500 million marks to buy just enough German government notes (paying 8.3 percent) to yield income equal to the required payments on your borrowed marks. You place the government notes in an irrevocable trust, guaranteeing that the interest and principal on your debt will be paid. Presto! You are allowed to remove the debt from your balance sheet. But you haven't used up all of your borrowed marks; the remainder is clear profit, and it doesn't show on your balance sheet either.

In February 1984, the practice of defeasance was called into question by the Financial Accounting Standards Board (FASB), a court-like regulatory agency that issues standards for corporate accounting procedures. The FASB ruled out some elements of international defeasance deals. But since more than $5 billion worth of defeasance deals had already been made by U.S. companies (among them PepsiCo and Sterling Drug), there was immediate controversy over whether the new accounting rules should stand. With so much money involved, defeasance seems unlikely to be outlawed altogether. But companies are likely to exercise caution in arranging such deals until the issue is resolved.

SOURCE: "An Accounting Shift That Has the Financial Community Reeling," *Business Week,* April 2, 1984, p. 96.

---

balance. Since there is no tangible asset that can be added to correspond to the pension liabilities, a new intangible asset must be created, similar to the "goodwill" concept we have already discussed. What is more worrisome to the corporations affected, however, is the size of the new liabilities involved: for Chrysler they would be 91 percent of its net worth, for Bethlehem Steel they would be 67 percent, and for TWA, 19 percent. Another problem is that the new liability threatens to alter the critical relationship among the various elements of the balance sheet—a relationship that is of much concern to those who provide funds to corporations. Creditors and investors may not be happy with the result.[5]

OWNERS' EQUITY

The investment of the owners of a business is listed under owners' equity. Presentations here vary with the form of business organization. Sole proprietorships list owners' equity under the owner's name, with the amount (assets minus liabilities). Partnerships list each partner's share of the business separately. Since our balance sheet is for a corporation, it gives the amount of common stock that is outstanding—meaning the amount that is in the hands of shareholders. (If a company also issued preferred stock, it would be listed separately.) The amount listed represents the investment that was paid into the corporation by the stockholders when the stock was issued.

The **retained earnings** of a corporation are *the total earnings of all previous periods, including the current period, reduced by amounts distributed as dividends.*

THE EFFECTS OF INFLATION ON THE BALANCE SHEET

Although double-digit inflation cast a pall over the whole economy in the late 1970s and early 1980s, by 1983 it seemed to have slowed to a bearable 3 to 4 percent a year for a number of quarters in a row. But apparently it was the recession of 1981–82 that reduced inflation; as of this writing, many people still fear that inflation may come back as the economy resumes its growth. And whatever path actual inflation may take, the problem of "inflation mentality"—which leads managers and workers to devise strategies to cope with inflation—will be with us for a long time.

Thus, it's important for us to look at the effects inflation has on the balance sheet of a corporation. Typically, a corporation has a variety of assets that have been purchased with dollars of various "values." Indeed, a corporation's assets represent such a mix of dollar values that looking at them has been compared to sorting out the relative values of foreign currency. We'll survey some of the ways businesses deal with this problem below.

Inflation and inventory

The effects of inflation on the value of inventory can be complicated. Inventory that was purchased at a variety of times and with a variety of old dollars is sold for today's dollars. During periods of high inflation, this generally means that by the time you try to restock your shelves with revenues from sales, the cost of inventory will have gone up. If you didn't raise prices a month ago, or a few months ago, in anticipation of this problem, you may actually have lost money on every sale. On the other hand, when inflation is low, inventory costs generally don't fall, but competition may stiffen and your competitors may try to undercut your prices. You may have to take a hard look at your own selling prices to see if you can lower them and still make a profit.

To show just how disastrous inflation can be for a company's inventory evaluation, we'll use a simple example. Suppose that Steve Stomper, owner of Chopper City, orders $10,000 worth of motorcycles at the beginning of the year. The bikes are delivered late in the spring for sale that summer. By summer, those same motorcycles now cost 10 percent more because of inflation. So you *might* think that before he has even sold the cycles, Stomper has made $1,000. But Steve uses a normal markup on cost of 8 percent for his motorcycles: he sells them for a total of $10,800 ($10,000 cost + 8 percent of $10,000, or $800, = $10,800), which gives him a reported profit of $800. But when Steve orders another shipment of motorcycles, he finds that the price is now $11,000 or more. Steve's sales haven't even provided him with enough dollars to replace the sold motorcycles.

Constant dollars and current value

Recent rulings from governmental agencies, and the Financial Accounting Standards Board's pronouncements on inflation accounting, give a corporation the opportunity and obligation to reflect the effects of inflation on long-lived assets and inventory by using one of two methods—the *constant-dollar method* or the *current-cost method*. Constant-dollar adjustments use a base year and adjust the figures on the basis of the government-computed consumer price index (CPI). The current-cost method works a little differently: essentially, it refers to the cost of replacing assets or inventory. Take, for example, a truck that originally cost $5,000 and has been depreciated at $1,000 per year for four years. The truck may now cost $12,000 to replace, so the current cost at the end of the fourth year would be $2,400 (one-fifth of $12,000).

THE INCOME STATEMENT

In a candy store, the shopkeeper earns income the moment you plunk down your 40 cents for a Hershey bar. But in a larger business, one that sells business computers, for example, a certain amount of time elapses between (1) the moment salesperson and customer clink glasses in agreement on a deal,

(2) the point when the computer is on the customer's loading dock, (3) the time the customer installs the machine, and (4) the time the customer actually pays for it.

At what point do we say that the computer vendor has earned its income? Accountants are in agreement, first of all, that it is not necessary for the vendor to wait until the customer actually pays his bill to record a sale. Why? It is quite common for vendors to extend credit to their customers by putting the customers' accounts into an accounting category that is an asset—namely, the accounts receivable category—and thus they can logically record the sale before they have the cash in hand. On the other hand, accountants agree that it is too soon to report a sale if the customer has merely agreed to accept delivery of a computer in six months. But between these two extremes there is much room for disagreement.

The questions raised have to do with the flow of income *over time*—how much is coming in per month or per year, versus how much is being paid out. This type of "inflow and outflow" problem is something accountants study by means of a document called an **income statement,** which *shows how a business's revenues compare with expenses over a given period of time*. This statement lists all the **revenues** (or sales), *the amounts received or to be received from customers for goods or services delivered to them*. It also lists **expenses,** *the costs that have arisen in generating revenues*. And finally it *subtracts expenses from revenues,* to show the *actual profit or loss of a company,* a figure known as **net income.** While, as we have seen, the balance sheet is a snapshot of a company's financial position on a particular day, the income statement summarizes financial transactions over a period of time, usually a year.

Figure 2 shows the income statement of Apple Computer, Inc. Let's look at its parts in some detail.

REVENUES

The revenues of a business usually come from sales to customers, fees for services, or both. Other kinds of revenue may be rents, commissions, interest, and money paid by other firms for the use of the company's patents.

Two alternative methods of recording revenues

It makes no difference whether the sales are for immediate cash or are "on account" and collected later, if a company is on an **accrual basis**—meaning that *all sales revenues are recorded in the year the sales are made,* even if the customer does not pay until the following year. Similarly, *expenses are reported in the year in which the associated revenue is reported*—an accounting method that is based on the matching concept.

A business run on a **cash basis,** however, *records revenue only when money from sales is actually received. Expenses are recorded when they are paid.* Manufacturers and retailers use the accrual system. On the whole, service businesses—such as laundries and restaurants—and professionals—such as doctors and lawyers—often operate on a cash basis.

No business manager is unaware that with the accrual method you have to pay taxes on income you haven't even collected yet. Some companies actually have to borrow money just to pay their tax bill, and for them, the advantages of cash-based accounting are obvious—the company doesn't have any tax liability until cash is actually collected. In the old days, the IRS routinely allowed firms to switch from accrual to cash whenever they wanted to. But it was forced to crack down on this practice in 1982 after high interest rates provoked a flood of such switches. Now the cash method can be used only by certain service-type businesses, where there are no physical goods flowing into the warehouse and over the counter to define the "accounting event."

What difference does having to use the accrual method make to businesses like the motorcycle dealership we talked about? Using the accrual method, the dealer who has taken in $5,000 in cash and $3,000 in accounts receivable has to report the whole $8,000 as income. And if he pays out $4,000 in expenses while holding another $1,000 as accounts payable, he must charge both against income, leaving a taxable income of $3,000 ($8,000 minus $5,000). If he had been allowed to use the cash method, his taxable income would have been just $1,000. In a 50 percent tax bracket, that would have meant a $1,000 tax savings (he would have paid $500, as opposed to $1,500).

FIGURE 2

Consolidated Statements of Income of
Apple Computer, Inc., 1981 through 1983

Three years ended September 30, 1983 *(In thousands, except per share amounts)*	1983	1982	1981
Net sales	$982,769	$583,061	$334,783
Costs and expenses:			
Cost of sales	505,765	288,001	170,124
Research and development	60,040	37,979	20,956
Marketing and distribution	229,961	119,945	55,369
General and administrative	57,364	34,927	22,191
	853,130	480,852	268,640
Operating income	129,639	102,209	66,143
Interest, net	16,483	14,563	10,400
Income before taxes on income	146,122	116,772	76,543
Provision for taxes on income	69,408	55,466	37,123
Net income	$ 76,714	$ 61,306	$ 39,420
Earnings per common and common equivalent share	$ 1.28	$ 1.06	$ .70
Common and common equivalent shares used in the calculation of earnings per share	59,867	57,798	56,161

Gross sales versus net sales

Gross sales, *the total dollar amount of goods sold,* doesn't give the entire revenue picture. In the normal course of business, there are deductions from gross sales—and these may be considerable. For example, customers are likely to return goods, for which they get refunds. Cash discounts, offered to customers to speed their payments, also reduce gross sales. *After such discounts are deducted from gross sales, the remainder is called* **net sales.**

COST OF GOODS SOLD (COST OF SALES)

For any goods a retailer or wholesaler sells, it must pay certain costs. A manufacturer, for instance, must take into account the added expense of producing the goods. Let's see how the cost of goods sold is calculated in two kinds of businesses—retailing and wholesaling businesses and manufacturing businesses.

Retailers and wholesalers start by evaluating inventory on hand at the beginning of the year. Purchases made during the year (less discounts) are then added to this figure. These sums make up the total cost of goods available for sale. To find out the cost of goods sold, the cost of inventory still on hand at the end of the period is deducted.

Manufacturers, in contrast, must first total the costs of producing goods, including labor, raw materials, and factory expenses. These costs are then added to the cost of inventory of finished goods on hand at the beginning of the year. The cost of inventory (finished goods not sold) at the end of the year is then subtracted, yielding the cost of goods sold.

STEPS FOR FIGURING NET INCOME

Now that we have examined revenues and cost of goods sold, let's see how net income is figured.

Figuring gross profit

The first step in determining net income is to deduct *the cost of goods sold from net sales,* to obtain the **gross profit** (or **gross margin**). An important figure for management to compare against previous income statements, the gross profit should cover all operating expenses and still leave some profit for owners and money for reinvestment.

Figuring operating income

The next step is to deduct from gross income a figure known as **operating expenses**—*all the costs of operations that aren't included in the category, costs of goods sold.* The remainder is a figure known as **operating income.**

Operating expenses consist of selling expenses (marketing expenses) and general expenses. **Selling expenses** are *incurred through marketing and distributing the products the company buys or makes for sale.* They include salaries of salespeople, advertising, sales supplies, insurance for the sales operation, depreciation of the store and other sales equipment, and all miscellaneous sales-department expenses, such as utilities and maintenance. **General expenses** *arise out of overall administration of a business.* They include office salaries, depreciation of office equipment, insurance covering office operations, supplies, and so on.

Net income: the "bottom line"

Net income, representing the actual profit or loss of a company, sums up the results of the company's operations. From the operating income two deductions are made, interest and income taxes. The resulting figure, net income, is the all-important "bottom line" of the income statement—the item that shows the profit or loss for a particular period. By comparing the net income for one year with the net income for previous years, owners, creditors, and investors can form judgments about the firm's performance and its future prospects.

THE EFFECTS OF INFLATION ON THE INCOME STATEMENT

As we saw above, inflation is likely to give our friend Steve Stomper of Chopper City some problems with his balance sheet. But the problems it creates for Steve's income statement may be more serious. This is especially true if he is applying for a loan or if he has investors interested in the business, since in these circumstances it's essential to present an accurate picture of the profits Steve's business makes. The first question a business owner like Steve has to answer, when he's figuring his profits, is how inflation affects the cost of the goods he has sold.

The effects of inflation on the cost of goods sold

We've seen how inflation can affect the inventory value, and the debt position, of Chopper City. In times of high inflation, the motorcycles may actually increase in value between the time they are ordered and the time they are sold. Furthermore, the current value of the entire stock is a hodgepodge of various prices paid at various times. Let's pursue that point a bit further to see how inflation affects the cost of goods sold.

Stomper still had five motorcycles he bought in the winter for $2,000 each. In the spring, he bought another five bikes. They were exactly the same as the ones already in stock, but this time he had to pay $2,200 apiece for them. During Chopper City's back-to-school sale, he sold five bikes for $3,000 each, or $15,000. Does Stomper assume that these cycles were the five he bought in the winter? If so, his gross profits will be $5,000. Or does he decide that the cycles he sold were the ones purchased most recently? If so, his gross profit will come out to only $4,000. This is obviously a decision that will affect how attractive Steve's company will look to a potential buyer, lender, or investor. Table 3 shows how the two approaches might be represented. Note that if Steve reports the higher profit ($5,000), he'll also

TABLE 3 How Inflation Affects the Cost of Goods Sold

SALE OF FIVE "WINTER" BIKES		SALE OF FIVE "SPRING" BIKES	
Sales	$15,000	Sales	$15,000
Cost of goods sold (5 bikes at $2,000 each)	10,000	Cost of goods sold (5 bikes at $2,200 each)	11,000
Gross profit	$ 5,000	Gross profit	$4,000

TABLE 4 How Different Methods of Costing Inventory Affects Taxes

SALE OF FIVE "WINTER" BIKES		SALE OF FIVE "SPRING" BIKES	
Sales	$15,000	Sales	$15,000
Cost of goods sold	10,000	Cost of goods sold	11,000
Gross profit	$ 5,000	Gross profit	$ 4,000
Taxes (at 40 percent)	2,000	Taxes (at 40 percent)	1,600
Net income	$3,000	Net income	$2,400

have to pay more income taxes. Assuming that the tax rate is 40 percent, he would pay the amount shown in Table 4.

LIFO and FIFO

Whether Chopper City's gross profit is $4,000 or $5,000 will depend on which method of costing inventory Stomper uses—LIFO or FIFO. **FIFO** means *"first in, first out."* It's a method that treats inventory costs as if they were on a conveyor belt traveling through the balance sheet. The costs that Stomper enters in the books as the units are purchased are assigned in the same order to the units as they are sold. (This is the method Steve will be using if he figures that he has sold the $2,000 "winter" bikes.) **LIFO** means *"last in, first out."* It's like stacking inventory costs in a box. When a layer of costs is at the bottom, it can't be reached until all the layers above it are removed. (This is the method Steve will be using if he figures that he has sold the $2,200 "spring" bikes.)

What are the pros and cons of the two methods? In times of high inflation, LIFO produces a larger cost of goods sold, a lower ending inventory, and lower profits. This arrangement usually results in lower taxes. FIFO inventory costing, in contrast, means that ending inventory is higher and goods sold are lower in cost. Therefore the profit—the difference between that lower cost and the inflated selling price—is greater, so taxes are higher. Firms are allowed to switch from FIFO to LIFO, but they cannot switch back without proving that they have a business reason, rather than just a tax-avoidance motive. Under LIFO, firms are allowed to provide readers of their financial statements with additional details that help them estimate what the firms' earnings *would* have been under FIFO.

In inflationary times, many firms feel that FIFO, by determining profits from an unrealistically low cost of goods sold, taxes them on "phantom" profits—earnings that are not really profits, but merely represent money needed to restock the shelves at tomorrow's prices. These firms often opt for LIFO to lower their "paper profits" and thus their cash payments for taxes. How do investors react to lower reported profits? Many academic researchers have concluded that this tactic doesn't cause investors to lose interest in the company's stock. When the investors read "LIFO" in the firm's financial statements, they understand that the company's real cash earnings haven't fallen in comparison to those of a similar firm using FIFO. They realize that, in fact, the firm that lowers its taxes actually holds *more* real cash.[6] (We have talked about this "efficient market hypothesis" in more detail in Chapter 15.)

The effects of inflation on earnings

Since inflation can affect all of a company's financial records, you might expect that it would affect the company's earnings. Just how much earnings are affected is not always obvious. However, we can make this general observation: the dollars of revenue are new dollars and are worth less than the old dollars used to buy equipment and supplies; therefore, expenses, as they appear on the financial statements, will be understated (in today's terms) and profits will be overstated. The damage to the financial integrity of the company occurs when dividends and taxes are paid on these overstated profits. Since future supplies will cost more—perhaps more than the price for which the goods were sold—dividends and taxes may have to be paid out of capital. One reason the Securities and Exchange Commission now requires companies to report financial results adjusted in terms of the CPI (that is, in constant dollars) is to allow investors to make judgments about the way the company has performed without having to look at a picture that's distorted by inflation.

At the time of this writing, some experts were suggesting that the FASB set aside the inflation-reporting requirements: companies found the requirements expensive and time-consuming to comply with, and investors did not pay much attention to them. But other experts cautioned that whether the rate of inflation is 4 percent, 8 percent, or 16 percent, it's not really possible to gauge the well-being of a company unless you bear inflation's impact in mind. For example, let's say you look at a company's five-year earnings per share history and see this:

1978	1979	1980	1981	1982
$1.00	$1.10	$1.21	$1.33	$1.46

Does this mean the firm had an impressive steady 10 percent increase in earnings each year? Or that they grew somewhat, alongside a 5 percent inflation rate? Or that they stood still in real terms but at least kept up with a 10 percent inflation rate? Or, worse, that they failed to keep pace with a 12 percent inflation rate, so that today's earnings are actually worth less in real terms? The fact is that the earnings pattern is meaningless if you don't know the inflation rates behind it.

Or, what if you see that one of your company's divisions is earning much more than another, although both are producing exactly the same product? You wonder why the second division has such high costs. Before you decide to close it down, however, you take a closer look at its depreciation. You find that the second plant is much newer than the first, and thus its cost reflects the higher, post-inflation building cost. If one-twentieth of a plant's cost is being subtracted each year for depreciation, then the plant purchased at inflated prices will require a larger charge against earnings than the plant purchased at pre-inflation prices. At the same time, when the plants wear out and it's time to replace them, you will not have put aside nearly enough money by depreciating the cost of the old, lower-priced plant, so the higher profits reported at that plant were really an illusion.

In cases like these, any system that measures inflation reasonably well is closer to reality than one that ignores inflation altogether. How unrealistic are data that are not adjusted to reflect inflation? If AT&T's depreciation, for example, had been adjusted to reflect true current replacement costs, the 1982 earnings of AT&T would have fallen from $7 billion to $1.5 billion; for Exxon they would have dropped from $4 billion to a $300 million loss; and for 29 of the Dow 30 they would have declined from a total of $31 billion to $14 billion.[7]

USING RATIOS

Besides revealing a good deal in themselves, the balance sheet and the income statement can be made to yield further clues to the present health and future prospects of a business when information from them is analyzed in terms of ratios. **Ratios** are simply *arithmetical relationships between two amounts*. The ratio between 1,000 fans at a rock concert, for example, and 100 security guards protecting the featured group is:

$$\frac{1,000}{100} = \frac{10}{1}$$

or 10 fans for every 1 guard. (The relationship can also be expressed as 10:1.)

TESTING OF THE PROFITABILITY OF A BUSINESS

One way of using ratios is to set up relationships between specific items from the income statement and the balance sheet, to show how profitable a business is. Potential investors are, of course, interested in the profitability of a business, and managers are particularly concerned with it, since any change in profitability means that something has changed in the way the business operates or perhaps in the market it attempts to serve.

Take, for example, the Hungry Tiger restaurant chain. When Hungry Tiger was on the verge of insolvency, its current president, Alan Redhead, was a waiter. He and a group of fellow employees felt they had the nuts-and-bolts knowledge to steer the operation to profitability. And they did. As a manager, Alan Redhead developed such a detailed grasp of costs that one year he increased profits by 15 percent simply by eliminating linen tablecloths (half from the cost of linen and half from related labor).[8] To turn the operation around, he had to keep an eye on some crucial ratios, which we'll discuss below.

FIGURE 3

CHRYSLER COMES OUT OF THE WOODS:
An "at-a-glance" summary of Chrysler's return to financial health.

This little "at-a-glance" summary, of a type often seen in newspapers, gives people who are interested in a particular business some crucial information from that firm's balance sheet and income statement. Shown here is a summary for Chrysler. It shows how the automaker's financial picture changed from 1983 to 1984, as it began to recover from the significant losses it had suffered in the early 1980s.

Using the summary, you can figure some important ratios. Chrysler's *return on equity*, for example, had begun to climb by 1984: in 1983 it was 14.82 percent, but in 1984 it was a healthy 35.69 percent. *Return on sales* had begun to bounce back too, moving from 5.55 percent in 1983 to 14.34 percent in 1984. But the *debt to equity* was still weak: it was 4.92 percent in 1983, and only 2.96 in 1984. Chrysler's past losses were still having a negative effect on the company's retained earnings (earnings are an element of equity).

Return on equity

One important indicator of profitability is **return on equity,** *the net income a business makes per dollar of*

HOW TO READ AN ANNUAL REPORT

On these pages is a passage from an ad created for International Paper Company as part of their campaign "The Power of the Printed World." Written by *Newsweek* columnist Jane Bryant Quinn, it tells you where to look in an annual report to get important information—fast. You'll need to know how to read annual reports in your future career, whether you're thinking of investing in companies, becoming a supplier for them, or just applying for a job. And you'll probably have no difficulty reading them now that you're familiar with basic accounting concepts.

Interestingly, Quinn's advice is to start at the back of the report rather than the front—because the back is where two crucial items, the accountant's report and the footnotes, are located. Only after you've looked there, she says, should you turn to the information that's in the body of the report.

Start at the back

First, turn back to the report of the *certified public accountant*. This third-party auditor will tell you right off the bat if Galactic's report conforms with "generally accepted accounting principles."

Watch out for the words "subject to." They mean the financial report is clean *only* if you take the company's word about a particular piece of business, and the accountant isn't sure you should. Doubts like this are usually settled behind closed doors. When a "subject to" makes it into the annual report, it could mean trouble.

What else should you know before you check the numbers?

Stay in the back of the book and go to the *footnotes*. Yep! The whole profits story is sometimes in the footnotes.

Are earnings down? If it's only because of a change in accounting, maybe that's good! The company owes less tax and has more money in its pocket. Are earnings up? Maybe that's bad. They may be up because of a special windfall that won't happen again next year. The footnotes know.

For what happened and why

Now turn to the *letter from the chairman*. Usually addressed "to our stockholders," it's up front, and *should* be in more ways than one. The chairman's tone reflects the personality, the well-being of his company.

In his letter he should tell you how his company fared this year. But more important, he should tell you *why*. Keep an eye out for sentences that start with "Except for. . ." and "Despite the. . ." They're clues to problems.

Insights into the future

On the positive side, a chairman's letter should give you insights into the company's future and its *stance* on economic or political trends that may affect it.

While you're up front, look for what's new in each line of business. Is management getting the company in good shape to weather the tough and competitive 1980's?

Now—and no sooner—should you dig into the numbers!

One source is the *balance sheet*. It is a snapshot of how the company stands at a single point in time. On the left are *assets*—everything the company owns. Things that can quickly be turned into cash are *current assets*. On the right are *liabilities*—everything the company owes. *Current liabilities* are the debts due in one year, which are paid out of current assets.

The difference between current assets and current liabilities is *net working capital*, a key figure to watch from one annual (and quarterly) report to another. If working capital shrinks, it could mean trouble. One possibility: the company may not be able to keep dividends growing rapidly.

Look for growth here

Stockholders' equity is the difference between total assets and liabilities. It is the presumed dollar value of what stockholders own. You want it to grow.

Another important number to watch is *long-term debt*. High and rising debt, relative to equity, may be no problem for a growing business. But it shows weakness in a company that's leveling out. (More on that later.)

The second basic source of numbers is the *income statement*. It shows how much money Galactic made or lost over the year.

Most people look at one figure first. It's in the income statement at the bottom: *net earnings per share*. Watch out. It can fool you. Galactic's management could boost earnings by selling off a plant. Or by cutting the budget for research and advertising. (See the footnotes!) So don't be smug about net earnings until you've found out how they happened—and how they might happen next year.

Check net sales first

The number you *should* look at first in the income statement is *net sales*. Ask yourself: Are sales going *up at a faster rate* than the last time around? When sales increases start to slow, the company may be in trouble. Also ask: Have sales gone up faster than inflation? If not, the company's *real* sales may be behind. And ask yourself once more: Have sales gone down because the company is selling off a losing business? If so, profits may be soaring.

(I never promised you that figuring out an annual report was going to be easy!)

Get out your calculator

Another important thing to study today is the company's debt. Get out your pocket calculator, and turn to the balance sheet. Divide long-term liabilities by stockholders' equity. That's the *debt-to-equity ratio*.

A high ratio means that the company borrows a lot of money to spark its growth. That's okay—*if* sales grow, too, and *if* there's enough cash on hand to meet the payments. A company doing well on borrowed money can earn big profits for its stockholders. But if sales fall, watch out. The whole enterprise may slowly sink. Some companies can handle high ratios, others can't.

You have to compare

That brings up the most important thing of all: *One* annual report, *one* chairman's letter, *one* ratio won't tell you much. You have to compare. Is the company's debt-to-equity ratio better or worse than it used to be? Better or worse than the industry norms? Better or worse, after this recession, than it was after the last recession? In company-watching, *comparisons are all*. They tell you if management is staying on top of things.

Financial analysts work out many other ratios to tell them how the company is doing. You can learn more about them from books on the subject. Ask your librarian.

But one thing you will *never* learn from an annual report is how much to pay for a company's stock. Galactic may be running well. But if investors expected it to run better, the stock might fall. Or, Galactic could be slumping badly. But if investors see a better day tomorrow, the stock could rise.

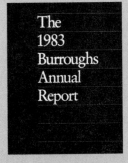

shareholders' investment. Hungry Tiger's return on equity has been 29 percent, compared with 17 percent at Denny's, and 20 percent for its rival, Chart House.[9]

We set up the **return-on-equity ratio**—the *ratio between net income and total owners' equity*—using information from the balance sheet and the income statement. Imagine a shop for jeans called Denim Den, which has netted $12,000 in income on an equity base of $99,000. The ratio (expressed as a percentage) would be:

$$\frac{\text{Net income}}{\text{Owners' equity}} = \frac{\$12,000}{\$99,000} = 12.1\%$$

How good is this particular return? There is no agreed-upon ideal return. Clearly, however, 12.1 percent isn't good when money market funds are yielding 12 percent. For the most part, managers and investors evaluate return on equity by comparing it to the ratio for similar businesses.

One might expect that a corporation would declare dividends to its stockholders based on its return on equity; if the company is making, let's say, 12.1 percent of income per unit of equity, shouldn't the stockholders receive dividends right up to this amount? Not necessarily. The corporation may decide to plow a portion of the earnings back into the business, so the business can grow in the future. This course of action, however, is not without benefits to the stockholders; the portion of the earnings that goes back into the business increases their equity.

Return on sales

Another important indicator of profitability is the net income a business makes per unit of sales, which can be determined by setting up a *relationship between net income and net sales*—the **return-on-sales ratio.**

Let's say that Denim Den's sales last year were $175,000. The ratio can be set up as follows:

$$\frac{\text{Net income}}{\text{Net sales}} = \frac{\$\ 12,000}{\$175,000}$$

By dividing the $175,000 net sales into the $12,000 net income, we can arrive at a percentage, 6.9 percent, which is the Denim Den's return on sales. This figure, when compared to the percentages of other companies in the same business, can give a potential investor a valuable warning of inefficiency—or reassuring knowledge that the store is doing well. In this case, Denim Den is doing well: most retail stores average only a 2 to 5 percent return on sales.

TESTING THE ABILITY OF A BUSINESS TO PAY ITS DEBTS

There is always some risk involved when one business grants credit to another or when an investor buys stocks or bonds. But these risks can be minimized by using ratios based on information from the company's balance sheet and income statement.

Ratios a short-term creditor needs to know

The **current ratio,** for example, is used to test how well a company is able to pay its short-term debts. It's expressed as *current assets divided by current liabilities.* Suppose, for instance, that the Open Road, a small custom motorbike outfit in Los Angeles, had current assets of $127,000 and current liabilities of $33,000. The current ratio would be set up as follows:

$$\frac{\text{Current assets}}{\text{Current liabilities}} = \frac{\$127,000}{\$\ 33,000} = 3.8$$

This means that the business has $3.80 of current assets to meet every dollar of current liabilities. How safe is a 3.8 ratio? To answer this question, analysts will compare a company's current ratio with the average for that type of business. As a rule, though, a company with a current ratio of at least 2.0 is considered a safe risk for short-term credit.

The **acid-test ratio,** also called a **quick ratio,** *shows the ability of a company to meet its short-term debts with its cash, marketable securities, and receivables.* Some analysts consider it a better indication of a company's ability to pay its immediate debts because, unlike the current ratio, inventories are left out of the equation. The acid-test ratio for the Open Road would look like this:

$$
\frac{\text{Cash} + \text{Marketable securities} + \text{Accounts receivable} + \text{Notes receivable}}{\text{Current liabilities}}
$$

$$
= \frac{\$15,000 + \$5,000 + \$51,000 + \$15,000}{\$33,000}
$$

$$
= \frac{\$86,000}{\$33,000}
$$

$$
= 2.6
$$

The Open Road isn't in bad shape at all, since some analysts consider a ratio of 1.0 to be reasonable. If the company were pressed for cash and inventory was moving sluggishly, it would still have $2.60 in quick assets to meet each dollar of current liabilities.

An inventory turnover ratio would tell potential investors how fast the inventory was turned into sales. The quicker the better is the general rule.

Using the income statement, the **inventory turnover ratio** *is computed by dividing the average inventory for a period into the cost of goods sold.* Where inventories are fairly constant, averaging the inventories for the beginning and the end of the year would be accurate enough. But if there are high and low inventory seasons not represented by the beginning- and end-of-year inventories, all the month-end inventories for the year should be averaged. Since the Open Road's inventory is more or less constant, the January and December figures are used. Its turnover is:

$$
\frac{\text{Cost of goods sold}}{(\text{Inventory, Jan. 1} + \text{Inventory, Dec. 31})/2}
$$

$$
= \frac{\$88,000}{(\$41,000 + \$37,000)/2}
$$

$$
= 2.3
$$

This means that the average inventory was converted (turned over) into sales every 159 days (365 days divided by 2.3). As a potential investor you would be interested in this information because it tells you that the Open Road's average monthly inventory can be turned into at least $39,000 in cash and probably more, depending on the store's markup. The "ideal" turnover varies with the type of operation. A grocery store's turnover would be much faster, usually around 16.

Ratios a long-term investor needs to know

Long-term loans can be tested for their safety in much the same way. Before handing over the large amount that long-term financing entails, it's best to determine whether or not the potential debtor has put enough money into the business to act as a protective cushion for your loan.

A **debt-to-equity ratio** can help answer that question. Creditors are protected by a low ratio of debt to equity. Only if the business loses more than the amount of the owners' equity would the creditors suffer a loss. The debt-to-equity ratio of the Open Road is:

$$
\frac{\text{Total liabilities}}{\text{Owners' equity}} = \frac{\$57,000}{\$99,000} = 0.58
$$

This means that if the assets of the Open Road could be disposed of at the amounts recorded in its balance sheet, the creditor's investment is $0.58 for each dollar of equity. If the ratio goes above 1, debts exceed equity and the business may be relying too heavily on debt.

Of course, none of these ratios is a magic formula. Investments can and do go wrong despite the cheery picture sometimes suggested by the equations. Ratios reduce risk; they don't eliminate it.

THE BUDGET

In addition to assessing what has been happening in a business, accounting involves planning for the future. That's where the **budget** comes in. It's a *financial blueprint for a given period of time* (often one year) *that structures future plans on a framework of estimated revenues and expenses.* Since working out a budget forces a company to determine how much money

TABLE 5 Breakdown of a Typical Master Budget

TYPE OF BUDGET	FUNCTION	SOURCES OF INFORMATION
Sales budget	To estimate future sales (units to be sold and expected unit price)	Study of past sales and estimates of future business conditions (often obtained from salespeople via sales managers)
Production budget	To estimate number of units needed to fill anticipated sales and leave inventory over at end of budget period	Projected sales added to number of units expected to be on hand at end of period, minus number of units on hand at beginning of period
Cost-of-goods-sold budget	To determine cost of goods sold	Estimates of cost of materials used in manufacture of units, cost of labor, overhead expenses (light, insurance, property taxes, etc.)

will be coming in and what costs will be entailed, it simultaneously becomes a controlling as well as a planning operation.

Since the budget is a guideline to what will take place over a lengthy period of time, a great deal of careful thought must go into its planning. Conse-quently, the master (or operating) budget, which is an overall estimate of revenues, costs, and expenses, is based on several subbudgets, including the sales budget, the production budget, and the cost-of-goods-sold budget. These are described in more detail in Table 5.

CHAPTER REVIEW

Accounting is a system of princi-ples and techniques for recording, presenting, and analyzing the fi-nancial operations of a business or other organization. Accounting reports help managers keep track of accounts receivable and paya-ble, thereby serving a control function. They provide investors and creditors with a way of ana-lyzing a business.

Public accountants operate inde-pendently of the businesses they serve and monitor the businesses' financial reports. Nonpublic ac-countants serve a single business in one of a number of specialized areas. Both types of accountants depend on two basic accounting concepts. One is the accounting equation:

Assets =
Liabilities + Owners' Equity

The other is double-entry book-keeping, which keeps the account-ing equation in balance by offset-ting any change in one part of the equation with a change in another part so as to keep track of the two monetary effects of every transaction.

The most important financial re-ports are the balance sheet and the income statement. The bal-ance sheet shows in detail the kinds and amounts of assets, lia-bilities, and owners' equity at a specific time. The high inflation rates of recent years have created difficulties in accurately reporting the value of assets and inventory on balance sheets. The income statement reports the accumulated revenue and expense transactions that result in either a profit or a loss over a specific period, gener-ally one year. The income state-ment, too, is affected by inflation,

which may distort the true cost of goods sold and the true earnings of a company.

Financial statements are analyzed and interpreted through the use of ratios—the arithmetical rela-tionships between amounts shown on such statements. They provide information about an organiza-tion's ability to meet short-term debt, to pay off long-term debt, and to give an adequate return on investment.

A budget is a plan that estimates the revenues and expenses of an organization for a specific period of time. The process of budgeting usually involves formulating an overall plan (or master budget) for the whole company and spe-cialized plans for departments or other business units.

KEY WORDS

accounting (464)

accounting statements (464)

receivables (464)

payables (464)

public accountants (465)

certified public accountants (CPAs) (465)

nonpublic (corporate) accountants (465)

assets (466)

liabilities (466)

owners' equity (466)

accounting equation (466)

double-entry bookkeeping (466)

balance sheet (468)

calendar year (468)

fiscal year (468)

cash (468)

marketable securities (468)

accounts receivable (468)

notes receivable (468)

inventories (470)

prepaid expenses (470)

fixed assets (property, plant, and equipment) (470)

depreciation (470)

intangible assets (471)

goodwill (471)

current liabilities (471)

accounts payable (471)

notes payable (471)

accrued expenses (471)

long-term liabilities (471)

leases (471)

mortgages (471)

unfunded pension liabilities (471)

retained earnings (473)

income statement (474)

revenues (474)

expenses (474)

net income (474)

accrual basis (474)

cash basis (474)

gross sales (476)

net sales (476)

gross profit (gross margin) (476)

operating expenses (476)

operating income (476)

selling expenses (476)

general expenses (476)

FIFO (477)

LIFO (477)

ratios (479)

return on equity (479)

return-on-equity ratio (482)

return-on-sales ratio (482)

current ratio (482)

acid-test ratio (quick ratio) (482)

inventory turnover ratio (483)

debt-to-equity ratio (483)

budget (483)

REVIEW QUESTIONS

1. Summarize the basic role of the accountant.

2. What is the difference between a public accountant and a nonpublic accountant?

3. Why is it important that the two sides of the accounting equation be kept in balance?

4. Name and describe the three types of assets and the two types of liabilities listed on a balance sheet.

5. What is the difference between an income statement and a balance sheet?

6. Describe the effects that inflation can have on a balance sheet and on an income statement.

7. What are the two main uses to which ratios can be put, and how does each of the various ratios fulfill its function?

CASE 1

DAYS INN'S EXPANSION PLANS

You're a security analyst and broker, looking for some hot new investment ideas for your clients. You've come upon a motel chain named "Days Inn," and are trying to decide whether this firm has the sound financial foundation and rosy prospects you require for one of your "buy" recommendations. You're looking for high profitability, great growth potential, and stability (reasonably low risk). You also want to see a strong "concept"—the idea that defines the company's niche in a crowded market. You can't put a concept in the bank, but a strong market niche often goes along with strong accounting fundamentals.

You are pleased with the Days Inn concept: a chain of budget motels catering to the Disneyworld traffic. This means 18 motels in the amusement park's Orlando, Florida, home (making Days Inn the largest provider of lodging in the area), 49 scattered around Florida, and 255 more strewn along the interstate highways linking Disneyworld to the Northeast and the Ohio valley. Quite a setup! And Days Inn established its lead early, buying these properties back around 1972 when Disney's popularity took off.

Days Inn has an extremely impressive profit record. Since 1978, revenues have grown at 15 percent annually, to $250 million for fiscal year 1983. Pretax profits have risen twice as fast, to $15.5 million last year. Operating income for the first nine months of 1983 more than quadrupled, to a record $11 million, on a mere 12 percent gain in sales. During this period, the firm also earned $6.4 million from the sale of six of its motel properties that were past their peak. With total assets of $625 million, most of them in real estate, many more such gains may be in store. And you learn that Days Inn is in the most profitable market segment: average profits for budget hotels are 25 percent of pretax earnings, compared to 5.1 percent for the hotel industry as a whole.

High margins are won by keeping costs low. Payroll costs for budget hotels average 20 percent, while they are 35 percent for the industry as a whole. Administrative costs are only 19 percent (compared to 24 percent for all hotels), and marketing costs are shaved as well. Days Inn is planning to keep marketing costs low by clustering its facilities in target areas. It keeps architectural fees low by using the same design for all its far-flung units. Unlike their full-service competitors, Days Inns do not have large lobbies and meeting rooms or fine restaurants. Without the overhead cost of such public space, room rentals can be kept low and still leave ample room for profits. The key to profits, of course, is selling rooms, and your research shows that average occupancy rates for the budget segment of the hotel business are higher than average; they stood up well during the recession.

Is Days Inn a good growth prospect? Though the road-to-Disney market is fast approaching saturation, Days Inns' growth plans look interesting. The firm's president and chief executive speaks ambitiously of plans to increase total rooms by 30 percent, to 59,000 by 1988. He is confident that the formula of good accommodations at a reasonable price will work in other parts of the country. He has his sights set first on California— a destination popular with tourists, and one where budget-motel occupancy rates have been 75 percent compared to 69 percent nationwide.

But how likely is the firm to carry off such an ambitious scheme? Will Days Inn have access to the capital needed—an estimated $400 million over a six-year period? Debt now stands at $330 million, more than six times equity, so the chance of raising a significant amount through loans is slim. Even if the banks were willing to make the loans, it would be very risky to increase leverage further. Motel chains often finance expansion by selling franchises and taking on joint venture partners. Days Inn tries to avoid these alternatives, to avoid having to split profits.

And what about competition? You find that competition is closing in from all angles. As Days Inn expands into new regions, it will have to battle with the entrenched regional chains. The major middle-level chains, including Holiday Inn, are trying to muscle their way into the budget market. If the regionals don't expand now, they will forever remain regionals—while the majors, with

their sophisticated computer reservation and billing systems, grab the national market for the cost-conscious traveler.

Says one competitor, "Nobody's inventing anything new in this business. It's strictly a question of who has the best product for the price in the right markets." Days Inn is going for new markets by seeking out suburban and airport locations rather than just the traditional roadside. And it estimates that its effective management strategies can undercut competitors' prices by 30 percent.[10]

1. According to your analysis, are Days Inn bonds a good investment for your clients?

2. Days Inn is now entirely owned by the Day family. It is thinking of going public, and estimates the firm's market value at $550. Will you recommend the new issue to your clients?

3. What numbers help you make these decisions? What considerations cannot be quantified by numbers?

CASE 2

A DELICATE BALANCE

Broadview Financial Corporation, a Cleveland savings and loan association, was losing money. At the same time, it had some real estate investments that were worth more than the value presented on last period's balance sheet. Broadview wanted to show the gain on its real estate holdings as soon as possible, to offset some of its reported loss.

For many years, Broadview had used Peat, Marwick and Mitchell as its auditor, and had maintained a good relationship with them. But that year, 1982, there was a clash of opinion. Peat, Marwick auditors felt that it would be more proper to spread that property gain over the life of the real-estate investment project. But Broadview felt strongly about the need to show the profit immediately. So it fired Peat, Marwick, hired Deloitte, Haskins and Sells, and reported a real estate profit as intended. But when year-end rolled around, DH&S came to precisely the same conclusion as its predecessors. "We're very sorry," they said in accounting-ese, "but you'll have to tick that 1982 loss up from $16.8 million to $25.4 million."

Did Broadview, then, go to the trouble of switching auditors for nothing? Did its leverage in hiring and firing auditors have no effect on the financial statements that it ultimately presented to its shareholders? Indeed, no. There is some ambiguity and flexibility in auditing practices, and in this case they worked to the company's favor. What happened was that Peat, Marwick had already observed during its 1981 audit that Broadview's net worth was dangerously low. They agreed to certify the financials, or give Broadview a "clean bill of health," only on the condition that a warning to investors be attached. This so-called "emphasis paragraph" stated that Broadview's net worth was likely to fall below the level required by federal regulators during the coming year. The emphasis paragraph was a fairly

mild warning. Peat, Marwick *could* have chosen to give a sterner warning, by giving what is known as a "qualified opinion." Investors interpret qualified opinions to financial statements as a significant danger signal, and it is quite common for the firm's stock to fall after such an audit report. In fact, the concept of the "emphasis paragraph" came into use as a way to provide a less severe warning to shareholders, and so evoke a less severe reaction.

During the year 1982, Broadview's capital did fall below the regulatory benchmark. At this point, it would have been reasonable to assume that the firm's 1982 statements would receive a "qualified" rather than an "unqualified" opinion. But Deloitte did not take this step; it settled for an emphasis paragraph, as Peat, Marwick had done the year before. Thus, even though Deloitte took a tough stand on Broadview's real estate profit, some observers felt Deloitte had still allowed Broadview to pressure it for favorable treatment.

Because the psychological distinction between a qualified opinion and an emphasis paragraph is so sharp in investors' minds, an auditor choosing between these two labels is in a very delicate situation. If the qualified opinion causes investors to lose confidence and abandon the firm, the auditor can be accused of causing the firm to go under. The warning, in essence, becomes a self-fulfilling prophecy. On the other hand, the firm may pull through and dismiss the auditor that gave it such harsh treatment (perhaps publicly stating some other reason for switching accountants).

But if the auditor decides to give the wobbly firm the benefit of the doubt by issuing the less severe warning (the emphasis paragraph), what happens if that firm's financial condition takes a nosedive? The auditor can be accused by shareholders of failing to do a thorough evaluation. At best, a CPA firm's reputation is at stake, and it can suffer severe embarrassment. This had happened to Peat, Marwick a year earlier: it gave an unqualified report to the Penn Square Bank shortly before the bank failed. At worst, auditors can be sued by shareholders of bankrupt firms for failing to give adequate attention to the hard facts about their client.[11]

1. If you had worked for Peat, Marwick, would you have stood out against the client's desire to recognize a gain, knowing the chances that the client might dismiss the auditing firm? What factors would you have taken into consideration?

2. If you were an auditor at Deloitte, Haskins and Sells, would you have given Broadview a qualified opinion, or an unqualified opinion with an emphasis paragraph? What additional information would have helped you decide?

3. One observer has asked, "Does an emphasis paragraph mean it's a cheap clean opinion? Or is it a cheap qualified opinion?" What do you think about this question?

4. If you were a stockholder in a company that had just received an unqualified opinion, would you feel assured that your investment was sound? What other clues would you look for? How would you react if you noticed that your company was firing its auditors frequently?

HOW COMPUTERS ARE USED IN BUSINESS 17

Every year, *Time* magazine chooses a "Man of the Year" as the subject of a cover story. The magazine selects people like Anwar Sadat, the Ayatollah Khomeini, and Lech Walesa—individuals who have had a profound impact on the world around them. But in 1982, *Time*'s "Man of the Year" wasn't a human being. It was a machine—the computer. The computer in its present form was invented less than forty years ago, but it has rapidly become essential to business, government, science, communications, and other major aspects of modern life.

What exactly is a computer? How do computers work, and how are they used? We will explore these questions in this chapter and the chapter that follows (Component Chapter F). In this chapter, we will survey the ways businesses work with computers; in Chapter F, we will look into computer components and programs a little more deeply.

CHAPTER FOCUS

After reading the material in this chapter, you will be able to:

- cite the principal components of a computer's hardware
- distinguish hardware from software
- name the four main types of computers
- name six essential business functions that computers can carry out
- describe the main functions of management information systems (MIS), and discuss two problems in developing such systems
- describe what a decision support system (DSS) involves
- list three business functions that can be carried out on a microcomputer

 When English textile worker Samuel Slater stepped ashore in New York City in 1789, disguised as a farm boy, he carried in his head the plans for one of his ex-employer's unique cotton-spinning machines. Slater emigrated illegally, and it was illegal to export the machine's design: the British government wished to preserve its monopoly on the mechanical manufacture of cotton yarn and cloth. But within two years a Rhode Island spinning mill was operating with machines patterned on the pirated plans, and the American industrial revolution had begun.[1]

Perhaps the most important product of this revolution in modern times has been the computer. Like a textile machine in one sense, the computer weaves the threads of technical and business data into a fabric of useful information. Some of this information is so vital that our government prohibits the export of certain American-made computers or their plans. And just as Slater's spinning mill created a new industry and showed Americans that machines could outproduce human hands, so the computer has launched the new industries of microelectronics, robotics, and data processing, and has enhanced our efficiency and productivity in factories and offices.

It is probably fair to say that most American businesses today employ computers in some way. They may own computers themselves, or they may use computers owned by outside data-processing services to perform specific tasks. Between 1982 and 1986, U.S. businesses are expected to spend $1 trillion on computerized information handling.[2] Computers are used not only to carry out routine functions such as cost accounting, payroll preparation, and inventory control, but also to perform more complex tasks such as economic analysis, sales forecasts, and the study of "What if?" questions. In some businesses, computers are found only in special data-processing departments; but in more and more firms, desktop-sized "personal computers" are making computer power available to any manager who wants to work with these machines. Computers also regulate heating, cooling, and lights in many office buildings: one Chicago real estate management firm, for instance, was able to halve its electric bills in ten buildings by computerizing the buildings'

lighting systems and thermostats.[3] Computers are also used in factories, as we have noted in Chapter 6: for instance, thanks to computer-aided design and manufacturing (CAD/CAM), Boeing Commercial Aircraft Company cut the time needed to build a wing-joint attachment from two weeks on one airliner model to eighteen hours on a later version.[4]

It's hard to discuss the use of computers unless we have at least an overall understanding of how they operate. So, before we talk about computers in their business settings, let's take a quick look at the machinery inside the impressively styled box. We'll make some preliminary observations here; the following chapter, Component Chapter F, discusses the workings of computers in more detail.

INTRODUCING THE COMPUTER

Given the computer's amazing abilities, many people fear that computers are more "intelligent" than human beings. But actually, computers are not "intelligent" at all; they are only unusually fast and precise—and they have an extraordinary ability to remember massive amounts of detail. All any computer can really do is add, subtract, multiply, and divide numbers, and compare and remember them. These few fundamental operations, conducted in countless combinations at tremendous speed, are the essence of all the computer's enormously varied applications.

The computer can answer a highly complex question such as, "How large a Social Security benefit is a retired person owed this month?" or "How can a car be restyled to weigh less, yet still offer protection in a collision?" It would be very expensive, however, to program a computer so that the machine itself could analyze such a problem and map out a solution. Usually, a human being does these jobs instead. The computer's specialty is data processing.

WHAT IS DATA PROCESSING?

Data are the *raw facts and figures, meaningless in themselves, that a computer must be given in order for it to answer a question.* For example, the date and amount of each check you have written during the last month are data. Processing these facts and figures simply means handling them according to a strict plan, so that a collection of random data is transformed into an organized pattern of information such as: "You have overdrawn your bank account." (That distressing conclusion might cause you to cry, "Computer error!" but thanks to the high quality of their construction, computers make remarkably few mistakes.) Computer **data processing,** in other words, means *performing specific operations on data to achieve a desired objective.*

PARTS OF THE COMPUTER SYSTEM

People sometimes talk about using a computer to "crunch numbers." This expression suggests that the computer can process data as crudely as a paper mill pulps logs. But in truth, the computer operates more like a railroad switchyard. It stores, retrieves, sorts, and shifts units of data, somewhat as if they were boxcars being linked onto trains bound for specific destinations.

The hub of a computer system is its **central processing unit (CPU)**—*the command and control center of the computer.* The CPU directs and controls the operation of all components on the computer system, performs calculations, and provides short-term storage of instructions and data that are used by the controlling and calculating elements. Outside the CPU, but connected to it, will be one or more devices used for **secondary storage**—an *external, but attached, "memory" bank that holds data for future processing.* (No computer's CPU could possibly keep the schedules and seating assignments of all the nation's airlines, for example, but a computer reservation system can book flights on the basis of data that are recalled from secondary storage.) Also outside the computer, but connected to it, are **input and output devices,** *devices used to enter data into the computer, and devices used to transmit processed data from the computer to the user.* The most familiar input device, perhaps, is the keyboard, but devices also exist for optical, audio, and other forms of input. One of the most familiar output devices may be the printer; but there are also output devices that drive magnetic tapes, and other forms. Familiar, too, is the video screen, which serves as both an input and an output device.

All these devices, as well as the CPU, are classified as **hardware**—*physical equipment related to the computer, including the computer itself and its related secondary storage and input/output devices.* Fascinating breakthroughs in hardware occur almost monthly, as manufacturers develop new ways to make computers faster, more efficient, and easier to use. (We discuss hardware in more detail in Component Chapter F.)

THE COMPUTER PROGRAM

To carry out any task, the computer must follow a logical sequence of steps and choices, and the user must give the computer a chain of brief commands instructing it how to execute these steps and choices. This chain of commands is called the **computer program**—*an ordered sequence of statements that guides the computer in performing a specific set of tasks.* Like a recipe for baking a gourmet chocolate cake, a program outlines step by step the operations a computer must perform to accomplish its assigned job correctly. Computer programs are written in **programming languages**—*systems of code by which commands or statements in English can be represented in a form that the computer can read and obey.*

Collectively, *computer programs* are known as **software.** Many corporations and government agencies have staffs of programmers who write software tailored to their employers' particular needs. Computer programs can also be bought ready-made, part of a software market worth $6 billion in 1983 and including everything from financial-analysis programs to video games.[5] Experts predict that this market will grow to $15 billion by 1986, and that some 1.5 million computer programmers will be needed to supply it by 1990, about three times as many as there are today.[6]

One reason there is such a great demand for programmers is that computer software requires much labor-intensive checking to ensure that it has no potential "bugs," or errors. Hundreds of programmers, for example, are needed to "debug" the 500,000 commands that guide flight computers aboard the space shuttle—a job that takes them months to complete.[7] Recently, software has been written that enables computers to program themselves in a limited way; but even this approach does

As robots move out of the factories, they may bring even more profits to their makers. Androbot Inc.'s "Topo" is a mobile, programmable personal robot that can teach as well as socialize and pass the hors-d'oeuvres.

KINDS OF COMPUTERS: FROM SUPERCOMPUTERS TO MICROS

Since the computer industry is in a state of tremendous change, it is not very useful to present rigid definitions of the four major types of computers—supercomputers, large-scale computers, minicomputers, and microcomputers. Instead, these four types can be considered as if they were on a scale (see page 494), with the computers with the highest processing capacity (the supercomputers) at one end, and those with the most limited processing capacity (the microcomputers) at the other. These four categories are useful ways of thinking about these machines and the settings in which they are used. But the distinctions between the four categories are constantly shifting: what minicomputers used to do five years ago, for example, microcomputers can do today.

not entirely eliminate programming errors. As the familiar saying goes, "garbage in, garbage out"—and computers are just as capable of inputting garbage as people are.

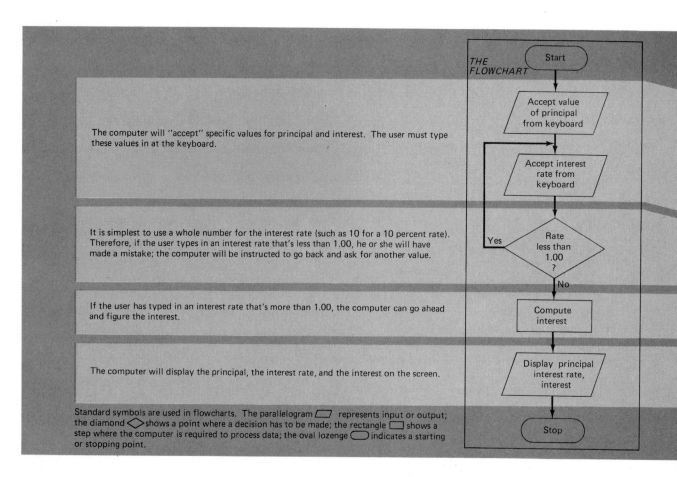

THE FLOWCHART

Start

Accept value of principal from keyboard

The computer will "accept" specific values for principal and interest. The user must type these values in at the keyboard.

Accept interest rate from keyboard

It is simplest to use a whole number for the interest rate (such as 10 for a 10 percent rate). Therefore, if the user types in an interest rate that's less than 1.00, he or she will have made a mistake; the computer will be instructed to go back and ask for another value.

Rate less than 1.00 ? — Yes / No

If the user has typed in an interest rate that's more than 1.00, the computer can go ahead and figure the interest.

Compute interest

The computer will display the principal, the interest rate, and the interest on the screen.

Display principal interest rate, interest

Stop

Standard symbols are used in flowcharts. The parallelogram ⬭ represents input or output; the diamond ⬦ shows a point where a decision has to be made; the rectangle ▭ shows a step where the computer is required to process data; the oval lozenge ⬭ indicates a starting or stopping point.

Supercomputers are *the fastest type of computer*: they work up to 200 times more quickly than general-purpose large-scale business computers, and sell for $5 million to $15 million each. In the past, supercomputers have been used mainly in engineering and research, for scientific problems involving billions of calculations. They have been used to design nuclear weapons, explore fusion energy, forecast weather, and break secret codes. They have also been used in some industries for such tasks as designing aircraft wings, and for interpreting the underground vibrations echoing from blasts set off to detect oil deposits.

Until recently, virtually all supercomputers were made by two American companies, Cray Research Inc. and Control Data Corporation; in 1983, there were only seventy-five of these machines in the world. But by mid-1984 Japan had borrowed American designs and improved on them, forging

A robot that can climb onto a pickup truck (this one is Odetics' "Functionoid") will find multiple uses in construction sites and other outdoor workplaces.

ahead in the race to develop more flexible, easier-to-use supercomputers. Though supercomputers will still be used for scientific purposes, Japan's new machines also promise to be more accessible for general business use.

Large-scale computers are *big, powerful computers capable of supporting powerful peripheral devices.*

THE PROGRAM (Written in the BASIC programming language)

```
10   REM    THIS PROGRAM CALCULATES SIMPLE INTEREST
20   REM    INTEREST = PRINCIPAL * RATE / 100
30   REM    RATE IS EXPRESSED AS A PERCENT
            (WHOLE NUMBER)


40   INPUT  "ENTER THE PRINCIPAL"; PCPAL



50   PRINT  "THE INTEREST RATE SHOULD BE EXPRESSED"
60   PRINT  "AS A WHOLE NUMBER"

70   INPUT  "ENTER THE RATE OF INTEREST"; RATE



80   IF  RATE < 1.00 THEN 50



90      ITR = PCPAL * RATE / 100



100  PRINT  "PRINCIPAL    ";PCPAL
110  PRINT  "RATE         ";RATE
120  PRINT  "INTEREST     ";ITR



130  END
```

Lines 10, 20, 30: These "REM" or "Remark" statements tell what the program will do and how the interest is to be computed.

Lines 40 and 70: The two "Input" statements instruct the computer to ask the user to type in values for principal and interest. (The computer will print, or display, "Enter the principal" and "Enter the rate of interest" on the screen).

Lines 50 and 60: Before the user types in the interest, a reminder will appear on the screen: the interest rate should be expressed as a whole number such as 10 (for 10 percent).

Line 80 instructs the computer to go back to line 50 and re-"PRINT" the reminder if the user has typed in an interest rate that isn't a whole number.

Line 90 tells the computer to figure the interest, using the formula "Interest = principal times rate divided by 100."

Lines 100, 110, and 120 tell the computer to display the results on the screen.

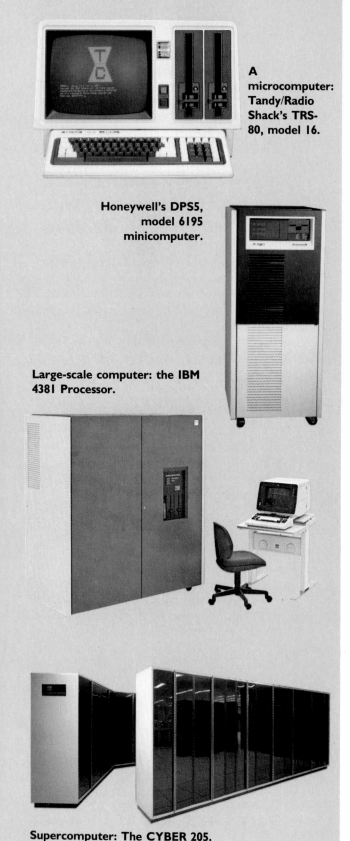

A microcomputer: Tandy/Radio Shack's TRS-80, model 16.

Honeywell's DPS5, model 6195 minicomputer.

Large-scale computer: the IBM 4381 Processor.

Supercomputer: The CYBER 205.

(Peripheral devices include external input/output devices and secondary-storage devices; we discuss them in detail in Component Chapter F.) Large-scale computers generally cost several hundred thousand dollars apiece. Federal agencies have almost 20,000 large-scale computers; many are dedicated to a single large task, such as census tabulation or weather forecasting. Over one-fourth of all Social Security, military pension, and other federal benefits are paid by large-scale computers that electronically credit payments directly to the recipients' accounts, rather than issuing checks. This shortcut saves taxpayers some $30 million yearly in handling and postage costs.[8] Commercial banks are also major users of large-scale computers; with the aid of these machines, the banks shift more than $500 billion daily into and out of major accounts.[9]

The term *mainframe* is often loosely used as a synonym for "large-scale computer." But "mainframe" is actually not a good substitute: its technical meaning is "central processing unit" (one specific part of the computer's machinery). The term *mainframe* was originally used as a marketing lure by companies, such as Amdahl, that manufactured mainframes and certain other computer parts that could be directly substituted for IBM equipment. The marketing phrase was "plug-compatible mainframe"—meaning that the purchaser could unplug IBM's equipment and plug in Amdahl's instead.

Minicomputers are *computers of intermediate size and cost.* The name *minicomputer* is confusing: it makes these machines sound small, but those in use at the time of this writing were about as large as refrigerators. In mid-1984, minicomputers were used heavily in mid-size companies, frequently as the brains behind networks of desktop terminals. Many executives were using terminals wired to minicomputers to retrieve, exchange, and file information electronically at their desks. Secretaries in some companies used terminals wired to minicomputers, too: they might, for instance, type letters and reports on terminals that could correct spelling errors. Research departments were using terminals that could make business statistics easier to interpret by automatically converting them into graphs and charts.[10]

The **microcomputer,** also known as the "micro" or the **personal computer (PC)**, is *the smallest and* *least expensive type of computer.* Microcomputers generally resemble typewriter keyboards teamed with small TVs. Some versions, which have built-in data-display screens, are portable and small enough to fit under an airplane seat; some will even slip easily into a briefcase. Micros are widely used in small businesses; even in large businesses that have large-scale or minicomputers, individual personal computers are seen on some managers' desks. And the relatively low cost of personal computers—often less than $2,000—is also turning them into consumer items for use in the home. At this writing, more than 4 million American families owned personal computers and used them to play video games, to do office and school work, or even to bank and shop at home electronically.[11] In 1975, when the personal computer was first introduced, fewer than 600 were sold. In 1983, sales topped 8 million units, and personal computers are predicted to be a $7 billion annual market by 1988.[12]

One factor in the rapid evolution of supercomputers, large-scale computers, minis, and micros has been the development of the "chip," a microelectronic device that contains hundreds of thousands of circuits and is so small that it's easiest to pick it up with tweezers. The chip has revolutionized electronic storage of information: one model can store the text of 110 typewritten pages in an area half the size of a dime.[13] Another key development has been that of **microprocessor,** or *computer on a chip,* which houses many of the main circuits of a computer in one compact unit. Since parts can now be smaller, room-sized machinery can now be icebox-sized; icebox-sized machinery can now be desktop-sized—and so on. The microprocessor also acts as the tiny brain of the microcomputer. (We talk more about chips, circuits, and microprocessors in Component Chapter F.)

COMPUTERS IN BUSINESS SETTINGS: THE USE OF DATA-PROCESSING SYSTEMS

One reason computers are so interesting is that we don't yet know all the functions they can perform for us. Fifteen years ago, most users thought of computers primarily in terms of the time they could cut out of long, repetitive calculating tasks. Then came word-processing applications that could save time with written material—form letters, labels from long mailing lists, standard contracts in which just a few items need to be individualized. More recently, users have become excited about the computer's ability to translate complicated, hard-to-read tables and other detailed data into visual form—in bar graphs, pie charts, and other graphics whose message can be read at a glance. Today, experts are exploring the frontiers of "artificial intelligence"—equipping computers with stored knowledge that can help human beings make difficult multistage decisions. Tomorrow—the possibilities are enormous.

So, in business settings, users have changed the tasks they assign the computers as their own understanding of the potential of the machines developed—and as the machines became more technologically sophisticated. But the whole computer revolution started with routine processing of basic accounting data, and computers are still used for this function in almost every American business.

DATA PROCESSING: ACCOUNTING AND RELATED MANAGERIAL FUNCTIONS

If you know the language of accounting, you can read the story of a business in its numbers—its daily or weekly sales, it purchases large and small, its costs for salaries, advertising, and other expenses, its cash on hand, its debts and the debts owed to it by others. All these items, recorded in numerical form and categorized in the balance sheet and the income statement, reveal the business's state of health and prospects for the future. And these items must, of course, be tracked every day with great care.

In the past, bookkeepers and accountants recorded all this numerical data by hand; when reports and summaries were needed, they found the relevant data, did the calculations, and formatted the resulting information step by step—using pen and ink, calculating machines, and typewriters. Today, businesses commonly use computer systems to track the numbers, record them in the appropriate categories, and summarize or analyze them when necessary.

THE JAPANESE COMPUTER INDUSTRY: HIGHLIGHTS AND TRENDS

Competition is the name of the game in the computer industry today. Most of the competition thus far has been among companies in the United States, where computer technology was born. But after thirty years of growth, the industry is maturing, and foreign competitors now want a piece of that very large market. Not surprisingly, Japan—the country that swept into the automobile and electronics markets in the 1960s and 1970s—is leading the charge in this latest battle.

By some standards, Japan offers no real threat yet. Fujitsu, the largest computer manufacturer in Japan, ranks only ninth among such manufacturers internationally. But by other standards, the possibilities for growth and power are there. As a potential exporter, Japan has a solid base. All Japanese computer makers taken together constitute the second largest group in the world—after American companies. As a market for computer products, Japan also ranks second, again behind the United States. Nearly $30 billion was spent there on data processing and telecommunications in 1981, and that figure is expected to double by 1986.

PERSONAL COMPUTERS

Within Japan itself, computer makers are fighting strenuously to capture the personal computer market. The reason has to do with the complexity of Japan's written language, which is made up of thousands of characters (not just a few alphabetical letters like our own). No typewriter has ever been able to efficiently generate all those Japanese characters, so communication in Japanese offices has required handwritten letters and memos. But with just fifty keys, the personal computer can construct and have printed out about 7,000 characters. The gain in office efficiency is substantial, and so Japanese office managers are lining up to buy PCs—some of them models that sell for as much as $6,000.

IBM: HOW "BIG BLUE" IS DOING IN JAPAN

Surprisingly, IBM—the Goliath of the computer industry worldwide—has been beaten out in this market by a Japanese company only one-tenth its size and is being pursued closely by two other Japanese firms. The reason, IBM claims, is that "Big Blue" cannot match the distribution network of its Japanese competitors. In Japan, computers are sold through thousands of retail stores, which contract with one manufacturer to sell that manufacturer's products exclusively. In the past, IBM's approach has been to have its salespeople make calls on individual firms. Only recently has IBM begun to contract outside dealers, such as liquor wholesalers who can sell IBMs to their customers (liquor retailers) as an efficient way to keep track of inventory.

IBM faces other problems, too, in its battle for the Japanese market. Japanese competitors have slashed prices on mainframes, for example, and have offered customers unlimited postsale service. Their strategy has been to forgo some profit now to gain a larger share of the market. IBM has counted on instant name recognition to make its sales; but it may have to match those aggressive Japanese methods if it wants to stay in the game.

CHIP MANUFACTURING

The same Japanese tactics that are giving IBM so much trouble in Japan are beginning to have an impact on the world market as well. One of the prizes being fought over is control of the sale of chips—and here, too, Japanese firms are willing to give up short-term profit to get more market share. But the key to winning here is not distribution but production: demand for chips so greatly exceeds supply that whoever can produce the most is likely to come out on top. So Japanese chip makers are pouring back more than 25 percent of their sales revenues into new plants

and equipment—almost twice what U.S. producers are willing to invest.

One reason the Japanese have been able to invest so much is that Japanese government policy allows the rates for loans to remain very stable, even in recessions. In the United States, by contrast, borrowing money becomes very expensive when the economy takes a dip, and expansion plans have to be shelved until the rates come down. The ability to plan and carry out long-term investment plans is a major plus for the Japanese.

And Japan may soon have another advantage in the production of chips—widely available supercomputers. In order to design memory chips, scientists must simulate the circuitry via computers. Only supercomputers have the capacity to carry out the very complex simulations needed for advanced design. Japanese companies are producing many of these supercomputers, at government-subsidized prices, for universities, where future research is likely to be carried out. In contrast, U.S. researchers often have to plead for time on commercially owned supercomputers, since most universities can't afford the investment.

SOFTWARE

In the battle for domination of the chip market, then, the Japanese government has helped its domestic firms in two ways—by pursuing policies to keep interest rates low and by subsidizing the research needed to develop the technology. These same government-business ties may help Japan penetrate the world market for software. Today the Japanese are strong in the sale of only two items of software—video games and engineering and scientific applications. Neither of these requires much translation to be used in non-Japanese-speaking countries, so both have been readily exportable. But the largest part of the market is in business applications, and that is where Japan's computer firms are training their sights now.

The Japanese government is again offering a helping hand. For one thing, Japan's Ministry of Interna-

tional Trade & Industry (MITI) is establishing research labs to work on software development. For another, independent software developers are getting low-interest government loans and tax breaks. The government is even considering a revision of copyright laws to make it legal to copy parts of existing programs without paying the original developers. If this revision becomes law, Japanese programmers will be able to build on some American programs instead of starting from scratch.

Some may consider such assistance unfair. The Japanese claim that it is the only way for them to catch up in a market that has been dominated so long by U.S. firms. And they are quick to point out that it is not government aid alone but innovativeness and hard work that are gaining them a place in the world market for computers. Japanese workers have always been well trained, so they have turned out better-than-average products. Moreover, the productivity rate of Japanese workers has usually exceeded that of American workers because Japanese firms have been willing to invest in sophisticated tools. For example, Japanese programmers may be 10 percent to 15 percent more productive than American programmers because they have the latest program-development aids.

There is much to be learned from Japan's strategy for winning a share of the world's computer market. Is it time for the U.S. government to form a closer partnership with business? When U.S. businesses make plans, should they be encouraged to place less emphasis on short-term profit? Should worker training and reinvestment in plant and equipment be higher priorities in America? These are questions that Americans must answer if they want their country to maintain its competitive position.

SOURCE: "Japan's Push to Write 'World-Class' Software," *Business Week*, February 27, 1984, p. 96; Lee Smith, "IBM's Counteroffensive in Japan," *Fortune*, December 12, 1983, p. 97; "A Supercomputer Gap Has U.S. Scientists Up in Arms," *Business Week*, November 28, 1983, p. 109; "How the Japanese Are Muscling In on U.S. Chipmakers," *Business Week*, April 30, 1984, p. 50.

Six key data-processing functions

Computers speed up data processing tremendously. But they still carry out six essential business functions that the bookkeepers of a hundred years ago did by hand—sales and order entry, inventory control, monitoring of accounts receivable, monitoring of accounts payable, payroll, and the keeping and updating of the general ledger. As you'll see in the descriptions that follow, these functions are connected to each other to provide a continuously updated picture of the company's financial position.

SALES AND ORDER ENTRY A good place to start our tour of a business's essential data-processing functions is the sales and order entry system. In department stores and many supermarkets, customers' orders are recorded right at the point of sale, by a computerized cash register or terminal that feeds the data to a central data bank (usually housed in a large computer, either at the store or at a central facility). Other businesses may use a system whereby customers' orders are received by mail or phone, and the data are entered by a clerk. The clerk records the customer's name, the goods he or she wants, and the quantity desired. (This step is known as "processing" the order.) The sales and order entry system may also include procedures for screening bad credit risks.

INVENTORY CONTROL The inventory control system is usually designed to mesh with the computerized sales and order entry system. As the sales and order entry system records the customer's order, the inventory control system checks whether the goods are in stock. If the goods are in stock, the system will automatically subtract that quantity from inventory and print instructions to send the goods to the customer; it may also signal the accounts receivable system to bill the customer.

Businesses must also keep records of raw-materials inventory; as we noted in Chapter 6, production departments in manufacturing companies often use sophisticated computerized systems to keep raw materials flowing to work stations in the production department as smoothly and economically as possible.

ACCOUNTS RECEIVABLE The accounts receivable system keeps track of customers' purchases; it sends bills to customers and records payments as they come in, automatically deducting the payments from the customers' account balances. Timely, accurate billing can improve a company's financial position considerably.

ACCOUNTS PAYABLE A similar (but "mirror-image") system, the accounts payable system, tracks the money the business owes to *other* businesses for all its purchases—raw materials, office supplies, insurance, and all the other goods and services it needs to operate. When Supplier A sends an invoice, the accounts payable system verifies that the bill is legitimate, writes a check to Supplier A, and subtracts the amount from the company's balance.

PAYROLL The payroll system resembles the accounts payable system somewhat in that it tracks payments that are owed—in this case, to the company's employees. The computerized payroll system calculates each employee's deductions for taxes, insurance, Social Security, and so on, and writes each employee's paycheck. In addition, it communicates with the general ledger system (see below).

GENERAL LEDGER The general ledger system is a "master accounting system" for the company; it tracks accounts payable, accounts receivable, transfers of funds between departments, travel advances, and all the other transactions that may take place. The balance sheet and the income statement are generated from the general ledger system.

OBTAINING REPORTS VIA COMPUTER

If a company can use computers to enter and update its basic financial data, it will be ahead of the game. But it can really gain by using computers to generate reports on the data—summarizing the data, analyzing them, and putting them in an instantly readable format, in far less time than it would take human beings to do. Following are a few examples:

■ The inventory control system can be programmed to

generate reports on the supply of various inventory items. It can also list those items that move the fastest, those items that move the slowest, and those items that are on back order.

■ The accounts receivable system can deliver sales analysis reports that highlight the products that sell best and those that sell least. It can also report on current accounts and accounts that are past due.

■ The accounts payable system can give a financial manager a list of all the bills that are due on a given date. It can also prepare a check register, showing the suppliers to whom the checks were issued, the invoice numbers involved, and the amount, date, and number of each check.

These reports may be particularly handy, for example, when managers are faced with preparing their yearly budgets. The manager can obtain from the computerized system reports on the past year's expenditures—for example, for salaries, equipment, and raw material; using this information, the manager can project his or her budget needs for the year to come. Likewise, managers can obtain market analysis reports on recent sales of specific items; using these reports, the manager can make forecasts of future sales.

MIS: MANAGEMENT INFORMATION SYSTEMS

Recent years have seen an important change in the organization charts of a number of American businesses: what used to be known as the "data-processing department" has in many companies been renamed "MIS," or (somewhat redundantly) the "MIS department." **MIS** stands for **management information system**—*a structure of people, machines, and procedures designed to generate an orderly flow of relevant information for use in management decision making.* The trend toward MIS is connected with an increased awareness on the part of American managers of the crucial role information plays in their everyday activities.

Take, for example, an incident in the day of a production manager for a company that makes clock-radios. The manager has just found out that, because another firm has canceled its order, her

supplier of radio cases can deliver 5,000 additional cases at a discount—if the production manager can take them off the supplier's hands by Tuesday. She *may* be able to save her company $10,000. But will she be able to use the extra radio cases on the shop floor—will the radios be ready by then? She needs information—fast. She needs to know the production department's schedule status this week, the number of radios she has on reserve, and the current costs of storing and insuring radio cases down in the warehouse. Only if she can get these facts right away, in the form she needs, can she make this crucial decision.

Decisions like this have always been tough, but they're even riskier today, because they remain valid for shorter lengths of time. To make them, managers need accurate information that can be obtained fast. Such information is the key to their remaining competitive in the marketplace.

FUNCTIONS OF MIS

Gathering information, analyzing it, and reporting it is the job of MIS. From both inside and outside the organization, the MIS system collects data—facts, statistics, opinions, or predictions—and organizes them so that they can be stored and retrieved. Not

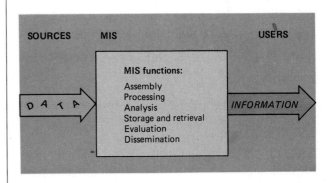

FIGURE 2

THE MIS CONCEPT:
Converting data into information

Quantities of data pour into the MIS department every day. To produce its "product"—information—the MIS must manipulate that data in various ways, often with the aid of computers.

all of this data is actually useful to the managers; a lot of it may be too detailed, or perhaps even irrelevant. So the MIS must pull out, from the flood of data that pours in every day, those pieces of data—and only those—that managers really need. The end product is **information**—*data that is relevant to the manager in making decisions.*

It's important to note that not all components of the MIS need be computerized. A computer is not needed, for example, to write up the results of a new-product focus group and distribute them to marketing managers. But computers are a useful tool in MIS: they make it easier to collect, summarize, and analyze many types of data.

THE DATA BANK AND THE DATA BASE

Any company has the potential material for a **data bank:** *a body of raw data that the MIS can assemble, record, store, and retrieve.* Most companies have data such as:

- personnel data (name, Social Security number, and so on)
- inventory data (part number, units on hand, and so on)
- tax data
- sales data
- accounting data

But the challenge for MIS managers is to convert all this raw material into a real **data base**—*a centralized, manageable system containing all of the organization's data resources.* Creating a usable data base doesn't just mean putting all the data from the company's different departments into one place. It also means coordinating all the personnel and procedures the entire company uses to gather data—from the factory, to the warehouse, to the accounting department. Furthermore, development of a data base includes coordinating all the methods the MIS managers will use to analyze the data. They may use simple mathematical methods, such as ways to calculate sales representatives' average sales, or they may use more complicated statistical techniques.

Only when the MIS managers have set up a smoothly functioning data-base system can they go on to further steps, such as: *processing data* (editing and summarizing it); *analyzing data* (computing percentages and ratios); *evaluating data* (determining how accurate, or even believable, it is); and *disseminating information* (routing it to the managers who need it).

PROBLEMS IN MIS

In an ideal world, all the data a company needed, both internal and external, would be stored electronically in one big system, to which various people in the company would have access. But even the best MIS manager can't always create such a dream system. Why not? Because no two MIS users want exactly the same information. Though all the managers need information urgently, different levels of management want, and generate, different kinds of data.

Management levels and their information needs

It's often said that a company's structure is like a pyramid. Divided horizontally, it narrows from a large number of workers at the base, through a smaller number of middle managers, to the few executives (or one president) at the top. In addition, most businesses are split vertically, with different divisions performing such functions as research, production, marketing, and accounting. If you could view the pyramid from above, you'd see something like a spiderweb—a complex of horizontal and vertical lines centered around the top.

When it comes to information, *lower operating managers*—for example, production supervisors and office managers—tend to need details, so they can monitor day-to-day operations. They're steady customers for the type of specific information that will help them plan scheduling and keep track of materials inventory, accounts paid, and sales and work efforts. In turn, the detailed results of these managers' work are fed back into the data base.

Middle managers often need an overview of what the lower operating managers have been doing: for example, they may need the computer to digest the production supervisors' daily input and make it available again in partly summarized form, as with daily production summary reports. Middle managers are often responsible for short-term decisions on a weekly or monthly basis. Their job is a tactical one: they have to plan and control things like cash flow, productive capacity, and inventory requirements. To do so, they have to be able to see what's going on in some detail, but they don't have to count paper clips or vacation hours.

Top managers must make strategic, long-term decisions about the company's overall objectives and operations: they have to set policy for important matters like mergers, new product development, or new plant locations. They need information in extremely summarized form, so that they can discuss four or five major issues at one meeting, if necessary. Top managers may also have a special need for external information, ranging from market studies (will buyers prefer clock-radios or clock-TVs?) to information on states' tax structures and pollution rules for new factories. (Middle and lower managers may also need external information, but less often; top managers are most concerned with trends and the overall business picture.) Such external information can be obtained from many *outside data banks,* extensively cross-indexed libraries on topics ranging from airline schedules to commodities futures. These resources, available by telephone or satellite hookup, can be indispensable to data-hungry decision makers.

Data needs in different divisions

Not only is it almost impossible for one MIS system with one data base to fulfill all the needs of different levels of a company's management, but different divisions may also require different types of information, presented in different forms. Different divisions also put different data into the data base: Personnel's input for one specific worker might involve his pension status or number of vacation days per year, while Manufacturing's input might involve the number of clock-radios he assembles per hour. The challenge for MIS managers is to get the various departments to input their data in a consistent fashion, so that the central computer can recognize it and integrate it into one large data base that will be accessible to all users of the system.

Few MIS managers are lucky enough to start such a system from scratch. A company is likely to have a collection of existing information systems and subsystems—perhaps a large-scale computer in the accounting department, a mini for Marketing's mailing list, a few micros on managers' desks. The MIS manager has to try to link all these systems, or at least make sure they don't work against one another.

DECISION SUPPORT SYSTEMS (DSS)

We've seen that a big problem for managers is the need to make quick decisions among different and risky alternatives, and that speedy access to the data base can be essential for managers who need to learn about the competition, the market, or their own company's situation. A branch of MIS known as **decision support systems (DSS)** is designed to meet this need and to provide such access. Unlike more traditional MIS methods, DSS is *a system for providing management information that uses interactive computer terminals*—terminals that are online (hooked up to the central processing unit), so that the user can input data, have the CPU process those data, and receive the resulting output, right on the spot. A traditional MIS might, for example, send out a preformatted computer report to various departments once a week. But a DSS lets managers ask questions and get answers whenever the need arises. A marketing manager might sit down at a terminal and ask the price of the smallest clock-radio the company makes, and find out its inventory status, any time he or she needed to do so.

THE USE OF MODELS IN MIS

Decision makers also need the best possible predictions concerning *what would happen if* they chose A over B. If they cut clock-radio prices by 20 percent, would the added sales outweigh the decreased profit? Would a new, automated factory increase productivity enough to pay for itself?

The computer can do these complex calculations incredibly quickly. Two of the tasks of MIS managers are to analyze typical business situations

THE SOCIAL IMPACT OF COMPUTERS IN BUSINESS: USES AND ABUSES

Computers are machines, and most machines have both good and bad uses and side effects. Just as the automobile, a transportation convenience, can be a murder weapon in the hands of a drunk driver, the computer can do harm as well as good. A retired couple who rapidly receive their Social Security checks, thanks to computers, may also get fifty pieces of computer-generated junk mail. More seriously, a computer may make it possible for a criminal to break into a bank and steal more than Bonnie and Clyde ever did, while safely sitting at a terminal miles away.

PRIVACY AND SECURITY ISSUES

One of business computing's most dangerous drawbacks is unethical data processing or data-base use, that may lead to *invasion of privacy*. Never have so many organizations known so much about so many individuals as they do today. In this electronic age, it seems that everyone has a "file" on you—your college, your bank, your phone company. There's nothing inherently wrong in this; your credit-card company has a right to know what you've charged, and whether you're late in paying your bills. (You gave them that right when you accepted the card.) Two questions, though, are cause for concern: do they know more about you than they need to, and are they telling anyone else? If you apply for a loan, it makes sense for the creditors to check your bank balance or credit history. But what if, like many organizations, they also interview your neighbors, trying to determine your "character"? Is it relevant to your financial affairs that you once threw a party that kept grumpy Mrs. Johnson awake next door? That you charged a keg of beer at Scott's Liquor Store (never mind that you paid for it as soon as the bill came)?

An amazing amount of information, whether relevant or not, will become part of your permanent file. (And you'd better hope it will be entered correctly: mistakes such as an operator's hitting 2 instead of 5,

for "His boss rates this applicant's trustworthiness, on a scale of 1 to 5," are far easier made than found and fixed.) Once it's there, it's likely that a great many people will be able to read it. There's the bored worker or prankster who reads people's files at lunchtime; more often, there are companies that sell their data bases to, or share them with, other institutions—companies you may have never heard of and have no interest in.

Even firms that don't share their data bases freely are subject to lack of *data security*. Besides everything else, an MIS manager has to worry about competitors' raiding the data base by simply dialing a phone; several well-publicized incidents in 1983, when teenage "hackers" broke into banks, hospitals, and government computer systems, dramatized the current low level of data protection. The problem is that security often conflicts with convenient, decentralized computer use. Safer systems are possible, but a Pentagon-style system with daily-changing passwords and special keys for hardware and auxiliary devices would bring business to a stop.

IMPACT ON WORKERS' LIVES

The *psychological effects* of the computer boom on employees vary. Some companies report that employees are not happy when computers enter their offices. Executives may be unwilling to spend the hours required to master desktop microcomputers, clerical workers may stage sick-outs, and there have even been cases of sabotage by workers who felt computers undermine their skills, their value as employees, or their self-worth. Others fear computer-caused *unemployment,* and not without reason. Draftspersons, for instance, may be laid off when their firm installs a CAD/CAM system.

However, not all employees dread the arrival of computers in the workplace. Clerical workers, for instance, are often delighted with word processors, which make their work easier and make them more productive than typewriters and correcting fluid do.

Advantages and disadvantages notwithstanding, computers are here to stay. Businesses will be concerned with using them efficiently. We should all be concerned with using them wisely.

(such as a change in sales or an increase in costs) to find the underlying patterns, and to design complex mathematical models that represent them. For example, if you sell 10,000 more clock-radios, you'll obviously make X dollars more revenue—but you'll also need M dollars more to pay for materials, Q dollars to pay W more workers, an extra Z for rent, and so on. Doing the calculations for one such "what if" might not take too long. But analyzing twenty different possibilities (What if you sell 20,000 more clock-radios? Or 10,000 fewer, saving on materials and workers?) would keep you doing math while competitors passed you by. Some MIS systems use "canned" programs built around mathematical models for common business questions; other MIS's, particularly in large corporations, have staff programmers who put together the mathematical models themselves. In either case, all the executive usually has to do is plug in the "what if" number, and the computer zooms through the math and whips out the bottom line—at lightning speed.

Some of the most complex decision support systems include *simulation models* for entire hypothetical situations—say, "What if we built a new plant in Minnesota?"—where there are thousands of variables, from local labor costs to local weather (in Minnesota, for example, fierce winters might keep delivery trucks off the road). Chemical Bank uses models in making real estate decisions; AT&T uses models of their long-distance system for help in routing calls; GM uses computerized models of their cars to predict performance characteristics.

USING MICROCOMPUTERS IN BUSINESS

The steam engines that powered the industrial revolution of the nineteenth century were huge machines that only wealthy manufacturers could afford. But desktop microcomputers, which many experts believe are the most important tools in the information revolution, are getting smaller, more powerful, and more affordable every month. Since microcomputers first appeared in the mid-1970s, costs have gone way down, while performance has gone way up. At the time of this writing—which may be ancient history by the time you read it, given the incredible changes in this industry—micros were offering large amounts of storage, remarkable speed, and clean, colorful graphics. They put power on managers' desktops that a large computer room and ten times the money couldn't match five years ago.

With such power at such prices, it's no wonder that businesses are in the midst of a computer explosion. These days, a company that has a big, complex MIS system, with a central large-scale computer or mini, connected to a number of terminals in other departments, may also have a number of independent micros—"stand-alone" or single-user computers. Micros can do many of the same kinds of work that a complex MIS can. Micros themselves can store data and make them available; they can be hooked into outside data banks to give managers information on tax schedules, stock quotes, and market surveys; they can even help their users answer the same kinds of "what if?" questions that are handled by larger MIS's. A few examples:

- Andrew M. Lewis, president of Best Products Company (the largest U.S. catalogue showroom retailer), uses his Franklin 1000 personal computer for personal scheduling, phone messages, electronic mail, word processing, and making financial models.

- Fred P. Hochberg, senior vice-president for marketing at Lillian Vernon Corporation (a mail-order company), uses his computer to study order trends and plot sales curves. By tracking the timing of response rates to determine the best week for sending out catalogues, Hochberg says, he recently saved Lillian Vernon $100,000.

- Ben W. Heineman, president of Northwest Industries Inc., the $3 billion Chicago-based conglomerate, can instantly call up detailed information on current or past performance of Northwestern subsidiaries, along with comparative industry statistics and economic information from outside data bases. Often, by examining details of his business he would not have seen in the past, Heineman spots something out of the ordinary—an odd inventory level, for example, or an unusual pattern in production. He is thus prepared to ask searching questions of a subsidiary president.

Like any other computers, micros have to be "fed" programs that tell them the detailed steps they must carry out to solve any given problem. We're going to talk about some of the micro programs that

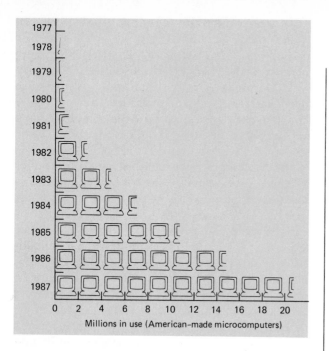

FIGURE 3

THE SPREAD OF MICROS:
"Desktop" computers' rapid growth in the U.S. market

Micros' phenomenal spread is due in part to their increasing use in large companies. One out of five micros bought now goes to a big company, and 50 percent of the micros bought in retail stores land in companies listed among the FORTUNE 500.

are most commonly used for business applications. These programs are generally recorded on disks; when the user wants to work with the program, he or she loads the contents of the disk electronically into the computer. (Recently, computers have also been developed that have certain programs permanently stored in memory.)

SPREADSHEET ANALYSIS

One of the most popular micro applications, *spreadsheet analysis,* uses the same concept as some of the "what if" models that are used in MIS. Spreadsheet analysis takes advantage of the computer's talent for rapid calculations ("number crunching") to let the user think through imaginary situations, or just to take the drudgery out of things like updating the company softball team statistics after every game.

What is a spreadsheet?

A spreadsheet is simply a table of rows and columns. You can set up a spreadsheet by hand—you don't need a computer. The *cells* of the spreadsheet, the points where the rows and columns intersect, are filled with numbers that the user may change at will. (These numbers are sometimes referred to as *variables.*)

A spreadsheet might be used, for example, to calculate a payroll. The sample spreadsheet in Figure 4 contains rows for workers' names; it has columns for the workers' hourly wages, and for the number of regular and overtime hours they have worked. Typically, the person who makes up the payroll already knows what numbers go in these columns. But he or she *doesn't* know what to put in the column for the employees' total pay.

This calculation can take up a lot of the payroll clerk's time if it is done manually. Paula Chang, for instance, put in her regular 40 hours at $10 an hour, but she also worked 6 hours overtime. If she earns time and a half for those hours, that'll be $15 × 6, or $90 overtime, added to her usual $400 paycheck. A payroll clerk could figure that out, but it's time-consuming. Worse, the clerk will have to start all over again if anything changes. What if Chang worked 37 regular and 11 overtime hours? What if her wage is raised to $12.50 an hour? What if her overtime pay changes from time and a half to time and three-quarters? In each case, the payroll clerk would have to go back and figure it out again. Multiply this aggravation by 100 employees and you've really got a problem.

Tackling the spreadsheet with a computer

Once again, the computer comes to the rescue. There are programs available, designed especially for use with micros, that instruct the computer to set up information in the form of a spreadsheet or table. The first and best-known spreadsheet program, VisiCalc, has been challenged by rivals like Multiplan and SuperCalc in recent years, but they all work the same way.

All you have to do is complete *most* of the table by filling in the rows and columns with the values

FIGURE 4

SPREADSHEET ANALYSIS PROGRAMS:
The software solution to a chronic business problem

EMPLOYEE'S NAME	WAGE	REGULAR HOURS	OVERTIME HOURS	REGULAR PAY	OVERTIME PAY	TOTAL PAY
[ALGEBRAIC VARIABLE LABELS] →	W	R	O	$X = WR$	$Y = 1.5(WO)$	$Z = X + Y$
Paula Chang	$10.00	40	6	$400.00	$90.00	$490.00
Lewis Bond	$7.50	32	5	$240.00	$56.25	$296.25

HANDWRITTEN SPREADSHEET

Setting up a spreadsheet by hand takes time—especially to do the calculations.

SAME SPREADSHEET, ENTERED INTO THE COMPUTER

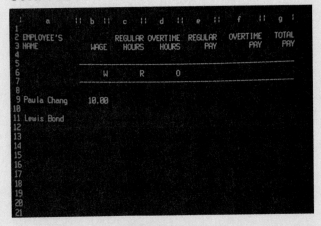

A spreadsheet analysis program prepares the computer to accept values in pre-established spreadsheet cells. The cells are identified by column and row labels: the "Wage" column, for example, is identified by the label "W," so Paula Chang's wage would be entered into cell "Paula Chang - W."

ZIPPING THROUGH THE CALCULATIONS

The spreadsheet program also asks the user for the basic mathematical operations that are to be performed. This user has stated that to compute an employee's regular pay (**X**), the computer must multiply that employee's wage (**W**) by his or her regular hours worked (**R**).

Once each employee's wage, regular hours, and overtime hours have been entered into the computer by typing on the keyboard, the computer calculates regular pay—and overtime pay and total pay—in an instant. Better yet, if you change any of the data (for instance, if you change all the employees' wages to $15 an hour), the computer will redo all the calculations in a jiffy.

you already know, such as your employees' wages and the number of hours they have worked. You also tell the computer, in general, what mathematical calculations to perform (such as: overtime pay = 1.5 × regular pay). Then, the computer cranks out the calculations for you and produces the answer: each worker's total pay. If any value changes for Paula Chang, the clerk can plug in that value and the computer will quickly redo the calculation. If the clerk wants to calculate another employee's pay, all that's needed is to plug in the values for that employee. And simply relabeling a column—changing overtime to time and three-quarters, for instance—will modify the entire spreadsheet, changing the pay figures for a whole list of workers.

This saves an immense amount of time, and it's just a small example. Many businesses need much larger tables—spreadsheets more than fifty columns wide, in some cases—with far more complex formulas. Even so, the computer can deliver the bottom line as fast as you can change the variables. More than anything else, that's the advantage of electronic data processing over paperwork—no matter how many times you change your mind, the machine does the dirty work for you instantly, over and over.

WORD PROCESSING AND COMPUTER GRAPHICS

Two other popular micro applications, *word processing* and *computer graphics*, are like spreadsheet programs in that they do something you can also do with pencil and paper, but they do it faster—making much faster first drafts, and almost immediate second or third ones.

Word processing

A word-processing program turns a computer into a high-speed, high-tech typewriter. It lets you type faster, because there's no need to hit the return key or move the carriage at the end of each line; a word that's too long to fit on the end of a line will appear unbroken at the beginning of the next one. Much more important, though, it lets you go back and make changes. You can take out a word in the previous paragraph, for example, or put a new sentence between two old ones, or swap one paragraph for another paragraph that's several pages farther on. When you are satisfied with the words on the screen, you can have the machine print out the material—just once, with no need to retype all the versions and revisions.

Word processing has been welcomed by novelists: imagine being able to rename the hero of a 300-page romance with one command, changing every "John" in the manuscript to "Charles." But word processing got its start and is still most popular in business. Using word processing, a realtor can use a standardized contract to type one lease for 100 renters, with different names, addresses, and figures mixed with otherwise identical text. And computerized form letters, generated with computerized mailing lists ("You may already be a winner!"), can be sent out in a jiffy with word processing.

Computer graphics

Computer graphics do what company art departments have done for years: they translate pages of fine-print information into charts and graphs that give viewers a quick visual summary. It's much easier for a viewer to scan a pie or a bar chart, finding the biggest slice or tallest bar, than to compare items in a long column of numbers.

The computer, however, beats the fastest artist. Tell the computer the same thing you'd tell the art department—how many slices are in your pie chart, each slice's identifying name or label, and the number or percentage that goes with it—and the computer will draw the chart in a few seconds. Then, if you change one element or variable, the computer will instantly redraw the graphic, as many times as you like. (The human artist would have had to start all over again, and might reasonably have complained and demanded overtime.)

As we noted in Chapter 6, CAD/CAM (computer-aided design and manufacturing) is sweeping the nation's design departments and factories. The computer lets designers make changes in designs as fast as they can think of them—stretching or shrinking a car's wheelbase, an airplane's fuselage, or a shampoo bottle's neck, and making dozens of models and sketches without pencil, eraser, or drafting table.

Word processing, one of microcomputers' most popular applications, can take a lot of the frustration out of writing letters, term papers, and other forms of text. You can say goodbye to laborious reworking and retyping—the word processing program lets you change words and rearrange chunks of material in an instant. The "reverse video" shown here (dark characters on light background, instead of the usual light characters on dark background) is handy for highlighting specific parts of the text.

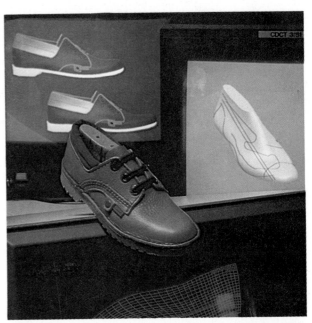

CAD/CAM (computer-aided design and manufacturing) isn't just for high-tech products like machine tools and supersonic jets. The Clarke Company uses it to design shoes: here you see an early stage (right) and a visualization of the finished product (left).

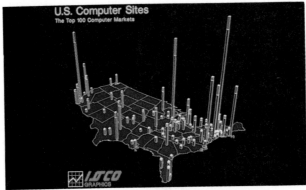

Business graphics programs: a way to cope with multi-page tables and other hard-to-scan text material. The program transforms dense quantitative data into bar graphs (like this three-dimensional one), line graphs, pie charts, and other quickly readable visual formats. Business graphics are useful in meetings and presentations; the individual sitting alone at the terminal will find them a lifesaver too.

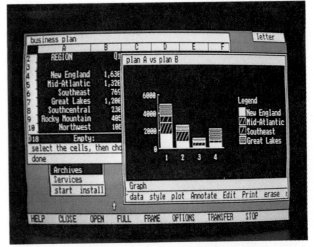

Integrated software saves time and aggravation: it lets your spreadsheet program, for example, "talk to" your business graphics program, so that you can transfer data between the two programs right on the spot. Without integrated software you might have to re-enter the same data at the keyboard for each application.

508 TOOLS OF BUSINESS

CHAPTER REVIEW

American businesses today are relying increasingly on computers. Computers merely add, subtract, multiply, divide, compare, and remember numbers; but they perform these tasks with amazing speed and accuracy.

Computer hardware includes the central processing unit (CPU) and devices for secondary storage, input, and output. To perform any task, the computer must be guided by a program; collectively, computer programs are known as software. The four major types of computers are supercomputers, large-scale computers, minicomputers, and microcomputers (personal computers).

Computers first established themselves as remarkable time savers in performing the essential data-processing functions—sales and order entry, inventory control, accounts receivable and payable, payroll, and maintaining the general ledger. Recently, many companies have transformed their data-processing departments into MIS's (management information systems)—structures of people, machines, and procedures designed to generate an orderly flow of relevant information for use in management decision making. An MIS collects raw data and organizes them into a centralized data base. It is difficult to create only one information system for any company, because its different levels of management and its different divisions need and generate different kinds of data.

A branch of MIS known as the decision support system (DSS) uses terminals that are hooked up to the CPU, so that managers can ask questions and get answers whenever the need arises. Some DSS's include simulation models to help executives evaluate hypothetical "what if" situations.

Even a business with a complex MIS may also use a number of "stand-alone" microcomputers on individual managers' desktops.

These micros can perform many of the functions that larger computers carry out; some of the most popular applications of micros are spreadsheet analysis, word processing, and computer graphics.

KEY WORDS

data (490)

data processing (491)

central processing unit (CPU) (491)

secondary storage (491)

input and output devices (491)

hardware (491)

computer program (491)

programming languages (491)

software (491)

supercomputers (493)

REVIEW QUESTIONS

1. Are computers more "intelligent" than human beings? Why or why not? What are the basic operations that a computer can perform?

2. What is a computer program? Discuss some of the reasons why demand for programmers is so great today.

3. What are the four major types of computers and the characteristics of each? Why should we think of the computer types as being on a scale, rather than define them rigidly?

4. What are the essential data-processing functions that a computer can perform effectively?

5. What is an MIS? What is its purpose? What is the difference between a data bank and a data base?

6. Why is it difficult for an MIS manager to create one system to serve his or her entire company?

7. How does a decision support system benefit executives? Give a specific example of a "what if" situation, and explain how a computer could help to analyze it.

8. Why are microcomputers being used more and more in businesses today?

9. What is spreadsheet analysis? Give an example of a situation in which spreadsheet analysis could be used.

10. What are word processing and computer graphics? What are the advantages of each? Can you think of any disadvantages? Explain your answer.

CASE 1

PUTTING A CAP ON COMPUTER SPENDING

Buying computers used to be the exclusive right of a company's data-processing department. But now, all that is changing—for two reasons. First, computers are becoming smaller and cheaper, and their purchase can easily be budgeted for by departments other than data processing. Second, office automation requires not just computers but word processors and telecommunications equipment, and very often data-processing personnel do not have the necessary expertise to be knowledgeable buyers of these other pieces of equipment. Responsibility for purchasing has therefore been dispersed throughout the company.

According to one estimate, for every $1 spent by a company's data-processing department for computer equipment, another 30 cents is spent by various other departments. In 1982, for example, about $78 billion was spent by U.S. corporations for central data-processing operations; perhaps another $23 billion was spent for personal computers, word processors, and the like by personnel, marketing, finance, and other department heads.

With that much money at stake, companies are beginning to set up systems for controlling costs. One way to do this is to charge data-processing costs on a department-by-department basis instead of as a company-wide overhead cost. The reasoning behind this so-called "charge-back system" is that department heads will become more aware of costs and less willing to waste money on unnecessary purchases.

Another plan allows department heads to purchase data-processing services and equipment either in-ternally or from outside computer service companies and sellers that are approved by top management. For example, at General Electric, 20 percent of the company's data-processing needs are met outside the company. Individual department heads thus have considerable discretion on how to meet their computer needs, though they don't have unlimited freedom to purchase whatever they want.

Giving managers a choice of where to purchase services has two advantages. First, outsiders present internal data-processing departments with some competition, which may keep costs down. Second, having a restricted list of outside suppliers lessens the chance that the company may end up with incompatible computers.

In the modern business world, computers have always been a big cost of doing business. Today, more than ever, managers face the challenge of keeping those costs under control while encouraging continued office automation.[14]

1. Is it desirable to leave some control over data processing and computer purchases in the hands of individual department heads? Why or why not?

2. Do you think the charge-back system will tend to make department heads more aware of the costs of information processing? Or will it simply make them use computers less?

3. How might allowing department heads to choose between using the company's own data-processing department and an outside computer service tend to make the company's data-processing department run more competitively?

CASE 2

CAUTION: PCs AT WORK

Personal computers are now at the forefront of the information revolution in business. For a relatively small investment, they promise to give managers an incredibly flexible tool for analyzing data. But they also have drawbacks. With so many managers now using them—an estimated 400,000 by 1985—the micros may be overwhelming executives with information. The old computer industry adage—"garbage in, garbage out"—still applies. Unless businesses exert some control over the information that gets to managers, the resulting analyses are likely to be useless.

There appear to be three principal problems. First, two managers in the same company looking at the same problem can come up with radically different answers. Executives using PCs often get their data from outside their companies, because that information is unavailable inside. The PCs the executives are using may be incompatible with the mainframe in the data-processing department. Or data may be stored in the main computer in a way that only the technical specialists in the data-processing department can get to it. The data-processing specialists may be unwilling—or unable, because of costs—to retrieve the information needed by many possible users.

A second problem can arise if the programs executives use to manipulate data on personal computers are not standardized. Sometimes executives may use their own programs to "massage" the data they have. The information may then come out doctored to meet the managers' own needs, and no one is able to check the results. When the executives leave, no one may know the programs they used to, say, track the sales of their departments; critical corporate information can be lost.

Personal computers contribute to still another problem—duplication of work effort. Two managers may actually be doing the same work on their personal computers without knowing it. The resulting waste of time and corporate money is highly inefficient.

The simplest solution to these problems is to discourage managers from bringing in and using their own PCs. With this alternative, the data used in analyses could be centralized, the programs used could be standardized, and duplicated management effort could be eliminated. But personal computers may already be too widespread for this to be a workable answer.

A less drastic solution is to discourage micro users from developing their own programs for handling data. The data-processing department would be charged with developing the software for all PC users in a company. North American Philips corporation has tried this plan; it now offers its executives a variety of financial, accounting, and marketing programs.

But in itself, this answer is incomplete since it doesn't deal with the problem of executives' using outside data. The key to this problem is to find a more direct way of tying PCs to one another, and to the mainframe in the data-processing department. This process of establishing links, or "networks," is now under way, but the technology for accomplishing it may not be perfected for another five years. Currently the software that can handle this problem is very expensive—$50,000 on up. Not many companies are willing to make that kind of investment.

According to one analyst, the computer networks of the future will be like mayonnaise—"an invisible ingredient that somehow integrates all the other elements." Finding the right recipe, at a reasonable cost, is the main objective of the experts who want to control the information revolution today.[15]

1. Construct arguments for both sides, regarding the first alternative—discouraging people from using PCs.

2. How might people in the data-processing department react to being asked to develop software for personal computers that aren't in their department?

3. Suppose you buy software that links PCs to mainframes. What security problems might this entail?

4. In terms of costs, how might the network option stack up? (Consider the initial cost; but also consider how this option might enable you to spread the cost of expensive peripherals, such as a high-priced printer, over several PCs, instead of buying a separate printer for each PC.)

HOW COMPUTERS WORK F

Did you know that if the airplane had matched the spectacular development of the computer in the last twenty-five years, a Boeing 767 jetliner would cost $500 today, and would be able to circle the earth in 20 minutes on five gallons of fuel? The swift development of computers has given us one of the near-miracle stories of modern technology. The first electronic computers astounded people not only with their quick calculations—several thousand per second—but also with their huge scale and expense: they were room-sized, and they seldom cost less than $1 million. Today, however, some of their hundred-dollar descendants will fit into a shirt pocket, and offer calculating speed measured in millionths of a second or better.

The technical side of computers—what their components are, how they have changed, and how they may change in the future—will be our subject in this chapter. We'll discuss not only individual computers but also systems whereby computers are connected to each other and to other data-handling devices.

CHAPTER FOCUS

After reading the material in this chapter, you will be able to:
- describe the kind of task computers do best
- indicate how the binary system converts data into electrical impulses
- list at least five major advances in the development of the computer
- cite the functions of the four major parts of a computer—the CPU, primary storage area, secondary storage devices, and input/output devices
- name the most common secondary storage media and input/output devices
- define and distinguish online processing systems, timesharing, and distributed data processing
- name three types of transmission services
- distinguish PBX and LAN office automation systems
- describe two problems complicating the choice of a computer today

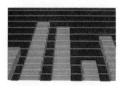 At some time in their careers, nearly all employees in a business—from the clerk up to the president—have probably faced at least one dull, time-consuming task and been grateful that computers exist to take over the dirty work. Jobs that humans would consider intolerably mindless, computers do without difficulty—particularly tasks that are sharply defined. Preparing mass mailings of business letters, for example, would be far more tedious if done manually by a secretary. But the computer can direct a printer to type thousands of letters: the letters are identical, except that the computer assigns each an individual name and address, calling them up from electronic storage within the machine itself. The computer can also carry out enormous but repetitive calculations, such as tallying monthly billings for millions of credit-card holders. And complex comparisons that might take an unassisted business manager days or even weeks to make—such as comparing year-to-year sales of a company's products by volume, price, and sales region—can be done in hours or minutes with computer power.

The number of instructions that are required to direct a computer to prepare mass mailings, set up form letters and credit card billings, and analyze business problems is enormous—often topping several trillions. The central processing unit (CPU), introduced in Chapter 17 and discussed in detail later in this chapter, is the part of the computer that directs the operation of the machine to accomplish these tasks. The CPU operates electronically: that is, it works by sensing the flow of electrical impulses through pathways known as circuits.

COMPUTER CIRCUITS

A **circuit** is *the path of an electric current;* when engineers draw a diagram of a circuit, they generally include various electronic devices that help direct the flow of electricity within that circuit. Every time a command or a unit of data is fed into a computer, electrical pulses race through an elaborate network of circuits within the machine—at nearly 186,281 miles per second, the speed of light. The history of the development of computers, from the giant machines of the mid-1940s to today's desktop and lap-sized models, is really the history of the development of increasingly small and complex arrangements of circuits.

WHAT COMPUTER CIRCUITS DO

Anyone who has taken piano or typing lessons knows how difficult it can be to make a machine perform converting or transforming operations the way a piano or typewriter converts the touch of your fingers into music or words on paper. Yet the computer can process all kinds of data into information. How it does this is ingeniously simple.

First, we have noted that the computer performs its operations electronically, with pulses of electricity. To regulate the incredibly swift traffic of these pulses, every circuit contains microscopic electronic switches—a computer has millions of these—that turn the pulses on and off as directed by the program that is guiding the computer. This switching action steers pulses from circuit to circuit in electrical currents that flow in a "go or no go" fashion, like water channeled by locks through the canals of an irrigation system. Ultimately, any computer operation (such as adding 3 + 4) boils down to millions of on-off choices, made almost instantly.

Second, the computer's use of on-off choices lends itself to a very simple means of representing all things in a numeric or "digital" form. "Off" can be represented by the digit 0, and "on" by the digit 1 (or vice versa). Therefore, any number or letter or other representation of an entity may be expressed as a series of "offs" and "ons" or 0s and 1s—the digits of the binary number system. Just as the decimal number system uses ten as its base, the binary number system uses two as its base. In computer parlance a binary digit is termed a "bit"; bits are the fundamental units of data processing, and all things the computer can do can be reduced to representations in the binary system.

The binary system of representing letters and numbers is not new; as you may know, Lincoln's eloquent Gettysburg Address was telegraphed across Civil War America with just the electrical dot and dash of Morse code! Similarly, a computer can encode symbols, an alphabet, or even the information communicated by a photograph or a symphony, into electrical pulses. Stored permanently in the memory of most computers is a special program called a **compiler,** *a computer program that translates other computer programs into machine-language programs.* The compiler automatically translates incoming data and the everyday language of other programs into numerical form.

Most computers combine their electrical pulses into groups of eight, sixteen, or thirty-two bits. Constantly rearranged as if they were cards in an automatic shuffler, the "on" (for 1) and "off" (for 0) pulses of even the simplest computer can form enough varied patterns of bits to represent uniquely and numerically each letter, number, and punctuation mark in the English language. For the computer that typeset this book, transforming electronic data into printed information was literally as easy as switching it around.

THE DEVELOPMENT OF COMPUTER TECHNOLOGY: FROM ENIAC TO THE BIOCHIP

A serious topic of debate among philosophers in the Middle Ages was how many angels can fit on the head of a pin. In 1970, computer-circuit designers conducted an experiment based on this question. They inscribed the head of a pin with 100,000 tiny drawings of angels, the size of the switches that were then used in computers. Today, the same space could accommodate *1 billion* angels.[1]

More than any other factor, the shrinking size of electronic components is responsible for so spectacularly multiplying the speed and capabilities of computers and slashing their cost. Take, for example, the contrast between the first successful electronic computer, ENIAC, and its descendants today. ENIAC—the Electronic Numerical Integrator and Calculator—was completed in 1946. Its components, laid side by side at two-inch intervals, would have covered a football field; they cost nearly $500,000 to assemble, and could perform 5,000 computations a second.[2] Today, five times as much circuitry as ENIAC contained can be imprinted on a flake of silicon crystal smaller than a contact lens, to

FIGURE I

WHEN IS A "I" NOT A "I"?

Binary numbers and how they can represent data

BINARY CODE

0001 1 in this position represents 1

0010 1 in this position represents 2, since values increase by multiples of 2 as they move to the left

0100 1 in this position represents 4

1000 1 in this position represents 8

Therefore, to represent the value 3 we have the following:

0011 that is, 2 + 1 = 3

And to represent the value 13, we have:

1101 that is, 8 + 4 + 1 = 13

ASCII CODE

ASCII code (American Standard Code for Information Interchange) is an 8-bit code that works on the basic principles of binary code. Here is how the letters A, B, and C are represented in ASCII:

1010 0001   represents A
1010 0010   represents B
1010 0011   represents C

Each 8-bit unit used to code data is called a byte.

make a computer on a chip that costs about $150 and can calculate 200 times as fast as ENIAC ever could.[3]

EARLY PROGRESS IN COMPUTER DESIGN

The first major advance in computer technology after ENIAC was the invention, in 1947, of the **transistor**—*a compact electronic switch for controlling electric current.*[4] Transistors were smaller, cooler, and more dependable than the vacuum tubes in early computers, and they used less power. Gradually, transistors replaced vacuum tubes. And gradually, engineers began shrinking the transistor, launching a drive toward miniaturization that is still under way.

In 1959 came another advance—the **integrated**

A

B

Although advances in computer design have come thick and fast during the past two decades, the computer's evolution actually spans well over 200 years. Among its forebears are the devices shown here. (A) The "difference engine," a mechanical device invented by Charles Babbage in 1812. The "engine" was supposed to calculate logarithmic tables without human help and print the results. Much to Babbage's regret, however, the parts could not, at that time, be machined accurately; so Babbage could not complete the full-scale steam-driven model. (B) The electrical census machine developed by Dr. Herman Hollerith to tabulate the data of the 1890 U.S. Census. This machine's basic storage device was a card with twelve rows and eighty columns, punched according to the Hollerith code. Punched cards are still in use today— and the Hollerith code is still used too. (C) The Mark I, an electromechanical computer developed by Howard Aiken in 1944. For input, punched paper tape was used; for output cards. The Mark I was noisy and not very efficient—it took three seconds to perform a multiplication. (D) The ENIAC (Electronic Numerical Integrator and Calculator) developed by J. Presper Eckert and John W. Mauchly in 1946. This huge machine could multiply two figures in three-thousandths of a second, but it was awkward to operate and had no internal memory. ENIAC often broke down, and it had to be rewired each time its program was changed.

C

D

circuit, or **IC.**[5] Nicknamed the **"chip,"** the IC is a *device that combines miniature transistors and other components on a thin sliver of silicon.* By eliminating the miles of copper wiring that slowed the flow of electricity in earlier computers, the chip slimmed down computing machines and explosively increased their calculating speed. Electrical pulses travel the tiniest distances between a chip's transistors, and switching operations in present-day computers typically take only 50 billionths of a second.[6]

ADVANCES IN CHIP TECHNOLOGY

With the advent of the IC, engineers realized that a chip combining 1,000 circuits would do more work, in less time, than one with only ten circuits—and would do it for about the same price. By the end of the 1960s, this insight led to a new wave of miniaturization called **large-scale integration (LSI)**—*the assembly of many circuits with different functions on one inexpensive chip.* Moreover, scientists found that by mounting several thousand LSI chips on circuit boards, it was feasible to create a small but complete computer. Even more advances were made in miniaturization—*refinements in LSI technology* known as **VLSI,** or **very large-scale integration.** Demand for chips skyrocketed, and within a decade the United States was annually selling chips worth $6 billion to computer manufacturers worldwide.[7]

The microprocessor

The first generation of chips had a major flaw: they were not multipurpose devices. The circuitry of a chip designed to turn out a factory payroll could not also monitor inventory or govern conveyor belts. This drawback was overcome in 1971 by the development of the **microprocessor**—*a computer on a chip.* The microprocessor is a silicon chip so tiny that an ant can carry it; it may have 500,000 or even more transistors, and it is designed to perform the fundamental arithmetic and logic operations that are the basis of electronic computing.[8] At a price of as little as $5, the microprocessor is incredibly cheap.[9] Better yet, it is programmable—one can alter its function simply by storing new instructions in its memory circuits, as if the microprocessor were a full-size computer.

The microprocessor's low-cost flexibility gives the device almost limitless application, from guiding missiles to activating children's toys. Microprocessors allow some microwave ovens to be programmed to start and stop in accordance with stored instructions for as many as eighty recipes.[10] Almost all cars built in the United States today contain a microprocessor programmed to control engine performance, and General Motors boasts only half-jokingly that it is the world's largest computer maker.[11] The computer on a chip tunes radios, regulates pacemakers, directs robots, and performs thousands of other tasks. By one estimate, there are now more computers on our planet than people![12]

Memory chips

Spreading even faster than the microprocessor is the **memory chip**—*a complex of microelectronic circuits that are used as the primary storage device in computer systems.* Currently, Japanese companies dominate the production of the largest-selling memory chip;

This Intel microprocessor, or "computer on a chip," is small enough to be carried by an ant. Yet it holds 30,000 transistors; it can store complex instructions and can make hundreds of thousands of calculations per second.

they view the chip in all its forms as a strategic commodity. American manufacturers consider the chip the crude oil of the computer age; they have challenged Japan with even more advanced memory chips. These advanced chips, they hope, will expand their share of the $16 billion international chip business.[13]

Chips of the future

Computer chips have been doubling in complexity every year for more than twenty years, and engineers who once dreamed of cramming 8,000 transistors on a slice of silicon now foresee a billion-transistor chip by this century's end.[14] Designing the circuits of this new chip will be comparable to mapping all the streets and freeways of 2,000 major cities on the head of a pin.[15] Manufacturing further generations of chips beyond that will be truly daunting, unless the chips can reproduce themselves—and, in fact, scientists actually predict that it will be possible to make *biochips,* constructed of self-assembling chains of proteins. With molecule-scale chemical switches, a biochip the size of a pea might contain the equivalent of a million billion transistors. It could be used to implant a computer into the human body, able to compensate for damaged or defective human nerves and muscles—a benefit for the physically handicapped.[16]

The impact of biochips would be dramatic, but probably no more so than that of microprocessors and memory chips. Teamed together, these micromiracles not only make computers smaller, faster, and cheaper, but they are also making computer power as commonplace and unnoticeable as electric power. It will be no surprise if one day we can steer cars or adjust our lights and thermostats by verbal command, or receive checkups from tiny medical computers circulating in our veins—and think nothing of it!

COMPUTER HARDWARE

A computer system is a complex of circuits, wires, and cabinets. These physical components are termed computer hardware—all those devices that permit data to be entered into a computer system, manipulated within the system, and returned to the user. All computer systems—supercomputers, large-scale systems, minicomputers, and microcomputers—have similar components: they have hardware for input, processing, seecondary storage, and output.

THE CENTRAL PROCESSING UNIT (CPU)

The CPU—the computer's command and control center—has two subareas, the control unit and the arithmetic and logic unit (ALU).

The control unit

The **control unit** is the *component that supervises and coordinates the computer's operations.* The control unit consults programmed instructions that have been placed in the computer's storage areas and uses these instructions to decide what data the computer should store, recall, or display—and where, when, and in what order. The control unit also manages the computer's arithmetic and logic functions. With strings of electrical pulses darting very rapidly through the computer, the machine would literally get its signals crossed if it lacked a control unit to act like the train dispatcher of a railroad switchyard.

The arithmetic and logic unit (ALU)

Another area of the CPU is the **arithmetic and logic unit (ALU)**—*the computer circuits that perform computations and logic operations.* The ALU performs arith-metic operations—addition, subtraction, multiplication, and division. It can also compare two numbers or encoded letters and symbols—to determine whether they are identical, and if not, how they differ. (These comparisons are its logic operations.) Although the ALU performs incredibly quickly, ALUs in most computers do their work piecemeal. New internal organization technology has been developed, however, that allows ALUs in some computers to do all the steps of an arithmetic or logic operation simultaneously: these ALUs are like factories where all the employees work at once.

PRIMARY STORAGE

Part of every computer's anatomy is the **primary storage area**—*a group of chips where the computer can momentarily store or retrieve the data it needs.* Magnified, these memory chips reveal rows and columns of transistors that can hold data bits in the form of electric charges. The transistor grid of a memory chip suggests an array of post-office letterboxes, and its well-ordered architecture makes finding or filing a data bit at a specific "address" as simple as pigeon-holing a postcard in the proper box at the post office.

As a computer works, its CPU continuously "checks in with" the primary storage area, trading data with it in less than a millionth of a second.[17] At times, the CPU "reads" stored data bits—representing, say, program commands. The CPU may also "write," or file in the primary storage area, data bits that express an incoming instruction. Or, it may temporarily store a subtotal that has been generated by the ALU—in effect, jotting the intermediate results of a computation on a scratchpad.

Computer data storage is usually measured in terms of the **byte,** *a unit of data equal to eight bits.* Years ago, computer engineers became accustomed to working with storage areas in which it was possible to store 1,024 bytes of data (symbolized by the letter K, meaning 2 to the tenth power or 1,024). Today, the "memory" chip in a small computer has sixty-four times that amount of storage, or 65,536 bytes (64K). That's more than 65,000 memory addresses for data storage. If that many actual postcards were laid end to end, they would stretch for almost five miles![18]

FIGURE 2

HOW COMPUTERS WORK 519

A TYPICAL MAINFRAME SYSTEM: Central processing unit (CPU) plus peripheral devices

(Right) Mainframe systems are configured in various ways, but most include certain basics: the **CPU** (center of picture), tape drives (at the back, on the right), disk drives (foreground), on-line workstations (this system has three), and at least one printer (front workstation). In this particular system, the **CPU** is a "dual processor"—two processing units integrated with each other. This system also has a group of small computers (at the back, on the left) whose sole function is to monitor the big computer. And another intriguing feature: this room isn't as chilly as most computer rooms have to be, because these Honeywell machines have their own built-in cooling system.

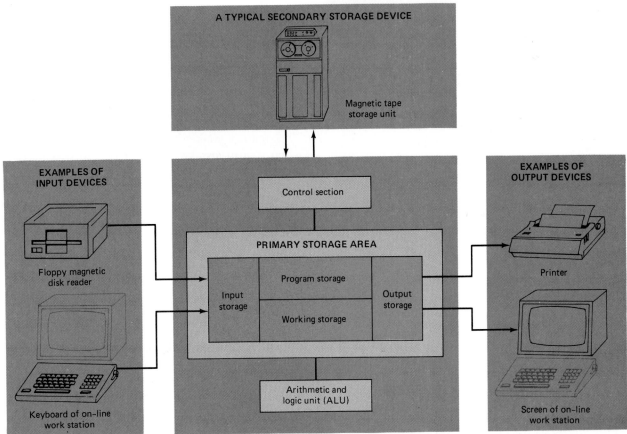

A TYPICAL SECONDARY STORAGE DEVICE

Magnetic tape
storage unit

EXAMPLES OF
INPUT DEVICES

Floppy magnetic
disk reader

Keyboard of on-line
work station

Control section

PRIMARY STORAGE AREA

Input
storage

Program storage

Working storage

Output
storage

Arithmetic and
logic unit (ALU)

EXAMPLES OF
OUTPUT DEVICES

Printer

Screen of on-line
work station

CENTRAL PROCESSING UNIT (CPU)

Above, a schematic diagram of the typical mainframe system. Primary storage in the **CPU** includes separate areas for input, output, programs, and data the computer is working on at the moment.

You may have heard of "RAM" and "ROM" (random-access memory and read-only memory). Want to know the difference? **ROM** contains crucial instructions such as those for starting up the computer. It is programmed in for keeps: it can be "read only," never erased. **RAM**, on the other hand, contains instructions for the computer task of the moment. **RAM** gets filled via the keyboard or a secondary storage device; if you turn off the electricity, whatever is in **RAM** will be lost.

SECONDARY STORAGE DEVICES

A computer would be deaf and dumb if it consisted only of the CPU and the primary storage area. What rescues it from splendid isolation are **supplementary** or **peripheral devices**—*auxiliary equipment in a computer system, including input and output devices and devices for secondary storage.* Secondary storage, the category we will consider first, is an area in which there have been some intriguing technological advances.

Punch cards

One of the earliest secondary storage media, or vehicles, was the punch card, which is still used in certain applications. Made of stiff paper, the punch card has hundreds of locations in which holes may be punched (to be read by the computer as 1's) or left untouched (to stand for 0's). In recent years, punch cards have largely been replaced by other secondary-storage media: as computer systems increased in power, they could have more tape and disk devices attached to them on-line.

Magnetic disks

Typically, an airline reservation system uses magnetic disks as a secondary-storage medium. These disks resemble record albums; they are coated with microscopic metal particles magnetized to represent data, and they are stacked roughly an inch apart in packs of several disks. A computer system may include an input device known as a *disk drive,* by which data stored on disk can be fed into the computer. As the disk spins (at nearly 60 miles per hour), an access device known as a *read/write head* is maintained at a position that is just above the disk's surface, searching out or filing data from the disk.

For small computers, including personal ones, secondary storage takes the form of a *floppy disk:* a flexible, magnetized plastic platter ranging in size from 3.25 to 8 inches across, and sealed in a protective jacket. Activated singly in a disk drive, a "floppy" can feed a computer all or part of the data stored on it. Larger computers may use the rigid, 8-inch aluminum *hard disk,* a multiple-platter magnetic storage medium. Groupings of data, such as individual personnel records, are stored on the disk in *random order:* the location, or address, of any element of data stored on the disk is independent of the location of any other element. Disks are thus a form of *random-access storage memory.*

Magnetic tape

Until recently, reels of magnetic tape similar to that used in a cassette player offered more storage capacity than any competing technology, and magnetic tape is still the most economical storage medium. A computer system may include an input device known as a *tape drive,* by which data stored on tape can be fed into the computer.

Groupings of data (again, individual personnel files are a good example) are stored on tape in *sequential order:* they are stored one after another according to some plan (they may be in alphabetical order, for example). To locate a specific data element (say, Fay Freeman's personnel file), it is necessary to start at the beginning of the tape and go all the way through to the F's and finally to Fay's file. This feature makes tape a less attractive medium when it is necessary to gain access to specific data quickly: for example, tape would not be desirable in an airline reservation system. But it presents no drawback in large files maintained as lists. The Social Security records of millions of Americans are stored in sequential order, for example.

Optical disks

Recently, newly perfected *optical memory disks* have surpassed tape's storage ability. A laser beam can create and read billions of microscopic marks on a twelve-inch plastic and metal optical memory disk, representing as much data as can be held on twenty-five reels—about twelve miles—of one-inch magnetic tape.[19]

INPUT AND OUTPUT DEVICES

How does the user feed data and programs into the computer, and how does the computer feed data and programs back to users when they are needed? A number of input and output devices are available for these purposes.

Input devices

One approach to input is to load data and programs into the CPU from a secondary-storage device such as a disk drive or a tape drive. Alternatively, the user may enter data and programs via an optical input device, an audio input device, or one of the newer devices such as a light pen or a graphics tablet. (See the photo gallery on page 522 for examples of these forms of input.)

The most commonly used input device, however, is the keyboard. Computer keyboards resemble those of typewriters, but they have extra keys for special commands. Tapping a key sends an electrical pulse through the machine. Depending on the way the keyboard is set up, the pulse may represent (in code) a letter, a symbol, or a number. Some keys may even be set up so that they give the machine specific instructions: one particular key, for example, might send a command to the CPU to interrupt its execution of a program. Some keyboards are part of the computer's frame, while others are detachable.

One of the specialized keys on a computer's keyboard is often labeled "Return" or "Enter." Only when this key is struck does a computer process the data it has received from other keys. One reason computer manufacturers build in this delay is to allow the computer operator to review the data, on a screen linked to the computer or built into it.

Output devices

One of the most familiar output devices is the printer, which prints words and numbers on paper. Printers come in a number of forms (see the photos on page 523); a printer to go with a personal computer, which will produce high-quality output, may cost almost as much as the computer itself. Also available are audio devices that produce computer output in the form of sounds—beeps, music, recorded voice messages.

Computer output can also be fed back onto magnetic tapes or disks for storage. As we have noted, data stored on a disk or tape as a set of magnetic fields can be converted by a disk drive or tape drive to electrical pulses that can be fed into a computer. Just as easily, electrical signals from the computer can be translated back into patterns of mag-

netism, when the flow of data is reversed and information moves from a computer to a disk or tape for storage.

The screen: input plus output

In a sense, the computer's screen serves as both a mirror and a window. It can be used to monitor and reflect data that is being entered into the computer from the keyboard and from other sources, such as floppy disks. The user can look at the screen and see whether this data needs revision. If it does, the changes can be typed on the keyboard and immediately displayed on the screen. Thus, a newspaper editor working at a screen can shift, copy, add to, or erase elements of a reporter's story, and follow each of these changes as it happens. An engineer working at a high-resolution color graphics monitor can command geometric shapes to rotate, shrink, merge, and so on, to produce the crisply outlined cross-section of an airplane wing.

The screen can also provide insight into the computer's internal memory and into what is happening to data as it is processed inside the machine. If the computer is alphabetizing a mailing list, for example, and suddenly stops, the user can type in a command that tells the screen to "call up" and display the commands that are in the computer's mailing-list program. This way, the operator can check them and possibly make corrections. Once the mailing list is completed, the user can type in a command that tells the screen to summon the list up for review, too.

The modem

A peripheral device that's especially useful with the personal computer is the **modem,** *a communications device that enables computers and their support devices to communicate over ordinary telephone lines.* One of the functions of the modem is to convert computer electrical pulses into sounds that can be transmitted over a telephone line; another is to translate such telephone tones back into computer signals. Connected to a telephone with a modem, a PC can "talk" to another computer across town or across country, vastly enlarging its usefulness. Properly programmed, it can dial a computerized information

A

B

C

D

(A) On many micros, the keyboard serves as the input device. But on this machine, the user can also enter commands by touching specific parts of the screen.

(B) Some computer systems include a "mouse"—a small box with push buttons that rolls on desk or table top. By pushing the mouse on the desk top, the user can move the cursor—the pointer on the screen that indicates the area of the screen where the user is working. Pushing a button on the mouse initiates a specific command.

(C) This designer is using an input device known as a light pen. As the user moves the light pen over the image, its outlines are entered as data into the computer system's memory.

(D) Optical reading systems scan light patterns and convert them to computer-readable electrical pulses. This scanning window decodes the Universal Product Code on grocery items.

(E) This plotter, connected to a terminal that's specially adapted for graphics, "paints" a printed copy with a computer-driven pen.

(F) The computer at this work station is connected to a printer. Printers come in several varieties: among them are the fast, inexpensive dot-matrix printer, which strikes the paper with tiny pinpoint-size hammers, and the slower, more expensive, but usually higher-quality daisy-wheel printer, which has a wheel of characters that spins around and is struck by a hammer for each character.

network and obtain and display data such as airline schedules—or headlines and articles from *The Wall Street Journal* and other major newspapers. A modem-equipped PC can even answer the phone, to take instructions from a human caller or to receive files and programs from another computer. Professional and business people find this feature particularly attractive, because the PC can make and take calls unattended, at any time of day or night.

OFFICE AUTOMATION AND LONG-RANGE DATA COMMUNICATIONS

Up to this point we have explored the components of an individual computer system, such as might be installed in a company's data processing department or sit on a manager's desk. Equally important, however, are the components that go into more complex computer systems—systems whereby a computer is linked to other computers, or a computer is linked to other data-handling machines. Today, data can be transmitted a few feet or a thousand miles away with tremendous speed among desktop and large-scale computers, telephones, long-range communications devices, and peripheral devices such as facsimile machines and printers.

ONLINE SYSTEMS, TIMESHARING, AND DISTRIBUTED DATA PROCESSING

In one form of data communications, individuals and companies hook their computers up to outside data bases such as Compuserve or Lexis, which allow the users' computers to act as terminals with access to a central bank of information. Another familiar example of long-range data communications can be found in airline reservation systems like American Airlines' Sabre, developed with IBM in the late 1950s. When a Pittsburgh travel agent sells a ticket for seat 14C on December 12's flight 601, the airline's central data base is updated; if, a moment later, a Denver customer asks about seat 14C, she'll find it's reserved.

E

F

Networks such as Sabre are known as **online processing systems,** or *systems that process data interactively:* all terminals have immediate access to a constantly updated source (to "read" data from it), and have immediate input as well (to "write" data into it). In the fastest online systems, **real-time systems,** the system *can receive and process data quickly enough to affect some ongoing physical activity.* The strength of a real-time system is its timeliness, its ability to deliver up-to-the-minute information. Giant real-time networks help air-traffic controllers monitor the crowded skies; as a plane leaves the area watched by one ground computer, it's passed to another ground computer like the baton in a relay race. Another mammoth computer network links U.S. military bases and radar stations worldwide with commanding officers up to the president.

In other networks, speed is less crucial but individuals may want to do more with the data at various points—a terminal operator may want to actually work with the data, for example, not just send and receive it. Many businesses and colleges with these types of needs use **timesharing systems.** Here, *several terminals share access to a central processing unit, but the processing tasks are done one at a time for the various terminals.* The CPU in a timesharing system is like a waiter serving several tables: it does part of one terminal's job, then works for the next terminal for a moment, then gives some attention to the third user, and so on, eventually circling back to the first and starting over. Since computers are so fast—they spend most of their time waiting for you to press a key, with long, boring stretches between even the fastest typist's hitting two letters—most timesharing users don't notice the delay. For most jobs, each of five students using a school district's minicomputer might believe no one else is on line.

More and more, though, timesharing's cost advantage is being offset by falling microcomputer prices—this year's CPU costs less than last year's plain terminal. The next step in large-scale systems is **distributed data processing (DDP),** an approach involving *a network of many computers (usually of different sizes) spread over a geographical area and connected by telecommunications.* Each link in a DDP system can compute independently (some may run terminals of their own), but all the links can share programs, data, electronic mail, or other information. Many national and global businesses have distributed data processing systems.

HOW DATA IS TRANSMITTED OVER LONG DISTANCES

Large-scale data communications systems, whether real-time, timesharing, or distributed, are useless without a way to tie the parts together. The distances involved—from one end of a university campus to another, or from Seattle to Paris—are too big for the machines in the system to be physically connected with cables. Instead, the information they process has to be transmitted via services that act as go-betweens.

Some of these "go-between" transmission services are familiar to nonbusiness communicators. They include *common carriers*—public phone and telegraph networks such as AT&T's and Western Union's; and *specialized common carriers,* which add services such as satellite broadcasting or microwave circuits reserved for data transfer. MCI Communications Corporation, for example, began as a specialized carrier, offering microwave data transfer to businesses; it now competes with AT&T in long-distance voice transmission.

Then there are *value-added carriers,* which lease transmission facilities from common carriers but perform extra functions in handling customers' data. GTE Telenet, for instance, takes data that comes in by phone, temporarily stores it, and organizes it into compressed "packets" for faster transmission (a service that helps lower customers' phone bills). After high-speed shipment, the data is reassembled into the original form at an office near its destination. Other value-added carriers provide ways to convert data that has to be transmitted between incompatible machines; they may also provide error checking and correction to make sure that the data isn't garbled along the way.

OFFICE AUTOMATION

Even if it's only a connection between three or four desktops and a mini down the hall, a data communications system can boost office productivity immensely. Besides having all the computing advantages mentioned above, an office with such a system (an "automated office," in today's jargon) benefits from electronic mail and message distribution. Memos are more likely to get read when they come to the receiver electronically. And employees can say goodbye to annoying "telephone tag" ("While You Were Out: Bob S. returned your call, made while he was out. Please call again, though he'll be out this afternoon").

Networks for office automation

Comparatively small businesses will account for a good many of the firms that are expected to have a micro network in the next few years. Many of these networks won't span global distances, but only a few floors of an office building. At this writing, two sets of initials—PBX and LAN—were fighting for small-scale-network dollars.

The first option, the **PBX (private branch exchange),** is a *system for sending data over telephone wires.* Like home computerists on local "bulletin boards," some companies have been using phone lines and modems to call other computers, as well as central data banks like Dow Jones's. This system is simple and economical, but dialing numbers and establishing links one at a time is awkward and time-consuming. One solution is to use a PBX, the computer-age successor to the switchboard. PBXs programmed for speed dialing, call forwarding, and similar functions have increased office productivity for some years; the newest units, marketed by companies like Rolm Corporation and AT&T, are able to handle data as well as voice transmission, and can even merge the two into a high-speed stream as value-added carriers do.

The PBX's main competitor is the **local area network (LAN),** *a system in which computers and other equipment are hooked up directly without phone lines.* LANs are much faster and more powerful than PBXs, but they require more planning and expense: there may be a limit to the different brands of machinery a LAN can handle, and running cables through the walls or floors is difficult and expensive. Despite these problems, however, over 10,000 local area networks are in use, with offices claiming the lion's share (factories, colleges, and laboratories have some). Though no single LAN has become an accepted standard, Xerox Corporation's Ethernet, which uses coaxial cables and special interfacing

devices, is currently popular. Also widely used is Datapoint's ARCnet, as sold by Tandy Corporation/Radio Shack: ARCnet can join up to 255 TRS-80 computers.

The problem of compatibility

Both carriers and DDP customers have to keep a wary eye on data coming from different machines or traveling through different machines at different speeds. Getting micros and large-scale computers to "talk" to each other, for instance, has become one of data communications' top priorities: one of the biggest of today's markets is for hardware and software that will help companies overcome compatibility problems.

The micro equipment war

Until recently, most automated offices have used word processors and/or terminals hooked up to large-scale computers or minicomputers elsewhere in the company. But now, thanks to its low price, wide availability, and ease of use, the stand-alone personal computer is now widely used in place of these other desktop machines. The personal computer can perform most of the functions of the word processor and the terminal, and more. As a result, many companies are witnessing a three-way battle between different internal departments—their office automation, telecommunications, and data processing departments—because each department may want to control the purchasing of personal computers. Technicians who run companies' central data processing departments have lost control to the users of the PCs, who may be spread throughout the company. According to one estimate, 85 percent of the purchases of desktop computers were made by users outside the data processing establishment in 1982.[20]

Problems still face companies joining the micro trend. Peripherals such as software, printers, and added memories can push the price of a PC up above $20,000. Moreover, the technology is still rudimentary for networks that can link stand-alone computers together. Still another problem is the widespread confusion about the variety of products that manufacturers of different kinds of technology are offering. Personal computer makers such as

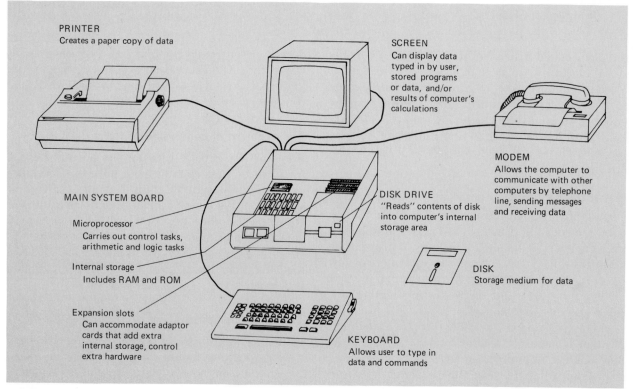

FIGURE 3

A TYPICAL PERSONAL COMPUTER SYSTEM:
A microcomputer plus some commonly used peripheral devices

The personal computer system includes some of the components found in larger computer systems (compare this system with the one shown in Figure 2).

Apple are adding features that let their desktop machines "talk" to large mainframes; makers of big computers such as Burroughs and Data General are broadening their product line to include PCs and connecting equipment; makers of terminals and word processors are offering souped-up "smart" terminals and word processors with added data processing functions; and telecommunications companies are marketing computerized private branch exchanges and combination telephone terminals that can move both voice and data signals. All these options make it harder for companies to figure out which equipment to buy. At this point there is no standardization, and a company may not be able to connect one brand of equipment it already owns to other machines it is thinking of buying. In the next few years solutions to these puzzles may begin to appear.

CHAPTER REVIEW

Computers perform repetitive tasks with enormous speed. They can do this because their circuits transmit electrical current at the speed of light. Millions of switches turn the current on and off. The resulting electrical pulses represent data by means of the binary system, a numerical code consisting of 1's and 0's.

Rapid progress in miniaturization has been largely responsible for spectacular advances in computer speed and capability as well as shrinking sizes and costs. These developments began with the appearance of the transistor (a compact electronic switch) and continued with the invention of the integrated circuit or chip (a set of transistors and other components on a sliver of silicon). Advances in chip technology then produced large-scale integration (very complex chips) and the microprocessor, or computer on a chip, as well as memory chips capable of storing enormous quantities of data.

A computer's hardware consists of several components. The central processing unit (CPU) is the computer's command center; it includes the control unit and the arithmetic and logic unit. Computers also house a primary storage area. Supplementary (peripheral) devices include equipment for secondary storage and input and output devices. Secondary storage media include punch cards, magnetic disks, magnetic tape, and optical disks. The most common input device is the keyboard, and a common output device is the printer; the screen can be used for both input and output, as can the modem, which connects the telephone to the computer.

Recent advances in technology have enabled the high-speed electronic transfer of data among computers and other data-handling equipment—a phenomenon called data communications on a large scale and office automation on a small scale. Types of data communications systems include online processing systems, timesharing, and distributed data processing (DDP). Data may be transmitted over long distances by common carriers, specialized common carriers, and value-added carriers. Office-automation systems include the PBX (private branch exchange) and the LAN (local area network).

The explosion in the number and type of computers available today has caused two problems. One is compatibility—making different models able to communicate with one another. A second problem is competition—both within companies for control of the purchasing decision and among manufacturers and sellers for share of the market. Because of competition, the decision as to which equipment to buy has become very complex.

KEY WORDS

circuit (514)

binary system (514)

bit (514)

compiler (514)

transistor (515)

integrated circuit (IC) (chip) (515–516)

large-scale integration (LSI) (516)

very large-scale integration (VLSI) (517)

microprocessor (517)

memory chip (517)

control unit (518)

arithmetic and logic unit (ALU) (518)

primary storage area (518)

byte (518)

supplementary (peripheral) devices (520)

modem (521)

online processing systems (524)

real-time systems (524)

timesharing systems (524)

distributed data processing (DDP) (524)

private branch exchange (PBX) (525)

local area network (LAN) (525)

REVIEW QUESTIONS

1. What kinds of tasks do computers do better than humans?

2. Explain how data, the computer's electrical circuits, and the binary code are linked.

3. What technological developments have been milestones in the history of the computer? Describe the devices that have made computers progressively smaller and cheaper.

4. What are the basic components of a computer system? What do they do?

5. What are the major types of secondary storage media?

6. Which computer devices can be used for input? output? both input and output?

7. What is the major difference between online processing systems and timesharing?

8. How do the PBX and LAN office-automation systems differ?

9. What problems do businesses face today in choosing new computers?

CASE 1

CLINCHING THE PERSONAL COMPUTER SALE

Computers are now a permanent feature of business life, and the selling of computers has become a big business in itself. With the invention of micros, computers have become available for small businesses and for personal use. But the people who want to buy personal computers are a different breed from traditional business buyers.

For one thing, personal computer buyers often have less knowledge than their corporate counterparts. They may come to a store with little or no idea of how they are going to make use of their computer. The salesperson's job then becomes one of educating customers. But how much time can a seller afford to spend on this process? After all, a salesperson's time is worth money. Should he or she take the time to explain the capabilities of several models and demonstrate them, or should the buyer simply be taken over to a rack of magazines and told to purchase a few, read up, and come back?

The answer to that may depend on how likely the salesperson thinks the buyer is to purchase a micro—and that's another difference from the corporate customer. When salespeople call on corporate clients, they are reasonably certain of serious intentions. Not so with the personal computer prospect, who may only be looking for a cheap and easy way to get information and have no intention of buying. Salespeople may have to spend a lot of time qualifying the customer—finding out how serious he or she is.

Personal computer buyers and corporate clients are alike in two important ways: both can be very cost-conscious, and both expect follow-up support after the sale. But the corporate customer may be more realistic about factoring follow-up services into the initial cost of the computer. In contrast, buyers of micros will very often pull out an ad from a discount or mail-order house and expect the salesperson to match the price shown in the ad. They forget that low-price firms do not offer the services of full-price stores, such as instruction in running the computer and advice on how to get it running properly when a glitch develops.

Sellers of personal computers face many other problems that sellers of large computers do not. Because micro buyers are often first-time users, they may call for assistance again and again. Sometimes, the buyer isn't even the ultimate user, so the salesperson has to spend time educating two clients—the one who comes in and expects hours of demonstration and instruction before making the purchase, and the frantic secretary who calls in after accepting delivery and asks, "What do I do with it?"

How much support should sellers offer after a sale has been made? The answer varies from store to store. For some personal computer users, the postsale education process can be the most important part of the deal. But it's only fair, say personal computer salespeople, that customers should expect to pay if they anticipate a lot of follow-up.[21]

1. If you were a personal computer salesperson, how would you handle the customer who came to you with no idea of what he wanted to use a computer for? How would you deal with the customer who wants to talk technical but who seems to have no serious intentions to buy?

2. Demonstrations of different models and programs are useful for people who fear computers. But such demonstrations cost the store money. Would a demonstration be worthwhile for someone interested in a $50 program? For someone interested in a $700 business package?

3. Which kind of follow-up instruction do you think would be best for the unsophisticated computer buyer—four or five hours of formal classroom instruction or an hour or two of hands-on instruction by the person who made the sale?

4. Buyers who lack knowledge are particularly vulnerable to unethical sales practices. What is unethical about each of the following practices?
a. Using a lot of technical language in making a sale
b. Saying "yes" to all the customer's questions without promising to demonstrate
c. Cutting corners on telling customers about all the equipment they need—just to get the sale

CASE 2

COMPUTER SECURITY: ANOTHER ANGLE

The loss of a data base through competitors' raids is only one security problem MIS managers face. Another nightmare they must cope with is a wipeout of their data due to some unforeseen disaster. Such disasters aren't all that uncommon. Mazda Motors Corporation recently lost a large mainframe when a roof collapsed during a heavy winter storm. And Paychex, a New Jersey payroll company, was nearly put out of business when a disgruntled employee broke into its computer facilities one holiday and destroyed all its computer records.

The destruction of computer records can pose serious problems. Almost all record keeping is done by computer today. Even small companies, which cannot afford their own computer operations, give over their record keeping to computer service companies. When disaster struck Paychex, for example, that company was holding the payroll and tax records of 1,300 other companies—which together employ over 95,000 workers.

When such vital information as level of inventory, production rates, interest paid, or taxes owed is lost, no company can stay afloat for long. In fact, according to the Minnesota Graduate School of Business Administration, most banks would go belly-up in two days after a computer failure. Distributors and manufacturers would take slightly longer—3.3 and 4.8 days, respectively. And the fallout from such a failure would not necessarily be limited to the affected company. The California Bankers' Association notes that the loss of one bank's data

center due to an earthquake would hurt the state's economy after three days, the U.S. economy after five days, and the world economy after seven days.

Many businesses, alert to the dangers of a computer disaster, have begun to plan ahead. At present there are two ways to safeguard computer data and avoid going under. One is to store duplicate computer records in special facilities, some of them located in remote underground caves and mine shafts that are safe from many natural disasters. The caves often have special rooms with air conditioning and telecommunications equipment, where computers could be brought in and run. In the event of a disaster, computers and personnel would be rushed to the site for immediate re-startup. But what if backup computers could not be found quickly enough? A second plan that some companies have opted for is to buy "hot sites"—centers where computers stand ready for use. Such backup sites have been used at least twice in the past to save small companies struck by natural disasters.

Despite their proven effectiveness, storage facilities and hot sites do have drawbacks. For one thing, they can be expensive. Some companies spend up to $7,500 a month for the right to use a hot site if an emergency strikes. Computer rooms that are ready to receive computer equipment are less expensive—$200 to $1,000 a month—but they are also more risky, since equipment may not always be available when needed.

Besides the expense, there is the problem of transporting personnel to the new sites and housing them, perhaps for several months. Would employees agree to such a disruption in their lives, especially if they were single parents who had to find substitute caretakers for children on a moment's notice?

No real large-scale emergency has ever tested the effectiveness of current backup plans. Whether such plans give a false sense of security is an open question.[22]

1. What sorts of information do banks, distributors, and manufacturers store in computers?

2. Why do you think banks would go under so quickly following a computer disaster? If you were a bank president, how would you plan for such a disaster?

3. Many large data banks—on which many companies depend for their information—are located in California near earthquake-prone sites. Should there be disaster plans for data banks? Who should be responsible for this planning?

4. What are the major drawbacks of current disaster plans? Can you think of any alternative plans that might either prevent disasters from happening or aid in rapid recovery after one has struck?

PERSPECTIVES ON SMALL BUSINESS USING BUSINESS TOOLS

Every small-business owner is inevitably involved with manipulating numbers. He or she needs reports on dollars invested, returns on investment, sales, payroll expenses, inventory, and countless other items. But few self-employed people have any expertise or formal schooling in accounting, business mathematics, or the use of computers. "I'll never get involved in the records," the small entrepreneur is frequently heard to say. "That's what I have an accountant for."

This attitude has certain merits, but it leaves two questions unanswered. First, is your accountant the best person for your particular company? And second, are you making the most effective use of your accountant's services? Let's explore some ideas that help answer these questions.

LEARNING TO WORK WITH AN ACCOUNTANT

Speak your accountant's language

The first point we need to emphasize here is that you'll need to become familiar with the accounting terminology that's presented in Chapter 16 of this text, and to develop an understanding of accounting principles through books and education. Without this knowledge, you won't be able to develop a working relationship with accounting professionals. You need to speak their language. The more you try to bridge the gap between yourself and your accountant, the greater your chance of receiving good, timely advice.

Choose well and ask questions

Next, choose an accountant who is knowledgeable in your business area. When you're talking to an accountant you think you might like to work with, ask a few pointed questions such as "How many small businesses do you handle?" and "How many of them are in my particular line of work?" The more experience your accountant has in your marketplace, the more meaningful the advice you receive will be. If your accountant has a basic familiarity with your problems, you will save many dollars in unnecessary research costs.

Hire a problem solver

Your accountant should be a problem solver, not a problem finder. Almost anyone can locate a problem area, but not everyone is able to formulate a set of procedures or organize a plan of action that will solve the problem. Your accountant should also be willing to consult a specialist if a unique problem arises.

Share basic attitudes

Find an accountant who shares your attitude on the interpretation of the law. There are many government agents who cannot agree on the meaning and application of the law themselves! Approaches vary widely, and it's important for you to work with an accountant who shares yours.

Accounting services

Finally, you need to look at the five types of accountants and accounting services that are available to the small-business owner:

1. Certified public accountants who are also attorneys (CPA-attorneys). These are highly qualified specialists in complex areas of estate planning, corporate taxation, and numerous other areas.

2. Certified public accountants (CPAs) and public accountants (PAs). These accountants are licensed by the state to practice the profession of accounting. They are trained to prepare, analyze, and report the financial aspects of any business in a manner that is acceptable to the government.

3. Enrolled agents, who are enrolled to practice before the IRS tax court, and have passed rigorous tax exams that neither lawyers nor CPAs are required to take. They are considered tax experts. However, they are not required to continue their education after they have passed the exam, so you have to take on faith that they remain in touch with new legislation and new ideas. But enrolled agents charge less than CPAs, and their work may be excellent. (If a person has a CPA title, there's still no guarantee he or she does high-quality work!)

4. Bookkeeping services that post business transactions to accounts and produce monthly financial statements. People who run such services need not have a college education in accounting, nor are they required to pass an exam to show competency or to enroll in courses to expand their knowledge. A person in this

group may provide valuable services, at a cost far lower than a CPA would charge. Some bookkeeping services have clients who recommend them highly. But they are usually not equipped to provide sophisticated management-planning services.

Many small businesses have solved the problem of accounting services by engaging a reputable bookkeeping service to perform the weekly posting to accounts, and a CPA or qualified accountant to prepare the monthly financial statements. They thus have the best of both worlds: the knowledgeable advice of a qualified professional, and the competent but less costly services of bookkeepers to handle the routine posting to accounts.

5. Tax specialists who operate only during the tax season. These people offer no advantages to a small business owner. You are in business 365 days a year, and you need specialists who are there when you are.

YOUR ACCOUNTING RECORDS

Your accounting records and financial statements indicate the financial health of your business. If your firm's profit-and-loss statement is properly prepared in a timely manner (monthly), by using computer programs like Visicalc (see Chapter 17), it will show the exact ratio of your sales to your expenses. This ratio will tell you if your business is meeting its financial goals. A small business must carry its own weight from the very beginning; if there is nothing left on the bottom line for the owner, how long will it survive?

The profit-and-loss statement and the balance sheet are of critical importance as business barometers. Many small businesses begin operation without any financial statement during the initial three- to six-month start-up period, but this is an almost certain invitation to failure. You must use financial statements from the beginning and on a regular basis. (Once a month is the accepted frequency for any new business, and during any critical growth period.) This way, if you see a problem area developing, you can make adjustments to put the business back on the track.

Special accounting reports

Besides the standard financial statements such as the balance sheet and the profit-and-loss statement, several other tools are critical to financial planning. This planning is even more important today because of high interest rates and reduced availability of loanable funds.

CASH-FLOW PROJECTION A small business must have an effective cash-management system in order to have enough cash to meet cash expenses. To effectively manage your cash, you should pay careful attention to planning the cash supply, controlling the cash flow, and investing any surplus cash.

One of the best business tools available to the small business is the cash budget. This budget is also known as the cash forecast, cash projection, cash-flow budget, or cash plan. The purpose of this budget is to plan the supply of money necessary to meet daily, weekly, or monthly cash needs.

An excellent form to use for this purpose is SBA Form 1100, Monthly Cash Flow Projection. Instructions are on the reverse side of this form and are easy to follow. A related form for making profit-and-loss projections is SBA Form 1099, Operating Plan Forecast (Profit and Loss Projection). This form also has instructions on the reverse side. A big advantage of both forms is that

they are commonly used to make projections to support loan applications and are well known by most lending institutions.

Many firms extend credit, so it is very important to know the status of your accounts receivable. A tool available for this function is aging of accounts receivable.

AGING OF ACCOUNTS RECEIVABLE Your balance sheet may indicate the dollar amount of your accounts receivable, but this is only a small part of the information you need. It's also important for you to know how long these bills have been outstanding. Most bills are due in 30 days; you need a report designed to indicate the length of time each account is overdue, and the amounts of money that are overdue 60 days, 90 days, and 120 days. Such reports are known as aging reports.

Other types of aging reports indicate aging by product line and aging by market area. If you need to increase your cash flow, this kind of report will tell you the areas to attack first.

SALES ANALYSIS A sales analysis breaks down your total sales into specific categories—product line, salesperson, market area—indicating strengths and weaknesses as they begin to develop. It also enables you to compare the current period's performance with performance in any previous period, so you can calculate the percentage of increase or decrease.

Another tool to control cash is calculation of the breakeven point, which is reached when the total revenue is equal to total costs. Some costs, such as property taxes, are fixed; they do not vary with sales. Others, such as production costs, are variable; these fluctuate in proportion to sales. Two formulas helpful in computing the breakeven point are:

$$\text{Breakeven} \atop \text{(Sales)} = \frac{\text{Total Fixed Costs}}{1 - \left[\dfrac{\text{Average variable cost per unit}}{\text{Average revenue per unit}}\right]}$$

$$\text{Breakeven} \atop \text{(Units)} = \frac{\text{Total Fixed Costs}}{\text{Selling price per unit} - \text{Variable cost per unit}}$$

Any dollar sales or number of units sold above the breakeven point are profits and below the breakeven point are losses.

Surplus cash that results from careful cash management should be invested to generate funds for future operating periods. As a small-business owner, you can consult a banker or an independent financial planner to help with investment decisions.

Another business tool now readily available to the small-business owner is the computer.

USING COMPUTERS

When they were first introduced, computers were very large and very expensive. They required special rooms, and were frequently difficult for the average person to operate and understand. Now, there are literally hundreds of low-cost (under $10,000), flexible microcomputers, which are all suitable for small business use. The tremendously increased availability of computers has caused the selling prices of computer hardware to drop steadily over the last few years. Competition is heavy, and small businesses can buy a lot for their money.

In the area of software (the programs that run the computer), the market has changed dramatically,

too. Standard software packages for word processing, financial analysis (Visicalc), and all the accounting applications (payroll, inventory control, and so on) have been developed and will run on most of the available models. This huge, though still incomplete, increase in software compatibility, along with falling hardware costs, has sparked the interest and opened the pocketbooks of thousands of small companies. More and more entrepreneurs have begun to use computers to cut labor costs, control inventory, monitor production, alert accounting to past-due accounts, and keep track of new customers. And these are only a few of the capabilities of these "new-age devices." Other new applications exist in every business.

The growth in available compatible software and lower hardware costs are expected to continue through the 1980s and 1990s. The question for the small-business owner is not whether to buy a computer, but when. Before you make a final decision, you should undertake a very careful analysis. Let's discuss the steps in the decision process.

Where will you use the computer?

First, think about the areas of your business that you might want to computerize. Accounts payable, accounts receivable, payroll, production control, and inventory control are only a few areas you may want to consider.

Let's look at a typical payroll problem. Suppose you own a manufacturing company that employs twenty-five assemblers working on a piecework basis. Calculating the payroll is a complex business, and errors may occur. Such a situation is bound to create unhappiness among the employees, affecting their morale and their productivity. Under the circumstances, the payroll would seem to be an ideal place to start a computerization analysis.

Determine the cost

The most realistic way to justify the expense of a computer is to calculate the dollars it will save. The computer must carry its own weight in the company. If it's simply bought as a status symbol, it may eat into profits and even ruin the business.

Let's look at one payroll example. How much does it cost you to process your payroll now? Let's say it takes two full days per week of your office manager's time. Her hourly rate is $8.50. Two full days is 16 hours. $8.50 multiplied by 16 hours is $136.00. Add a 30 percent burden to cover her overhead and fringe benefits, and the total becomes $176.80 per week. Multiply the $176.80 by 52 weeks, and divide the answer by 12 months, and you arrive at a monthly cost of $766.13.

Now, calculate the work necessary to compute the quarterly government reports. You estimate the approximate time per quarter to be four days, or 32 hours of the office manager's time; 32 times $8.50 equals $272.00, to which you again add 30 percent, for a quarterly cost of $353.60. Divide this figure by the three months in the quarter, and the monthly cost factor is $117.87. You now have a monthly cost of $884.00 ($117.87 + $766.13) to calculate the entire payroll manually.

Now, let's say that an efficient computer program could easily process the payroll in 25 percent of the time. Twenty-five percent of $884.00 is $221.00. The difference between $884.00 and $221.00 is $663.00. This $663.00 is an estimate of the savings to the company by using a computer for the payroll only. A $10,000 total computer system could be leased on a five-year basis for about $480.00 (including all maintenance) per month. Therefore, it is obvious that a savings exists if all our estimates are correct. So we are able to justify its cost.

Or are we? Two additional points remain that are usually forgotten:

1. What is your office manager going to do with the extra time? There may well be other jobs in the company that the office manager could handle, such as collecting past-due accounts. But if her time can't be effectively used, re-evaluate the problem.

2. How much would it cost to write the computer program to compute this unique piecework payroll, or is there a standard piecework payroll program that can be used or modified? You probably can find a suitable one for less than $1,000, plus $500 for modification. This software cost erodes your savings quite heavily. Unexpected costs can and will seriously hamper business profits and cash flow. So let's look further.

Set up a list of priorities. What other procedures might you want to computerize? You should select two or three additional areas and make the same cost comparisons for them as you did for your payroll. You must be able to prove a cost savings in reduced labor and other direct expenses.

When you're thinking about computerizing, don't tell your employees any sooner than necessary. They're likely to fear that their jobs will be eliminated; unfortunately, there is a general feeling that computers reduce the number of jobs available. This is not necessarily so. If computer programs are designed properly, they frequently enable a firm to increase its efficiency and thus handle more business. The increase in business will usually support more employees, not fewer. Some employees will need to receive new training on the computer, but this will only enhance their value as workers.

In analyzing the potential cost savings offered by a computer, never use a time frame of more than five years. The computer must prove itself in that length of time, because new technology will provide improved products within that period. And once you have purchased your first computer, every computer-marketing organization in the country will rush to tell you why you need to upgrade to an even newer type of equipment. Eventually, you'll follow their advice.

Consider for a moment the concept of obsolescence. The trend in the computer industry of the 1980s is one of rapid technological change in all areas. The growth rate is so fast that whatever you buy, lease, or rent, your system could be outdated by a more advanced or faster approach within six months. So how do you decide? You choose the system (hardware and software) that will best meet your requirements at the best all-around price—in other words, the one that will give you the most value for your money. Don't worry too much about the future. As long as the computer you select will do your job for five years, you have made the right decision. Then— as long as the computer works, does the job, and spare parts are available—use it until it no longer serves its function. Obsolescence is really a marketing term, a way to convince companies they need to buy newer, more efficient, and possibly more expensive models. Sometimes the change is for the better, but frequently it only helps the profits of the computer company.

Choosing a vendor

Before you sign a contract with any vendor, be sure of two things: the vendor's reputation, and the availability of service for both the hardware and the computer program (software). If the computer and the program come from different vendors, make sure that all parties are clear on their obligations and that these obligations have been spelled out in writing.

Require your potential vendor(s) to submit the following information and perform the following tasks:

1. Submit a detailed proposal outlining all the specifications of both the hardware and the programs.

2. Provide an actual demonstration, showing how the computer will perform the job you want done, or a very similar one. You need to acquire a feel for the operation of the computer, and you need to see how easily the computer will perform the various tasks you require.

3. Indicate in writing all the technical and training support that will be provided, and all the costs and responsibilities to be shouldered by the parties involved. As a business owner, you are making a major purchase; the vendor must make a commitment too.

4. Provide the names, addresses, and phone numbers of other people who are using the equipment you are considering. You should call these people and get their opinion of the equipment and the vendor's services.

Any vendor who refuses or hedges on any of these requirements should be ruled out immediately. None of these requests is unreasonable; each would be considered a normal requirement by any knowledgeable computer manager in a large firm.

Last, do not make the final payment until all equipment is delivered and running to your satisfaction. This clause should be in any agreement.

PART SIX

THE ENVIRONMENT OF BUSINESS

Anyone who wonders how government and the law might affect business should consider the recent furor over consumers' videotaping of TV programs for private use. Two movie studios claimed that home videotaping of movies shown on TV was equivalent to stealing the studios' prints, and they insisted on compensation from video machine makers. In 1984, the Supreme Court decided such taping did not violate present copyright laws. But now, movie studios are asking Congress to revise those laws: the situation has worsened, they say, since renting cassettes of recent popular movies has become so inexpensive (as little as $1 a night). Advertisers, too, feel home videotaping should be restricted:

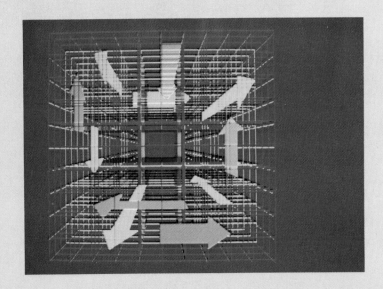

they fear that consumers will press the fast-forward button
and bleep out their commercials.

Does government have a responsibility to protect business
in situations such as this? What are the laws that protect business?
And what laws prevent businesses from taking certain actions?
These are some of the questions we will examine in Part 6.

☐ Chapter 18, **Business Law and Ethics,** reviews the legal and
ethical considerations that apply to businesses.

☐ Chapter 19, **Government and Business,** broadens the
discussion by showing how government both restrains and
supports business activities.

BUSINESS LAW AND ETHICS 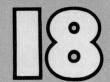 18

Is a computer company acting illegally if a machine it sells turns out to be a competitor's equipment? If a car's poor design contributes to your injuries in a crash, can you seek damages? Should a company be able to obtain legal protection from its creditors if its business goes sour? And what happens if a TV set you buy on the installment plan is stolen from your home a week later—are you still bound to pay all the monthly payments?

These are some of the questions we discuss in this chapter. Though, as you'll learn, there is no special law for business, the public nature of private enterprise often leads to issues that can best be resolved by legal precedent or written law. It also leads to tough ethical problems; we'll look at these as well.

CHAPTER FOCUS

After reading the material in this chapter, you will be able to:

- describe the overall purpose of common law, statutory law, public and private laws, and the Uniform Commercial Code
- state the six conditions that must be met for a contract to be valid and the three remedies for a broken contract
- cite the powers and duties of business agents
- state three violations covered by tort law
- specify the ways in which real and personal property are transferred
- distinguish voluntary from involuntary bankruptcy, and discuss reasons for resorting to bankruptcy proceedings
- describe the ethical issues surrounding conflict of interest and company secrets

In March 1981 the Paradyne Corporation of Largo, Florida, a manufacturer of information-processing equipment, won a $100 million federal contract. This agreement, which required Paradyne to supply a computer network for the Social Security Administration, was a major coup for the company, and its stock jumped from $37 to $48 a share. Paradyne's annual report characterized the agreement with Social Security as "a major step in the company's ability to undertake large system contracts."

Unfortunately for both Paradyne and the federal government, the equipment the company eventually delivered was not precisely what it seemed. The main microprocessing unit, supposedly Paradyne's new P-8400 line, proved to be the product of a rival company, Digital Equipment Corporation. Apparently, engineers at Paradyne had taken apart the Digital Equipment machine, put "Paradyne" labels on its parts, and put the newly assembled machine into a Paradyne cabinet. Even worse, what was supposed to be an "encryptor," an accessory machine that would scramble confidential information, turned out to be, according to the government, "an empty box with blinking lights"! Instead of the sophisticated piece of equipment the contract demanded, the device was a simple electrical circuit labeled "Paradyne P-2811 encryption device." The only working parts of the "encryption device" were its flashing lights.[1]

The Paradyne fraud illustrates only one of the several types of legal issues that will be discussed in this chapter—issues centering around the types of activities businesses are permitted by law to carry out in our society. All businesses, like all individuals, must obey the **law**—*the rules made by elected legislators and by judicial decisions that a society enforces to assure its existence and to function smoothly.* The law protects businesses against those who act against society's interest, and it spells out accepted ways of performing many essential business functions—along with the penalties for failure to comply. Thus the law promotes the survival of business but will allow no individual business to operate except within legal boundaries.

Not all the choices businesspeople face are within the sphere of law at all; some raise ethical or moral questions that become the focus of much uncertainty and disagreement. In this chapter we'll look at some of the major legal guidelines that businesspeople must follow and also at some of the crucial ethical issues that come up in the course of business activity.

TYPES OF LAW

All laws apply to society at large; none are specifically "business laws." But the two major kinds of law—common law and statutory law—affect business significantly.

COMMON LAW

Common law is sometimes called the "unwritten law" because it does not appear in legislative acts. Instead it is *based on the precedents established by judges' decisions.* A new decision may be based on a previous judicial ruling; or through a new interpretation, another precedent may be set for future judges to follow.

Common law began in England many centuries ago and was brought to America by the colonists. The continuity of common law was, and still is, guaranteed by the doctrine of **stare decisis** (Latin for *"to stand by decisions"*). What the stare decisis doctrine means is that judges' decisions establish a precedent for deciding future cases of a similar nature.

STATUTORY LAW

Much of the common law finds its way into **statutory law,** *laws created by government statutes.* (A **statute** is *a law that is written and passed by a state or federal legislature.*) In fact, the common law has been incorporated into statutory law to such a degree that today the difference is often indistinguishable. We take for granted, for instance, that the products we buy from reputable companies contain what the labels say they contain. If you bought a goose-down coat and then found out the first time you cleaned it that it was actually filled with reprocessed polyester, you could sue the coat manufacturer for misrepresentation. Although this is an old concept in common law, it has also been incorporated in more specific forms in the state and federal legislation governing fraudulent and misleading advertising that is enforced by the Federal Trade Commission.

What if there is a conflict between common law and statutory law? Generally, statutory law prevails.

THE UNIFORM COMMERCIAL CODE

As we know, laws governing the same subject matter often vary widely from state to state; such variation could make things very difficult for companies doing business in more than one state. It was to ease this problem that the Uniform Commercial Code (UCC) was developed. The UCC is a form of statutory law. It covers a number of areas of commercial law, including laws concerning sales contracts and warranties. The UCC has been adopted in its entirety in forty-nine states, and about half of it has been adopted in Louisiana.

PRIVATE LAW AND PUBLIC LAW

Both common law and statutory law can be further classified as either private law or public law. **Private law** *concerns itself with wrongs to individuals;* **public law** *covers wrongs to society.* In the following sections we'll focus on private law, emphasizing common and statutory law of major importance to business.

CONTRACTS

One legal agreement fundamental to many kinds of business is the contract. We can broadly define a **contract** as an *exchange of promises enforceable by law.* Few people realize how many business and personal transactions involve contracts.

CONDITIONS FOR CONTRACTS

The law of contracts deals largely with identifying the exchanges that can be classified as contracts. In the United States all of the following conditions must be met for a promise to be considered a valid and binding contract:

1. *An offer must be made.* One party must propose that an agreement be entered into by both parties. The offer can be oral or written: a salesperson telephones or writes a prospective client, telling the client he or she can purchase materials at a certain price. Or it can be in the form of an act: the telephone company offers to provide service by the act of placing a pay phone on a street corner. In any case the offer must be specific enough to make clear the intention of the offering party.

2. *Acceptance of the offer must be voluntary.* Don Corleone, the Godfather of film and novel, frequently made people "an offer they couldn't refuse." Luckily for him, he did not depend on the law to enforce the promises gained by these offers, for an ability to refuse is a prerequisite for a valid contract. *The courts will not uphold a contract if either the offer or the acceptance was obtained through what is termed "duress or undue influence."* This rule is known as the **principle of mutual acceptance.** Both parties must enter into a contract freely.

3. *Both parties must give consideration.* A promise binds legally only when each party gives something of value to the other. This *item of value,* or **consideration,** may be money, goods, services or the forbearance (giving up) of a legal right. The central idea behind this requirement is that bargaining should take place and that each party should get something for giving something.

The relative value of each party's consideration does not matter to the courts. If people make what seems to be a bad bargain, that is their affair. Consideration is legally sufficient when both parties receive what they thought was sufficient when making the agreement.

4. *Both parties must be competent.* The law gives to certain classes of people only a limited capacity to enter into contracts. These are minors, the insane, and the intoxicated. In most states, people so classi-

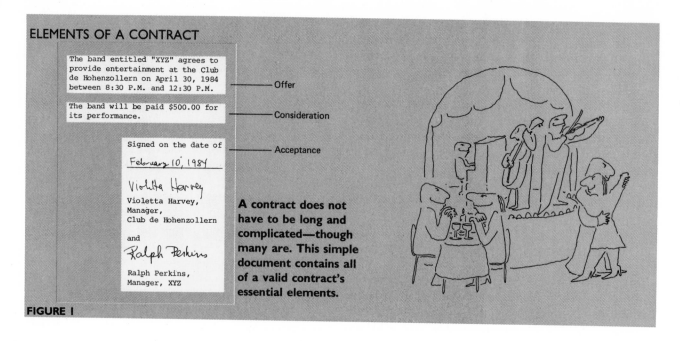

ELEMENTS OF A CONTRACT

> The band entitled "XYZ" agrees to provide entertainment at the Club de Hohenzollern on April 30, 1984 between 8:30 P.M. and 12:30 P.M. — Offer

> The band will be paid $500.00 for its performance. — Consideration

> Signed on the date of — Acceptance
>
> February 10, 1984
>
> Violetta Harvey
>
> Violetta Harvey, Manager, Club de Hohenzollern
>
> and
>
> Ralph Perkins
>
> Ralph Perkins, Manager, XYZ

A contract does not have to be long and complicated—though many are. This simple document contains all of a valid contract's essential elements.

FIGURE I

fied can make agreements only for the necessities of life: food, clothing, shelter, and medical care. There is little variation among states on the matter of contracts with the drunk or insane, but minors are a special category. The age of majority is established by state law. In most states it is eighteen; in some, it is twenty-one. In addition, many states have adopted the Uniform Minor Student Capacity to Borrow Act. This law allows a lender to enforce an educational loan made to a minor, provided that the lender possesses a statement indicating that the borrower has been accepted for enrollment at a specific school.

5. *The contract must be legal.* The law will not enforce a promise that involves an illegal act. For example, a gangster cannot get help from the courts to enforce a contract to deliver illegal drugs at a prearranged price.

6. *The contract must be in proper form.* Although many contracts can be made orally, by an act, or by a casually written document, in certain situations the law requires that a prescribed form be followed for a promise to be considered a valid contract. The statute of frauds requires that the transfer of goods worth $500 or more be put into writing. The written form is also required for all real property contracts and for contracts that cannot be fulfilled within one

year, such as installment-purchase agreements. When the law requires a written document, any change in the agreement must also be written.

A contract need not be long; all the elements of a contract can be contained in a simple document, as shown in Figure 1.

WHAT HAPPENS IF A CONTRACT IS BROKEN?

Most valid contracts are obeyed by both parties. Each does what was promised, and the contract is dissolved by being carried out. Sometimes a contract will not be fulfilled because both parties agree to end it. Occasionally the law will excuse one party from meeting an agreement. (For example, bankruptcy frees a person from credit agreements, and death or serious illness is a valid excuse for not fulfilling a contract for personal services.) But *where one party has no legal excuse for failure to live up to the terms of a contract,* the other party can claim **breach of contract.**

The essence of a contract is that the law will enforce the promise made. Three enforcement alternatives—discharge, damages, and specific performance—are open to a person whose contract has been breached by the other party. We can illustrate the protection afforded by law with a hypothetical example. Nick Santo, a builder, contracts to buy 2,000 feet of pine board from the Zeller Lumberyard. The contract stipulates that the price for the board is to be $2 per foot and that delivery must be made by January 25. But on January 10 the lumberyard calls Santo and tells him that another contractor has offered to buy all of the yard's lumber at $2.50 per foot. Zeller tells Santo that he must pay the higher price or wait until February 15 for delivery. The builder has the following options:

1. *Discharge.* When one party violates the terms of the agreement, the other party is under no obligation to continue with his or her end of the contract. In other words, the second party is discharged from the contract. Santo is free to buy his wood from another lumberyard. If Zeller goes ahead and delivers the wood at the later date, Santo does not have to accept it.

2. *Damages.* A party has the right to sue in court for damages that result from the other party's failure to fulfill a contract. The damages awarded usually reflect the direct loss of profit resulting from the nonperformance. If Santo had to pay another yard a higher price to get lumber, he would be entitled to collect the difference from Zeller, plus court costs. If Zeller's failure to deliver the wood as contracted caused Santo to lose a large contract or a good customer, the court might force Zeller to pay damages far exceeding the value of the wood itself.

3. *Specific performance.* A party can be compelled to live up to the terms of the contract if money damages would not be adequate. If, for instance, Zeller had agreed to sell not pine board but one-of-a-kind wood paneling from a sixteenth-century Spanish castle, Santo could demand specific performance of the contract.

RECENT CHALLENGES TO CONTRACTS

Contracts are basic to business: if they could not be relied on, business would rapidly grind to a halt. In the past few years, however, the long-established tradition that contracts are inviolable has come into question in certain instances. In the case of the Washington Power Supply System (Chapter 14), for example, the Washington State Supreme Court allowed a group of utility companies to avoid their contractual obligations. And in 1983 Continental Airlines declared bankruptcy and asked the court to void its contracts with labor unions (we will consider bankruptcy below).

A striking—and perhaps ominous—example of this new challenge to the "bindingness" of contracts is that of several gas pipeline companies—among them Tenneco, Columbia Gas Transmission, and InterNorth—that have attempted to back out of contracts to buy large quantities of natural gas following a sharp decline in demand for gas. The companies that sold the gas (some of the nation's largest oil companies) countered that the gas glut was caused by changing market conditions—an occurrence for which contracts cannot be broken. They charged that the pipeline companies had simply planned poorly—and now just wanted an easy way out. At present, the issue remains in the courts.[2] But many observers have expressed fears that if the pipeline companies win, many more contracts may be open to challenge. A one oil company executive put it, "It will be a sad day when a knowledgeable seller and buyer can't make a contract that will stand up."[3]

AGENCY

These days it seems that nearly every celebrity has an agent. Baseball players' agents sign up their clients to do beer commercials; authors' agents sell their clients' manuscripts to the publishers that offer the largest advances; actors' agents try to find choice movie and television roles for their clients. These partnerships illustrate a common legal association known as **agency,** which *exists when one party, known as the principal, authorizes another party, known as the agent, to act in his or her behalf.* The principal usually creates this relationship by explicit authorization, either orally or in writing. If, for instance, you telephone a stockbroker and ask her to buy stock for you, she is then empowered to act as your agent. In some cases—where a transfer of property is involved, for example—the *authorization must be written* *in the form of a document* called **power of attorney,** which states that one person may legally act for another. In some situations agency can be created simply when one person allows someone else to act in his or her behalf. The principal can't subsequently deny that an agency relationship existed, even though no oral or written authorization was ever actually expressed.

Agency is of critical importance to business because it allows delegation of the authority to enter into a contract. Under the law, the principal is liable for any contracts made by an agent so long as the agent is acting within the scope of his or her authority. Equally important, the principal may also be held liable for wrongdoing on the part of an agent. In a classic 1973 case, for instance, the manager of a small grocery store in Minnesota sued the National Biscuit Company (Nabisco) because one of its agents, a salesman named Lynch, had assaulted him. Lynch's aggressive conduct had already been the subject of complaints from several stores. On the occasion in question he got into a furious argument with the store manager and beat him up.

In the subsequent lawsuit, Nabisco argued that the assault resulted from personal antagonism, not from anything legitimately related to business, and therefore the company should not be held responsible. The court concluded, however, that since the assault not only occurred while Lynch was officially on duty but also stemmed from a dispute clearly related to his job as an agent for Nabisco, the company was indeed liable for the harm done to the store manager.[4]

TORT LAW

In the mid-1970s Rockwell International, a manufacturer of airplanes and spacecraft, decided to lease some computer equipment from OPM Leasing Services, Inc. Attracted by the thought that OPM could save them money, Rockwell officials signed agreements with the firm over several years. Unfortunately, it did not read its leasing agreements carefully, nor did it monitor the monies paid out to OPM as closely as it should have. OPM was eventually exposed as a swindler: it had overbilled for services, sent in multiple bills for the same computer, and defrauded not only Rockwell International but nearly a score of banks and other financial institutions. In the investigation that followed OPM's bankruptcy and the conviction of its officers for fraud, it came to light that an official at Rockwell had been friendly with one of the principals of OPM and had continued to give the firm Rockwell's business when he knew (or should have known) that the firm's dealings were suspect. Rockwell, unfortunately, never got back most of the money that OPM had made off with.[5]

Business conduct such as that of OPM Leasing is clearly a violation of the law—a law that belongs in the category known as torts. A **tort** is *an act, not involving a contract, that results in injury to another person's body, property, or reputation, and for which that other person is legally entitled to compensation.* Tort law covers both intentional and unintentional acts. The OPM fraud we described was clearly intentional; so are **libel**—*defamation of another person's character*—and the infringement of patents and copyrights. You cannot, for example, claim that your competitor in the home-appliance business refuses to make service calls if in fact he does make them. You cannot manufacture the Never-Slip Can Opener without having an agreement with its patent holder. Nor can you use another company's trademark without running into a tort-law minefield.

PRODUCT LIABILITY

Your own negligence, even if it is not deliberate, may also make you liable under tort laws. If, for example, a customer in your garden-supply store cuts a finger on a lawnmower blade, you can be sued. And under the concept of **product liability,** *a manufacturer is held liable for injuries caused by a defective product even if he or she was not negligent or did not know that the product was dangerous.*

One classic product-liability case was that of the Ford Pinto. Pintos manufactured from 1971 through 1976 were found by the government to have improperly designed fuel systems that were likely to spill fuel and catch fire in a rear-end crash. Ford responded by recalling the cars for repairs and settling damage suits brought by the families of

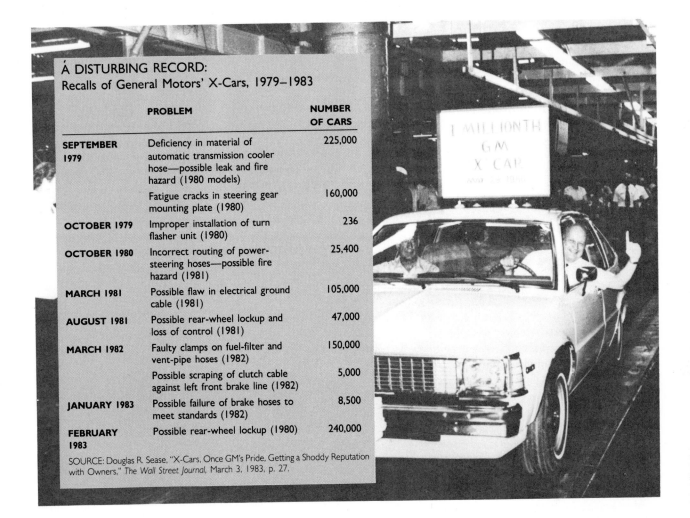

A DISTURBING RECORD:
Recalls of General Motors' X-Cars, 1979–1983

	PROBLEM	NUMBER OF CARS
SEPTEMBER 1979	Deficiency in material of automatic transmission cooler hose—possible leak and fire hazard (1980 models)	225,000
	Fatigue cracks in steering gear mounting plate (1980)	160,000
OCTOBER 1979	Improper installation of turn flasher unit (1980)	236
OCTOBER 1980	Incorrect routing of power-steering hoses—possible fire hazard (1981)	25,400
MARCH 1981	Possible flaw in electrical ground cable (1981)	105,000
AUGUST 1981	Possible rear-wheel lockup and loss of control (1981)	47,000
MARCH 1982	Faulty clamps on fuel-filter and vent-pipe hoses (1982)	150,000
	Possible scraping of clutch cable against left front brake line (1982)	5,000
JANUARY 1983	Possible failure of brake hoses to meet standards (1982)	8,500
FEBRUARY 1983	Possible rear-wheel lockup (1980)	240,000

SOURCE: Douglas R. Sease, "X-Cars, Once GM's Pride, Getting a Shoddy Reputation with Owners," *The Wall Street Journal*, March 3, 1983, p. 27.

those who had died in fiery Pinto accidents. But in 1980, after a crash in which three young women were burned to death in a Pinto, Ford was charged with "reckless homicide." Prosecutors argued that Ford, by knowing of the hazards in the Pinto's design and declining to change it, had recklessly caused the women's deaths. Although Ford was eventually found not guilty of reckless homicide, the negative publicity clearly emphasized the seriousness with which liability cases are taken.

A recent troubling case for General Motors has been that of the X-car, introduced in 1979 and plagued since then with a series of defects. Most serious have been charges that the brakes in the X-cars may cause the car's rear wheels to lock, resulting in a dangerous skid. Several multimillion-dollar damage claims have been filed by accident victims and their families, alleging that X-car brake malfunctions led directly to a fatal or serious crash. And in August 1983 the National Highway Traffic Safety Administration (NHTSA) sued GM to force it to recall more than a million X-cars to repair the brakes. If that weren't enough, the government's General Accounting Office promptly charged that NHTSA had known about the X-car brake problem for years and had failed to do anything about it. Whatever the result of the battle of words (and lawyers) over the X-car, the negative publicity has certainly hurt what GM thought was the most promising addition to its product line in years.[6]

PROPERTY LAW

Anyone interested in business must know the basics of property law. **Property** is *anything of value that can be owned.* The law recognizes two types of property, real and personal. **Real property** is *land or anything more or less permanently attached to land.* **Personal property** is *anything that can be owned other than land.* A piece of marble in the earth is real property. When it is cut and sold as a block, it becomes personal property.

The law deals with many aspects of property. Here we shall concentrate on the transfer of interest in property.

TRANSFER OF REAL PROPERTY

Two types of documents are important in the transfer of real property: deeds and leases.

Deeds are important to businesspeople who must buy land or buildings for factory, office, or store space. A **deed** is *a legal document by which an owner gives an interest in real property to a new owner.* A deed is not a contract and requires no consideration to be valid.

A **lease** is *a document used for a temporary transfer of interest in property. The party that owns the property is* commonly called the **landlord.** *The party that occupies or gains the right to occupy the property* is the **tenant.** A lease is granted for a specific period of time, during which the tenant pays rent to the landlord in periodic installments. There is no limit on the length of time for which a lease may be granted; ninety-nine-year leases are not uncommon. A long lease allows a business that lacks sufficient capital to buy real property to enjoy the stability normally associated with ownership.

TRANSFER OF PERSONAL PROPERTY

A permanent transfer of personal property, such as a car, a TV set or a check, is technically a transfer of **title,** or *legal possession of the property and the right to use it.* The property transferred may be something intangible, like a check, which is transferred by endorsement. Or the property transferred may be a tangible item, which is transferred via sale.

When does a sale occur?

The question may sound like an easy one, but in a legal sense, it is sometimes difficult to answer. Legally, a sale involves the transfer of title by the *owner,* or **vendor,** in exchange for consideration from the buyer. A sale is therefore a contract and is subject to some interpretation.

The issue that needs interpretation is the exact time when title passes from the vendor to the buyer. Sometimes the time of transfer is easily established. In the typical cash-register sale, for example, title passes when the clerk accepts the customer's money and hands over the goods. Any loss before the transaction is the seller's, and any loss afterward is the buyer's. In certain situations, however, the transfer does not take place immediately, and this small legal detail can make a big financial difference. Let's look at a few such situations:

WHEN DOES TITLE PASS ON AN F.O.B. SHIPMENT? A sales contract may call for goods to be shipped F.O.B. (free-on-board) point of origin. In this case, title passes to the buyer at the time and place of shipment. Thus, if you buy a Chevrolet from a dealer F.O.B. Detroit, you will have title when the auto is placed on a train or truck in Detroit. Damage to the car en route to its destination is your responsibility.

WHEN DOES TITLE PASS IN A C.O.D. SHIPMENT? When property is purchased C.O.D., title is not transferred until the buyer accepts the goods. But as soon as you hand over payment for goods delivered to your door, the loss is yours, even if the goods prove to be damaged when you open the package.

WHEN DOES TITLE PASS IN AN INSTALLMENT PURCHASE? When property is purchased on installment, title passes when the buyer takes possession of the property. If, for example, you buy a stereo set on credit, you must pay the full purchase price after delivery, even if the set is stolen or damaged before you've finished paying for it.

You'll find it useful to think over these distinctions carefully.

BANKRUPTCY

In November 1982, just after stocking its stores with goods for the holiday season, HRT Industries, Inc., filed for bankruptcy. HRT, operators of chain discount and shoe stores, had experienced a downturn in sales and had been unable to pay its creditors for a few months. The creditors were angry—not only because they had just delivered to HRT large orders of goods for which they might never be paid, but also because this was the second time in less than ten years that HRT had gone bankrupt. (The firm, under a different name and with a slightly different organization, had gone bankrupt in 1974.) HRT's critics charged that the company's condition was not bad enough to justify a bankruptcy filing, and that the company was using bankruptcy as a strategy to help it survive a dip in sales.[7]

As the HRT example suggests, bankruptcy is not what it used to be: an ordeal so stigmatizing that it meant the personal ruin of an individual or the financial obliteration of a business. Today, companies do survive bankruptcy—indeed, as we shall see, some companies seem to be turning to bankruptcy as a survival tool in the competitive corporate world. Whatever its terms, **bankruptcy** is *the legal procedure by which a person or a business, unable to meet financial obligations, is relieved of debt by having the court divide the assets among the creditors.* Some companies, of course, do go out of existence altogether after a bankruptcy. The late 1970s and early 1980s saw a great number of such business failures, when inflation, recession, and high interest rates pushed many marginal firms over the brink.

Occasionally bankruptcy proceedings are *initiated by a firm's creditors; this is called* **involuntary bankruptcy.** Far more common is **voluntary bankruptcy,** in which *the debtor begins the proceedings in court.* Why would a business go bankrupt voluntarily? Why not just wait until the creditors' lawyers come knocking at the door? By entering voluntary bankruptcy, a company seeks legal protection and permission to reorganize itself—the idea being that the company can streamline itself by cutting costs drastically and continue operations with a new, slimmer figure. This is what HRT had in mind when it entered bankruptcy. A case like HRT's is commonly known as a "Chapter 11"—from the section of the bankruptcy code that permits distressed companies to reorganize while continuing in business.

The problem with this proceeding is that the cumbersome obligations that the company may most want to shed are legal contracts such as collective-bargaining agreements and leases on stores and office space. While the debtor company may see bankruptcy as an orderly legal proceeding leading to a necessary reorganization, creditors, unionized employees, and others may see it as an unfair attempt by the company to weasel out of its legal—or even moral—obligations. Since the bankruptcy code no longer requires that a company be utterly insolvent before filing as bankrupt, critics have argued that many companies that take the Chapter 11 route today don't really *need* to do so. Bankruptcy has become but one more management technique.

One case that prompted angry debate over abuse of the bankruptcy laws is that of the Manville Corporation. Manville, a producer of asbestos and building materials, filed for bankruptcy in August 1982, claiming that it could not afford to pay the costs of settling the many lawsuits filed against it by former employees who became ill with asbestosis after working in Manville plants. While the company is protected by the courts (as it still is), it cannot be sued by any more asbestosis victims. Critics have charged that Manville used bankruptcy as a means to shirk its moral obligation to pay settlements to its injured ex-workers. And, ironically, since filing for bankruptcy, Manville's business has been doing very well—which has only provoked more outrage over the company's conduct.[8]

Similar objections were raised when Continental Airlines entered bankruptcy in the fall of 1983. Continental immediately canceled its union contracts, sharply lowering wages and salaries and requiring pilots (among others) to work additional hours. Some public officials and businesspeople have been disturbed by these recent bankruptcy cases, and it has been suggested that the bankruptcy laws may need some amending to prevent abuses. Creditors and disgruntled employees have to live with the unpaid bills and slashed paychecks that follow in a bankrupt company's wake; yet unless that company stays in business, it will be unable to honor any claims at all, so there *are* two sides to the question.

FOREIGN BRIBES: AN AMERICAN MORAL DILEMMA

Texas Senator Lloyd Bentsen has called it a "massive handicap to American exports." Some of America's top business executives, responding to a General Accounting Office survey, said it has put them at a "competitive disadvantage." What is the cause of their irritation? The Foreign Corrupt Practices Act.

The **Foreign Corrupt Practices Act (FCPA)** in 1977 *outlawed the payment of bribes by American businesses to foreign officials.* Congress passed this law after the Securities and Exchange Commission revealed that Lockheed, Gulf Oil, and other very large American corporations were making generous contributions to foreign officials in return for lucrative contracts—a practice that patently violates traditional American moral standards, as well as domestic laws.

Senator Bentsen and other opponents of the FCPA aren't suggesting that bribery should be legalized. In fact, some business executives have found that the law has its advantages. According to the director for the U.S. Chamber of Commerce, "Most businessmen don't like these payments because of the expense and because they generally have a high sense of morals."

Nevertheless, the FCPA is often mentioned as a major trade disincentive. Pragmatic executives and government officials base their objections to the law on its cultural bias and its ambiguity. France, Japan, and Korea have no formal restrictions against such payments, they say, and in trade with Taiwan, the Philippines, and Indonesia, the law puts them at a disadvantage because it interferes with trade in countries where personal compensation is an accepted part of the business process.

Critics also claim that the FCPA is poorly worded and doesn't distinguish clearly between permissible "facilitating payments" (the legal term for payoffs to low-level officials for doing their jobs) and outright bribery to win contracts. As a result, many perfectly legal transactions are inhibited. Especially vulnerable to this effect are smaller businesses that can't channel negotiations through foreign representatives, as large multinational companies can.

Several bills to amend the FCPA have been introduced in Congress, and at least some changes in the act are expected to be approved. A *Business Week* survey in 1983 found that 69 percent of the business executives polled found fault with the law. Particularly burdensome is the FCPA's requirement that corporations record all international transactions, which is a paperwork headache. (On the other hand, without careful records, it would be difficult for the government to enforce the antibribery provisions of the act.) Another change advocated in the poll (by 65 percent of those questioned) is that "grease payments" be permitted in countries where they are customary. But again, there is a danger that small "grease payments"—to get goods through customs, for example—may turn into the bribes of old. In fact, 55 percent of those polled by *Business Week* agreed that "unless the law is very tough, what starts out as petty payments can turn into major bribes of important officials to get the business order."

Even if the FCPA is amended, there will be those in business who will be opposed to it as an unreasonable standard in the international marketplace, who will stick to the old adage, "When in Rome, do as the Romans do." More thoughtful businesspeople may counter that we've come a long way from the days when Rome was in its glory, and perhaps if we require American businesses to operate ethically at home, we should apply the same standard abroad.

SOURCE: *Dun's Review,* January 1980, p. 8, and March 1980, p. 8; *New England Business,* October 1, 1980, pp. 22–24; *Business Week,* April 6, 1981, p. 131; *New York Times,* May 21, 1981, p. 1; "The Antibribery Act Splits Executives," *Business Week,* September 19, 1983, p. 16.

THE SCOPE OF BUSINESS ETHICS

Business ethics concerns itself with *the relationship between business goals and practices and the good of society.* A businessperson behaves ethically when his or her actions serve the good of society. Every corporation serves a number of different "publics." Each has responsibilities to employees, customers, stockholders, and neighbors. If a company serves all its publics well, it will provide a safe workplace and fair pay for its employees, it will produce a well-made product at a fair price, it will pay a dividend to its stockholders, and it will do its best to avoid damaging the environment.

Of course, companies have their ethical weaknesses, just as individuals do. Sometimes companies may violate their responsibilities by accident—for example, when a toy manufacturer unknowingly sells a hazardous product. Unfortunately, however, in many instances companies know exactly what they are doing when they violate the law or otherwise engage in unethical business behavior. Take, for example, what happened in 1983 when three executives of one of the nation's largest testing concerns, Industrial Bio-Test Laboratories, were found guilty of having submitted faked data to the government on hundreds of chemicals present in consumer products. According to federal investigators, IBT had concealed the presence of harmful substances in many of the products it tested—for example, a swimming pool chlorinator so toxic to the bladder and kidneys that it wiped out an entire test-animal group. Apparently IBT, working under contract to the large chemical manufacturers, had turned in tests that showed dangerous products to be "safe" in order to please its corporate clients.[9]

Why do violations of ethics occur? A 1980 study by *Fortune* magazine reported that of more than 1,000 major corporations observed in the past ten years, 11 percent had been involved in at least one major delinquency in the United States. The most common violations were bribery, criminal fraud, illegal political contributions, tax evasion, and criminal antitrust violation (such as price fixing). According to the *Fortune* study, business widely perceives these crimes as "victimless."[10] They are, moreover, almost universally considered to be "no worse than what everybody else does." In a highly competitive business atmosphere, it is extremely tempting to resort to bribery, for example, when it seems to hurt no one and when it will enable one to gain a financial edge over a competitor. In many cases, corruption seems to pay—and it should be noted that when companies are caught paying bribes or fixing prices, penalties are often fairly low. There can be no doubt that there is considerable temptation to engage in unethical behavior, especially when a large sum of money—or even the future of one's business—is involved, and when the rewards of ethical actions would seem smaller than those of unethical actions. Nevertheless, companies are becoming increasingly concerned about their business conduct. Let us now look at two "gray areas" of ethical concern—they involve behavior that is not strictly illegal—that are frequently at issue today.

CONFLICT OF INTEREST

Conflict of interest—a situation in which a person or business stands to benefit financially from a business decision that should be made objectively—can arise in many settings, from the fairly trivial to the very serious. College coaches choosing athletic shoes for their teams, for example, are routinely offered large bonuses of money, free shoes, and other incentives by shoe manufacturers seeking to outfit the team.[11] (Presumably the coach should choose the best shoe, regardless of "freebies.") Businesses that suspect some internal wrongdoing have been known to ask their own law firms to investigate the matter. (The law firm would seemingly have a strong incentive to produce findings acceptable to its client.) This very thing happened in 1978 when Citicorp asked Shearman & Sterling, its own law firm, to investigate possible improper foreign-currency transactions made by its banking unit, Citibank. Shearman & Sterling's report cleared Citibank of violating U.S. law, but foreign penalties and taxes on the bank ultimately amounted to $10.5 million.[12]

To avoid conflict-of-interest problems, individuals and businesses sometimes rule themselves out of situations in which they may be tempted to make self-enriching decisions. Members of the president's

Credit-card companies, magazine publishers, and direct-mail marketers routinely sell names and addresses of their customers to other organizations for their direct-mail campaigns. Is this practice an invasion of privacy?

Businesses that provide gifts and free services to public officials often expect political favors in return. Should public employees accept such offerings?

Many competing businesses try to learn their rivals' secrets by analyzing or taking apart their products. Would you support a law forbidding this practice?

"All in favor of going ahead with the Dingaling Brothers Circus acquisition?"

Is it ethical to serve on the board of directors of a firm whose business is related to your own or one with which your company does business?

cabinet who have business interests or own stock, for example, often sell these assets or place them in a blind trust (one managed by others) while they are in office. In this way, officials can be free of suspicion that their regulatory decisions are made for their own gain rather than the good of the public.

COMPANY SECRETS

In the highly competitive international computer market, the developer of a successful new model can make millions—even put its less innovative competitors out of business. In 1982 Hitachi Ltd., seeking to speed up the development of its new computer line by copying IBM's research, resorted to an obviously illegal tactic: theft. In February 1983, Hitachi pleaded guilty in federal court to charges that its

agents had attempted to steal top-secret computer designs from IBM.[13]

In the Hitachi case, the ethics—in fact, the legal questions—were fairly black and white. But many issues involving trade secrets inhabit a gray area. For example, what if Hitachi had merely bought one of IBM's machines, taken it apart, and copied its design? Today, technology exists by which computer engineers can analyze and copy even a tiny silicon chip—a process known as "reverse engineering." This procedure is legal, and is apparently widely used by computer manufacturers. Or what if Hitachi had hired the IBM engineer who had devised the trade secrets it sought? Most companies seek to protect themselves from such raids on employees—for example, research staff members may be asked to sign agreements promising not to reveal secrets if they go to work elsewhere. But no such protection is ever ironclad.

CHAPTER REVIEW

Businesses, like individuals, must obey the law—the rules approved and enforced by a society that help it to function smoothly. Common law is based on the decisions of judges, which shape precedents to be followed. Statutory law is created by government bodies, but in the United States it is derived in large part from common law. Businesspeople are most concerned with private law, especially law dealing with contracts, agency, liability, property, and bankruptcy.

A contract is a promise enforceable by law. To be considered valid, it must meet the following conditions: an offer must be made, acceptance must be voluntary and mutual, both parties must give consideration, the parties must be legally competent, the purpose must be legal, and the form must be correct. Recent challenges to the binding effect of contracts have caused concern.

Agency is a relationship whereby a principal authorizes an agent to act in his or her behalf. Agency can be created through power of attorney or by conduct.

A tort is an act that, while not involving a contract or an agency relationship, injures another person in some way and entitles that person to compensation. Libel, infringement of patents and copyrights, and product liability are all covered by tort laws.

Real property is land or anything permanently affixed to land. Personal property is everything else subject to ownership. A deed permanently transfers interest in real property; a lease conveys temporary interest. Title to personal property is transferred most often by sale or endorsement.

A business that can no longer meet its financial obligations may declare bankruptcy. Bankruptcy proceedings begun by the business itself are called voluntary. Involuntary bankruptcy comes about when the creditors of a business initiate court action. Shaky businesses have been known to make use of the bankruptcy law simply to avoid their obligations and thus stay afloat.

Business ethics concerns itself with the relationship between business practices and the interests of society. Violations of ethics often occur in highly competitive industries because it is felt that such violations hurt no one and are necessary if the company is to compete effectively.

KEY WORDS

law (538)
common law (538)
stare decisis (538)
statutory law (538)
statute (538)
private law (539)
public law (539)
contract (539)
principle of mutual acceptance (539)
consideration (539)
breach of contract (540)
agency (541)
power of attorney (542)
tort (542)
libel (542)
product liability (542)
property (544)
real property (544)
personal property (544)
deed (544)
lease (544)
landlord (544)
tenant (544)
title (544)
vendor (544)
bankruptcy (545)
involuntary bankruptcy (545)
voluntary bankruptcy (545)
business ethics (547)

REVIEW QUESTIONS

1. What is the difference between law and ethics? Why is an understanding of both important to the businessperson?

2. List and explain the six conditions that must be met for a contract to be valid.

3. What happens if a contract is broken? How has the force of contracts been challenged?

4. How is agency created? What can't an agent do for the principal?

5. What is tort law?

6. What is meant by the concept of product liability? Why is it important to produce a safe product?

7. When does title pass in an F.O.B. sale? A C.O.D. sale? An installment sale?

8. Describe the process of bankruptcy, taking note of changes in the law since 1979. How do businesses sometimes turn these laws to their advantage?

9. Why are businesspeople tempted to engage in unethical conduct, and what can be done to prevent this?

CASE I

CORPORATE WRONGDOING AT EXXON

Exxon Enterprises, a division of Exxon Corporation, was set up by its parent concern just over a decade ago. Its purpose was to develop profitable new business sidelines for Exxon, the giant oil company. In 1983 two separate cases came to public attention involving alleged theft of corporate secrets by Exxon Enterprises. Apparently some employees of the firm, under pressure to come up with new product ideas, had sought to steal them from other companies.

In the first case two Exxon employees had called on a computer software company, Continental Data Systems, posing as potential customers. They were, they said, consultants to a law firm seeking to buy a law-oriented software system from Continental Data. After sitting through a lengthy sales presentation, the two "customers" borrowed a confidential software manual from the Continental salesman, promising to return it in forty-eight hours. Instead, they kept it for two and a half weeks and had it copied. And within a few months Exxon Office Systems (the division of Exxon Enterprises that is concerned with computerized office equipment) began offering a law-oriented

software program virtually identical to that outlined in Continental Data's manual. Shortly thereafter, Exxon tried to hire the Continental Data representative who had lent them the company's manual. He not only turned down the Exxon job offer—he went to the police. The Exxon employees involved in the affair have since been fired, and the two who posed as customers to obtain the confidential manual from Continental Data have been charged with theft of trade secrets.

In the second case, Exxon is accused of having illegally gathered information from a Union Carbide plant in Greenville, South Carolina, by paying a contractor employed by Union Carbide. The contractor, Steve Burnette, allegedly was asked by an Exxon consultant, Alex James, to give James drawings of the Union Carbide plant. (Burnette, who was installing insulation at the plant, had access to much of it.) Burnette also charges that James asked him to remove samples of one of Union Carbide's new products, carbon fiber, so that it could be examined in an Exxon-financed lab. Then, when Exxon started building its *own* plant near Greenville, Burnette was hired to insulate the building—and was allegedly "paid" for his earlier undercover work by being allowed to submit grossly inflated invoices to Exxon for his work. In turn, it is alleged that James received kickbacks as part of the deal. The apparent wrongdoing was uncovered when a new purchasing agent hired by Exxon, Wilton Gregory, began questioning Burnette's invoices. The upshot of this case? By the time the alleged crimes were brought to light, the statute of limitations had expired. Burnette alleges that Exxon offered him $500,000 to hush the matter up. (Exxon denies the charge, but it has not tried to recover the money paid to Burnette on the basis of his fraudulent invoices for work in their plant. And as for the new plant, it never operated and is now for sale.) Wilton Gregory, the conscientious employee who informed his superiors of the wrongdoing, was fired. He has since sued Exxon, charging the company with improperly firing him and with engaging in fraud and deception.[14]

1. In both cases, which of the actions described are actually illegal? Which probably aren't illegal but are still unethical?

2. Why do you think that Exxon chose to fire the employee who reported the wrongdoing?

3. What problems may be caused for a company when it fires employees who report misdeeds?

4. Why do you think that the Exxon employees might have been tempted to engage in espionage? (Hint: the parent company had poured $1 billion into Exxon Enterprises.)

5. What are some *legal* ways that Exxon's employees might have used to come up with new product ideas?

CASE 2

CORPORATE ETHICS: SOME INTRIGUING FINDINGS

In the fall of 1983 *The Wall Street Journal* commissioned a Gallup poll of business executives and members of the general public on the subject of business ethics. One focus of the poll was "what belongs to the company and what to the employee?"—and different answers to this question were given by the executives and the public.

The survey asked questions describing a number of familiar ethical dilemmas that arise in business. Suppose, for example, that a supplier of your company offers you a case of liquor at Christmas. (You, the purchasing agent, are supposed to choose suppliers on an ethical basis.) Should you take the liquor? Seventy-nine percent of the executives said no, but only 29 percent of the general public agreed. How about cheating on income tax? Is it wrong for a business executive not to declare $2,500 of interest income on his or her tax return? Ninety-five percent of business executives thought it was wrong, but only 75

percent of the general public thought so. Is it wrong to steal an ashtray from the office? Ninety percent of the executives thought it was, but only 62 percent of the general public agreed. Similar results were obtained on most of the survey questions: the business executives generally applied stricter moral standards than did the general public.

The pollsters also asked the executives whether they ever felt guilty about taking advantage of certain corporate perquisites. Apparently, some did: 39 percent had ethical reservations about eating at a very expensive restaurant on an expense account; 32 percent about taking a spouse on a business trip at company expense; and 28 percent about flying first class at company expense. It is interesting to note, however, that most of the executives who expressed such reservations were not in a senior enough position to be entitled to such perquisites. Those who were entitled to the luxuries had far fewer reservations about accepting them.[15]

1. How do you stand on the questions asked in this poll? Explain your responses.

2. Why do you think that the executives reported stricter standards than the general public?

3. Why do you think that only a minority of the executives questioned expressed reservations about using corporate perks?

4. Do you think that the executives reported their own reactions to the pollster honestly?

GOVERNMENT AND BUSINESS

One issue hotly debated by both sides in the 1984 presidential election involved the role that government should play in aiding American business. Should the government commit itself to revitalizing the nation's faltering smokestack industries? In view of Chrysler Corporation's successful recovery after receiving federal loans, this viewpoint has its merits. Should the government throw its support behind the high-tech industries of the future with research-and-development grants, exemption from antitrust barriers, and other favorable treatment? Only this government aid, some said, would enable our industries to compete with the state-subsidized enterprises of Japan, Europe, and the developing countries.

Or should government keep its hands off business? Traditionally, the viewpoint of U.S. business has been that business will develop best on its own, although selected businesses have always sought favorable treatment, such as loans (in the case of Chrysler), price supports (in the case of the tobacco industry), and protection from foreign competition (in the case of the steel, automobile, and clothing industries).

In this chapter we'll look at some of the major areas in which business and government interact and consider the pros and cons of government's activities in the business area.

CHAPTER FOCUS

After reading the material in this chapter, you will be able to:
- cite several advantages and disadvantages of government deregulation for business and the public
- list six laws by which the government restricts monopolies, and cite their major provisions
- explain why the government supports some "natural" monopolies
- describe the provisions of the Robinson-Patman Act that regulates retail pricing
- name four revenue-raising taxes and at least two regulatory taxes
- describe the purposes of business lobbies and political action committees (PACs)
- distinguish copyrights, trademarks, and patents

Many people think of government and business as natural antagonists. In some respects, as we shall see, this is true, but increasingly both sides are seeing the advantages of being partners. Consider the U.S. space program. For the first time since the moon walk, the government seems ready to launch a major new push into outer space. This time business and industry will be there right alongside the astronauts. President Reagan has called for "a more permanent presence in space" for this country—partly to beef up defense with a new generation of weapons, but also to undertake commercial ventures in cooperation with business.

Since the early days of the space program, government rockets have lifted communications satellites into orbit for private firms. But now private companies are taking over the job of marketing satellite launches. The first commercial products made aboard a spaceship—tiny plastic beads used for medical research—will soon be put on sale. Other such ventures are in the works, ranging from low-cost "getaway specials" (private research experiments on board shuttle flights) to full-scale partnerships between the National Aeronautics and Space Administration (NASA) and business. If NASA's plans for a $20 billion permanent space station, manned by a crew of six or seven, can get funding from Congress, factories in space may become commonplace by the turn of the century. This proposed space station provides an excellent example of how business and government are learning to work together.

Whereas in its early days NASA designed its own space projects and then hired private contractors to build them to its specifications, now it starts by consulting the business community. Before building the proposed space station, NASA canvassed possible commercial users to see what services and equipment they wanted and then launched a hard-sell campaign to drum up trade for the planned space system. "Rather than design a space station and then try to figure out specific uses for it," said NASA Administrator James M. Beggs, "we are taking the opposite tack: nailing down the needs of the users."[1] Its industry contacts aren't a one-way street either: support from business leaders may help NASA persuade Congress to fund its costly new program.

In an ideal world, such examples of government-business partnership would be the norm. Both sides would work together to serve the public and to forge the strength of the nation. Such is not the case in the world we live in. This chapter will discuss the areas of agreement and disagreement between government and business—what works well and what doesn't, and why.

BUSINESS AND GOVERNMENT: A RECIPROCAL RELATIONSHIP

As the NASA venture shows, the business-government relationship is not always one of government domination. Sometimes government needs the expertise of the business community. More and more, both sides are working together as equals. Finally, government can provide business with a wide range of assistance. Let us look at the ways government and business serve one another before considering the conflicts.

GOVERNMENT'S DEPENDENCE ON BUSINESS

In its day-to-day operations, the government needs all kinds of manufactured products—from Army uniforms to jet fighters to computers. These products must all come from the business world—and many industries depend on government contracts for a large portion of their income. Although many of the government's needs are as simple and cheap as ballpoint pens and typewriter ribbons, many are extraordinarily sophisticated and expensive. For example, the surveillance systems now used by the military to locate foreign submarines—ultrasensitive listening devices involving the most advanced computers—cost several billion dollars and came from IBM, Western Electric, Hughes Aircraft, and other large corporations. At least three

How deeply should the government get involved with companies' private troubles? Many observers in 1980 thought Uncle Sam had made a mistake, when the U.S. government granted struggling Chrysler a giant financial bailout. But Chrysler was back on its feet by mid-1983. Jubilantly, Chairman Lee Iacocca returned the loan—seven years ahead of schedule.

aircraft makers are working on designs for a new, experimental helicopter—a streamlined, light-weight workhorse jammed with sophisticated electronic equipment—that the Army wants to build in the 1990s.[2] Similarly, on a much smaller scale, state and local governments must turn to private industry for everything from new office buildings to fire engines.

GOVERNMENT AND BUSINESS AS EQUALS

Of course, government is not always in the position of having to plead for help when it turns to business. Very often the two cooperate as equals. The National Alliance of Business (NAB), for instance, an independent nonprofit corporation founded by business leaders, works in partnership with government—as well as with labor, education, and community groups—to reduce the unemployment problems of the economically disadvantaged by encouraging private businesses to provide them with training and jobs. This cooperative venture helps to whittle away at a social problem that constantly plagues government, and at the same time it benefits businesses by providing a readily available labor pool.

NASA's efforts to line up joint ventures for its proposed space station include some spectacular examples of such partnerships. A three-year-old Florida company, Microgravity Research Associates, is basing its entire business on space research. It signed up for a joint research venture with NASA in hopes of eventually producing defect-free semiconductor crystals in a sterile, gravity-free space lab. St. Regis Paper is looking into the possibilities of using space-based sensors to monitor its vast forest lands. A host of firms doing biochemical research want to use space labs to create high-purity products. All these companies hope to use NASA for a boost into space, and the government agency, in turn, needs these customers to help pay the freight for developing its space systems.[3]

GOVERNMENT ASSISTANCE TO BUSINESS

Government helps business in many ways. If a company needs marketing information, it can obtain it from such agencies as the Census Bureau, the Small Business Administration, and the departments of Commerce and Labor; the information is wide-ranging, up to date, and free. If a company needs advice on tax matters, it can get free guidance from

FIGURE 1

UNCLE SAM AT THE CONTROLS:

Some government agencies and the industries they regulate

The Environmental Protection Agency (EPA) is charged with integrating and coordinating an attack on environmental problems, to protect the public health and welfare. It sets standards and enforces compliance with regard to air and water pollution, solid-waste disposal, pesticides, radiation, and noise.

The Federal Power Commission (FPC) regulates interstate electric rates. It has jurisdiction over interstate transmission lines, sale of electric utilities, and transmission of natural gas by pipeline.

The Interstate Commerce Commission (ICC) regulates the rates and trade practices of companies engaged in interstate commerce. It is concerned with transport by rail, water, and motor vehicles.

The Federal Communications Commission (FCC) regulates interstate telephone, telegraph, radio, and television communications. It sets rates for wire communication and community area television and licenses commercial broadcasters and assigns them frequencies.

the Internal Revenue Service. If it is involved in a labor dispute, it can turn to federal mediators and arbitrators. And a business can get more direct help in the form of loan guarantees, which the federal government has made available to businesses ranging in size from the corner pizzeria to the Chrysler Corporation.

State governments, too, provide much-needed services and advice, including free employment services and, occasionally, financial aid. In fact, direct financial help to business in the form of tax breaks, subsidies, and loans has become a weapon in the competition among state governments as they work to retain and attract jobs. New York and several other states are setting up industrial research parks centered around public universities. Such programs especially benefit high-technology companies in computers, electronics, and biotechnology, and they are being built in states hoping to develop their own local "Silicon Valleys" to replace jobs lost in declining smokestack industries.

GOVERNMENT REGULATORY AGENCIES: THEIR IMPACT ON BUSINESS

Government and business may often help each other, as we have just seen. But companies sometimes find that government restricts certain of their business activities. Government regulations, as we have noted in earlier chapters, are enacted by regulatory agencies created by Congress to protect public health and safety, prevent competitive abuses, and advance a host of other public goals. Some of these regulatory agencies have existed for decades. (See Figure 1.)

In recent years some political and economic observers came to the conclusion that government was too involved in regulating business and industry. These critics pointed out that in many regulated industries—such as the airlines—the competitive spirit was being killed. When rates and rules were set by a government agency, small companies didn't stand a chance against large companies. Moreover, the regulations set up by the government agencies very often increased costs, pushing up the price that consumers had to pay for products and services. Many people began to wonder: if the costs exceed the benefits derived by the consumer, should the regulations continue? Such questions gave rise to a call for some deregulation in government-business relations. Deregulation began during Jimmy Carter's administration, but it wasn't until after Ronald Reagan was elected in 1980 that deregulation went into effect on a large scale.

Most people agree that the results so far have been mixed. There has been major upheaval in some industries that had been protected from the rigors of competition. For example, as soon as the Civil Aeronautics Board (CAB) stopped setting fares and allocating airline routes, new air carriers sprouted up to serve heavily traveled air corridors. Several of the major carriers were forced to cut prices to keep customers and to drop less popular air routes that were no longer profitable. As a result, some smaller cities lost air service entirely, and some established airlines began to teeter near bankruptcy. On the other hand, fares were cut sharply on popular routes and several new airlines are thriving today. Much of the turmoil in this industry will subside as the airlines adjust to the new, deregulated environment. In time, say supporters of deregulation, air travel will be less costly and more efficient.

The cost-benefit approach to deregulation has been a controversial issue, especially as it has been applied in environmental areas. For example, the Reagan administration has held that if it costs $100 million or more to equip smokestacks with scrubbers, regulators should first measure those costs against the benefits of cleaner air before requiring factories to install the expensive equipment. Opponents of deregulation argue that, because the benefits of cleaner air or safer workplaces are intangible, they are harder to measure than costs. Cost-benefit analysis has also led the National Highway Traffic Safety Administration (NHTSA) to drop plans requiring air bags for cars produced in 1986 and to reduce its standards for crash resistance in bumpers. Staff cutbacks and looser rules at the Occupational Safety and Health Administration (OSHA) have meant less protection for workers who face on-the-job hazards. For a time the Environmental Protection Agency (EPA) was not aggressive in forcing polluters to clean up toxic waste dumps. Opponents of deregulation tend to drum up support when they cite problems in such sensitive areas.

The upheaval in government regulation is also giving rise to new ways of writing and enforcing the rules: the aim is to encourage businesses to take part in negotiating rules that will be acceptable to all parties. For example, the Federal Aviation Administration (FAA), which oversees air safety, has experimented with holding preliminary talks with affected parties, rather than simply imposing its rules from Washington. This new procedure is more open than the typical rule-making approach taken by most regulatory agencies. To help draft new regulations governing cockpit crews' flight time and rest periods, the FAA brought together representatives from large airlines, small commuter lines, pilot unions, and consumer groups and encouraged them to discuss the new rules extensively. Previously, three FAA proposals since 1975 had been shot down by objections from one group or another; but these groups, by bargaining, were able to reach an agreement in just three months. Other agencies are planning similar attempts at regulating by negotiation, both in the writing of rules and in carrying out negotiations out of court to settle violations.[4]

More time is needed before a final judgment can be made on the effects of deregulation. When deregulation benefits society without endangering it, deregulation works. But deregulation is likely to remain controversial in the sensitive areas of public health and worker safety.

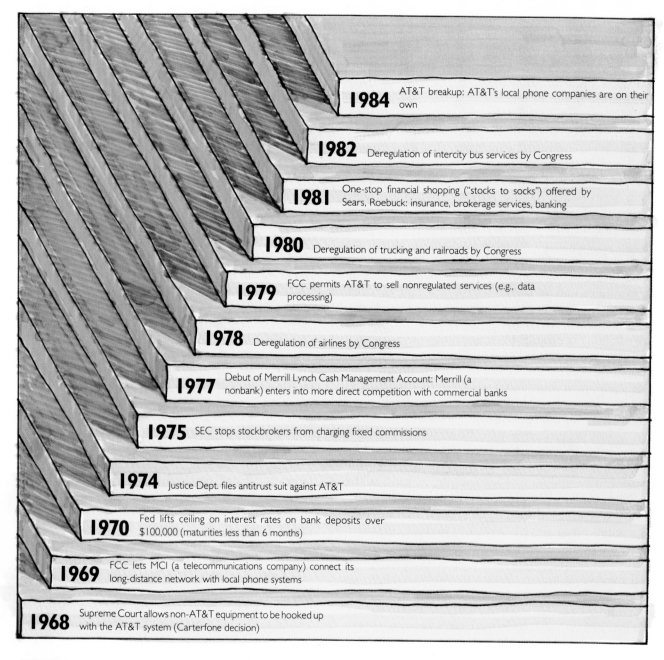

1984 AT&T breakup: AT&T's local phone companies are on their own

1982 Deregulation of intercity bus services by Congress

1981 One-stop financial shopping ("stocks to socks") offered by Sears, Roebuck: insurance, brokerage services, banking

1980 Deregulation of trucking and railroads by Congress

1979 FCC permits AT&T to sell nonregulated services (e.g., data processing)

1978 Deregulation of airlines by Congress

1977 Debut of Merrill Lynch Cash Management Account: Merrill (a nonbank) enters into more direct competition with commercial banks

1975 SEC stops stockbrokers from charging fixed commissions

1974 Justice Dept. files antitrust suit against AT&T

1970 Fed lifts ceiling on interest rates on bank deposits over $100,000 (maturities less than 6 months)

1969 FCC lets MCI (a telecommunications company) connect its long-distance network with local phone systems

1968 Supreme Court allows non-AT&T equipment to be hooked up with the AT&T system (Carterfone decision)

FIGURE 2

STEPS TOWARD DEREGULATION:
Significant laws and decisions, 1968–1984

The move toward deregulation started slowly, less than two decades ago. Now it's gaining force— revitalizing the finance, telecommunications, and transportation industries. The result, some experts believe, is a boost for the overall economy: fast, efficient transport and communications help economic growth, and a freer financial system encourages the flow of capital to the most productive businesses.

GOVERNMENT REGULATION OF NONCOMPETITIVE PRACTICES

The government's regulation of noncompetitive practices, which has developed over the course of almost one hundred years, is the oldest and most widely accepted form of government regulation. As we saw in Chapter 3, business was given a free hand in the period of rapid industrialization after the Civil War. Some of the most ruthless practices in this ruthless age took place in the railroad industry. Train schedules during the 1870s often gave no consideration to customer convenience; the company could run all of its trains at maximum load and maximum profits—a plan that was good for the railroad but bad for the public.

Because of the high visibility of these unfair practices, the railroad industry was the first to feel the force of citizens' resentment. The wealth and power of the railroads were great enough to counteract public opinion for some time, but finally an organization of midwestern farmers, the National Grange, managed to win passage of a few laws that regulated railroad practices. Though most of these laws were later found to be unconstitutional, they were a milestone in American history. They led to the passage of a congressional act to regulate commerce in 1887, known as the **Interstate Commerce Act.** This key act set up *the first U.S. independent regulatory commission.*

Aimed squarely at the railroads, the Interstate Commerce Act was hailed as a sure means to put an end to abuses by such industries for all time. The hoped-for relief did not materialize, since the law contained too many weaknesses and loopholes to be effective for long. The legislation did, however, lead to the establishment of the Interstate Commerce Commission (ICC), a federal agency that regulates interstate shipping rates.

LAWS RESTRICTING MONOPOLIES

Beginning with the Interstate Commerce Act in 1887, the body of government regulation grew, expanding to control monopoly in other industries and to protect the consumer.

The Sherman Antitrust Act

The principal tool of the monopolist was the **trust,** which is established when *one company buys a controlling share of the stock of competing companies in the same industry.* (One of the most notorious trusts was Rockefeller's Standard Oil Trust, established in 1882.) In industries dominated by trusts, competition was stifled and prices and profits climbed. Because of public outrage at this situation, Congress passed the **Sherman Antitrust Act** in 1890. The new law *declared that trusts and conspiracies "in restraint of trade or commerce" were illegal.* The vaguely worded provisions of this act, however, again left loopholes large enough to permit many of the offending monopolies to stay powerful. Congress therefore turned to further legislation to combat the growth of trusts.

The Clayton Act

The **Clayton Act** (1914) *amended the Sherman Antitrust Act, clearing up wording and forbidding specific actions that Congress saw as leading to monopoly.* Among the forbidden practices were **tying contracts—***forcing buyers to buy unwanted goods along with goods actually desired;* setting up **interlocking directorates,** where *members of the board of one firm sit on the board of a competing firm;* acquiring large blocks of competitors' stock; and establishing discriminatory prices, other than discounts made "in good faith."

With that last proviso—"in good faith"—Congress once again failed to state its purposes clearly. The Clayton amendments, like the act they were designed to amend, were simply too vague to do any real damage to monopolies.

The Federal Trade Commission Act

In the light of the difficulties the lawmakers were encountering, observers believed it might be advisable to try another approach—to outlaw unfair trade practices by very general laws and then establish a powerful federal commission that would continue to look for specific abuses. In 1914 President Woodrow Wilson pressed successfully for passage of a bill incorporating this concept, which would make up for the weaknesses of the Sherman and Clayton acts. The result was the **Federal Trade Commission Act.**

This act, with its deliberately vague wording, *stated that "unfair methods of competition in commerce are hereby declared illegal."* In addition, it set up a five-member commission empowered to define, detect, and enforce compliance with this and the Clayton Act. The Federal Trade Commission (FTC) is still very much in evidence; it acts on complaints made by business and also takes action on its own initiative. A violator is given thirty days to answer a charge of unfair practice. If the commission is not convinced that the violator's excuses are valid, it issues a "cease and desist" order, requiring the violator to stop the offensive practice. The effectiveness of the FTC depends, however, on the five people running it. Consequently, enforcement has ranged from very tough to not tough enough.

The years have brought with them new provisions to strengthen the original act. In 1938 an amendment called the **Wheeler-Lea Act** *expanded FTC jurisdiction to include practices that injure the public generally, in addition to those that specifically harm competitors.* It also declared illegal false advertising of foods, drugs, cosmetics, and therapeutic devices. And it gave the FTC the authority to increase the fines it imposes if a cease-and-desist order isn't obeyed within sixty days.

The Celler-Kefauver Act

In 1950 the **Celler-Kefauver Act** finally closed one of the most glaring loopholes in the Clayton Act, which had prohibited anticompetitive mergers only if they were made by stock acquisition. The new act *forbade anticompetitive mergers by other means as well, including acquisition of assets.* Other provisions of the 1950 amendment *gave the FTC general authority to approve mergers before they took place.* As a result, companies that wish to merge have to describe their plan to the FTC, which then furnishes an opinion on the merger's legality.

ANTITRUST TODAY

The 1970s saw two more major antitrust laws enacted. The first was the **Antitrust Procedures and Penalties Act** (1974), which *increased the fines for vio-*

lation of Sherman Act provisions to $100,000 for individuals and to $10 million for corporations. It also made violation of the law a felony rather than a misdemeanor, with a maximum jail sentence of three years. In 1976, the **Antitrust Improvements Act** *required premerger notification for companies, and it also empowered attorneys general at the state level to bring suit on behalf of injured consumers in their states.* These acts were accompanied by a flurry of suits aimed at breaking up **conglomerate mergers**—*mergers between firms in unrelated industries* (a restaurant chain and a mattress manufacturer, for example).

Currently, political leaders' attitude toward antitrust enforcement has been changing to reflect the more complex realities of today's competition, both within the United States and internationally. Now, mergers may not be considered undesirable simply because of the size of the resulting combination. In 1982 the Justice Department updated its guidelines on which mergers it would oppose. The department is now using a new formula, which measures not only the size of the firms that wish to merge but also the number of firms serving those firms' market: only if the resulting (newly merged) firm would be able to swallow up more than a certain proportion of the total market will the Justice Department view the merger as truly threatening to competition. Very few merger cases, and no complex monopoly suits, have been filed recently. Instead, the Justice Department has been focusing its antitrust enforcement resources on "garden-variety" anticompetitive practices: for example, cases against companies that rig bids on highway construction projects have increased, and several business executives have been jailed in such cases.

Nothing has symbolized the changes in antitrust enforcement better than the announcement, in mid-January 1982, that the Justice Department had ended two if its biggest antitrust cases. One case was simply dropped: it was a massive and complex case, filed in 1969, that had charged IBM with monopolizing the computer industry. The second, as we noted in Chapter 2, was settled. The eight-year-old action against AT&T that sought to divest it of its twenty-three operating companies and Western Electric (its manufacturing arm) was concluded: AT&T agreed to spin off the local phone companies, but it was allowed to keep Western Electric, and it gained freedom to compete in such fields as computers and data communication.

In part, the shift in focus in antitrust regulation stems from the pressures of worldwide competition and inflation. The crisis in the U.S. auto industry strikingly illustrates this point. In the 1960s there was a great deal of support for antitrust action against General Motors, but the rise of foreign competition and the simultaneous decline of American auto makers' fortunes have made such a step unthinkable. By 1984 foreign competition had so eroded GM's dominance of the domestic market that the FTC approved a joint venture with Toyota that would enable GM to build a competitive small car in the United States. The Justice Department has also approved a merger of the nation's third and fourth largest steel companies (a merger it had originally rejected) to help the domestic steel industry fight foreign competitors.

Another reason for allowing large firms to stay large is the greatly increased cost of research and development. Today, only the largest firms can afford to invest the huge sums of money that are needed for research. Thus, economists have urged that we allow large firms and joint ventures to come into being when their near-monopoly status is likely to yield good results—in this case, when it seems likely to bring about technical innovation. The Reagan administration supports that view: it encouraged a consortium of twelve U.S. electronic firms to band together in joint research projects to compete with government-subsidized research abroad, and other R&D joint ventures are likely to be permitted in the future.

GOVERNMENT REGULATION OF NATURAL MONOPOLIES

The law has never considered all monopolies to be harmful to the public. In fact, in certain industries, competition may even hurt the consumer. Such businesses, called **natural monopolies,** are those that *provide services that it would be unnecessary or impractical to duplicate.* Public utilities, for example, are

natural monopolies. Consider what would happen if two electric companies were competing for business in your community: rates would actually be higher than they are now. Why? The biggest factor in the cost of electricity is the company's investment in generators and wiring. When the government allows one company to monopolize electricity production, that company can spread the cost of capital equipment over the greatest possible number of customers—and reduce the cost to each customer.

Before the antitrust suit against AT&T, many experts considered telephone service a natural monopoly. But in the last few years, technological changes have made it relatively cheap and easy for other companies to compete in the telecommunications business. For example, once microwave and satellite transmission replaced costly wires to connect distant cities, competitors could offer long-distance service for less than AT&T charged. Of course, some telephone users fear that service could deteriorate without the protective apron of Ma Bell. This dilemma illustrates the difficult trade-offs in deciding whether to permit a monopoly: AT&T's existing equipment works well and is built to last, though some of it is not state-of-the-art. If AT&T had been left alone, might the company have been reluctant to push for technological improvements? On the other hand, with the system broken up, will service be less efficient and will local rates soar? Only time will tell if our phone system would have been better left a protected natural monopoly.

Though natural monopolies are indeed monopolies, there are limits on what they can charge their customers. The government has enacted a wide range of legislation to control these businesses and others that are powerful for similar reasons. Control is vested in a number of specialized public service commissions at the federal, state, and local levels, which keep an increasingly strict eye on the pricing and planning activities of the utilities they regulate (see Figure 1). The public service commissions are particularly watchful over the power companies, on which consumers are so completely dependent.

Nearly every state also has regulatory commissions that control statewide natural monopolies. Local public utilities, however, are often regulated by the communities they serve.

U.S. CONTROLS ON HIGH-TECH TRADE: TECHNOLOGICAL IMPERIALISM?

One of the Reagan administration's priorities in international trade has been to stem the flow of computers and other sophisticated electronics equipment to the Soviet Union. Fearing that these devices might find military applications, the government has supported several laws that give the Defense Department the power to veto sales of high-tech items even to our allies, and for an indefinite period—even after they have been sold abroad. For example, a Briton who bought an IBM computer from the British distributor of IBM equipment could not sell the computer without U.S. Defense Department approval. The government's worry is that once these devices are out of the country, they might be sold to the Soviet Union through intermediaries.

U.S. business leaders, eager to export high-tech equipment, have opposed tight controls on their sales abroad. But an even louder chorus of disapproval has come from our allies, in particular Great Britain. English business leaders have disputed the right of the U.S. government to control the sales of computers once they have been sold in England. The British Secretary for Trade and Industry, Norman Tebbit, has characterized the regulations as attempts to "impose [U.S.] laws on people in other countries, inside *their* homes and *their* businesses." What he is objecting to is the U.S. assertion that it has the right to control American-made goods indefinitely.

Critics in Britain and other European countries have charged that Washington's policy is not only an unfair extraterritorial extension of U.S. law, but a clever way to protect American business interests. Such tight control, they argue, helps U.S. companies continue to dominate the international high-tech market. U.S. business leaders deny this charge, and in fact most of them have lobbied against the regulations as unwelcome government interference in trade.

What the outcome of this international wrangling will be is still not known. A similar dispute, over the Europeans' right to sell equipment containing U.S. components to the USSR for use in its gas pipeline, erupted in 1982. Although this disagreement was eventually settled, it left much resentment of U.S. policy among Europeans. As one European has said of the brewing high-tech dispute, "It could make the row over the Siberian gas pipeline look like tiddlywinks."

SOURCE: "Angry Charges of U.S. High-Tech 'Imperialism,'" *Business Week*, February 27, 1984, p. 50; "High-Tech Exports: Sparks Are About to Fly," *Business Week*, April 2, 1984, pp. 30–31.

REGULATION OF RETAIL PRICES

As we've seen, the primary goal of the Sherman, Clayton, and Celler-Kefauver acts, and most of the FTC acts, was to limit anticompetitive practices on the manufacturing end of industry. Firms that dealt directly with individual customers on the retail level were considered too small to threaten competition; thus for a time they remained unregulated by the federal government, except in matters connected with advertising. Then, as the nation struggled to free itself from the Depression of the 1930s, a new type of marketing enterprise—giant retailing businesses, such as chain merchandisers and discount houses—came on the scene. These enterprises could buy in huge quantities and sell cheaply to millions of customers. To protect small retailers and wholesalers against uncurbed monopoly among these marketing enterprises, Congress passed the Robinson-Patman Act in 1936.

The **Robinson-Patman Act** amended the sections of the Clayton Act dealing with price discrimination. It *aimed to outlaw discrimination against buyers as well as sellers, by providing that no seller could make a* *price concession*—that is, mark down its prices—*to any one buyer without giving all other buyers the same concession on a proportional basis.* This rule applied to concessions for advertising as well as price concessions. The act also forbade suppliers to offer any quantity discounts that might tend to lessen competition. The only permissible quantity discounts were those that reflected decreased costs; and if a seller offered a discount on this basis, all purchasers of an equal quantity of goods had to receive the same discount.

How did these provisions actually affect retailing? In one case in Utah, the Robinson-Patman Act saved the day for a pie company. When the Utah Pie Company began producing its wares, it had three main competitors: Pet Milk, Continental Baking, and Carnation, all giant marketers that produced their pies outside the state. Despite this formidable competition, Utah Pie began to win an increasing share of the market. In an effort to halt this growth, the three larger companies lowered their prices in the Utah market while holding the prices of their pies constant in other geographic areas—and succeeded in substantially reducing Utah Pie's share of the market. Thanks to the Robinson-Patman Act, however, the three food giants were found guilty of price discrimination in an attempt to destroy a competitor, and were obliged to discontinue their discriminatory pricing policy.[5]

The Utah case involved price discrimination across geographic lines. Another antitrust principle governs instances where a manufacturer tries to control the price that retailers charge for its product. That's known as vertical price fixing, because it involves prices up and down the distribution chain. Such arrangements had been ruled automatically illegal under the Sherman Act. But in a recent case before the U.S. Supreme Court, the Reagan administration argued that one form of vertical price fixing, called resale price maintenance, actually enhanced competition. The administration supported the argument of Monsanto Company that it shouldn't have to pay $10.5 million in damages for cutting off a distributor of one of its herbicides, a discounter who didn't offer full service to customers. The administration's economists saw some competitive benefits in Monsanto's desire to maintain the quality of its products by precluding such discounting; the distributor, on the other hand, said it had been penalized for price cutting. It remained to be seen whether the Supreme Court would accept the Reagan administration's argument or stick to the traditional view that vertical price fixing always stifles competition.[6]

TAXATION

Nobody likes taxes: that fact was driven home to elected officials in California in 1978 when voters there approved Proposition 13, which sharply curtailed escalating property taxes. Proposition 13 and similar legislation in more than a dozen other states were heralded as a "tax revolt." Advocates of lower taxes in these areas argued that government at all levels was spending way beyond its means; to stop spending, they decided to apply a tourniquet to the flow of tax dollars that nourished those growing government budgets, using laws like Proposition 13 to impose limits on how fast local taxes could grow. Some states linked tax increases to the inflation rate, others to growth in personal income.

The highly publicized tax revolt mostly cut taxes on property. But numerous other taxes are enacted by governments: on income, on retail sales, on luxury goods and many other items. If government didn't get its revenue from one source, some observers pointed out, it could always tap another. As a result, some business groups that generally support lower taxes didn't join in the citizens' tax revolt. In Ohio, for example, retail merchants actually came out *against* a cut in income taxes because they feared the state would just turn around and hike sales taxes—which, of course, would be bad for the retailers.[7]

The tax revolt slowed during the recession of the early 1980s as states scrambled for funds to close budget deficits. If the revolt returns, as some new voter initiatives have suggested it may, citizens this time will have to face more difficult choices. How much should government spend? Who should pay for needed public services? How do changes in taxes affect individuals and businesses? Should taxes be used to achieve goals other than raising money, such as controlling trade and checking undesirable economic trends? All these issues surrounding taxes affect business in different ways. Here we'll discuss the most important ones.

REVENUE COLLECTION

Someone has to foot the bill for government, and that is the purpose of the five major revenue-producing taxes we pay: Social Security, individual income, corporate income, property, and general sales. We discussed Social Security in Chapter 8. Now let's look at the four other taxes and their impact on business.

Individual income taxes

The individual income tax strongly affects business practices. Most small businesses are partnerships or sole proprietorships, and for tax purposes their profits are considered to be the personal income of the owners. Also, the law requires all employers to withhold from their employees' pay a percentage of earnings equivalent to the individual income tax rate. This withheld money is periodically forwarded to the federal, state, and local tax agencies to be credited to the employees' tax accounts. Although the money so collected comes strictly from the employees, the company pays all expenses of administering the pay deductions, and these costs can be high for a large company. Furthermore, what individuals pay in taxes they might otherwise have invested in stocks and bonds or deposited in savings accounts, thereby making money available for business expansion.

Property taxes

Because business is a large owner of property, it naturally pays a large portion of the property tax in communities that aren't primarily residential, particularly when the tax emphasis is on the value of buildings. A twenty-story office tower, for instance, is worth far more than a filling station. In addition, commercial property is usually taxed at a higher rate than houses and farms.

Sales taxes

Businesses don't pay a general sales tax on merchandise they buy for resale. The sales tax does affect business, however, in that it increases the prices customers have to pay, and thus it may make the merchandise less attractive. Also, as with personal income taxes, the business is required to collect the sales tax and to pay the accounting expenses associated with that operation.

Corporate income taxes

A corporation pays tax on profits similar to that paid by an individual. The federal tax rate for corporations is 15 percent of the first $25,000 in income; 18 percent in the $25,000–$50,000 range; 30 percent in the $50,000–$75,000 range; 40 percent in the $75,000–$100,000 range; and 46 percent of income over $100,000. Many large companies, however, never pay the 46 percent rate; in fact, on average, business is taxed at only 35 percent. How is this possible? Many tax laws have provisions to encourage businesses to grow and invest more: for example, a business can take tax credits for investing in new equipment and can write off aging property rapidly. The idea is that a growing company will produce more, hire more people, and earn more, which in the long run will supply more tax dollars. Some industries can use more of these incentives than others, so their "effective tax rates" are even lower: large banks have reduced their taxes to only about 2 percent of their income. Each year, corporate taxes make up an even smaller share of the federal government's annual tax "take"—less than 7 percent in 1983, compared to 23.2 percent in 1960.[8]

Some public officials, including President Reagan, think the best way to reform the corporate income tax is to abolish it. They cite a problem known as "double taxation" of corporate profits: first, the company pays corporate income tax on its earnings, and then shareholders are required to pay taxes on corporate earnings distributed as dividends. Other experts have suggested removing from the law provisions and incentives that favor some businesses over others. So far, however, little has been done on either score. Meanwhile, the government is cracking down on companies that exploit gray areas in the tax laws and on firms that play the "audit lottery"—that is, underpay their taxes, hoping their returns won't be audited by the IRS. A 10 percent penalty is now imposed if a company underpays its tax without also filing a separate statement in support of its questionable claim. (Filing the support statement would alert IRS auditors to examine the tax return more closely,

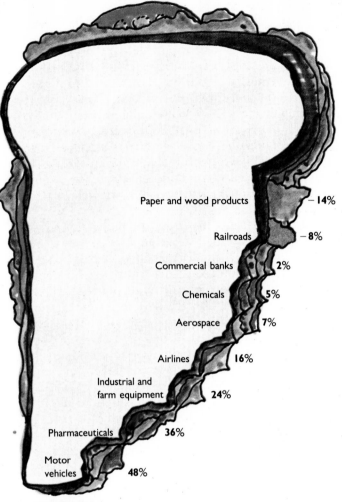

Paper and wood products — 14%

Railroads — 8%

Commercial banks 2%

Chemicals 5%

Aerospace 7%

Airlines 16%

Industrial and farm equipment 24%

Pharmaceuticals 36%

Motor vehicles 48%

FIGURE 3

THE UNEVEN TAX BITE:
Effective tax rates as percentages of the incomes of
selected industries, 1981

**Industries vary widely in their ability to take
advantage of tax breaks. Certain capital-intensive
smokestack industries, such as paper and wood
products, can take fast write-offs for equipment; banks
can deduct interest payments on money they borrow
to buy tax-exempt municipal bonds. But are these
variations helpful to our economy? Some economists
have doubts about this question. They fear the
patchwork of tax breaks may be causing corporate
investment to flow in directions that are not
necessarily the best for the whole economy.**

of course.) Many companies object to the penalty:
they think they shouldn't be penalized for honest
disagreements over complex, little-understood tax
questions.[9]

Many state and local governments also impose
corporate income taxes, but at lower rates. And
since most of this country's large corporations also
operate abroad, they must pay income taxes in foreign countries as well. The tax system and corporate
income tax rate of a country thus influence a business's decision to operate in that country. It should
be noted that the U.S. government allows American
corporations a **tax credit,** *an amount deducted from the
money on which they're taxed here,* for taxes paid to a
foreign government.

REGULATORY AND RESTRICTIVE TAXATION

Regulatory and restrictive taxes produce revenue,
but that is not their main purpose. Instead, some are
levied because they allow government to temper
potentially harmful practices; others are imposed to
protect American business against foreign competition.

Excise taxes

A number of items are subject to **excise taxes**—*taxes
intended to help control potentially harmful practices or to
help pay for services used only by certain people.* The
United States imposes excise taxes on the making of
gasoline, tobacco products, liquor, firearms, tires,
automobiles, sugar, and fishing tackle. Excise taxes
are also levied on certain services of national scope,
such as air travel and telephone calls. In addition, all
states levy excise taxes on gasoline and liquor, and
some impose them on the sale of luxury items, such
as furs and fine jewelry.

Income from federal excise taxes must be used
for a purpose related to the tax. The gasoline tax,
for example, goes toward funding road-building
projects. Through the gasoline tax, the burden of
paying for the roads is in large part borne by those
who use them most.

Through taxes on cigarettes and liquor, the
government tries to discourage people's use of these
substances. (Needless to say, the method has not entirely succeeded.) Some excise taxes, such as those
on legally produced narcotics and firearms, are
so small that they're almost purely regulatory.
Through the existence of these taxes, the govern-

ment can place rigid controls on their manufacture and, it's hoped, their use.

Excise taxes are imposed on either the manufacturer, the retailer, or both. Ultimately, however, the consumer pays these taxes, since they are often hidden in the prices of goods. Because goods with these hidden taxes are often subject to the general sales tax as well, the consumer is hit twice.

Customs duties

Goods brought into this country are subject to *import taxes*, or **customs duties.** These taxes are selective; they vary with the product and its country of origin. Designed to protect American business against foreign competition, customs duties have the effect of raising the price of imports to a level comparable to similar American-made merchandise. Customs duties have been used with increased frequency as a weapon in foreign policy, the goods of friendly nations being taxed at rates below those of indifferent or openly hostile countries.

HOW BUSINESS COMMUNICATES WITH THE GOVERNMENT: LOBBYING AND PACs

"Mr. Businessman Goes to Washington" might be the name of Hollywood's remake of the classic small-town-boy-in-the-national-capital film. It also aptly describes a heightened concern among corporate executives and small businesses alike that, more than ever before, decisions in Washington affect business at home. So, businesses have created new, more effective ways to ensure that their views will be considered by elected officials and regulators.

To influence Congress, individual companies set up **lobbies**—*groups of people whose aim is to persuade legislators to vote according to the interests of the group's sponsor.* Before AT&T was broken up, it was well known on Capitol Hill for a flock of lobbyists dubbed "shepherds" for their guardianlike protection of Ma Bell's interests. Each one of these lobbyists was assigned to monitor an individual representative or senator as he or she went through the debate on bills affecting the phone company: the lobbyist stood by, always ready to remind the legisla-

tor how the folks back home felt. Business also bands together in organizations dedicated to pushing common interests in Washington. The Chamber of Commerce, the most powerful and most tightly organized lobby group in Washington, issues research reports that help shape public debate. A group of high-level corporate executives, the Business Roundtable, is frequently consulted before the president or Congress acts on an economic policy matter.

Businesses also make contributions to candidates to help fund their increasingly expensive election campaigns. Campaign finance laws prohibit corporations from giving donations directly, but corporations can operate through political action committees (PACs) that solicit funds from certain employees. The PACs control large sums. Many individual companies have their own PACs, but the largest PACs represent trade associations. The biggest donor in the 1982 congressional elections, for example, was the National Association of Realtors PAC, which gave more than $2 million to congressional candidates. The American Medical Association was second, with $1.6 million.[10]

The law limits the amount a single PAC can give to any one candidate. Thus, few individual officeholders are beholden to PACs. The idea of a PAC contribution isn't to "own" a candidate, but to ensure access for one's point of view. (In fact, though PACs typically support incumbents rather than challengers, sometimes a PAC will contribute to both sides in an election.) PAC supporters say PACs provide a legitimate way for citizens to maintain contact with elected officials. But critics of the contributions complain that business PACs can band together to make or break a candidate. They also argue that the abundance of PAC money raises the costs of campaigning, so that only those who curry favor with the wealthy PACs can afford to run for office.

Opponents of PACs would eliminate the PACs by providing public funding for congressional candidates. Opponents like Common Cause, which describes itself as the citizens' lobby, insist that PACs corrode the democratic process. The reform proposals so far haven't gained sufficient support to pass both houses of Congress, but some candidates, such as Gary Hart and Walter Mondale in the 1984 presidential primaries, have begun to refuse to accept PAC contributions.

COPYRIGHTS, TRADEMARKS, AND PATENTS

Your favorite television show is aired at 8:00 P.M., but you've got a dinner date. So you switch on a videocassette recorder, program it to record the show, and return home at 10:00 to watch a self-made rerun. A commonplace scenario, right? Well, not long ago the companies that made TV shows might have accused you of violating the copyright laws.

Copyright is one of three ways in which federal law protects certain exclusive business rights. The others are trademarks and patents. In the VCR example, the creative artists who made the program owned a copyright that gave them the right to control use of their material by others. But in early 1984 the U.S. Supreme Court ruled that home videotaping doesn't violate that exclusive copyright because it isn't done for commercial gain.

Disputes over these protections make for some protracted, tenacious, and high-stakes legal battles. The issues can be diverse:

■ An inventor who sold the rights to a patented engine-cooling system to one auto manufacturer finds that others are using it without paying him.

■ Two scientists have developed a revolutionary new way of splicing genes to make new organisms, but others claim the procedure can't be patented because the inventors didn't apply for protection in time.

■ A professor names his new board game "Antimonopoly." The makers of the original Monopoly game sue to block an infringement of their trademark.

How are these kinds of controversies resolved? Each dispute involves its own special facts and circumstances. But the general rules are easier to explain.

COPYRIGHTS

Copyrights protect the creators of literary, dramatic, musical, artistic, and other intellectual works. Any printed, filmed, or recorded material can be copyrighted. The **copyright** *gives its owner the exclusive right to reproduce ("copy"), sell, or adapt the work he or she has created.* The Registrar of Copyrights, Library of Congress, will issue a copyright upon an application from the creator or from someone to whom the author has granted the right to reproduce the work. (A book, for example, may be copyrighted by either the author or the publisher.) Copyrights issued after 1977 are valid for the lifetime of the creator plus fifty years. Copyrights issued prior to 1977 are good for seventy-five years. Copyright law also covers reproduction by xerography, videotape, and magnetic storage.

TRADEMARKS

A **trademark** *is any word, name, symbol, or device used to distinguish the product of one manufacturer from those made by others.* McDonald's golden arches are one of the most visible of modern trademarks. Brand names can also be registered as trademarks. Examples are Exxon, Polaroid, and Chevrolet. If properly registered and renewed every twenty years, a trademark generally belongs to its owner forever. Among the exceptions are popular brand names that have become **generic terms,** meaning that they *describe a whole class of products.* A brand-name trademark can become a generic term if the trademark has been allowed to expire, if it has been incorrectly used by its owner (as in the case of Borden's ReaLemon lemon juice, which the Federal Trade Commission in 1976 ruled was being used by Borden to maintain a monopoly in bottled lemon juice), or if the public comes to equate the name with the class of products (e.g., yo-yos).

PATENTS

A **patent** *protects the invention or discovery of a new and useful process, an article of manufacture, a machine, a chemical substance, or an improvement on any of these.* Issued by the U.S. Patent Office, a patent grants the owner the right to exclude others from making, using, or selling the invention for seventeen years. After that time, the patent becomes available for common use. On the one hand, patent law guarantees the originator the right to use the discovery exclusively for a relatively long period of time, thus encouraging people to devise new machines, gadgets, and processes. On the other hand, it also ensures that rights to the new item will be released eventually. Other enterprises may be able to make use of it more creatively than its originator.

COMPUTER COPYRIGHTS

One of the hottest new products in the early 1980s was the Apple II home computer. The California-based company that manufactured the machine grew almost overnight from a two-man operation in a garage to a multimillion-dollar business. Success has its imitators, however, and Apple soon found itself competing with numerous computer clones of its popular model. One copycat machine, the Franklin Ace, performed exactly like an Apple.

So Apple took Franklin to court. It argued that special instructions for its Apple II, embedded on a silicon chip in a string of electronic impulses, were as fully protected by copyright as words on a printed page. The legal issue was a novel one. There was a special law that ensured copyright protection for computer programs that performed specific tasks, such as calculating a payroll or alphabetizing a list of names; but no one knew whether the complex coding on a computer chip, called an operating system, qualified for copyright protection.

The judges ultimately ruled for Apple, and Franklin settled the case by paying $2.5 million in damages. The decision could be an important trend setter in the complex new terrain of computer copyrights and patents.

CHIP PIRATES

If operating system programs can be copyrighted, what about the computer chips themselves? Ordinarily, physical devices are protected only by patents. But patents take a long time to obtain. In the meantime competitors can perform what amounts to electronic plagiarism: they can study the chip's design under a microscope and produce one of their own. By the time the original company obtains its patent, its chip may be obsolete.

Against this uncertain legal background, American and Japanese manufacturers, who are fighting bitterly over the lucrative market for microprocessor chips, have traded accusations of chip piracy. Computer piracy can take on all the intrigue of buccaneer days.

Apple sent a team of detectives scouring through Taiwan to track down imitation Apple computers built in Asia. IBM nearly provoked a trade war with Japan when it accused Hitachi of sending spies to steal its secret computer plans. (In fact, many computer companies prefer to protect their products by secrecy and tight internal security, rather than relying on laws that haven't caught up with the computer age.) One U.S. firm, Intel Corporation, took on two Japanese chip makers in court. One chip maker settled, and the other case is still unresolved. Unlike the Apple case, the chip questions have not been settled: no judge has cleared up the legal uncertainty surrounding the international chip wars. Meanwhile, the American companies hope Congress will write a new law protecting their chip designs.

THE DEBATE OVER COPYING SOFTWARE

Copyright disputes over computer software also reach into the home. Many home computer programs can be easily copied onto a blank disk. To many software companies, of course, a copied program is an unsold program; so one of them sued a southern California rent-a-program store, charging that the business was an open invitation for renters to spread copied programs among their friends. The matter hasn't been resolved.

The software industry has mixed feelings over the copying issue: though most firms urge users to make a backup copy for safekeeping, others sell deviously designed disks that are difficult to copy. Some in the computer industry fear that this piracy paranoia is bad for business: computer users who want to make sure they've got a backup handy may be unwilling to buy the "copy-protected programs." Some products, like the IBM Personal Computer, thrive on the wide availability of compatible software—IBM expressly made the plans for its PC's internal design widely available, just so that the smaller software houses could create a wealth of software for the machine, thus helping to make the machine more attractive to a wide variety of users. In the view of computer experts who advocate openness, any high-tech industry that stifles innovation with excessive secrecy is doomed to stagnation.

CHAPTER REVIEW

Government and business depend on each other in many ways: government needs the products and services of business, and business needs the help of government agencies in the form of information, advice, and loan guarantees. Often, business and government can work cooperatively.

Regulatory agencies of the federal government restrict certain business activities in order to protect public health and safety, prevent competitive abuses, and advance other public goals. Under the banner of "deregulation," many of these agencies have recently been easing their restrictions, often on the basis of a controversial "cost-benefit" approach. Critics claim that while business may benefit from this approach, it is actually very costly in ways that are not readily measurable, as in damage to the environment. On the other hand, some forms of deregulation have been attacked as being hurtful to business—as, for example, deregulation in the transportation industry, which has spurred fierce competition and has caused some companies to fail. Another approach, regulation by negotiation, has received a more positive response.

Over the past century Congress has taken steps to restrain monopoly and other noncompetitive business practices that weaken free enterprise. Important antitrust laws are the Interstate Commerce Act (1887), the Sherman Antitrust Act (1890), the Clayton Act (1914), the Federal Trade Commission Act (1914), the Wheeler-Lea Act (1938), the Celler-Kefauver Act (1950), the Antitrust Procedures and Penalties Act (1974), and the Antitrust Improvements Act (1976). Recently, however, the government has begun to focus on ways to keep U.S. companies competitive in a world of increased foreign competition and global inflation. The result is that big companies are no longer being attacked merely for being big.

Sometimes monopoly is considered to be in the public interest. Natural monopolies, such as public utilities, are regulated by commissions at the federal, state, and local levels. To protect small retailers and wholesalers against marketing monopolies, Congress enacted the Robinson-Patman Act (1936) to regulate retail prices.

Government also interacts with business by exercising its taxing powers. There are two major forms of taxation: revenue-raising and regulatory. Revenue-raising taxes include Social Security, income taxes, sales taxes, and property taxes. Regulatory taxes, such as excise taxes and customs duties, not only produce revenue but also help to equalize tax burdens, restrict potentially harmful practices, and protect American business.

To advance their interests, companies send lobbyists to Washington and support influential business research and policy groups. They also make huge campaign contributions through political action committees (PACs).

REVIEW QUESTIONS

1. How do business and government help each other?

2. What is the cost-benefit approach to deregulation? Why has it been criticized? What are the pluses and minuses of deregulation in the transportation industry?

3. Describe some of the abuses that led to the passage of the Interstate Commerce Act and the Sherman Antitrust Act.

4. List the major antitrust laws and briefly describe their purposes.

5. What are natural monopolies and why are they regulated?

6. What are the revenue-collecting taxes that affect business?

7. Give an example of a regulatory tax and state how it works.

8. Describe the ways in which business tries to wield influence among legislators and regulators.

KEY WORDS

Interstate Commerce Act (559)

trust (559)

Sherman Antitrust Act (559)

Clayton Act (559)

tying contracts (559)

interlocking directorates (559)

Federal Trade Commission Act (559–560)

Wheeler-Lea Act (560)

Celler-Kefauver Act (560)

Antitrust Procedures and Penalties Act (560)

Antitrust Improvements Act (560)

conglomerate mergers (560)

natural monopolies (561)

Robinson-Patman Act (562–563)

tax credit (565)

excise taxes (565)

customs duties (566)

lobbies (566)

copyright (567)

trademark (567)

generic terms (567)

patent (567)

CASE 1

WHEN THE STATES DO THE REGULATING

The Reagan administration, as part of its effort to decrease unnecessary federal interference in business, instituted a policy known as "regulatory federalism." In this approach, states were encouraged to take over the regulatory functions of the federal government. At first many businesspeople warmly welcomed this loosening of federal regulations. Citing the ease with which they could deal with state officials (compared with the complexities and delays in dealing with Washington), they looked forward to a regulatory climate more comfortable to business.

More recently, however, a number of corporate executives have called for a return to federal regulation. The problem? It has proved far more difficult for certain industries to deal with fifty sets of state regulations than with one set for the entire country.

Take, for example, the laws concerning the labeling of chemicals, which require companies to list all ingredients of their products on the labels. Some states have strict labeling laws, some don't—so some drug companies now must maintain separate product inventories for those states that have strict laws. Likewise, several states have "lemon laws" to protect buyers stuck with poorly built cars—forcing car manufacturers to replace the faulty cars. Certain states have enacted pollution control laws far more stringent than federal standards, requiring businesses in their states to invest heavily in waste treatment and disposal. The state of Virginia recently adopted a tight code of fair practice for the securities business—even though the same code had been abolished in a federal deregulation effort. Other laws have required businesses to buy American-made goods (or even state-made goods). Although some states have tried to loosen regulation (for example, permitting banks to diversify into other fields, such as insurance), the general impact of state regulation has been to confront business with regulations that are stricter and that vary from state to state.

Concerned by this confusing—
and constantly changing—
situation, a number of business
spokespersons have asked the federal government to get back into
the regulation business. New federal regulations have been requested in the securities business,
in the field of product liability, in
hazardous waste disposal, and in
chemical labeling. As of this writing, the federal government
seems likely to accommodate the
demands of these industries.[11]

1. Why do you think the loosening of
federal regulations has led to stricter
state regulations?

2. How might stricter regulations in
just a few states inconvenience a corporation doing business nationwide?

3. Are there some areas of business
that you believe should be regulated
at the federal level? Which areas, and
why?

4. This case suggests that federal regulation is not always bad for business.
Describe some advantages of federal
regulation of business.

CASE 2

ANTITRUST AND PAY TV: YOU BE THE JUDGE

Since 1948 movie studios have
been forbidden to control the
exhibition of the movies they
make. In that year's famous "Paramount case," the Supreme Court
ruled that the studio could not
run its own movie theaters, nor
could the studio force independent theaters to take grade B movies from Paramount in order to
get the A movies they wanted to
show. These practices, according
to the court, were a violation of
the nation's antitrust laws. But the
Paramount case involved only
movie theaters—not the showing
of movies on cable or subscription
TV. Since pay-TV showing is an
increasingly important factor in a
movie's success, movie studios
have sought a way to join forces
with the tube.

One such effort, under consideration at the time of this writing, is
an enterprise called Nova, a joint
venture by Columbia Pictures,
CBS, and Home Box Office.
Nova films would presumably be
put together by Columbia, have
their pay-TV runs on HBO, and
eventually be shown on the regular CBS network. The Justice
Department may decide that the
Nova plan is a legitimate joint
venture—or it may decide that
the deal is a violation of the antitrust law. A similar pay-TV entity,
Premiere, which involved four
movie studios, was put out of
business by a court decision in
1981. The court in this case decided that Premiere would have
the effect of reducing competition
in the TV-movie industry. A similar charge might stick against the
Nova venture, particularly since
one of the partners, HBO, already dominates the pay-TV market—so much so that it's been
called "the IBM of pay TV."

In another case that challenges
antitrust laws a merger has been
proposed between Showtime and
The Movie Channel, two pay-TV
channels. Since The Movie Channel is operated by companies that
include two movie studios and
Showtime is a unit of Viacom, this
merger may also be on shaky antitrust ground.[12]

1. In your opinion, is the Nova venture likely to increase competition—or
is it an agreement between competitors that will produce the opposite effect?

2. Does Nova represent an attempt by
a movie studio to get back into the
movie exhibition business, despite the
1948 Paramount decision?

3. Are there significant differences
between showing a movie on TV and
in a theater, such that movie studios
should be allowed to operate pay-TV
networks?

4. Will ventures such as Nova freeze
competition out of the pay-TV market? If so, what might be the bad effects?

PERSPECTIVES ON SMALL BUSINESS LEGAL AND GOVERNMENTAL ASPECTS

Since most small businesses have very few managerial or technical employees, they must turn to professionals for help. This section discusses important sources of this assistance: lawyers and the Small Business Administration.

FINDING THE RIGHT LAWYER

The small-business owner must seek the best qualified legal help available. Where should you start your search? First, you could ask your CPA or fellow entrepreneurs about lawyers they have used. You certainly should not make a random choice through the Yellow Pages. Whenever possible, a good referral is always the best source.

However, don't overlook attorneys' advertisements in newspapers. These ads may help you identify attorneys who specialize in the legal areas where you need help.

Once you have made your initial choice, you need to ask the attorney some probing questions about your particular case. Be sure to ask something like, "Do you regularly handle cases similar to this one?" (Even a business specialist may be unfamiliar with your particular problem. You don't want yours to be the first such case your attorney has handled. You're paying by the hour, and the learning process can be expensive.) Ask, "Are these types of cases an important aspect of your practice?"

(Maybe the last time the attorney handled a case like yours was ten years ago. You want to know whether the attorney is familiar with *current* aspects of your problem.) And ask, "Have you been successful on this type of case in the past?" (You must have someone with a successful track record in your area of concern.)

These are important questions. Ask them, and any others you can think of. It's your business and your money; you deserve the facts and the best opinion available. Remember, if for any reason your attorney handles your case in an incompetent manner, you can demand compensation in court. All practicing lawyers are protected by errors-and-omissions insurance to cover their oversights—a fact that's not generally known. The real trick will be to find an attorney that will aggressively sue another attorney.

ETHICS AND YOUR BUSINESS

Does a small business need ethics? Our response is an absolute *yes!* And the best one-word summary of an appropriate ethical code is *honesty.* Honest to customers in service, in quality of product, in all aspects of business dealings with the public. Usually the survival of a small firm is due largely to the uniqueness and quality of its service or product. Most of its clients may be consumers who are dissatisfied with the impersonal service and mass-produced goods provided by larger firms. In

fact, word-of-mouth advertising is definitely essential to the growth of any small business. It is generally assumed that each new customer has at least five friends or associates who are influenced by each other's actions. For each new customer who is satisfied, five others will patronize your company, and you will begin to develop a loyal customer base.

This building process will continue as long as customers are satisfied with your product or service—and no longer. And the reverse of this process can have a devastating effect. When you lose a customer by failing to stand behind your product, that dissatisfied former customer will spread the bad word. This kind of adverse publicity can doom a small firm.

All successful small-business owners attribute a major portion of their success to word-of-mouth advertising. Other forms of advertising and image building are of course essential to success, but the goodwill created by treating each customer fairly and honestly is the basic foundation on which small businesses survive.

TRADEMARKS, BRAND NAMES, AND OTHER FORMS OF COMPANY IDENTIFICATION

Your brand name, company name, and other forms of company identification must project an accurate picture of your firm or product.

When you choose a brand name, special advertising identification, and your company's name, you will need legal protection. Be aware that some types of advertising material must be copyrighted, and that brand names and trademarks must be registered. These inexpensive procedures provide essential protection. Start by obtaining copyright forms, available from the Library of Congress, Washington, D.C. If you need trademark information, you'll find it in a booklet available from the U.S. Department of Commerce.

Incorporation

When a business is incorporated, it is protected throughout its existence within the state in which it is incorporated. The name may also be reserved in other states if the corporation meets their individual requirements. Carrying out this procedure is called "qualifying to do business" in each state. The costs and requirements vary with each state.*

Statement of fictitious business name

The name of a unincorporated business can be protected by the county in which it is located if its owner files a statement of fictitious business name. The names of the owner and the company ("John Doe dba [doing business as] Super Squeegee Service"), and their address, are filed at the county seat and are published for three weeks in the public-notices section of the local newspaper of record. This procedure will

*Small Business Administration pamphlet Management Aids No. 6.003, *Incorporating a Small Business*, is very useful.

protect a business name for five years; it must be repeated at five-year intervals as long as the business exists.

Patents

A patent is the exclusive right to make and sell a product, a method, a composition of chemical substances, or a computer program. The patent is issued by the U.S. Patent and Trademark Office, and it takes about two years, at least, to receive one. You must apply before the idea or product is released for sale, or you may lose some basic rights to even receive a patent.

Unfortunately, in order to keep your patent, you must defend all infringements in court or you will lose the exclusivity. It is critical that you seek the services of a capable patent attorney during the initial stages of development. Patent laws are tricky, and you need an expert in this area.

Copyrights

Copyrights protect all written matter and works of art—including all artwork and writing used in advertising, promotion, package design, and sales and operating manuals. Computer programs may also be copyrighted. To receive copyright protection, you must do the following when the work or material is made public: include the symbol ©, the year of publication or when first made public, and the name of the owner of the work. In order to have your copyright federally registered, you must submit an application with the Copyright Office of the U.S. Library of Congress. Failure to file promptly for federal registration can prevent recovery of statutory damages and attorneys' fees.

Trademarks

A trademark is a symbol, word, or phrase that represents your product or service in your company literature, advertising, promotion, and manuals. Any company logos or shapes (like McDonald's golden arches) can and should be trademarked. After you have used the symbol, word, or phrase in the marketplace, you may apply for a trademark from the U.S. Patent and Trademark Office. When granted, you will receive exclusive rights to its use.

You may need the help of a trademark attorney, who will conduct a private computer search of all federal and state registrations to be sure your trademark can be granted exclusivity. The search may cost more than $500, but it will be worthwhile if you have big plans for your company.

Two common-law protections

"TRADE DRESS" UNFAIR COMPETITION This refers to the way a product is "dressed up" (packaging, labels, and so on). Your distinctive package or product designs are automatically protected, even if you don't apply for a copyright or trademark. As soon as you publicize your unique packaging, you are protected. Naturally, you must sue someone who steals your designs, and you are required to prove the pirated designs are close copies of yours.

TRADE SECRETS Any information or documents that are meant to be concealed from outsiders are automatically protected. Items that are kept secret, such as customer lists, blueprints, and formulas, qualify. Ownership of these secrets exists when they are created, and registration is not required. Anyone stealing these secrets can be sued, and damages will be charged by the courts. To qualify, however, these items must be kept secret and must be very difficult to learn about.

UNCLE SAM AND SMALL BUSINESS

Generally, all parts of statutory and common law apply to all businesses. Very small businesses, however, are free from certain aspects of statutory law: companies with fewer than eight employees are not required to comply with the regular reporting procedures of the Occupational Safety and Health Administration (OSHA); and companies with fewer than fifteen employees need not initiate the affirmative action programs that would otherwise be required under the Equal Employment Opportunity Act (EEOA).

These types of exceptions for the smallest of small firms have been a feature of government legislation for years. Regulation is especially costly to small companies, because they lack funds to grind out the paperwork that regulations require. The new mood of Washington is to cut red tape; however, only time will tell how long this will last.

The Small Business Administration

For the small-business sector, the most important of all government agencies is the Small Business Administration (SBA). The SBA was created in 1953 to assist the small firm with its unique financial requirements. Since that time, dozens of programs have been developed to provide services for the millions of firms classified as "small."

Let's proceed with a detailed discussion of some of the SBA services.

FINANCIAL ASSISTANCE Generally speaking, the SBA provides loans to small businesses that are unable to obtain funds from conventional sources. Among the loan programs are:

1. "Guaranteed" loans, in which the SBA guarantees up to 90 percent of a loan obtained from a conventional bank to help a small business to finance construction; to purchase equipment, facilities, machinery, supplies or materials; and to acquire working capital.

2. Economic-injury loans to assist businesses suffering from a natural disaster declared by the president or the Secretary of Agriculture.

3. Disaster loans to help disaster victims to rebuild homes or business establishments damaged in SBA-declared disaster areas.

4. Small business investment company loans (SBICs), which provide venture capital and long-term financing to small firms for expansion, modernization, and other business purposes. Special consideration is given to small firms owned and managed by socially or economically disadvantaged persons, generally defined as black Americans, American Indians, Spanish-Americans, Asian-Americans, Eskimos, and Aleuts. Vietnam military service may also be considered a contributing factor in economic and social disadvantage, according to SBA publications.

Management assistance is part of the SBIC package, and it is also not uncommon for SBICs to accept partial equity or ownership in companies in exchange for money and assistance.

SURETY BONDS The SBA is committed to making the bonding process accessible to small contractors who find that bonding is unavailable to them elsewhere. The agency is authorized to guarantee to a qualified applicant up to 90 percent of the losses incurred under the bid, payment, or performance bonds issued to contractors.

PROCUREMENT ASSISTANCE With the help of the SBA, thousands of small businesses have received as much as one-third of the total federal procurement budget. Special federal procurement specialists are available through the SBA to provide the following services to small firms:

1. Aid in preparing bids.

2. Aid and special considerations in obtaining prime contracts and subcontracts.

3. Directions to government agencies that may be able to use the small business's products and services.

4. Placement of small businesses on bidders' lists.

5. Provision of certificates of competency (COC) that authorize small businesses to perform contracts, following on-site inspections.

6. Making small businesses' names available, through the agency's regional procurement source files, to large firms and government agencies that are attempting to locate small firms that can provide specialized services.

7. Workshops conducted throughout the country to inform small businesses about opportunities for contract work with government agencies.

8. Many kinds of technological assistance, from technical assistance on

internal problems to help in obtaining federal research and development projects.

9. Contracting "with other Federal Departments and agencies to supply their goods, services, and construction needs and then subcontract[ing] the actual performance of the work to small business concerns which are owned and controlled by socially or economically disadvantaged persons."*

MANAGEMENT ASSISTANCE The SBA provides a number of services that are designed to help solve small-business owners' management problems:

1. Individual counseling by the SBA's Management Assistance staff.

2. The Small Business Institute (SBI). Perhaps you have an SBI program at your school. Several hundred of the leading business schools participate in this important program, which prepares more than 6,000 consulting reports each year. The SBI, using college seniors or graduate students, provides confidential and professional management assistance to small businesses under the supervision of business professors. There is no charge to the small business. It is a program where both the students and the small business benefit: the students receive an opportunity to put their classroom knowledge and skills to work, while the business receives the kind of quality consulting services it might not otherwise be able to afford.

After an initial meeting, students and the owner(s) agree upon specific needs and services and begin work doing such activities as marketing surveys, feasibility studies, or cash-flow analyses. Upon completion, students make recommendations to the client firm that it may accept, reject, or modify. The client also will receive a written report. If your school has an SBI program, why not see how you can participate? Thousands of students have found the SBI program to be a particularly worthwhile and satisfying experience, and it has taught many students the skills they need to open their own small business.

3. The Service Corps of Retired Executives/Active Corps of Executives (SCORE/ACE). Under these programs, volunteer retired executives visit a small firm on request, to study its problems and to recommend solutions.

4. Small Business Development Center (SBDC). A rapidly growing program of small-business assistance is the SBDC, which provides management and technical assistance, business information and statistical data, entrepreneurial-skills training, and access to existing sources of government assistance for small businesses located within the service area. It is a center for accessing community resources and is staffed by professionals who can help the client determine the most appropriate type of help.

5. Conferences, workshops, clinics, courses, and publications to help small-business owners upgrade their general management know-how.

MINORITY SMALL BUSINESSES Special help is available to members of socially or economically disadvantaged minority groups who want to own and operate small businesses. This help is extended to women as well as to those groups named earlier. The numerous programs that exist are coordinated by field representatives in regional offices and in numerous district offices.

The future of the SBA

Small business is a very significant contributor to our nation's economy. More than 30 percent of the U.S. labor force is employed in small business, and this percentage is rising. Growth areas such as financial services, construction, wholesale trade, and retail trade are dominated by small business. This dominance is particularly strong in service industries, which employ almost a million more people than the manufacturing sector (which has traditionally been dominated by big business).

The SBA has contributed to this growth through management assistance, financial support, and creation of business opportunities, a contribution that is expected to increase in future years.

SUMMARY

This concludes the six-part section "Small Business Perspectives." We hope that it has given you some special insights into the problems and opportunities of starting your own small business. Despite the difficulties, most small-business owners find that their business gives them a unique satisfaction not attainable from working for someone else. Perhaps your own business will give you this satisfaction also—not too far into the future.

*Small Business Administration, "SBA: What it Does," Publication OPI-6, p. 13.

CAREERS IN MANAGEMENT

Title	Job description	Requirements	Salary* and advancement prospects	Outlook through 1990	Comments
TWO-YEAR PROGRAM					
Bookkeeper	Maintains financial transactions for organization; computes and mails statements; operates calculating and bookkeeping machines.	Community-college training, plus co-op office experience with bank, retail store, or similar organization. Some accounting courses necessary. Computer courses desirable.	$11,500 to $14,000. Supervisor, assistant manager, night auditor.	Very good	Excellent training for learning about an organization. Advancement limited without four-year degree.
Management trainee	Training position; requires learning many assigned duties. Usually participates in work assignments under close supervision in sales, finance, personnel, production, and similar departments.	Community-college training, plus good potential for growth.	$13,000 to $16,000. Assignment to any department where candidate shows potential.	Excellent	Usually involves substantial investment by employer, so candidates with "good potential" usually chosen.
General clerk	In small company, writes and types bills, statements, and other documents. Answers inquiries; compiles reports.	High-school diploma minimum. Community-college degree desired. General clerical skills required, plus aptitude for office work.	$10,000 to $11,500. Clerk-supervisor.	Good	Good starting point for learning and growing with a solid organization.
Food supervisor	Trains and supervises employees in preparing and serving food in fast-food or institutional enterprises. Oversees sanitary conditions.	Community-college degree plus specialized courses in food management. Experience (part-time, summer, or co-op) necessary.	$10,000 to $13,500. Food and beverage manager; director of food service, restaurant manager.	Excellent	An excellent field for one who will work long and hard in a fast-growth industry.
Travel consultant	Arranges travel and tours for leisure and company business. Sometimes accompanies tours. Extensive telephone communications. Knowledge of flight and train schedules and of tourist areas.	Community-college degree. Best opportunities come through co-op or summer work. Ability to handle detail important.	$11,500 to $13,500. Tourist bureau manager; owner of travel agency.	Good	A good way to combine interest in travel with job. It's not all glamour, however.
Interviewer (employment agency)	Interviews candidates for local employment in clerical jobs.	Community-college degree with good common sense. Ability to screen people and match them with jobs. Must know requirements of jobs to be filled.	$11,000 to $13,000. Personnel manager, employment agency.	Good	Good entry-level position for personnel work in business or government.
Insurance adjuster	Investigates claims for loss or damages filed with insurance companies. Interviews and negotiates with claimants, witnesses, police, physicians, and hospital personnel. Inspects accident areas and property damage.	Community-college degree minimum. Four-year degree desired. Usually requires some travel.	$13,000 to $15,500. Head, claims department; district claims manager.	Fair	No-fault insurance has seriously curtailed this activity in some states.
FOUR-YEAR PROGRAM					
Management analyst	Researches selected projects and assists top executives in improving organizational and management decisions. Analyzes policies and practices, and recommends improvements.	Four-year degree. Willingness to probe deeply into facts and figures to find better solutions to problems. Must be good at detail and report writing.	$16,000 to $21,000. Project leader; head of research; line position in management, production, sales, etc.	Very good	Good place to learn about major units of an organization. Can make good personal contacts.
Manpower planning specialist	Plans an organization's needs in terms of human resources available or required. Knowledge of consumer needs; production capacity; prices, costs, and product development.	Four-year degree. Ability to forecast the future on basis of data found and analyzed. Computer courses desirable.	$16,000 to $20,000. Plant personnel supervisor; labor-relations representative.	Very good	Good entry-level position for personnel work.
Management trainee	Participates in actual work in department such as production, sales, personnel, and engineering, under close supervision. Upon completion of program, enters any of above departments in line job.	Four-year degree. Must have good management potential, as employer spends large amount of money on training program. Computer courses desirable.	$15,000 to $20,000. Supervisor of small departments in personnel, data processing, production, etc.	Very good	Excellent way to start in large organization. Trainee has opportunity to see many career options before making a commitment.

*Represents starting salary range

Title	Job description	Requirements	Salary* and advancement prospects	Outlook through 1990	Comments
Manufacturing supervisor (production foreman)	Responsible for or assists with operations within the manufacturing and assembly divisions of a company. Duties include cost control, reporting systems, meeting production schedules and work standards, etc.	Four-year degree plus summer work experience in manufacturing. Practical work experience, plus ability to handle people, are essential.	$16,000 to $21,000. General supervisor (general foreman); plant supervisor (plant foreman).	Excellent	One of the best starting points for a career in manufacturing. Shortage of good people in this field. Leadership ability required.
Personnel representative	Hiring and processing hourly-rated and salaried personnel. Experience gained in recruiting, placement, salary administration, job analysis, and employee counseling and training.	Four-year degree. Knowledge of many jobs and their requirements. Ability to deal with people. Part-time or summer work experience invaluable.	$15,000 to $18,500. Supervisor of employment, salary administration, employee benefits, and safety.	Good	Key job for getting a start on career in personnel or labor relations.
Traffic manager	Plans, develops and administers passenger and freight traffic programs. Analyzes tariffs, rates, regulatory requirements, and transportation needs and practices. Negotiates rates, routes, etc.	Four-year degree. Special courses in transportation desirable. Work experience with common carrier desirable.	$18,000 to $22,000. District manager.	Excellent	Good opportunities for aggressive, entrepreneurial individuals.
Food supervisor	Supervises employees and operations of large food organization. Determines menus, food preparation, and distribution in college, business, or government cafeteria, large restaurant, or hospital.	Four-year degree with specialty in food management. Evidence of supervisory ability necessary.	$15,000 to $17,000. Food director; dormitory manager; restaurant manager.	Excellent	Fast-growing business lacking in college-trained personnel. Good potential for self-employment later.

MBA PROGRAM

Title	Job description	Requirements	Salary* and advancement prospects	Outlook through 1990	Comments
Financial analyst	Conducts statistical analyses and interprets data on investments, yield, stability, and future trends. Performs analyses of financial institutions, such as banks, savings and loan companies, and brokerage houses.	Four-year degree in management or accounting, with MBA in management. Internship or experience with financial house desirable.	$27,500 to $30,000. Manager or partner in investment company.	Excellent	Dealing with "big money" opens doors for great potential development.
Operations research analyst	May be assigned to work as an individual or part of a project team to simulate manufacturing operations, provide market and production analyses and forecasts, and develop energy-crisis and fuel information.	Four-year degree in management or general business with MBA in management. Experience with computer desirable. Ability to compile reports a necessity.	$28,500 to $32,000. Head, operations research; director of management; director of operations.	Excellent	Forecasting is becoming increasingly important and complicated. Sharp people with MBA in management have a great future.
Personnel administrator	Plans and carries out all policies pertaining to personnel activities in small organization. Handles workman's compensation, employee benefits, salaries and wages, labor negotiations, training, and records.	Four-year degree in management or personnel, with minor in labor relations. MBA in management, with two years' experience in personnel administration.	$22,000 to $24,000. Manager, director, or vice president of personnel	Very good	Work experience in as many fields as possible (while attending school) is very good training for personnel work.
Manager (hotel)	Supervises personnel and manages one or several hotel operations. Formulates policy on advertising, operations, services, and maintenance of facilities. Coordinates services such as banquets, catering, and restaurant.	Four-year degree in management, plus experience in managing housing and food-service units. MBA good for executive management opportunities.	$16,000 to $17,500. Regional director; national director; or vice president.	Excellent	With Americans becoming highly mobile, this industry has great growth potential.
Industrial relations analyst	Serves as specialist in labor relations, preparing data for management to use in negotiations. Interprets labor contracts and recommends changes. Determines costs of options under consideration for labor contract.	Four-year degree in management or labor relations plus MBA in management or labor relations.	$23,000 to $27,500. Labor relations negotiator; manager, labor relations	Very good	Labor relations become more complex with each year that passes. The need for greater expertise in this field is unlimited.

*Represents starting salary range

CAREERS IN MARKETING

Title	Job description	Requirements	Salary* and advancement prospects	Outlook through 1990	Comments
TWO-YEAR PROGRAM					
Media specialist	Keeps records of clients' advertising for ad agency and computes costs. Records media used. Determines cost of advertising space in competing areas, factoring in size and population of city, space rates, and frequency of publication.	Two-year associate degree in marketing minimum. Part-time or summer work experience in newspaper, radio, or TV.	$11,000 to $13,000. Account representative.	Fair	Highly competitive career path, with outstanding financial rewards for those who make it.
Assistant buyer—retailing	With buyer, selects and orders merchandise from showings of manufacturing representatives for resale. Checks invoices and return of merchandise, and authorizes payment for merchandise. Sets prices for merchandise.	Two-year associate degree in marketing, plus co-op or part-time experience in retail store.	$11,000 to $12,500. Buyer.	Very good	Good base for future career in retailing.
Sales manager trainee	Trainee for supervision of retailing department. Displays, advertises, and sells items such as furniture, clothing, and hardware. Maintains inventory control and requisitions merchandise as needed.	Two-year associate degree desirable, plus ability to supervise part-time and full-time employees.	$11,000 to $12,500. Department manager to store manager.	Very good	With larger chain organizations, willingness to make frequent geographic moves is necessary for continued success.
Travel agency representative	Arranges travel and tours for leisure and company business; coordinates and sometimes accompanies tours. Extensive telephone communication.	Two-year associate degree desirable.	$10,000 to $12,000. Tourist bureau manager or owner of travel agency.	Very good	A good way to combine interest in travel with job. It's not all glamour, however.
Sales—real estate	Lists, sells, and sometimes rents property. Solicits property listings and sells to clients. Draws up contracts such as deeds or leases, and negotiates selling price, loans, and mortgages.	Two-year associate degree in marketing, plus aggressive and persistent personality.	Commission. Sales manager or broker.	Very good	Requires great tenacity. Those who are successful do very well financially. Supplemental real-estate courses helpful.
Sales—insurance	Sells insurance to new and present clients, recommending amount and type of coverage. Develops contact lists and explains features of policies based on needs of client.	Two-year associate degree, preferably in marketing, plus desire to succeed in nontangible sales (considered by many to be difficult).	Commission (or salary plus commission for training program). Sales manager to agency manager.	Very good	Professional life insurance salesperson should get a C.L.U. (Certified Life Insurance Underwriter) certificate.
Sales—automotive	Promotes sales of motor vehicles, tires, and parts; uses advertising, sales, and promotion techniques in advising dealers about increasing sales volume. Analyzes dealers' records to help improve sales records.	Two-year associate degree in marketing, plus dynamic personality and interest in motor vehicles. Considerable travel involved.	$12,000 to $16,000. Usually starts with smaller dealers, and advances to working larger accounts.	Good	Additional courses and knowledge in accounting, marketing, and advertising helpful.
Traffic agent	Sells tickets, i.e., air, railroad, bus; supervises cargo handling. Handles customer complaints.	Two-year Associate degree.	$11,500 to $13,000. Traffic manager.	Good	Good starting position for career in transportation.
FOUR-YEAR PROGRAM					
Market researcher —interviewer —editor —statistician —analyst	Performs one or several of the following duties: secures information from consumers; writes and proofreads survey material; analyzes and interprets data; collects secondary data for compilation of final report on project.	Four-year college degree, with emphasis on marketing, math, or advertising. Computer courses desirable.	$17,000 to $19,000. Field supervisor; project supervisor.	Good	Mathematical aptitude helpful.
Salesperson—retailing trainee	Sells apparel, appliances, cosmetics, tools, etc. Answers questions pertaining to goods for sale. Arranges displays. May coordinate advertising and inventory control. Resolves customer complaints.	Four-year college degree in marketing or merchandising desired.	$13,500 to $16,500. Department manager.	Excellent	Excellent training ground for management, buyer position. Must be self-starter.

*Represents starting salary range

Title	Job description	Requirements	Salary* and advancement prospects	Outlook through 1990	Comments
Salesperson —computer —food products —pharmaceutical —petroleum —chemicals	Sells appliances, computers, clothing, etc. to individuals, businesses, or government agencies. Demonstrates items, and prepares estimates, credit terms, and trade-in. May collect payments.	Four-year college degree in marketing desirable. Specialist training in product line necessary and usually available in training program.	$15,000 to $23,000 (commission sometimes part of total income). District sales manager.	Excellent	Aggressive, highly motivated, and "self-starting" persons usually do well in this field.
Salesperson —securities	Provides clients with information on stocks, bonds, and market conditions; history and prospects of corporations. Transmits buy and sell orders to trading division as customers wish. Develops portfolios for clients.	Four-year college degree in marketing preferred. Strong academic background in economics helpful. Lengthy training required.	$15,000 to $19,000. Manager, partner.	Excellent	Unlimited opportunities for persistent, personable, knowledgeable person. Must have good numerical ability.
Public relations	Produces publicity or information services for organizations through the media, such as radio, TV, etc. Writes new releases and scripts and takes ad photos. Participates in community and civic programs.	Four-year college degree in marketing. Ability to communicate via the written and spoken word essential. Outgoing personality.	$14,000 to $16,000. Supervisor, manager, or director of public relations, depending on size of firm.	Fair	Entry-level jobs difficult to find in this field. Best access is through utilization of writing or verbal skills.
Media analyst	Keeps records for clients on media, computing cost of space used and ad program. Determines costs of various media, factoring in size and population of city, space rates, and kind and frequency of publication.	Four-year college degree in marketing. Supplemental courses in advertising and computer desirable.	$14,000 to $16,000. Account executive.	Fair	Job involves routine work in early stages, but is one of best ways to enter this field. Highly competitive.
Methods analyst	Develops new systems for effectively applying electronic equipment to existing office procedures. Investigates work done, size of staff, working conditions, etc. Recommends changes based on investigation.	Four-year college degree in marketing or advertising.	$17,000 to $20,000. Account executive.	Fair	Very difficult area to break into due to supply/demand ratio. Excellent potential for big income.
Account executive trainee	In ad agency, the account executive represents the agency to the client; within the agency, he or she is the client's representative. Must have excellent selling abilities; must know client's business and market.	Four-year college degree in marketing or advertising	$17,000 to $20,000. Account executive.	Fair	Very difficult area to break into due to supply/demand ratio. Excellent potential for big income.

MBA PROGRAM

Title	Job description	Requirements	Salary* and advancement prospects	Outlook through 1990	Comments
Technical sales	Sells highly technical equipment such as generators, computers, jet engines, turbines, structural materials, etc. to customers, usually involving high-dollar volume.	MBA in marketing, with engineering undergraduate degree.	$26,500 to $30,000. Sales manager.	Excellent	A combination of non-technical (sales) and technical (engineering) abilities required.
Traffic manager	Supervises shipments of cargo and passengers; establishes schedules and coordinates all activities associated with scheduling, movement of cargo and passengers; supervises traffic agents and clerks.	MBA desired, specializing in marketing or transportation.	$25,500 to $29,000. Director or vice president of traffic.	Excellent	There is a shortage of highly qualified personnel in this field; it will experience rapid change in near future.
Assistant advertising manager	Under the direction of the manager, may work in any or all of the following: 1. Research 2. Production 3. Writing 4. Layout supervision 5. Media sales	MBA specializing in marketing or advertising.	$24,000 to $27,000. Advertising manager.	Good	Competition keen for most jobs. Great potential for those who can make it.
Assistant marketing manager	Under the direction of the manager, supervises all phases of the marketing of a product, from its conception to market design to advertising to sales.	MBA specializing in marketing. Must know how to use computer as a tool.	$25,000 to $27,000. Marketing manager.	Very good	Statistical and analytical aptitude beneficial.

*Represents starting salary range

Title	Job description	Requirements	Salary* and advancement prospects	Outlook through 1990	Comments
TWO-YEAR PROGRAM					
Insurance (claims adjuster)	Investigates claims for loss or damages filed with insurance companies. Interviews parties involved. Inspects accident areas and property damaged; negotiates settlements; attends legal hearings.	Community-college degree minimum. Four-year degree desired. Usually requires some travel.	$14,000 to $16,000. Head, claims department; district claims manager.	Good	No-fault insurance has seriously curtailed this activity in some states.
General clerk	In small company, writes and types bills, statements, etc. Answers inquiries; compiles reports. May supervise part-time employees. Handles clerical responsibilities for office.	High-school diploma minimum. Community-college degree desired. General clerical skills required, plus aptitude for office work.	$9,500 to $11,500. Clerk-supervisor.	Good	Entry into government; good starting point for learning and growing in a stable occupation.
Junior auditor (county government)	Under county auditor, records deeds and similar legal instruments, keeps record of county accounts, compiles and transfers fiscal records as directed, prepares financial statements.	Minimum of two-year associate degree in finance or accounting.	$12,000 to $13,500. Auditor.	Very good	Responsibilities vary greatly, depending on size of government office.
Credit authorizer	Authorizes credit charges against customer accounts. Verifies or denies credit requests. Prepares credit cards or charge-account plates.	Two-year associate degree in finance or accounting.	$10,500 to $12,000. Credit supervisor.	Very good	
Bank clerk	May: 1. Sort checks, etc. 2. Post and process accounts 3. Keep interest files 4. Handle mortgages; maintain tax records and insurance on customers' property	Two-year associate degree in finance or accounting	$11,000 to $13,000. Various bank supervisory positions, usually in loans, mortgages, personnel, etc.	Very good	Good entry-level position for career in banking.
Loan counselor	Analyzes loan contracts and attempts to obtain overdue installments; receives and records payments; prepares reports on delinquent accounts; answers loan inquiries. May represent employer in legal proceedings.	Two-year associate degree minimum, specializing in finance or accounting.	$12,000 to $18,000. Branch manager.	Very good	
Bank teller	Cashes customer checks; handles deposits and withdrawals; receives and issues receipts; issues and collects cash, checks, and other notes.	Two-year associate degree in finance or accounting. Courses in banking helpful.	$11,000 to $13,500. Chief teller.	Very good	Ability to handle precise, detailed work necessary.
Securities salesperson	Contacts client for purchase and sale of securities; executes orders for clients; furnishes information on investments to clients; encourages sales.	Minimum of associate degree. Additional courses in banking, finance, and economics helpful.	$12,000 to $18,000 (commission sales common). Branch manager.	Good	Licensing by state required.
FOUR-YEAR PROGRAM					
Finance specialist (credit)	Analyzes credit data to estimate degree of risk involved in extending credit or lending money to individuals or firms; visits firms to determine condition of facilities; prepares reports and suggests credit limitations.	Four-year college degree in finance or accounting. Internship desirable.	$16,000 to $19,000. Manager, credit department.	Excellent	High grade-point average helpful.
Senior credit analyst	Analyzes financial data, provides credit information on customers; transcribes balance sheets into reports. Writes credit reports on customers, providing information on operating, depository, and borrowing figures, etc.	Four-year college degree with major in finance or accounting. Internship in accounting is desirable.	$16,000 to $19,000. Chief credit analyst.	Excellent	High grade-point average helpful.

*Represents starting salary range

Title	Job description	Requirements	Salary* and advancement prospects	Outlook through 1990	Comments
Accountant (public)	Provides a variety of accounting services to clients either as an individual or a member of a firm. Employees with public accounting firms generally seek certified public accountant status while employed.	Four-year college degree in accounting or finance. Computer courses a must.	$18,000 to $23,000. Senior accountant and then to partner.	Excellent	Affords opportunity for highly diversified experience with many organizations. High grade-point average helpful.
Accountant (industrial)	Installs and maintains accounting system. Handles bookkeeping: maintains accounting controls over inventories and purchases. Audits contracts, orders, and vouchers. Prepares tax returns.	Four-year college degree in accounting or finance. Additional courses in computers, taxes, and economics highly desirable.	$17,500 to $22,500. Assistant comptroller.	Excellent	Excellent opportunity for career path to top management in organization.
Credit reporter	Investigates history and credit status of individuals and businesses applying for credit, insurance, and jobs. Contacts trade and credit associations, banks, employers, and personal references to verify data.	Four-year college degree in finance or accounting desired. General business degree sometimes acceptable.	$17,500 to $19,500. Credit manager.	Very good	
Operations research analyst	Conducts logical analyses of management problems and formulates mathematical models of problems for solution by computer. Develops proposals to afford maximum probability of profit in relation to risk.	Four-year college degree in finance, operations research, or computer science (nontechnical)	$24,000 to $28,000. Project leader, operations research.	Excellent	

MBA PROGRAM

Title	Job description	Requirements	Salary* and advancement prospects	Outlook through 1990	Comments
Actuary	Examines problems in health, life, casualty, and social insurance, annuities, and pensions. Determines mortality, accident, sickness, disability, and retirement rates. Constructs probability tables; calculates premiums.	MBA in finance or statistics with undergraduate degree in mathematics or computer science (nontechnical) desired.	$27,500 to $32,000. Manager.	Excellent	Excellent potential for top people.
Financial analyst —computers —sports —retailing —insurance	Analyzes investments program for businesses; interprets data concerning investments, their price, yield, and stability trends. Sets forth current and long-range trends in investment risks and measurable economic influences.	MBA in finance required	$26,000 to $31,000. Director of Investments.	Excellent	Excellent potential for growth.
Stockbroker	Gives data to clients on stocks, bonds, market conditions, history, and prospects of companies or government bonds. Transmits buy and sell orders on stocks and bonds for clients. Develops portfolio of selected investments for client.	MBA in finance desired, but not necessary.	$16,000 to $22,000 (commission sales). Manager, branch office.	Excellent	Must have broker's license for state in which one works.
Commercial loan analyst	Evaluates applications for commercial lines of credit in banking organization. Analyzes customers' financial status, credit, history of payment on other credit, and property evaluation to determine feasibility of making loans.	MBA in finance	$24,000 to $26,500. Mortgage loan officer.	Excellent	

*Represents starting salary range

CAREERS IN COMPUTERS AND DATA PROCESSING

Title	Job description	Requirements	Salary* and advancement prospects	Outlook through 1990	Comments
TWO-YEAR PROGRAM					
Procedures analyst (data processing)	Analyzes requirements for information, evaluates the existing system, and designs new or improved data-processing procedures. Outlines the system and prepares specifications that guide programmer.	Two-year associate degree minimum, with four-year degree in business desired.	$14,000 to $16,000. Team leader; supervisor, data processing.	Excellent	For persons wishing to follow a career path in this field, additional education above the two-year degree is highly recommended.
Programmer (data processing)	Charts the logic of the computer programs specified by the systems analyst. Programmer also codes the logic in the language of the computer, debugs the resulting program, and prepares program documentation.	Minimum of two-year associate degree in data processing or business. Aptitude for math desirable.	$13,000 to $15,000. Systems analyst.	Excellent	Additional education recommended for advancement in data processing career path.
Unit record equipment operator	In a relatively uncomplicated data processing system, may operate the following: 1. Tabulating equipment 2. Sorter 3. Collator 4. Reproducer 5. Accounting machine 6. Keypunching	Two-year associate degree in data processing or business preferred.	$11,000 to $14,000. Supervisor.	Very good	
Computer operator	Beginning level for entry into the computer field. Operates the computer according to relatively uncomplicated operating procedures set forth in the computer-operator instruction manual.	Two-year associate degree in data processing.	$11,000 to $15,000. Programmer.	Excellent	
Forms designer	Designs, drafts, and prepares master copy for new or modified forms and prepares instructions for their use. Records information concerning form origin, function usage, cost, and inventory.	Two-year associate degree in data processing or business desired. Some knowledge of business procedures and systems preferred.	$11,000 to $15,000. Forms analyst or supervisor.	Good	Some sales ability desired, as person in this position must work with clients in designing forms.
Systems analyst	Analyzes business procedures and problems to refine data and convert to a programmable form for processing. Studies data-handling systems to evaluate effectiveness and designs new systems.	Two-year associate degree minimum, with four-year degree in data processing preferred. Part-time work in data processing helpful.	$16,500 to $18,000. Team leader or supervisor.	Excellent	Four-year degree enhances promotion prospects in this field.
Reports analyst trainee	Under supervision, examines and evaluates purpose and content of business reports to develop new reports or improve existing ones. Works as a kind of efficiency expert.	Two-year associate degree minimum, with four-year degree preferred. Good analytical mind required.	$13,000 to $15,000. Report analyst.	Good	Good way to learn a lot about an organization for future career growth. Additional education recommended.
FOUR-YEAR PROGRAM					
Associate systems programmer	Under direction of software supervisor, performs detailed software design, coding, debugging, and start-up on industrial control and monitoring systems; writes compatible process control programs.	Four-year college degree computer science (nontechnical), accounting, math, statistics, or operations research.	$19,000 to $23,000. Systems programmer.	Excellent	Computer-knowledgeable people are much in demand.
Technical writer	Generates use-oriented software documentation. Reviews, proofreads, and coordinates production of documentation, assists writers in running programming examples, and coordinates various service groups.	Four-year college degree in computer science, statistics, or math. Programming experience desirable.	$18,000 to $20,000. Supervisor.	Very good	Opportunities especially good in high-tech organizations.

*Represents starting salary range

582

Title	Job description	Requirements	Salary* and advancement prospects	Outlook through 1990	Comments
Scientific programmer	Develops mathematical methods for use in solving design problems, analyzes mathematical and statistical systems, and develops various computer techniques.	Four-year college degree in computer science, math, or statistics.	$24,000 to $27,000. Senior scientific analyst.	Excellent	Computer-knowledgeable people are much in demand.
Information systems specialist	Helps develop computer systems for corporations. Designs and implements computer systems, working closely with professionals in engineering, construction, finance, and administration areas.	Four-year college degree in computer science, business administration, or engineering.	$23,000 to $28,000. Project leader or supervisor.	Excellent	
Applications analyst	Supports marketing activity. Responsible for software system installations and maintenance, programmer consultation, and liaison between customer and various in-house software groups.	Four-year college degree in business, statistics, data processing, or math.	$20,000 to $25,000. Sales representative or senior analyst.	Excellent	Special courses by company at home office are a usual part of training program.
Programmer	Assignments may include: coding, modification, or maintenance of computer program to meet program/system specifications; correcting program malfunctions; testing and debugging programs to insure correct logic.	Four-year college degree in computer science, statistics, or math. Programming experience helpful. Courses in programming important.	$17,500 to $20,000. Various levels of programmer, and then to supervisor.	Excellent	
Systems analyst	Prepares systems through: system/program flowcharts; code structures and search arguments; file design and report formats, etc. Works on system documentation, file conversion, and parallel testing.	Four-year college degree in computer science preferred. Statistics or math degree may be acceptable.	$19,000 to $24,000. Various levels of systems analyst; then to supervisor.	Excellent	Excellent growth potential.
Computer systems software specialist	Functions as a problem-solver, working with operating systems, compilers, and utility programs. Job includes the installation and maintenance of highly complex software provided by outside sources.	Four-year college degree in computer science, math, statistics, or accounting.	$20,000 to $25,000. Various levels of software specialist; then to supervisor.	Excellent	Excellent growth potential.

MBA PROGRAM

Title	Job description	Requirements	Salary* and advancement prospects	Outlook through 1990	Comments
Applications engineer	Performs general microcomputer applications work, including support of specialized application areas, writing application notes, assisting customers with problems, and doing product planning.	MBA plus electrical engineering or computer science (technical) undergraduate degree, with emphasis on logic/circuit design (hardware).	$25,000 to $32,000. Supervisor of operating unit.	Excellent	MBA highly desirable for future growth in organization.
Product marketing engineer	Responsible for market and account penetration for manufacturer of semiconductor memories and microcomputers. Works with sales and support groups in setting pricing, products, product mix, and timing.	MBA plus undergraduate degree in electrical engineering, computer science (technical), or related field.	$26,000 to $32,500. Supervisor of operating unit.	Excellent	MBA highly desirable for future growth in organization.
Applications analyst (sales)	Provides sales information for marketing. Begins in postsales analyses; is responsible for software installations and maintenance, programmer consultation, and liaison with customer and employer software groups.	MBA plus BS in computer science (technical), math/statistics, or engineering.	$25,000 to $30,000. Branch manager or supervisor of technical unit.	Excellent	MBA highly desirable for future growth in organization.
Computer applications engineer	Formulates mathematical models of systems, and controls analog or hybrid computer system to solve scientific and engineering problems. Prepares reports for staff and articles for publication.	MBA plus undergraduate degree in math, computer science (technical) or electrical engineering with computer courses mandatory.	$27,000 to $35,000. Project leader.	Excellent	High aptitude for solving mathematical, engineering, or science problems necessary.

*Represents starting salary range

CAREERS IN THE FEDERAL GOVERNMENT

Title	Job description	Requirements	Entry level salary* and advancement prospects	Outlook through 1990	Comments
TWO-YEAR PROGRAM					
Worker's compensation specialist	Performs routine clerical responsibilities involving processing of claims for worker's compensation.	Associate degree or high school diploma with two years experience.	$12,367 (GS4 rating) Advancement prospects open; depends on experience and ability.	Good	Those with an associate degree may feel underemployed, but this is a good place to enter this field.
Clerical stenographer	Perform various typing, filing, shorthand, and related clerical duties.	Associate degree in clerical studies. Shorthand or speedwriting skills required. High school diploma with two years experience also acceptable.	$12,367 (GS4 rating) Advancement prospects open.	Very good	Excellent entry-level position for secretarial career.
Junior assistant	Performs various receptionist and clerical duties; assists supervisor in carrying out various assignments.	Associate degree in general studies or two years minimum working experience.	$12,367 (GS4 rating) Advancement prospects open.	Fair	
FOUR-YEAR PROGRAM					
Internal Revenue officer	Handles variety of services including accounting, auditing, public complaints, and routine investigative matters.	All majors acceptable. Opportunities greatest for those with minimum of six hours accounting.	$12,837 (GS5 rating) Advancement prospects open.	Very good	About 950 openings available annually.
Internal Revenue agent	Performs all kinds of investigative and general management functions.	Accounting majors, with best opportunities for those in top $\frac{1}{4}$ of class. Must be willing to travel. Must be in upper 25 percent of class to start at GS7.	$13,837 (GS5 rating) $17,138 (GS7 rating) Advancement prospects open.	Very good	Highly competitive but opportunities for promotion make this a "best bet" for accounting graduates. About 750 jobs open each year.
Personnel specialist	Handles various phases of personnel, including classification, salary analyses, interviewing, benefits, recruiting, and research.	All majors, preferably with degree in personnel or labor relations. Employment experience with hourly-rated or clerical employees helpful for entry-level position.	$13,837 (GS5 rating) Advancement prospects open.	Fair	Stable field with substantial competition for the 300 jobs that become available annually.
Social insurance administrator	Handles all facets of social insurance administration.	All majors, with accounting, management, personnel, and general business having edge.	$13,837 (GS5 rating) Advancement prospects open.	Field has stabilized after recent expansion.	Positions available nationwide. Especially good for those seeking long-range careers in Social Security.
Accountant (Auditor)	Provides a variety of accounting services to various agencies of government. May audit contracts, orders, and vouchers.	Four-year college degree in accounting. Internship in public, industrial or government accounting highly desirable. Must be in top of class to rate GS7.	$13,837 (GS5 rating) $17,138 (GS7 rating) Advancement prospects open.	Very good	Competition is keen. Excellent starting point for long-range career in government. Apply well in advance of graduation date. Average annual openings number 450.
Claims examiner	Handles claims for such agencies as Social Security Administration and Veterans Administration.	Four-year college degree desired. Any major acceptable. Must be able to relate well to people.	$13,837 (GS5 rating) Advancement prospects open.	Very good	Highly competitive. Apply well in advance of graduation date. Average annual openings number 1,260.
Economist	Performs various economic analyses of projects in labor, agriculture, industry econometrics, material resources, finance, and transportation.	Four-year degree in economics; advisable to consider advanced degrees for best long-range career opportunities.	$13,837 (GS5 rating) Advancement prospects open.	Good	Most jobs in Washington, D.C., though some are available nationwide. Highly competitive. Average annual openings number 450.

*Represents starting salary effective January 1, 1984. Check local Post Office for latest starting salaries.

Title	Job description	Requirements	Salary* and advancement prospects	Outlook through 1990	Comments
Financial institution examiner	Makes periodic fiscal examination of financial institution records to insure compliance with government regulations.	Accounting, management, or business-related majors acceptable. Minimum of twelve credits in accounting and willingness to travel. Major employers would be Federal Home Loan Bank Board and Federal Deposit Insurance Corporation.	$13,837 (GS5 rating) Advancement prospects open.	Good	Average annual openings number 300.

MBA PROGRAM

Title	Job description	Requirements	Salary* and advancement prospects	Outlook through 1990	Comments
Accountant	Classifies and evaluates financial data, records transactions in financial records, develops and installs new accounting systems, and prepares and analyzes financial statements, records, and reports.	MBA in accounting; four-year degree in accounting with experience or CPA.	$20,965 (GS9 rating) Advancement prospects open.	Very good	Excellent potential for those with proper credentials for career in government. Excellent experience for later entry into business.
Budget analyst	Analyzes relative costs and benefits of alternate courses of budget and program action, checks the propriety of obligations and expenditures, establishes standard rates and charges to customers of industrially funded activities.	MBA in business administration, economics, accounting, or related degree field. Undergraduate degree should be in accounting or finance.	$20,965 (GS9 rating) Advancement prospects open.	Good	Excellent potential for those with proper credentials for career in government. Excellent experience for later entry into business.
Examiner —savings and loan —farm credit —investment company	Makes examinations and audits of savings and loan associations, cooperative banks, investment institutions, national banks, and other financial organizations to determine financial soundness, compliance with regulatory laws and provisions, and integrity of accounts.	MBA in business administration, economics, accounting, or related degree field. Undergraduate degree should be in accounting or finance.	$20,965 (GS9 rating) Advancement prospects open.	Good	Excellent potential for those with proper credentials for career in government. Excellent experience for later entry into business.
Management analyst	Provides advice and service to management in such areas as planning, policy development, work methods and procedures, work force utilization, organizational structures, distribution of assignments, and delegation of authority, with the objective of improving managerial effectiveness.	MBA in business administration or management science.	$20,965 (GS9 rating) Advancement prospects open.	Very good	Excellent potential for those with proper credentials for career in government. Excellent experience for later entry into business.
Logistics management specialist	Performs staff work in planning and coordinating logistical support activities to provide the money, labor, material, facilities, and services needed to support a specific mission.	MBA in materials and logistics management or related degree field.	$20,965 (GS9 rating) Advancement prospects open.	Very good	Excellent potential for those with proper credentials for career in government. Excellent experience for later entry into business.
Financial analyst	Performs analytical and evaluative studies to determine the accuracy and adequacy of security filings in reflecting soundness of corporate organization. Evaluates the soundness of loans, grants, or other provisions of capital or credit.	MBA in finance, business administration, economics, or accounting.	$20,965 (GS9 rating) Advancement prospects open.	Very good	Excellent potential for those with proper credentials for career in government. Excellent experience for later entry into business.
Realty specialist	Advises, plans, directs, or performs such duties as acquiring real property by purchase, lease, or exchange; manages real property and disposes of real property for sale, lease, grant, or exchange.	MBA in business administration or management science, plus knowledge of real estate principles, practices, and markets.	$20,965 starting salary (GS9 rating) Advancement prospects open.	Good	Excellent potential for those with proper credentials for career in government. Excellent experience for later entry into business.

*Represents starting salary effective January 1, 1984. Check local Post Office for latest starting salaries.

APPENDIX II
RESEARCH, STATISTICAL ANALYSIS, AND REPORTS

Marketers use sophisticated information-gathering methods and interpretation techniques to get a clear view of the size of the market; production, marketing, and distribution costs; and many other factors. Without such research, manufacturers might make some very costly errors. They might even bring out a new product for which there is no demand.

In this appendix we'll take a look at some of the basic techniques marketers use in their research, and we'll discuss some of the mathematical tools they use to interpret their data.

STATISTICS: THE BASIC TOOL OF RESEARCH

A **statistic** is *an item of factual information expressed as a number.* Statistics are often expressed as *percentages:* an inflation rate of 17 percent, for instance. Examples of statistics include the batting averages of ballplayers, the number of highway deaths in a year, and the number of ice-cream cones eaten in August. All these numbers are **data**—*factual information presented in statistical form.*

Statistics describes more than just items of numerical information. It is a mathematical discipline concerned with *methods of collecting, analyzing, interpreting, and presenting numerical information.* Statistics is a theoretical field, but it has many practical applications—in sports, government, health care, and many other areas besides business. Business managers use statistics to increase or create markets, improve efficiency, maintain standards, and so on.

In the sections that follow, we'll survey some of the statistical approaches managers use most frequently. First we'll look at methods of doing research—that is, methods of obtaining basic information about the questions under study. And then we'll look at mathematical techniques used to summarize, analyze, and interpret this information.

BASIC RESEARCH METHODS: WHAT ARE THE MAJOR SOURCES OF DATA?

There are two main ways to classify the information that managers need for decision making. One way is to group data according to the places where they can be located. The other, more common method is to classify information according to the reason it was gathered.

DATA GROUPED BY LOCATION

Data grouped according to location can be either internal data or external data. **Internal data** include *information that is available in the records of the company's own invoices, purchase orders, personnel files, and the like.* **External data** comprise *information obtained from sources outside the records of the business itself.* These sources may include government agencies—say, the Census Bureau—and nongovernment sources such as trade associations and trade periodicals.

DATA GROUPED BY PURPOSE

Data grouped by purpose can be either primary or secondary. **Primary data** consist of *information gathered for the study of a specific problem.* **Secondary data** consist of *information previously produced or collected for a purpose other than that of the moment.* The government and trade organizations are the major sources of secondary data.

Businesspeople usually examine secondary data first, because they often have three advantages over primary data:

1. *Speed.* Secondary-data sources, such as *A Guide to Consumer Markets,* put out by The Conference Board, provide information at a moment's notice.
2. *Cost.* Collecting primary data can be an expensive process. For the cost of a membership in an organization, a business can have the results of all the group's research at its disposal.
3. *Availability.* The owner of a business can hardly expect the owner of a competing firm to make information available. Trade associations and the government, on the other hand, collect information from all firms and make it available to everyone.

Secondary data do have some drawbacks, however. The information may be out of date—or it may not be as relevant as it first seems. And it may be that the company or agency that collected the data may not be as impartial as it should be. Furthermore, the source may lack expertise: the survey may not be broad enough to cover the targeted geographic area or income group, or questions may be phrased in such a way that the respondents can guess the "correct answers," that is, what the researcher wants to hear.

HOW RESEARCHERS OBTAIN PRIMARY DATA

There are several techniques for gathering primary data, and they all involve original research. Let's take a look at some of these methods, which both small businesses and multinational corporations use to find answers to their problems.

SAMPLING

A **sample** is *a small part of a large group—of people or other items.* (In statistical language, *the group from which a sample is drawn* is known as a **population** or **universe.**) Researchers can use data from a properly selected small sample to draw conclusions or make forecasts about the population from which the sample was drawn. For instance, if 10 out of 100 people sampled by the Inquire Corporation—a research organization—on Monday night are watching a specific program, then it is probably safe to assume that 10 percent of the whole TV-watching population in that geographical area is watching that program, provided that the sample was selected to represent the population fairly.

The most common method of selecting a sample is **random sampling.** *A group of items or individuals is chosen from a larger group in a way that gives all items or persons in the group an equal chance of being selected.* Simple methods of random selection include drawing names from a hat, taking every tenth name from a list, and so on.

Sampling is useful in a number of business situations. If, for instance, a college bookstore in an urban area has ordered 1,000 T-shirts imprinted with the school's name, the T-shirt manufacturer can use sampling to determine whether the men's and women's clothing stores in that city also would like to stock the T-shirts. It is highly impractical for the manufacturer to call the 234 stores that, according to the Yellow Pages, carry this kind of merchandise. Instead, he or she can sample the 234 stores by calling the first 10 men's shops and women's shops listed in the phone book. The 20 stores represent a random sample because they are listed alphabetically—not by size, location, type of customer, or any other factor that might affect their interest in the T-shirts. A good response from those 20 stores would indicate that many of the other 214 stores would be interested in the T-shirts, too.

The major limitation of the sampling method is that the population to be sampled has to be small enough and sufficiently concentrated geographically so that a list of all the names or items it includes is available or can easily be prepared. To draw a sample from all the clothing stores in the United States would be much too large and expensive a task. But other sampling techniques can be used in such instances. It's sufficient for our purposes to note that random sampling is a very effective technique when used in limited populations.

Probability: The principle behind random sampling

Probability is *the likelihood, over the long run, that a certain event will occur in one way rather than in another way.* For example, we know that if we flip a coin, the likelihood of throwing "heads" is $\frac{1}{2}$, or 50 percent—because a coin has only two sides—and the likelihood of throwing "tails" is also 50 percent. In a series of ten tosses, we would expect to throw "heads" about five times. We *could* throw "heads" ten times, but it would be very unlikely.

How does a businessperson use probability in everyday business operations? Suppose the sales manager of a department store finds that out of 1,000 letters from customers, about 50 letters, or 5 percent, are complaints. On any day when 100 letters arrive from customers, then, the sales manager expects that about 5 of them will be complaints. If complaint letters suddenly increase to 20 or 30 percent, he or she might suspect that one, or both, of the following two things has happened: someone has tampered with the customer correspondence file, or something has gone wrong with the store's operations and the customers don't like it. In either case, a sudden shift in probability will put the sales manager on the alert.

OBSERVATION

Observation is *the technique of watching or otherwise monitoring all incidents of the particular sort that the investigator wants to study.* An example of observation is the use of cameras and videotape to study the way in which employees do their work. Another example is the use of a counting mechanism to record the number of cars that drive on a given street (the information would be used, say, by the traffic department).

SURVEY

Businesses often must know *why* employees or potential customers behave the way they do. The simplest way to find out is to ask them, and that's where surveys come in. The investigator may use a **questionnaire,** or *list of questions,* either mailing it to the **respondents** (*the people who are answering the questions)* or getting their answers via face-to-face or telephone interviews. Respondents may be questioned once or a number of times.

EXPERIMENT

In an **experiment** the investigator tries to *find out how one set of conditions will affect another set of conditions by setting up a situation in which all factors and events involved can be carefully measured.* An experiment differs from ordinary observation in that the experimenter can deliberately make changes in the situation to see what effect each change has. *A changeable factor in a situation (or in an experiment)* is called a **variable.** Experiments are often conducted in laboratories, where variables can be easily controlled. For example, a scientist studying the effects of crowding on mice could, in the laboratory, control the size of the cages, the number of mice in each cage, and so on. But some experiments, like the one

described in the next paragraph, can be performed in an ordinary social setting.

An experimenter usually tries to observe two separate but similar groups. One group is exposed to a specific variable and the other is not. (*The group that is not exposed to the variable is called the* **control group.**) To find out whether students do better on tests if they are allowed to get up and stretch, for example, a professor might allow students in one group to go out in the corridor one by one during tests but require the control group to remain seated at all times. At the end of the term, the professor could compare the test scores of the two groups of students. If the group allowed to leave the room does better, the relaxed testing environment (the variable) might be considered helpful to students. But if the control group did better or if the two groups did equally well the easygoing approach would not be considered advantageous.

ANALYZING DATA: KEY NUMBERS TO WATCH

Suppose you have obtained a body of numerical data through one of the methods we have just described. As you go about the task of analyzing this data, what types of numerical information might you look for—or develop—that would be particularly useful to you? We'll look at some answers to this question in the section that follows.

AVERAGES

One way to take data and present it in an easily understood way is to find the average. The **average** is *a number typical of a group of numbers or quantities.* For example, a personnel manager may want to know the average wage of workers in each labor classification in order to present the officers of the corporation with a forecast of future labor costs when a new union contract is negotiated. Or a marketing manager may want to know the average age of potential consumers of a new product in order to slant advertising toward that age group. The most widely used averages are the mean, the median, and the mode.

THE MEAN

The statistic most often thought of as an average is the **mean,** *the sum of all the items in a group, divided by the number of items in the group.* The mean is invaluable when comparing one item or individual with a group. For example, if a sales manager wants to compare the performance of his salespeople during a certain week, the mean would give a simple figure for comparison.

To find the mean, the manager first lists the members of his sales staff together with their sales for the week:

Salesperson	Sales	
Wilson	$ 3,000	
Green	5,000	
Carrick	6,000	
Wimper	7,000	*Mean*
Keeble	7,500	*Median*
Kemble	8,500	
O'Toole	8,500	*Mode*
Mannix	8,500	
Caruso	9,000	
Total	$63,000	

Then he divides the total sales by the number of salespeople so that the mean is

$$\frac{\$63,000}{9} = \$7,000 \text{ in sales}$$

The advantages of the mean are ease of comprehension and speed of computation. One disadvantage of the mean, however, is that it gives a distorted picture when there is an extreme value. For instance, in the above example, if Caruso's sales for the week were $27,000, the mean for the nine salespeople would be $9,000 ($81,000 divided by 9), clearly not a helpful statistic, as eight of the nine salespeople would have sold less than the mean. Obviously, additional methods of summarizing data are necessary.

THE MEDIAN

When items or numbers are arranged from lowest to highest, the **median** *is the midpoint, or point at which half the* numbers are above, half below. If the number of items is odd, the figure can be arrived at by inspection. In the above example, the median is $7,500. There are four figures above it and four below. If there is an even number of items—say, ten salespeople instead of nine—the midpoint would be the mean of the two central figures.

The median is easy to find, and it is a great time saver when items that are difficult to measure can be arranged in order of size. It also avoids the distortion caused by extreme values and is thus more typical of the data. In the study of salespeople's performances, if Caruso's sales were $27,000 instead of $9,000, the median would not be affected.

The chief disadvantage of the median is that many people do not understand what it means. Moreover, it can sometimes be cumbersome to arrange items in order of size when there are many of them.

In business, however, the median is a useful measure, especially when management needs an average that is not affected by inclusion of extremely large producers or spenders in a given category. For example, if it is necessary to know the average amount spent on advertising by retail grocers, the figure used would probably be the median; the amounts spent by the big chains would not distort the average.

THE MODE

The **mode** is *the number that occurs most often in any series of data or observations.* The mode answers the question: "How frequently?" or "What is the usual size or amount?" In the sales manager's study above, the most frequently recorded amount, the mode, is $8,500.

One important use of the mode is to supply marketing people with information about common sizes of shoes and clothing. If you were the owner of a shoe store you would *not* want to stock four pairs of every shoe size in each style. You might find, perhaps, that for every forty pairs of size eight sold, only two of size twelve were sold.

Like the median, the mode is not influenced by extreme values. The mode should not be used, however, when the total number of observations is small or when a large group is subdivided into many small groups. In such cases, a significantly repeated value may not exist. And there *is* no mode if a number does not appear more than once.

INDEX NUMBERS

In business, it is often important to know how the sales or industrial production of one period of time compares with that of another. To conveniently express this comparison, an index number is used. An **index number** is *a percentage usually used to compare such figures as prices or costs at one period of time with those figures at a base or standard period.*

Let us say that an oil company wants to keep an index on the number of workers it employs. It chooses as a base year 1982, when it employed 5,000 workers. In 1983, employment slipped to 4,900 workers. In 1984, it surged ahead to 5,300 workers.

The index numbers for the years 1983 and 1984 are obtained by dividing the base-year figure into the current-year figure and then multiplying by 100 to change the resulting decimal into a percent.

$$\frac{\text{Current-year employment (1983)}}{\text{Base-year employment}} = \frac{4,900}{5,000}$$
$$= 0.98, \text{ or } 98\%$$

$$\frac{\text{Current-year employment (1984)}}{\text{Base-year employment}} = \frac{5,300}{5,000}$$
$$= 1.06, \text{ or } 106\%$$

These figures tell us that employment was off 2 percent in 1983 but up 6 percent in 1984.

One of the best-known index numbers is the Consumer Price Index, used by economists to track inflation. Others include the Dow Jones Industrial Average, which gauges ups and downs in the stock market, the index of Industrial Production, and the Wholesale Price Index.

TIME-SERIES ANALYSIS

Executives must often consider what has caused the changes in their business activity that the statistics indicate. Suppose, for instance, that a department store's monthly index of sales shows an increase of 6 percent for December. Before the sales manager can decide whether to increase the sales force, inventory, and advertising budget, he or she must know what underlies the change. Time-series analysis can help uncover the reasons.

A **time-series** (or **trend**) **analysis** is *the examination of data over a sufficiently long period of time so that regularities and relationships can be detected, interpreted, and used as the basis for forecasts of future business activity.* Such an analysis generally explains change in terms of three factors: seasonal variations, cyclical variations, and secular (or long-term) trends in business growth.

Seasonal variations are *regular annual changes in sales or other items.* For instance, the demand for ice cream is always higher in August than in December. Two other examples are increased store sales before Christmas and the rise in sales of snow tires when the mercury drops.

Business executives can sometimes use their knowledge of seasonal variations to open up new markets in slack seasons. Makers of tea, for example, noticed that tea drinking fell off sharply at the end of winter. But management wanted to maintain a constant labor and sales force; they wanted to neither hire extra workers in peak seasons nor lay off workers in slack periods. So tea manufacturers successfully promoted iced tea to keep sales—and thus production—more evenly distributed throughout the year.

Over a period of several years (often four), the economy goes through a fluctuation known as the **business cycle,** which is a familiar example of medium-term **cyclical variation.** The business cycle begins with **prosperity,** *a period of high income and employment,* in which businesses grow and there is a large amount of construction. Then follows a **recession,** during which *income, employment, and production all fall.* If sufficient corrective measures—usually by government regulation—aren't taken, depression sets in. A **depression** is *a radical drop in business activity with consequent high unemployment and frequent business failures.* Generally, a depression is followed by **recovery,** characterized by *a rise in production, construction, and employment.* The cycle then usually begins again. Government spending, wars, and inflation may temporarily disrupt this pattern, but eventually the cycle's phases are likely to return to normal. A **secular** (or **long-term**) **trend** is *a pattern of growth or decline in a particular business industry, or an* *economy as a whole, over a long period,* usually twenty to thirty years. Secular trends may result from population growth, availability of capital, new inventions and production methods, changes in consumer habits and spending patterns, and so on. One familiar secular trend has been the decline in the demand for rail travel since the development of the automobile and airplane. Another is the upward trend the drug companies have been enjoying because of increased interest in health care. Managers study secular trends to plan for the future, compare their company's growth with that of other firms in the same industry, and set up standards for their own performance.

INTERPRETING DATA: STUDYING CAUSE AND EFFECT

As noted earlier, a changeable factor in a situation (or in an experiment) is called a variable. Sometimes a *relationship, or* **correlation** *exists between two or more variables.* When data show that changes in one variable (for instance, the election of a particular president) appear to be accompanied by changes in another variable (such as the stock market), we may presume that some correlation exists. Each election in this case would be called the **independent variable,** since it is *an event that is controlled by outside factors* (here, by the voters). The health of the stock market would be called the **dependent variable,** because it *changes as the independent variable changes.* Correlations of independent and dependent variables can be positive or negative. The correlation is *negative* if the election seems to trigger a *drop* in stock prices. If stocks go *up,* the correlation is *positive.*

WHAT IS THE SIGNIFICANCE OF A CORRELATION?

Finding a correlation does *not* mean that one can predict or even control future events. A correlation merely shows that two variables change at the same time—*not* that change in one actually causes change in the other. Even though the stock market plunged when a certain man was elected, for instance, there was no evidence that his election *caused* the market to drop.

There's a danger in relying upon an apparent relationship between variables to predict business activity. For example, a large department store noticed that its sales seemed to be positively correlated with the Dow Jones Industrial Average: an increase in the stock price index was regularly followed by a similar increase in the store's sales. After several years, however, the correlation suddenly turned negative; when the price index went up, the store's sales inexplicably went down. Statisticians soon found the reason. The Dow Jones Industrial Average and the store's sales were both dependent variables related to a *third* variable, the state of the economy as a whole. When the economy started to decline, the correlation of the economy with store sales remained strong (both went down). But the economy's correlation with stock prices was weaker and subject to time lags. Stock prices even rose temporarily at certain points during the period of low prosperity. So the store managers realized that watching stock prices would not help them predict how well their business would do; there was no real cause-and-effect relationship between the two.

STATISTICS AND HONESTY

Figures don't lie, as the saying goes. But it's also true that the people who collect and present figures are not always as straightforward as they might be. Statistical findings can sometimes be manipulated or juggled to make them appear in the best possible light. One such tactic is to provide precise, impressive-sounding statistics (called "semiattached figures") that may actually prove very little. For instance, an advertising agency can claim that a half ounce of an antiseptic killed 31,108 germs in a test tube in eleven seconds. But an antiseptic that kills germs in a test tube may not in fact work in the human body. Or there may be so many thousands of germs in a comparable portion of the human anatomy that 31,108 is just a drop in the bucket.

Another juggling technique is the "shifting base." Suppose a store offers $10 Christmas gifts in October and urges customers to buy right away to "save 100 percent." Save 100 percent of what? The store plans to increase the price to $15, so the saving would be 100 percent of the *markup,* not of the present price. The store is not being entirely honest in telling customers what *base* the percentage was figured on.

PRESENTING DATA

Even the most carefully planned and painstakingly prepared statistical research project may be a total waste of time if the information is poorly presented. Written reports that highlight key research results must be clear and easy to follow. And it's often helpful to use tables and graphs. Such visual aids can be crucial in helping managers get a clear picture of the situation.

THE PROPER BUSINESS REPORT FORM

A good business report has six basic parts:

1. The *title* should be a brief description of the report as a whole rather than a catchy headline. The names of the report's authors and the date go under the title.
2. The *introduction* should briefly state the subject of the report, the research techniques that were used, and the nature of the specific problem to be solved.

3. The *conclusions*—the answers to the problem outlined in the introduction—should be presented concisely.
4. *Recommendations*—suggestions on how the company might deal with the problem—should be practical, specific, and derived from the conclusions.
5. The *body of the report* should present data to back up the conclusions and recommendations.
6. *Appendixes* (which contain data not directly related to the problem), *notes* (which give additional information on points made in the body), and *sources* (which tell the reader where the information in the report was obtained) all go at the end of the report.

TABLES AND GRAPHS

A **table** is commonly used to present data when there is a large amount of precise numerical information to convey. (See Figure 1.) A **graph** or **chart** is usually a diagram or picture showing the relationship of one set of data to another. Depending on the data, the needs of the reader, and the kind of impact desired, the data may be presented in at least five different forms: the **line graph** (Figure 2a), the **bar chart** (Figure 2b), the **pictogram** (a variation of the bar chart), the **circle chart** (Figure 2c), and the **statistical map** (Figure 2d).

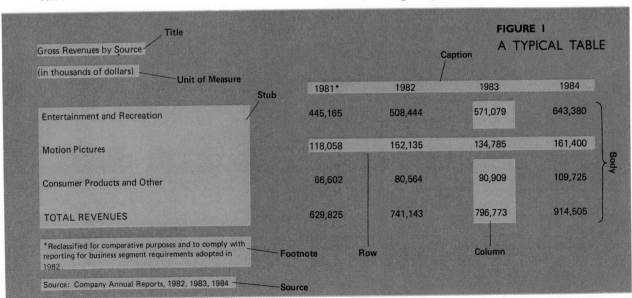

FIGURE 1
A TYPICAL TABLE

Gross Revenues by Source — Title

(in thousands of dollars) — Unit of Measure

	1981*	1982	1983	1984
Entertainment and Recreation	445,165	508,444	571,079	643,380
Motion Pictures	118,058	152,135	134,785	161,400
Consumer Products and Other	66,602	80,564	90,909	109,725
TOTAL REVENUES	629,825	741,143	796,773	914,505

*Reclassified for comparative purposes and to comply with reporting for business segment requirements adopted in 1982. — Footnote

Source: Company Annual Reports, 1982, 1983, 1984 — Source

TYPES OF GRAPHS

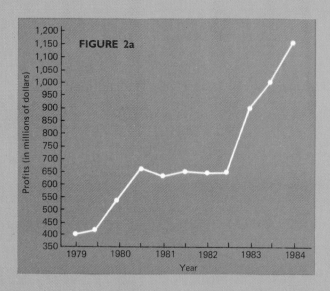

The line graph is a line connecting points. Line graphs clearly show trends, such as an increase in profits.

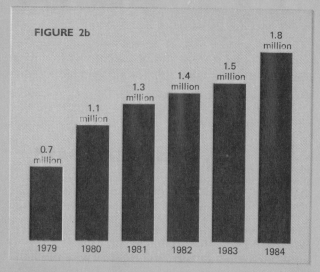

The bar chart uses either vertical or horizontal bars to compare information. Because of its simplicity, the bar chart is often used; it may be made fairly accurate by the use of graph paper.

The pictograph is a variation of the bar chart, in which pictures representing the data are substituted for the bars. Pictographs are good attention-getters, but some accuracy is sacrificed.

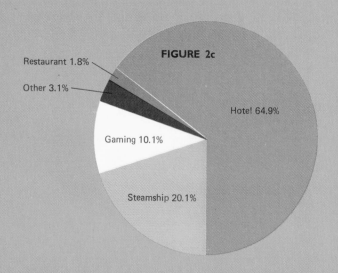

The circle chart, commonly referred·to as a pie chart, often takes the form of a pie divided into slices. The circle shows the relationship of slices as percentages of the whole circle, or 100 percent. A circle chart provides a vivid picture of the relationships shown, but it is not good for very precise data.

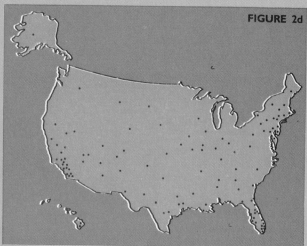

The statistical map shows quantities by variations in color, texture, or shading, or by the concentration of dots. Here each dot represents a specific unit of sales. The heavier the concentration of dots, the greater the sales.

REFERENCES

Part introductions

PART 1: Thomas C. Hayes, "Hard Decisions Ahead for the New Chief of Levi Strauss," *The New York Times*, April 15, 1984. PART 2: "Changing a Corporate Culture: Can Johnson & Johnson Go from Band-Aids to High Tech?" *Business Week*, May 14, 1984, pp. 130 ff. PART 3: Winston Williams, "Personality Change for P. & G." *The New York Times*, March 23, 1984. PART 4: Jeff Blyskal, "Up from Pancakes," *Forbes*, January 30, 1984, pp. 70 ff. PART 5: "How Giant Food Harnesses High Tech to Fatten Supermarket Profits," *Business Week*, December 5, 1983, p. 120. PART 6: Richard Stengel, "Decision: Tape It to the Max," *Time*, January 30, 1984, p. 67; Aric Press and Lucy Howard, "A Blank Tape for Hollywood," *Newsweek*, January 30, 1984, pp. 57 ff.; Aljean Harmetz, "Hollywood Thriving on Video-Cassette Boom," *The New York Times*, May 7, 1984.

Chapter introductions

Component Chapter A: "It Ain't Easy," *Forbes*, November 7, 1983, p. 152. Chapter 5: Tom Nicholson, "GM Plans a Great Divide," *Newsweek*, January 9, 1984, pp. 68 ff. Chapter 6: "How Just-in-Time Inventories Combat Foreign Competition," *Business Week*, May 14, 1984, pp. 176D ff. Chapter 7: Agis Salpukas, "Changing American's Rules," *The New York Times*, April 29, 1984. Component Chapter C: "'Computer People': Yes, They Really Are Different," *Business Week*, February 20, 1984, pp. 66 ff. Chapter 8: Robert Reinhold, "Life in High-Stress Silicon Valley Takes a Toll," *The New York Times*, January 13, 1984. Chapter 9: "To Market, To Market," *Newsweek*, January 9, 1984, p. 70. Chapter 10: Janet Guyon, "General Foods Gets a Winner with Its Jell-O Pudding Pops," *The Wall Street Journal*, March 10, 1983. Chapter 12: Claudia Ricci, "Children's Wear Retailers Brace for Competition from Toys 'R' Us," *The Wall Street Journal*, August 25, 1983. Chapter 13: Kirk Johnson, "Guitars Are Down, but This One's a Star," *The New York Times*, April 29, 1984. Chapter 14: "Robots Are Making a Big Undersea Splash," *Business Week*, March 5, 1984, pp. 90B ff. Chapter 15: "Market Volume (N.Y.S.E.)," *The New York Times*, March 23, 1984; and data from New York Stock Exchange. Component Chapter D: Eric N. Berg, "Crocker's Loan Crisis," *The New York Times*, April 29, 1984. Chapter 16: Paul B. Brown and Steve Kichen, "The Class of 1983: Breaking the Barriers", *Forbes*, November 7, 1983, pp. 168 ff. Chapter 17: *Time*, January 3, 1983.

Chapter 1

1. Pamela Sherrid, "Good News on the Productivity Front," *Forbes*, October 10, 1983, pp. 124 ff. **2.** Ibid. **3.** U.S. Department of Commerce, Bureau of the Census, *Statistical Abstract of the United States, 1982* (Washington, D.C.: Government Printing Office, 1983), p. 528; and General Motors Corp. **4.** *1983 USA Oil Industry Directory* (Tulsa: Penn Woll Publishers, 1983), p. 5; and *Standard & Poor's Industry Surveys*, April 1983, vol. 2, p. M83. **5.** Paul Blustein, "Poisoned Image: Dow Chemical Fights Effect of Public Outcry over Dioxin Pollution," *The Wall Street Journal*, June 28, 1983. **6.** Rachel Carson, *Silent Spring* (Boston: Houghton Mifflin, 1962). **7.** National Academy of Sciences. **8.** "How the EPA Plans to Live with Cancer Risks," *Business Week*, August 8, 1982, pp. 84B ff. **9.** Philip Shabecoff, "Tacoma Gets Choice: Cancer Risk or Lost Jobs," *The New York Times*, July 13, 1983; and Melinda Beck and Richard Sandza, "A Life-and-Death Choice," *Newsweek*, November 21, 1983, pp. 45 ff. **10.** Philip Shabecoff, "E.P.A. to Reverse Easing of Water Rules," *The New York Times*, November 1, 1983. **11.** Michael Posner, "Anatomy of a Missouri Nightmare," *Maclean's*, April 4, 1983, pp. 10 ff. **12.** "All Used Up with No Place to Go," *Business Week*, March 14, 1983, pp. 142F ff. **13.** Ibid. **14.** "Emergency Ruling Set by Job Agency on Asbestos Peril," *The New York Times*, November 3, 1983. **15.** Ibid. **16.** Upton Sinclair, *The Jungle* (New York: New American Library, 1973). **17.** Ralph Nader, *Unsafe at Any Speed; The Designed-In Dangers of the American Automobile* (New York: Grossman, 1965). **18.** Tom Nicholson with Christopher Ma, "Onward, Consumer Soldiers," *Newsweek*, April 25, 1983, p. 56. **19.** "The Exploding Markets for Environmental Audits," *Business Week*, June 6, 1983, pp. 92B ff. **20.** John Diebold, "Management, Circa 1990," *Enterprise*, February 1983, pp. 10 ff. **21.** Sonia L. Nazario, "Insurer Wants to Sell the Grand Ole Opry, Riling Tennesseeans and Country Musicians," *The Wall Street Journal*, April 8, 1983; and Eric N. Berg, "Grand Ole Opry Finds a Buyer," *The New York Times*, July 2, 1983. **22.** "Black-Gold Rush," *Time*, November 29, 1982, p. 63; "A Billion-Barrel Find," *Newsweek*, November 29, 1982, p. 84; Ken Wells, "Stormy Seas: A Major Oil Discovery Off Santa Barbara Riles Town, Sparks Lawsuits," *The Wall Street Journal*, May 4, 1983; and Frederick Golden, "Pouring Oil on Troubled Waters," *Time*, January 30, 1984, p. 81.

Chapter 2

1. "Click! Ma Is Ringing Off," *Time*, November 21, 1983, pp. 60 ff. **2.** Joyce G. Fox, "Some Grocers Think Limited," *Venture*, May 1980, pp. 26 ff. **3.** U.S. Department of Commerce, Bureau of the Census, *Statistical Abstract of the United States, 1982* (Washington, D.C.: Government Printing Office, 1983), p. 528 (hereafter cited as *Stat. Abstract*). **4.** Ibid. **5.** "Partnership Seeks to Fill Void in the Sale of Small Computers," *The New York Times*, March 7, 1983; and Tom Kempf, "ISO PROFILE: Network 1," *ISO World*, April 25, 1983, p. 30. **6.** "The Last Day in the Life," *Time*, December 22, 1980, p. 23. **7.** *Webster's New Collegiate Dictionary* (Chicago: Encyclopaedia Britannica Education Corp., 1970). **8.** *Stat. Abstract*, pp. 528 ff. **9.** Norman Thorpe, "Bitter Contest for Control of World Airways Is Seen as Threat to Ailing Carrier's Survival," *The Wall Street Journal*, July 12, 1983; and "Struggle for Control Pits Officials Against Each Other," *The Wall Street Journal*, June 28, 1983. **10.** Richard L. Hudson, "New SEC Rules Forcing Activist Holders to Alter Strategies in Corporate Contests," *The Wall Street Journal*, September 2, 1983. **11.** Roy Rowan and Thomas Moore, "Behind the Lines at the Bendix War," *Fortune*, October 18, 1982, pp. 156 ff. **12.** Randall Smith, "GAF Proxy Defeat Reflects Revolt by Impatient Institutional Holders," *The Wall Street Journal*, May 12, 1983; and "In Bitter GAF Proxy War, Dissident Gains from Management's Errors," *The Wall Street Jour-

nal, April 28, 1983. **13.** "Basic Problems: Steel Merger Proposal May Signal a Shakeout in Heavy Industries," *The Wall Street Journal,* September 30, 1983. **14.** "Greyhound: A Big Sell-Off Leaves It Built for Better Speed," *Business Week,* July 25, 1983, pp. 88 ff. **15.** "IBM Buys Another Key to the Automated Office," *Business Week,* June 27, 1983, pp. 27 ff. **16.** "High-Tech Companies Team Up in the R&D Race," *Business Week,* August 15, 1983, pp. 94 ff. **17.** Suzanne Daley, "2 Restauranteurs in Chelsea Realize a 24-Table Dream," *The New York Times,* October 3, 1983. **18.** Tim Metz and John D. Williams, "Pickens's Mesa Group, Gulf Wage Stiff Campaign for Proxy Victory," *The Wall Street Journal,* November 23, 1983.

Chapter 3

1. For this idea, we are indebted to Bradley R. Schiller, *The Economy Today,* 2nd ed. (New York: Random House, 1983). **2.** Eric Pace, "Paperbacks: Gloomy Scenario," *The New York Times,* January 13, 1983; and Thomas Weyr, "Rise and Fall of the Blockbuster," *Publishers Weekly,* September 9, 1983, pp. 26 ff. **3.** Ralph E. Winter, "Firms' Recent Productivity Drives May Yield Unusually Strong Gains," *The Wall Street Journal,* June 14, 1983; "$23 Million Program Begins at Mead Plants," *Paper Trade Journal,* September 15, 1983; and "Mead Slates Expansion Outlays of $23 Million," *The Wall Street Journal,* August 11, 1983.

Component Chapter A

1. William Baldwin, "Golden Fleece," *Forbes,* August 1, 1983, pp. 110 ff; "Tultex Net Up 26.4% in 2nd Quarter," *Daily News Record,* July 14, 1983; and "Fitness Binge Boosts Tultex; 12% Gain in Net Seen," *Daily News Record,* August 24, 1982. **2.** Charles P. Alexander, "The New Economy," *Time,* May 30, 1983, pp. 62 ff. **3.** "A Rising Tide of Protectionism," *Newsweek,* May 30, 1983, p. 26. **4.** William Bowen, "How to Regain Our Competitive Edge," *Fortune,* March 9, 1981, p. 74. **5.** The Statistical Office of the United Nations, *The Yearbook of International Trade Statistics 1967*

(New York: United Nations, 1969), pp. 12 ff. **6.** *Readers Digest Almanac and Yearbook 1984* (Pleasantville, N.Y.: Readers Digest, 1984), p. 198. **7.** *Fortune,* July 1957, Supplement "International 500," p. 20. **8.** Jean-Jacques Servan-Schreiber, *The American Challenge* (New York: Atheneum, 1968). **9.** "The International 500", *Fortune,* August 22, 1983, p. 170. **10.** George Thomas Kurian, *The New Book of World Rankings* (New York: Facts on File, 1984), p. 96. **11.** Alexander, "The New Economy," p. 62. **12.** *Ibid.* **13.** "Detroit Falls Far Short in Its Effort to Match Japan's Smaller Autos," *The Wall Street Journal,* November 1, 1983. **14.** Charles P. Alexander, "Roaring Out of the Doldrums," *Time,* November 14, 1983, pp. 82 ff. **15.** Robert H. Hayes and William J. Abernathy, "Managing Our Way to Economic Decline," *Harvard Business Review,* July–August 1980, p. 67. **16.** Robert B. Reich, *The Next American Frontier* (New York: Times Books, 1983). **17.** Alexander, "The New Economy," p. 63. **18.** Lawrence Minard, "Can Europe Catch Up?" *Forbes,* July 4, 1983, pp. 84 ff. **19.** Darby Miller, "Videotex: Science Fiction or Reality?" *Byte,* July 1983, p. 42. **20.** "Phillips' High-Tech Crusade," *Business Week,* July 18, 1983, pp. 152 ff. **21.** "America's Hidden Problem," *Business Week,* August 29, 1983, p. 66. **22.** Barry Bluestone and Bennett Harrison, *The Deindustrialization of America* (New York: Basic Books, 1982). **23.** U.S. Department of Commerce, Bureau of the Census, ST 990, December 1983, p. 64. **24.** "Should Export Controls Be a Political Weapon?" *Business Week,* September 12, 1983, pp. 68 ff. **25.** "U.S.–China Textile Pact," *Dun's Business Month,* September 1983, p. 30. **26.** Opinion Research Corporation, "Issues Facing Business—The Public's Priorities for Action," *Public Opinion Index,* February 1983. **27.** "Chrysler's New Protection Machine," *Fortune,* June 27, 1983, pp. 29 ff. **28.** Herbert Stein, "Don't Fall for Industrial Policy," *Fortune,* November 14, 1983, pp. 64 ff. **29.** Standard & Poor's Industry Surveys, April 1983, p. A15. **30.** Lester C. Thurow, "The Road to Lemon Socialism," *Newsweek,* April 25, 1983, p. 63. **31.** *The New York Times,* March 1, 1984. **32.** *Business America,* February 20, 1984. **33.** "The U.S. Tries to Tame a Rampaging Dollar," *Business Week,* August 15, 1983, pp. 102 ff. **34.** "Dollar Fever Infects the World," *Business Week,* June

27, 1983, pp. 90 ff. **35.** Annual Report of Citibank, 1981. **36.** Geraldine Brooks, "Here's a Trade War That May Stretch Your Imagination," *The Wall Street Journal,* September 9, 1983; and U.S. Department of Commerce, Bureau of the Census, Census of Manufacturers 1982, Preliminary Report Industry Series MC 82-1 (P) Report #30A-5(P) "Fabricated Rubber Products, NEC" #3069 pp. 1 ff. **37.** John R. Emshwiller and Neil Behrmann, "Restored Luster: How De Beers Revived World Diamond Cartel after Zaire's Pullout," *The Wall Street Journal,* July 7, 1983; "Why De Beers Can't Stop Buying Diamonds," *Business Week,* June 14, 1982, p. 48; and Neil Behrmann, "De Beers May Be Cutting Diamond Output in Renewed Bid to Support Ailing Market," *The Wall Street Journal,* April 8, 1982.

Component Chapter B

1. *Moody's Industrial Manual,* vol. 1, (New York: Moody's Investors Service, 1974), p. 356. **2.** Laura Rohmann, "A One-Man Show," *Forbes,* September 26, 1983, pp. 72 ff. **3.** Walecia Konrad, "Changing Gears," *Forbes,* May 9, 1983, p. 180. **4.** Stanley W. Angrist, "Betting the Company," *Forbes,* April 25, 1983, pp. 109 ff. **5.** Erik Larson, "Osborne Takes Little of the Blame for Fall of His Computer Company," *The Wall Street Journal,* October 13, 1983. **6.** John R. Dorfman, "Jigsaws, Money and Freedom," *Forbes,* June 6, 1983, p. 114. **7.** "Sweet Success: Mrs. Fields Cookies goes East," *Fortune,* February 7, 1983, p. 9. **8.** SBA News Release, March 1983. **9.** State of Small Business: A Report of the President, p. 50. **10.** "Small Business' Big Clout," *Dun's Review,* March 1980, p. 70. **11.** Kathleen A. Hughes, "In New York, You Can Get Candy That Resembles People You Know," *The Wall Street Journal,* May 5, 1983. **12.** Paul B. Carroll, "Dungeons and Dragons Game Propels Firm to Success, But Growing Pains Lie Ahead," *The Wall Street Journal,* January 7, 1983; and Heywood Klein, "After Success of Dungeons and Dragons, TSR Fights Poor Management, Uneven Growth," *The Wall Street Journal,* November 25, 1983. **13.** Paul B. Brown,

"Standing in the Sunshine," *Forbes*, September 26, 1983, p. 118; and Isadore Barmash, "Tech Hifi Tries Discounting," *The New York Times*, November 16, 1983. **14.** Charles P. Alexander, "The New Economy," *Time*, May 30, 1983, pp. 62 ff. **15.** Ellen Home, "President Counters Democrats' Charges on Economic Plan," *The Wall Street Journal*, February 1, 1984. **16.** Alexander, "The New Economy." **17.** Jon Levine, "Money for the Asking," *Venture*, June 1983, pp. 34 ff. **18.** "The State of Franchising in the Economy," *Restaurant Business*, March 15, 1981, p. 89. **19.** Myron Magnet, "Here Come McDentists," *Fortune*, February 21, 1983, pp. 135 ff. **20.** Ray Kroc, *Grinding It Out: The Making of McDonald's* (New York: Berkley Publishing, 1978), pp. 125 ff. **21.** Virginia Inman, "How Nutri/System Developed Indigestion from Its Acquisitions," *The Wall Street Journal*, October 14, 1983. **22.** Dedra Hauser, "Avanti Motor Is Revamped by New Owner," *The Wall Street Journal*, November 7, 1983; and Jenny L. King, "The Old Order Changeth at Avanti," *Automotive News*, July 25, 1983, p. 12. **23.** "Do-It-Yourself Chips: A New Case of Startup Fever," *Business Week*, March 21, 1983, pp. 134 ff.; Joel Kotkin, "The Third Wave: The Comeback of Semiconductors," *Inc.*, February 1984, pp. 57 ff.; and Howard K. Dicken, "Semi-Smart: The Faster, Cheaper, Smaller World of Semiconductors," *Computerworld*, November 7, 1983, p. ID1.

Chapter 4

1. Steve Kichen, "Thunder Road," *Forbes*, July 18, 1983, pp. 92 ff.; Alice M. Greene, "Motorcycle Builder Revs Up Quality," *Iron Age*, May 2, 1983, pp. 60 ff.; and "Harley's Guardian Angel," *Business Week*, April 18, 1983, p. 44. **2.** Roy H. Harris, Jr., "Organizer Plans a No-Frills 1984 Olympics for Los Angeles amid Strong Objections," *The Wall Street Journal*, January 10, 1983; Tom Callahan, "Eve of a New Olympics," *Time*, October 17, 1983, pp. 72 ff.; and Joseph L. Galloway, "The Olympic Games Get Back to Basics," *U.S. News & World Report*, January 30, 1984, pp. 47 ff. **3.** Laura Landro, "Highflier's Fall," *The Wall Street Journal*, July 25,

1983; "What Sent Atari Overseas," *Business Week*, March 14, 1983, pp. 102 ff.; "Zapped: Losses and Layoffs at Atari," *Time*, June 13, 1983, p. 50; Gary Hector, "Atari's New Game Plan," *Fortune*, August 8, 1983, pp. 46 ff.; "Atari Realignment of Management Set," *The New York Times*, January 24, 1984; and "Rupert Murdoch's High-Stakes Gamble on Warner," *Business Week*, January 23, 1984, pp. 106 ff. **4.** "How Bob Pritzker Runs a $3 Billion Empire," *Business Week*, March 7, 1983, p. 64. **5.** "Turnover at the Top," *Business Week*, December 19, 1983, p. 110. **6.** "A Silicon Valley Wizard's Life in Five Fast Lanes," *Business Week*, October 17, 1983, p. 208. **7.** Stratford P. Sherman, "Muddling to Victory at Geico," *Fortune*, September 5, 1983, p. 72. **8.** "Why They're Jumping Ship at Intel," *Business Week*, February 14, 1983, pp. 107 ff.; and Willian M. Bulkeley, "Losing Its Flash," *The Wall Street Journal*, May 10, 1983. **9.** James MacGregor Burns, *Leadership* (New York: Harper & Row, 1978), p. 4. **10.** Walter Kiechel III, "Wanted: Corporate Leaders," *Fortune*, May 30, 1983, pp. 135 ff. **11.** Thomas J. Peters and Robert J. Waterman, Jr., *In Search of Excellence* (New York: Harper & Row, 1983), pp. 75 ff. **12.** Allan A. Kennedy and Terrence E. Deal, *Corporate Cultures: The Rites and Rituals of Corporate Life* (Reading, Mass.: Addison-Wesley, 1982). **13.** "Mead Data Central Begins Offering New York Times Database Online," *Editor & Publisher*, April 23, 1983, p. 97; and T. C. Taylor, "Mead Data Lays It on the Line," *Sales & Marketing Management*, April 6, 1981, pp. 42 ff. **14.** Monica Langley, "Wrong Number: AT&T Manager Finds His Effort to Galvanize Sales Meets Resistance," *The Wall Street Journal*, December 16, 1983.

Chapter 5

1. "TRW Leads a Revolution in Managing Technology," *Business Week*, November 15, 1982, pp. 124 ff.; "TRW Vidar Restructures Sales Organization," *Telephony*, March 30, 1981, p. 36; and Janice Drummond, "Vidar Plans 'Orderly' Retreat from Digital Switch Business," *Telephony*, December 14, 1981, p. 11. **2.** Ibid. **3.** Jim Brokaw, "Dr. Pepper, Sealtest and the Wood Brothers," *Motor Trend*, March 1974, p. 102. **4.** "The Shrinking of Middle Management," *Business Week*, April 25, 1983, pp. 54 ff.

5. Ibid. **6.** "Apple Takes on its Biggest Test Yet," *Business Week*, January 31, 1983, pp. 70 ff.; Rachael Wrege, "Lisa's Design," *Popular Computing*, March 1983, pp. 96 ff.; David E. Sanger, "For Apple a Risky Assault on I.B.M.," *The New York Times*, January 23, 1984; and Michael Moritz, "Apple Launches a Mac Attack," *Time*, January 30, 1984, pp. 68 ff. **7.** John A. Byrne, "Nuts-and-Bolts Bosses," *Forbes*, September 26, 1983, pp. 129 ff.; and John S. McClenahan, "New Marching Orders for M.B.A.'s," *Industry Week*, August 8, 1983, pp. 49 ff. **8.** Stanley W. Angrist, "Classless Capitalists," *Forbes*, May 9, 1983, pp. 122 ff.; and Dick Silverman, "Gore-Tex Mounts Major Expansion," *Footwear News*, August 9, 1982, p. 66.

Chapter 6

1. Gene Bylinsky, "The Race to the Automatic Factory," *Fortune*, February 21, 1983, pp. 51 ff. **2.** Ibid. **3.** Ibid. **4.** Ibid. **5.** "Production Problems Become More Manageable," *Business Week*, April 25, 1983, pp. 70 ff. **6.** Ibid. **7.** "Quality: The U.S. Drives to Catch Up," *Business Week*, November 1, 1982, pp. 66 ff. **8.** Ibid. **9.** Jeremy Main, "Ford's Drive for Quality," *Fortune*, April 18, 1983, pp. 62 ff. **10.** Ibid. **11.** "Quality Circles," *The Wall Street Journal*, February 3, 1983. **12.** Dennis Kneale, "Commodore Hits Production Snags in Its Hot-Selling Home Computer," *The Wall Street Journal*, October 28, 1983; James E. Braham, "Commodore Takes Off the Gloves," *Industry Week*, February 6, 1984, pp. 15 ff.; Andrew Pollack, "Commodore's Woes Mount," *The New York Times*, February 1, 1984; and "Commodore Disk Lack Hits Software Sales," *Electronic News*, December 5, 1983, p. 62. **13.** James Cook, "Comes the Revolution!" *Forbes*, October 24, 1983, pp. 43 ff; and "Cincinnati Milacron Plans Epi Si Manufacturing Plant," *Electronic News*, November 14, 1983, p. 70.

Chapter 7

1. "High Tech Lures Union Organizers," *Business Week*, April 11, 1983, pp. 101 ff. **2.** Carey W. English, "Embattled Unions Get Their Act Together,"

U.S. News & World Report, October 17, 1983, pp. 95 ff. **3.** William Serrin, "Union Membership Falls Sharply; Decline Expected to Be Permanent," *The New York Times,* May 31, 1983.
4. Carey W. English, "For Unions, Another Crack at Public Employees," *U.S. News & World Report,* November 7, 1983, pp. 89 ff. **5.** *Fortune* Panel, "Are the Unions Dead, or Just Sleeping?" *Fortune,* September 20, 1982, pp. 98 ff.
6. Serrin, "Union Membership Falls Sharply." **7.** *Fortune* panel, "Are the Unions Dead?"; data from Bureau of Labor Statistics, "Major Collective Bargaining Settlements in Private Industry, First 9 Months 1983," *USDL News,* October 28, 1983, p. 8, Table 3. **8.** Dale D. Buss, "Out of Sync: Many Auto Workers Bitterly Blame UAW for Recent Givebacks," *The Wall Street Journal,* May 13, 1983. **9.** "High Tech Lures Union Organizers." **10.** Ibid.
11. Ibid. **12.** Ibid. **13.** *Fortune* panel, "Are the Unions Dead?"; data from National Labor Relations Board.
14. "Why Clerical Workers Resist the Unions," *Business Week,* May 2, 1983, pp. 126 ff; and Barbara Aarsteinsen, "NLRB Orders Equitable to Bargain with Union," *Journal of Commerce,* May 18, 1983, p. 5A. **15.** James Strong, "Trade Unions Gamble That Pay Freeze Will Create Jobs," *Chicago Tribune,* June 1, 1983. **16.** Dean Rotbart, "American Airlines Gets Tentative Accord on New Contract with Flight Attendants," *The Wall Street Journal,* July 7, 1983; and "What Labor Gave American Airlines," *Business Week,* March 21, 1983, pp. 33 ff. **17.** (Press release, no date): Sherwood Ross Associates, 1069 National Press Building, Washington, D.C., 20045.
18. John Hoerr, "Why Labor and Management Are Both Buying Profit-Sharing," *Business Week,* January 10, 1983, p. 84. **19.** Dale D. Buss, "Lifetime Job Guarantees in Auto Contracts Arouse Second Thoughts Among Workers," *The Wall Street Journal,* April 18, 1983.
20. Ibid. **21.** Ibid. **22.** "Bell System's Breakup Is Jarring the Unions," *Business Week,* May 30, 1983, pp. 76 ff.; and "The Sudden Uncertainties of Working for Bell," *Business Week,* June 20, 1983, p. 26. **23.** Ibid. **24.** Jeremy Main, "Anatomy of an Auto-Plant Rescue,"

Fortune, April 4, 1983, pp. 108 ff.
25. Joann S. Lublin, "Unions and Firms Focus on Hand Disorders That Can Be Caused by Repetitive Tasks," *The Wall Street Journal,* January 14, 1983.
26. Ibid. **27.** "When Plant Gates Close," *Forbes,* July 18, 1983, p. 10; and "Closing Shop," *The Wall Street Journal,* April 12, 1983. **28.** Laurel Sorenson, "Chapter 11 Filing by Wilson Foods Roils Workers' Lives, Tests Law," *The Wall Street Journal,* May 28, 1983.
29. Bill Saporito, "Unions Fight the Corporate Sell-Off," *Fortune,* July 11, 1983, pp. 145 ff. **30.** Ibid. **31.** Howard Banks, "Who Guards the Public Interest?" *Forbes,* April 11, 1983, pp. 39 ff.; Kenneth Labich, "A Steel Town's Bid to Save Itself," *Fortune,* April 18, 1983, p. 103 ff; "The Next Step for Weirton's Workers," *Business Week,* March 28, 1983, p. 39; and William Serrin, "Employees to Buy Huge Steel Works in $66 Million Pact," *The New York Times,* March 14, 1983.
32. "Labor: No More Mr. Nice Guy," *Business Week,* August 29, 1983, pp. 18 ff. **33.** Robert S. Greenberger, "Striking Back: More Firms Get Tough and Keep Operating in Spite of Walkouts," *The Wall Street Journal,* October 11, 1983. **34.** "USW Asks Members to Withdraw Funds from Mellon Bank," *The Wall Street Journal,* June 2, 1983.
35. English, "Embattled Unions Get Their Act Together." **36.** "Next!" *Forbes,* July 18, 1983, p. 149; and "Paper Avoids a Replay of J. P. Stevens," *Business Week,* June 27, 1983, pp. 33 ff. **37.** Stephen B. Goldberg and Jeanne M. Brett, "An Experiment in the Mediation of Grievances," *Monthly Labor Review,* March 1983, pp. 23 ff.
38. Daniel Seligman, "Who Needs Unions," *Fortune,* July 12, 1982, pp. 54 ff; and *Fortune* Panel, "Are the Unions Dead?" **39.** Ibid. **40.** Ibid. **41.** Leonard M. Apcar, "Greyhound's Tentative Pact with Strikers Includes Important Concessions by Union," *The Wall Street Journal,* December 5, 1983; Steven Flax, "Pay Cuts Before the Job Even Starts," *Fortune,* January 9, 1984, pp. 75 ff; and "Bus Stop: A Strike Halts Greyhound," *Time,* November 14, 1983, p. 89.
42. Allan Dodds Frank, "Comes the Mouse," *Forbes,* August 15, 1983, pp. 54 ff.

Chapter 8

1. A. F. Ehrbar, "Grasping the New Unemployment," *Fortune,* May 16, 1983,

pp. 106 ff. **2.** James W. Walker, *Human Resource Planning* (New York: McGraw-Hill, 1980), p. 4. **3.** Marilyn Chase, "Problem-Plagued Intel Bets on New Products, IBM's Financial Help," *The Wall Street Journal,* February 4, 1983. **4.** Carl Camden and Bill Wallace, "Job Application Forms: A Hazardous Employment Practice," *Personnel Administrator,* March 1983, pp. 31 ff.
5. Data from Equal Employment Opportunity Commission. **6.** Robert S. Greenberger, "Federal Shift in Hiring Rules Stirs Criticism," *The Wall Street Journal,* March 15, 1983. **7.** Robert Pear, "Rights Commission Abandons Policy on Racial Quotas," *The New York Times,* January 18, 1984. **8.** "GM Settles Up," *Time,* October 31, 1983, p. 92.
9. "The Handicapped Test Their Rights in Court," *Business Week,* May 19, 1980, pp. 142B ff. **10.** Ibid.
11. Gopal C. Pati and John I. Adkins, Jr., "Hire the Handicapped—Compliance Is Good Business," *Harvard Business Review,* January–February 1980, pp. 14 ff.; and data from Office of Federal Contract Compliance Programs.
12. Ibid. **13.** "Technology Is Opening More Jobs for the Deaf," *Business Week,* May 9, 1983, pp. 134 ff. **14.** U.S. Department of Commerce, Bureau of the Census, *Statistical Abstract of the United States 1979* (Washington, D.C.: Government Printing Office, 1979), p. 400.
15. U.S. Department of Labor, *Employment and Earnings, December 1983* (Washington, D.C.: Government Printing Office, 1983), p. 8, Table III; and Bureau of Labor Statistics, *Perspectives on Working Women* (Washington, D.C.: Government Printing Office, June 1980), p. 2.
16. U.S. Census Bureau, *Money Income of Households, Families, and Persons in the U.S., 1981.* (Washington, D.C.: Government Printing Office, 1981), Series P-60, No. 137, Table 55. **17.** Donald J. Petersen and Douglas Massengill, "Sexual Harassment—A Growing Problem in the Workplace," *Personnel Administrator,* October 1982, pp. 79 ff. **18.** John Curley, "More Executive Bonus Plans Are Tied to Company Earnings, Sales Goals," *The Wall Street Journal,* November 20, 1980. **19.** John Perham, "Upsurge in ESOPS," *Dun's Business Month,* February 1983, pp. 76 ff. **20.** Survey

Research Center, Economic Policy Division, Chamber of Commerce of the U.S., *Employee Benefits 1981* (Washington, D.C.: Chamber of Commerce of the U.S., 1981). **21.** Jane Mayer, "Kodak Workers Offered Package to Leave Firm," *The Wall Street Journal*, January 5, 1983. **22.** Data from U.S. Chamber of Commerce, Survey Research Center. **23.** "A Debt-Threatened Dream," *Time*, May 24, 1982, p. 19. **24.** Bureau of Labor Statistics, "Occupational Injuries and Illnesses in 1982," *USDL News*, November 4, 1983, p. 1. **25.** Joann S. Lublin, "Occupational Diseases Receive More Scrutiny Since the Manville Case," *The Wall Street Journal*, December 20, 1982. **26.** Jim Montgomery, "Law Firm Sets a Rapid Pace in Bank World," *The Wall Street Journal*, June 30, 1983. **27.** Joann S. Lublin, "Firing Line: Legal Challenges Force Firms to Revamp Ways They Dismiss Workers," *The Wall Street Journal*, September 13, 1983; and William S. Waldo, "'Wrongful Discharge' Suits: Judiciary Playing with Fire," *Los Angeles Times*, April 3, 1983.

Component Chapter C

1. "The Old Foreman Is on the Way Out, and the New One Will Be More Important," *Business Week*, April 25, 1983, p. 74. **2.** Elton Mayo, "Hawthorne and the Western Electric Company," in *Classics in Management*, ed. Harwood F. Merrill (New York: American Management Association, 1960). **3.** Abraham H. Maslow, "A Theory of Human Motivations," *Psychological Review*, July 1943, p. 370; and *Motivation and Personality*, 2nd ed. (New York: Harper & Row, 1970). **4.** Douglas McGregor, *The Human Side of Enterprise* (New York: McGraw-Hill, 1970). **5.** William G. Ouchi, *Theory Z: How American Business Can Meet the Japanese Challenge* (Reading, Mass.: Addison-Wesley, 1981). **6.** "A Work Revolution in U.S. Industry," *Business Week*, May 16, 1983, pp. 100 ff. **7.** Ibid. **8.** John Holusha, "Detroit's New Labor Strategy," *The New York Times*, May 13, 1983. **9.** Kevin P. Helliker, "Two Years After Buying Continental Air, Texas Air's Chief Still Facing Resentment," *The Wall*

Street Journal, September 8, 1983. **10.** Jeremy Main, "Ford's Drive for Quality," *Fortune*, April 18, 1983, pp. 62 ff; and "Ford Uses Employee-Involvement Groups to Improve Quality," *Automotive News*, February 28, 1983, p. 4. **11.** Dan Shannon, "Productivity: Quality Circles for Supermarkets," *The New York Times*, April 18, 1982. **12.** Heywood Klein, "Interest Grows in Worksharing, Which Lets Concerns Cut Workweeks to Avoid Layoffs," *The Wall Street Journal*, April 7, 1983; and "Motorola's Transformation," *Dun's Business Month*, August 1983, p. 60. **13.** Dale D. Buss, "High-Tech Track: Retraining of Workers for Automated Plants Gets Off to Slow Start," *The Wall Street Journal*, April 13, 1983. **14.** Ibid. **15.** Carol Hymowitz, "Culture Shock Affects Steelworker Who Switched to White-Collar Job," *The Wall Street Journal*, June 1, 1983. **16.** Paul A. Engelmayer, "Worker Owned and Operated Supermarket Yields Financial Success, Personal Rewards," *The Wall Street Journal*, August 18, 1983. **17.** Carol Hymowitz, "Tradition-Bound Alcoa Develops Training to Challenge Concern's Old-Boy Network," *The Wall Street Journal*, November 15, 1983; and Daniel J. Cuff, "Executive Shifts Are Set for Alcoa," *The New York Times*, February 18, 1983. **18.** Dale D. Buss, "GM vs. GM: Unions Say Auto Firms Use Interplant Rivalry to Raise Work Quotas," *The Wall Street Journal*, November 7, 1983.

Chapter 9

1. "Atari Turns to a Marketing Magician," *Business Week*, July 25, 1983, p. 26. **2.** Thomas C. Hayes, "Selling Computers like Soap," *The New York Times*, July 27, 1983. **3.** Janet Guyon and Erik Larson, "New Apple Chief Expected to Bring Marketing Expertise Gained at Pepsi," *The Wall Street Journal*, April 11, 1983. **4.** Fred Ferretti, "Cabbage Patch Kids: Born for 'Adoption' at a Price," *The New York Times*, January 16, 1984. **5.** "Sony's Slippage," *Fortune*, July 25, 1983. **6.** "Swanson Spices Its Menu," *Business Week*, April 18, 1983, pp. 41 ff.; and L. Langway, L. Rotenberk, J. Young, E. Williams, and T. Jackson, "Frozen Foods Get Hot Again," *Newsweek*, May 23, 1983, p. 42. **7.** June Kronholz, "A Living-Alone Trend Affects Housing, Cars and Other Industries," *The Wall Street Journal*, November 6, 1977. **8.** Landon Y. Jones,

"The Baby Boom Consumer," *American Demographics*, February 1981, p. 39. **9.** William C. Freund, "The Looming Impact of Population Changes," *The Wall Street Journal*, April 6, 1982. **10.** Reginald Stuart, "'Old Old' Grow in Numbers and Impact," *The New York Times*, June 22, 1983. **11.** John Herbers, "Industrial Flight from North," *The New York Times*, April 12, 1983. **12.** Larry Long and Diana DeAre, "The Slowing of Urbanization in the U.S.," *Scientific American*, July 1983, pp. 33 ff. **13.** "Smaller Cities Led Increase in Population from 1970–80," *The New York Times*, July 8, 1983. **14.** John Herbers, "Major Cities Ringed by Suburbs Yielding to Sprawl of Small Metropolitan Areas," *The New York Times*, July 8, 1983. **15.** "Why Procter & Gamble Is Playing It Even Tougher," *Business Week*, July 18, 1983, pp. 176 ff.; and Damon Darlin and Bill Abrams, "New Ingredients: Procter & Gamble Co. Starts to Reformulate Tried-and-True Ways," *The Wall Street Journal*, March 30, 1983. **16.** Aaron Bernstein, "Time to Make a Move," *Forbes*, February 14, 1983, p. 90. **17.** Myron Magnet, "Coke Tries Selling Movies Like Soda Pop," *Fortune*, December 26, 1983, pp. 119 ff. **18.** John Koten, "Giving Buyers Wide Choices May be Hurting Auto Makers," *The Wall Street Journal*, December 15, 1983.

Chapter 10

1. Mark Potts, "Soft-Drinks Wars Get Bitter with Sweetener Debut," *The Washington Post*," July 14, 1983; "Coke's Big Marketing Blitz," *Business Week*, May 30, 1983, p. 58. **2.** Ibid. **3.** "Smoke Detectors Face Cloudy Future," *The New York Times*, November 10, 1980; and "Better Luck Next Time," *Forbes*, August 20, 1979, p. 113. **4.** *Home Furnishing Daily*, August 15, 1983, p. 34. **5.** Jeremy Main, "Help and Hype in the New-Products Game," *Fortune*, February 7, 1983, pp. 60 ff. **6.** Ibid. **7.** Ibid. **8.** William L. Shanklin and John K. Ryans, Jr., "Is the International Cash Cow Really a Prize Heifer?" *Business Horizons*, March–April 1981, p. 10. **9.** Paul Hemp, "A Lot Rides on a Good Name," *The New York Times*, September

7, 1983. **10.** "Move Over, Cap'n Crunch: Pac-Man and His Pals Are Taking Over," *Business Week,* July 18, 1983, p. 174. **11.** "Box Rebellion," *Time,* June 13, 1983, pp. 51 ff. **12.** Steven J. Marcus, "Tin Can Battles Challengers," *The New York Times,* October 3, 1983. **13.** Pamela G. Hollie, "Repackaging: Team Triumph," *The New York Times,* February 7, 1983. **14.** *Standard and Poor's Industry Surveys,* October 1983, p. B 86. **15.** "A Deposit Law That Is Rattling Glassmakers," *Business Week,* May 30, 1983, p. 90B. **16.** "Mattel Struggles to Fix Its Product Woes," *Business Week,* May 9, 1983, pp. 76 ff. **17.** Christopher Gilson and Leon Schiffman, *Marketing* (New York: Random House, Inc., unpublished). **18.** Robert Guenther, "Windham Hill Records Prospers by Producing Soft Jazz for Music Lovers Who Can't Stand Rock," *The Wall Street Journal,* December 13, 1983; Cynthia Kirk, "Windham Hill on a Roll," *Variety,* February 8, 1984; and Jack McDonough, "March (to the Bank) to the Beat of a Different Drummer," *Esquire,* April 1984, pp. 237 ff. **19.** Damon Darlin, "Faced with More Competition, P&G Sees New Products as Crucial to Earnings Growth," *The Wall Street Journal,* September 13, 1983; and "P&G Dives into Orange Juice with a Big Splash," *Business Week,* October 31, 1983.

Chapter 11

1. Dennis Kneale, "Advertisers Use Music Groups to Reach Young Consumers," *The Wall Street Journal,* July 28, 1983. **2.** Lee Smith, "The Lure and Limits of Innovation," *Fortune,* October 20, 1980, p. 84. **3.** Christy Marshall, "Ad Spending Seen Climbing 13.8%," *Advertising Age,* December 19, 1983, p. 3. **4.** Pat Sloan, "'Made in America' Greets Shoppers," *Advertising Age,* December 19, 1983. **5.** Data from the Newspaper Advertising Bureau. **6.** Sandra Salmans, "Big Gains for Radio Networks," *The New York Times,* June 9, 1983. **7.** Ibid. **8.** *Broadcasting/Cablecasting Yearbook 1983,* p. A2. **9.** Marc Gunther and Noel Gunther, "And Now a Word from Pay Radio," *Washington Journalism*

Review, July/August 1983, pp. 64 ff. **10.** *The World Almanac Book of Facts 1982* (New York: Newspaper Enterprise Association, 1982), p. 429; and A. C. Nielsen Company. **11.** Data from A. C. Nielsen Company; and *Broadcast Advertising Record.* **12.** Jane Mayer, "Big TV Advertisers Found to Be Looking Beyond the Networks," *The Wall Street Journal,* July 11, 1983. **13.** Data from Cable Bureau of Advertising; and National Cable Television Association. **14.** Laura Landro, "MTV Music Channel Rocks Teen-Agers, But Big Advertisers Haven't Tuned In," *The Wall Street Journal,* August 24, 1983. **15.** Richard P. Kern, "1984 Survey of Selling Costs: Something Old, Something New," *Sales & Marketing Management,* February 20, 1984, pp. 12 ff. **16.** Data from Direct Mail Corp. **17.** Sandra Salmans, "Advertising: All Sci-Fi's Are Not All the Same," *The New York Times,* June 8, 1983. **18.** *Advertising Age,* March 16, 1983, p. 1; and U.S. Department of Commerce, Bureau of Industrial Economics, *1983 U.S. Industrial Outlook* (Washington, D.C.: Government Printing Office, 1983). **19.** U.S. Department of Commerce, Bureau of the Census, *Statistical Abstract of the United States, 1982–1983* (Washington, D.C.: Government Printing Office, 1983), p. 386. **20.** Kern, "1984 Survey of Selling Costs." **21.** Data from Direct Selling Association publication, *What Are They Saying About Direct Selling?* **22.** Anne Bagamery, "Please Make Me Feel Special," *Forbes,* March 28, 1983, pp. 88 ff. **23.** Anna Quindlen, "About New York: King Kong Is Returned To 34th St. Perch," *The New York Times,* April 6, 1983; and Carolyn Sykes and Jack Mays, "The King Kong Event," *PR Casebook,* November–December 1983, pp. 26 ff. **24.** Michael Millenson, "Tylenol Sales Rebound, Approach Pre-Tragedy Levels," *Chicago Tribune,* April 22, 1983. **25.** "What Makes Manny Hanny Run?" *Business Week,* August 22, 1983, p. 55. **26.** "Retailing May Have Overdosed on Coupons," *Business Week,* June 13, 1983, pp. 147 ff.; and Jennifer Alter and Nancy Giges, "Industry Losing $350 Million on Coupon Misredemption," *Advertising Age,* May 30, 1983. **27.** Bill Abrams, "Some New Ads May Rekindle Burger Battle," *The Wall Street Journal,* March 4, 1983. **28.** Philip H. Dougherty, "Advertising: Optimism at Last on Spending," *The New York Times,* July 14, 1983. **29.** Ronald Alsop, "Du Pont Steps Up

Promotions to Prove Its Selling Ability," *The Wall Street Journal,* December 1, 1983; and "Du Pont Sets Two-Pronged Effort for Spring Antron Promotion," *Modern Floor Coverings,* March 1983, p. 12. **30.** Richard A. Shaffer, "Software Firm Taps Market for Education," *The Wall Street Journal,* November 15, 1983; and Bob King et al., "ComputerWare: The Mass Retailing of Computers, Software, and Videogames," *Retailing Home Furnishings,* October 10, 1983, p. S1.

Chapter 12

1. Robert Lindsey, "Home Box Office Moves in on Hollywood," *The New York Times Magazine,* June 12, 1983, pp. 31 ff. **2.** "Why Manufacturers Are Doubling as Distributors," *Business Week,* January 17, 1983, p. 41. **3.** Bill Seporito, "Super Valu Does Two Things Well," *Fortune,* April 18, 1983, pp. 114 ff. **4.** *Neiman-Marcus Christmas Catalog,* 1983. **5.** Claudia Ricci, "J.C. Penney Goes After Affluent Shoppers, But Store's New Image May Be Hard to Sell," *The Wall Street Journal,* February 15, 1983. **6.** "The Synergy Begins to Work for Sears' Financial Supermarket," *Business Week,* June 13, 1983, pp. 116 ff. **7.** Isadore Barmash, "The 'Off-Price' Retailing Boom," *The New York Times,* April 5, 1983. **8.** Ann M. Morrison, "The Upshot of Off-Price," *Fortune,* June 13, 1983, pp. 122 ff. **9.** Claudia Ricci, "Discount Business Booms, Pleasing Buyers, Irking Department Stores," *The Wall Street Journal,* May 3, 1983. **10.** Standard & Poor's *Industry Surveys,* October 1983, p. R176. **11.** Toni Mack with Jessica Greenbaum, "A Marriage of Convenience," *Forbes,* February 14, 1983, p. 102. **12.** Standard & Poor's *Industry Surveys,* October 1983, vol. 2, p. 122; and *Advertising Age,* June 13, 1983, p. 34. **13.** Data from L. L. Bean. **14.** John Curley, "Catalogs Are Getting Thin, Specialized," *The Wall Street Journal,* September 13, 1982. **15.** Barbara Rudolph, "Shades of Discontent," *Forbes,* July 18, 1983, p. 50. **16.** Sandra Salmans, "The Trials of Owning Just One Movie Theater," *The New York Times,* June 27, 1983. **17.** Agis Salpukas, "Pan Am's Marketing Error," *The New York Times,* January

4, 1983. **18.** Janet Guyon, "Supermarkets Change to Lure More Shoppers," *The Wall Street Journal*, November 14, 1983; Bill Saporito, "Shopping-Cart Battle in Winn-Dixieland," *Fortune*, October 3, 1983, pp. 206 ff; and Evelyn Bash, "Tampa: Winn-Dixie and Publix Tie for No. 1 Spot," *Supermarket News*, September 26, 1983, p. S32. **19.** Douglas R. Sease, "You Can Buy a Car at $49 Over Invoice, But It'll Take Time," *The Wall Street Journal*, September 21, 1983; and Richard A. Wright, "$49-Over Dealer Angers Rivals Anew," *Automotive News*, October 10, 1983, pp. 1 ff.

Chapter 13

1. Steve Swartz, "Auto Rebuilder Finds It Takes Lots of Money to Make Money," *The Wall Street Journal*, August 22, 1983. **2.** "Struggling to Cope Without Snow," *Business Week*, July 4, 1980, p. 66. **3.** Mary Williams, "Fresh Idea, Optimism, Luck Helped Running-Wear Maker," *The Wall Street Journal*, June 27, 1983. **4.** Ibid. **5.** American Banking Association, Washington, D.C. **6.** Robert Sobel, *The Fallen Colossus: The Penn Central and the Metamorphosis of American Capitalism* (New York: Weybright and Talley, 1976). **7.** Stanley W. Angrist, "It Pays to Be Patient," *Forbes*, February 14, 1983, pp. 82 ff.; "Going the Distance on the Slopes," *The New York Times*, March 25, 1984; and Jeffrey Arlen, "C. B. Vaughan's Race to the Summit," *Daily News Record*, February 2, 1984. **8.** Thomas J. Lueck, "Coleco Can't Savor a Success," *The New York Times*, December 9, 1983; "A Christmas Deadline Looms for Coleco's Computer," *Business Week*, October 17, 1983, pp. 44 ff.; and "Trouble in the Cabbage Patch: Why Investors Are Down on Coleco," *Business Week*, January 9, 1984, p. 93.

Chapter 14

1. Thomas C. Hayes, "MGM, Its Image Bruised, Is Straining to Find Hits," *The New York Times*, January 30, 1983. **2.** "U.S. Steel's Debt-Shrouded Future," *Business Week*, October 18, 1982, pp. 154 ff. **3.** Robert L. Simison, "AMC Is Raising $500 Million via Loans, Stock Offer, Planned Sales of AM General," *The Wall Street Journal*, March 24, 1983. **4.** Standard & Poor's Corporation, *Standard Corporation Descriptions*, February 1978, pp. 4836 ff. **5.** Joan Lulkovich and Frank Nasella, "The Market Place: Municipal Volume Sets Record of $81.2 Billion," *Credit Markets*, January 3, 1984, p. 5. **6.** Tamar Lewin, "Power Group Says It Cannot Pay Off $2.25 Billion Debt," *The New York Times*, July 26, 1983; and "The Fallout From 'Whoops,'" *Business Week*, July 11, 1983, pp. 80 ff. **7.** Irwin Ross, "What's New About This Boom," *Fortune*, May 30, 1983, pp. 50 ff. **8.** Tim Carrington, "Many Firms Capitalize on Rallying Market by Quickly Issuing a Flood of New Securities," *The Wall Street Journal*," August 27, 1982. **9.** Richard A. Shaffer, "Software Firms Going Public, Letting Investors in on Boom," *The Wall Street Journal*, August 26, 1983. **10.** Eric N. Berg, "Mattel Reports Losing $156.1 Million in Quarter," *The New York Times*, September 9, 1983. **11.** *Control Data 1979 Annual Report*, p. 23. **12.** *IBM 1979 Annual Report*, p. 27. **13.** Lawrence Ingrassia, "Sign of the Bull: Recent Increase in Share Prices Has Led to Flurry of Stock Splits, Stock Dividends," *The Wall Street Journal*, January 27, 1983. **14.** Robert J. Flaherty, "The Case for Kodak," *Forbes*, December 1, 1977, p. 122. **15.** "A Leveraged Buyout: What It Takes," *Business Week*, July 18, 1983, p. 194. **16.** Pamela G. Hollie, "Off-Price Retailers Go Public," *The New York Times*, November 8, 1983; "Syms Plans Initial Offering of 3,125,000 Common Shares," *The Wall Street Journal*, August 10, 1983; and "Sy Syms Going Public; To Sell 17.7% of Stock," *Daily News Record*, August 3, 1983. **17.** "Wall Street's Buyout Craze," *Newsweek*, December 19, 1983, pp. 70 ff.; "Billion-Dollar-Plus Buyback at Metromedia," *Broadcasting*, December 12, 1983, p. 33; and "Is Metromedia a Bargain at $1.5 Billion?" *Business Week*, December 19, 1983, p. 31.

Chapter 15

1. Data from New York Stock Exchange; and "Market Volume (N.Y.S.E.)," *The New York Times*, March 23, 1984. **2.** *The New York Times*, March 23, 1984. **3.** R. Foster Winans, "Stock Prices Posted Substantial Gains in 1983 but Wall Street Is Moving Cautiously into 1984," *The Wall Street Journal*, January 3, 1984. **4.** Data from Securities Data Corporation, Inc. **5.** Data from Securities and Exchange Commission; and New York Stock Exchange. **6.** Yla Eason, "Nasdaq's New Prominence," *The New York Times*, May 3, 1983. **7.** Michael Blumstein, "Big Board's Electronic Gains," *The New York Times*, August 29, 1983. **8.** Ibid. **9.** Ibid. **10.** Data from New York Stock Exchange. **11.** "The Small Investor Is Back," *Newsweek*, May 23, 1983, p. 58. **12.** "Welcome Back: The Small Investor Returns," *Time*, December 12, 1983, p. 52. **13.** Eason, "Nasdaq's New Prominence." **14.** Yla Eason, "Financial Futures: A Hot New Act," *The New York times*, April 24, 1983. **15.** Michael Blumstein, "Amex Carving a New Niche," *The New York Times*, September 8, 1983; and Hilary Rosenberg, "NYSE vs. AMEX vs. OTC: A Bitter Triangle," *Financial World*, January 24, 1984, p. 16. **16.** Steven Greenhouse, "Memorable '83 Market Moves," *The New York Times*, January 3, 1984; and "Tale of the Tape," *Time*, January 9, 1984, p. 52.

Component Chapter D

1. Data from Board of Governors of the Federal Reserve System. **2.** *The New York Times*, April 27, 1984. **3.** Data from Board of Governors of the Federal Reserve System. **4.** Winston Williams, "The Explosion in Bank Deposits," *The New York Times*, May 1, 1983. **5.** G. Christian Hill, "So Far, Money-Market Accounts Aren't Cutting Bank, S&L Profits," *The Wall Street Journal*, February 15, 1983. **6.** Gary Hector, "The Banks Invade Wall Street," *Fortune*, February 7, 1983, pp. 44 ff.; and data from American Banking Association. **7.** Robert A. Bennett, "Changing Ways at Citibank," *The New York Times*, April 21, 1983. **8.** Ibid. **9.** "That #*!% Float," *Time*, May 16, 1983, p. 59. **10.** Nancy L. Ross, "Top Firms Enter Planning Area as Deregulation, Competition Spur Financial Proliferation," *Washington Post*, November 6, 1983; and Nancy Rivera, "Deregulation a Mixed Blessing for S&L Industry," *Los Angeles Times*, November 20, 1983. **11.** Robert A. Bennett, "BankAmerica in Search of Itself," *The New York Times*,

October 30, 1983; Victor F. Zonana, "Stirring Giant: BankAmerica Corp., Seeking a Turnaround, Seems to Gain Ground," *The Wall Street Journal*, January 27, 1984; and Geoff Brouillette, "BankAmerica Has 15% Fall in '83 Profits," *American Banker*, January 20, 1983, pp. 3 ff.

Component Chapter E

1. Douglas McLeod, "Insurance Guarantees Rain Won't Dampen Baseball Club's Profits," *Business Insurance*, May 16, 1983, p. 3. **2.** Eckardt C. Beck, "Hazardous Waste Disposal—Most Firms Urgently Need to Review Loss-Control Programs," *Business Insurance*, June 20, 1983, pp. 17 ff. **3.** Bill Densmore, "Premium Hikes Force Dow to Halt Bendectin Production," *Business Insurance*, June 20, 1983, p. 1. **4.** Sandra Salmans, "Time Inc. Declines by 13.9%," *The New York Times*, October 20, 1983. **5.** "An Ounce of Prevention," *Chain Store Age*, October 1983, p. 90. **6.** "Iron-Man Insurance," *Forbes*, October 10, 1983, p. 8. **7.** "ABC Insures the 1984 Games," *Fortune*, January 10, 1983, p. 8. **8.** Jerry Geisel, "Product Liability Suits Jump in '80, Court Report Says," *Business Insurance*, October 6, 1980, p. 1. **9.** "A Legal Time Bomb for Corporations," *Business Week*, June 16, 1980, p. 150. **10.** Leonard Sloane, "Worker Insurance Evolution," *The New York Times*, December 6, 1983. **11.** Data from Council of New York State Workman's Compensation Board. **12.** Sanford Jacobs, "Business Disruption Coverage Is Inadequate at Many Firms," *The Wall Street Journal*, October 3, 1983. **13.** John D. Long and Davis W. Gregg, eds., *Property and Liability Insurance Handbook* (Homewood, Ill.: Richard D. Irwin, 1965), pp. 829 ff. **14.** Goldie Dietel, "The Changing Face of Life Insurance" (Advertising Supplement), *Forbes*. **15.** Ibid. **16.** Information from Health Insurance Association of America. **17.** "How to Size Up Your Company," *Business Week*, May 12, 1980, pp. 136 ff. **18.** Data from Health Insurance Association of America. **19.** Dietel, "Changing Face of Life Insurance." **20.** Louis S. Richman, "Health Benefits Come Under the Knife," *Fortune*, May 2, 1983, pp. 95 ff.; and *1982–1983 Sourcebook of Health Insurance Data*, p. 8. **21.** Lorrie Gawla, "Employer Sponsored PPO's Attract Attention," *Business Insurance*, June 6, 1983, p. 1. **22.** Data from Insurance Institute. **23.** *Life Insurance Factbook*, *1983*, p. 5. **24.** Ibid., p. 48. **25.** Christopher Power, "Pension Raiding, 1983 Style," *Forbes*, June 20, 1983, p. 130. **26.** Jerry Geisel, "Two States Approve Unisex Legislation," *Business Insurance*, June 13, 1983. **27.** "Sex and the Insurance Policy," *Business Week*, February 7, 1983, p. 83. **28.** Eric N. Berg, "Major Corporations Ask Workers to Pay More of Health Cost," *The New York Times*, September 12, 1983; Barry Stavro, "Sick Call," *Forbes*, October 24, 1983, p. 116; "GM Revises Benefit Plan," *American Medical News*, June 11, 1982, p. 8; and George Ruben, "Auto Industry Update," *Monthly Labor Review*, October 1983, p. 38. **29.** Adapted from study materials for the Associate in Risk Management designation, awarded by the Insurance Institute of America, Malvern, Pennsylvania.

Chapter 16

1. "The NBA's Ingenious Move to Cap Players' Salaries," *Business Week*, October 31, 1983, pp. 81 ff. **2.** "Light Touch," *Forbes*, September 12, 1983, pp. 134 ff.; and "D'Lites of America," *Nation's Restaurant News*, July 18, 1983, p. 35. **3.** Gregory Stricharchuk, "More Ailing Concerns Are Firing Auditors in Hopes of Keeping Bad News from Public," *The Wall Street Journal*, May 12, 1983. **4.** Current Population Survey, Employment and Earnings, January 1983; and American Institute of Certified Public Accountants (AICPA), *Annual Report 1982–83*. **5.** "New Rules Would Jeopardize the Healthier Look of Pension Funds," *Business Week*, September 12, 1983, p. 126. **6.** John L. Grant, "Inflation's Full Impact on the Bottom Line," *Business Week*, February 7, 1983, p. 8. **7.** Janet Bamford, "Out of Sight, Out of Mind?" *Forbes*, July 4, 1983, p. 133. **8.** Michael Cieply, "Mutiny in the Galley," *Forbes*, September 12, 1983, p. 126; "Hungry Tiger Profits Rise 25% for Third Quarter," *Nation's Restaurant News*, August 2, 1982, p. 4; and "Hungry Tiger to Buy 12-Unit Castagnola's," *Nation's Restaurant News*, March 14, 1983. **9.** Ibid. **10.** "Days Inns: Looking for a Berth in a Crowded National Field," *Business Week*, October 31, 1983, pp. 70 ff.; and Loretta Ivany, "Days Inns: A Budget Formula Turns to Gold," *Lodging Hospitality*, October 1983, p. 72. **11.** Gregory Stricharchuk, "More Ailing Concerns are Firing Auditors in Hopes of Keeping Bad News from Public," *The Wall Street Journal*, May 12, 1983; and Richard Greene and Christopher Power, "Banking on Real Estate," *Forbes*, March 28, 1983, p. 41.

Chapter 17

1. *World Book Encyclopedia*, vol. 17 (Chicago: World Books, 1982), p. 414. **2.** *Electronic Market Data Book 1983* (Washington, D.C.: Electronic Industries Association, 1983), p. 74. **3.** Ibid. **4.** National Science Foundation, *Research Briefings*, December 1983, p. 5. **5.** *Electronic Market Data Book 1983*, p. 70. **6.** Ibid. **7.** Allen Boraiko, "The Chip: Electronic Mini-Marvel That Is Changing Your Life," *National Geographic*, October 1982, p. 456. **8.** *Electronic Market Data Book 1983*, p. 80. **9.** Boraiko, "The Chip." **10.** Paul Fiondella, "Videogram: A Designer's Description," *Popular Computing*, November 1983, pp. 114 ff. **11.** *World Almanac and Book of Facts 1984* (New York: Newspaper Enterprise Association, 1983), p. 70. **12.** International Data Corporation, cited in William M. Bulkeley, "Microcomputers Gaining Primacy, Forcing Changes in the Industry," *The Wall Street Journal*, January 13, 1983. **13.** "Semiconductor Computer Plans," *The New York Times*, February 2, 1983. **14.** "Taking control of Computer Spending," *Business Week*, July 12, 1983, pp. 59 ff.; and Richard A. Immel, "The Automated Office: Myth Versus Reality," *Popular Computing*, May 1983, p. 125. **15.** William M. Bulkeley, "Firms Linking More Users to Mainframes," *The Wall Street Journal*, September 19, 1983; Bro Uttal, "Linking Computers to Help Managers Manage," *Fortune*, December 26, 1983, pp. 145 ff.; David Gabel, "The Mainframe Connection," *Personal Computing*, June 1983, p. 131; and "How Personal Computers Can Backfire," *Business Week*, July 12, 1982, pp. 56 ff.

Component Chapter F

1. Dr. Edward A. Wolf, Director, National Research and Resource Facility for Submicron Structures, Cornell University, Ithaca, New York 14853.
2. Christopher Evans, *The Micro Millennium* (New York: Viking Press, 1980), p. 51; and Allen Boraiko, "The Chip: Electronic Mini-Marvel That Is Changing Your Life," *National Geographic*, October 1982, p. 421.   3. Boraiko, "The Chip."   4. Ibid.   5. Ibid., p. 425.
6. *Electronic Market Data Book 1983* (Washington, D.C.: Electronic Industries Association, 1983), p. 126.   7. Ibid., p. 2.   8. Boraiko, "The Chip," pp. 431, 434. The half-million figure is 1983 "state of the art" for commercially available microprocessors.   9. *Electronic Market Data Book 1983*, p. 67.   10. Ibid., p. 84.   11. Ibid., p. 91; and Anthony V. Gagliardi, Manager of Public Relations, General Motors Technical Center, Warren, Michigan 48090.   12. This estimate was derived by Dataquest, a San Jose, California, market research firm, and was published in the *The Wall Street Journal* in late 1981.   13. "Chip Wars: The Japanese Threat," *Business Week*, May 23, 1983, p. 81.   14. Arthur L. Robinson, "One Billion Transistors on a Chip?" *Science*, January 20, 1983, pp. 267 ff.   15. Ibid.   16. Boraiko, "The Chip," p. 444.   17. Robin Bradbeer, Peter De Bono, and Peter Laurie, *The Beginner's Guide to Computers* (Reading, Mass.: Addison-Wesley, 1982), p. 37.
18. Ibid., p. 37   19. *Electronic Market Data Book 1983*, p. 126.   20. "Computer Shock Hits the Office: A Wild Proliferation of Desktop Units Is Confusing Everyone," *Business Week*, August 8, 1983, pp. 46 ff.   21. Michael Rogers, "How Computer Salesmen Size You Up," *Physician's Assets*, March–April 1983, pp. 13 ff.; and Gus Hedburg, "The Computer, the Future and You," *Money Guide/Personal Computers*, 1984, p. 10.   22. Andrew Pollack, "Computer Disaster: Business Seeks Antidote," *The New York Times*, August 24, 1983; "They Also Serve," *Forbes*, August 1, 1983, pp.

139 ff.; and Richard A. Immel, "Data Security: Threats to Company Data Are Real but Controllable," *Popular Computing*, May 1984, p. 65.

Chapter 18

1. Thomas E. Ricks, "Paradyne Faces Fraud Charges Over U.S. Job," *The Wall Street Journal*, March 28, 1983; and "Unhappy, Engineers May Have Launched the Paradyne Probe," *Data Communications*, August 1983, p. 50.
2. "Tenneco Is Doubtful of Getting U.S. Help in Natural Gas Suits," *The Wall Street Journal*, November 14, 1983.
3. "A Stunning Challenge to the Sanctity of Contracts," *Business Week*, August 22, 1983, pp. 76 ff.   4. *Lange v. National Biscuit Company*, 211 N.W. 2d 783 (Sup. Ct. Minn., 1973).   5. Doron P. Levin, "Poor Controls at Rockwell Helped Make It a Fraud Victim, Report Says," *The Wall Street Journal*, August 18, 1983; and "The OPM Scandal Unmasked," *Datamation*, September 1983, p. 34.   6. "The Tangled Story Behind the X-Car Suit," *Business Week*, August 22, 1983, pp. 31 ff.   7. "A Retailer's Chapter 11 Has Creditors Enraged," *Business Week*, May 9, 1983, pp. 71 ff.; and "Hide and Seek: Bankruptcy in America," *Economist*, May 21, 1983, p. 102.   8. Thomas J. Lueck, "Manville Thriving in Bankruptcy, Shielded from Asbestos Lawsuits," *The New York Times*, August 25, 1983; and Anna Cifelli, "Management by Bankruptcy," *Fortune*, October 31, 1983, pp. 69 ff.   9. Bill Richards, "Papers from Trial of Former IBT Officers Raise Many Questions on Product Safety," *The Wall Street Journal*, May 13, 1983.   10. Irwin Ross, "How Lawless Are Big Companies?" *Fortune*, December 1, 1980, pp. 56 ff.   11. Steve Swartz, "Athletic-Shoe Concerns' Payments to College Coaches Draw Criticism," *The Wall Street Journal*, July 26, 1983.   12. "Should Law Firms Investigate Their Own Clients?" *Business Week*, July 11, 1983, p. 59.   13. David B. Tinnin, "How IBM Stung Hitachi," *Fortune*, March 7, 1983, pp. 50 ff.   14. Steve Mufson, "Troubled Waters: Exxon Employees Face Accusations of Stealing Ideas of Other Firms," *The Wall Street Journal*, November 9, 1983; and G. Felda Hardyman, Mark J. DeNino, and Malcom S. Salter, "When Corporate Venture Capital Doesn't Work," *Harvard Business Review*, May–June 1983, pp.

114 ff.   15. Roger Ricklefs, "On Many Ethical Issues, Executives Apply Stiffer Standard Than Public," *The Wall Street Journal*, November 1, 1983; and Gallup Organization, Princeton, N.J., "*The Wall Street Journal* Survey of Business Ethics," October–November 1983.

Chapter 19

1. Arlen J. Large, "Mission Possible: Will U.S. Space Station's Crew Ever Find Happiness? Maybe So, If the Space Station Is Ever Launched," *The Wall Street Journal*, October 27, 1983.
2. Howard Banks, "Cleared for Takeoff." *Forbes*, October 10, 1983, pp. 35 ff.
3. "While the Price Lasts," *Forbes*, October 10, 1983, p. 179.   4. "Rule Making by Consensus Passes Its First Test," *Business Week*, November 14, 1983, p. 194K.   5. Russell C. Warren, *Antitrust in Theory & Practice* (Columbus, Ohio: Grid, 1978), p. 332.   6. Stephen Wermiel, "Supreme Court Set to Review Big Trust Case," *The Wall Street Journal*, September 30, 1983.   7. "The Taxpayer Rebellion Is Coming Back," *Business Week*, September 19, 1983, p. 33.
8. Data from Internal Revenue Service.
9. "Treasury's Sneak Attack on Big Business," *Business Week*, August 22, 1983, pp. 106 ff.   10. "Record $189 Million Was Raised by PACs for 1982 Election," *The Wall Street Journal*, January 6, 1983.   11. "State Regulators Rush in Where Washington No Longer Treads," *Business Week*, September 19, 1983, pp. 124 ff.; Michael Oreskes, "U.S. and State at Odds Over Banking Law," *The New York Times*, March 21, 1984; and John Herbers, "Cities Spurning Washington in Bid to Reassert Authority," *The New York Times*, February 19, 1984.   12. William Harris, "No, No, Nova?" *Forbes*, May 23, 1983, pp. 40 ff.; and Stephen J. Sansweet, "A New Movie Studio Starts Work: It Seeks Credibility, Tries to Break Hollywood Mold," *The Wall Street Journal*, May 23, 1983.

ILLUSTRATION CREDITS

Chapter 1

Page 2: ROBERT V. ECKERT, JR./EKM-Nepenthe. **Page 5:** A, CHARLES STEINER/Picture Group; B, Courtesy of AT&T Bell Laboratories; C, JONATHAN GOELL/The Picture Cube; D, DAN MCCOY/Rainbow. **Page 6:** GEORGE MORAN and Vantage Art, Inc., based on information from Bureau of Labor Statistics. **Page 10:** HARRY WILKS/Stock, Boston. **Page 16:** A, MICHAEL MELFORD/Peter Arnold; B, MICHAEL PHILIP MANHEIM/Photo Researchers; C, TOM MYERS/Photo Researchers; D, BRAD BOWER/Picture Group. **Page 18:** GEORGE MORAN. **Page 21:** Vantage Art, Inc., based on information from Census Bureau, Bureau of Labor Statistics.

Chapter 2

Page 26: JIM PICKERELL. **Page 29:** MIKE QUON and Vantage Art, Inc., based on information from *Statistical Abstract of the United States, 104th Edition* (Washington, D.C.: Government Printing Office, 1984). **Page 32:** GEORGE MORAN. **Page 35:** SALLY BLAKEMORE and Vantage Art, Inc. **Page 40:** STUART LEEDS, based on information from *Newsweek*, November 28, 1983. **Page 42:** CINDY CHARLES/Gamma-Liaison.

Chapter 3

Page 46: PETER B. KAPLAN. **Page 51:** (left and right): Vantage Art, Inc. **Page 52:** Vantage Art, Inc. **Page 53:** ALAN CAREY/The Image Works. **Pages 54–55:** GEORGE MORAN. **Page 56:** Vantage Art, Inc. **Page 57:** SALLY BLAKEMORE, based on information from Bradley R. Schiller, *The Economy Today* (New York: Random House, Inc., 1980), p. 193. **Page 59:** A, DENNIS BRACK/Black Star; B, DIEGO GOLDBERG/Sygma; C, BRYCE FLYNN/Picture Group. **Page 62** (photos): Left, New York Public Library Picture Collection; center, and right, The Granger Collection. **Page 63** (photos): Left, Courtesy of General Motors Corporation; right, WILLIAM JAMES WARREN/West Light. **Pages 62–63** (graphics): Vantage Art, Inc., based on information from *Statistical Abstract of the United States, 104th Edition* (1984).

Component Chapter A

Page 70: ALAN PORTER. **Page 73:** Vantage Art, Inc., based on information from Interindustry Forecasting Project, University of Maryland. **Page 76:** JERRY MCDANIEL, based on information from "How Japan Guides Industries," *The New York Times*, May 18, 1983. **Page 78:** ANDREW POPPER/Phototake. **Page 79:** SALLY BLAKEMORE, based on information from "Executives Split on Saving Smokestack Industries," *Business Week*, April 18, 1984, p. 18. **Pages 80–81:** SALLY BLAKEMORE, based on information from Prof. John Ryans. **Page 84:** J. P. LAFFONT/Sygma. **Page 85:** SALLY BLAKEMORE, based on information from "Making Industrial Policy," *Newsweek*, October 24, 1983, p. 98. **Page 87:** GEORGE MORAN.

Component Chapter B

Page 94: CAROL PALMER/The Picture Cube. **Page 96:** Above, courtesy of Delta Airlines; below, courtesy of McDonald's Corporation; right, courtesy of International Business Machines Corporation. **Page 99:** LIONEL DELEVINGNE/Picture Group. **Page 101:** GEORGE MORAN. **Page 102:** GEORGE MORAN. **Page 108:** A, DIANA CHURCH; B, RICK BROWNE/Picture Group; C, JACK CURRAN. **Page 109:** D, all courtesy of Orbital Sciences Corporation, Vienna, Virginia. **Page 111:** SALLY BLAKEMORE.

Chapter 4

Page 122: JOHN BRYSON/The Image Bank. **Page 124:** GEORGE HALL/Woodfin Camp & Associates. **Page 127:** GEORGE MORAN and Vantage Art, Inc., based on information from *Management by Objectives* by George S. Odiorne (Belmont, California, Fearon-Pitman Publishers, 1965). **Page 128:** KEN REGAN/Camera 5. **Page 129:** GEORGE MORAN. **Page 132:** Left, HARRY BENSON; right, THOM O'CONNOR. **Page 133:** Left, RICK BROWNE/Picture Group; right, MARIANNE BARCELLONA. **Page 135:** Vantage Art, Inc. **Page 136:** SALLY BLAKEMORE and Vantage Art, Inc. **Page 137:** SALLY BLAKEMORE and Vantage Art, Inc.

Chapter 5

Page 146: HANK MORGAN. **Page 150** (photo): TIM CARLSON/Stock, Boston. **Pages 150–151** (graphic): Vantage Art, Inc. **Page 152:** (left) MIKE QUON; (right) Vantage Art, Inc. **Page 153** (photos): Courtesy of Time, Inc.; (graphic) Vantage Art, Inc. **Page 157:** STUART LEEDS. **Page 158:** Vantage Art, Inc. **Page 159:** Vantage Art, Inc. **Page 160:** SALLY BLAKEMORE.

Chapter 6

Page 164: PETER MENZEL. **Page 168** (photo): HANK MORGAN/Rainbow. **Pages 168–169** (graphic): JERRY MCDANIEL. **Page 170:** CHUCK ROGERS/Black Star. **Page 174:** MARTIN LUBIN and Vantage Art, Inc. **Page 176:** Vantage Art, Inc. **Page 177:** Vantage Art, Inc. **Page**

178: Courtesy of Nissan Motor Manufacturing Corporation, U.S.A. **Page 179:** *New York Post* photo by LOUIS C. LIOTTA.

Chapter 7

Page 184: ALAN PORTER. **Page 186:** Library of Congress. **Page 187** (left): LEWIS HINES Collection, International Museum of Photography at George Eastman House; (right) AP/Wide World Photos. **Page 189:** STUART LEEDS and Vantage Art, Inc., based on information from "The Rise and Fall of Big Labor," *Newsweek*, September 5, 1983, pp. 50 ff. **Page 196:** ALAN REININGER/Contact Press Images. **Page 202:** Vantage Art, Inc.

Chapter 8

Page 208: SHEPARD SHERBELL/Picture Group. **Page 211:** GEORGE MORAN. **Page 216:** Vantage Art, Inc., based on information from Census Bureau, Bureau of Labor Statistics. **Page 219:** H. YANAGUCHI/Gamma-Liaison. **Pages 220–221:** Vantage Art, Inc., based on information from U.S. Chamber of Commerce, 1982. **Page 223:** GEORGE MORAN.

Component Chapter C

Page 230: CHIP MAURY/Picture Group. **Page 233:** GEORGE MORAN. **Page 235:** GEORGE MORAN. **Page 236:** AP/Wide World Photos. **Page 240:** ADRIANO HEITMANN/Archive Pictures. **Page 241:** CHARLES GUPTON/Southern Light. **Page 242:** LESLIE WONG/Archive Pictures.

Chapter 9

Page 252: ALAN PORTER. **Page 255** (top): Courtesy of EXXON Office Systems; (bottom): Courtesy of John Deere & Company. **Page 256:** MARTIN LUBIN and GEORGE MORAN. **Page 257** (top): DAVE SCHAEFER/The Picture Cube; (middle): JOHN LEI/Stock, Boston; (bottom): JOEL GORDON. **Page 259:** Vantage Art, Inc. **Page 260:** Vantage Art, Inc., based on information from *Statistical Abstract of the United States, 104th Edition* (1984). **Page 263** (top left): courtesy of Colgate-Palmolive Company; (top right): courtesy of American Motors Corporation; (bottom left): courtesy of Sony Corporation of America; (bottom right): courtesy of Ricoh Corporation, photo by PETE TURNER. **Page 265:** Vantage Art, Inc. **Page 266:** JERRY MCDANIEL.

Chapter 10

Page 272: ALAN PORTER. **Page 274:** Vantage Art, Inc. **Page 275:** ISADORE SELTZER. **Page 276:** SALLY BLAKEMORE and Vantage Art, Inc., based on information from *Merchandising*, March, 1983. **Page 279:** SALLY BLAKEMORE and Vantage Art, Inc. **Page 281:** A, Courtesy of Minnetonka, Inc., Minneapolis; B, courtesy of American Can; C, MARK ANTMAN/The Image Works; D, courtesy of BrikPak, Inc., A Tetra Pak Company; E, F, and G, courtesy of American Can. **Page 284:** Vantage Art, Inc. **Page 287:** Vantage Art, Inc.

Chapter 11

Page 292: WILL REGAN/International Stock. **Page 294** (left): SAM EMERSON/Sygma; (right): Focus on Sports. **Page 295:** Vantage Art, Inc. **Page 297:** Vantage Art, Inc., based on information from *Statistical Abstract of the United States, 104th Edition* (1984). **Page 299** (left): Courtesy of Wendy's and Dancer Fitzgerald Sample, Inc.; (right): BILL NATION/Sygma. **Page 300:** G. RANCINAN/Sygma. **Page 303:** GEORGE MORAN. **Page 304** (top left): Courtesy of Air Atlanta. Ad by Cargill, Wilson & Acree; (right): Courtesy of Lucite Paint, Olympic Stain; (bottom left): Courtesy of Canon U.S.A., Inc., Calculator Division. Ad by DYR, Inc., Dentsu Young & Rubicam. Creative Director, Shojiro Yanagi; Art Director, Hiro Shibata; Copy Writer, Mike Macina. **Page 305** (top): Courtesy of Revlon, Inc.; (bottom left): Courtesy of Butlers/Malings Shoes; (bottom right): Created for Lawry's Foods, Inc. by Dailey & Associates. **Page 306:** KATHY BENDO.

Chapter 12

Page 318: CHUCK O'REAR/West Light. **Page 320:** Vantage Art, Inc. **Page 321:** Vantage Art, Inc. **Page 325:** GEORGE MORAN. **Page 327:** A, A. BERLINER/Gamma-Liaison; B, C, and D, BARBARA ALPER. **Page 330:** MARTIN LUBIN and Vantage Art, Inc., based on information from Direct Marketing Association. **Page 333:** Vantage Art, Inc., reprinted from "Physical Distribution: Key to Improved Volume and Profits," *Journal of Marketing*, 29 January 1965, p. 66, published by the American Marketing Association. **Page 335:** MIKE QUON and Vantage Art, Inc.

Chapter 13

Page 348: ERIK LEIGH SIMMONS/The Image Bank. **Page 352:** Vantage Art, Inc. **Page 353** (top): PAUL WALDMAN; (bottom) MIKE QUON and Vantage Art, Inc. **Page 354:**

Vantage Art, Inc. **Pages 366–367:** SALLY BLAKEMORE, based on information from Irwin Ross, "The Race Is to the Slow Payer," FORTUNE, April 18, 1983, pp. 75 ff.

Chapter 14

Page 372: KEN BROUSSEAU/EKM-Nepenthe. **Page 384:** GEORGE MORAN. **Page 388:** G. GORMAN/Sygma. **Page 389:** MARTIN LUBIN, based on information from New York Stock Exchange and Prof. Robert Eskew, Purdue University (personal communication).

Chapter 15

Page 394: KEN KARP. **Page 400:** BARBARA ALPER. **Page 401:** Courtesy, The New York Stock Exchange. **Page 402:** Vantage Art, Inc., based on information from New York Stock Exchange. **Pages 405, 406, 407, and 408** (all figures): Vantage Art, Inc. Reprinted by permission of The Wall Street Journal © Dow Jones & Company, Inc., 1984. All rights reserved. **Page 410:** SALLY BLAKEMORE and Vantage Art, Inc., based on information from Futures Industry Association, Washington, D.C.

Component Chapter D

Page 414: ALAN PORTER. **Page 417:** SALLY BLAKEMORE and Vantage Art, Inc., based on information from Federal Reserve Statistical release, May 10, 1984. **Page 419:** Vantage Art, Inc. **Page 420:** MIKE QUON. **Page 425:** Vantage Art, Inc., based on information from Robert A. Bennett, "Deregulation Alters Banking," *The New York Times*, December 5, 1983. **Page 429:** JERRY MCDANIEL, based on information from Robert A. Bennett, "Inside Citicorp: The Changing World of Banking," *The New York Times Magazine*, May 29, 1983.

Component Chapter E

Page 436: KILBY/Uniphoto Picture Agency. **Page 439:** GEORGE MORAN. **Page 441:** NYPL/Picture Collection. **Page 442:** GEORGE MORAN. **Page 445:** ABRAMSON/Gamma-Liaison. **Page 446:** MIKE QUON. **Page 448:** Vantage Art, Inc., based on information from *The New York Times*, March 5, 1984.

Chapter 16

Page 462: ALAN PORTER. **Page 469:** Reprinted by permission of Apple Computer Inc. **Page 475:** Reprinted by permission of Apple Computer Inc. **Page 479:** SALLY BLAKEMORE and Vantage Art, Inc., based on information from Chrysler Corp. quarterly report, March 1984. **Pages 480–481:** Jane Bryant Quinn, "How to Read an Annual Report," from advertising campaign titled "The Power of the Printed Word," © 1981, International Paper Company. Annual reports shown courtesy of Boise Cascade Corporation, Johnson & Johnson, The Boeing Company, Levi Strauss & Company, Weyerhaeuser, The Coca-Cola Company, Xerox, AT&T, and Burroughs Corporation.

Chapter 17

Page 488: CHUCK O'REAR/ West Light. **Page 492** (photo): Courtesy of Androbot, Inc., photo by TOM CHARGIN. **Pages 492–493** (graphic): Vantage Art, Inc., based on information from Profs. Peter Ginter and Andrew Rucks, University of Alabama (personal communication). **Page 493** (photo): MARK S. WEXLER. **Page 494** (top): Courtesy of Radio Shack, A Division of Tandy Corporation; (center right): Courtesy of Honeywell; (center left): Courtesy of International Business Machines Corporation; (bottom): Courtesy of Control Data Corporation. **Page 499:** Vantage Art, Inc., based on information from Keith K. Cox and Ben M. Enis, *The Marketing Research Process* (Pacific Palisades, Calif.: Goodyear Publishing Co., 1972), p. 19. **Page 504:** Vantage Art, Inc., based on information from International Data Corporation. **Page 505:** MARTIN LUBIN. **Page 507** (top left): BILL GALLERY/Stock, Boston; (bottom left): Courtesy of ISSCO Graphics; (top right): JERRY MASON/Science Photo Library—Photo Researchers; (bottom right): RICK BROWNE/Picture Group.

Component Chapter F

Page 512: HANK MORGAN. **Page 515:** Vantage Art, Inc. **Page 516:** All courtesy of International Business Machines Corporation. **Page 517:** Courtesy of North American Philips Corporation. **Page 519** (photo): Courtesy of Honeywell; (graphic) Vantage Art, Inc. **Page 522:** A, Courtesy of Hewlett-Packard Company; B, RICK BROWNE/Picture Group; C, DAN MCCOY/Rainbow; D, Courtesy of International Business Machines Corporation. **Page 523:** E, Courtesy of Hewlett-Packard Company; F, EDITH G. HAUN/Stock, Boston. **Page 526:** Vantage Art, Inc.

Chapter 18

Page 536: ALAN PORTER. **Page 540:** Vantage Art, Inc., and GEORGE MORAN. **Page 543** (photo): AP/Wide World Photos; Table based on information from Douglas R. Sease, "X-Cars, Once GM's Pride, Getting a Shoddy Reputation with Owners," *The Wall Street Journal,* March 3, 1983. **Page 548:** GEORGE MORAN.

Chapter 19

Page 552: JOAN LIFTON/Archive Pictures. **Page 555:** AP/Wide World Photos. **Page 556:** JERRY MCDANIEL. **Page 558:** SALLY BLAKEMORE, based on information from "Deregulating America," *Business Week,* November 28, 1983, pp. 80–81. **Page 565:** SALLY BLAKEMORE, based on information from Joint Committee on Taxation for the year 1981 (cited in *The New York Times,* March 20, 1983).

GLOSSARY/INDEX

A

absolute advantage   the economic advantage a country has when it can produce a given product more cheaply than other countries can.

absorbable risks   risks that can be covered by insurance but that, for one reason or another, are assumed or absorbed by a business itself. 441–42

accountability, 154

accountants, 464–65

accounting   a system of principles and techniques that permits bookkeepers or computers to record, classify, and accumulate sales, purchases, and other transactions. Accounting also provides ways to present and interpret this information so that a company's past performance, present condition, and future planning can be clearly and efficiently evaluated. 463–87

budget in, 483–84

computers in, 495–98

constant-dollar vs. current-cost method of, 473

double-entry bookkeeping in, 466–67

inflation and, 473

key concepts in, 466–67

nonpublic (corporate), 465

public, 465

ratios in, 479–83

small businesses and, 530–33

accounting cycle   a sequence of procedures by which the transactions of a business are recorded and classified, over a specific time period; includes posting transactions to specific accounts, tallying the accounts, closing the books, and transferring totals to financial statements.

accounting equation   the equation stating that assets equal liabilities plus owners' equity. 466

accounting statements   summaries of a business's operations during a given time period and its financial position at the end of that period. 464

accounts payable   debts that are due in thirty days or less. 471, 498

accounts receivable   the money that is owed to a company for items or services it has sold. 352, 361–62, 458, 468, 498

accrual basis   an accounting method in which all sales revenues are recorded in the year the sales are made. 474

accrued expenses   expenses incurred for which bills have not yet been received and recorded. 471

acid-test ratio (quick ratio)   a ratio showing the ability of a company to meet its short-term debts with its cash, marketable securities, and receivables. 482–83

acquisitions, 38

actuaries   persons employed by an insurance company to compute expected losses and calculate the cost of premiums. 444

advertising   any paid form of nonpersonal presentation made by an identified sponsor through a mass communication medium on behalf of goods, services, or ideas. 294–305

creative strategy in, 302

evaluation of, 304–5

media, 297–301

media planning in, 302

regulation of, 312–14

self-regulation in, 314

small businesses and, 343–44

types of, 296–97

advertising agencies, 303

advocacy or controversy advertising   ads that address hotly debated public issues. 296–97

affirmative action   the active recruitment of minority group members, based on some demonstration of availability, in order to train them for jobs. 20–21

age discrimination, 214

agency   in law, that which exists when one party, known as the principal, authorizes another party, known as the agent, to act in his or her behalf. 541–42

agency shop   a shop requiring nonunion workers who benefit from agreements negotiated by the union to pay dues to that union. 192

agent   a party who acts in behalf of another party (the principal), who has authorized him to do so.

Agriculture Department, U.S., 107

Airbus Industrie, 82

air travel industry, 11

Alaskan pipeline, 40–41

alien corporation   a corporation that has been organized in a foreign country but operates in the United States.

Allied Corporation, 37

Amalgamated Clothing and Textile Workers Union, 199

amalgamation, 38

American Airlines, 193

American Challenge, The (Servan-Schreiber), 73

American Express, 39, 426

American Federation of Labor–Congress of Industrial Organizations (AFL-CIO), 188, 193, 199

American Medical Association (AMA), 18, 314, 566

American Stock Exchange (Amex), 397–98

American Telephone & Telegraph Corporation (AT&T), 77, 194, 218, 220

breakup of, 18, 28, 40, 560–61

lobbying by, 566

ants who meet a state's requirements for education and experience and pass an examination prepared by the American Institute of Certified Public Accountants. 465

chain of command the relationship between different levels of employees within an organization. 153–54

chain stores a group of centrally owned and managed stores that sell similar goods.

Chamber of Commerce, 221–22

channel of distribution (trade channel, marketing channel) the sequence of marketing agencies (such as wholesalers and retailers) through which a product passes on its way from the producer to the final user. 320–32

conflicts in, 330–32

direct, 320–21

middlemen in, 321–30

chart *see* **graph or chart**

chartists, 403

chattel mortgage an agreement, often part of a loan agreement, that the movable property purchased through the loan belongs to the borrower, while the lender has a legal right to take possession of the property if payments are not made as specified in the loan agreement. 362

check an order to a bank to release the amount of money specified. 417

Chicago Board of Trade, 408

chief executive officer (CEO) the person who is responsible for setting down the policies of a company, under the direction of its board, and for supervising the officers who carry out those policies. 36

China, People's Republic of, 81

Chrysler Corporation, 11, 157, 195, 448, 479, 555

CIO (Congress of Industrial Organizations), 188

circle chart (pie chart) chart that often takes the form of a pie divided into slices, using the sizes of the slices to indicate percentages of the whole circle, or 100 percent. 592–93

circuit the path of an electric current. 514

circular flow the pattern whereby the economy carries goods and services one way and money the other. 55–57

Citibank, 88, 428–29

Citicorp, 547

Citizen/Labor Energy Coalition, 18

Civil Aeronautics Board (CAB), 557

Civil Rights Act of 1964 historic law forbidding discrimination in employment. 20, 191, 213, 215, 218

Civil Rights Commission, 214

Civil Service, 215

classical theory of motivation the view that money is

the sole motivator in the workplace. 233–34

Clayton Act of 1914 an act amending the Sherman Antitrust Act, clearing up wording and forbidding specific actions that Congress saw as leading to monopoly. 559–60

closed corporation corporation owned and controlled by a small number of stockholders.

closed shop a shop in which union membership is a condition of employment. 192

COBOL (Common Business-Oriented Language) a computer programming language used in business data processing.

C.O.D. shipment, 544

coinsurance a form of property insurance requiring the purchaser to buy coverage equal to a certain percentage of the property's value.

Coleco Industries, 254–55

collateral a valuable item or items that can be seized by a lender should the borrower fail to repay a loan. 361–62, 376

collective bargaining a process of negotiation involving unions and management. 186, 201–3

Commerce Department, U.S., 107

commercial banks, 425

commercial goods, 255

commercialization, 278

commercial paper a company's promise to pay back a stated amount of money on a stated date within 3 to 270 days from the time the loan is issued. 355, 363–64

commissions payments based on sales made. 220

committee organization an approach to organizing a company's internal structure, in which a group of individuals hold authority and responsibility together.

commodities raw materials. 407–8

commodity exchanges exchanges that specialize in trades involving raw materials (commodities). 407–8, 410

common carriers, 524

Common Cause, 566

common law law based on the precedents established by judges' decisions. 538–39

common stock stock whose owners have last claim on distributed profits; shares of ownership in a company. 350–51, 381, 384–86

communication the transferring of information. 139–40, 232, 248–49

communications industry, 11

Communications Workers of America (CWA), 186, 194

comparable worth, 21

comparative advantage the advantage a country has if it can produce a specific product more cheaply and more efficiently than it can other products.

comparative advertising, 313

compensating balance a substantial portion of an un-secured loan that is kept on deposit with the lend-ing bank in order to protect the lender and in-crease the lender's return on the loan. 362–63

compensation the payment of employees for their work. 218–20

competition, 8–9

compiler a computer program that translates other computer programs into machine-language pro-grams. 514–15

compulsory arbitration arbitration in a labor-manage-ment dispute, required by a third party such as the government (both labor and management are re-quired to submit).

computer-aided design (CAD) the use of computer graphics in the design of products. 167–69

computer-aided manufacture (CAM) the use of com-puters to control production machines. 167–69

computer-assisted instruction (CAI) instruction via computer, using programmed sequences.

computer graphics, 506–7

computer hardware, 491, 513–23
circuits in, 514–15
compatibility of, 525–26
described, 491, 518–23
forebears of, 516
input and output devices, 491, 520–23
keyboards, 521
primary storage area in, 518
secondary storage devices, 491, 520

computer program an ordered sequence of statements that guides the computer in performing a specific set of tasks. 491–92

computers, 4–6, 129–30, 489–529
automation and, 166–69
copyrights and, 568
costs of, 532–33
data communications and, 523–24
history of, 515–18
introduction to, 490–95
inventory and, 176–177
Japanese industry and, 166, 242, 496–97
kinds of, 492–95
mainframe, 494
MRP and, 176–77
office automation and, 523–26
off-price retailing and, 327–28
organization and, 156
privacy and, 502
promotion and, 310–11

psychological effects of, 502
reports obtained via, 498–99
safety and, 224
small businesses and, 105–6, 532
social impact of, 502
spreadsheet analysis with, 504–6
strikes and, 200
use of, 495–99
vendors of, 533
word processing and, 506
see also **MIS**

concept testing, 278

conceptual skill the ability to understand the relation-ship of parts to the whole. 140–41

conciliation bringing a neutral third party into a labor-management dispute to facilitate negotiation.

conflicts of interest, 547–48

conglomerate merger a union of two or more corpo-rations whose operations are unrelated. 39, 560

consideration in contract law, an item of value given to make a contract legally binding. 539

Consolidated Edison, 214

consumer goods goods and services which ultimate buyers purchase for their own use. 257

consumer market, 255, 257–64
buying psychology in, 262–64
18- to 34-year-old group in, 259–60
location of, 260–61
over-65 age group in, 260
profiles of consumers in, 257–64
ultimate vs. organizational, 262

consumer movement, 7, 17–19

Consumer Price Index (CPI) a measure of the aver-age price changes for selected goods and services from month to month.

Consumer Product Safety Commission a federal agency created in 1972 to monitor the safety of products sold to consumers. 18

containerization the use of large standard-sized sealed containers for shipping merchandise; these are packed and sealed at the factory, loaded on trucks, and then reloaded on railroad flatcars, ships, or planes without disturbing the contents. 333

Continental Air, 240, 545

contingencies, 133

contingent business interruption insurance coverage that protects against loss of business due to an in-terruption in the delivery of essential supplies. 445

continuity the amount of time spanned by a given media schedule and the timing of the ad messages. 303

ment, marketing, accounting management, and media research, as well as creative services.

functional job analysis, 211–12

functional organization (departmentation by function) those specialists who are given direct authority in their particular areas of expertise. 158–61

fundamental analysis an approach to stock selection that involves careful examination of a company's history, current financial position, and prospects for the future. 403

futures trading trading in commodities for future delivery. 408

G

GAF Corporation, 37

games and sweepstakes, 312

Gantt, Henry L., 175

Gantt charts, 175–76

Garrino, Gian Luigi, 356

general accounting, 351

General Agreement on Tariffs and Trade (GATT) a multinational agreement that sponsors negotiations for lower tariffs and encourages the elimination of nontariff barriers to imports (such as quotas). 79–80

general expenses the expenses arising from the overall administration of a business. 476

General Foods, 273

general ledger, 498

General Motors, 11, 17, 33, 38, 100, 284, 561
  EEOC complaint against, 214–15
  JIT approach used by, 179
  organizational reform of, 147, 165
  UAW and, 194
  X-car of, 543

general obligation bond a bond backed up by a municipality's taxing power. 380

general partner or partners partners who have unlimited liability for the firm's debts. 32, 117

Generally Accepted Accounting Practices (GAAP) guidelines used by the accounting profession in reporting business transactions.

generic products products packaged in plain black-and-white boxes, bags, or cans bearing only the name of the product. 280

generic terms terms that describe a whole class of products. 567

geographic and demographic editions editions of national magazines that are aimed at narrower audiences on the basis of region and occupation. 298

Germany, West, 78

Glass Packaging Institute, 283

Glass-Steagall Act of 1933, 425–27

Goldwater, Barry, 28

goods, 4, 7–9

goodwill a company's reputation, especially in its relations with its customers; regarded as an intangible asset. 471

Goodwill Industries, 8

government, 10–17, 54, 553–71
  borrowing by, 390
  business assisted by, 555–56
  business needed by, 554–55
  discrimination and, 20
  fiscal policy and, 62
  inflation and, 64–65
  labeling and, 283
  lobbying in, 566
  natural monopolies and, 561
  noncompetitive practices regulated by, 559–61
  retail prices regulated by, 562–63
  small businesses and, 106
  see also regulatory agencies; taxes

grapevine the unofficial lines of communication in an organization, bypassing the formal chain of command. 161

graph or chart usually a diagram or picture showing the relationship of one set of data to another. 592–93

Gray, Carolyn Doppelt, 98

gray market, 327

greenhouse effect, 14

grievance mediation an arrangement whereby a neutral third party meets with both sides and attempts to steer them toward a solution to the problem. 203

grievances disagreements that arise from changes in working conditions or from decisions made by lower-level managers. 202

gross national product (GNP) a dollar figure that lumps together the total dollar value of the goods and services produced by the economy over a given period of time. 58, 62–63

gross profit (gross margin) the amount remaining after the cost of goods sold is deducted from net sales. 476

gross sales the total dollar amount of goods sold. 476

group life insurance a master life-insurance policy covering a group of company employees or a group of people in an organization.

group norms standards of behavior that all the members of a given group accept. 239–41

group process, 238–41